The "Four Hundred"

ALLEN, MR. FRED H.

APPLETON, MR. AND MRS. F. R.

ASTOR, MR. AND MRS. JOHN JACOB

ASTOR, MR. AND MRS. WILLIAM

BALDWIN, MISS

BALDWIN, C. C.

BALDWIN, C. C., JR.

BALDWIN, MISS LOUISE

BARBEY, MRS.

BARBEY, MISS

BARCLAY, MR. AND MRS. JAMES L.

BAYLIES, MR. AND MRS. EDMUND L.

BEND, MISS AMY

BEND, MISS BEATRICE

BENTINCK, MRS. CAVENDISH

BERRYMAN, MISS

BISHOP, MISS

BISHOP, HEBER

BOWDOIN, MRS. GEORGE S.

BOWDOIN, MRS. TEMPLE

BRONSON, MR. AND MRS. FREDERIC

BROWN, HAROLD

BROWN, WILLIAM HAROLD

BRYCE, MR. AND MRS. LLOYD

BULKELEY, EDWARD

BURDEN, MISS

BURDEN, MR. AND MRS. I. TOWN-
SEND

BURNETT, GEN. AND MRS.

CAMERON, THE MISSES

CAMERON, DUNCAN

CAMERON, SIR RODERICK

CANNON, MR. AND MRS. HARRY

CARROLL, MR. AND MRS. CHARLES

CARY, MR. AND MRS. CLARENCE

CHANLER, MR. AND MRS. WIN-
THROP

CHANLER, THE MISSES

COOPER, MR. AND MRS. EDWARD

COSTER, CHARLES HENRY

COSTER, WILLIAM B.

COTTENET, RAWLINS

CROSBY, MISS

CROSBY, COL. J. SCHUYLER

CROSS, MR. AND MRS. JAMES

CRUGER, MR. AND MRS. S. VAN RENSSELAER

CUSHING, MISS EDITH

CUSHING, MR. THOMAS F.

CUTTING, MR. AND MRS. BAYARD

CUTTING, MR. W. BAYARD, JR.

CUTTING, MRS. BROCKHOLST

CUTTING, F. BROCKHOLST

CUTTING, ROBERT L., JR.

CUTTING, WILLIAM, JR.

DANA, MR. AND MRS. PAUL

DEFOREST, MR. AND MRS. GEORGE B.

DELAFIELD, MISS

DEPEW, MR. AND MRS. CHAUNCEY M.

DEPEYSTER, MR. AND MRS. FREDERIC J.

DYER, MR. AND MRS. ELISHA, JR.

ELLIOTT, MR. AND MRS. DUNCAN

FISH, MR. AND MRS. HAMILTON, JR.

FISH, MR. AND MRS. STUYVESANT

FORBES, H. DECOURCEY

FRANCKLYN, MR. AND MRS. C. G.

FRELINGHUYSEN, THEODORE

FURMAN, J. C.

GOELET, MR. AND MRS. OGDEN

GOELET, MR. AND MRS. ROBERT

GRANT, MISS

GREENE, MISS

GREENE, ALISTER

GRISWOLD, FRANK GRAY

GURNEE, AUGUSTUS C.

HADDEN, ALEXANDER M.

HADDEN, JOHN A., JR.

HALL, MISS

HALL, MR. AND MRS. VALENTINE G.

HAVEMEYER, MR. AND MRS. CHARLES F.

HAWKES, ROBERT F.

HEWITT, MR. AND MRS. PETER COOPER

HOFFMAN, MISS

HOFFMAN, CHARLES F.

HONE, ROBERT, JR.

HOWARD, MR. AND MRS. THOMAS

HOWLAND, MEREDITH

IRVIN, MR. AND MRS. RICHARD

IRVING, LANGDON

ISELIN, MR. AND MRS. COLUMBUS

ISELIN, ISAAC

JAFFRAY, MISS

JAFFRAY, MRS. WILLIAM

JAY, COL. AND MRS.

JONES, MISS BEATRIX

JONES, MR. AND MRS. F. RHINELANDER

JONES, SHIPLEY

KANE, MR. AND MRS. DELANCEY

KANE, MISS ELIZABETH

KANE, JULIAN

KANE, S. NICHOLSON

KANE, WOODBURY

KERNOCHAN, MR. AND MRS. FREDERICK

KERNOCHAN, MR. AND MRS. J. P.

KIP, COL. AND MRS.

KIP, MISS

KNOWLTON, MISS

KOUNTZE, MR. AND MRS. LUTHER

LANIER, MR. AND MRS. JAMES

LEARY, ARTHUR

LEITER, MISS

LIVINGSTON, MISS CLARISSA

LIVINGSTON, EDWARD

LIVINGSTON, EDWARD DE PEYSTER

LIVINGSTON, MR. AND MRS. HENRY B.

LIVINGSTON, MRS. MATURIN

LUSK, MISS

MARCH, CLEMENT

MARIÉ, PETER

MARSHALL, MR. AND MRS. CHARLES

MARTIN, MR. AND MRS. BRADLEY

MARTIN, F. TOWNSEND

MCALLISTER, WARD

MCALLISTER, MISS

MCVICKAR, MR. AND MRS. H. W.

MILLS, MR. AND MRS. OGDEN

MOORE, MR. AND MRS. CLEMENT C.

MORGAN, MISS ANNE

MORRIS, MR. AND MRS. NEWBOLD

MORRIS, MISS EVA C.

MORTIMER, MR. AND MRS. RICHARD

MUNN, CHARLES

NELSON, MRS. FREDERICK

NEWBOLD, MR. AND MRS. THOMAS

OELRICHS, MR. AND MRS. CHARLES M.

OLIN, STEPHEN H.

OTIS, JAMES

OTIS, MISS

PARKER, JAMES V.

PENDLETON, MR. AND MRS. FRANCIS KEY

PENDLETON, MRS. WILLIAM A.

PERRY, MISS

PETERS, RICHARD

PIERSON, GEN. AND MRS. J. FRED

PIERSON, MISS

PORTER, MR. AND MRS. BENJAMIN C.

POST, MR. AND MRS. CHARLES A.

POST, EDWARD C.

POST, MR. AND MRS. GEORGE B.

POTTER, CLARKSON

POTTER, MR. AND MRS. H. N.

POTTER, MISS JULIAN

RANDOLPH, MISS CORA

REDMOND, GOOLD H.

RHINELANDER, T. J. OAKLEY

RICHARDS, ROBERT KERR

RIPLEY, MR. AND MRS. S. D.

RITCHIE, JAMES W.

RIVES, MR. AND MRS. GEORGE L.

ROBERT, MR. AND MRS. CHRISTO-PHER

ROBBINS, MR. AND MRS. HENRY P.

ROBINSON, D. T. L.

ROBINSON, MR. AND MRS. DOUGLAS, JR.

ROBINSON, RANDOLPH

ROCHE, MRS. BURKE

ROGERS, MRS.

ROGERS, MISS

ROOSEVELT, MR. AND MRS. JAMES

RUTHERFORD, MR. AND MRS. LEWIS

SANDS, MISS

SCHUYLER, GEN. AND MRS. PHILIP

SHEPARD, MR. AND MRS. EDWARD MORSE

SHEPARD, MISS

SHERMAN, MR. AND MRS. WILLIAM WATTS

SLOAN, MISS ADELE

SLOANE, MR. AND MRS. WILLIAM D.

SMITH, J. CLINCH

STEVENS, MR. AND MRS. BYAM K.

STEVENS, MISS ELIZABETH

STEWARD, LISPENARD

STEWART, MR. AND MRS. WILLIAM RHINELANDER

STOKES, MR. AND MRS. ANSON PHELPS

STURGIS, MR. AND MRS. FRANK K.

SUYDAM, MR. AND MRS. WALTER LISPENARD

TAILER, EDWARD NEUFVILLE

TAILER, MISS

TALLEYRAND, MARQUISE DE

TIFFANY, BELMONT

TOOKER, G. MEAD

TOOKER, MISS

TWOMBLY, MR. AND MRS. HAMILTON MCKOWN

VANDERBILT, MR. AND MRS. CORNELIUS

VANDERBILT, GEORGE W.

VAN RENSSELAER, MRS. A.

VAN RENSSELAER, MISS ALICE

VAN RENSSELAER, MISS MABEL

VARNUM, GEN. JAMES M.

WATERBURY, MR. AND MRS. JAMES M.

WEBB, GEN. AND MRS. ALEXANDER S.

WEBB, ALEXANDER S., JR.

WEBB, MR. AND MRS. W. SEWARD

WEBB, MISS CARRIE

WELLES, MR. AND MRS. BENJAMIN

WELLS, MR. AND MRS. W. STORRS

WETMORE, MISS

WETMORE, GOV. AND MRS. GEORGE PEABODY

WHITEHOUSE, MR. WORTHINGTON

WHITNEY, MR. AND MRS. WILLIAM C.

WHITTIER, MRS. C. A.

WILKS, MATTHEW ASTOR

WILLING, BARTON

WILLING, MISS

WILMERDING, MISS GEORGIANA L.

WILSON, GRACE

WILSON, MR. AND MRS. ORME

WILSON, RICHARD T., JR.

WINTHROP, MR. AND MRS. BUCHANAN

WINTHROP, MISS

WINTHROP, EGERTON

WINTHROP, F. B.

WYSONG, MR. AND MRS. J. J.

WHO KILLED SOCIETY?

"Who killed Cock Robin?"
"I," said the Sparrow,
"With my bow and arrow,
I killed Cock Robin."

"Who saw him die?"
"I," said the Fly,
"With my little eye,
I saw him die."

—Unknown, "The Death & Burial of Cock Robin"

WHO KILLED SOCIETY?

by CLEVELAND AMORY

HARPER & BROTHERS, PUBLISHERS, NEW YORK

91X.3
A82Aw

WHO KILLED SOCIETY?

Copyright © 1960 by Cleveland Amory

Printed in the United States of America

All rights in this book are reserved. No part of the book may be used or re-
produced in any manner whatsoever without written permission except in the
case of brief quotations embodied in critical articles and reviews. For information address Harper & Brothers, 49 East 33rd Street, New York 16, N.Y.

C-L

Library of Congress catalog card number: 60-15314

For My Mother,
Leonore Cobb Amory

CONTENTS

Forty-eight pages of photographs, by Slim Aarons, Jerome Zerbe and others, can be found in groups following pages 88, 248, and 408.

THE "FOUR HUNDRED"　　　　　　　　　　Front endpaper
COATS OF ARMS　　　　　　　　　　　　　Back endpaper

PART ONE　　　TITLE SEARCH

I. SOCIETY—*From the First Settlers to the International Setters*　3

II. ARISTOCRACY—*From Codfish to Coats of Arms*　59

III. CELEBRITY—*The Arbiters Are Biting: From Gibson Girl to Glamour Girl*　107

IV. SOCIAL SECURITY—*Clubs and Titles: From the Union Suit to the Windsor Knot*　189

PART TWO　　　FAMILY CIRCLE

V. NEW ENGLAND AND THE OLD SOUTH—*From Cabots, Lowells and Adamses to Byrds, Randolphs and Lees*　249

VI. NEW YORK, PHILADELPHIA AND POINTS WEST—*From Roosevelts, Du Ponts and Biddles to Ryans, Mellons and Phippses*　314

VII. MIDWEST, SOUTHWEST AND FAR WEST—*From Rockefellers, McCormicks and Fields to Big Fours and Little Fours*　368

VIII. FULL CYCLE—*From Jewish Grand Dukes Back to Astors, Vanderbilts and Whitneys and the Last of the Firsts*　442

PART THREE   THE PEOPLE'S CASE

IX.   MONEY, MANNERS AND MORALS   517

ACKNOWLEDGMENTS AND INDEX   553

PART ONE

TITLE SEARCH

Her mother was a Shaw and her father was a Tompkins,
Her sister was a bore and her brother was a bumpkins.
  Oh, Soci-, oh, Soci-, oh, Soci-i-i-i-ety!

Her flounces were of gold and her slippers were of ermine,
And she looked a little bold when she went to lead the German.
  Oh, Soci-, oh, Soci-, oh, Soci-i-i-i-ety!

For my part I never saw where she kept her fascination,
But I thought she had an awful conceit and affectation.
  Oh, Soci-, oh, Soci-, oh, Soci-i-i-i-ety!
                    —Julia Ward Howe, "The Sociomaniac"

The pedigree of honey
Does not concern the bee;
A clover, any time, to him
Is aristocracy.

                    —Emily Dickinson, *Poems*

Authors and actors and artists and such
Never know nothing and never know much . . .
People who Do Things exceed my endurance;
God, for a man that solicits insurance!

                    —Dorothy Parker

Hark! The herald angels sing—
Mrs. Simpson pinched our King.
          —Anonymous (English School Children, Christmas, 1936)

CHARLES DANA GIBSON

I

SOCIETY—*From the First Settlers to the*

International Setters

"MERCY! Society isn't a knit thing any more. It's everybody and his brother!"

The speaker was a lady who died in November, 1960, whose name was unknown to probably ninety-nine percent of even the most avid readers of Society pages and social news. Nonetheless, she was, and indeed had been for more than half a century, perhaps the most powerful single individual in that strange and mysterious force known as American Society. For her job, which she always called "position," had been, during all of that time, nothing less than editor and almost sole arbiter of a strange and mysterious little black book—the *Social Register.**

* This writer interviewed Mrs. Barry in 1957 but agreed to withhold publication of the interview until 1960.

3

Her name was Mrs. Edward C. Barry, and there is irony enough in the fact that this will, as the saying goes, "mean nothing" to Society. It is even more ironic, however, that this *Register*, which still presumes to tell not only the sheep from the goats but also the sheep's Married Maidens and Dilatory Domiciles—not to mention the fact that they are Gentiles, for the *Register* has often, and accurately, been accused of anti-Semitism—should have been for so long run by someone whose own "Married Maiden" name, Miss Bertha Eastmond, would to Society mean even less than nothing. And then there is perhaps the final irony of all—particularly in view of the fact that the *Register* seemingly lays such stress on "Family"—that Miss Eastmond's father was a humble railroad lineman.

Such ironies are, however, part and parcel of the whole picture of what passes, or perhaps has passed, for American Society in general. Mrs. Barry, in some contrast to so many others who have spent their lives propping up something they have never really understood, was not only a simple person but a modest one to boot. Formerly of Summit, New Jersey, she was long married to a Vermont lawyer and divided her time between Wilmington, Vermont, and, of all places, Tangerine, Florida. Not only had she never listed her own name in her *Register*, let alone her unprepossessing if not dilatory domiciles, but she had never given a single interview in her life—"unless," she said prophetically to this writer, "you count this one." Furthermore, from 1900 to 1960, all attempts to get information from her on the part of virtually all newspapers and magazines, varying from *Fortune* and *Vogue* to *Confidential* and *Whisper*, had ended in failure. In 1955, for example, the magazine *Life*, having failed in its effort to interview her, attempted to photograph her; and in so doing, they put her house in Tangerine in a virtual state of siege. Mrs. Barry and her husband barricaded the doors, locked and pulled down the shades of the windows, and stayed inside for a day and a night. The next morning, when provisions were beginning to run out, Mr. Barry called police and the forces of the magazine were dispersed in a brief but decisive front-lawn battle.

Among other things, *Life* missed a good picture. For Mrs. Barry was a memorable-looking person. A rather birdlike little woman but at the same time a handsome one, she was of extremely advanced years—yet even here secrecy and mystery were her watchword, as they have been in the running of her book. "I have many ages," she said in 1957. "I went over to the hospital for a blood count a while ago, and when they asked me how old I was, I said, 'You did me a year ago. Can't you add?' "

The strange and mysterious history of the *Social Register* would seem, by itself, a saga of the decline and fall of American Society. For all intents and purposes, of which it had many, it was started in 1887 by Louis Keller of Summit, New Jersey, a bumptious and rather affected little man who was the son of a patent lawyer and, in his own right, a gunsmith, a farmer, a dairyman, a bicycler and a golfer. Besides the *Register*, he founded such enterprises as the Baltusrol Golf Club, the League of American Wheelmen, the Wat Nong Dairy, and his so-called "Baltusrol and Pacific Railroad"—a one-locomotive system which ran, when it did, between Summit, Baltusrol and Newark. Keller was also, in the words of a former Calumet friend of his, "a gentleman, but just"—the latter, unfortunately, in its colloquial adverbial rather than adjectival sense. As for Mrs. Barry, then Miss Eastmond, also of Summit, New Jersey, she came into the picture as—at least so all accounts to date have had it—his secretary.

This report Mrs. Barry would neither confirm nor deny. "Oh," she said, with a knowing smile, "is *that* what they say? Well!" Married to a Vermonter of not only modesty but wit—"I was the best lawyer in town," he says, "until they got another"—she spent her summers at a Vermont farm so secluded that many of their neighbors did not even know of her work. As for the neighbors who did, they were philosophical. "The Barrys are simple, quiet, nice people," said one, "but it's a hell of a place for them when you come right down to it. God, around here we don't even have zoning!"

In latter days Mrs. Barry's work consisted of corresponding by letter and occasionally by telephone with the quaint and rather rundown-looking office of the Social Register Association—at the ironically far from "social" address of 381 Fourth Avenue—and in turn having its correspondents in different cities, most of whom are meagerly paid ex-Society editors, correspond with her about marriages, divorces, births, deaths, graduations from college, etc., all of which were dutifully clipped out of Society pages and sent to her. These correspondents were also supposed to keep in touch with Mrs. Barry for various socially suicidal crimes, such as going on the stage, publicly criticizing the *Register*, marrying somebody who is not in it or divorcing somebody who is. Up until comparatively recently, however, there has been no question, which Mrs. Barry, albeit modestly, made no bones about, that Mrs. Barry was definitely the sole boss. No one can be listed, even in San Francisco, in any other way than by applying to the New York office—a relatively easy procedure for a Gentile, provided it is accompanied by five letters from people already in—and such applications through the years have been invariably okayed or rejected by Mrs. Barry herself. In the same way no one could be, without her approval, delisted.

From such a woman, particularly in view of the seriousness which outsiders accord her *Register*, might be expected a rather thorough knowledge of American social history, genealogy and social perspective. Unhappily, apart from an abiding faith in a kind of curious, "Four Hundred"-vintage prominence and a vast distaste, seemingly, for any prominence since, Mrs. Barry had as little perspective, or so it seemed to this interviewer, as her modest background would indicate. Her farmhouse was piled with newspaper and magazine articles about the *Register*, almost all of which were critical and literally all of which, she maintained, were almost totally inaccurate. One even had the distinct feeling when talking with her that she regarded herself as presiding over a dying institution. In view of this, it is not surprising that of late years a good deal of her time was spent in worrying about her own future, as well as that of the *Register*—in other words, wondering who, in view of the anonymity in which she had lived, would write her obituary. "I wrote to a man in Washington about it a while ago," she said in the year 1957, a little sadly, "who at least knows *something* about me, but I haven't heard from him." As an example of the kind of thing she felt that "literally nobody knows" about her, she told us that when Keller was on his deathbed in 1922— "Literally," she said, "he could hardly speak"—she bent down and heard him whisper, "I count on you. Keep the *Register* running right."

In Mrs. Barry's firm opinion, this "has not been done." Furthermore, since in her view the *Register* is in many respects the last stand not only of Society as it once was but also, in her firm opinion, as it still should be, this is a great pity. For a while, she believed, the *Register*, if not Society in general, went swimmingly. Keller's nephew and heir, Charles Keller Beekman, a mild-mannered lawyer from Milburn, New Jersey, took over, and together with Mrs. Barry ran the *Register* to its 1925 peak, at which time it had twenty-one individual city volumes as compared to today's bare dozen. Mrs. Barry remembered that Beekman almost invariably told her on "difficult" cases to "use your own judgment." Finally, though, Beekman succumbed and Mrs. Barry made no bones about the cause. "Literally," she said, "he was hounded to death. He didn't enjoy being bothered about who was in and who was out the way some of them do now."

It is no secret that in the years since Beekman's demise Mrs. Barry had never seen eye to eye, or rather escutcheon to escutcheon, with the *Register*'s other heirs, the law firm of Beekman and Bogue. Mr. Bogue, too, is now unfortunately deceased, and this writer, at least, in telephoning to the firm, spoke to a very pleasant young man named Mr. Weiss. "I don't think anyone has any real interest in it any more," Mrs. Barry concluded, sighing, "except to—well, I better not say. But they've gone far afield—*far afield*," she repeated emphatically, "if you know what I mean. Insignificant people are getting in all over, even in Summit!"

By Summit, of course, Mrs. Barry meant Summit, New Jersey, not "at the Summit," in its 1960's usage. Nonetheless, since even a brief poll of "Old Summit"—in other words, the old-time Society of Summit, New Jersey—demonstrates that Summit itself regarded Mrs. Barry as none too significant—a quotation such as "No, Old Summit doesn't know her," is perhaps typical—Mrs. Barry's own indictment of Society as depicted in her own *Register* is not without irony in its own bailiwick. It is, therefore, probably as good a starting place as any for a more general inquest into the matter of who killed Society. For in the initial phase of our inquest we should certainly make clear that not only did Mrs. Barry, as our first witness for the prosecution, know, in that age-old Society phrase, "whereof she speaks," but she also knew, firsthand, of murder. Her own father, who was a Civil War captain before his railroad days and who was for many years separated from his wife, was finally, by a mental patient in Dayton, Ohio, shot and killed.

Other witnesses for the prosecution are not hard to find. Indeed, from Maine to California one hears an almost unbroken cry of woe that Society isn't—and even occasionally ain't—what she used to be. Nor is the subject confined to America. In fact, one lady of advanced years, living abroad, got so excited about the matter that she became something of a Mrs. Malaprop. "It is," she solemnly assured us, "a world wild thing." However exaggerated this seems, the fact remains that only yesterday, it appears to the Old Guard of today, there was definitely and definitively such a thing as Society. Furthermore, this was something definite and definitive not only to this Old Guard, but also to lesser people. It was deferentially and without today's self-consciousness reported on the Society pages—in the days when there still were Society pages—and it was comfortingly, if occasionally obsequiously, pictured in the rotogravures—in the days when photographers were not sought after and fawned over but, instead, occasionally "permitted" to take a picture. And, if this Society was more than occasionally gossiped about, still there was no such thing as today's gossip column.

There was, of course, the late *Town Topics*, but this was finally stopped—still another proof of the strength of Society itself. Indeed, so strong was this Society that it was, for better or for worse, piously promoted by virtually everybody who was anybody—in the days, of course, when this was not literally everybody. People who were out wanted to get in and people who were in did not, as so many do today, want to get out. All in all, it was a Society which was generally admitted, even by those who did not know what it meant, to mean a great deal. More than two centuries ago it was defined by Lord Chesterfield, in the country whence it came, as "good company . . . that company which all the people of the place call, and acknowledge to be, good company, notwithstanding the objections which they may form to some of the individuals who compose it." In America it had similar definitions, for if, again, Americans disapproved some of the individuals, they approved the idea, and particularly in America, as Don Marquis once said, "an idea is not responsible for the people who believe in it."

What might be called the "Stately Quo" of England did not, of course, transfer itself without some difficulty to the not so stately "States." Nonetheless, the Americans did their unlevel best, and the Society idea soon did not lack for definition, at least in the major cities. If one were a Bostonian, for example, one defined this Society idea by saying that in Philadelphia one asked who a person was, in New York one asked how much he or she was worth, and in Boston one asked what did he or she know. On the other hand, if one were a Philadelphian, one reversed the distinctions of Boston and Philadelphia. But all over the country the idea was the same, and if the late William Black exaggerated when he said "the American young man spent five-sixths of his waking time in asking himself if he was a gentleman," surely Mrs. John King Van Rensselaer did not when she said the "entertainments and ceremonies of Society were given more space than the proceedings of the Congress." For, as William Dean Howells once noted, "Inequality is as dear to the American heart as liberty itself," and it is only a step from this to arrive at something which passes muster for a Society definition of America: that all men may be born equal but most of us spend the better part of our born days in trying to be as unequal as we can.

And today, or yesterday, or perhaps even the day before yesterday, it is this very idea which, in the opinion of the few, has been challenged by the many. For almost overnight, it appears to these few, Society has, as an entity, been destroyed, dispatched and done in. At the same time, if there is still something going on which calls itself Society, that fact is, to these few, irrelevant, immaterial and inconsequential. Furthermore, there is, to these same few, clearly no question of either second-degree murder or even manslaughter. It is murder in the first degree—willful, premeditated and with malice aforethought.

Indeed, one can easily go a step further and imagine an arraignment, complete with all necessary writs, warrants and habeas corpuses. For such an inquest, one should have not only professional witnesses, such as Mrs. Barry, but also amateur ones. Fortunately for the case for the prosecution, these are not lacking—in fact one of the chief complaints about present-day Society, in comparison to previous eras, is that it is no longer amateur. Almost all the old-timers of today will tell you that they remember when Society was amateur in the real sense of the word—a lover of the arts—in the days before it became corrupted by an age turned pro, into a word meaning nonproficiency and hence poor. "Donkeys' ages ago," the late Mrs. Margaret Emerson, who died in 1959, used to say, "there was just as much the Age of the Amateur in Society as there was in anything else—perhaps more so." Mrs. Emerson, the mother of Alfred Gwynne Vanderbilt as well as of the country's first Glamour Girl No. 1, Gloria ("Mimi") Baker, believed, like so many other leading ladies of her generation, that she had lived through greater changes in one lifetime than had occurred in any previous social era. Among these changes, and not the least of them, is what happened to Society itself. "In my life," Mrs. Emerson gently concluded, "I saw the death of Society, and, if you ask me, 'it was murder!' "

Mrs. Emerson was philosophical—less so was one of her friends, who once solemnly assured us that the world had, socially speaking, changed more from the time of her girlhood to her old age than it had from the time of Julius Caesar to her girlhood. Such a comment is obviously food for thought, and so is the fact that to conduct any kind of indictment for the murder of Society, one finds so many complainants that, in deference to the subject under indictment, one is almost immediately forced to restrict them to *grandes dames*.

One of the foremost of these for close to half a century was un-

doubtedly New England's reigning dowager, Mrs. Augustus Hemenway, of Boston, a sister of Boston's late Bishop Lawrence. She died
in 1960 at the incredible age of 103. For almost a quarter of a century
she had been the only living member of her own Society, one which
she founded more than half a century ago, called The Society of
Those Still Living in the House They Were Born in. In her last
years she had, moreover, many other signal honors heaped upon
her. On her 100th birthday President Eisenhower sent her special
greetings, and a year later, when a fire broke out on her place on
Green Street, Milton, she not only took control of the situation but
confidently directed the fire-fighting operations. Such a woman's
views on Society were always worth hearing.

"Society," Mrs. Hemenway told us, shortly before her 100th
birthday, "is a Nineteenth Century word in a Twentieth Century
world. It is a word that can't be defined in the new world any more
than I can. It's gone with the wind—kaput—kaflooey." To Mrs.
Hemenway the modern world, which she defined as "a world of
M.C.'s, maître d's and all your other New Yorkese," was simply
unintelligible. And she was far from alone in this feeling; there were,
and indeed still are, other *grandes dames* in almost every city in the
country in thorough agreement with her. Even in far-off Houston,
the late Mrs. "Mimi Bird" King, grandmother of the present Sheppard King, ex-husband of belly-dancer Samia Gamal, would have
found kinship with Mrs. Hemenway. For the last years of her life
Mrs. King refused to read any modern newspapers at all. Instead
she had kept newspapers of twenty years before; these she reread
every day.

As of the 1960's, living *grandes dames* are hardly less adamant.
Mrs. William Woodward, Sr., of New York puts it in her character-
istically frank and democratic language. "The past was lousy," she
says, "in some ways, and it was small. In the old days it was Mrs.
Astor and Mrs. Vanderbilt and Mrs. Belmont and there you were.
It was all well defined. When Mrs. Belmont gave a dinner and Mrs.
Oelrichs came, they weren't speaking and, after dinner, the two
coteries went into separate rooms. And, if Mrs. Clews hadn't been

'taken up' by Mrs. Belmont, she would have been nothing. But she was—and so everything was all right. It was boring, a lot of it, and it may seem rather silly now—I remember dear old Harry Case telling me he'd run a block to see a girl's ankle—but just the same there was style. They were the Old Guard and now there just ain't no such thing."

Since to many people Mrs. Woodward herself represents Old Guard, there is, of course, irony here. Prominent long before the tragic shooting of her only son, she was born one of New York's famous Cryder triplets and was long married to one of New York's best-known bankers. Nonetheless, it's typical of Mrs. Woodward that she disowns such exalted rank. "No," she says, "I'm not Old Guard. We were poor and we weren't pretty. But my mother was very publicity-conscious and dressed us all alike and things like that, so we were pretty well known. Of course, in those days there wasn't any press the way there is today—just *Town Topics*—but there was a real Old Guard and they really had power. Now there isn't any Old Guard and the power they represented is all gone."

One New Yorker, formerly of Boston, who feels that along with the decline and fall of the Old Guard has gone the decline and fall of human values is Mrs. Chester Burden. Founder of one of New York's most famous debutante and party agencies, she combines, in a way, not only Boston and New York but also an amateur and a professional viewpoint. "Then people were different," she says. "They were fascinating and charming—men like Dana Gibson and his wife, Irene Langhorne. He was the most attractive man, bar none, I've ever met, and Irene—well, you just can't describe her. She *was* the Gibson Girl, and she *stood* so beautifully. It was distinction, that's all. Nowadays, distinction isn't what people want. It's finished."

In hearty agreement with these sentiments is New York's Mrs. Kimball Colby, a Roman Catholic *grande dame*, who was one of the few whose "calling list" was commandeered by the late Louis Keller for his *Social Register*. "There's just too few of us left," she says. "My children come into the room, kick their shoes off and behave like nothing. As for their children—mercy! In my day we wore laced shoes to help our ankles. This new generation will have terrible ankles." Mrs. Colby, who feels that Society in general has lost "all sense of proportion," still feels that Catholics have come a long way in what's left of Society but still have to combat prejudice. She even admits she has herself been part of this prejudice. "When Anne McDonnell was married to Henry Ford, dear old Mrs. Livingston and I had to stand on the street and watch them come out of the church. But it was all right—we deserved it." The only thing Mrs. Colby does not feel is all right is the kind of person who feels she is "understanding" the Catholics by saying, "Well, my cook says—" To these Mrs. Colby has a stern answer. "I suppose you'd ask your cook," she says, "which corner of the visiting card to turn down."

Chicago's Mrs. G. Alexander McKinlock, in recent years a year-round resident of "Vita Serena," her cottage at Palm Beach, is another ageless *grande dame*—in 1960 she was nearing 100—who feels that the Good Old Days of Society and gracious living are gone. "In the old days," she says, "everything was private. There were private houses and private parties and private balls and private yachts and private railroad cars and private everything. Now everything is public—even one's private life. In the old days we were taught self-control, even down to our expressions. Don't 'look out loud' I can remember being told, and I didn't. Now nobody has time for control or manners or anything. Everything's in such a hurry. Look at the *Saturday Evening Post*. It comes on *Tuesdays*. And people are like puppy dogs. They get married for a few minutes."

In Philadelphia, Mrs. Barclay Scull says it is useless even to try to find the old families. "Most of the Biddles and Cadwaladers now," she says, "are either in front of bars or behind bars." And the Quaker City's Mrs. A. Atwater Kent, Sr., a lady who in happier days cut one of the largest swaths in Society history, now feels the whole thing has come full cycle. "Today," she says, "the higher up you are the lower you are."

Such a sentiment is even echoed by probably the most distinguished of all this country's *grandes dames*, Washington's Mrs. Nicholas Longworth. Daughter of President Theodore Roosevelt and the famous "Princess Alice" of White House turn-of-the-century days, Mrs. Longworth modestly describes herself as "less wit than mimic, more wit than wise" and declares that "I have no sense of humor, just a sense of irony." Nonetheless, the lady who once said that the late Calvin Coolidge looked as if he had been "weaned on a pickle," has almost equally sharp words on the subject of what has happened to Society. "It shouldn't have happened to a dog," she says. "Society's absolutely nothing any more—or it's less than nothing, because it's just a word in the newspapers. The only people who know what it means don't use it because it doesn't mean anything any more. In the old days it was a tribal thing and it had a perfectly good point for its time. Now, either everybody's in or nobody, and anyway, it doesn't make much difference because, nowadays, the whole thing is just a question of what I call 'gilded slumming!' "

In Middleburg, Virginia, Miss Charlotte Noland, great-grand-mistress of Foxcroft, long recognized as *the* of America's private girls' schools, represents the seventh generation of her family to live on her property (she founded Foxcroft in 1914) and yet she now feels that in one generation the whole world has changed. "The 'Get-rich-quick' killed Society," she says. "In the old days they made fun of the people who were trying to keep up with the Joneses. Now nobody dares make fun of it because everybody does it. It just can't be done either. You can't put everybody on one level. They weren't born that way and they weren't meant to be that way. I don't care how many Russians or Chinese are in the world. It hasn't happened since the beginning of the Bible."

Out in California a lady who demands to be anonymous—"Out here," she says, "anonymity is the only distinction left"—concludes the discussion. "Just the other day," she says, "everybody knew who everybody *was*. Now nobody knows who anybody *is*—let alone was—which is probably lucky. We're all prisoners. You can't get anybody to do anything any more, and if you do you're sorry. We live in a servants' world and the servants won't even let us use the word. I don't know just when Society died, or who killed it, or what they killed, but it's gone all right, and it probably didn't have much of a funeral either. Even the funerals aren't what they were. The last one I went to had people in the front pew that I wouldn't have to my funeral over my dead body."

As a grand jury of *grandes dames*, ladies ranging in age from high seventies to low hundreds, the above represents a fair cross section—and if cross they are about the present state of Society, the fact remains that their comments are no less strong than those of the male contingent. Up in Newport, for example, Schuyler Livingston Parsons, who has been called the "last of the extra men," boils the matter down to a boiled shirt. "I simply cannot remember," he says quietly, "when I had a white tie on last." In Boston, Godfrey Lowell Cabot, at the age of 99 either chairman of the board or president of, among other things, Godfrey Lowell Cabot, Inc., Cabot Company, Cabot Carbon Company, and Cabot Shops, Inc., is perhaps the tersest of all. "Society today," he says, "bah."

At St. Simon's Island, Georgia, Newell Tilton, seasonally of Tuxedo, Newport, Palm Beach and Southampton, and the last of the species once known as *arbiter elegantiarum*—in the days, of course, before arbiters became biters only—delivers a formal obituary. "In my generally ignored opinion," he says, "there is no such thing as Society any more any where any time any how. The family standard is at half staff and the gold standard isn't either gold or a standard. The people who really are Society don't want to be associated with the ones who just think they are—so the ones who just think they are, are the only ones left. The whole thing's gone to hell in a hack."

In view of the sternness of these complaints, it is not surprising that many complainants have gone further and have named for the murder of Society actual suspects. Some, indeed, have even named each other. Lady Astor, for example, the former Nancy Langhorne and a sister of the late Gibson Girl, Irene, unhesitatingly nominated the Duchess of Windsor. The Duchess, at the time "feuding" with Elsa Maxwell, promptly named Miss Maxwell. Miss Maxwell, not to be outdone, named a rival of hers, whom, since she said she dislikes giving publicity to those she dislikes, she named anonymously.

Some nominated inanimate objects such as the times, while others blamed taxes. Some even nominated whole groups of people. For example, Sherman Billingsley, despite the fact that he was nominated himself, named "all the 'dese, dem and dose' girls who finally hook some guy and then spend the rest of their lives talking with marbles in their mouths." On occasion there were sharp turnabouts. Nominated for "manslaughter," for example—and a surprising number of women were named for this honor rather than the outright murder of Society—was Eleanor Searle, the ex-Mrs. Cornelius Vanderbilt Whitney No. 3. Eleanor, herself, nominated *Mr.* Whitney.

Young people generally worried little over the demise. "I don't know who killed what," says William Blair, Jr., scion of the distinguished Chicago Family, "but I'd like to call him up and congratulate him." On the other hand, the elder contingent were both distressed about the loss and definite about the cause. Out on Mackinac Island, W. Stewart Woodfill, courtly Victorian patriarch of the world's largest resort hotel, says gruffly, "Three things killed Society—the automobile and bad manners and no sense of history." As if to prove his thesis, he allows no automobiles on his island, devotes a large part of his life to the restoration of historic landmarks, and also owns the country's largest collection of canes. "No, *no*," he groans, "not *canes*, walking sticks, walking sticks! Don't you know *anything!*"

Most definite of all was Richard Lounsbery, distinguished New York clubman and speaker for inherited wealth; his grandfather owned the original farm on which the Kern County Land Company started and also discovered, along with George Hearst, the Homestake mine. "What killed Society," he says sternly, "is men marrying terrible women and no birth control and the United States government. The United States government makes the old robber barons look like children. The United States government robs every man, woman and child, every living, breathing moment from the day of their birth to the day of their death, and then if they've got anything left, they take that too."

In any case, as of the 1960's, a poll of voters' preferences for the murderers of Society, listed under their specific indictments, ran as follows:

I. *Murder in the First Degree*
   (1) With Deliberation, Premeditation and Malice Aforethought:
   >The Servant Problem
   >The Bureau of Internal Revenue
   >Hollywood
   >Franklin Delano Roosevelt
   >William Randolph Hearst, Sr.
   >The Duchess of Windsor
   >The Duke of Windsor
   >Walter Winchell
   (2) Without Deliberation, Premeditation or Malice Afore-thought, but Committed while Engaged in Another Felony:
   >Too Much Money (Wrong People)
   >Too Little Money (Right People)
   >"Quick" Money
   >Prohibition
   >The Depression
   >The Nightclub
   >Café Society
   >The Common Man
   >The Working Girl
   >World War I
   >World War II
   >The Cold War
   >Henry Luce
   >Harry Truman
   >Cholly Knickerbocker
   >Jack Paar
   >Antony Armstrong-Jones
II. *Murder in the Second Degree*
   With Design to Effect Death but without Deliberation, Premeditation or Malice Aforethought:
   >The Telephone
   >The Automobile
   >The Airplane
   >The Sputnik

The Red Russians
The White Russians
Mrs. Roosevelt
The Roosevelt Boys (except John)
Joseph P. Kennedy
The Kennedy Family
The Kelly Family
Sherman Billingsley
Serge Obolensky
Aristotle Onassis
John Jacob Astor VI
Cornelius Vanderbilt V
Cornelius Vanderbilt Whitney

III. *Manslaughter in the First Degree*
While Engaged in the Commission of a Misdemeanor:
Glamour Girl No. 1's
Poor Little Rich Girls
Cinderella Girls
Chorus Girls
Girls Smoking
Girls Drinking
Brenda Frazier
The Cushing Sisters
Barbara Hutton
Gloria Vanderbilt
"Cee-Zee" Guest
Liz Whitney
Eleanor Whitney
Mary Lou Hosford Whitney
Bobo Rockefeller

IV. *Manslaughter in the Second Degree*
(1) By a Person Committing a Civil Trespass:
Elsa Maxwell
Perle Mesta
Gwen Cafritz
Mme. Jolie Gabor
Mlle. Zsa Zsa Gabor
All Gabors (except Magda)
(2) In the Heat of Passion by the Use of a Dangerous Weapon
or by Cruel and Unusual Means:
Society Singers

Bermuda Shorts
Dorothy Kilgallen
(3) By any Culpable Negligence, such as Negligent Use of
Machinery, Care of Animals, etc.:
The Newport Jazz Festival
Southampton
Hope Hampton
The April in Paris Ball
The Diners' Club
Gamble Benedict

The complainants and witnesses for the prosecution make, as of
the 1960's, such a strong case, together with actual suspects, that the
case for the defense is, seemingly, a difficult one indeed. Without
stretching the point, however, one can easily picture the lawyer for
the defense making, in a sense, no defense while at the same time
making the strongest defense possible. For such a courtroom scene
one indeed imagines the lawyer for the defense arising and saying
he admits all the prosecution has charged. He even duly notes all
complaints. At the same time he asks only that something else should
be noted. This is, in fact, that for a long time people have been
saying that Society isn't what it used to be—for so long, indeed, that
one wonders, occasionally, when it ever was. Let us, for example—
and we now put ourselves in the position of the lawyer for the
defense—having admitted that Society as of the 1960's had its
shortcomings, try to pinpoint when it had no such failings. Let us
attempt, in short, to see when was Society when Society was—in
other words, when everything, socially speaking, was as it should be:

> In the general picture of this modern day, the smart and the
> near-smart, the distinguished and the merely conspicuous, the
> real and the sham, and the unknown general public, are all mixed
> up together. The walls that used to enclose the world that was
> fashionable are all down. Even the car tracks that divided cities
> into smart and not-smart sections are torn up. . . . There is no-
> where to go to see Best Society on Parade.

That is in 1950—from the introduction to the seventy-seventh
edition of *Etiquette*, by Mrs. Price Post, better known as Emily.

Once named by Ward McAllister, author of the "Four Hundred," as one of the ten ladies in New York who could gracefully cross a ballroom floor alone, Mrs. Post wrote the above at a time when the phrase "Café Society" was coined, as she said, "to apply to an unclassifiably mixed group of restaurant and night club habitués," and she felt that her words were "as applicable" in 1950 as they were when they were written. Since 1950 had its shortcomings, let us look again:

> There is no longer any real Society. Nowadays the only quali-
> fication for membership is to own, or rent, a dress suit—and soon
> we won't even do that. The individual man is passing, and it is no
> longer even smart to belong to a club. As for the individual
> woman, she is no longer even a woman, let alone an individual. In
> another fifty years we'll all dress alike, talk alike, smell alike and
> love alike. It won't be any fun.

That is 1945, and the speaker, late in his career, is the late Frank Crowninshield, the last of Society's acknowledged "arbiters." Editor *elegantiarum* of his magazine *Vanity Fair* and once called by one of the workers in his vineyard, Clare Boothe, the "last of the species known as 'gentleman,' " Mr. Crowninshield was, as we shall see, far from the last to complain of Society—even going backward. Let us go back another five years and have another late look—this time at New York's debutante parties of the so-called "Glamour" era:

> Those debutante parties in New York are the rendezvous of a
> gang of professional idlers—parasites, pansies, failures, the silliest
> type of sophomores, young customers' men from Wall Street
> and hangers-on. They are the very riff-raff of social New York who
> would exploit a child like Scottie with flattery and squeeze her
> out until she is a limp colorless rag. In one more year she can cope
> with them. In three more years it will be behind her. This year she
> is still puppy enough to be dazzled. She will be infinitely better off
> here with me than mixed up with that sort of people. I'd rather
> have an angry little girl on my hands for a few months than a
> broken neurotic for the rest of my life.

That is none other than the late F. Scott Fitzgerald himself, like the late Frank Crowninshield, speaking late in his career. This is

1940, and he is firmly of the opinion that his daughter, Scottie, would be better off in Hollywood with him than in New York—certainly, in view of the tragic neuroticism of Fitzgerald's own later life in Hollywood, a stern opinion of New York Society, particularly when we realize that Fitzgerald is talking about the very Society that he himself had once found so attractive. We are beginning to find out that even among the people who are so identified with their eras that they are credited with naming them, there is a noticeable difference between Society in distant retrospect and Society in immediate prospect. But now another five years:

> Because of the swift change in the current of events, Society has today grown out of its old formulas. The great social leaders of the nineties and the early hundreds have vanished. Money, rather than family, is the watchword which now opens the gates. If one wishes to be in Society one must have money and spend it —let Society feed on it, drink on it and gamble on it. Then one can be anything, go anywhere and do most anything one wants. For the truth is that today Society is bored with itself.

This is none other than the late Lady Mendl, Elsie de Wolfe, inventor of interior decorating and the lady who brought, not only to America but also to a whole Victorian world, her credo of "suitability, simplicity and proportion"—The time is now 1935, and the place is her autobiography, *After All.* But let us go on, even before her "after":

> Wholesale invasion of the best circles by the *nouveau riche* and the hordes of hangers-on is making places like Palm Beach no more exclusive than Coney Island. Newport, the last stronghold of the élite, has the moneyed intruder at the gates. At least one gentleman whose revenues are derived from the new and profitable industry of bootlegging has pushed the social football to the one-yard line. He may get through. Undesirables are penetrating everywhere.

That one is 1929 all right—at the height of the great boom. It is from an article entitled "The Price of Prestige," by the late Mrs. Jerome Napoleon Bonaparte. Mrs. Bonaparte once advertised for

Alfred Knopf that she never read anything but a Borzoi book. She
evidently wrote more widely, for this article appeared in the late
Collier's magazine. By now we are back over a quarter of a century:

> It is a far cry from the stately patrician Society that New York
> knew in pre-Revolutionary times to the loose, rather indiscriminate
> social circle of today. . . . To members of the old regime, who
> valued names above notoriety and lineage above bank books, New
> York Society as the average person uses the term today, is not
> composed to any great extent of either the socially elect or of
> New Yorkers. It is not that the old families, who were once all
> of Society, remain in Brahminlike aloofness from the people who
> today share in the life of the city's many times multiplied Four
> Hundred. But the proportions of Society itself have changed. The
> qualifications for admission have broken down or been altered.
> Society is no longer a unified entity.

That was from Mrs. John King Van Rensselaer's *The Social
Ladder*, and we are now back to 1924. Mrs. King, whose uncle-in-
law, Archibald Gracie King, was the first gentleman in New York
to give a ball elsewhere than under his own roof—at Delmonico's in
1870—was also the first girl to drive a pony phaeton up Fifth Avenue by herself and was branded "fast" for so doing. But she was by
no means by herself when it came to social complaints:

> Who are the leaders of New York Society today? Who are
> the present officers of the Minute Men? Who comprise the na-
> tional committee of the Bull Moose party? Where are the snows
> of yesteryear? Those questions are just as sensible. What is New
> York Society? There is no such thing. It isn't an entity any more.
> It has no fixed limits, as it once had. It hasn't had a leader since
> Mrs. William Astor's day. There are people in New York who
> are socially prominent. But they have no actual rank in Society
> because there isn't any Society.

When we get back to "Mrs. William Astor's day" (i.e., from
1880 to her death in 1908) we shall see what we shall see. But here
we are still talking of the 1920's—the quotation is unsocially titled
from *Jazz and Gin* from the socially titled Mr. Frederic Van de
Water. It is obvious, if we are going to get anywhere, even in

reverse, we must go back more rapidly than by five-year plans. Let us try again:

> Society, as I first remember it, was based on the old families. . . . They represented several generations of education and standing in the community. They had traditions running back not infrequently to the first white settlement and the days of Elizabeth and James. . . . The persons who now fill Society, as depicted in the depressing phrases and strange language considered suitable to the subject by the daily press, are for the most part the modern, very modern plutocrats who are widely different from their modest predecessors of the middle of the nineteenth century. . . . These newcomers have absorbed, in fact they are in large measure the *fons et origo* of the Society columns of the newspapers, which they fill with their performances, with their entertainments, their expenditures, their marriages, their divorces, and their scandals.

Here, speaking in his *Early Memories*, 1913, is the late Senator Henry Cabot Lodge, grandfather of the present Henry Cabot Lodge, Jr. Son of a Boston merchant, and a Salem Cabot, he was the man perhaps most responsible for scuttling the League of Nations, and, always a severe man socially, once fenced himself off with barbed wire from his own brother-in-law at the "Cold Roast Boston" resort of Nahant. Nonetheless, on the subject of American Society he knew indeed whereof he spoke. But let us try an even longer retrospective view. This time a look at Newport and New York:

> I often look back to those quiet days of Newport with positive regret. Then it was a place where one went to meet friends, not to make them; culture and charm were the passports into Society, but now wealth seems to be the Golden Key which unlocks most doors in this place of rich men's houses. Bellevue Avenue, with its mêlée of expensive cars and expensive owners, is as artificial as the unnatural-looking clumps of hydrangea which is Newport's favorite flower. What a contrast to the dignified Avenue as I remember it! But it is an age of change, and Newport has shared the universal fate. . . . In New York Society the older families never allowed the turmoil of outside life to enter their social scheme. The best houses were absolutely restful, and the present generation will never know the charm and tranquillity which was manifest

whenever people like Mrs. Schermerhorn, Mrs. William Astor, Mrs. John Jacob Astor, Mrs. Belmont and Mrs. Paran Stevens entertained their friends.

Here, in 1913, is a gentleman speaking of "universal change" at a time which is generally regarded today as the heyday of the Golden Age. The quotation is from *Things I Remember* by Frederick Townsend Martin, a gentleman who was at that time called, as the late Frank Crowninshield was later to be called, "the last of the arbiters of a crumbling Society." But if Mr. Martin was wrong about change in Society, he was right about there being a change in times, for the year 1913 saw, of course, the passage of the Sixteenth Amendment, authorizing Congress to impose taxes on incomes, "from whatever source derived." But let us deduct still more years:

> Were I not afraid of appearing to strike to excess the so-called pessimistic note, I should really make much of the interesting, appealing, touching vision of waste. . . . The show of the case today—oh, so vividly and pathetically!—is that New York and other opulence, creating the place (Newport) for a series of years, as part of the effort of "American Society" to find out, by experiment, what it would be at, now has no further use for it—has only learned from it, at immense expenditure, how to get rid of an illusion. . . . Newport is only one of these mistakes; and we feel no confidence that the pompous New York houses, most of them so flagrantly tentative, and tentative only, bristling with friezes and pinnacles, but discernibly deficient in reasons, shall not collectively form another. It is the hard fate of new aristocracies that the element of error, with them, has to be contemporary—not relegated to the dimness of the past, but receiving the full modern glare, a light fatal to the fond theory that the best society, everywhere, has grown, in all sorts of ways, in spite of itself. We see it in New York trying, trying its very hardest, to grow, not yet knowing (by so many indications) what to grow *on*.

And that, of course, given away by his trademark style, is none other than Henry James. Speaking in 1906, in *The American Scene*, he brings us back a full half century. Where is Mrs. Astor's restful day? Apparently there is no rest for the social weary. And, it appears, we are just beginning. For now let us turn, from the sublime to the ridiculous, even farther back, to a far different kind of write-up:

> I sympathize deeply with my friend Ten Broek Van Rotterdam, who says Society is going to the dogs—that is the Knickerbocker side of it, and "Good Gawd! dear boy, what other side is there?" Look at the list. How many of the swellest of the swell today were anything at all twenty years ago—fifteen years ago even? Where were the Vanderbilts, socially, even five years ago? The Astors had just fifteen years the social start. The Vanderbilts in fifteen more will have come up to an equality, and I prophesy they will eventually lead, partly because there is more gold on the young male, and more brass on the young female side of their house. Where, indeed, are the Knickerbockers now? Even twenty years ago, they led, they directed, they swayed social festivities with an undisputed sceptre; they were in, and all others were out; the Astors themselves, but twenty years ago, meekly accepted the patronage of the wife of the last Patroon, of the great Livingstons, of Suydams, of Van Courtlandts, Stuyvesants, De Peysters, Lispenards, de Reuters, Schermerhorns and Van Blatherskites. Now persons whom they would never have condescended to meet lord it over all, while they—poor decayed splendor!—sit in grim state in cheap boarding-house parlors and dream of the days forever dead to them, of the glory that never, never shall be theirs again. Well, why not? Who were the Knickerbockers, anyway? How many distinguished men has the whole tribe produced? They came, and were great only in their own little fussy Dutch opinions; they have gone, and there is not a mourner. What they were, let us judge by the few miserable little paupers trotting around the ragged edge of society now with nothing under heaven to thank God for but a name, and that part being forgotten. Hoopla! In fifteen years more most of the ups will be down. But, meantime, Lord! how we apples swim!

That is, of all things, 1887—a "Chat from the Clubman" in the most famous of all Society journals, the late *Town Topics*. This paper, published under the awful auspices of the late, unlamented "Colonel" Mann, was the predecessor of today's "gossip" column. But even with such trouble in the 1880's we must keep to our task, and in our flight another backward turn of the clock brings us, if not a different note, at least a welcome change in style:

The New York of Newland Archer's day was a small and slippery pyramid, in which, as yet, hardly a fissure had been made or a foothold gained. At its base was a firm foundation of what Mrs. Archer called "plain people," an honorable but obscure majority of respectable families who had been raised above their level by marriage with one of the ruling clans. People, Mrs. Archer always said, were not as particular as they used to be; and with old Catherine Spicer ruling one end of Fifth Avenue, and Julius Beaufort the other, you couldn't expect the old traditions to last much longer.

Here, unmistakably, is the greatest social stylist of them all, the one and only Edith Wharton, and, though the names are fictitious, Mrs. Wharton's fiction was no stranger to truth. This selection is from *The Age of Innocence*, a novel which had the distinction of naming its age—the New York of the 1870's—although it was not published until half a century later. By now we are nearing another postwar period:

It is undeniable that changes, and changes not for the better, have been taking place during the last few years in American social life in every quarter of the Union. . . . Since the conditions of things during the war enabled men to amass fortunes in an incredibly short time, and the discovery of oil in almost worthless lands gave them suddenly immense value, the "shoddy" and "petroleum" element has been prominent in circles composed of wealthy persons inclined to scatter their money profusely for the purpose of display. These leaders of gayety flutter in the admiring gaze of the stupid and ignorant masses. . . . It is very easy to create a sensation in New York, or any other large city. Where there is a display of unbounded wealth, such old-fashioned articles as morality and good taste are often despised.

This is 1868, from a book entitled *Queens of American Society* by Mrs. E. F. Ellet. Even the oil folks, it appears, are not new but, at least as far as new riches go, old folks indeed. And, in still another complaint, money was again the root of all equality:

How New York has fallen off during the last forty years! Its intellect and culture have been diluted and swamped by a great flood-tide of material wealth . . . men whose bank accounts are all they can rely on for social position and influence. As for their ladies, not a few who were driven in the most sumptuous turnouts, with liveried servants, looked as if they might have been cooks or chambermaids a very few years ago.

Here is the recently unearthed diary of George Templeton Strong, New York gentleman and scholar. Strong kept his diary from 1835 to 1875. For fifty years after his death, its four and a half million words were a family secret; not for another quarter of a century was publication permitted. It has since become one of the most famous and valuable American diaries. As for this entry, it is 1864, four years after the outbreak of the Civil War. From the Southern side of the fence there was hardly more reassuring news:

> Free Society! We sicken at the name. What is it but a conglomeration of greasy mechanics, filthy operatives, small-fisted farmers, and moon-struck theorists? All the northern, and especially the New England states, are devoid of Society fitted for well-bred gentlemen. The prevailing class one meets with is that of mechanics struggling to be genteel, and small farmers who do their own drudgery, and yet are hardly fit for association with a southern gentleman's body servant.

That is a part of an article from the Muscogee (Georgia) *Herald*, which was reprinted by the New York *Tribune* on September 10, 1856. By now we are back more than a full century, and, by way of celebration, let us take a look at an item inspired by what was then, as now, the favorite reading of Society—the obituary page:

> Died yesterday, Mr. James Roosevelt, in the eighty-eighth year of his age; a highly respectable gentleman of the old school, son of Isaac Roosevelt, the first president of the first bank of New York, at a time when the president and directors of a bank were other sort of people from those of the present. Proud and aristocratical, they were the only nobility we had—now we have none.

In this case, the date of the "now" is 1847; the source is the celebrated *Diary of Philip Hone*. Hone's diary, like Mr. Strong's, was not written with a view to publication, but Hone maintained it from 1828 to within five days of his death, which occurred in

1851, four years after this entry. Once mayor of New York and one of the founders of the Union Club, Hone himself could see both sides of every question—even of Society. But if New York Society was, in Hone's day, the worse for wear, let us have a look at the Golden West:

> The stream flows inland, and those who are here today are gone tomorrow, and their places in Society filled by others who ten years back had no prospect of ever being admitted. All is transition, the waves following one another to the far West, the froth and scum boiling in advance.

That is another diarist speaking, the irrepressible Captain Frederick Marryat. Unlike Strong and Hone, Marryat was not American but English. But his novels of the 1830's were almost as widely read in the States as in England. In any case, the date is 1839, his book *A Diary in America*. But, if there was "froth and scum" in the West, there was also trouble in the East, right in the middle of the White House:

> The old man [President Jackson] stood in the center of a little circle, about large enough for a cotillion, and shook hands with everybody that offered. The number of ladies who attended was small; nor were they brilliant. But to compensate for it there were a throng of apprentices, boys of all ages, men not civilized enough to walk about the room with their hats off; the vilest promiscuous medley that ever was congregated in a decent house; many of the lowest gathering around the doors, pouncing with avidity upon the wine and refreshments, tearing the cake with the ravenous keenness of intense hunger; starvelings, and fellows with dirty faces and dirty manners; all the refuse that Washington could turn forth from its workshops and stables.

The speaker is the historian George Bancroft; the date is 1831. He writes of one of the famous levees of that democrat of Democrats, Andrew Jackson. And, at the same time, for a more detached view of the country as a whole, let us turn to another source:

> And now, after a lapse of a little more than sixty years [from the beginning of the Revolution], the aspect of Society is totally altered; the families of the great landed proprietors are almost all

commingled with the general mass. In the state of New York, which formerly contained many of these, there are but two who still keep their heads above the stream; and they must shortly disappear. The sons of the opulent citizens have become merchants, lawyers, or physicians. Most of them have lapsed into obscurity. The last trace of hereditary ranks and distinctions is destroyed; the law of partition has reduced all to one level.

Here, writing of his trips which began in 1831, is the Frenchman, Alexis Charles Henri Maurice Clérel de Tocqueville; his *Democracy in America* was destined to become a classic. And, lest anyone believe that anti-Semitic prejudice is a new issue in Society, let us turn to the first in a long line of British critics:

> We went to a party last night at Mrs. Van Rensselaer's, the Patroon's . . . The outer room was, as usual, bare of furniture except for the awful range of seats next to the walls, to me all the more formidable and dull because of the difficulty of any gentleman inserting himself in the room, and as the truth ought to be told I must confess that the ladies I have yet met are very dull companions, so exceedingly commonplace. I am afraid you will think that I affect to like no society except that of gentlemen. As far as this country is concerned I must plead guilty to the charge, but I deserve the reproach no further. I am extremely amused with the motley company we meet here, Senators, lawyers, actors, editors of newspapers, one of them a Jew, all placed indiscriminately at table and all joining equally in the conversation.

The writer of this letter was understandably bitter. Born Margaret Hunter, on the day of George Washington's death, she later married Basil Hall, grandson of the Lord Selkirk whose silver plate had been raided by John Paul Jones. Jones, however, later returned the plate. Mrs. Hall's *Outspoken Letters* (1827-1828) were never taken back; instead they were promptly published. Meanwhile, in case anyone shall believe that such a Society phenomenon as the servant problem also is a new issue, let us turn to another foreigner:

> The servants are generally negroes and mulattos; most of the white servants are Irish; the Americans have a great abhorrence of servitude. Liveries are not to be seen; the male servants wear

frock coats. All the families complain of bad servants and their impudence, because the latter consider themselves of an equality with their employers. Of this insolence of servants I saw daily examples.

This is from *Travels in North America* by a German, Karl Bernhard, Duke of Saxe-Weimar-Eisenach. He arrived in gaslit New York in 1825. But, to return to a native son, let us again look more generally:

As might be expected, the general Society of New York bears a strong impression of its commercial character. In consequence of the rapid growth of the city, the number of families that may be properly classed among those which have long been distinguished in its history for their wealth and importance, bears a much smaller proportion to its entire population than that of most other places. . . . It is not difficult to see that Society in New York, in consequence of its extraordinary increase, is rather in a state of effervescence than settled, and, where that is the case, I presume you will not be surprised to know, that the lees sometimes get nearer to the surface than is desirable.

That is a native of the natives, no less than the old Indian writer James Fenimore Cooper himself. His reference to the "Lees" has, of course, nothing to do with the distinguished Southern family of that name. Here Cooper uses it in the sense of that which settles from a liquid; sediment or dregs. His book, *The Travelling Bachelor*, which was written in defense of America from foreign attacks and was not published until 1828, was concerned with the early years of the Nineteenth Century and so brings back almost to George Washington's day.

With all the opulence and splendor of this city, there is very little good breeding to be found. We have been treated with assiduous respect; but I have not seen one real gentleman, one well-bred man, since I came to town. At their entertainments there is no conversation that is agreeable; there is no modesty, no attention to one another. They talk very loud, very fast, and altogether. If they ask you a question, before you can utter three words of your answer, they will break out upon you again, and talk away.

This is no less than Bostonian John Adams, second President of the United States, commenting on New York, where he spent a month en route to the Continental Congress in the fall of 1774. And, again, we find the age-old story:

> At this time, the furniture and expenses of every tradesman now equal those of the merchant formerly; those of the merchant surpass those of the first rate gentleman; those of the gentleman, the old lords, &c. All other nations have each their favorite luxury; as the Italian his pompous palace, the Frenchman his fine suit, the Pole his splendid equipage, the German his capacious cellar, the Spaniard his bead roll of titles, &c. But our taste is universal; & there is scarce a little clerk among us, who does not think himself the outcast of Providence, if not enobled by his salary, fees, etc., to outlive the rich man in the Gospel.

This date is 1747; the source, a burgomaster's admonition against "the Prevalence of Luxury." Lest anyone need still further proof that, if there is anything new under the sun, it does not come under the head of Society, let us take a last look at New England. There was the devil to pay in, of all places, Boston:

> The Courte expresses its utter detestation that men and women of meane condition, education, and calling, should take uppon them the garb of gentleman by wearinge of gold or silver lace, or buttons or poynts at their knees, or walke in great boots, or women of the same ranke to weare silke or tiffany hoods or scarfs.

This is the Massachusetts Bay Court speaking. The date is 1651, and we are now back well over three centuries. And, obviously, we are also back where we started from. So, with a bow to the inevitable, let us end at the very beginning and see what sort of men started all the trouble in the first place:

> All this time we had but one Carpenter in the Countrey, and three others that could doe little, but desired to be learners: two blacksmiths, two saylers, & those we write labourers were for the most part footmen, and such as they that were Adventurers brought to attend them, or such as they could perswade to goe with them, that never did know what a dayes worke was, except the Dutch-men and

Poles, and some dozen other. For all the reast were poore Gentlemen, Tradesmen, Serving-men, libertines, and such like, ten times
more fit to spoyle a Common-wealth than either begin one or but
helpe to maintaine one. For when neither the feare of God, nor the
law, nor shame, nor displeasure of their friends could rule them here
[in England], there was small hope ever to bring one in twentie
of them ever to any good there [in Virginia].

And that, finally, is the story of the colony of Jamestown, 1607,
by the one and only Captain John Smith himself, the full title being,
*The Generall Historie of Virginia, New England & The Summer
Isles Together with The True Travels, Adventures and Observa-
tions, and A Sea Grammar by Captaine John Smith, Sometimes
Governour in those Countryes and Admirall of New England.*

In view of such testimony it would be a bold deponent who would
predict, in any given year, the end of Society, much less declare, in
any given year, its outright murder. For if, as our brief excursion into
history has shown us, people have complained about Society not
being what it used to be for some 350 years, the stark, inescapable
conclusion seems to be that Society, as such, never was—or at
least never was in the entire White life of the country. As for the
Red life, even here the record is none too sanguine. Henry Hudson,
voyaging onto Manhattan Island in 1609, invited a picked group of
"chiefe men"—presumably the top drawer of Indian Society—to
dinner on board his *Halve Maen*, or *Half Moon*. Whereupon, it is
recorded, a sizable contingent of them promptly partook too heavily
of the beverages provided, and afterwards both they and other red
men started more serious trouble. Thus, while we are searching for
homicide, or perhaps even suicide, we should not arbitrarily rule
out the possibility of massacre.

There is, however, another stark, inescapable conclusion here.
This is that, if Society never existed in any form which was not
regularly and severely criticized, we already have, in a sense, our
corpus delicti—which is not, as so often thought, the body of the
victim, but rather the body of evidence, or basic facts necessary

to the commission of the crime. These facts, in the opinion of present-day complainants, we have aplenty, and if we also had the same facts all the way back to Captain John Smith, that still does not change the basic charge. We still have our *corpus* all right—it is just rather more *delicti* than we might have thought.

Unwittingly, we would also seem to have provided our motive. For while it is quite clear that Society in America has always been, to those who are not in it, a bad thing, it is equally clear that, to those who are in it, there is no such thing as Society at all—or at least there is no such thing in comparison to former days. So obviously there was, on the part of these inmates, boring from within —unhappily in all senses of the word. And, if Society was in truth dispatched, destroyed and done in, then it is far from immaterial, irrelevant and inconsequential to point out that the crime was in all probability an inside job. It might, of course, have been committed by someone who, once in, wanted out, or it might have been committed by someone who, once out and then taken in, ran, in his or her disillusionment, amuck.

We must, however, suspect everything, even motives, and particularly complaining ones. For, while a relative newcomer like Miss Elsa Maxwell may declare, as she often has, that to complain about Society is to prove you are out of it—a view which should have served to keep down the complaints—actually, as we have seen in our 350-year excursion, the exact reverse is true. Moreover, as not only history but also as any true *grande dame* will tell you, it always has been true. One presents, as it were, one's calling card by one's complaint. For example, to say that present-day Society is fine, great shape, wonderful people, etc., is tantamount to an admission that one has never known better and one's calling card, or card of admission, is—or at least once was—the fact that one *has*, that one belonged before the present. Otherwise, one is obviously open to the charge of being newly arrived, or, as the French put it, *nouveau*, *parvenu* or even *arriviste*. And that, of course, is, socially speaking, far worse than being suspected of murder.

By the use of those French words we have, without malice aforethought, brought up still another point. For if we must be suspicious of American suspects, we must be equally on guard against foreigners. This is because, while our American suspects may have, as we have seen, bored from within, there is no question but that a host of foreigners have, since the beginning, bored from without. Indeed, the possibility of a foreign angle to our social homicide beggars the International Set itself. For without the deference of American Society to all things British—from the Court to the English accent —and without its dependence on all words French—from the *élite débutante* to the *soignée grande dame*, from the *chic fiancée* to the *décolletée divorcée*, from the *savoir faire* and the *au fait* of the *haut monde* to the *pas comme il faut* and *faux pas* of the *nouveau riche*—it is very doubtful if it could have made any headway at all, let alone have got up enough steam to get itself murdered. Indeed, one may say, without fear of domestic contradiction, at least, that American Society has, from the very beginning, acted British, talked French, and behaved like the Devil.

Any inquest into the murder of Society should properly begin with an examination of the word—and it soon appears that what has happened to this word is by no means the least interesting of the things that have happened to Society itself. Only a generation ago the newspapers boasted not only *bona fide* Society pages but also whole sections which were often almost entirely devoted to the goings on of Society. Now not only have these goings on, figuratively speaking, gone, but also we have no real Society pages, in the old sense, at all. Some newspapers, it is true, still do use the word, among them such a distinguished journal as the *New York Times*, but exactly what they mean by the use of the term—particularly in the sense of who does and who does not come under its heading —would seem to be a difficult problem. The *Times*, for example, is one of the few journals which do not give in to the racial or creedal prejudices of what might be termed its "Old Guard" Society-page readers—proof positive of which came on September 12, 1954, when, for the first time in *Times* history, a Negro girl was given, on the Society page, under "Weddings," a "spread story with photo" —in other words, the full treatment.*

Outside of New York, where, ironically, there is a good deal more, rather than less, Society in the old sense, the majority of papers have given up on the word entirely and now call their Society pages "Women's pages" and put whatever Society they might think they have under "Women's News." Whether this is for lack of interest on the part of male readers or a curious belief that Society has, like Christine Jorgenson, changed gender, the fact remains that this is one of the most extraordinary and little-noticed changes which have taken place in journalism in recent years. So stealthily has the whole thing been done that a view such as that expressed by the assistant managing editor of the Indianapolis *News* is perhaps typical. "We still use the word 'Society' on our interoffice memos and stuff," he says, "but we've dropped it entirely for the paper. It's always just 'Women' now."

As for Charleston, South Carolina, where Society in the old sense is still not only old but also news, publisher Peter Manigault of the *News & Courier* has very much the same kind of story to offer. "We still refer to the presiding lady as 'Society Editor' and loosely to her office and her section in the paper as 'Society.' But since about World War II, the designation in the index card sometimes on the page has been 'Women's News.' There seems to have been no great deliberation about the change—it just struck somebody that since more and more copy about cooking, dressmaking, etc., was being carried, 'Society' just wasn't accurate." And out in California, where the job is unquestionably a most difficult and thankless one, the Los Angeles *Times* has thrown up its hands at the whole thing and now lumps the entire question under the word "Family"—a solution

* The couple were married in the chantry of St. Thomas Church by Dr. Brooks. The bride, Louise Ann Dickson, the daughter of Mr. and Mrs. David Augustus Dickson of Portland, Maine, is a graduate of Radcliffe College, where she was president of the student government association and a Phi Beta Kappa. The groom, James Theodore Irish, Jr., of Mount Airy, Pennsylvania, is a graduate of Bowdoin and also studied at the University of Florence. The groom's father and two sisters of the bride—one in New York and one in East Lansing, Michigan—are doctors.

which, if nothing else, is perhaps reminiscent of the definition of Los Angeles Society on the part of the late Miss Ethel Barrymore. "Los Angeles Society," she once said, "is anybody who went to High School."

The same newspapers which have such doubts about the word "Society"—whether because of concern for its present-day meaningfulness or because of increased concern for "social" conscientiousness—have no such doubts about the rest of the Society vocabulary. Adjectival and adverbial uses of the word have, paradoxically, suffered no such eclipse as the noun from which they were derived, and phrases like "socially prominent" and even "socially impeccable" abound in almost every kind of newspaper write-up, from gossip columns to obituaries. And yet, if these phrases mean anything, surely they should be subject to the same suspicion as their root. Beyond this, if sins are committed in the name of these phrases, let us look for a moment at what sins are committed in associated words and phrases—phrases such as "well bred" and "well born," "well connected" and even "to the manner born." Here it is immediately apparent that we are dealing with a one-way street. For if our democracy still permits these phrases, it most certainly does not countenance their opposites. Whoever today, for example, would be so bold as to tell someone he was "badly bred," "badly born" or "badly connected"? Furthermore, if our democracy has allowed such phrases to traffic in one direction, it will not grant them the right to proceed without humor. Thus, as long as a half century ago, we find Mark Twain defining "good breeding." "It consists," he said, "in concealing how much we think of ourselves and how little we think of the other person."

All these phrases, part and parcel of the vocabulary not only of newspaper Society editors but also of the Society *grandes dames*, are, of course, in one way or another almost totally suspect. Thus "well born," which long ago Seneca defined as "one who is by nature fitted for virtue," has become, in our social vocabulary, someone whose family was a member of Society. Yet we have already demonstrated that one man's Society is another man's *hoi polloi—*

which is at least one non-French word which made the grade despite the fact that it would, as of the 1960's, hardly be understood, let alone recognized by the very people it was originally intended to designate.

The phrase "to the manner born" is a particular stickler—in fact, so consistently do so many people spell the word, Shakespeare to the contrary, "manor" that only a short time ago lexicographer Charles Early Funk had to make a public reminder that Hamlet said "manner." "When you use the phrase," Dr. Funk said sternly, "bear in mind that it refers to a habit or practice, a custom of the people; it has nothing to do with rank or aristocracy or high estate, as would be implied by the word 'manor.' "* Unfortunately, Dr. Funk was not in time to correct the writing, in 1899, of *The Theory of the Leisure Class* by Thorstein Bunde Veblen. "The ways of heredity are devious," Veblen wrote, "and not every gentleman's son is to the manor born."

Finally, as for the phrase "well connected," this would seem to fit the modern idea of having contacts perhaps better than the old-fashioned idea of having family connections. Certainly its earlier usage seems almost as dated today as the famous Baltimore story, best told by Francis Beirne, of Baltimore's late Rebecca Shippen. Born a Nicholson and descended from the Lloyds of Wye House, Mrs. Shippen was asked by a friend of hers if it had ever occurred to her that if Our Lord had come to Baltimore she would never have met Him—since His Father was, after all, a carpenter. "But, my dear," replied Mrs. Shippen, "you forget. On His Mother's side He was well connected."

In several other cities similar "well connected" stories exist, notably in Boston, where there is the story of the small Hallowell boy who went over to the Saltonstall house, across Brush Hill Road, for his first overnight visit. That evening the Saltonstalls, fearing homesickness, left their young visitor's door open and were almost imme-

---

* Hamlet, in Act I, Scene 4, explains to his friends a royal drinking custom, then adds, "But to my mind, though I am a native here and to the manner born, it is a custom more honored in the breach than in the observance." His phrase has, it might be added, been similarly so honored.

diately surprised to hear him, in a man-to-man Boston voice, start his prayers. "Our Father who art in Heaven," he said, "Saltonstall be Thy Name." Thinking the boy was nervously upset, the Saltonstalls did nothing about it until breakfast the next morning. Then, apologetically, they admitted they had overheard his prayer and asked if he always said it like that. "Oh, no," he replied politely, "in my house I always say, 'Hallowell be Thy Name.' "

In Pittsburgh, of all places, the story translates only slightly differently. There, in deference to the "social" suburb of Sewickley and more particularly to the famous family of Nevin, the boy begins his prayer, "Our Father who art a Nevin." And in this same city, where not even Sewickley outranks the awesome "Heights," Mrs. James B. Davis adds the further intelligence that, while teaching Sunday school there, she distinctly heard one child singing, not "Glory to God in the Highest" but simply "Glory to God in the Heights." To a child in Pittsburgh the thought that the Almighty could live anywhere else was apparently unthinkable.

Turning to more mundane usage, we find an equal multitude of semantic sins in our social vocabulary. What, for example, do we mean by as simple a word as "snob"? We mean, it seems, a person who looks down on someone else. And yet there are three, and only three, defensible derivations of the word. The first is the simplest: that it was, like so many social words, derived from a contraction of the French *sans noblesse*. The second is the first dictionary definition of the word: "a person having no wealth or social rank; one of the common people"—a definition which comes from the fact that "snob" originally meant a shoemaker or cobbler, then later came to mean a person ashamed of that lowly estate. The third theory is that the word originated in Cambridge University where it was slang for anyone not a gownsman—or, in other words, a townsman—and where, according to legend, a boy wrote after his name "S.N.O.B." to signify that he was *sine* (without) nobility. All three meanings are close to the exact opposite of our one and only present usage—still another irony of the social vocabulary.

For a final irony, let us look at a well-integrated—or perhaps we should say well-segregated—part of the "snob" vocabulary, the word "exclusive." So often used in connection with clubs that it has—as indeed have so many words—all but lost its meaning, the word is the bane of America's "private," or, as they now prefer to call themselves, "independent" schools. In any case, it was perhaps most lastingly defined by the late Austin O'Malley. "Exclusiveness," he once said, "is a characteristic of recent riches, high Society and the skunk."

Now that we are over these hurdles, let us take another group of Society phrases, perhaps the most overworked group of all—phrases such as "old family," "good family," or even "nice family." What, we may ask, do we mean by these?

Once again it becomes immediately apparent that while our democracy will permit them—in fact, it uses them *ad nauseam*—it will not countenance their reverse. In other words, we never hear phrases such as "new family," "bad family," or, to balance "nice family," perhaps "naughty family." But, since "nice family" is actually a euphemism for a family both "old" and "good" and since both "old" and "good" family apparently mean, to users, the same thing, we are once more back to the same kind of phrase as "socially prominent" or even "socially impeccable." But what *does* it mean? Does it mean, for example, that someone's family goes back many generations? It seems it does not, for all of us, presumably, go back many generations—indeed, literally all of us, save the illegitimate, had recognizable fathers, grandfathers, great-grandfathers, and so on *ad* Adam. Such phrases must refer, then, back to some social distinction. Thus we are forced, unwillingly or not, to a definition. A good family, it seems, is one that used to be better.

One thing is certain. Such phrases as "old family" and "socially prominent" do not mean social distinction or prominence of demonstrably long duration. To illustrate, let us take the case of *Life* vs. the Society of the Cincinnati—*Life* being the magazine and the Society being something which has nothing to do with the city of Cincinnati except that both were named in honor of the Roman dictator who returned to plowing after rescuing the Army. The Society of the Cincinnati has a membership which entails direct descent from the officers of the Continental Army. Besides this distinction, there is another qualification—there can be only one representative descending from each of the originals who were eligible in 1783. Founded in that year by Generals Heath, Steuben and Knox, the Society chose as its patron Louis XVI, boasted George Washington as its first president, Alexander Hamilton as its second. It has long been regarded as the oldest, longest lasting, and easily the most distinguished attempt to set up an Aristocracy in America. At present there are something over 1,500 members. Yet when in the summer of 1956, at Newport, the Cincinnati was holding its triennial convention and *Life* had sent representatives, including one of its leading photographers, to do a "Life Goes to a Party," the magazine gave up the assignment in a matter of hours. "They just weren't social enough," said one of the magazine's representatives. Later asked what he meant, the young man, in the time-honored manner, elucidated: "There were not any people with a ranking social status or prominence who talked at cocktails while a group of proper-looking people gathered around and hung on every word."

If ancestral distinction back to 1783 is not "social," let us next see if present-day users of the word mean *original* social distinction. Again it seems they do not. For it is quite apparent that the F.F.V.'s (First Families of Virginia), the D.A.R.'s (Daughters of the American Revolution), the S.M.D.'s (Society of Mayflower Descendants), laudable as they may or may not be, do not by any stretch of the invitation mean that their present-day descendants are members of present-day Society. Nor even do they mean, ironically enough, that their ancestors were. In the case of the Society of the Cincinnati we were at least dealing with George Washington's officers. In the case of the other three Societies, we are dealing with something else. "Almost without exception," said the late Dixon Wecter, "the first permanent settlers in America—F.F.V.'s, *Mayflower* passengers, Knickerbockers and Quakers—were drawn from the middle and lower classes, from the aggressive, the dissenter, the ne'er-do-well, the underprivileged and the maladjusted. . . . As has often been said, 'Dukes don't emigrate.' "

The historian meant, of course, they didn't then—later, as we shall see, America was to have rather more dukes than Europe had dukedoms. But, of the original *Mayflower* group of 1620, including 100-odd passengers, the majority were people of such humble origin in comparison to later arrivals that they gave rise to at least two of the most venerable of all Boston stories. As one goes, Mrs. Harrison Gray Otis was asked if her family came over on the *Mayflower*. "Oh, no," she replied, "we came over on the second boat. We sent our servants on that." The other story is credited, among others, to Boston's great Mrs. Jack Gardner, who was once bored to rebuttal by a visitor who launched into a family history of having had ancestors on the *Mayflower*. "Indeed," arched Mrs. Gardner, "I understand the immigration laws are much stricter nowadays."

Both stories have, ironically, much historical truth to back them up. For it was indeed the "second boat," the *Arbella*, which brought to the Plymouth Colony, among other passengers, the country's first Whitney, as well as such a distinguished Boston forebear as "Sir" Richard Saltonstall—the latter to start the only family in America to boast ten unbroken generations of Harvard men.

Actually, and in severe point of fact, of the forty-one men who signed the famous Compact in the cabin of the *Mayflower*, though eleven were addressed as "Mr." and a handful could claim "Master," not a single one bore the title of "Gent." And, of original passengers, no less than eighteen were included under the designation "Family Servants and Young Cousins." Charles M. Andrews, in *The Fathers of New England*, puts the matter in no uncertain terms. "A group of English emigrants," he said, "more socially insignificant could hardly be imagined. . . . Their intellectual and material poverty, lack of business enterprise, unfavorable situation and defenseless position in the eyes of the law, rendered them an almost negative factor in the later life of New England."*

---

* Frank Stoddard, in his excellent book, *The Truth about the Pilgrims*, points out that "servants" in the Seventeenth Century did not have the

These are harsh words, of course, and they not only fail to do justice to the Pilgrims who were, as a group, perhaps the greatest of all this country's heroes, but they are also inaccurate about the actual accomplishments of the Pilgrims. These Pilgrims, ironically often blamed for the excesses of intolerance of Boston's Puritans, from whom they were very different, number among their signal accomplishments the first teaching and practicing of the separation of church and state, the first practicing of freedom of religious worship, the first trial by jury extending to all people, the first abolishing of primogeniture, the first recognition of the rights of women, the first system of free public education and, indeed, the introduction of almost all of our system of equality. Furthermore, such anti-Pilgrim historians significantly fail to account for the fact that a great many distinguished latter-day citizens are *Mayflower*-descended—including Boston's Adams family, Mrs. Ralph Waldo Emerson, Henry Wadsworth Longfellow, Ulysses S. Grant, the first Mrs. Jefferson Davis, William Howard Taft, J. P. Morgan, George F. Baker, the first Mrs. John D. Rockefeller, Jr. (Abby Aldrich), and Franklin Delano Roosevelt. Even Sir Winston Churchill was descended from the brother of a *Mayflower* passenger.

Nonetheless, in the Society "social" sense—or, for that matter, in the First Family-founding sense—there is accuracy to the charge that the first permanent settlers in New England were drawn, generally speaking, from the middle and lower classes, and they were so drawn in the days when classes were much more clearly defined than nowadays. Also, this fact is now recognized by most dispassionate historians, including Bradford Smith, descendant of the greatest of the Pilgrim Fathers, William Bradford. "They were all working men," he says, "tailors, merchants, wool combers, weavers, sawyers, hatters, carpenters. . . . The false notion that they were noblemen . . . is especially ironic in view of the fact that the chief

---

modern meaning or connote necessarily a social inferiority or menial position, that a servant frequently ranked only a little below the rank of his master and that the term might convey that he was a companion as well as a servant. Occasionally, Mr. Stoddard would seem to protest a little too loudly, but the book is, at least, a necessary antidote to Andrews.

distinction of the Pilgrims and their claim to our continual veneration is that they established a caste-free government of free men,
making no attempt to duplicate the system of degree and station
which existed in England and by which the leaders, if they had
been smaller men, might well have hoped to advance themselves
in the new world."

Mr. Smith is justly proud of the fact that his distinguished ancestor was, as he says, "a self-made man in an age of privilege." A
similar down-to-earth view is held by Walter Merriam Pratt, Governor General of the General Society of Mayflower Descendants.
As of 1960 his Society consisted of some 11,000 members, and, he
says humorously, "Some three or four hundred thousand could be,
but they just don't know it." Mr. Pratt, who is descended from a
man who brought over two "servants" on the boat, does know it;
furthermore, he is under no illusion of his "S.M.O.'s" being today's
"Society." "The Mayflower Society," he says, "is not interested in
the wealth of its members, or their social standing, or their politics.
The Pilgrims believed in the equality of all men."

Turning south to Virginia for a second illustration, we find
roughly the same not so "gentle" story. In the original Jamestown
expedition of 1607 there were 35 "Gentlemen" listed out of 105
men, and of the 295 men who were actually counted founders of
Jamestown, 92 were classified on contemporary records as "Gentlemen." But both figures can be misleading, for, as Louis B. Wright
says, "Of the background of most of the settlers who were careful
to sign themselves 'Gent.' we know next to nothing. . . . The cold
truth is that the English origins of nearly all of the colonists, even
those who founded aristocratic families, are unknown. . . . Though
the First Families of Virginia may have in their veins the bluest
blood in all England, the proof of their descent will rarely stand in
either a court of law or a council of scholars."

The late James Truslow Adams once said, "There was not a
gentleman of leisure in Virginia until well after 1700—unless he
were a jailbird or a redskin." A very few early Families, notably
the Fairfaxes, Peytons and Throckmortons, boasted genuine Eng-

lish titled connections. More, like the Lees, Carys and Randolphs, not only came later but also have less well-established ties. But by far the majority, families like the Carters and the Byrds, were frankly mercantile. Although Southern genealogists have done their unlevel best to prove, for example, that a word like "goldsmith," the humble occupation of the father of William Byrd, was "an old expression for banker," Virginia's own Clifford Dowdey is more objective about F.F.V's. "Of the original band of 105 who landed in Jamestown," he says, "not one left a descendant in Virginia; and of the less than 200 survivors of the nearly 800 who came in the first and most perilous period (1607-1610), not five by record left descendants in Virginia. These descendants, however well-connected and personally elegant, are not listed in that roll of the ruling planter Families (Carters, Randolphs, Harrisons, Lees, etc.) who loosely comprise the royalty known as the F.F.V.'s. For F.F.V. does not mean the First Families who came to Virginia. It means the First Families who achieved power *after* the settlement had been won."*

Here again the historical has been translated into the humorous, for a favorite Virginia story concerns a young man whose family had come over on the fourth boat having quite a run-in with a lady whose family had come over on the first. The young man had gone north and had apparently made good in a rather large way. Returning, loaded with his good fortune, he was so thoroughly objectionable that the first-boat lady could not stand it. "Why, I remember you all," she drawled, "when you all had just one pair of shoes to your name." Replied the young man, sternly, "And I

---

* The starving of the Jamestown colony, before the arrival of Gates' ship, in the midst of the "land of plenty" is still one of the strangest stories in the annals of America. Even admittedly pro-Virginian Marshall Fishwick, in his admirable *Virginia; A New Look at the Old Dominion*, does not spare the grim story. "Starving settlers ate boots, shoes, or any other leather, and were 'glad to make shift with vermin.' . . . Men 'licked upp the bloode which had fallen from their weake fellowes.' One demented wretch killed his wife and ate her before the murder was discovered. With sardonic Elizabethan humor, Captain Smith thought the episode worth commenting on when he wrote his history. 'Whether she was better roasted, boyled, or carbonado'd, I know not,' he speculated. 'But such a dish as powdered wife I never heard of.' "

remember you all. You all asked what they were." A rather more
brief version of the F.F.V. story is credited to the late Will Rogers,
who was once accosted by a lady who boasted lengthily of being
an F.F.V. "I, madam," he said, "am an 'L.F.A.' " What on earth, the
lady wanted to know, was that? Replied Rogers, "A Last Family of
Arkansas." Rogers was apparently also up to facing the Society
of Mayflower Descendants—as witness his well-worn story of
answering the woman who claimed her ancestors came over on
the *Mayflower*. "My ancestors," he said, "met the boat."

For still another Southern irony, in the matter of early Society
and First Families, let us look even farther south—all the way to
St. Augustine, Florida, the oldest city in the entire country. St.
Augustine was founded in 1565, half a century before Jamestown
and Plymouth, and more than a century before Manhattan. Yet
who has ever heard of any family, North or South, boasting descent
from there? Still looking at the South, the ancestry of the proud
city of New Orleans is a particularly interesting story. Plagued in
its early days by a shortage of women, the King of France dispatched in 1721 eighty-eight women from the houses of correction
in Paris. For several years he continued to send "correction girls"
until in 1728 came the famous "casket girls"—a group of better-
class girls, albeit many were girls from orphanages, who arrived,
each with a little "casket" of clothing and personal effects. The
late Robert Tallant tells their story:

> As the first respectable, unmarried women to arrive in New
> Orleans the "casket girls" were besieged by so many suitors that
> duels were fought over them, or sometimes, with the persuasion
> of the Ursuline nuns, who had the girls in their charge, were
> drawn by lots cast by lonely bachelors. For generations afterwards
> all New Orleanians were to boast of direct descent from the *filles
> à la cassette*, rather than from the correction girls, a boast that be-
> came as proud and as general as an Anglo-Saxon American's that
> his ancestors all arrived on the *Mayflower*. Not too many years
> ago a mathematically-minded New Orleanian estimated that if all
> such claims were correct each "casket girl" bore one hundred and
> sixty-two children!

Finally, let us turn to New York and take a look at the earliest white settlers of Manhattan. They comprised some thirty-odd families of Walloons, who came over in 1623 in the *Nieu Neder-landt*, and they were perhaps most thoroughly, if not best, described by Augustus Van Buren in the *Proceedings of the New York Historical Society*. "Most of them," he said, "could neither read nor write. They were a wild, uncouth, rough, and most of the time a drunken crowd. They lived in small huts, thatched with straw. They wore rough clothes, and in the winter were dressed in skins. They were afraid of neither man, God, nor the devil." The late Mr. Van Buren concluded that "they were laying deep the foundation of the Empire State." One can draw one's own conclusion about the depth of the claim regularly made by the late Walter P. Chrysler, in each succeeding edition of *Who's Who*, that he was descended from Tuenis Van Dolsen, the first male child born in New Amsterdam. Abraham Lincoln was more modest. "I don't know who my grandfather was," he said. "I am much more concerned to know what his grandson will be."

If users of such phrases as "good family" and "old family" and "socially prominent," do not, as we have illustrated, apparently mean ancient or original social distinction, then what kind of social distinction do they mean? Many years ago Ward McAllister gave it as his opinion that "it takes three generations to make an American gentleman." But even if the late Ward was right, what, we might interrupt to ask at this point, ever happened to the fine old Pittsburgh saying, attributed to Andrew Carnegie, of "shirtsleeves to shirtsleeves" in three generations? And, speaking of Carnegie, what about money? A century ago Josh Billings declared that "men ain't apt to be kicked out of good Society for being rich," and surely even a cursory reading of social history will demonstrate, if not the truth of that, at least the truth of its reverse—that money may not always have been able to get a Family into Society, in one generation, that is—but lack of it has almost always been able to get one out.

Many years ago, for example, New York saw the old "telephone exchange" Families, the Beekmans, the Schuylers and the Rhine-

landers, give way to the Astors, the Vanderbilts and the Whi
Such once all-powerful Knickerbocker Families as the Stuyve
the De Peysters, the Van Burens, the Van Cortlandts and the van
Rensselaers, as well as the old English Families associated with them
in the early days of "patroonship" in the Hudson River Valley—the
Jays, Pells and Livingstons—all have pathetically small representation
in the 1960's so-called Society. So many of these Families, who, in
happier days, looked down socially on families who were "in trade"
are fated in the end to have their names used for trade only. Thus, of
more than two hundred listings in the current New York telephone
directory for the once-proud Jay family, all but a handful are
commercial, and of sixty-five Stuyvesant listings every single one is
commercial—for the simple reason that there is not a single living
direct descendant of Governor Peter Stuyvesant's once very
"First" Family.

In the case of the First Families not being first, New York is no
exception. Boston saw the Hancocks, Otises and Quincys fade
before the Cabots and Lowells, and if a few Saltonstalls and
Adamses and Forbeses showed fiscal stability—as well as pro-
creative ability—they were the Boston exception, not the country's
rule. In Philadelphia, the Willings, Rushes and Chews passed in a
sort of poetic review before Biddles, Cadwaladers and Pews. And
again, if there was stability among the so-called *"Qu'est-ce que sait?"*
Cassatts, there had to be against the onrushing Wideners, Wanamakers and Drexels, not to mention—which the press most certainly
did—the Stotesburys and the Kents, or, for that matter, the Kellys.

Among insiders, of course, there were distinctions within distinctions. In Boston it was the Lowells and not the Lodges—though
the latter are often accorded the honor, because of the name Henry
Cabot Lodge—who spoke to the Cabots. The Cabots, as we know,
spoke only to God. In Philadelphia, because of the latter-day prominence of the Biddles, it was said that "When a Biddle gets drunk,
he thinks he's a Cadwalader." It was also said that so keen is a
Philadelphian's ear that he can distinguish between *the* Cadwaladers
—with one "l" only—and the "other" Cadwalladers.

But these were minor matters in the larger picture of the ephemeral nature of "social" prominence. Moving west, the pattern is, if anything, even clearer. In Detroit the Newberrys, Algers and Jays were overwhelmed by the Fords, Dodges and Chryslers, and if a few old-timers remember the days when "the Ford could go everywhere except in Society," it was the Model T, not the A and the V8—or certainly not the Thunderbird—that failed the grade.

Out in St. Louis, where, as the saying went, the word "debutante" was drowned crossing the Mississippi, that fair city nonetheless saw Pulitzers, Anheusers and Busches overwhelm the old French Creole families like the Chouteaus and Peugnets, Cabannes, Desloges and Garesches. Indeed, the St. Louis telephone book, which recently even made a mistake in the spelling of Cabanne, now lists, under that once proud name, only one Cabanne, a Methodist Church and an employment agency. Under Chouteau there are three names, Auguste, Jr., James M. and Pierre, and, while Auguste Chouteau, Jr., represents the eighth in direct descent of that name from the Family founder, the fact also remains that the number of Chouteau "Trade" names is constantly growing.*

In Cleveland there was a move from Mathers to Cases to Boltons to Hannas to Humphreys; there is also a story of a grandson of the "original" Samuel Mather who had a grandson named Gwinn whose house bore the famous entrance sign, GWINN. "My mother always wondered," says Clevelander Peter Greenough wistfully, "if the exit sign said, 'Gwout.'" In any case, it might well have, for the time will undoubtedly come, in Cleveland Society, when the Gwinns will be, indeed, the "Gwouts." As for Cincinnati, once upon a social climb—actually the year was 1888—an uncharitable British visitor divided the city's Society into the "Stick-'ems" and the "Stuck-'ems" —in other words, between the wealthy butchers and the retired pork packers. Extreme as this may seem, the fact remains that both Dallas and Houston have been divided, in point of time, between cotton and oil, into the "Cotton Rich" and the "Rotten Rich."

Finally, if Chicago could go "from Potter Palmers to potted

---

*Cabanne is not pronounced the French way, Ca-bán, but rather St. Louisized to Cabin-y.

palms to pot," so could Atlanta, Georgia, go from Crackers to Coca-Cola, or far-off San Francisco go from "Big Fours" to "Little Fours" to *petits fours*. If such brief designations work hardships on such families as Atlanta's Inmans and Ormes—who were hardly "Crackers," even if Candlers and Woodruffs were indeed Coca-Colas—it perhaps works even more of an injustice on such prominent Southern families as the Gwins and Ritchies, Otises and Osgoods, Redingtons and Poulterers, who were, in the social settlement of San Francisco, a leavening influence on the Crockers and Hopkinses, the Stanfords and Huntingtons, the Parrotts and Alexanders, etc. Yet, generally speaking, the designations are accurate, and even in such a social melee as Los Angeles it is possible to view the passing parades, from the old boulevard names (Pico, Figueroa and Sepulveda) to the "Freeways"—in all senses of the word—and on to the other streets (like the well-oiled Dohenys) and even to the hotels (Hilton and Kirkeby), not to mention, which in the old days newspapers didn't, the newspaper names like Otis and Chandler. As for the really old Los Angeles Families, such as the Garniers and the Dominguez, they have been all but forgotten entirely. Indeed, Western Society in general was perhaps most memorably, if all too rudely, reminded of its rough-and-ready roots when the late Governor Dan Thornton of Colorado told a dinner in Denver that he was sick and tired of the whole question of whether or not Society had anything to do with First Families. "I don't want to hear anything more in this State about First Families at all," he said, "and if I do, may I remind you that our First Families were miners married to whores."

Back in Manhattan only a generation ago, in 1924, Mrs. John King Van Rensselaer noted that the "most prominent families in published accounts of New York social events" were the Vanderbilts, the Astors, the Morgans, the Davidsons, the Belmonts, the Lamonts, the Vanderlips, the Villards and the Goulds. Yet there "endured submerged," she declared, at least a dozen ladies she knew "whose families had directed the social life of New York for ten generations." Among this social flotsam, modestly excluding herself,

Mrs. Van Rensselaer named Mrs. Gouverneur Morris, Mrs. James Gore King, Mrs. Sumner Gerard, Mrs. George Wickersham and two Mrs. Iselins. In contrast to these, not a single of "the most prominent families in published accounts" ran back in Society, she said, to the Revolutionary era and only one ran back as far as the Civil War. And that one she was none too kindly about. "The first John Jacob Astor," she said sternly, "born in Walldorf, Germany, came to New York in 1783 as a piano merchant." If Mrs. Van Rensselaer seems cross at this point, it might be noted that the historian James Parton was equally stern. He gave Astor's name as Ashdor and declared he was "the son of a jovial, good-for-nothing butcher." Furthermore, not only Parton but other historians agree that eleven years after Astor's arrival there was born, in 1794, on Staten Island, of the fourth generation of "miserably poor squatters," the fourth of nine children of a Dutch farmer and ferryman, a young man who spelled his name—when he got it right—Cornelius Van Der Bilt.

To this day, to an Old Guard which is now more submerged than even Mrs. Van Rensselaer could have imagined, the Vanderbilts remain symbols, not of the Old but of the New—and there is scarcely an old Family of genuine social pretensions who does not boast at least one elderly member who remembers having in her childhood been reminded of that fact. Mrs. Huntington Tappin, of the famous social agency, Tappin and Tew, recalls that, as a debutante, she was not allowed to attend the coming-out party of Consuelo Vanderbilt, later Duchess of Marlborough. "The Huntingtons," she was told, "do not go to the Vanderbilts." As for the late dancing master, William de Rham, he remembered that when he was a child in Newport his mother only very reluctantly allowed him to play with *any* Vanderbilt. And his mother, as a girl, had not been allowed to play with *the* Mrs. Vanderbilt. "Grace Vanderbilt," *her* mother had told her, "is *nouveau*." And the late Herman Rogers recalled that as a boy at his place at Hyde Park he was perfectly free to play with the Roosevelts but was warned of possible contamination from the Vanderbilts. "You may be nice to them," his mother said, "but don't get involved."

Altogether, it seems rather remarkable that the Vanderbilts ever had anybody to play with.

When we come at long last to the word "Society" itself, we find few people, in the world of the 1960's, who will even attempt a definition under the old standards. One, however, is Mrs. George Henry Warren, president of the Society for the Preservation of Newport Antiquities and a lady who stands almost alone, like Horatius, at the Mount Hope Bridge, guarding that ancient but honorable resort citadel. "Society," she says briskly, "is a banding together of people of similar taste for their mutual pleasure." This definition is impersonal but definite. On the other hand, when one asks Miss Alice Brayton, a spinster who has retired from Newport to a farm near Portsmouth, one receives a definition which is personal but indefinite. "I want to know people who don't want to know me," she says. "They want to know people who don't want to know them, and so on ad infinitum. That is Society."

Other definitions are more startling. "Society!" exclaims Mrs. Margaret Case, of *Vogue* magazine. "I don't know what the damn thing means, and what's more I don't think anybody else does either." If this was vague for *Vogue*, the one and only Carmel Snow, High Priestess of Fashion, of *Harper's Bazaar*, was positively bizarre. "If you mean, does it mean anything," she says, "the only meaning it once had is meaningless now."

Across the country, opinions differed, but not by much. In Boston, Mrs. Robert Herrick turned 84 in 1960; she started as a girl of 15 doing social work with a small "s" at Hull House with Jane Addams. "Now," she says, "I'm a 'socially prominent woman,' with a big 'S'—whatever that means—but it's finished. Society's finished and the whole Boston thing is finished." Mrs. Ogden Reid, of Wisconsin and New York, has seen an equal change but is less totally concerned. "I have always resented the word 'Society,' " she says. "In the old framework it meant something, I suppose, but I don't think it does in the new—and I'm glad of it." Mrs. Clark Williams of Tennessee, who has lived in New York since 1897, concurred with Mrs. Reid. "Society is an arbitrary word," she says, "that each generation picks out to exclude other people." On the other hand, Mrs. Charles Suydam Cutting, of New York and New Jersey, disagreed. "Society, my foot!" she says. "Everybody knows what it *was*, but nobody knows what it *is*, for the simple reason that it isn't anything now, that's why." This same sentiment was echoed, albeit more gently, by Miss Jessie Jerome Fanshawe, last of the surviving Four Hundred social secretaries and a lady who in the spring of 1959 retired at the age of 83, with the feeling that her occupation had also. Miss Fanshawe shepherded three full generations of social sheep—and "some goats too," she adds. Nonetheless, her own background was impeccable; her grandfather and the grandfather of Sir Winston Churchill were brothers. "Mercy!" she begs. "What do I think Society is nowadays? What *can* you think? The whole world's changed. You're better off not thinking about it." Mrs. William H. Tew, of Tappin and Tew, concludes the New York round table. "I can't tell you what it is," she says, "but I can certainly tell you what it is not!"

Out in Bernardsville, New Jersey, Mrs. B. Sumner Welles was totally baffled. "I read the 'Society' columns," she says. "I read them faithfully. But I just don't know who these people are. I don't even know what connection they are to anybody Sumner and I know." In Wilmington, Mrs. L. Mulford Taylor had not only a definitive definition of Society but also a new nomination for Society's murder. "In the old days," she says crisply, "Society was culture and education. Now it's money. Drinking and smoking did it." In Philadelphia, Mrs. Livingston Biddle asked a question herself. "Who can define Society," she asked, "in a day when you need a blueprint to know your own Family?" And, in Baltimore, the perspicacious Eleanor Arnett Nash, sister of poet Ogden Nash, advises looking beneath the surface. "Society here," she says, "is a small group of people who have, to avoid pseudo-Society, gone underground." Pressing on to Washington, D. C., we went to the country's foremost columnist. "Society?" repeated Walter Lippmann. "It's the elite—only the trouble is the elite aren't the elite any more. Nobody gives a damn about an Adams except another Adams." On the other hand, Mrs. Perle Mesta had no ready definition. "I really don't think," she says a little desperately, "Society is anything any more—except in its most liberal sense. I have the very oldest Bostonians to my party and even they like the liberal." Moving south to Richmond, for a more elderly Guard view, we found one of the country's most charming of all Southern *grandes dames,* Mrs. Douglas Southall Freeman. "I would like to say it meant something," she told us gently, "but I honestly don't think it does—not even in Richmond. You might try Charleston, though. That's Charleston, South Carolina, of course—not West Virginia."

In Charleston we found Sam Stoney, arbiter in the gentle Southern tradition and head of the South Carolina Historical Society. "I can look out one window," he said, "and see the house where I was born. I can look out another and see where my first South Carolina ancestor owned a plot of land. That was in 1680. But even here you've got Society *à la carte* and you've got Society *à la mode.* And both of them are a long way from the Blue Plate Special."

Our next call was on Mrs. Everette DeGolyer, *grande dame* of Dallas, Texas, and the wife of the late dean of petroleum geologists. "I'll tell you what he used to say," she said. "He said Texas was too new for Society in the old sense—the Dads were too close to the dirt and the Moms were too close to the washtubs." And out in Phoenix, Arizona, at her Arizona Maine Chance Farm, Mrs. Florence Nightingale Graham, better known as Elizabeth Arden, was perhaps the most discouraging of all. "I don't think Society means a thing any more," she said, "I've even noticed it with the horses."

Among Society editors there was wide disparity of opinion—even, on occasion, in just one opinion. For example, Russell Edwards, Society editor of the *New York Times* and a man who has either edited or written all the Society news that's fit to print for three decades, declared firmly that there were two meanings of the word. "One," he said, "is your Old Guard, your old families who control the wealth, cultural institutions and traditional functions.

The other is the group which sets the pace in fashion, in genteel living and entertaining—they also are Society, but the fact remains they include some of the first group too."

In the Midwest, two Society editors of more than thirty years' standing, Mrs. Margaret Ruhl, of the St. Louis *Post-Dispatch*, and Miss Louise Davis, recently retired from the Cleveland *Plain Dealer*, support the general confusion. "I haven't got the faintest idea what it means," says Mrs. Ruhl. "I remember once Father Edward Dowling defining Society as 'the commercial use of leisure time,' but as far as I'm concerned it's just a word that came down the river on a flatboat and we got stuck with it." Miss Davis, of the "eastern" Midwest, agrees, albeit to a lesser extent. "In the old days it was a stratum," she says, "like whipped cream. And that isn't healthy today. In the old days, though, I went to them. Later they came to me."

Down in Miami, Miss Helen Wells, Society editor for twelve years of the Miami *Herald*—"But that's several generations down here," she says—is even more definitely undefinitive. "It's a hodge-podge—and, furthermore, it's a moving hodgepodge. People who never made good at home make very good here, and I say more power to 'em." In Milwaukee, Wisconsin, where Society is not only confusing enough but also has the added confusions of having "socially prominent" families by the dozens of Millers, Moellers and Muellers, we received, in lieu of a definition, a story. At the end of a long day a lady who said she was a Mrs. Miller called assistant Society editor Jean Dessel. "Which Mrs. Miller," asked Mrs. Dessel, wearily, "*are* you?" "Don't you know?" snapped her caller. "The rich Mrs. Miller on Newberry Boulevard."*

Turning, in some desperation, for further definition to the Inter-

---

* Such a story is not so "Midwestern" as might be supposed. Thomas Lamont, son of the late chairman of the board of J. P. Morgan & Company, recalls, after graduating from the Columbia School of Journalism, a stint on the AP in New York. An item came in that a Mrs. So-and-so of such-and-such an address on Fifth Avenue had died. Lamont wrote it up and put it in the slot. When the city editor got it, he read it, then, ahead of the name, wrote "Socialite." "How," asked Lamont, "do you know she's a socialite?" "Well," said the editor, "look at the address—Fifth Avenue."

national Set, we next accosted Mr. Noel Coward, in Jamaica. "I have always believed," he said wryly, "more in quality than in quantity, but whether that's Society in America or not, old boy, I wouldn't know." We next tried the founding father of New York's White Russian Set, George Schlee, husband of the famed designer, Valentina, long-time squire of Greta Garbo and perennial International Setter. "I looked for Society in the dictionary," he said, in his characteristic waggish manner, "and the only thing I found was something 'as in social intercourse.' " Serious, for a moment, Schlee compared Society to oil on water. "It's an ability," he said, "to float in spite of everything—and the biggest in spite, in my opinion, has been the servant revolution. Even if you can afford them you don't want them. They forced out-of-home entertaining. In the old days in St. Petersburg where I grew up, it would have been just as unthinkable to entertain outside of your own house as it would be for the President of the United States to walk down Pennsylvania Avenue naked."

For further explanation we turned to another distinguished White Russian, the famed Prince, who prefers to be just plain "Colonel," Serge Obolensky, a social specialist who has, among other accomplishments, successively restored the social status of no less than half a dozen New York hotels, including the Plaza, the St. Regis, the Sherry-Netherland, the Ambassador, the Astor and the Drake, as well as way stations in between. "Society," he says, after several weeks' consideration, "is the elite of any town or any country. It doesn't matter where they come from. They are there. They are the personalities—authors, politicians, diplomats, journalists, inventors— the whole galaxy of people of social importance, intelligence and purpose!"

Somehow we had never thought of Society as "purpose," but in any case the good Colonel's observations are tempered and brought down to specifics by another International Setter and social specialist in the hotel field—the elegant Frenchman, M. Claudius Philippe. "Society in America?" he repeats. "Well, of course there are the people who wear their own gold-plated crowns—the artists, writers and so forth—but the only sense Society in America makes, in one sense, is dollar and cents." Since M. Philippe had just raised from his ninth—and most criticized—"April in Paris" ball the incredible sum of $202,000 for charity, he knows whereof he speaks. However, the final fillip of the International Set was delivered, not by M. Claudius Philippe but by Baron Hubert Panz of the Schloss Mittersill Club, Salzburg, Austria. "What is not Society in America?" he says. "Is it not to go to your Greenbrier Hotel in your Spring Festival and to bet $5,000 on the Duke of Windsor's team and to sit only a couple of tables from the Henry Fords? Is that not Society, no?"

The good Baron would seem to have asked his own answer. In any case, back in London we turned to a lady who has probably seen, in a shorter time, more Society on both sides of the Atlantic than any other—Fleur Cowles Meyer. This extraordinary lady, after cutting a wide swath in the social picture in America, after a severe illness and a divorce from *Look*, *Flair*, *Quick* and Gardner Cowles, recently went on to start all over again in London. Now, married to London's charming lumber baron, T. Montague Meyer, her famous Albany House apartment has become, if not a salon, at least one of the most prominent meeting places of both English and American social figures. Her definition of Society was the briefest of all we encountered. "Society," she said simply, "is interesting people." Miss Cowles' husband, on the other hand, gave us the most philosophical of all our definitions. "Let's be basic," he said. "The fact is that, despite all the arguments against it, there will always be Society in any country, or for that matter, any planet. If there are three people on an island, one of them will say he got there first—and so he is Society. Pretty soon another one will climb up a hill and build a big house and say *he* is Society. And finally, the third one will climb up a tree and corner all the coconuts and claim *he* is Society. Who is Society? Obviously all of them are: The first has family, the second has prominence, and the third has money."

After some deliberation, then, we come for our own definition of Society to something like this: to anyone who made his social reputation a generation earlier, someone who made it a generation later is socially suspect. It is not a strong definition which makes use of the word it defines, but one is working, after all, with a word which, as we have seen, means very little under the best circumstances and certainly almost nothing, or at least something very different, unless it is spelled with a capital letter. Turning to Webster, one finds no definition for Society with a capital "S"—indeed, one finds no mention of the capital "S" word at all. Under "society" with a small "s," however, under definition No. 7, one finds the brief notation: "The members of the wealthy fashionable class"— a definition which sounds reasonable enough until one begins to challenge the word "class" and to remember that it is something that, on the one hand, America is not supposed to have and, on the other, something which, as in the case of the late Franklin Roosevelt, it is nonetheless possible to be a traitor to.

In contrast to Webster, in the large Oxford dictionary wealth is not mentioned, but, "with defining or limiting adj.—esp. *good* society" one finds the following: "The aggregate of leisured, cultured, or fashionable persons regarded as forming a distinct class or body in a community; *esp.* those persons collectively who are recognized as taking part in fashionable life, social functions, entertainments, etc." Here at least the word "class" is hedged and to some extent modified. Then, for the first listed example of usage of the word, one finds none other than Lord Byron himself—*Don Juan* 1823:

> Society is now one polish'd horde
> Form'd of two mighty tribes, the *Bores* and *Bored*.

That, surely, is hard news—to think Society was already boring when, to the dictionary's way of thinking at least, it had just begun. But we can take some measure of solace from the fact that Lord Byron was obviously referring to English Society. And our previous peregrinations have taught us, if nothing else, that where Society is concerned a little patience is not only a virtuous thing but also a necessary one. To persevere, let us try the second entry from the Oxford. This one is from Thackeray, *Barber Cox* 1840:

> The paragraphs in the papers about Mr. Coxe Coxe . . . had an effect in a wonderfully short space of time, and we began to get a very pretty Society about us.

Here at last, with a capital "S" supplied, we are beginning to get somewhere, for it now becomes apparent that since earliest days Society has always, to a greater or lesser extent, depended upon publicity. Furthermore, it is now also apparent that herein lies its chief point of contrast, not only with a recognized nobility—which, of course, America does not have—but also with something which America may or may not have, as we shall shortly see: an Aristocracy. As far back as 1902 this contrast was sternly stated in England's *Blackwood's Magazine*. "Nowadays," it said, "Society and Aristocracy are two totally different things. The Aristocracy care not to be identified with those odious people one sees in the newspapers."

It would seem, then, in view of the confusion that for some 350 years has reigned supreme in America on the subject, that the only thing dated about that article—and perhaps its sole shortcoming for application to America—is its title, "The Anglo-Saxon Society Woman."

II

ARISTOCRACY—*From Codfish to Coats of Arms*

THE WORD "Aristocrat" comes from the Greek *aristos* (best) and *kratia* (rule). Originally it meant "government by the best citizens," but Webster now allows, after definition No. 4—"a privileged ruling class or nobility"—definition No. 5—"Those considered the best in some way." And, if Webster seems vague at this point, it would seem to be so with good reason, for even the confusion over the word "Society" pales before the word "Aristocracy." Here in America people cannot even agree on the pronunciation, let alone the meaning, and the *ar*-istocrats who pronounce it a-*ris*-tocrats, have never seen dictionary to dictionary or, for that matter, Family to Family, with the a-*ris*-tocrats who pronounce it *ar*-istocrats. Nonetheless, this has in no way limited the use of the word, for if there is one thing certain about Aristocracy, it is that Americans have always dearly loved it, and one rarely picks up a newspaper without

seeing at least one advertisement concerned with it—from automobiles to hotels. Indeed, the use of the word runs the gamut from
asparagus—which is known as the "Aristocrat of Vegetables"—to the
call girl, who as recently as 1958 was called "the Aristocrat of the
World's Oldest Profession."

Actually, as the Encyclopaedia Britannica has pointed out, there
is nowadays little justification for the word even from "a purely
governmental point of view." "In no case," it says sternly, "does the
sovereign power in a state reside any longer in an aristocracy, and
the word has acquired a social [*sic*] rather than a political sense as
practically equivalent to 'nobility.' "

Both Webster and the Encyclopaedia nonetheless believe that the
American Aristocracy, if there is such a thing, is, if not a nobility, at
least "practically its equivalent." Yet, surely, the country did not start
out, as we have seen from a discussion of our first settlers, as having
an Aristocracy. And, as of 1776, no less an authority than Adam
Smith stated, "No oppressive aristocracy has ever prevailed in the
colonies." From 1776 onward, however, it would appear that the
aristocratic idea—we can hardly, under our democracy, call it an
ideal—refused to be downed. Indeed, hardly was the Revolution
over when Colonel Lewis Nicola proposed that George Washington
become "King George I"—a suggestion to which Washington, to
his democratic credit, refused to become a party. Nonetheless, in
1789, before the opening of Congress in New York, a large group
of admitted "Aristocrats" of their day—including James Madison
and Richard Henry Lee from Virginia and Thomas McKean and
William Bingham of Philadelphia—did attend a party at the house
of Dr. Edward Shippen in Philadelphia. And at this party, Rufus
Wilmot Griswold recalls, in his aptly named book, *The Republican
Court*, the question of the hour was a title for "Mr." Washington:

> Soon after the company were assembled, the Chief Justice asked
> Mr. Madison if he had thought of a title for the President. Madison
> answered that he had not, and added, that in his opinion no title
> except that of President would be necessary or proper. "Yes,
> sir," replied McKean, "he must have a title, and I have been exam-

ining the titles of the princes of Europe to discover one that has not been appropriated; 'Most Serene Highness' is used, but Serene Highness without the word 'Most,' is not; and I think it proper that our Chief magistrate should be known as His Serene Highness the President of the United States."

Later there was another dinner meeting in New York, which was reported by Griswold, on the authority of General Muhlenberg:

General Muhlenberg states that Washington himself was in favor of the style of "High Mightiness," used by the Stadtholder of Holland, and that while the subject was under discussion in Congress he dined with the President, and, by a jest about it, for a time lost his friendship. Among the guests was Mr. Wynkoop, of Pennsylvania, who was noticeable for his large and commanding figure. The resolutions before the two Houses being referred to, the President, in his usual dignified manner, said, "Well, General Muhlenberg, what do you think of the title of High Mightiness?" Muhlenberg answered, laughing, "Why, General, if we were certain that the office would always be held by men as large as yourself or my friend Wynkoop, it would be appropriate enough, but if by chance a president as small as my opposite neighbor should be elected, it would become ridiculous."

On April 23, 1789, committees were appointed by both Houses of Congress on the question of Washington's title search. The House of Representatives, led by such stalwarts as General Muhlenberg, stood foursquare against, but in the Senate, South Carolina's Ralph Izard and Virginia's Richard Henry Lee stomped for "Excellency" and "Highness," respectively, while Boston's John Adams, of all people, also refused to give in to just "plain" President. "There are," he said, "presidents of fire companies and cricket clubs," and he even went so far as to suggest titles for all of Washington's staff— that the Sergeant-at-Arms be called "Usher of the Black Rod" and that Washington's cook be called "Steward of the Household."*

---

* Even as Vice-President John Adams had become worried about his own title—as President of the Senate. "When the President comes into the Senate," he asked, "what shall I be? I cannot be President then. No, gentlemen, I cannot, I cannot. I wish gentlemen to think what I shall be." On another occasion, when the nature of Aristocracy was being debated in the New York Constitutional Convention, a speaker rose and said tauntingly, "I would refer

In any case, on the 14th of May, 1789, the Senate made one last try with the title "High Highness the President of the United States of America, and Protector of Their Liberties," but, once more rebuffed by the lower House, settled, at long last, for "President"— a title so bare that, it is recorded, "on at least one occasion Washington was refused lodgings at a village inn upon the assumption that he was the President of Rhode Island College."

All through the post-Revolutionary period there were giants of —as they were called even then—the "old Aristocracy." There was, for example, Boston's first King of the merchant princes, Colonel Thomas Handasyd Perkins, who, asked by George Washington to become his Secretary of the Navy, refused, stating that he had more ships than the American Navy and thought he would better serve the country by minding his own property. In Boston, too, if there was "Society" in the form of "King" John Hancock, who spent half a million dollars—a huge fortune in those days—in just ten years after the Revolution, there was also "Aristocracy" represented by Harrison Gray Otis, tall, strikingly handsome with coal-black hair and nose thin and patrician. In 1830, on the day fixed for the organization of Boston's present-day city government, he sent word to the members of the city council that he was ill and wished them to convene at his Beacon Hill residence. There were protests from the other members that a municipal inauguration should not be held in a private home—but held there it was. In Connecticut there was the "second" Oliver Wolcott, of whom it was said that "no Family in all the continent had preserved through its American generations a purer fame." Philadelphia had, as we have seen, perhaps more Aristocrats than any other city, and, moving south, there were Cavalier Aristocrats all the way from Baltimore to Charleston. Indeed, it was Charleston's Ralph Izard who, though an Aristocrat through and through, refused in London to be presented at Court, because, he said, he would never "bow the knee to mortal man." In Tidewater, Virginia, home of Aristocrats, there was the Harrison family of the

---

the gentlemen for a definition of it to the Hon. John Adams, one of our *natural aristocrats.*"

famed Berkeley Hundred, oldest and greatest of Virginia Plantations, and in scarcely less celebrated Tidewater, Maryland, there was the peerless Charles Carroll of Carrollton, scholar, gentleman and Aristocrat to his fingertips—of whom Lord Brougham wrote:

> Charles Carroll's family was settled in Maryland ever since the reign of James II and had during that period been possessed of the same ample property, the largest in the Union. It stood, therefore, at the head of the aristocracy of the country; was naturally in alliance with the government; could gain nothing while it risked every thing by a change of dynasty; and therefore, according to all the rules and prejudices and the frailties which are commonly found guiding the conduct of men in a crisis of affairs, Charles Carroll might have been expected to take part against the revolt, certainly never to join in promoting it. Such, however, was not this patriotic person. He was among the foremost to sign the Declaration of Independence. All who did so were believed to have devoted themselves and their families to the furies. As he set his hand to the instrument, the whisper ran round the hall of Congress, "There go some millions of property!" And there being many of the same name, when he heard it said, "Nobody will know which Carroll it is," as no one signed more than his name; and one at his elbow, addressing him, remarked, "You'll get clear —there are several of the name—they will never know which to take," he replied, "Not so!" and instantly added his residence, "of Carrollton."

And finally, last but not least, was the Revolution's Aristocrat of Aristocrats, Alexander Hamilton himself. Called by the envious Adams "the bastard brat of a Scotch pedlar," he was actually the illegitimate son of a relatively unsuccessful Scottish merchant and a brilliant and beautiful daughter of the French Huguenots. And he grew to a physical manhood that matched his political beliefs. "Graceful and debonair," says Claude Bowers, "elegant and courtly, seductive and ingratiating, playful or impassioned, he could have fitted into the picture at the Versailles of Louis XV, or at the dinner table at Holland House. No one born in the atmosphere of courts could have looked the part more perfectly." From such a man, born the lowliest of the low, came the highest expression of Aristocracy

America was ever to know. "His sympathies were always aristocratic," says his most partisan biographer, and his ideal of government was the "rule of gentlemen," on the logical theory that these, with a certain prestige to maintain, were more jealous of their honor and above the vulgar strivings for mere place.

Early in the Nineteenth Century came the "rage for democracy," and Aristocracy took a turn for the worse. As early as 1808 John Adams noted the coming trend: "We have one material which actually constitutes an aristocracy that governs the nation. That material is wealth. Talents, birth, virtues, services, sacrifices, are of little consideration with us." By the middle of the century, in the North at least, confusion about the word reigned supreme. Just a hundred years ago, for example, in 1859, John Bartlett, of *Familiar Quotations* fame, found the word "aristocratic" "strangely misapplied in those parts of the country where the population is not dense." "The city," said Bartlett, "in the surrounding towns, is deemed 'aristocratic.' The people in the villages consider the inhabitants of the towns 'aristocratic' and so on." And yet this was a fairly new development, for James Fenimore Cooper, returning from abroad, noted in his *Redskins* (1846) that "the word 'aristocratic' I find since my return home, has got to be a term of expansive signification, its meaning depending on the particular habits and opinions of the person who happens to use it." Even before this, the word was giving trouble. Latter-day New Englanders, for example, who take severe pride in their descent from the celebrated "codfish aristocracy," have had, on occasion, to be reminded that the term originated in the late Eighteenth Century as a term of opprobrium; it denoted, of course, a class of *nouveau riche* who had acquired wealth from the codfishing industry. And not until a hundred years later was it socially hallowed in Wallace Irwin's stanza:

> Of all the fish that swim or swish
> In ocean's deep autocracy,
> There's none possess such haughtiness
> As the codfish aristocracy.

Codfish and cash to the contrary, it was some time, even in America, before what Carlyle called the "Aristocracy of the Feudal Parchment" gave way to what he also called the "Aristocracy of the Moneybag." Even when it did, many Americans would have agreed with England's Lord John Manners who said, "Let wealth and commerce, laws and learning die—but leave us still our old nobility." For if America was without a nobility and could not, even in the Nineteenth Century, define the word "Aristocracy," it could at least contrast it with the word "Society." This contrast, of course, involved first and foremost the question of ancestral distinction. For Aristocracy, even in America, demanded some kind of ancestral distinction, although, as we shall see, the distinction was often monetary rather than a matter of birth. Society, on the other hand, might have some form of ancestral distinction but it also might not. In almost all cases it had a far lesser number of generations to go on—and in some cases, as evidenced by the gossip columns of a later day, it would seem to have only a future generation.

Second only to the question of ancestral distinction was the question of publicity. To the true Aristocrat, publicity, particularly in its later, more virulent forms, was a creature of the Devil. "Society," said the late Dixon Wecter a quarter of a century ago, "is the overt manifestation of caste. It is active, conspicuous, articulate, specialized." Aristocracy, on the other hand, might be defined as the reverse of every one of Mr. Wecter's adjectives. In other words, it is—or perhaps we should say, it should be—covert, passive, inconspicuous, inarticulate and unspecialized. Even in later "Four Hundred" days the same contrast obtained. "A château by Hunt," continues Wecter, "a box at the Metropolitan, a pair of opera glasses by Lemaire, a C-spring carriage, a pair of spanking bays to drive through Central Park, a yacht with rosewood panelling and marble pilasters in the saloon . . . to own them was to belong to Society."

To belong to the Aristocracy, however, one needed none of these things. One might have them—or better still have *had* them—but one also might not want them. Above all, one did not talk about having them, having had them or, worst of all, having the news-papers talk about one's having them. And, finally, ingrained in Aristocracy was the pious belief that "blood," if not the newspapers, "will tell."*

So strong is the enmity between Aristocracy and Society that the whole history of either one of them might well be written as the story of the warfare between the two. When all was said and undone, however, there would still be for the Aristocrats—if vic-torious they should be—a final irony. For, incomprehensible to most of them as it would seem, the fact remains that the American Aris-tocracy was once, of course, American Society. It might have been a day when the highly publicized social figures were of entirely different caliber than those of a later day. They might, for example, have been members of Colonial or Provincial Councils, Doctors of Divinity, early-day merchant princes or scholarly "elders." They might have been any of these, or even others, and the publicity media of the day might have been, instead of the newspaper, the town meeting or for that matter the pulpit—but the fact remains that they were, once, the people of "social" prominence. And thus it behooves the Aristocrat to remember that, look down on Society as he has and undoubtedly always will, there is always the possi-bility of his one day facing, like Harmodius the Aristocrat of ancient Greece, the American counterpart of Iphicrates, the shoe-maker's son. And facing him he would hear the age-old rebuttal: "My nobility begins in me, but yours ends in you." Or, translated from latter-day France, the Aristocrat might face the Society coun-terpart of Napoleon's Marshal Junot. The latter was sneeringly

---

* One is reminded of Marceline Cox's definition of heredity—"the thing a child gets from the other side of the family." However, Ashley Montagu, in his book *Human Heredity*, says that the whole idea of "good" or "gentle" blood is one more in the long list of ironies in our "social" or even "aristo-cratic" vocabulary. "The term 'blood relationship,'" he says, "and its Anglicized Latin equivalent 'consanguinity,' meaning the condition of being of the same 'blood' or relationship, by descent from a common ancestor, enshrine the belief that all biological relationships are reflected in, and are to a large extent determined by, the character of the blood. This venerable error, along with others, requires correction. . . . Blood has nothing whatever to do with the transmission of heredity."

asked by one of the old regime about his ancestry. "I am," he replied in an answer that has echoed down the ages, "my own ancestor."

There is irony too in the fact that even in our own day the Aristocrat can best be found, in sizable numbers, if not in Society at least in *a* Society—in particular, in the Aristocrat's all but patented patriotic Societies like the Cincinnati, Colonial Dames, Colonial Wars, D.A.R., etc. For, while these are, as we have seen, not necessarily today's "Society," they are assuredly, indeed even genealogically, yesterday's—which makes them, of course, today's Aristocracy.

Take, for example, an Aristocrat such as New York's Lawrence Phelps Tower, a gentleman who descends from no less than thirteen *Mayflower* passengers. President of the U.S. Flag Foundation, he is Deputy Governor of the Order of Founders and Patriots, a member of the Board of Governors of the Society of Mayflower Descendants, past Secretary General of the General Society of Colonial Wars in America, as well as a member of the St. Nicholas Society, the Pilgrims of the U.S., and the Society of the War of 1812. "It's harder to have it than not to have it," he says philosophically. "When you haven't got it, you can do what you please. But when you've got it up there," he adds, pointing a finger skyward, apparently to indicate distinguished ancestors above, "you just feel you can't do a damn thing to let any of them down." Once asked if he didn't feel he was living on his ancestors, Tower replied. "Living *on* them? I should say not. I'm trying to live up to them."*

The Tower genealogy, published in 1894, was undoubtedly the most elaborate one, in cost, ever assembled—its price, in 1894 dollars, was an even $50,000. When, however, it was presented to the late Charlemagne Tower, who at age 24 had just had his own first child and faced many financial problems, he was frankly baffled. "I only

---

* Living up to rather than living on distinguished ancestry has become the motto of at least one patriotic Society—the Descendants of the Signers of the Declaration of Independence. There are chapters of the Signers in each of the thirteen original states, and Massachusetts boasts at least two members who bear the same names as their Signer ancestors—Robert Treat Paine and Oliver Wolcott.

wish to God," he wrote on a card accepting the volume, "I knew where I was going as well as where I came from."

The total aristocratic population embodied by all the patriotic Societies would be an extraordinary number of people—particularly if joined with the even larger number of people who could belong but have never taken the time to have their genealogical requirements filled out. Best known of all, of course—albeit not always known for good—is the Daughters of the American Revolution, which was not only nothing to start with, it was actually less than nothing. When the Sons of the American Revolution was founded in 1876, it voted to exclude women—whereupon, the aroused Daughters in 1890 formed their own organization and have ever since wagged, in all senses, the dog.

Women showed the same more-than-mere-male sticking power in the South, where, as of 1906, the United Confederate Veterans, who also excluded women, had 412 of 569 local chapters in arrears and were, according to General Stephen Lee, "lost beyond recovery." Rising from the ashes, however, the United Daughters of the Confederacy became an almost unbelievably powerful organization. "Only the bravest of men," says Marshall Fishwick, "dare cross the path of the U.D.C., which in 1958 could boast of over a hundred Virginia chapters and 5,000 dues-paying Confederacy-proud members." Some towns, he declares, "which were only railroad whistle stops," supported two U.D.C. chapters "carrying on a friendly but brisk rivalry." As for California, as far back as 1850—far older than the D.A.R.—there was the Society of California, formed to preserve from generation to generation the immortal "days of old, days of gold, days of '49!"

From the beginning, the Daughters of the American Revolution were often accused of attempting to establish an Aristocracy based on ancestry and to welcome as members only descendants of officers or other well-placed Revolutionists. This charge has, however, been repeatedly denied, and the fact is that, of the four founding Daughters, two were government clerks—one, though a grandniece of George Washington, was a clerk in the Dead Letter Office—and another was a boardinghouse keeper whose rooms rented for $1.25 a day. Furthermore, the Daughters point with pride to the fact that one of their most distinguished latter-day recruits, Mrs. Dwight D. Eisenhower, is a descendant of a private soldier. And when one of their most controversial officers of the 1920's, Mrs. Alfred J. Brousseau, went to London and was presented at Court—bowing, as one writer put it, "her 100 percent American knees"—she quickly made amends by a patriotic postscript. "Let it be here recorded," she wrote, "that one is not compelled to make concessions with one's 'democratic spirit' in the unique and delightful experience. The question is merely one of orientation and for a brief time becoming a part of and enjoying the highest social honor that one nation can bestow upon a guest from another country."

In contrast, the Society of the Cincinnati is, as we have seen, nothing if not an hereditary Aristocracy. It forthrightly demands descent "from Officers Only" and furthermore demands descent in the male line only—or, as the quaint wording of 1783 has it, "that the original member is to be the propositus from whom succession is to be derived, and that the collateral branches are those collateral to the original member, and the succession should be through the direct male line, and not through females, until all the male lines have become extinct." And any sort of extinction is far from envisaged—as witness the Cincinnati Society *Verses*, written by William Linn Keese in 1889:

The acorn of the Oak was sown in Seventeen Eighty-three;
We sit tonight beneath the shade of our ancestral tree;
The storms of time have swept the boughs, and many a branch
    is bare,
But stoutly still the old tree stands in Freedom's bracing air.

The axe can never level it, the blast may do its worst;
'Tis rooted in the heart of man, and that must perish first;
Its branches are those human ties that link us one and all,
And, shone upon by Freedom's Sun, the tree can never fall.

Then let us inspiration draw from all that gave it birth;
May we forever clasp it round and glorify its worth;

"The Cincinnati," root and branch—this sentiment I give;
May Memory, Friendship, Honor be the sap to bid it live!

Probably the most difficult of all patriotic Societies to enter is the Order of the Founders and Patriots—not because of any so-called Society "exclusiveness" but because of what, genealogically, is demanded. The member must descend from a "Founder," a person living in the Colonies prior to 1700, and descend, in the same line, from a "Patriot," a man who fought in Washington's army. Also difficult is the Philadelphia branch of the Society of Colonial Wars, where membership is not only limited, as in the case of the National Society of Colonial Wars, to descent from a Colonial soldier or sailor, but is also, arbitrarily, limited to two hundred members, making it a question not alone of one's own birth but, apparently equally important, someone else's death. As for the Society of Colonial Dames, this, like the Cincinnati, insists on descent from an officer in the Colonial Wars. This Society had, around the turn of the century, a *cause célèbre* and ultimate schism—one which occurred, amazingly enough, over the question of whether or not to admit the descendants of the illegitimate children of Benjamin Franklin. The group which wanted them finally broke off and formed their own National Society of Colonial Dames, meanwhile leaving the "plain" Colonial Dames committed to a new post-schism requirement, that a member must be "legitimately descended from some ancestor of worthy life who came to reside in America prior to 1750 and was efficient in the service of the country."

Curiously enough, one of the most difficult of all patriotic Societies to enter is the Society of the War of 1812. Even the Aztec Club, which dates to 1847 and was formed "to cherish the memories and keep alive the traditions of those officers who took part in the Mexican War of 1846, 1847 and 1848"—a Society which was so anxious to form that it did so before the war had even ended—is easier of ascendancy than the War of 1812. "You see," one member explained briefly, "very few people fought in it. It was a very unpopular war." On the other hand, on at least one occasion this war was fought all over again at a memorable banquet which occurred some years ago on the anniversary of the Battle of New Orleans. The scene was New York's famed Fraunces' Tavern, where Washington bade farewell to his officers, and an elderly member, increasingly in his cups, became increasingly distressed at the sight of a distinguished guest of the Society only a few seats from him —the British Consul General. Finally he could stand it no longer and, leaning across the table, addressed the visitor directly. "You know," he said grimly, "you *burned* Washington." "Really," replied the Britisher coolly, "I thought he died peaceably in bed."

All these patriotic and/or aristocratic Societies have, despite often unfavorable publicity, contributed much in the way of actual service—all the way from the remarkable work of the Association for the Preservation of Virginia Antiquities, being particularly active in the erection of monuments and the protection of historical antiquities, to such mundane matters as the establishment, on the part of the Founders and Patriots, of the city of Washington's first cafeteria for working people. And all the Societies have also had, in recent years, an increasing demand for their charity right at home. Whether this is due to a rule of thumb of the American Aristocracy —that the "old" Families are not necessarily the rich Families—or to a new sort of Gresham's law—that bad Society drives good Aristocracy out of circulation—the fact remains that almost all of the Societies have, of late, been forced to look after an extraordinary number of indigent members and wives as well as institute college scholarships and school-essay prizes. A few years ago the Society of Mayflower Descendants went a step further and initiated the idea of a daughter of the Society being able, for the price of two $30 tickets, to "come out" at the annual Mayflower dinner dance—which is probably the most aristocratic and least expensive method of debut since Society began.

Despite these modern exigencies, the Societies still feel strongly about the hereditary principle. Even the D.A.R., for all of its claims of a private in Washington's army being as worthy in its eyes as a general, still adds a rider to its membership qualification that "the applicant is personally acceptable to the Society." Several other

Societies have even sterner ideas on the subject. The Colonial Daughters of the Seventeenth Century, for example, which asks only the general qualification of an ancestor who "rendered service between 1607 and 1700," also demands "a woman of good moral character and reputation." And if the high-sounding Order of Colonial Lords of Manors in America demands descent "from a recognized Patroon, Seigneur or Lord of a Manor of the New Netherlands," it remains for the far more plebeian Military Order of Foreign Wars to add the injunction that its members must be "of the Caucasian Race." Among such upper-crustacean groups as the Holland Society, Huguenot Society, and the Pilgrims of the U.S. —the latter, incidentally, has nothing to do with the *Mayflower* but fosters good will between Britain and America—probably the most "social" in the Society sense is New York's St. Nicholas Society. Founded in 1835, it demands that one have an ancestor in New York State prior to 1785; then also adds, as a membership criterion, that one also be "qualified in other respects to join a Society composed of gentlemen."

So gentlemanly indeed are the patriotic Societies that it was a *cause célèbre* to all of them when the news came, in New York in 1955, that an elderly member of one of the Societies—at first no one knew which—had shot and killed his wife in a restaurant. As the intelligence concerning the crime became clearer, it appeared that the guilty party was, as the Society regulars have it, "a Colonial Wars." Then, and only then, did the deed burst into the open, and two members of a Society which shall be nameless were heard discussing it. "It was murder all right," said one quietly, then raising his voice slightly, he added, "and it was Colonial Wars too." Then, fairly raging at the enormity of it all, he exclaimed, "But do you know where he did it? In a Schrafft's, for God's sake—a *Schrafft's!*"

Perhaps nothing better illustrates the eternal warfare between Aristocracy and Society, or, for that matter, the eternal internecine warfare within Aristocracy itself, over the matter of birth vs.

money, than the simple question of the words "lady" and "gentle-man." To the true Aristocrat who abhors the modern sun of pub-licity—possibly for altruistic reasons but equally possibly because it once shone on him and now passes him by in favor of Society— there is but one definition of a lady. And this is one which in today's Society seems almost as extinct as today's Society seems—namely, that a lady's name should appear in the papers three times: when she is born, when she marries, and when she dies. That saying crops up, credited to at least one *grande dame*, in almost every Family of any aristocratic pretensions from Maine to California.

Out on Long Island, for example, Mrs. E. Coe Kerr, who was brought up, as she remembers, not to "get her name in the paper under any circumstances," finally got used to seeing her friends' names and decided that, *faute de mieux*, as she might have said, it was nowadays *au fait*—in other words, okay. Then one day, when her cook was out and she was in her kitchen—where so many latter-day Aristocrats seem to find themselves—she was engaged in such a menial task as wrapping papers for her garbage pail. Folding a paper neatly for a base for her pail, she looked at it and suddenly, to her horror, saw her friend Mrs. William Paley. "There she was," she says, "looking me right in the eye, 'Babe' Paley, the Best Dressed Woman in the world, in my garbage pail! I've never gotten over it, and I never will."

In fairness to Mrs. Paley, one of Boston's famed Cushing sisters and the wife of the man who almost singlehandedly built the Colum-bia Broadcasting System, it should be said that there is less and less likelihood of such a thing happening again—recently Mrs. Paley has led more and more the firmly anti-publicity life of a Long Island Aristocrat. Still, the story is close to a textbook example of an Aristocrat's view of modern Society where the word "lady" is concerned. Equally aristocratic is the touching definition of a lady as related by a Southerner named Mrs. Fort Elmo Land. The attri-butes of a lady, she remembers, as handed down to her by her mother, involved just four "S's"—simplicity, sympathy, sincerity and seren-ity.

Today, however, to the Aristocrat at least, it would seem that the word "lady" in contrast to the plain word "woman" has lost, if nothing else, its contrast. As Russell Lynes has noted, "You have never heard of a 'lady' going to the 'women's room.' It is always vice versa. It is 'ladies' day' at the ball park, women who used to be called 'salesgirls' are now 'salesladies,' and there are also 'ladies of the evening,' which seems to me to be pushing the word a little further than absolutely necessary."

Even Mr. Lynes admits that he has been unable to come up with any definition for the word other than one which also involves the "gentleman"—a lady, in other words, is one who makes a man behave like a gentleman—and thus the traditional association of the "lady" with the one who was once her "lord" is gone with the wind. And the fact remains that she has gone down, to some extent at least, by being placed on a par with her gentleman. For, if we still accord the word "lady" more dignity than we do her modern counterpart, it seems we do so more out of gallantry in the modern sense than chivalry in the ancient. Lastly, a speech such as that never-to-be-forgotten one at Tuxedo Park, when the aristocratic "Congresslady" of the area, Katherine St. George, addressed first "ladies of the Park," looking to one side, and then, looking to the other, "and Women of the Village," seems indeed as dated as—well, as Tuxedo Park itself.

Actually, the original meaning of "lady" was "bread kneader," and if the dictionary adds, "See DOUGH," it refers, we add sternly, to bread only. For a long time the invention of the word "gentlewomen"—as a substitute for "lady"—was ascribed to Cincinnati and Washington's late Nicholas Longworth, but Boston's Dr. Oliver Wendell Holmes used it long before him, and in England the word goes far back. Nonetheless, if this word has had hard sledding, so too has the "lady" herself. The late H. L. Mencken noted that if English newspapers still referred to "lady champions" and even "lady actors," in the United States the word was, as contrasted with "women," definitely out of favor. And, many years before Mencken,

Wisconsin's Ella Wheeler Wilcox had issued a stirring plea for democracy in this regard:

> Give us the grand word "woman" once again,
> And let's have done with "lady"; one's a term
> Full of fine force, strong, beautiful and firm,
> Fit for the noblest use of tongue or pen;
> And one's a word for lackeys.

The late Mrs. Wilcox would seem to have been granted her wish. But what about the erstwhile lady's erstwhile "gentleman"? The Oxford dictionary defines him as "a man of gentle birth"—from the Latin *gen*—but not only have evil times apparently overtaken the word "gentle," they would also seem to have overtaken the entire word. For not long after their first definition of the word, the "New" Oxford people note rather sadly—"Now chiefly *Hist.*"

But is it chiefly historical? Surely we use the word as a mark of some aristocratic distinction, even in these new-fashioned times. Craigie's *Dictionary of American English*, for example, currently defines the "gentleman" as a "man of superior social standing"— and even here, disregarding the word "social," the gentleman is at least "superior." And, if nowadays "gentleman" only rarely precedes "scholar" in the old-fashioned phrase "gentleman and scholar," it still follows, albeit a little self-consciously, every Service Officer in the phrase "officer and gentleman." As far back as 1777 one finds George Washington writing to a friend about his choice of officers. "Take none," he said, "but gentlemen." John Adams went even further. "People in all nations," he said, "are naturally divided into two sorts, the gentlemen and the simplemen. The gentlemen are generally those who are rich, and descended from families in public life."*

Two centuries ago Thomas Fuller said, "Manners and money make

* In the old days a gentleman was "a man of property," usually not engaged in any business at all and often not even in a profession. In Virginia, in 1673, Marshall Fishwick recalls that James Bullock, a York County tailor, raced his mare against a horse belonging to a Mr. Matthew Slader but never collected his winnings. The county court judged the race illegal, "it being contrary to Law for a Laborer to make a race, being a sport only for Gentlemen." Indeed, the court went further and fined Bullock 100 pounds of tobacco and cash for his insolence.

a gentleman," and even before that George Herbert felt that "gentility was nothing but ancient riches"—two definitions which translate to America in the form of the old aphorism that to make the American gentleman it takes "three generations, plus one good guess in the stock market." And if, in the Twentieth Century, it was the "Society" Palm Beacher Charles Munn who said, "A gentleman is a man who has pronounced 'to-may-to' 'to-mah-to' for three generations," it was a self-made Boston pugilist, by the name of John L. Sullivan, who reproved a rowdy with not only a classic but also a most touching Americanism, "It don't cost nothin' to be a gentleman." The most lasting definition was undoubtedly Cardinal Newman's "one who never inflicts pain"—which was, of course, amended by Oscar Wilde to "one who never hurts anyone's feelings unintentionally." But Oscar Wilde also said, "A gentleman never looks out of the window," and a lady in a London police court once testified, "My husband is no gentleman—he puts on his trousers before his socks." All of which may have induced Noel Coward to abandon the gentleman altogether and praise the "gentleman's gentleman." "They're always," he said, "much more reliable than gentlemen."

There were several other lasting American contributions to the word besides Mr. Sullivan's. The broadest definition was that of Georgia's Robert Toombs. "We of the South," he contended, "are a race of gentlemen." Another remarkable definition was that of Thomas B. Reed, late Speaker of the House from Maine. A man who weighed between 250 and 275 pounds, he once took to task a reporter who questioned his quoted weight at 199. "No gentleman," he said, "ever weighs more than 200 pounds." Still another contribution was the definition of the late novelist, Corra May Harris. "According to my mild way of thinking," she once said, "it is not necessary for a gentleman to be bright." Then, too, there was the story of Mrs. Sidney B. Wood, Jr., reproving the table manners of the late racing driver, the Marquis de Portago. "Why can't you eat," she asked, "like a gentleman?" Replied the Marquis, "I don't have to eat like a gentleman, or drink like a gentleman or dress like a

gentleman or do anything like a gentleman. I was born a gentleman."
Replied Mrs. Wood gently, "In America we also like a gentleman
to behave like a gentleman."

It was, of course, Lord Chesterfield who noted that the vulgar
man has "freedom without ease," while the manner of a gentleman
has "ease without freedom." But it was Columbia's late Nicholas
Murray Butler who best translated this. "One of the embarrassments
of being a gentleman," he said, "is that you are not permitted to be
violent in asserting your rights." Yale's late William Lyon Phelps
declared that "the final test of a gentleman is his respect for those
who can be of no possible service to him." And *Vanity Fair's* late
Frank Crowninshield defined the gentleman as "a man who tries to
be some help to his fellows, who is considerate of women, of the
sick, the weak and the unfortunate." All of which comes down, in
the final analysis, to that simplest and best of all definitions of a
gentleman—a gentle man.

All these men, Butler, Phelps and "Crownie," were indeed "gentlemen and scholars." One cannot say as much for the American
contributors to the semantics of "gentleman" in the purely "social"
sense. Late in the past century, a professor of Harvard, by the
extraordinary name of Irving Babbitt, opened his first class of the fall
term with these words: "Probably none of you young men has ever
seen a gentleman." Since then the chances of such a sight, even at
Harvard, would, to the American Aristocrat at least, appear to
have lessened. Indeed, to today's Aristocrat, one measurement of
the steady decline of the word would be what has happened to the
word "gentleman" in combination with other words. The word
"gentlewoman," as we have seen, was close to a total casualty of the
Twentieth Century, yet a hundred years ago it actually outranked
"lady," and even a general magazine such as *Harper's* could say
firmly, "We scarcely know a truer test of a gentlewoman's taste in
dress than her selection of a shawl." As for the egregious phrase
"gentleman friend," that too is, to the younger set of today, a relic of
a bygone age—even before "beau," which also seems to be dis-
appearing. Other casualties of the Twentieth Century would seem

to be such combinations as the "gentleman farmer" and the "gentleman jockey." The former has not even been "taken up," as might be expected, by the tax-deductibly minded aristocratic farmer of nowadays; as for the latter, one has only to attend the Middleburg, Warrenton or Maryland Hunt to learn that "gentleman jockey" is no longer used—"except, of course," as we were told by those aristocratic Southern communities, "in the West." In the Middleburg races of 1957, for example, there was just one "gentleman jockey" —and he was called an "amateur rider."

Today it would seem, from the aristocratic point of view, that either everyone is a gentleman or no one. Furthermore, the trouble seems to be not only that we are not quite sure which but also that both are equally bad news. Just when all this began is not quite clear, but to the Aristocrat there is no question but that the Twentieth Century is clearly to blame. This writer's own father, for example, a man who admits to a stern prejudice in favor of any century previous to his own, is inclined to lay the whole thing to the dawn of 1900 itself. Although this is earlier than most Aristocrats would date it, the fact remains that as far back as 1892 *Vogue* magazine sternly inquired, "Now that the masses take baths every week, how can one ever distinguish the gentleman?" As if this were not enough, only a short time later Mark Twain added, "Soap and education are not as sudden as a massacre but they are more deadly in the long run." In any case, by the early part of the century the obituaries for the word "gentleman" were coming thick and fast. "A real gentleman," said Kim Hubbard in 1908—and the very fact that he had to use "real" is in itself revealing—"is at a real disadvantage these days." And as for today, one finds that even in what would be thought primarily objective circles, the word has an almost simon-pure nostalgic flavor. "When I was young," laments Somerset Maugham, "the conception of a gentleman had value. Now not only what it stood for but the word itself has become vaguely objectionable."

The 1930's were perhaps the heyday for obituaries of the word "gentleman." Edith Wharton in 1934 spoke of the "vanished American gentleman"—a type which, she said, "vanished with the conditions that produced it." She named as examples Bayard Cutting, Robert Minturn, John Cadwalader, George Rives, Stephen Olin and Egerton Winthrop. "They combined," she said, "a cultivated taste with marked social gifts. Their weakness was that, save in a few cases, they made so little use of their abilities. A few were distinguished lawyers or bankers, with busy professional careers, but too many, like Egerton Winthrop, lived in dilettantish leisure." Nonetheless, Mrs. Wharton found Egerton "in difficult moments, the surest of counsellors," and she concluded, "Even now that I am old and he has been so many years dead, it still happens to me, when faced by a difficulty, to ask myself, 'What would Egerton have done?' "

Only a year after Mrs. Wharton, Henry Dwight Sedgwick wrote an entire book devoted to gentlemen. Mr. Sedgwick, who died in 1957 at the age of 95, was not only a gentleman and lawyer himself, he was also the son of one. If the father was best known for his work *Sedgwick on Damages,* the son was best known for *In Praise of Gentlemen* or for his belief that the Twentieth Century had mortally damaged the ideal of the gentleman as "the guardian of leisure." "A revolution," he said, "has taken place in our statements, manners and moral opinions," and the core of this revolution he found to be "the reversal of the time-honored notion that the qualities which make a gentleman are qualities valuable to society."

Mr. Sedgwick refused to call his gentlemen a "class." Instead, he called them a Guild: "guide and mentor to the general mass of men, blinded and confused as they are in the hugger-mugger of workaday life." Then Mr. Sedgwick proceeded to outline his gentleman under six "Notes," as follows:

(1) Manners. "The old order was aware how large a part casual relations play in social life, how many a little makes a mickle. . . The old order understood how important is the outside of things."

(2) Style. "This quality is similar to that of manners, but it has a different shade of meaning, a different emphasis. . . . Whatever is noble, grand, rhythmical, subtle, whatever possesses measure or elegance, is the result of form. Form, when it is successful, has style."

(3) Modesty. "Another note of the old-fashioned gentleman was reticence upon matters of sex. . . . Such reticence the present generation, full of Freudian valiancy for truth, declares to be nonsense; matters which, in the days of my youth, Mr. Frederic Harrison printed in Latin in a footnote now stand in capital letters at the head of the chapter."

(4) Taste. "In old days, when quality was valued more than quantity, when the cult of beauty was both a privilege and a duty, taste was the finger post to what the aristocracy regarded as the mind's most permanent pleasure, the love of beauty. Now all this is changed. . . . The world's favorite axiom is that the needs of belly and back come before the delicacies of mind and the fastidiousness of the soul."

(5) Privacy. "What used to be considered the inalienable right of a man to keep himself and his affairs to himself is his no longer. It has not only ceased to be a right, but it has become a wrong done to the public. . . . The old adage that a man's house is his castle bears all the marks of the old regime. A castle to be sure! The very emblem of aristocracy, pride, privilege, privacy and inequality."

(6) Education. "Gentlemen of old studied the humanities. . . . This luxury of voyaging through the thought and literature of the classical world was not open to everybody; it was the appurtenance of property and privilege. Young patricians held a monopoly of opportunity, and, however imperfectly, they justified this prerogative by upholding the law of decorum, the value of form, the abiding pleasure in beauty, the worth of manners, style, dignity and reticence."

Mr. Sedgwick's words, let alone his ideas, seem at first blush far more dated today than they were when he wrote them. But Mr. Sedgwick's white paper on Aristocracy considered every facet of what he regarded as a great tradition. To him even that bane of Aristocracy, the word "dilettante," was praiseworthy. Derived from *dilettare* (to delight) and originally "a person who loved the fine arts," this word also fell from its once-high estate to become synonymous with "dabbler," "drifter" or "trifler." But Mr. Sedgwick, speaking for Aristocracy, would have none, as he would have said, of such modern folderol. Boldly he spoke out, as he had in praise of gentlemen, in praise of dilettante:

The dilettante, like an accomplished host, kept the Guild of Gentlemen together; he brought the whole company into mutual relations, into common sympathies and a common understanding; he re-formulated their ideals and renovated their traditions. . . . Specialization has, as we say, put the dilettante out of business; it loosed the cord that held the Guild of Gentlemen together, and so helped render it defenseless before the assaults of triumphant democracy.

With such sentiments many a modern Aristocrat would find himself in hearty agreement. And surely a little historical perspective will serve to show that Mr. Sedgwick's complaint is as old as America itself—in fact, it is in the mainstream of the American definition of Aristocracy. Ever since the emergence of the so-called "self-made man"—a birth which took place, according to Professor Irvin G. Wyllie, almost a hundred years before Mr. Sedgwick wrote his aristocratic obituary—the warfare between the Aristocrat and the self-made man has been as integral a part of America's social history as Society itself.*

Since the 1830's, through successive generations of San Francisco's Forty-niners, Montana Copper Kings, Chicago Packers, Pittsburgh Steelers, and Detroit Auto Magnates, the self-made man has been the butt of every conceivable joke on the part of the Aristocrat, and even as late as 1892, William Dean Howells placed him below Society. "The self-made man," he said, "can never be the Society equal of the Society-made man." Horace Greeley was even sterner. "I am a self-made man," a Congressman once proudly told him. "That, sir," replied Greeley, "relieves the Almighty of a great responsibility." And no less aristocratic was the comment of the distinguished political scientist Francis Lieber. "Self-made men, indeed!" he once exclaimed. "Why don't you tell me of a self-laid egg?"

For a whole century, humorists had, along with the Aristocrats, a field day. Josh Billings declared that "Self-made men are most

* Credit for the coining of the phrase "self-made" goes to Henry Clay, who, in 1832, was defending the protective tariff against charges that it would spawn an hereditary industrial aristocracy. "In Kentucky," he said, "almost every manufactory known to me is in the hands of enterprising, *self-made* men, who have whatever wealth they possess by patient and diligent labor."

always apt to be a little too proud of the job," while Kim Hubbard added, "No self-made man ever did such a good job that a woman didn't want to make a few alterations." And if one Aristocrat, Oliver Wendell Holmes, poet and doctor, was gentle: "It's a great deal better to be made that way," he said, "than not to be made at all," James Russell Lowell expressed the hope that someday America would decide that self-made men had not been "divinely commissioned to fabricate the higher qualities of opinion on all possible topics of human interest."

There were, of course, provocations—among them the mortal words of Uncle Dan'l Drew, *circa* 1879: "Book learning is something, but thirteen million dollars is also something, and a mighty site more." There was also the not so considered opinion of Commodore Vanderbilt. Following his famous *North Star* cruise to England, Lord Palmerston told a friend of his that it was a pity that a man of the Commodore's ability, as he gently phrased it, had not had more formal schooling. Told of this, Vanderbilt replied, "You can tell Lord Palmerston from me that if I had learned education I would not have had time to learn anything else."

At the other end of the business spectrum was the greatest of America's business Aristocrats, the late J. P. Morgan the Elder. He was an Aristocrat through and through—literally so, since it was not his father but his grandfather who first founded his fortune, in stagecoaches, in Hartford, Connecticut. Often quoted is Morgan's remark about a man who wanted to know how much a yacht cost. "If a man has to ask," replied Morgan, "he can't afford it." Less often quoted is his remark that "You can do business with anyone, but you can only sail a boat with a gentleman." Or, for that matter, his remark to a prospective yacht buyer that he should not consider it unless he numbered among his associates men who would be willing to spend time with him. "A yacht," said Morgan, "can be the loneliest place in the world."*

Carl Hovey estimated that for all the world fame of Morgan there

---

* At the same time, Morgan believed in limitation of his cruising guests. "With more than four," he said, "there's no real cruising." This count excluded, of course, the crew—which, on the *Corsair*, numbered some 85.

were not fifty people in Wall Street who had a speaking acquaintance with him. Once his son invited a Harvard classmate to spend
the night up the Hudson at Morgan's "Highland Falls," and suggested that since his father was coming up on the *Corsair* the friend
should join him. The friend did, and during the entire trip, he recalled, Morgan spoke to him only once—and that on his arrival,
"How do you do?" Yet Morgan told his son later, "That's a very
pleasant young man." In the same way, when Morgan was in Egypt,
an Englishman had been directed to take charge of the Morgan
party on a train trip across the desert. "In six hours," he said, "Morgan asked me only 'How do you do?'—and two terse questions
about the state of the desert." Yet, if he made no fuss over other
people, Morgan demanded no fuss in return. In London he became
so exercised over his employees who, in the class-conscious British
manner, bowed to him that he ordered them to desist on pain of
dismissal.

Like the true Aristocrat, Morgan had rigid standards of conduct,
both for himself and for other people, and if his code admitted the
double standard of the day where women were concerned, it admitted it only in the strictest privacy. When an associate whom he
had called on the carpet for some action protested that he had only
been doing what he, himself, had been doing for years "behind
closed doors," Morgan was adamant. "That, sir," he said, "is what
doors are for." On the other hand, when another man broke his
word on what would seem today a relatively trivial matter, Morgan
never spoke to him again, and yet the man was not only a former
close associate in business but a close relative as well. In today's New
York Society when people "feud," if at all, for publicity purposes
only, such a standard would seem to date to the Middle Ages.

On the subject of publicity Morgan was adamant. "He had," says
one of his former partners, "the instinctive shrinking from publicity
of the man of breeding." Despite his world-wide fame, he made no
speeches, never attended public meetings, gave the rarest and briefest
of interviews, avoided photographers on every possible occasion,
and generally ignored not only the press and public opinion but

also all politicians up to the President himself. "He seems to regard me," said his fellow Aristocrat Theodore Roosevelt after one conference, "as a rival operator." Retorted Morgan, upon hearing the remark, "If he had his way we'd all do business with glass pockets." Unflattered by praise, Morgan was equally unruffled by censure. He never wrote or signed an "autobiography" despite incredible offers and refused to countenance either any biography in his lifetime or, for that matter, even the attempt of his son-in-law, Herbert Satterlee, to make him give private interviews for posthumous publication. The closest he ever came to a public statement of his code was undoubtedly the occasion, during the Pujo Committee hearings, when Samuel Untermyer asked him whether commercial credit was based primarily on property or on money. "The first thing," thundered Morgan, "is character. A man I do not trust could not get money from me on all the bonds in Christendom."

Many other Aristocrats, both before and since, have had hard treatment after their deaths. But Morgan's was the hardest of all. For he was almost immediately made the scapegoat of the entire "muckraking" era—and this apparently, or for at least the main reason, because he was an Aristocrat. Just why this should have been a crime, when to have been "in Society" was not, was by no means the fault of the press alone. It was rather the end result of the almost total confusion of Aristocracy and Society. Ironically enough, many other social figures of Morgan's time escaped the muckrakers almost entirely, and some of them not only were far more culpable than Morgan of the excesses of the era but were also richer. Andrew Carnegie, commenting on Morgan's art collection, was surprised. "And to think," he said, "he wasn't even a rich man." By Carnegie's standards, Morgan was not. On his death in 1913, Morgan left $68,000,000, which was not only a smaller fortune than that of a Frick, a Harriman or a Mellon, it was far smaller than that of a Thomas Fortune Ryan or a Payne Whitney, and a mere pygmy compared to a Du Pont or a John D. Rockefeller.

One of Morgan's disciples, another scion of silence where publicity was concerned, was the late George F. Baker. Born to no Aristocracy, he nonetheless lived by its standards. In his entire life of 90 years, he gave two speeches, of half a dozen words each, and one interview. And yet he, too, all but paid with his reputation. Some years ago his grandson, George F. Baker III, was taken to the Dartmouth College Library, which the elder Baker had given, to view his grandfather's portrait. Young Baker was speechless. "I didn't know what to say," he says. "It wasn't even he."

Other examples of aristocratic anonymity are legion and exist in every city in the country. Frank Ashburn, of Brooks School, recalls that when he had completed his biography of Endicott Peabody, headmaster of Groton, and had sent it to him, the late "Mr." Peabody—he refused "Dr."—who was at that time 86 years old and "retired," had "no time to read the biography"—though it was the first and only one of him published—"for five weeks." "And then Mr. Peabody reported," says Mr. Ashburn, "that he had been grossly overestimated." Yet this all was entirely in character. Mr. Peabody bore one of the country's most aristocratic names—one which is pronounced by saying the consonants as rapidly as possible and ignoring all vowels, including the "y." Mr. Peabody came from Salem, a sterner city of Aristocracy even than Boston, where it was, as the saying went, "Peabody or nobody."

Outside of this country such distinctions were never understood nor, in all probability, ever will be. A Philadelphian who, many years ago, made a trip to China still recalls—"with wonderment," he says—the expression on a Chinese merchant's face while his friend, a Chew, explained to the Chinese "just what it meant to be a Chew in Philadelphia." One can only hazard that it must have been a somewhat similar expression to that which probably crossed the face of the late Kaiser Wilhelm of Germany when, in a burst of enthusiasm, President Theodore Roosevelt informed him of the engagement of his daughter, Alice, to Nicholas Longworth, and added, "Nick and I are both members of the Porc, you know."*

* Harvard's Porcellian Club is generally regarded as the *ne plus ultra* of college clubs. Started in 1791, it was once known as the Pig Club, from the fondness of two of its first members, Francis Cabot Lowell and Robert Treat Paine, for that delicacy in roasted form. Legend persists that it was a Porcel-

Curiously enough, Aristocracy, which is, then, in large measure the reverse of Society, is likely to manifest itself, if at all, only in this reverse. And this manifestation involves not only old possessions and even old clothes but also something more—or rather less. "As children," says Ambassador "Jock" Whitney, "we were the reverse of snobs, and we liked people in almost inverse proportion to their so-called 'social' position." Brought up in this reverse fashion also, a member of one of the so-called "poor" Whitneys has a sadder tale to tell. "I didn't even know we had money," she says, "until we didn't." In some instances aristocratic Families have even become self-effacing about one of the indices of Family—the Jr., III, V, etc., or II, IV and VI, if the same name is used for a nephew. Joseph H. Choate, Jr., for example, son of the great Society wit, Joseph H. Choate, named his son Joseph Choate III, but was pleased when the latter named *his* son Jonathan. "I told my son," he said, "enough is enough." In the same manner Huntington Hartford II named his son John Hartford. "I want him to make it on his own," he said, "be independent."

Perhaps the basic American social story—the one from which all others might be said to stem—is the one in which an aristocratic person says, or does, something which a person of secure position could do, or say, but one which a person of less secure position, or new-generation Society, could not. For example, let us take the famous story of Edith Wharton's husband hailing a butcher cart and riding down Newport's Bellevue Avenue in it. A Westerner— by that time any Westerners bore the brunt of all *nouveau riche* Society stories—took him to task. "Wharton," he said, "I hear you rode up the Avenue in a butcher cart. I wouldn't do that, if I were you." Replied Wharton, "No, if I were you, I wouldn't do that either." Translated to Virginia, the same Aristocracy is evident in the story of Mrs. William Meade Lewis, of the distinguished Lewis family of Lewis and Clark of Albemarle, Virginia, a lady who some years ago was wired by the *New York Times* to find out what

---

lian stroke of a Harvard crew of whom it was said, "He's democratic all right —he knows all but the three up front."

relation she was to Lady Astor, the former Nancy Langhorne. Promptly Mrs. Lewis wired back. "The Lewises were making history," she said, "when the Langhornes were making moonshine and the Astors were skinning rabbits." And finally, translated to present-day Dallas, Texas, the story becomes that of a man from "west Texas" who catches Dallas' "Harvard" lawyer, Tom Knight, in the middle of an "ain't." "If I were you, Tom," he said, "I wouldn't use that word." To which, of course, Knight replied, "No, if I were you, I wouldn't."

A similar version of this story exists in almost every city or, for that matter, area of aristocratic pretensions in the country. There are also, of course, versions in reverse. Robert Moses, for example, New York's great Park Commissioner, recalls that Judge Townsend Scudder once took him to a meeting of the Meadowbrook Club on Long Island, of which he was a charter member. "To the fox hunters in their red coats," Moses says, "Judge Scudder explained the Northern Parkway—whereupon the audience rose as one man and denounced us on the grounds the hounds would lose the scent as the foxes crossed the parkway. Governor Smith later suggested fox and hound underpasses." Hardly more extreme is the oft-told story of the radio business when an advertising agency approached the Du Pont company with the idea of a three o'clock Sunday afternoon program. The Du Pont people wanted none of it. "At three o'clock on Sunday afternoons," they said firmly, "everybody is playing polo."

There are also whole aristocratic cities, usually in close proximity to some now usually larger "Society" city. Port Huron, Michigan, where the Family fortunes in most cases antedate the Detroit auto fortunes, is one of these. Another is Santa Barbara, which is to Los Angeles, as one lady expressed it, "what it should be." Probably the best example, however, is San Antonio, Texas, which is, of course, pre-oil. Here Mrs. Franz Stumpf, representing not only five generations of Texas but also the "D.T.R."—Daughters of the Texas Republic—defines "top-drawer" San Antonio as "genteel people— people who don't need to be justified by anything." On the other hand, her friend, Mrs. Frank LaFlamme, born in Brooklyn and only fifteen years in San Antonio, disagrees. "It's money that counts. At the Chrysanthemum Ball there isn't a name there that anybody ever heard of twenty-five years ago." And writer Frank Conniff, visiting Texas, was in turn unimpressed by a Texan who boasted of four generations. "Where I come from," he said, "even the Irish have been there four generations."

Easily the most aristocratic of all American cities, and indeed the stern answer to any foreigner who claims that American Aristocracy is nothing but money, is Charleston, South Carolina. Once called the "Home of the Stranded Gentry," it is here that the first ball fired from the Battery on Fort Sumter is enshrined in a counting-house on Broad Street under a label stating that it started "The War of Northern Aggression." It is here also that the late modern Southern "merchant prince," Elliott White Springs, could take a visitor around the city and, asked if the odor which greeted him came from a nearby fertilizing plant, promptly shook his head. "No," he said, "it is merely the decaying Aristocracy." Outside of Charleston, in the town of Hartsville, Mrs. Elizabeth Boatwright Coker was showing a "Yankee" her collection of spode. "We have some too," said the Yankee proudly. "My great-great-grandfather was a sea captain from Salem, you know, and he brought them to us." "Ah," said Mrs. Coker gently, "but these were brought by gentlemen."

Charleston had begun, curiously enough, with actual warfare between herself and St. Augustine, Florida, oldest of all American cities, and to this day the walls which she put up against her rival remain as important to her as her great Families themselves—her Hugers and Legarés (pronounced you-gees and luh-grees), Prioleaus and Izards, Pinckneys and Pringles, Ravenels and Rutledges, Middletons, Manigaults, and the rest. In fact, says Samuel Gaillard Stoney, the walls will probably never be torn down, for they are the "spiritual bastions and battlements" which have seen Charleston through both her "bright, bitter days" when she ruled the South and the days when she became the "scapegoat of the Nation, the city that had lost the war," right up to her venerable present. "So

Tearing down the statue of George III on Bowling Green, 1776: America decides that all men are born equal—although some, of course, are more equal than others. . . .

The "Old House," Quincy, Mass., where four generations of Adamses lived. (Brown Brothers)

"Stratford Hall," home of four generations of Lees. (Brown Brothers)

In contrast—"Biltmore," home of George Washington Vanderbilt II, Asheville, North Carolina. (Courtesy of Biltmore)

John Jacob Astor I. (Brown Brothers)

Commodore Vanderbilt.

Virginia's "King" Carter.

Boston's Sir Richard Saltonstall.

Isaac Roosevelt—first Roosevelt politician and founder of the "Hyde Park" branch.

Eleuthère Irénée du Pont de Nemours.

Lambert Cadwalader,
"Epitome of the
Philadelphia
gentleman."

The three Straus brothers—Nathan, Oscar and Isidor—taken shortly before the death of Isidor on the *Titanic*, 1912.

John Randolph of Roanoke—the country's
No. 1 orator. (Corcoran Art Gallery)

Col. and Mrs. Charles Russell
Lowell, Jr.

Two great-grandchildren of Robert E. Lee unveil his portrait, West
Point, 1952. (Brown Brothers)

Baltimore's Betsy Patterson, who married
Jerome Bonaparte. Triple-head portrait by
Gilbert Stuart.

Mrs. John Jay. Her "Visiting List"
was the first.

Philadelphia's Anne Willing, who, at 16,
married William Bingham, the country's
richest man.

Virginia's Evelyn Byrd, who died of a
broken heart. From a portrait by Sir
Godfrey Kneller.

Ward McAllister, author of the "Four Hundred."

Oliver Wendell Holmes the Elder—poet and doctor. (Fabian Bachrach)

The Mrs. Astor. (Brown Brothers)

Leland Stanford, photographed in 1885.

Daughters of the American Revolution.

Mrs. Potter Palmer, Mrs. Honoré Palmer and Mrs. Frederick Dent Grant, daughter-in-law of President Grant, at the Lake Forest Fair, 1916. (Chicago Historical Society)

New York's famous James Hazen Hyde Ball—1905; (l. to r., standing) Mrs. Sidney Smith, P. A. Clark, Mrs. James Burden, Stanford White, James Henry Smith, Norman Whitehouse; (seated) Sidney Smith, Mrs. Stuyvesant Fish. (Museum of The City of New York)

Cast of play given in the '90's by Chicago's Friday Club; (l. to r.) Mrs. John Alden Carpenter, Mrs. Murry Nelson, Mrs. Lysander Hill, Mrs. Samuel T. Chase, Mrs. William Nitze, Mrs. Frank R. Fuller, Mrs. John Kales. (Chicago Historical Society)

Jennie Jerome, mother of Winston Churchill.

Lady Astor, the former Nancy Langhorne of Virginia.

Bessie Wallis Warfield, future Duchess of Windsor, at camp.

Consuelo Vanderbilt, future Duchess of Marlborough. (Brown Brothers)

The children of the late John D. Rockefeller, Jr.; (l. to r.) Abby (Mrs. Jean Mauzé), John D. III, Nelson, Laurance, Winthrop and David, and, in insert, their mother as a child.

The children of the late George J. Gould; (l. to r.) Kingdon, Marjorie, Jay, George J., Jr., and Vivian. The Gould chauffeur at the wheel. (Culver)

The last photo of the late E. H. Harriman and family; (l. to r.) Mrs. George Discon, Miss Mary A. Harriman, Miss Carol A. Harriman, Robert Goelet, W. Averell Harriman, Dr. Discon, Mr. Harriman and Mrs. Robert Goelet. (Brown Brothers)

The late Alfred Gwynne Vanderbilt drives his famous drag in London with his wife, the late Margaret Emerson, seated beside him. He went down on the *Lusitania*. (Brown Brothers)

Mrs. O. H. P. Belmont, the former Mrs. W. K. Vanderbilt, wheels Julia Ward Howe into a Newport suffragette meeting. (Brown Brothers)

Consuelo Vanderbilt sells peanuts on Labor Day at the Newport Casino. (Brown Brothers)

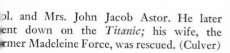

Col. and Mrs. John Jacob Astor. He later went down on the *Titanic;* his wife, the former Madeleine Force, was rescued. (Culver)

"Princess" Alice Roosevelt Longworth (front row, second from right) in Hong Kong in early 1900's. Her husband, the late Nicholas Longworth of Cincinnati, is at extreme left; lady with fan is Mrs. Newlands, the former Edith McAllister; Sen. Newlands, Nevada, behind Mrs. Longworth; man with beard, Frederick Huntington Gillett, Mass., member of House, 1893-1925. (Culver)

C. K. G. Billings' famous Horseback Dinner given in the Grand Ballroom of Sherry's (converted into a woodland scene) in 1903. The riders ate from small tables attached to the saddle pommels; during dessert the horses were given oat-filled troughs. (Museum of The City of New York)

Above, the late Pittsburgh "idler," Harry K. Thaw, who murdered Stanford White, and Evelyn Nesbit, the chorus girl Thaw married, claiming she had been "ruined" by White. (Max Haas)

J. P. Morgan the Elder—epitome of the Northern Aristocrat. (Edward Steichen)

if," says Stoney, "in her old age, she has suddenly found herself, like Queen Victoria, become almost holy, a place of pilgrimage for the grandchildren of men who would joyously have sown her ashes with salt, you must forgive her if she has walls."

As for the characteristics of the gentlemen themselves of America's purest Aristocracy, Mrs. St. Julien Ravenel, in her *Charleston: The Place and the People* (1906), has written what remains the definitive story:

> Some traits they had in common, traits springing from the creed of their race. They were brave, and truthful, and manly; to be otherwise would be disgrace. They were formal in address, but in society had the courteous ease of manner that comes from generations of assured position, and of living amongst one's peers.
>
> To women they were charmingly and carefully polite; it was always *chapeau-bas* in the presence of ladies. Mothers and wives were queens to sons and husbands; the slightest offence offered to them was cause of battle. The men were, it must be confessed, quick of temper, too prone to resent even a trifling wrong; both proud and passionate, but generous and liberal to a fault; faithful in friendship, but fierce in enmity.
>
> The lodestar of their lives was "the point of honour." A man's word must be *better* than his bond, because unguaranteed. A woman's name must never pass his lips except in respect; a promise, however foolish, must be kept. If he had wronged any man, he must offer his life in expiation. He must always be ready to fight for the State or for his lady. This was the unwritten law which made "the chivalry."

It was such a people who cheered, when, after the bombardment of Fort Sumter from the Battery at Charleston, shots from the Union side came back—showing the Fort was still fighting—for they had started what they firmly believed would be a chivalric war. And it was such a people who are now immortalized on the memorial tablet to the Confederate dead under the portico of St. Philip's: "Henry Augustus Middleton, Jr. Co. A. Haupton Legion, mortally wounded Manassas, Virginia, July 1861, aged 31 years . . . Edmund Shubroch Hayne, 18 years . . . Robert Woodward Rhett, 23 years . . . George Coffin Pinckney, 25 years . . . Charles Edwin Prioleau,

24 years . . . Washington Alston, 18 years . . ." and so on and on.

Today the Aristocracy of Charleston may best be viewed at the St. Cecilia Ball—in fact, not only the ball itself but also the whole St. Cecilia Society which runs it is undoubtedly the most truly aristocratic stronghold in America. St. Cecilia began in 1737, being originally an amateur concert society. Through its first century, however, ardor for concerts steadily diminished and ardor for balls grew more and more passionate. By 1822 the concert was abandoned altogether and the ball alone reigned in solitary splendor. Like the Baltimore Cotillon, which is still spelled with one "i" as a visible proof of Aristocracy—as well as the Philadelphia Assembly, with its almost equally modest aristocratic traditions—St. Cecilia is run entirely by men, the Society itself being a club which does nothing but run the ball once a year. Only elected members of St. Cecilia and their guests (all of whom must be passed on in advance) may attend the ball.

So rigid are the standards that the description of the requirements, as written by Mrs. Ravenel more than half a century ago—one of the rare times anything about the club was ever publicized—are still in force today:

> If a man's father or grandfather, or any of his immediate kindred, have belonged before him, there is little doubt that he will be chosen. Nevertheless blackballs (two suffice to exclude) have fallen, when the applicant was a notoriously unworthy scion of his family tree. If a new resident, or of a family recently brought into notice, there will be inquiry, perhaps hesitation, and a good backing will be desirable. But if he be of character and standing calculated to make his membership acceptable to the Society, he will be elected,— unless he has some adversary; then he may fail. The presenter of such a one will make careful examination into public feeling before subjecting his friend to mortification; and will withhold the letter if in doubt. When a man is elected, the names of the ladies of his household are at once put upon "the list" and remain there forever. Only death or removal from the city erases them,—change of fortune affects them not at all. "To be dropped from the St. Cecilia" is an awful possibility sometimes hinted at, but which (as far as known) has never come to pass.

To this day no actors or actresses may attend. Neither may any divorced woman—whatever the extenuating circumstances. On the other hand, a gentleman may attend if, after a divorce, he has not married again. A girl from "off," as it is called, or away from Charleston, may attend as a guest if her "Family background" passes the rigid committee check. However, if an "off" girl lives in Charleston for over a year, thus becoming in St. Cecilia's eyes a resident, she may never attend, no matter who asks her. Many times girls come to Charleston for eleven months, then quickly move away so that they may attend. As for a girl whose father is a member of St. Cecilia, if she has the misfortune to marry a man who is not a member, she may attend but neither her husband nor her children may do so.

The ball, held annually in a beautiful, historic, but rather shabby building, is never reported in newspapers or magazines. "They don't," said one member, "even dare ask to cover it." Even Charlestonians rarely mention the ball because of the touchiness of the subject. Nonetheless, on the night of St. Cecilia, an extraordinary number of people stay home with darkened drawing rooms in the hope that other people may think they are at the ball. There is probably no social function in America where money counts for less or where there is less monetary show, save, in true aristocratic proportion, in reverse. Ladies of St. Cecilia families may have only one St. Cecilia dress, but they wear it proudly for life. Gentlemen without even the money to afford a dinner jacket, let alone owning a white tie, have been known to attend the St. Cecilia in a dark-blue or black suit and black bow tie. That too is in the great tradition.

As for the ball itself, the rules are strict. It is a card dance—every dance of every lady is spoken for in advance—and only waltzes and slow fox trots are played. There is no South American music, albeit there is an occasional Charleston. Finally, although champagne is served at supper, there are no other alcoholic beverages served in the ballroom. Gentlemen may and occasionally do go into a room and drink a glass of wine, but ladies may not drink, not even wine, anywhere on the premises.

All in all, it is only fitting that such an Aristocracy in such a city should have provided what will undoubtedly always remain as the textbook story of the warfare between Aristocracy and Society. An elderly lady was being told by her grandchildren of the sights they had seen abroad. She listened with no comment until they came to the story of their trip to the Louvre. When, however, they reported the awe of all the tourists at the sight of the famous painting of Whistler's mother, she could contain herself no longer. "But *why?*" asked the old lady gently. "After all, she was only a *McNeill* of *North* Carolina!"

As Charleston provided the country's leading example of Aristocracy by city, so too did the South in general and Virginia in particular provide the greatest of all examples of Aristocracy in person. In fact, it provided the paragon of the whole Southern idea of Aristocracy by birth in contrast to the Northern idea of Aristocracy by wealth—one which we have already seen in the person of J. P. Morgan the Elder, New Englander and New Yorker. It provided it, of course, in the person of the late Robert E. Lee.

To this day, so great is the deference to Lee's name that Southern mothers of errant children or, for that matter, Southern "gentlewomen" running schools, control any and all matters of manners, morals, and mores by the mildest mention of this greatest of Southern heroes. "Whenever we did something bad," a lady from Lynchburg says of her school days, "the head mistress would quietly turn Lee's picture to the wall—and that was enough." This same sort of deference, on a more memorable scale, was demonstrated in 1919 when the then young Southern historian, Douglas Southall Freeman, was addressing the three hundred surviving Confederate veterans at the Soldiers Home at Richmond. The historian asked how many had ever seen General Lee. "A few held up their hands," it is recorded, "but most of them, as if to do his memory greater honor, rose to their feet, shoulders squared with pride."

Not a winner but a loser, not even the South's greatest general— in fact, there are books to prove (albeit wrongly) that he wasn't even a great general—with a youth of poverty, a young manhood of hard work and incredibly slow promotion—twenty-one years out of West Point he was still a Captain—with an invalid wife who had succeeded an invalid mother, with the death of a beloved daughter and without even a belief in Secession to begin with, Lee yet remains, to friend and foe alike, the all-time giant of American Aristocracy, the immortal embodiment of the Lost Cause and, as Christina Bond called him, "the realized King Arthur." And there is, indeed, no man in all American history who better deserves such praise as the man who all his life "disliked adjectives," never gave a single newspaper interview, and took to the bitter end the sole burden of the Southern defeat on his own shoulders. "It's all my fault," he said. "I thought my men were invincible." As a youth he had coal-black hair, coal-black eyes, an aristocratic, courtly bearing and a courteous, kindly manner. As an older man—he was 53 when the war broke out and 65 when, in 1870, he died—with his gray beard and hair, mounted on his beloved gray horse, "Traveller," he was an almost unbelievable sight. "Oh!" exclaimed a Northern girl, seeing him on the road to Gettysburg, "I wish he were ours!"

During the war the word "Yankee" was never used in his presence —not because he disliked Northerners but because others used it as a term of opprobrium which he would not countenance. Only once did his men refuse to obey him—when, in the battle of the Wilderness and the beginning of the end for the Confederacy, he rode too close, in their judgment, urging them forward. "Lee to the rear!" they shouted—and only when he had obeyed them did they obey him and return to the attack. At Appomattox he divided his own cash equally among his staff officers, and after that, in the true aristocratic tradition he alone, of all the generals on either side, refused to write his memoirs. "I should be trading," he said, "on the blood of my men."*

* The late General George Catlett Marshall similarly refused to write his memoirs of World War II, and, as those close to the General knew, his decision was primarily due to the example set by General Lee before him. Indeed, his veneration for his fellow Virginian and his desire to emulate him is held by many people as primarily responsible for the fact that General

Although his own fortune, never large, was gone, his beloved estate at Arlington sold for debts, he still refused even an honorary position as titular head of an insurance company which would have paid him $10,000 and saved Arlington. Finally, although he was offered virtually every conceivable high-paying and highly honored position, from Commander in Chief of the Rumanian Army to the Democratic nomination for the Presidency, he chose to become president of, at that time, the small and relatively impoverished Washington College at Lexington—later the famed Washington and Lee—where his salary was $1,500 a year.

Even as a soldier in the field, Lee had always stood first and foremost for character. One general, though excellent in combat, was demoted by him on the basis of lack of self-control. "I cannot have a man in control of others," Lee said, "who cannot control himself." After the war, to a mother who brought her child for his blessing, he said, "Teach him to deny himself." In the same spirit was his sole declaration of policy at Washington and Lee. "We have but one rule here," he told a prospective student, "that every man should be a gentleman."

Of all stories told at the College during Lee's brief tenure there, the favorite is the story of the sophomore who, carried away by the General's lecture about hard work where success is concerned, suddenly could contain himself no longer. "But, General," he blurted out, "you failed!"

For a second Lee's eyes blazed. Then, as quickly, they calmed. "I hope, my son," he said gently, "that you will be more fortunate than I."

Throughout their aristocratic history, Americans would seem to have ignored one definition of the word "gentleman"—one given by the great Blackstone, of common law fame. "A gentleman," he held, "is a man entitled to bear a coat of arms." But if Americans have ignored the definition they have not ignored the idea. Indeed, for

---

Marshall alone of all World War II leaders best exemplified character in the tradition of Lee.

the American, arms and the gentleman went, from the very beginning, hand in hand. Even the Indians apparently liked them. The very first traders gave royal arms, it is recorded, "only to headmen"— less than royal sufficed, evidently, for the average brave.

In the old days in England there was a law that the manufacturer of bogus arms should be docked of an ear. If the same law had ever been enforced in this country, the number of one-eared businessmen would make a small army. For in America, it seems, the boast of heraldry and the pomp of pedigree are very nearly everywhere— from Cadillacs to cans of baking powder. Cadillacs, for example, are embossed with six ducks—or swans—swimming westward. As for Chryslers, one of the crown-crested models is known as the Crown Imperial—possibly to distinguish it, in Detroit eyes, from the Crown Cromwellian. Even the lowly Chevrolet features the *fleur-de-lis*, while Fords are embellished with a coat of arms featuring a pair of lions *couchant*, right forepaw raised somewhat—in the imperious gesture of a policeman halting traffic.

There is, however, no halting America's armigerous appetite. Bottles of whiskey and perfume, boxes of candy, and even soap are apparently not only descended from gentlemen but also actually from kings. Throughout the land, hotels and restaurants pedigree everything from their dinnerware and crockery to their matchbooks. The symbol of the lordly Ritz hotels, for example, is the leonine head, and even lowly Schrafft's, so maligned by the Society of the Colonial Wars, has its armor—presumably to *vincit omnia*. Examination of the latter arms discloses a shield, regal in concept, with the letters in the center, surrounded by eight doves—or perhaps sea gulls —in full flight. Dexter and sinister are scrolls of fish tails—or mermaids' tails—and surmounting the whole is the figure of a lion, holding aloft a platter upon which rests a fowl which might be a roast duck. "All in all," says John McMaster, a stern student of business arms, "it is a coat to shake the College of Heralds to its foundations."

Actually, there is probably no subject in our whole social spectrum which has for so many years been so thoroughly revered and yet so thoroughly misunderstood and so widely misused. In the first place, the vocabulary of heraldry is itself so complicated that it has stopped many an earnest student of the art—or, as it really is, a quasi-science. And right at the beginning there are formidable ironies. Not the least of these is the fact that though heraldry has always had an almost irresistible fascination for women, the world of heraldry is a man's world. In fact, a woman, though an "heiress," in other words, a woman entitled to a coat of arms (it has nothing to do, to the dismay of so many interested women, with "heiress" in the property sense), cannot transmit her right to a coat of arms to her children at all—unless their father be, in his own right, an armiger (or "arms bearer"). For the laws of heraldry dictate that children inherit even their mother's coat only by their father's right. Furthermore, although one finds women cheerfully using their "crests"—which they think is another word for coat of arms—on everything from stationery to dinner plates, the crest is not a coat of arms but only a part of a coat of arms, and indeed is actually the one part (since it was worn only by heroes and men of high rank that they might better be distinguished in the field of combat) which may not be inherited by a woman at all. Only a queen or a peeress is ever allowed to display a crest—and then only in certain instances.

But the largest difficulty in the strange world of heraldry and coats of arms is the spuriousness of almost all source material. Not a single one of the major genealogical reference books, despite the affection for them on the part of the Families included, is even reasonably reliable where nonchallengeable coats of arms are concerned. This includes such standard references as the Gore Roll in New England, Bolton's American Armoury and Blue Book, the Magazine of American Genealogy, or, for that matter, the Abridged Compendium of American Genealogy; the last-named volume, incidentally, was edited by Frederick Virkus under the direction of the late Who's Who publisher, Albert Nelson Marquis. As for the hundreds of other genealogical "companions," from the days of Tiffany's—who started such a department in 1875—to the present hundreds of "authorities" who advertise that they will find "your own family's rightful coat," their claims are so ridiculous that though the chances of finding a coat of arms may be excellent—in fact, for a price, literally anyone may have a coat of arms—the chances of finding your own coat of arms, or even if you have a rightful coat, are infinitesimal.

Even books which should know better are literally crammed with inaccuracies. The late Frederick Curtis, in *Heraldry Simplified*, for example, got angrier about his subject than most authorities, but unfortunately he did not get any more accurate:

> A little knowledge thereof [of heraldry] suffices to show that a cross or crescent in any of its forms, is evidence that the original grantee of the arms had been engaged in the Crusades or Holy Wars, a *fleur-de-lis*, that he had been in the French Wars, whilst an escallop shell showed that he had journeyed to the Holy Sepulchre as a Palmer or Mendicant Friar: yet to the writer's knowledge both crescent and escallop have been selected, and are to this day borne by members of the Semitic race. In another case, a baton sinister, the mark of illegitimacy, is, or was, until attention was called thereto by the writer, borne by one who certainly had no right nor desire to carry such a mark of disgrace.

Here almost every single fact is incorrect. The cross meant no such thing—in fact, on most coats it has no religious significance at all. The *fleur-de-lis* is a mark of cadency and means nothing about where anybody has gone; so too is the escallop shell; the latter being pure design and indicates nothing in the way of any journey. And, as for the rather typical anti-Semitism prevalent in so much writing on the subject, the fact is that many distinguished Jewish families— as well as many undistinguished ones—have excellent coats of arms, the Sephardic Jews in particular having probably as high a proportion of recognized coats of arms as any other one group of people anywhere. Finally, as for the baton sinister and the illegitimacy, the actual mark of illegitimacy on coats of arms is the so-called "difference" and, far from being shaming, right down until fairly recent times illegitimacy bore no particular social stigma. Alexander Hamilton, for one example, had an excellent coat of arms. Even the amateur in the coat of arms field soon runs up against illegitimacy—

"There's a good deal of it," one distinguished gentleman in the field told us, "human nature being what it is"—and he soon learns, even where his own Family is concerned, to be more tolerant of it than the late Mr. Curtis, whose own coat, by his own temper, is undoubtedly suspect.

The days of the Four Hundred were particularly bogus times in this often entirely bogus field. In 1904, for example, the Rev. Dr. Nichols wrote, in *The Ultra-Fashionable Peerage:* "Mr. J. P. Morgan, Mr. E. D. Morgan and Mrs. Herbert Livingston Satterlee (J. P. Morgan's daughter) are scions of a dynasty of Welsh Kings, the founder of which was Gwynned Cymric, King of all Wales, 605 A.D. Mr. Morgan can by right use eighteen quarterings on his shield, but by choice shows only twelve." Here, again, the inaccuracy is startling. Mr. E. D. Morgan and Mr. J. P. Morgan were not related to begin with, and the latter, far from descending from a dynasty of Welsh kings, had, Aristocracy to the contrary, no recognized coat of arms at all. As for the quartering, the number of quarterings indicate nothing in the way of distinction—in fact, the continued quartering of shields was carried to such confusing extremes that it usually indicated the opposite.

But the Rev. Dr. Nichols was not a man who could be stopped easily. For all other members of the Four Hundred he had almost equally kind words of ancestor worship. "Mrs. John Jacob Astor," he said, was "one of the most far-descended ladies in the United States," and he went on to add, "Ogden Mills, Mrs. Vanderbilt, Mrs. Oscar Livingston, Mrs. James Francis Sullivan of Philadelphia, Mrs. Frank S. Witherbee, Lispenard Stewart, James Laurens Van Alen, Mrs. Royal Phelps Carroll and Mrs. Vanderbilt descend gracefully from Kings." As many other, possibly far less "far-descended" social historians have noted, here the Rev. Dr. Nichols did not pause long enough even to realize that he had gracefully descended Mrs. Vanderbilt twice in the same sentence.

Even as late as 1929—the date in itself has possibly some significance—a book entitled *Your Family Tree*, by the late David Starr Jordan and Miss Sarah Louise Kimball, conclusively proved that

Abraham Lincoln, Grover Cleveland and John D. Rockefeller were descended from King Henry I of France, that Ulysses S. Grant was descended from William the Conqueror, and that Calvin Coolidge and, of all people, Shakespeare were descended from Charlemagne, while William Howard Taft, J. P. Morgan and the author himself, David Starr Jordan, were descended from King David of Scotland. Here, of course, Morgan finds himself not descended from a Welsh king, but a Scottish one.

Farther back in point of time, however, the late Charles H. Browning founded an organization called the Colonial Order of the Crown "for such men who could trace their descent from Charlemagne." Four years later he wrote a book, *Americans of Royal Descent*, in which he attempted to prove not only that virtually all Americans of the Four Hundred were regally allied, ancestrally speaking, but several thousand lesser souls were also. Years later it remained for Dr. E. M. Best of McGill University to add the final fillip. "Every one of us is descended from William the Conqueror"—the only difficulty here being the fact that even the Encyclopaedia Britannica, while admitting the uncertainty of heraldry, makes the positive assertion that "nothing is more certain then that neither armorial banners nor shields of arms were borne on either side at Hastings."

William the Conqueror brings up a particularly absurd question in point of another fact—the plain and simple matter of the application of mathematics to the problem. As far back as 1899, genealogist William Stowell Mills estimated that anyone born in the last third of the Nineteenth Century could claim more than four thousand ancestors living in the last third of the Fifteenth Century. "If the number of generations were increased to twenty-five," he pointed out, "that is if the lines could be followed back to the year 1066, one could reckon more than thirty-three and a half million progenitors contemporary with William the Conqueror—the only trouble being," he adds dryly, that "such a number is approximately fifteen times as great as the population of Great Britain at that time."*

* Mills also adds: "There have been kings in all generations; therefore, if the arithmetical theory be correct—and, modified by certain conditions, it

Among other people whom such facts have never deterred are the individual Family genealogists, almost all of whom are almost invariably rank amateurs—in all senses of both words. Even more general Family histories are suspect in this regard. James D. McCabe, for example, states in his *Great Fortunes* that George Peabody, New Englander and later merchant of Baltimore, "came from an old Family which traced its descent back to the year of Our Lord 61, the days of the heroic Boadicea, down through the brilliant circle of the Knights of the Round Table." And yet the subtitle of the book reads, "Struggles and Triumphs of Our Self-Made Men"!

"Apparently everyone who writes a Family history," the late Dr. Arthur Adams once said, "feels obliged to include a coat of arms in the naïve assumption that every family has one—of which about one in a hundred is correct, and that is a high proportion." Dr. Adams died in 1960, after having been for thirty-five years guiding star and spirit of the New England Historic Genealogical Society; he was undoubtedly the country's foremost authority on the subject of coats of arms and was so recognized by London's College of Heralds. "People either think," he said, "that no American has a right to a coat of arms, which is not true, or that anybody of the same name as somebody who has a coat, is entitled to it—which is absurd. Coats of arms are family badges indicating descent from a common ancestor—a phrase that many of those who want coats don't like to begin with. The fact that they were used in certain classes of Society is merely an additional matter of interest. And not the least matter of this interest is the fact that most so-called 'Society' names do not have a genuine coat of arms at all—and, if they do, they have them in no higher proportion than other people."

In proof of his statement, Dr. Adams pointed out that the Astors and Vanderbilts, Whitneys and Adamses, Biddles and Cadwaladers,

---

cannot be questioned—every individual of this generation is a descendant of kings and queens. Had noblemen all been noble men, this belief that royal blood has coursed through every line of descent would be satisfying, even to the most fastidious, were it not for the other side of the picture, viz.: the descent of all from the low and vicious, for such there have been in all generations."

Cabots and Lodges, do not have genuine coats; on the other hand, there are plenty of Families by the name of Smith and Jones who do have good coats. Even our two outstanding examples of American Aristocracy fall short. In the case of J. P. Morgan, Dr. Adams recalled that the late James J. Goodrich, vice-president of the New England Historic Genealogical Society for many years, devoted a quarter of a century and a small fortune to proving the parentage of Morgan's first American ancestor—all to no avail. As for the peerless Robert E. Lee, Dr. Adams quoted Burton Hendrick. "The simple fact is that we do not know who Richard Lee (the American ancestor of the family) was; that is, we do not know the names of his father or mother, or the place and date of his birth."

On the other hand, Dr. Adams has shown that there are an extraordinary number of good coats held by Families with names which might not so indicate—names like Gooch and Gorsuch, Zeng and Zouch, Hesilrigge and Odingselle, not to mention Wyllys and van Wenckum, d'Abbadie and d'Anterroches. Throughout his life Dr. Adams spent many years studying the heraldry of other countries besides England. He regarded Scottish coats as the hardest to prove—they are, however, excellent coats, he felt, and their regulation is a matter of law. In Germany, too, it is a matter of a State regulation, and a German coat is considered "incomplete" if helm and crest are omitted. In France, in contrast, where there is no official source, just various societies, crests are regarded as so unimportant that many French families have coats but no crests. In Italy the Vatican maintains an heraldic office, and there are also Spanish coats, Dutch coats and Scandinavian coats. On the subject of Irish coats, in which, Dr. Adams said early in 1960, "there has been much interest lately," these are perhaps the easiest to prove; the only thing being demanded is evidence that the coat was in use for four generations.*

* Although there is a registered Kennedy coat, the well-known Kennedy family is not related to it. As for Irish names beginning with "Fitz" meaning "son of," these were originally used to denote an illegitimate son of a prince, and as recently as a year ago this writer, discussing coats of arms in Detroit with Thelma Tevis Schneider, of the Michigan Social Directory, was startled by

One of Dr. Adams' jobs throughout his career was that of constantly advising people, who wrote to him from all parts of the country, that there was nothing they could do about another person, even one of a different name, using their coats of arms. Unless a coat is registered as a trademark in the Patent Office, there is no government authority which can prevent any individual from using it for the simple reason that the government has not recognized coats of arms since 1776. On the other hand, in England, in 1957, the Court of Chivalry—a court which had not sat since 1737—sat on a case, with the Lord Chancellor presiding, involving a suit brought by the city of Manchester against an amusement park, which, said the city of Manchester, was wrongfully using its coat of arms. Furthermore, the fact that the Court had not sat for 220 years was held irrelevant, immaterial and inconsequential—and the amusement park was fined £100. The last case upon which the Court had sat, in 1737, involved a coat of arms and whether the person using it was "living in the manner in which a gentleman should live."

All in all, Dr. Adams felt that, while there had been some improvement since Four Hundred days, the ignorance on the subject of coats of arms in America was still appalling. One lady, for example, wrote to him about the meaning of her coat. "Of course," she began, "I know red means royalty . . ." Replied Dr. Adams, "You are wrong right there. Red means nothing—except that the person who first chose it thought it was a nice color for a coat." Another man, apparently due to the publicity over the Duchess of Windsor, wrote him that he had an ancestor who was "the brother of Lord Warfield" and even named the field of battle on which, he said, his ancestor had borne his coat. "I couldn't find the field of battle," Dr. Adams said, "any Warfield coat, or, for that matter, any Warfield." Actually, he added sternly, the Howard family in Maryland, from whom Wallis Warfield descends, not only had no genuine coat of their

---

her comment that when she first moved to Detroit her Eastern mother warned her against "Fitzes." "Be careful of Fitzsimmonses or Fitzgeralds or anything like that," her mother said. "They're all illegitimate, you know."

own, but, worse still, wrongfully used the coat of the great Howard family in England.

Such misappropriation in the field has apparently always been widespread. The Hancock family of Massachusetts used a coat of arms for several generations despite the fact that there was no evidence whatsoever that they had any right to it. On the other hand, there was a far less socially inclined Hancock family from New Jersey, most of whom never would have known they had a coat of arms, who were entitled to an excellent coat. Other paradoxes are equally striking. Among *Mayflower* passengers, Dr. Adams rated only Standish and Winslow as good coats. Bradford, Winthrop and indeed all the others were, he felt, not good. John Harvard had no coat, but Elihu Yale had a perfectly good coat. Among Presidents, George Washington had a good coat; in contrast, very few other Presidents did, including Eisenhower, Truman, Calvin Coolidge, Herbert Hoover or, for that matter, Ulysses S. Grant. "Nobody knows anything," wrote Dr. Adams sternly, "about the parentage of Matthew Grant, six generations ahead of Ulysses S." As for the Roosevelt Family, curiously enough, these also have no recognized coat—"although," said Dr. Adams, "there is something to be said for both sides," a statement which, considering the two sharp divisions of the family, would seem to be something of an understatement. On the other hand, the McCormick Family in Chicago has a recognized coat—"but," said Dr. Adams again, "I'm not satisfied with the evidence."*

The Rothschild coat is a good one, but, in contrast, the late John

---

* If Dr. Adams seemed unduly stern, it should be noted that he was equally so about his own family. No relation to Boston's "royal" Adamses, who as we have seen do not have coats, he was never able to prove the parentage of his own first American ancestor—"although," he noted wryly, "they had children which was pretty fair evidence, in those days, of marriage." Thus, he himself was never entitled to an inherited coat. In view of his extraordinary work in the field, however, the College of Heralds in London made a special grant, giving him an "earned" coat and furthermore made it retroactive to include descendants of his great-grandfather—an extremely unusual grant. "Many young people scoff at the whole thing," he said, "but I notice they become more interested when they have children themselves."

D. Rockefeller, Sr., had a genealogist work for many years on a two-volume history of the family and was never able to come up with an armigerous ancestor from whom all present Rockefeller armorial blessings would flow. Among other industrial families, the Du Ponts and the Phippses have recognized coats, but the Fords, the Deerings and hundreds more have tried and failed. The Chryslers have a good German coat, but, though the Dodge family received a grant some years ago, scholars now say that their inherited coat is a forgery—which, considering the device involved, one would think present-day Dodges would not dispute. For the Dodge coat, as used, clearly shows the curious figure of a woman's breast dispensing milk. Even this is hardly less extraordinary than the coat of arms once suggested for—and rejected by—the Crane plumbing Family in Chicago. The shield was divided into four parts, including, in each section, a sink, a bathtub, etc. Over all was a hand gripping the handle of a chain—with the inevitable motto, *"Après moi le déluge."**

Dr. Adams' parent organization, the New England Historic Genealogical Society, is today recognized as the leader among all genealogical organizations in the country. As far back as 1864 it appointed a Standing Committee on Heraldry under the chairmanship of the late William Sumner Appleton, Jr., of Boston. Mr. Appleton promptly laid down the rules that the Committee would not recognize any arms which had not been granted or confirmed by the College of Heralds and would not admit the right of anyone to use arms unless he could prove absolutely his descent from the Family whose arms had thus been granted or confirmed. Soon, however, albeit after the death of Mr. Appleton, the Committee decided that "in view of the history of heraldry in England," such rules were too rigid and noted, among other things, "There is no evidence that arms in the early days were granted by the Crown." They were, instead, the Committee continued, "adopted much as a tradesman adopts a

* In St. Louis this story translates to the distinguished Desloge Family, who are credited not only with an "Après moi le Desloge," but also with building an underground ballroom complete with statuary of many saints. Since the Family is the owner of the St. Joseph Lead Company, St. Louisians are fond of saying, "They've got every saint in there but St. Joe Lead!"

trade-mark, and, like trade-marks, while they were regarded as a species of private property, their use was governed by custom rather than by rule, and the rules, if any, were very elastic." And finally, though the Committee noted that "in the Seventeenth Century, arms, as a rule, were borne by those who had risen into the gentry class," it added that "in this respect the Committee labors under no delusion. The right to a coat of arms does not make a gentleman."

All of which, as with so many of our investigations, would seem to leave us back where we started from. But American Aristocracy, like American Society, has never been easily stopped, and in any case in 1928 the Committee on Heraldry of the New England Historic Genealogical Society began issuing what they called "A Roll of Arms"—which listed the names of those Families, in the order submitted for registration confirmation, entitled to coats. The first list, beginning with "Washington No. 1, Appleton No. 2, Bowen No. 3," etc., was published in 1928. This list contained 72 names and was followed in 1932 by a second list of about the same number— the interval being necessitated by the extraordinary volume of re-search needed to check every name. Ever since, at approximately five-year intervals, succeeding lists have appeared until, as of 1960, well over 500 names have been published—representing by far the most authentic and accurate listing of coats of arms ever attempted.*
However, as Dr. Adams pointed out in connection with the last issued list, there are hundreds—perhaps even thousands—of other good coats of arms which so far, for one reason or another, have not been submitted for confirmation. "And," Dr. Adams added wearily in a letter to this writer, "I suppose after you publish those names, we will have thousands of letters saying, 'Why, that's *my* name—then I *do* have a coat of arms.' "

Dr. Adams pointed out once more—but "without much hope," he admitted—that "you are *not* entitled to a coat of arms unless you can prove direct relationship to the Family of that name who received the arms." But, to anyone who fails to do so, he suggested in conclusion, that such a person might possibly find himself eligible

* The complete list, up to 1960, appears at the end of this book.

for the Society which Dr. Adams himself to the day of his death always regarded as the most distinguished of all those to which he belonged—the Society of the Descendants of the Illegitimate Sons and Daughters of the Kings of England. "There are between sixty and seventy members," he said, "and they meet once a year and have a hell of a time. They call themselves the 'D.R.B.'s for short— Descendants of the Royal Bastards. Charles I was the only King, you know, who didn't have a bastard. I myself have three or four bastard lines and I'm proud of every one of them."

CHARLES DANA GIBSON

III

CELEBRITY—*The Arbiters Are Biting: From Gibson Girl to Glamour Girl*

THE ACTUAL DATING of the passing of the Old Order, even to the most definite of Society complainants of the 1960's, is a difficult one. Some date it not long after they were born—with the death, in 1908, of *The* Mrs. Astor. Surely, they point out, since that time Society has never had a leader with anything like her autocratic authority. Even in her last years, when her mind had failed and she lived in solitary splendor at her Newport cottage of "Beechwood," she was a lady to conjure with. "Still erect," said the late Lloyd Morris, "still bravely gowned and jeweled, she stood quite alone, greeting imaginary guests long dead, exchanging pleasantries with ghosts of the utmost social distinction."

Other complainants choose a later date, one of their favorites being not a death but a birth. This date is the birth of so-called

"Café Society"—a delivery which occurred in 1919, on a cold February night, in the downstairs dining room of New York's Old Ritz. The late Cholly Knickerbocker No. 1, Maury Paul, was dining at the Ritz that night, and his eye chanced upon a group of people about to have dinner—a group which included, according to Paul's faithful secretary Eve Brown, Mrs. Allen Gouverneur Wellman (later Mrs. Harold Brooks), Joe Widener, Laura Corrigan, Whitney Warren, Jr., and one "assorted pair of Goelets." Miss Brown recalls Paul murmuring to himself, "Society isn't staying home and entertaining any more. Society is going out to dinner, out to night life, and letting down the barriers. Heavens—that I should see a Widener, a Goelet, a Corrigan and a Warren all together. It's like a sea-food cocktail, with everything from eels to striped bass!" In any case, the next morning Paul batted out, with his two-fingered typing, the phrase "Café Society," and the handwriting was, according to many old-timers, clearly on the wall for the old Society.

Still a third favored date for the passing of the Old Order is the tearing down, in 1942, of the old Cornelius Vanderbilt house—640 Fifth Avenue. Last of the great Vanderbilt mansions which once flanked Fifth Avenue, it was thereafter taken over by the late *Collier's* magazine—thus marking one more step in the triumphal march of the Fourth Estate over the Four Hundred. The house, built in 1881 by William H. Vanderbilt, son of the old Commodore himself, had remained what the late Frank Crowninshield called "the last stronghold of ceremonial Society in America," and if the late Mrs. Vanderbilt was far removed in both time and dignity from Mrs. Astor, still the fact remained that she was the last *The* Mrs. Vanderbilt and through her house's portals and salons had passed, as Crowninshield put it, "an unending phalanx of her friends —a long parade of such exalted figures as King Albert of the Belgians, the Queen of Spain, Lord Balfour, the Duke of Kent, Winston Churchill, the Crown Prince of Norway, the Prince of Wales, Theodore Roosevelt, Calvin Coolidge, Herbert Hoover and General Pershing."

Still a fourth favored demise for the Old was another Vanderbilt milestone—the death, in 1952, of Mrs. Hamilton McKown Twombly, last granddaughter of the old Commodore. And, although it is extremely doubtful if social history could be written at all if one disallowed such words as "late" and "last," "old" and "order," "last of the gentlemen" and "old school," etc., again the fact remains that this latter date, the passing of Mrs. Twombly, mid-Century as it is, is certainly a most socially acceptable date for the passing of the Old Order itself. For, among other qualifications, Mrs. Twombly was 98 years old.

For three-quarters of a century, in New York and Newport, and even, remarkably enough, in New Jersey—at "Florham," her incredible estate near the town of Convent—Mrs. Twombly had held what amounted to America's last Court. *The* Mrs. Vanderbilt, her niece-in-law, had held court contemporaneously, but of the two, to the inner circle, Mrs. Twombly's was the inner court. She was, in other words, Aristocracy, Mrs. Vanderbilt was Society, and they had, in the great tradition of the warfare between the two, little use for each other. To Mrs. Vanderbilt Mrs. Twombly occupied a position to which, however, over-reaching her public ambition, she could never privately aspire, and as for Mrs. Twombly as a "real" Vanderbilt, rather than a married one, there was no reason to acknowledge the existence of Mrs. Vanderbilt. She simply ignored her—which, in itself, in the face of Mrs. Vanderbilt's publicity, took some doing.

Throughout her reign, Mrs. Twombly had, like her beloved England, through thick and thin, muddled through—through two World Wars, two depressions, and even two booms. Visitors to "Florham" invariably carried away at least one cherished memory, and John Mason Brown, a literary ambassador to the Court on one of its last, long weekends, was no exception. He remembers one Sunday morning when Mrs. Twombly was returning from church, and the guests were assembled to greet her, as was their wont, in the foyer. In this foyer, besides the guests, stood the busts of twelve Roman Caesars. Mrs. Twombly returned all right, and as she stepped out of her violet Rolls-Royce and swept inside she wore a violet hat and carried, in violet gloves, a bunch of violets. "It was unforgettable," recalls Brown. "I even remember where I was standing. It was inviolate, too—right beside Caligula."

This was a thick time for "Florham," but there were thin times too. Another ambassador, who shall be nameless, recalls one among the thinnest. This occasion was a memorable Saturday night dinner party late in World War II when the ambassador hazarded to Mrs. Twombly the remark that the Court must have suffered many reverses in the form of its footmen being drafted for war. For some time Mrs. Twombly said nothing, then finally she sighed. "This week we lost four," she said, "from the pantry alone."

Even before this death sentence Mrs. Twombly had observed changing times. In 1935, then in her early eighties, she had gone west—to, of all places, Hollywood, California. The event was the wedding of her grandson and Flobelle Fairbanks, niece of Douglas Fairbanks, Sr. Although the reception contained, in deference to her, a sizable proportion of Eastern refugees and a well-turned-out delegation from Pasadena, Santa Barbara and even San Francisco, there was also, unavoidably, a large group of Hollywoodians. For some time Mrs. Twombly surveyed them, and then turned to a relative from New York. "In my day," she said quietly, "we had the celebrities. Now, if you please, the celebrities have us."

Of all the latter-day complainants of Society, Mrs. Twombly was perhaps the most gentle. She was also, many feel, the most accurate. And, in the final analysis, it would not be the least of the ironies of social history if Society, which has always set such store by whom it was having—to dinners, to balls and to operas—should have been, in the end, had. But to many people such would appear to be the case. And if Mrs. Twombly in 1936, at 82, was ahead of her time, back even before she was born, in 1828, our old friend, James Fenimore Cooper, also was ahead of his time—in *The Travelling Bachelor:*

In a country where wealth is constantly bringing new claimants for consideration into the arena of fashion (for it is, after all, no more than a struggle for notoriety, that may be more bloodless but is not less bitter than that of the gladiators), those who are in its possession contrive all possible means of distinction between themselves and those who are about to dispute their ascendancy.

By the Twentieth Century, it would appear, Mr. Cooper's "means of distinction" had fallen upon evil days. But his "struggle for notoriety" most certainly had not. On this score, in an interview with the late Mrs. Charles Dana Gibson, this writer asked Mrs. Gibson what was the greatest change in Society which had occurred in her lifetime (1873-1956). "In my life," said Mrs. Gibson, "I've seen the death of Society." One of the fabulous Langhorne sisters of Virginia—another being, of course, Lady Astor—Mrs. Gibson not only was chosen to lead the Grand March at the Patriarchs' Ball in 1893, but she also won world-wide fame as the model for her artist-husband's Gibson Girl. As such, in the Society homicide case, she turned out to be on two counts a star witness for the prosecution. "Why," she said, "there's nothing left *but* notoriety. In my day notoriety was recognized for what it was—you were known but you were known unfavorably. Nowadays, the word isn't even used. There's no need for it. A person who is unfavorably known is as famous—and often more so—than one who is known entirely favorably. They're all, in this awful modern word, 'celebrities.' We had what we called 'celebrities' too, but they were either people everyone knew anyway—people like my husband and Elisha Dyer and Dick Child and Dick Gilder and Edith Wharton and Henry James and Owen Wister, John Sargent and Peter Dunne, or else they were people like Paderewski and Nicholas Murray Butler and Edison and Agassiz—who were certainly people of some kind of social position. Of course, there were the others too, but one didn't have them for dinner. They came after dinner—to entertain."

One who remembers coming "after dinner" is Mrs. Irene Castle. One of America's best-known dancers and the first woman in this country to "bob" her hair, Mrs. Castle has lived for many years at her "Destiny Farm" ranch near Eureka Springs in the Ozarks. Before World War I, however, though already nationally famous, she had the experience of being invited, together with her husband Vernon, to a Long Island estate to dance. She recalls a long train ride during which, since she was dressed in skin-tight tights and was terrified of bagging her knees, she had to sit, stretched out, with her feet up. The Castles were met at the station by a chauffeur and driven to their appointment at exactly the specified time. Then for a full hour, before anyone except the servants greeted them, they waited down-stairs in a room "the size of a clothes closet," while the guests up-stairs leisurely finished their dinner—and once again, Mrs. Castle recalls, she sat with her feet out and up. After their act, she recalls, while Vernon had to dance with all the ladies present, "I was passed from gentleman to gentleman, like a football." Looking back on it all today, Mrs. Castle, now Mrs. Castle McLaughlin Enzinger, be-lieves that the new status of the celebrity is the largest social change which has taken place. "Celebrities of today," she says, "have no idea how socially unimportant you were in the old days."

One who led the early-day celebrity march into a more formid-able position in Society is the noted dress designer, Captain Edward Molyneux. He opened his Acacia Tree nightclub in Paris in 1921 and brought Clifton Webb and the Dolly Sisters over from America to open it. One of the latter was dressed in a red cloak with white ostrich feathers and white gardenias. "You were literally bowled over," Molyneux says. But the Captain also recalls being told that, when it came time for dinner, "You simply cannot have the Dolly Sisters and the United States Ambassador to dine at the same time." Nonetheless, he did so, and he also had Lord Derby and Elinor Glyn, and the party, he remembers, lasted until six o'clock the next morning. If Captain Molyneux is widely credited with beginning the "mixture of everybody," however, he is modest about it. "I guess I did start something," he says, "but I didn't realize I was doing it. I was nobody then. I had just opened my shop."

Out in Beverly Hills, Clifton Webb not only recalls Captain

Molyneux's party but also recalls his own social pioneering days. He remembers distinctly, for example, the first time he went out in Society *for* dinner and not *after* dinner. "I still remember the expression on one man's face," he says, "and later what he said. *'You here,'* he asked, 'at Mrs. Alexander's?' " Webb has lived to see the time when he considers the "mélange of today" as well handled, socially speaking, in Hollywood as it is anywhere else. "But if you want my nomination for the murderer of Society," he adds, "I'll give it to you—Elsa Maxwell."

Before getting on to Miss Maxwell's proper, or perhaps improper, place, it is first necessary to pause again for social semantics—in this case, for an examination of the word "celebrity." And again, as with the word "notoriety," with which modern neglect Mrs. Gibson took umbrage, we are faced with change, for there was a day when the word was used only impersonally—a person might *have* "celebrity," or fame, but it would have been as meaningless to say "a celebrity" as it would be today to say "a fame." But this change, too, cannot be charged to the Twentieth Century. It was under way a long time before that; in fact, as far back as 1836 the *American Quarterly Review*, speaking of John Jacob Astor I, said, "From an obscure stranger he has made himself one of the 'celebrities' of the country." It was still early enough, it is true, for the word to be used with quotation marks, but by mid-Century, in 1856, we find no less a "celebrity" than Emerson himself using the word, and without quotation marks, in *English Traits*. By the first part of the Twentieth Century the word was in full flower, as witness its use in 1908 in *Harper's Bazaar*, in an article entitled the very thing that so many old-time celebrities were annoyed about—"The Dinner Party":

> Guests must feel they are meeting *new* people, not unknown ones. . . . They will forgive you for putting them next to their worst enemy, but not their social inferior. One is exciting, the other an insult. . . . If one wishes to invite the Van Aspics in order to impress another guest, one must first find someone to impress the Van Aspics. One must find them a celebrity.

In order to impress the Van Aspics, Society would seem, to many present-day complainants, to have gone above and beyond the call of dinner. But, as was the case with our very first complainants, a little historical perspective is not out of order—even when considering what happened to the Old Order. First and foremost, there is the plain and simple fact that Society itself is, and always has been, a matter of publicity. Second and almost equally important is that the very people who complain about celebrities mark the end of the eras they liked, not by aristocratic figures but by celebrities. Even Mrs. Astor was herself a celebrity, particularly when compared with the more aristocratic, albeit equally autocratic, Mrs. Ogden Mills. So too was *The* Mrs. Vanderbilt a celebrity—the *The* alone marks her as such, and, even if it did not, she would still have been a celebrity among a Family which has always numbered a higher proportion of celebrities to total membership than any other American Family. If Mrs. Twombly considered herself, as indeed she did, "Old Family" and not "celebrity," she had merely made the upward move—which Grace Vanderbilt certainly never did—in the age-old progression from celebrity to Society to Aristocracy.

As for the sternest complainant of all, the late Mrs. Gibson, she herself was probably the best example of "Four Hundred" celebrity of anyone of her time. Indeed, for all the respect both the Society and Aristocracy had, and indeed still have, for her, she was also widely condemned among other people for—in her own words —"notoriety." Actually, of course, the whole "Four Hundred," as indeed it should have been, was itself regarded by the Aristocracy of its day as celebrity. This could hardly have been otherwise since it was originated, named, numbered and publicized by that celebrity of celebrities, Ward McAllister himself.

The history of American arbiters, one which is in reality a history of Society's celebrities, properly begins with Mrs. John Jay. Born Sarah Van Brugh Livingston, of New York's proud Livingston Family, she married John Jay in 1774. Traveling with him to Paris, where he was to perform outstanding service, she was so strikingly beautiful that, it is recorded, at one time her entrance into a French theatre caused the entire audience to stand, thinking she was Marie Antoinette. Returning to New York, where her husband became Secretary of Foreign Affairs, Mrs. Jay became the first recognized Queen-Arbiter of American Society and her "Dinner and Supper List from 1787 to 1788" was probably the first listing of social celebrities on record. Although the list is interesting today for the fact that it contains an Alsop, an Aaron Burr, a Cadwalader, a de Peyster, a Gerry, a Huger, a Pinckney, a Van Rensselaer, two Lees, five Van Hornes and seven Livingstons, it is notable also for the fact that there are a dozen doctors and clergymen on the list; in McAllister's "Four Hundred" list a century later, doctors would be down to one and clergymen would disappear altogether. But if her list was interesting, so too was Mrs. Jay herself. For of her, in contrast with the parade of arbiters who would follow her, it is recorded that "amid the gay Society of Paris and New York," she "preserved unimpaired her gentleness, amiability and simplicity"— and throughout her life she managed "with fidelity and womanly affection the duties of a daughter, sister, wife and mother."

If Mrs. Jay was Society's most lovable arbiter, the most unusual was assuredly McAllister's immediate predecessor—in many ways the most interesting, and certainly the largest, of all arbiters. On the first score, he was the sexton of a church; on the second, he weighed, at his peak, over three hundred pounds. His name was Isaac Hull Brown, he was born in 1812, and he started out as a carpenter—a trade which came to his great assistance at the most crucial moment of his career. This event occurred in 1860 when, at the ball for the Prince of Wales at the old Academy of Music, a great crush of people determined to get to the Prince at once—among them the hefty Brown himself—and a section of the floor collapsed. Despite his part in the overweighting, Brown, cool as always, saved the day. Throwing off his coat, he first extracted the people who had fallen down among the collapsed boards, then signaling for additional help,

directed a repair job which in fifteen minutes allowed the ball to
proceed as if nothing had happened.*

N. P. Willis declared that, despite Brown's weight and large
paunch, his manner "would well become the nobleman who is
Gold Stick in Waiting at the Court of Her Majesty." As sexton of
New York's Grace Church for thirty-five years, Brown was honored by a commemorative tablet placed there by "Members of the
Congregation who Gladly Recall his Fidelity, his Generosity and
his Stainless Integrity." But if this was praise unusual for an arbiter,
Brown was far more than just a sexton. "The Lenten Season," he
once said, "is a horridly dull season, but we manage to make our
funerals as entertaining as possible." Besides presiding at weddings
and funerals, Brown was soon branching out in all directions—even
to taking care of women who never went near Grace Church. "A
fashionable lady," the records recall, "about to give a gathering at
her house, orders her meats from the butcher, her supplies from the
grocer, her cakes and ices from the confectioner, but her invitations
she puts in the hands of Brown." Called the "connecting link between Society and the curbstone," he was in truth the entering
wedge of modern celebrity, and before his death his fame had spread
across the country—although, as he himself once modestly admitted,
"I cannot undertake to control Society beyond 50th Street."

In 1869, when George William Curtis divided Society into three
classes, he named first the rich, second the "good old Families," a
group which he said had been made by "some ancestor who had
been very rich and had kept the fortune in the Family," and third a
group which he did not name but said was "made up by sundry
French tailors, bootmakers, dancing masters and Mr. Brown." Not
the least of Brown's achievements was his organization of the so-

* During the interim, William Perrine recalls, Prince Albert Edward had
been taken into an anteroom, where he was "engaged so long in a conversation" with Fernanda Wood, daughter of the Mayor of New York, that the
dignified Duke of Newcastle thought "they had been alone quite enough."
In any case, he advanced toward them only to be stopped by the Mayor
himself—in the time-honored manner of American parents where royalty is
concerned. "Oh, Duke," the Mayor exclaimed, "let the young people alone—
they are enjoying themselves."

called "Brown's Brigade." A lifelong bachelor himself, Brown was in the great arbiter tradition and was keenly aware, even in those days, of the "extra men" problem; he had thus recruited and trained, for instant call, a group of a hundred or more young men. Suitable for debutante or dowager, they were, if not clubmen types, at least reasonable facsimiles of same and were mustered in and out for duty according to Brown's own special code of regulations for what he called "the camp-grounds of Society." It was not enough that they have "commanding figures" and be fashionably dressed; it was necessary that they should have "an ample supply of small talk at their tongue's end."

Like all arbiters, Brown grew increasingly arbitrary in his last years. When running certain *nouveau riche* parties uptown, he would stand at the door and on occasion warn Old Family members that they entered at their own risk. "This is mixed—very," he would say firmly. But, second only to Mrs. Jay, he was the best-beloved figure in the field of arbitrage, and after his death—which occurred in 1880 in the little town of Bradford, New York, where he was wont to spend his summers—his body was brought down to Grace Church and he was given a funeral of which he himself, in happier days, would have been proud. At these funerals Brown was accustomed to saying a few words extolling the noble qualities of the deceased—and interspersing a few remarks about the increasing laxity of social times—and since this was obviously impossible at his own funeral, a parishioner of Grace Church composed a poem for the occasion:

> Oh, glorious Brown! thou medley strange
>   Of churchyard, ball-room, saint and sinner;
> Flying by morn through Fashion's range,
>   And burying mortals after dinner!
> Walking one day with invitations—
> Passing the next at consecrations;
> Tossing the sod at eve on coffins;
> With one hand drying tears of orphans,
> And one unclasping ball-room carriage,
> Or cutting plum-cake up for marriage:

Dusting by day the pew and missal;
Sounding by night the ball-room whistle,
Admitted free through Fashion's wicket,
And skilled at psalms, at punch, and cricket.

If Brown had already paved the way for Celebrity Society, it was Ward McAllister, the most celebrated of all arbiters, who brought it to fruition. Born in Savannah, Georgia, in 1827, the son of a Southern jurist, Matthew Hall McAllister, who later went west during the Gold Rush and made a sizable fortune practicing law in San Francisco, Ward himself came east in 1853, to Washington, D.C. Here he married an heiress, Sarah T. Gibbons, but one who was so self-effacing that even at the height of his fame, in the 1880's and 1890's, few old-timers recall her at all. This was necessary, for McAllister, after a trip abroad where he boned up on court procedure, knowledge of wines and other foreign gifts, returned to New York to attach himself, in his almost unbelievably pompous way, to the lady he called his "one and only," his "Mystic Rose"—*The* Mrs. Astor.

With his Vandyke beard and his penchant for odd-looking clothes, McAllister was not personally the most prepossessing of figures. But, without the slightest hint of a sense of humor, he imparted such seriousness to his ideas, as well as to himself, that in the socially insecure times in which he lived he was soon taken extremely seriously even by people who should have known better. Following the Civil War, the great fortunes were piling up, and in default of anyone else, to Ward McAllister descended the honor of leading them out of the wilderness of just plain wealth into the promised land of highly decorated Society. He was at once a mixture of Southerner and Northerner, and in what sense he did make he combined seemingly the worst features of both—the insincerity of the Southerner and the rudeness of the Northerner. "Beauty before Brains," he would say, and "Mind before Money"—but actually, if he meant anything, it was more likely to be the opposite of what he said. However, in fairness it should be noted that at a time when most of his fellow gentlemen were engaged almost exclusively in making money, McAllister was at least doing something else; as they gave their days and nights to the counting tables, so he gave his days and nights to the dinner tables, and he soon had his own code of cookery, court etiquette and coats of arms. "The talent of and for Society," he once said, "develops itself as does the talent for art." Having divided Society into what he called "Nobs" —i.e., the Old Families—and the "Swells"—i.e., the newcomers— he was not the least averse to giving advice to the latter on how to become the former:

> If you want to be fashionable, be always in the company of fashionable people. As an old beau [sic] suggested to me, if you see a fossil of a man, shabbily dressed, relying solely on his pedigree, dating back to time immemorial, who has the aspirations of a duke and the fortunes of a footman, do not cut him; it is better to cross the street and avoid meeting him. It is well to be in with the nobs who are born to their position, but the support of the swells is more advantageous, for Society is sustained and carried on by the swells, the nobs looking quietly on and accepting the position, feeling they are there by divine right; but they do not make fashionable Society, or carry it on. A nob can be a swell if he chooses, i.e. if he will spend the money; but for his social existence this is unnecessary. A nob is like a poet,—*nascitur non fit;* not so a swell,—he creates himself.

In 1872, McAllister organized a ball committee of his so-called "Patriarchs"—a group of twenty-five men who, he said, "should have the right of inviting to each ball four ladies and five gentlemen, including himself and family." Also, he declared, "We then resolved that the responsibility of inviting each batch of nine guests should rest upon the shoulders of the Patriarch who invited them, and that if any objectionable element was introduced, it was the Management's duty to at once let it be known by whom such objectionable party was invited, and to notify the Patriarch so offending, that he had done us an injury, and pray him to be circumspect. He then stood before the community as a sponsor of his guest, and all Society,

knowing the offense he had committed, would so upbraid him, that
he would go and sin no more." In any case, he then named his "little
band," typically including himself, as follows:

John Jacob Astor	Royal Phelps
William Astor	Edwin A. Post
De Lancey Kane	A. Gracie King
Ward McAllister	Lewis M. Rutherfurd
George Henry Warren	Robert G. Remsen
Eugene A. Livingston	Wm. C. Schermerhorn
William Butler Duncan	Francis R. Rives
E. Templeton Snelling	Maturin Livingston
Lewis Colford Jones	Alex. van Rensselaer
John W. Hamersley	Walter Langdon
Benjamin S. Welles	F. G. D'Hauteville
Frederick Sheldon	C. C. Goodhue
William R. Travers	

Flushed with the success of his Patriarchs' Balls, as well as his
Family Circle Dancing Class—which critics have suggested was
necessitated by his having a homely daughter—McAllister, who was
by this time being called Mr. "Make-a-lister," next determined to
make a list of all Society. Since Mrs. Astor's ballroom held just 400
people, in 1888 he began to say that there were only that many in
Society. "If you go outside that number," he said, "you strike
people who are either not at ease in a ballroom or else make other
people not at ease." Sometimes, McAllister admitted, for "a large
ball" it was possible to go outside of the "exclusive fashionable set"
and invite "professional men, doctors, lawyers, editors, artists and
the like," but he didn't advise it often and in fact recommended it
primarily for New Year's Eve. Finally, after four years of titillating
the press and general public, McAllister released on the occasion of
Mrs. Astor's ball of February 1, 1892, to no less a journal than the
New York Times, his "Four Hundred." The list, which actually
barely went over three hundred names—though it included McAllister himself—is dominated, in men's professions, by bankers, lawyers,
brokers, real estate men and railroaders, although it does include
one editor (Paul Dana of the New York *Sun*), a publisher, albeit

also a patent agent (Charles Munn), an artist (Benjamin Porter), two architects (George Post and H. N. Potter), and two "visitors from Baltimore" (the Browns). It was the paucity of artistic representations that led one of the "Four Hundred," Mrs. Winthrop Chanler, to declare, "The Four Hundred would have fled in a body from a poet, a painter, a musician or a clever Frenchman." Later the so-called "King of the Dudes," Evander Berry Wall—who in 1888, in Saratoga, appeared in forty complete changes of costume between breakfast and dinner, added his intelligence. "Remember," he said, "that Broadway only cuts across Fifth Avenue—it never parallels it."

The story that *The* Mrs. Astor did make an attempt at what would later be called Café Society and invited to dinner Edith Wharton and J. P. Morgan is not, unfortunately, true. On the other hand, Edith Wharton's meeting with the "Four Hundred," as she recalled in *A Backward Glance*, was almost as good a story. The invitation, on the part of a "fashionable person," came about through a cousin who relayed the invitation that the lady inviting her to dine, explained, "It will be rather Bohemian, I'm afraid, but they say one ought to see something of those people." Great were Mrs. Wharton's expectations and she admitted she "racked her brains" to guess how her cousin could have made the acquaintance of "the very people I was still vainly longing to know":

> The evening came, we assembled in the ornate drawing-room . . . and I discovered that the Bohemians were my old friend Eliot Gregory, most popular of New York diners-out (but who had the audacity to write an occasional article in a review or daily paper), George Smalley, the New York correspondent of the London *Times*—and myself! To emphasize our common peculiarity we were seated together, slightly below the salt, while up and down the rest of the long table the tiara-ed heads and bulging white waistcoats of the most accredited millionaires glittered between gold plate and orchids. Such was Fifth Avenue's first glimpse of Bohemia, as personified by myself and two old friends!

But if the "Four Hundred" were not literary, they were indeed celebrities. From Maine to California they caught the public's fancy, and McAllister himself became as well known as a movie star of a later date. Mrs. Burton Harrison, for example, recalls a trip in 1892, just after the publication of McAllister's list, to the newly built Four Seasons Hotel at Cumberland Gap in Tennessee. Although McAllister did not make the trip, at one station James Brown Potter, taking a constitutional along the railroad track, was mischievously pointed out to a curious crowd by a Dr. Holbrook Curtis as McAllister—something which in itself gives some idea of the aristocratic attitude toward him. But the "gaping natives," Mrs. Harrison reports, were satisfied. "I want ter know!" remarked a butternut-garbed horseman in cowhide boots. "Wal, I've rid fifteen miles a-purpus to see that dude McAllister, an' I don't begrutch it, not a mite."

Actually, among the inner circle, McAllister's reputation waned rapidly after the publication of his list and his fatuous book, *Society as I Have Found It*. His public downfall, curiously enough, was Chicago. Prior to the World's Columbian Exposition of 1893, the Chicago Mayor announced that he would give everybody all over the country a "genuine" Chicago welcome. Replied McAllister, from New York, "It is not quantity but quality that Society people here want. Hospitality which includes the whole human race is not desirable." He also advised Chicago, gratuitously, "not to frappé their wines too much." This was too much for Chicagoans, who, according to Emmett Dedmon, promptly dubbed McAllister, "Head Butler," "New York Flunky" and "A Mouse Colored Ass." McAllister replied by taking Chicago to task for having their ballrooms in the attic approached by elevators. "Here in the East," he said, "we don't go to balls in private houses by climbing up a ladder or going up in an elevator."

McAllister never did go to the Fair, but his Chicago contretemps sealed his doom. All over the country he had become, if not a "Mouse Colored Ass," at least a "New York Flunky," and few people were surprised when he was discharged by a committee composed of Hamilton Fish, Elbridge Gerry and Colonel William Jay. "McAllister is a discharged servant. That is all," Stuyvesant

Fish curtly told the press. In 1895, McAllister died, and at his funeral only five of his beloved "Patriarchs" and less than a score of the "Four Hundred" bothered to attend. The general public, however, the people McAllister had always looked down on as beneath contempt, crowded and clamored for seats in the church. He was left without monument of any sort. In contrast, his brother, Hall McAllister, who led a rich and full life as a lawyer in San Francisco and was not known to the general public at all, had a street named in his honor and a bronze statue in City Hall.

After the death of McAllister there was not a single arbiter of major proportions who did not owe his position to the growing power of the press and publicity. There were, it is true, some wine merchants, such as New York's Harry Lehr, and some cotillion leaders, such as Boston's Samuel Hooper Hooper and Baltimore's Walter de Courcey Poulteney, but these were doomed to short reigns and were in any case severely limited in authority. Not so the arbiters who, seeing which way the wind was blowing, seized the power of the printed word.

First and foremost of these was the late Louis Keller. The son of a patent lawyer of rather vague French descent, he was born in New York in 1857. Unlike McAllister, whose position was relatively unassailable and who belonged to the Union Club, the best Keller ever made was the Calumet Club, which was a good crew cut below. Like McAllister, however, he took himself extremely seriously and was never troubled by a sense of either humor or objectivity—particularly about himself. Growing up on the fringe of Society, he was, like so many arbiters, fascinated by it. "The mind of Louis Keller," says one biographer, "never went beyond Society."

In person Keller was uninterested in girls, was sandy-haired and had a curious-looking drooping mustache and a squeaky, affected voice. He was also troubled, relatively early in life, with deafness. As a young man, he had looked around for various outlets for his talents. First he tried to be a gunsmith. Failing at this, he next had a go at dairy farming. Once again he failed. With the advent of the new British sport of golf, however, he had his first success;

laying out a course on his New Jersey farm, he established the Baltusrol Golf Club, and since he owned many of the bonds of his Calumet Club, he had no trouble in getting the members of the Calumet—who would later for the same reason support his *Social Register*—also to become members of his new club. Alongside, as a sort of practical joke, he established a one-engine railroad, known as his Baltusrol and Pacific, in which he also sold stock.

Keller's first venture into arbitrage was to found, rather typically, a gossip sheet. It was called *The American Queen and Town Topics*, and Keller lasted in its management just two years; afterwards, as *Town Topics*, it proved to be the predecessor of a later day's gossip columns. Then, in 1887, he launched what was to prove his most lasting success. Contrary to general belief, however, the *Social Register* was by no means a startling innovation. There had been a host of "Blue Books" and "Visiting Lists" before it. Indeed, Keller's first edition was inspired to the point of plagiarism by a volume which had come out years earlier called *Society-List and Club-Register*, which had been Maurice Minton's publication based on the visiting lists of his mother, Mrs. Charles Minton. In two ways, however, Keller proved himself shrewd. The first was that, as the son of a lawyer and a man who knew his way in and around the law, he somehow managed to protect his own *Register* from being copied, at the same time to protect himself from the charge—which was of course true—that he had copied others. The second way Keller proved himself was to establish, from the beginning, a strict policy of secrecy where his *Register* was concerned. The names of his "Advisory Board"—if indeed in the early days there was one— were never made public, and right away the office established a policy of never giving interviews, information or indeed intelligence of any sort. This policy was to prove a wise one—in more ways than one.

By the time of Keller's death in 1922, the *Register* was an established success. But Keller himself had been something less than that. His financial affairs were always carelessly handled, and his total property at the time of his death, exclusive of some $135,000 of

Social Register stock, included $13,000 in cash, eight old sack suits, one trunk of old shirts and underclothes and one 72-ton steam locomotive. Upon his death, the management of the *Register* fell apparently to his nephew, Charles Keller Beekman, who lived until 1941, but actually, as we have seen, was in the hands of his secretary, Miss Bertha Eastmond, later Mrs. Edward C. Barry.

In 1925 the *Register* reached its peak, numbering editions in twenty-one different cities. At this time, however, a reaction set in which has continued more or less unabated to the present day. The start of *Register* trouble was its invasion of the South. To his dying day, Beekman could never understand why, for example, Richmond refused the honor of being socially registered. Finally one day a Richmond lady told him. "Mr. Beekman," she said gently, "down here we know who's who without being told." The *Register* met with similar lack of success in its invasion of the Minneapolis-St. Paul area. First the office moved in a correspondent, chose a thousand or more names, and then mailed them all their *Registers* with a $5 due bill. Only 150 replies were received and the project was abandoned, the *Register* admitted, for "lack of interest." Detroit also proved a stumbling block, when Miss Sarah Burnham, of the local *Social Secretary*, declared, "I do not consider that the *Social Register* uses very good discretion." But the final blow in the Motor City came when Mrs. William A. McGraw also spoke her mind. "Why, it's perfect nonsense!" she said. "One person is every bit as good as another. Anyway, I spend half my time throwing invitations into the wastebasket."

Soon not only Minneapolis-St. Paul and Detroit, but also Providence, Richmond, Savannah, Atlanta and Charleston were abandoned for "lack of interest," and later it was found necessary to combine Philadelphia with Wilmington and Cleveland with Cincinnati and Dayton. By the 1950's, Cleveland was freed of the burden of Cincinnati and Dayton, but the *Register* itself was down to eleven editions. In the 1950's, also, two members of the secret "Advisory Board" undertook to search for a replacement as editor of the *Register* and had an interview with, of all people, an assistant editor of *Look* magazine. To this day the editor so honored has no idea why they came to her, but she has never forgotten the experience.

At first, she recalls, the men "beat around the bush" and were very "hush-hush." Then they finally admitted they needed a new editor and also that the office needed modernization; they said they had only one "badly battered typewriter" and that most of the addresses were still done by hand. By this time the young editor was beginning to have strong doubts herself about wanting the job, but she recalls that the men were determined to know everything about her; they even wanted to see her paintings and were vastly relieved, she says, when they learned they weren't abstract. Since she also wrote for *Look*, she naturally brought up the question, if she took the job, of her writing on the "outside." This caused some consternation. The men wanted to know exactly what kind of writing she might be doing. Each thing she mentioned caused increased consternation. Finally in desperation she asked them what kind of writing they thought she could do. "The best thing for you to be," one of the men said reflectively, "would be a lyric poet."

Since the editor was some distance removed from poetry, the interview was as good as over. "What finished it though," she says firmly, "was when the question of salary came up." Actually salary has been a sore subject in the *Social Register* family ever since the days of Keller. Although its correspondents in different cities are not overworked, they are meagerly paid, particularly since they are also expected to keep the New York office informed of all scandals that may breach the *Register's* curious moral code—which is easily Society's most difficult party line. Otherwise the work is not either heavy or, since all decisions are made in New York, demanding of judgment. They merely clip items, as we have said, concerning marriages, divorces, deaths, debutante lists, college graduations, etc. Nonetheless, even doing such tasks over the years, certain correspondents, despite the *Register's* pretensions to anonymity, have risen to become rather well known in their cities, among them Mrs. John J. Attridge in Boston, Miss Nannie Poor in Baltimore, Mrs. Walter Tuckerman and Miss Sallie Pickett in Washington,

D.C., Mrs. Louisa Sanborn Hill in Chicago and Mrs. Jacques Henrici in San Francisco.

Of these Mrs. John J. Attridge, who started working for the *Register* in 1907, easily rates as senior correspondent. Born Margaret Roche in 1876, the daughter of a carpenter and later the wife of the assistant register of deeds for Suffolk County, she inherited her job via an assistanceship to the late Boston *Herald* Society editor, Caroline Washburn. Nor has Mrs. Attridge ever had an easy time. A Roman Catholic herself, as was her boss, Mr. Keller, she is more associated with the Irish political element in Boston than the Yankee social, and yet has seen her *Register* include, as she admits, "very few Catholics" and, as far as she can recall, "no Jews at all." In all her fifty years, Mrs. Attridge never met Mr. Keller, Mr. Beekman, Miss Eastmond, or even any correspondent from any other city.

Mrs. Attridge received $150 for her first year's work in 1907; in 1957, her fiftieth anniversary, she received, again for the full year, $350. She is, however, philosophical about this. "It was about a dollar a day at the end," she says, "and after all I only worked about two minutes a day." Asked if she thinks the *Register* has any future, she says she very much doubts it. "I just don't think there is any Society any more," she concludes. "The First World War killed it. I've protested about many of the people who get in but it does no good, and look where the ones who do get in go. Look at the Sumner Pingrees. They're in the Boston *Register* all right, but their address is Central Ermita, Orienta, Cuba."

Through the years nothing has so fascinated Society editors—most of whom have no idea of the way the *Register* is run—as why certain names are dropped and others added. Actually, as anyone in the *Register* knows, getting in is primarily a matter of writing for an application and getting five or so letters of recommendation from people already in. As for being "dropped," many of the people who are dropped are omitted simply because they got tired of filling out the forms which the *Register* sends. For example, when a man who is in the *Register* gets married, a few days after the marriage he receives the following letter:

It has been brought to the Association's attention that Mr. ——
has married recently. Will Mr. —— therefore kindly inform the
Association of the date and place of his marriage and give the full
Christian and maiden name of the bride and the names of her
parents in order that the customary notice may be entered in the
Dilatory Domiciles.

If Mrs. —— was previously married will Mr. —— kindly give
her former married name and state whether she was a divorcee or
a widow and if the latter give the Christian name of her late husband.

The Association would also appreciate receiving some information regarding Mrs. —— as to her Family background and any
other particulars which would be of assistance.

The repetition of the word "Christian," as well as the phrase
"Family background," can be extremely irritating to sensitive bride-
grooms, and at least half of the newspaper stories about such-and-
such a person being "dropped" for marrying so-and-so can be
traced to just such a simple irritation. The bridegroom just did
not return the form, and the *Social Register* staff being what it is,
since the form was not returned, the bridegroom's name was, a
year later, removed. Then too a large number of people have spoken
out against the *Register* and are not listed because they do not choose
to be. Notable among these have been John Hay Whitney and
Alfred Gwynne Vanderbilt. After Stephen ("Laddie") Sanford
was dropped for marrying actress Mary Duncan, the late John
Sanford was so exercised that he told the *Register* in no uncertain
terms to take his entire family out and keep them out. The same
sort of ruckus prevailed when the *Register* dropped elderly broker
William C. Langley for marrying singer Jane Pickens. "This," he
said, "is no better than Communism."

Actually, to get excited about inclusion or exclusion marks one,
particularly in New York where the shortcomings of the *Register*
have long been recognized, as taking the book with a seriousness it
has never deserved. "It's just a silly book," says Jessie Jerome
Fanshawe, last of the surviving "Four Hundred" social secretaries.
"It never really did mean very much, and now it is absolutely

meaningless." In the New York edition, for example, one looks in vain for the very names which form the staple fare of almost all the Society columns—the Duke and Duchess of Windsor, Elsa Maxwell, Mrs. William Paley, Gloria Vanderbilt, Barbara Hutton, Doris Duke, etc. Even when it comes to people in the same immediate family, the *Register* can be extraordinarily cavalier. Among the Roosevelts, for example, Eleanor, John and Franklin D. Jr. are apparently social; Elliott and James are not. Among the Chryslers, Walter P. Chrysler, Jr., the late Mrs. Byron Foy, and Mrs. Edgar Garbisch were in; the late Jack Chrysler never was. Bernard Baruch, for another example, has always been in; his brother, Sailing Baruch, has always been out. And in another Jewish family—Jewish names are rare enough considering the population of New York— Ralph M. Strassburger has been for many years in the *Register;* his brother, Perry, has not.

Whatever field one chooses to look at, the only policy is obviously no policy. Again taking the New York edition, one finds Arthur Hays Sulzberger in, but Hearsts, Howards, Paleys and Sarnoffs out. Among people who, for no reason, have been sometimes in and sometimes out, are such celebrities as Charles Lindbergh and Henry Ford. James Farley, included in the Washington, D.C., edition when he was in Washington, has never made the New York edition although he has lived in New York for a quarter of a century. Polly Lauder, a niece of Andrew Carnegie, was in before her marriage to Gene Tunney; afterwards, although they led an extremely active Society life, they never made it. Averell Harriman is in the book; Thomas Dewey is out. The late John Marquand was first in and then, after a divorce, out; the late Emily Post was always in, while Amy Vanderbilt never has been. Alfred Knopf is not in the book, but Charles Scribner is. Even in the ministerial field the selection is curious: the Rev. Arthur Lee Kinsolving is in, but the Revs. Norman Vincent Peale, Harry Emerson Fosdick, and several hundred others are out. Sidney B. Wood, Jr., was out, apparently for entering the laundry business, while Philip Van Rensselaer was out because of gossip column mention of his closeness with Barbara Hutton; meanwhile, Stephen Rockefeller and the former Norwegian housemaid, Ann Marie Rasmussen, were immediately put in.

Out on the West Coast, the *Register* threw out Charles Alden Black, of San Francisco, for marrying Shirley Temple—a feat to some people about on a par with insulting the American flag. Cobina Wright, Jr., however, who later became one of the most famous Society debutantes in history, was thrown out at the age of nine. "I asked my daughter if she minded," says Cobina Wright, Sr., "and she said, 'Mommy, it's nothing but a telephone book.' And that's when she was *nine*, mind you."

The attitude of the *Social Register* toward celebrities of stage and screen is perhaps the most curious of all. Katharine Hepburn and Princess Grace Kelly are not in the *Social Register*, but Ann Eden Crowell, the ex-model who accidentally shot and killed her husband, William Woodward, is in. Also included was Mae Daw, an occasional musical comedy girl who married the son of Louis Kaufman. On the other hand, Earl E. T. Smith, in the *Register* when he was married to Consuelo Vanderbilt, was out when he married Florence Pritchett; in the same way Elizabeth Grant was in when she was married to the late William Hale Harkness and out when she married Robert Montgomery. George Richard was out for marrying actress Helen Mencken. Whitney Bourne and Jane Wyatt, formerly in the *Register*, were out when they went on the stage; later when Miss Wyatt went on television, she was back in. On the other hand, Kyle McDonnell, in when she was on TV and married to Richard Gordon, Jr., was out when she divorced him. Two stage personalities who have never run into any trouble were the late Ruth Draper and the present Cornelia Otis Skinner; apparently, to the *Social Register*, the only safe Society, where the theatre is concerned, is that of monologuists.

After the late Louis Keller, the mantle of arbitrage next descended on the first of a long line of what Tex McCrary was later to call the "Gentlemen of the Pressure"—as well as the greatest Society writer of what the late Lenore Corbett called the "Gossip Truth." Cholly Knickerbocker No. 1 was, as we have seen, the man who named Café Society. As for his own real name, it was Maury Henry Biddle Paul, and he was particularly fond of the third. He was a Philadelphian, but although he once claimed direct descent from Rolf, the Norse Conqueror (A.D. 860-932), he was never able to establish connections with the Biddles, at least to the latter's entire satisfaction.

The son of a real estate man, who in his turn had some difficulty in connecting himself with *the* Pauls, Maury was born in the Quaker City in 1890. He had three years at the University of Pennsylvania but never graduated. Instead, after a brief turn in a machine foundry and an attempt to sell Técla necklaces, he applied to the editor of the Philadelphia *Times* for a job as Society editor. Pompous and already inclined toward weight, both physical and otherwise, he irritated the editor and was promptly turned down. Undismayed, Paul began sending in to the paper a series of incorrect Society items. These he mailed on expensive notepaper, handwritten with different handwritings and with fake but correct-sounding signatures. The editor printed them all—whereupon Paul, after a decent interval, descended upon him once more and, clutching a handful of clippings, demanded to know the meaning of such "outrageous lies" about nice people. He was promptly hired.

In 1914, when the editor moved to New York to another paper, he took his new Society editor with him and Paul, whose career was singularly uninterrupted by such mundane matters as wars, promptly undertook to write four different Society columns in four different newspapers under such pseudonyms as "Dolly Madison," "Polly Stuyvesant" and "Billy Benedick." Then one evening in 1919, William Randolph Hearst himself, calling upon Miss Marion Davies, was irritated to find her engrossed in a rival paper. Demanding to know what she liked in it, she told him, "Dolly Madison." That very night Hearst called one of his editors and ordered him to "Get Dolly." Paul was hired, Margaret Case Harriman remembers, at a salary slightly larger than that received by the Chief Justice of the United States Supreme Court.

The comparison was curiously apt—and Paul soon became not only judge but also jury to Society not only in New York but, as his syndication spread, all over the country. Like all arbiters he loved lists, and as early as 1921 he divided Society into what he called "Old Guard" and "Café Society," as follows:

Old Guard	*Café*
Mrs. Charles B. Alexander	Mrs. John Aspegren
August Belmont	Mrs. Morgan Belmont
Mrs. Henry Clews	Mrs. Craig Biddle
R. Fulton Cutting	G. Louis Boissevain
Mrs. W. Bayard Cutting	Mrs. Jerome Napoleon Bonaparte
Mrs. John R. Drexel	Mrs. Nicholas F. Brady
Mrs. W. B. Osgood Field	Mrs. Edward N. Breitung
Stuyvesant Fish	Mrs. Gardner Brown
Mrs. Richard Gambrill	Mrs. William Proudfit Burden
Elbridge T. Gerry	Mrs. Lewis L. Clarke
Mrs. Ogden Goelet	Genevieve Clendenin
Mrs. E. Henry Harriman	Mrs. Sydney J. Colford, Jr.
Mrs. Francis Burrall Hoffman	Mrs. James W. Corrigan
Mrs. Henry Reese Hoyt	Mrs. Joshua Cosden
Rosina Sherman Hoyt	Mrs. Jean de St. Cyr
Mrs. Adrian Iselin	Elsie de Wolfe
Mrs. C. Oliver Iselin	Mrs. William Disston
Mrs. Arthur Curtiss James	Mrs. John R. Drexel, Jr.
Mrs. Walter B. James	Mrs. Joel Ellis Fisher
Mrs. Goodhue Livingston	Mrs. Frederick T. Frelinghuysen
Pierre Lorillard	Mrs. Preston Gibson
Clarence H. Mackay	Mrs. Jay Gould
Ogden Mills	Mrs. William Miller Graham
Mrs. J. Pierpont Morgan	Mrs. Arents Humphreys
Mrs. Frederick Pearson	Mrs. Edward F. Hutton
Edmund Randolph	Mrs. Louis G. Kaufman
Mrs. Whitelaw Reid	Mrs. Adolph Ladenburg
Mrs. Walter Rutherfurd	Julie Lentilhon
Mrs. John King Van Rensselaer	Mrs. W. Goadby Loew
Philip Rhinelander	Mrs. Charles M. McNeil
Mrs. William Jay Schieffelin	Mrs. Hermann Oelrichs

Old Guard	Café
Mrs. W. Watts Sherman	Mrs. James Lowell Putnam
Mrs. James Russell Soley	Princess Rospigliosi
William Rhinelander Stewart, Sr.	"Jack" Rutherford
Mrs. Henry A. C. Taylor	Mrs. John Sanford
Mrs. Hamilton McK. Twombly	Mrs. Preston Pope Satterwhite
Mrs. Cornelius Vanderbilt	Mrs. Morton L. Schwartz
Mrs. Frederick W. Vanderbilt	William Rhinelander Stewart, Jr.
The Dowager Mrs. Vanderbilt	Mrs. Edward T. Stotesbury
Mrs. George Henry Warren	Mrs. Cornelius Hoagland
Mrs. Whitney Warren	Tangeman
Mrs. Harry Payne Whitney	Mrs. Griswold Thompson
Mrs. Henry White	Marion Tiffany
Mrs. Forsyth Wickes	Reginald C. Vanderbilt
Mrs. Marshall Orme Wilson	Mrs. William K. Vanderbilt II
Mrs. Richard T. Wilson	Mrs. John Wanamaker, Jr.
Mrs. F. Egerton Webb	Mrs. Allen Gouverneur Wellman
Mrs. W. Seward Webb	Mrs. Ambrose Wetmore
Mrs. John J. Wysong	Mrs. J. Norman de R. Whitehouse
	Mrs. Joseph E. Widener
	Mrs. John N. Willys

Paul himself, as he freely admitted, was one of the most amazing snobs who ever existed even in a notably snobbish field. "You can't," he often said, "interest everybody in everybody." He has no interest in girls—"No woman," he once said, "is beautiful"—lived with his mother and, although surpassed in sartorial splendor by Lucius Beebe, cut no mean figure in that regard himself and loved to roll up his trouser legs on Fifth Avenue and demonstrate, to skeptical passers-by, his solid-gold garter clasps. But his snobbishness remained his ruling trait. Once when his secretary, the able Eve Brown, confided that she wanted to leave him but didn't want to "have to sleep with producers to get ahead," Paul laughed. "My dear child," he said, "nobody gives a damn who you sleep with. In this world, it's who you're seen dining with that counts."

The columnist was almost always seen with the Right People— whom he wrote up and down as his moods varied—but the difficulty was that he could never quite decide who the Right People were. In his early days he confined his writings primarily to the doings of Mrs. Vanderbilt, Mrs. O. H. P. Belmont, "the ancestral" Pells, etc., and "wondered dourly" what would happen when Mrs. Hermann Oelrichs, Mrs. Ogden Goelet, Mrs. George J. Gould, etc., had "passed into the great beyond." Then he began to have some doubts. "The foremost Families of today," he said—this was in 1926—"are the Rockefellers, Morgans, Astors, Vanderbilts, Goulds, Drexels, Kahns and Whitneys. Will they be consequential factors in Society fifteen years hence? I say 'No' with two or three exceptions." Next, as he went along, he was to calculate that "95 per cent" of the *Social Register* comprised the "dullest, dreariest and most colorless collection of so-called socialites" imaginable. Then, toward the end, he became convinced that, as he put it, "Being in Society is nothing more than a state of mind. . . . If you think you're in and give Society scribblers something to scribble about they'll help you with the— I wonder if I could call it—'deception.' " And finally, at the very end, he told Lyman Kendall that New York needed "new money and new faces. . . . I shall concentrate on new people. The newcomers of today are the Old Guard of tomorrow."

Vain and not above stooping to blandishments and advertising pressures, Paul had a flair which, if it wasn't quite charm, often passed as such in the circles he scribed. At times he had an almost appealing naïveté. Among his most famous features, for example, were his "Great Tragedies of Society"—features which bore titles such as "Suicides Stalk the Joneses of Long Island," "Cup That Cheer Wrecks Laura Biddle," "Polo Fall Drove Socialite Arthur Scott Burden Violently Insane." He loved these dearly and often would startle a group in his table-hoppings at El Morocco and the Colony by leaving them with the line, "Well, so long. If you hear of any good tragedies, let me know." At other times he had genuine wit, though it was usually buried in a morass of his favorite clichés, such as "oodles of ducats," "art of Terpsichore," "tinkling telephones," "Longuyland" and "Yours truly." It was Paul, for example, who, just before the Abdication, characterized the Duchess of Windsor's former husband, Ernest Simpson, as "The Unimportance of Being Ernest."

It was he too who wrote his own headline on a savage story of the late Joshua Cosdens: "Cosden Servants Strike in Middle of Dinner, Leaving Cosden Guests Face to Face with Starvation or, What Is Worse, Face to Face with Themselves."

To Paul's celebrity "creations"—Mrs. Harrison Williams, Mrs. William Rhinelander Stewart, Reginald Vanderbilt, George J. Gould, the "Miraculous Morgans" (the twins Gloria and Thelma), Beth Leary, Adele Astaire, etc.—he could do no wrong. But somehow even these people liked Paul best in the middle of his feuds—with Palm Beach, Lady Mendl, Laura Corrigan, Emerald Cunard and Mrs. Vincent Astor No. 1. Says Eve Brown:

> Maury disliked Marion Snowden Rospigliosi Reed Dresser, step-daughter of his good friend, Mrs. Robert Johnson, formerly Mrs. Snowden. He disliked Mrs. Nicholas Holmsen, to whose "Second Avenue background" he referred often. He disliked Muriel Richards, now Mrs. Warren Pershing, although he usually laid off her because he was a friend of her mother and her grandfather, the late Jules Bache. He disliked Mrs. Gilbert Miller, the daughter of Mr. Bache, because he considered her an insufferable snob. He disliked Marlene Dietrich. I recall that once, at a party where the guests included la Dietrich, Clifton Webb and other Hollywood "celebrities," if that is the word, Maury became so irritated that nobody was talking about him that he arose, stamped his foot petulantly, and said, "You're all such crashing bores and God-damned exhibitionists. Goodbye, please," and walked out.

The irony was of course that, before his death in 1942, Paul lived to see the world of "celebrities" overwhelm his Café Society the way he and it had overwhelmed the Old Guard. But he was by no means the only arbiter who presided, albeit unwillingly, over the dissolution. Another was his great and good friend, the remarkable Boston-born Lucius Beebe, late of New York and even later of Virginia City, Nevada. For if Paul coined the term Café Society, Beebe best described it, chronicling in a glorious rolling style not only the new but also the old—the day before the day in which he would much rather have lived. "I would rather be a bright leaf on the stream of dying civilization," he once said, "than a fertile seed dropped in the

soil of a new era." And, in 1936, Beebe succinctly described, in the
New York *Herald Tribune*, how Society and Celebrity had become
synonymous:

> The itch for personal publicity has proceeded to such lengths that
> patrons will come into a nightclub or bar and if they don't see
> Louis Sobol, Helen Worden, Jerry Zerbe or Molly Thayer or some
> other fashionable reporters or photographers, they simply don't
> check their wraps and move on somewhere else.

The generally recognized "last of the arbiters," however, was the
late Frank Crowninshield. A very different sort of man from Maury
Paul, he stemmed from one of New England's proudest Families.
Indeed, in the Eighteenth Century a Crowninshield merchant was
allied not only by business with Elias Haskett Derby, once King of
the merchant princes and the richest man in America, but also by
marriage with the venerable Peabody Family of Salem. Crowninshield's great-grandfather, Benjamin Crowninshield, was Secretary
of the Navy under both Presidents Madison and Monroe—at a time
when he personally owned more ships than the American Navy—
and Crowninshield's great-great-uncle built in 1816 the famous
Cleopatra's Barge, the first elaborate private yacht in America and
one so elegant that when it crossed the Atlantic it became to the Old
World one of the wonders of the New.

But the Crowninshield fortune had begun to run out by the time
Francis Welch Crowninshield was born, in a Paris hotel, in 1872.
In sharp contrast to Paul, who was suspicious of "foreigners" and
railed against them in his column, Crowninshield, whose father was
director of the American Academy of Rome, was a cosmopolite from
the start. Indeed, his formative years were about equally divided
between Rome and Paris, Boston and New York. His father was a
water-colorist and mural painter and, though he had a small independent income, was not particularly successful; neither for a long
time was his son. Crowninshield attended the University of Rome
for two years and at eighteen got a job with the publishing firm of
Putnam's. Later he was, in order, publisher of the *Bookman*, editor

of *Metropolitan*, editor of *Munsey's*, a literary agent in London and art editor of the *Century* magazine. At none of these jobs did he distinguish himself enough to be noticed outside of his business, as either editor or businessman, but he was soon recognized almost everywhere for his remarkable qualities as a human being. Debonaire and distinguished looking, he had an air, an elegance, a *savoir faire* and a cachet which not only set him apart from Maury Paul but also enabled him to bridge the gap of American Society in transition—from "Four Hundred" to "Smart Set." His opportunity to give full public vent to this bridging came about, of course, through his editorship of the famous magazine *Vanity Fair*.

Vanity Fair grew out of the old *Dress* magazine which Condé Nast, as publisher of *Vogue*, had purchased. The first issue, under Nast, appeared in 1913 and was called *Dress & Vanity Fair*. Nast, however, was dissatisfied with it and took it around to show his friend Crowninshield. The latter looked it over, then handed it back to Nast. "There is no magazine," he said, "which is read by the people you meet at lunches and dinners. Your magazine should cover the things people talk about—parties, the arts, sports, humor and so forth."

Almost immediately Nast asked Crowninshield to edit his magazine, and from the beginning *Vanity Fair* was a remarkable hit. Through it, the hinterlands of the country also passed from "Four Hundred" to a new Society—one that embraced the arts and theatre and Hollywood and indeed all of Crowninshield's "and so forths." *Vanity Fair* became, in fact, the central rendezvous of a Café Society without the Café, and in this regard Nast was himself almost as important an influence—with his elaborate penthouse parties—as was Crowninshield. In his later years Nast was wont to say that he once gave a party and since he couldn't leave out his friend Mrs. Vanderbilt and he couldn't leave out his friend George Gershwin, he had them both—and thus Café Society was born. Whether this version was as significant as Paul's dinner at the old Ritz is doubtful, but the fact remains that both versions occurred at approximately the same time, and so both foisted their influence, through the twin media of Paul's column and Crowninshield's magazine, all over the country.

To this day there are Crowninshields in Boston who regard Frank as an errant son. And, if Clare Boothe, then Brokaw, could call him "the last of the species once known as gentleman," the fact is that he could be criticized, albeit gently, even by some of his closest associates. "If a rich man has taste," Robert Benchley once said, "he is just as worthy in the eyes of Frank Crowninshield as a man who has no money at all. Crownie is like that in everything— broad-minded." And illustrator May Wilson Preston once toasted her boss: "Here's to Crownie, the victim of a profound, constant, but ever-changing sincerity." But if these were gentle slings and arrows, the praise which came his way from people in all walks of life more than balanced them. By his office staff he was loved with a fanatical devotion. Like most arbiters, a lifelong bachelor, he was defended by the girls who worked for him even on this score. "The reason he never married," says his long-time secretary, Miss Jeanne Ballot, "is simply that he couldn't. He felt as if he had to make every girl in the world feel as if she were the only girl in the world—and he almost did too."

If Crowninshield was the kindest and most lovable of all America's social arbiters, he was also the most humorous. "Married men," he once said, "make very poor husbands." And if Nast, at age 58, married a 24-year-old office girl and generally made something of a fool of himself, Crowninshield never lost either his dignity or his curiously powerful influence in making people conscious of the world of art and theatre on a social basis. Crowninshield had pioneered in this direction with publication, in 1908, of his brief satire, *Manners for the Metropolis:*

> At a very large dinner, the lady beside you is almost certain to be one who entertains generously and, as such, should be treated with a certain degree of politeness. Try to suppress, however, all sentiments purely human in their nature, such as pity, kindness of heart, sympathy, enthusiasm, love of books, music, and art.

These ridiculous sentiments are in exceedingly bad taste and should be used sparingly, if at all.

In discussing literature at a lunch or dinner, try to remember that there are but a very few fashionable authors. They are as follows: Mrs. Wharton, Colonel Mann, Mrs. Glyn, Robert Hichens, F. Peter Dunne, John Fox, Jr., and Billy Baxter.

After dinner, over the cigars, it is bad form for men to discuss any subject but stocks and motor cars.

Always be half an hour late for everything. Nothing is so tedious as waiting.

In criticizing a play or a novel be careful to avoid long and discriminating criticisms. You should either "knock" or "boost." Try to remember that there are only two kinds of plays or novels—they are either "bully" or "rotten."

At the theatre it is smart to "roast the show." Do not be afraid of wounding the feelings of your host and hostess. It is an even chance that they are more bored than you. If the actors seem to object to your conversation or show annoyance or impatience, try to remember that they are not, as a rule, well bred, and are ignorant of all the graceful little social conventions.

Here lay in a nutshell—or better still in Crowninshield's inimitable prose—the attitude toward the Four Arts of the majority of the "Four Hundred," the very group, of course, to which Crowninshield himself, by eminent domain, so eminently belonged. And yet after Crowninshield had done his work, and after publication of *Vanity Fair*, the group would never have the same attitude again. And, while *Vanity Fair* died in 1936 and Crowninshield himself in 1947, the revolution he had spearheaded—one which might be called the Revolt of the Classes—would proceed apace.

But it is perhaps not without significance that, in the direction of celebrities, this revolution had, long before Crowninshield's death, proceeded entirely too fast for his taste. For the man who founded the Coffee House Club to get away from the Knickerbocker Club, and who was all his life as at home at the Stork Club or "21" as he was at Mrs. Vanderbilt's, became so disenchanted with certain celebrities that he took to running, along with his famous "Hall of

Fame" feature, an even more famous feature entitled "We Nominate for Oblivion." Among these were King Carol and Queen Marie of Rumania, Belle Livingston, Raymond Duncan and Cornelius Vanderbilt, Jr. Once, indeed, one of his nominees for oblivion, the late Floyd Gibbons, complained that his treatment was manifestly unfair—only a few issues before, he pointed out, he had been enshrined in the magazine's Hall of Fame and then he found himself consigned to Oblivion. "Then," replied Crowninshield, "what are you grumbling about? You're all even." By the end of his life, too, he was disenchanted with the very Café Society he had done so much to bring to the fore; in fact, he spoke out on the subject, and in no uncertain terms, to Geoffrey Hellman:

> In the old days, Society was so snobbish and narrow and limited that artists and writers and playwrights were not sought after. Finally it was discovered that they were more amusing, so the narrow Society began breaking its neck to get into what was the forerunner of Café Society. It became chic to go to Alma Gluck's, Stanford White's, Bessie Marbury's, Augustus Thomas', Elsie de Wolfe's. That made a very charming Society. But finally Café Society drifted into barrooms and night clubs and lost its chic. The idea of Café Society was all right, all but the café. What actually ruined the whole goddam thing was alcohol and noise.

In 1941, James McKinley Bryant produced his *Café Society Register* in which he gave it as his opinion, in his introduction, that the term "had been too broadly used" and that Café Society was "not a class of people or a social stratum." Instead, he maintained, "it is a heterogeneous, sometimes nomadic group, that follow a certain mode of living." In any case, he came up with something close to three thousand names, starting with Miss E. Marie Abbett, of North Street, Greenwich, whose profession was unidentified, and ending with Mr. and Mrs. Adolph Zukor, of Hollywood, "film executive." Between them were seven Lehmans, five Vanderbilts, and a motley assortment of night and day people ranging from Mr. and Mrs. Winthrop Aldrich to Mr. and Mrs. David Windsor—after which, incidentally, was written "Duke of Windsor (Wallis Simpson)."

And, at the end of his introduction, Bryant had this observation: "The name of Café Society may die, but these people as a group will continue to make news in their professions and recreations."

In this he would seem to have been correct; the only addition one might make would be to note that what to one generation is Café Society is to the next generation real Society, and vice versa. And both are, of course, nothing but celebrities in the first place. Let us, for example, turn the question of a definition of Society over to the tender mercies of today's gossip columnists. "Most of the 'old Families' today," says Walter Winchell, "have either 'press agents' or 'praise agents.'" Leonard Lyons, commenting on the names in Cholly Knickerbocker's column, was almost equally blunt. "They can't be Society," he said, "*I* know them all." And, out in California, Mrs. Cobina Wright, Sr., told us that many years ago she had embarked on a column entitled "Society as I Find It." "I didn't find any," she says—and now writes a column entitled "Cobina Wright." As for Hedda Hopper, she at first protested she did not know anything about Society and was "just a working girl." Then she exploded. "Society," she said, "is people who would go to hell rather than not see their names in print!" Back in New York, Inez Robb, who served as the first "Nancy Randolph" for ten years starting in the twenties, declared that there's a "new influx after every war. I caught the reflex after the first war. Money was the foundation then—now it's Publicity." The present "Nancy Randolph," Julia McCarthy, archdeaconess of Society columnists, was even sterner. "Society is two things," she snaps, "publicity and more publicity." Frank Farrell, dining in New York's famous "21" restaurant, next gave his definition: "Society is '21' and the front room of Morocco— mostly '21.'" And, taking office in April, 1958, as Society Editor of the New York *World-Telegram and Sun*, Joseph Xavier Dever, having left a six-year tenure on the New York *Journal American*, declared that in his opinion the only Society in America today is a Society of Achievement. "Family background," he said, "is no longer the sole criterion of an individual's distinction."

The Cholly Knickerbocker who succeeded Maury Paul, and who

has from the beginning believed in not only a Society but also an Aristocracy of Achievement, went so far as to throw down the gauntlet. "Today is as good a time as then [Ward McAllister's day]," he wrote in 1953, "for establishing new standards of admission to American Society." He then proceeded to publish a list of 399 names—he left one for "the most deserving I've omitted"—which he said represented the "Aristocracy of Achievement in this country." He insisted, however, that every person on his list was (a) "a loyal American," (b) "a leader in his field of work," (c) "a man of excellent character," (d) "a man of culture and taste," and (e) "a whole man, blending his qualities harmoniously and in humility." Since his list included such controversial figures—at least from the point of view of his "character," "culture" and "humility" qualifications—as Al Capp, Joe DiMaggio, Sam Goldwyn, Joseph P. Kennedy, Perle Mesta, John Ringling North, Louella Parsons, Westbrook Pegler, Spyros Skouras and Cornelius Vanderbilt Whitney—there was some disagreement over the list, but few quarreled with Knickerbocker's summation, as published in *Esquire:*

> Here in America we have all the material necessary for creating a true aristocracy, a social leadership that would be the envy of the world. Unfortunately, all our previous attempts have been based on the European model, while what we ought to do is set out on our own, from our own criteria of accomplishment and culture.

Probably the most extraordinary definition we received was from one of the most famous, albeit anonymous, of press agents. "Society to me," he said, "is seven people." Asked to name these, he was quick. "Jack Astor, Gregg Sherwood, Barbara Hutton, Barbara Hutton's son, you know—what's his name?—Doris Duke, Winthrop Rockefeller and Vanderbilt." Next asked to name which Vanderbilt, the man was vague. "Any Vanderbilt," he said, "I don't give a damn." And, if seven people seem indeed close to the end of the line for Society, the fact remains that the *International Celebrity Register,* published in 1960, included, of American Society, names— in other words, people who made the book primarily because of Society—hardly more than that number. Yet the celebrity field has, in contrast to Society, grown to almost incredible proportions. When Earl Blackwell first listed his "Celebrity Service" in the telephone book a quarter of a century ago, his was the only entry under the word; in the 1960 telephone book there were twenty entries under it.

The *Celebrity Register* maintained in its introduction that it was not a "Blue Book" but a "do" book, and that as American Society had changed from "How-do-you-do" to "What-do-you-do," so the book represented not Society at all but Celebrity—not the family name but the name name, not who somebody was, in the sense of his or her antecedents, but who somebody *is* and presumably even *will be* in the sense of his or her descendants. Although it was admitted, in the latter instance, that there were, in some cases, reasonable grounds for doubt, the book would seem to have failed to realize, as indeed all the purveyors of Café Society and achievement lists failed to realize, that there is no difference between celebrity and Society and never has been since the days when John Jacob Astor I was first called a "celebrity." And, if the *Celebrity Register* has already proved itself a more accurate barometer of the times than the *Social Register*, this is not so much because of the word "celebrity" as because the *Social Register* stopped realizing, with its issue from approximately 1890, that American Society has from the beginning started with celebrity and then moved on to Society and Aristocracy.

To most people the idea that celebrity is, in reality, Society will come as something of a shock. Such people should realize, however, that what they think of as Society is actually Aristocracy, which, as we have seen, was once Society but now has graduated, by dint of at least one generation of prominence, into Aristocracy. A far better word than either celebrity or Society seems, to this writer at least, the word "Publi-ciety"—in other words, a combination of publicity and what people used to think of, in happier days, as Society. For good as the phrase "Café Society" was for its time and the phrase "Society of Achievement" for its time, the word "Publi-ciety" is the actual ogre under which, whether we like it or not, we all live today. It is a world in which the arbiter is the gossip columnist or, outside of the gossip areas, the Society columnist. He or she, and he or she alone, decides who, socially speaking, is who—and for the very reason that, in the words of Columbia's Professor Lyman Bryson, "The predominant American prestige symbol is the appearance of one's real or professional name in print, and its sound on broadcasts." To this one might add the appearance of one's picture in the newspaper or on television—or, in the words of C. Wright Mills, "The world of the celebrity . . . is now the American forum of public honor."

Once one has understood this world—and the realization that it has never been any different from the world of Society—then it becomes not at all difficult to explain the "position" of someone like Elsa Maxwell—which is in any other definition of Society literally incomprehensible. There was a time, in her more modest days, when Miss Maxwell wrote, in 1939: "Society as we know it must be in a very peculiar state indeed if I, a girl from Keokuk, Iowa, and a former vaudeville pianist, am acknowledged as one of its arbiters."

Although such modesty is refreshing, particularly in comparison with the later Miss Maxwell, there was, of course, nothing "peculiar" about it at all. Miss Maxwell was Publi-ciety in 1939, and she was Publi-ciety in 1959, and presumably will be Publi-ciety in 1979. And, exactly like all arbiters since the days of Louis Keller, her power is the power of the press. Actually in her case, while she writes a column and makes a certain number of television appearances, these activities are somewhat limited in scope. But since she is closely identified as a friend and companion of Mrs. William Randolph Hearst, Sr., people feel that if they cross her—which otherwise would certainly be enjoyed—they will bring down on their heads the whole Hearst press. Like most fears in the insecure world of Publi-ciety, this fear is groundless, but few people choose to test it.

This same explanation holds true for Miss Maxwell's ability to attract large numbers of foreign ambassadors to her parties. The position of ambassador has, of course, changed greatly from the days when he was a powerful political figure representing at many days' distance from his homeland his home government. Nowadays, if the matter is of real urgency, the heads of State can pick up a telephone; the ambassador's position is primarily a symbolic one and, even more important, a public relations job. Here, of course, is where Miss Maxwell comes in. If she chooses to invite, say, the Portuguese Ambassador to one of her parties, the Portuguese Ambassador is not only curious to meet such a highly publicized person but is extremely cognizant of the fact that she will write about him—and in the course of him—about his country.

Even as a self-appointed arbiter, however, Miss Maxwell has had a career which is not without interest. Born in Keokuk, Iowa, in 1883, she was the daughter of an insurance man who wrote a column for $10 a week for the New York *Dramatic Mirror*. It was a newspaper devoted to the performing arts, and Miss Maxwell has always maintained that she was actually born in a theatre box. In any case, her father soon moved his family to San Francisco. He had a prejudice against formal education, so he decided to educate his daughter himself; Miss Maxwell never even graduated from grammar school. At the age of 12, however, she was vastly interested in Society and apparently never forgot having been told by her family that they were "too poor" to be invited to a San Francisco party. This she usually refers to as a "Vanderbilt" party but it was actually a party given by San Francisco's Senator Fair for his daughter, Theresa, who later married a Vanderbilt. "I made up my mind there and then," she says, "that some day I would give great parties all over the world and that no one would give more parties with less Vanderbilts than I would."

Although the Vanderbilts have had their ups and downs in American social history, it seems possible that they might survive without attendance at Miss Maxwell's parties. Even so, the career of Miss Maxwell from that point of no return has been a remarkable one. She was, in order, a pianist in a nickelodeon, an accompanist for a vaudeville performer, a partner in two Paris nightclubs, a press agent for Monte Carlo, an aspiring actress, a columnist, and a lecturer. Once in the lobby of the Excelsior Hotel in Venice, in an altercation over the dining rights to Noel Coward, she engaged in a hair-pulling contest with the late Dorothy di Frasso. "Dorothy always did have," Miss Maxwell says of the incident, "a peculiar sense of humor." As for her own sense of humor, she gives it full credit for having been able to go so far on apparently—in one sense—so little. "I honestly believe," she says, "people were attracted by the gaiety I radiate as naturally as I breathe. As far back as I can remember I've always been like a little girl on Christmas morning."

Miss Maxwell's Christmas spirit seems to work both ways. She was not only one of the first to realize the potentials involved in being a columnist—Maury Paul gave her the first boost in this direction—but once she became one, she never let any grass grow under her feet in realizing these potentials. "Everything is given to me that I want," she has said. "Even the Waldorf gives me my suite for virtually nothing." On top of this, she has never made any bones about having a little cash too. "Four old friends," she has written, "Mrs. Hearst, Mrs. Jessie Donahue, Mrs. Eleanor Loder and Mrs. Margaret Emerson—who know I'm always strapped for ready money —give me substantial checks at Christmas or on my birthday." This writer, curious as to just why such a highly perspicacious lady as the late Mrs. Emerson kept on year after year giving to Miss Maxwell, and wondering indeed if Mrs. Emerson regarded it as charity, asked her about it. Mrs. Emerson was gentle. "In the early days," she said, "Elsa really did add a great deal to Society. She really was gay. She just got —-well, like they all do. But I just went on giving money to her anyway. I really don't know why. I always got everything I wanted myself, and I enjoy giving money—even, I guess, when I shouldn't."

Since 1907, outside of the Waldorf, the Drake and other hotels that benefit from her benefits, Miss Maxwell has never had a home. Whenever she feels the need of one for a party or some other reason, she "borrows" one, as she puts it; some years ago she was given one "in perpetuity." Neither has she ever had, outside of herself, any romance. Once she said there were only two men in the world with whom she could have had one—the late Aly Khan and Cole Porter—but apparently decided not to. On another occasion she told an interviewer she had never liked the idea of sex. "I wouldn't subject myself to it," she said. "It never interested me—I was never interested for one minute, ever. I married the world—the world is my husband. That is why I'm so young. No sex. Sex is the most tiring thing in the world."

When it comes to what might be loosely described as her writing, Miss Maxwell is one of the few authors who has literally written more than she has read. She averages close to an autobiography a year, some of them in styles amazingly different from her columns. Her change of pace, as a writer, is breathless, but even this is less interesting than her change of face. At first blasting Maria Callas as an inferior talent, she was soon so lavish in her praise of the diva as to cause raised eyebrows. With the Duchess of Windsor she carried on a long feud during which time she wrote that the Duchess "was not interested in anything except herself" and "I just don't like her." Then, after the difficulties in connection with the sale of the Duchess' autobiography, the Duchess was persuaded, for publicity reasons, to "make up" with Miss Maxwell. Although this caused the Duke some anguish, since Miss Maxwell is one of the very few women about whom he has been known to be extremely caustic, they did make up. Ever since then, Miss Maxwell's reportage of the Duchess would seem to be on the basis of, as Hollywood might say, an "I" for an "I."

Arbiters on the order of Miss Maxwell are rare in other cities, but they are by no means unknown. In Baltimore, for example, the most famous Society editor in that city's history was Dr. Frederick Taylor. For one thing he was, to begin with, a man—the only one in the city ever to hold a post which not only in Baltimore, but also elsewhere in the country, is universally consigned to women. For another thing he was, before his Society editing days, a *bona fide* doctor of medicine, as his father was before him. A member of an old Virginia Family, he was small in size but large in scope—and such an ardent Anglophile that "if a fog descended over Baltimore he would rush out into the street and take long breaths exclaiming in delight that it reminded him of London."

As might be expected from such a man, Dr. Taylor's lifelong model for his Society column was London's Court Circular. But *arbiter elegantiarum* he was, and no mistake, and along with a distinguished career, first on the Baltimore *News* and later on the *Sun*, he handled any and all problems of decorum and etiquette with ease. One unfortunate telephoned to inquire if, for his four-o'clock wedding, he could wear a tuxedo. "You would," thundered Dr. Taylor, "be as suitably dressed in your pajamas."

Unfortunately, when it came to his Society column itself, Dr. Taylor wrote in such a flowery, Old World style that it was, to a large percentage of his readers, unintelligible. Finally one day Dr. Taylor's publisher rather tremulously suggested that his column needed modernization and "pepping up." Dr. Taylor said nothing— always an ominous sign. The next morning, however, his column was indeed modern. "Anyone who lives in the Green Spring Valley," Dr. Taylor began, "has either to be a Stewart or a horse." That morning the publisher called again; he had decided it would be perfectly all right, he said, to have the other style after all.

But even Dr. Taylor paled before one of the most remarkable Society editor-arbiters in American social history. Her bailiwick was Cincinnati and her name was Marion Devereux; up until her death in 1948, she was to Cincinnati a combination of the late Mrs. Vanderbilt, Elsa Maxwell and Lizzie Borden. Born to the purple prose—her mother had preceded her as Society editor—she started as an assistant on the famed Cincinnati *Enquirer* in the 1890's. In 1910, at the age of 37 and on her mother's death, Marion took over. She was a lifelong spinster and was the admitted "Tsarina" of her city until 1939, when at the age of 66 she suddenly walked out of her office one day for a physical checkup and never came back. Although she did not die until nine years later, she lived her last years in almost complete retirement—which was the exact opposite of the way she had previously worked. For three decades she had ruled her city as no other town has ever been ruled by its Society editor. "There has never been anyone else quite like her in America," says Alvin Harlow, "and Cincinnati, for one, fervently hopes

there never will be again." As for James Maxwell, he puts it succinctly: "You just cannot imagine her. You have actually to read
what she wrote—and then remember that she probably wrote more
than any other Society editor who ever lived."

Like Miss Maxwell, Miss Devereux lived rent and other per-
quisites free—in her case, it was the Hotel Sinton, which of course
she relentlessly plugged. Reverential toward those who she decided,
apparently by the degree of their kowtowing to her, were "Old
Families," she was a fiend incarnate toward anyone who ignored her,
and who was, therefore, a "social climber." In her own office, Miss
Devereux, a small woman, had the legs of her guests' chairs cut
down in order that visitors might be properly impressed.

During her entire reign very few dared cross her. One who did,
however, and dared to give a party without consulting her, received
a telephone call in the middle of the night—a habit Miss Devereux
formed in order to keep people better in line. "How dare you give a
party without consulting me?" she asked. "Don't you know that
I am the social arbiter of Cincinnati?" Miss Devereux concluded,
Harlow recalls, by calling the other woman a "social highway
robber" and thereafter, when the woman's three children, in order,
were married, all three weddings were totally ignored in the
Enquirer.

In Marion Devereux, the strange and wonderful world of Society-
page language soared to heights never before seen or attempted to
be read. At the height of the Cincinnati "Season," a single weekday's
social news would, in the tender hands of Miss Devereux, be accorded sixteen full columns, or two pages—and never was so much
as a comma permitted to be changed, either by the managing editor,
editor or publisher, all of whom were mortally afraid of her. She
particularly enjoyed distinguished obituaries:

> Cincinnatians returning to town from far and near have taken up
> the interests of their customary routine where they were dropped
> with the summer exodus. These fateful threads which now are to
> be woven into the fabric of winter's work and play have led during
> the long vacation to sorrow as well as joy. Particularly is this so

in the death of well known citizens who have in that period slipped
the slender moorings which held the bark of life at anchor in the
terrestrial seas and have sailed out upon that uncharted main which
sweeps forever on.

First among these is Mr. Michael Myers Shoemaker, whose death
in Paris in August has left a sense of loss in the lives of his friends
which cannot soon be stilled. As an author, traveler, country gentleman and thorough man of the world, Mr. Shoemaker was known
the length and breadth of the seven seas.

A member of an old and distinguished American family, a descendant of great men of colonial days, without whom the siege
of Boston and other revolutionary episodes might have written a
very different finale with the pages of history, Mr. Shoemaker was
persona grata at most of the courts of Europe, where he numbered
among hosts of friends the elect of countless countries.

But Miss Devereux was also far from averse to weddings:

Mr. James Morgan Hutton, Jr. and Mr. William Griess added
to their other duties that of placing snowy ribbons down the central
aisle where these silken moorings formed a frail barrier between
the guests and the bridal party as it passed. Mr. Reginald Barnard
and Mr. Richard Mellon of Pittsburgh, a nephew of Secretary Mellon, led the way, followed by Mr. Closson, Mr. Hutton, Mr. Griess,
Mr. Jesse Sweetser of New York, who as all the world knows is the
amateur golf champion of the United States; Mr. Blackwell Shaffer
and Mr. Douglas Robbins of Middletown, an uncle of the bride,
who was a welcoming host for the guests from his own city as they
arrived. All these men are accustomed to the niceties of life and
their smartness and poise helped maintain the dignity and glamour
of the service. They wore gardenias in the coat lapels of their
afternoon dress, the gray gloves and spats which completed their
costumes not to mention their top hats worn at various rakish
angles on the way from the church to the club, being the dernier
cri of good form.

At the troth plight as the waning day sent its fading shaft of sunshine through the window of the chancel groined in stone its saints,
angels and madonnas seemed to come to life and mingle their own
gorgeous color with that of the tableau that surrounded the bride
and groom, and which, as the service wrought its impressive milestone in the lives of these young people, stood out like separate
panels of vivid design and captivating contrasts.

And, of course, because of the style, there were the inevitable, albeit unintended, *doubles entendres*. Often they were extremely embarrassing to the entire staff of the paper, but, again of course, not a word could be changed:

> Mr. and Mrs. Tom Conroy have been the center of many merry moments since their return from their honeymoon.

> Miss Ruth Harrison whose toilet of black satin was relieved by a touch of ermine.

> An hour of agreeable intercourse will follow this series of events, the membership being all cocked and primed to stay on to enjoy it.

Last but not least were the paragraphs which, puzzle as Cincinnatians would over them, not one ever knew what she meant:

> In nothing to the Philistines are the May Festivals more intriguing than in the boxes and the Audience. Last night these themes of and corridor and foyer were paramount to the carnal-minded devotee of these two yearly events.

One city which is almost entirely devoted to celebrity and Publi-ciety is Washington, D.C. Although the so-called "cave-dwellers," the "Old Families" with certain usually rather decayed Southern social roots, as well as the "Georgetown Set" and the "Chevy Chase Set," would be the first to deny it, there are few places in America where Aristocracy has so abdicated and where a high-powered celebrity Society runs rampant on a field of dexter and sinister cocktail parties. A few genuine old-timers, notably Mrs. Longworth, Mrs. J. Borden Harriman and Mrs. Marjorie Merriweather Post Close Hutton Davies May—all of whom were, of course, once celebrities themselves—have attempted to keep, if not the Old Order, at least some kind of order. But, among the Mestas and Cafritzes of today and the McLeans and Pattersons of yesterday, it has been a difficult battle—and this despite the reserve strength the Old Guard has been able to muster among such stalwarts as Mrs. Robert Woods Bliss and Mrs. Robert Low Bacon, as well as, of late, such youthful standouts as Mrs. Joseph Casey and Mrs. Garvin Tankersley (the former "Bazy" McCormick). Washington's Old Guard themselves are constantly caught up, amid a welter of some thirty-five Society editor-arbiters, in the very web they are trying to unweave. Ever since 1940, the nation's capital has proceeded socially at a breakneck pace, from Hot War to Cold War, from Hot Shoppes to cold canapés, and yet it has in reality never had even a Café Society; rather, it might be called Cafeteria Society.

Washington's No. 1 arbiter-hostess during Eisenhower days was undoubtedly Mrs. Wiley Buchanan, wife of the Chief of Protocol of the State Department and a lady fortified by her own family's large chemical fortune. Of perhaps the strangest arbitrage, however—for Washington has a way of changing socially with each election—has been the career of Carolyn Hagner Shaw. "Callie," as she is sparingly called, owes her position not only to her famous *Green Book* but also to the fact that her aunt and her own mother were social secretaries before her; in fact her aunt had the honor of serving in that capacity to Theodore Roosevelt. At age 14 young Callie left school to be about her mother's business, and growing up a tall slender woman, she became more and more convinced that Washington Society was a matter of neither wealth nor social position. "The desirable guests," she said, "are the ones in key political or governmental posts even if they sometimes are sprinkled with hayseed."

To help this "hayseed," Mrs. Shaw started her *Green Book* as long ago as 1930, and from the beginning ran it to suit herself. In 1960 she listed close to seven thousand names, and at that time was accepting about one in four of the four hundred applications which each year came her way. "The 'cave-dwellers,'" says Mrs. Shaw, "have been dwindling for some time. In the old days there was a definite blue-blood set. Now it's all jumbled up together." Mrs. Shaw had particularly difficult times, as might be expected, during the Truman administration. Once, she recalls, she stood transfixed with horror when she saw two men go down the receiving line and slap the President on the back. "And do you know how they greeted him?" she continues. " 'Hi, Harry.' That's all—just 'Hi, Harry.' "

"If you let the bars down too far," says Mrs. Shaw, "what have you got left?" Against such unanswerables, Mrs. Shaw has not only her *Green Book* but also a book entitled *Modern Manners*, as well as an etiquette column. When all these fail, she still has a large, highly insured file of every single person who has, ever since her *Green Book* started, applied for listing. In this there are contained not only all the pertinent and vital statistics of each applicant but also a curious set of initials to aid Mrs. Shaw in seating parties. In 1960 she decoded these for the benefit of Ami Stewart of *The Georgetowner:*

> We use the initials B.D. to warn of a person reported to have caused trouble as a "bad drunk." The symbol O.F. stands for "old fool," and refers to a man who may let his hands stray when near an attractive young woman. There are at present several prominent men in the O.F. category—one of them a Senator. Because of their rank they are compulsory guests at some parties. We always try to seat them next to older women and keep temptation out of their way.

Probably the most relentless Publi-cietist on the Washington scene is the famed Perle Mesta. The "Call Me Madam" of the Broadway musical, she has also been called everything from "The Hostess with the Mostest" (in that show) to "The World's No. 1 Party-Giver" (Harry Truman) and "The gayest person I know" (Louis Bromfield) all the way to "a Helen Hokinson character" (Mrs. Longworth), "silly" (Lady Astor), and "Mrs. Thing" (Mrs. J. Borden Harriman). Born in 1891 in Sturgis, Michigan, Perle, whose name was then spelled Pearl, was the daughter of a hotel and later oil man named "Billy Skirvin." She grew up in Oklahoma City, where her father struck it rather well, and in 1916 was sent east to "meet people." Among those she met was Pittsburgh's late George Mesta of the machinery company and in 1917 they were married. Returning to Pittsburgh, Mrs. Mesta had little success—something which she attributed to the fact that her husband had, before her time, been engaged to a girl from one of Pittsburgh's "Old Families." But it is perhaps equally attributable to the fact that to Aristocracy, either in Pittsburgh or in Timbuctoo, Mrs. Mesta would have been—and in fact would still be—anathema.

Mesta died in 1925, and Pearl, changing her name to Perle, was soon a familiar figure from Newport to Washington, and from there to Harry Truman, Luxembourg, Broadway, a television biography and a book autobiography. Although, like most highly publicized people, she claims she is basically shy, she has managed to overcome this; at her parties, although she serves modest portions of conversations, she rarely misses a trick. "I always try to play a party by ear," she says, "and I always try to give them something different." She does not take even one drink at her parties. "I have to keep my wits about me," she says.

More controversial even than Mrs. Mesta is Gwen Cafritz, her "newspaper rival," although actually they are rather inclined to ignore each other. Born Gwendolyn Detre de Surnay in Budapest in 1912, the daughter of a Hungarian physician and a Washington-born mother, young Gwen arrived in Washington in 1928. Meeting real estate man Morris Cafritz, who has for some years been reputed to be the highest taxed man in Washington, she married him and soon after built her showplace on Foxhall Road. Among other things, this house boasts a "supper club" downstairs, one which is lighted from beneath a glass floor. Mrs. Cafritz seldom throws stones, but her ambition and marriage have made her a lively target for them. Like so many hostesses before her time and since, she is accused of being a Mrs. Malaprop, of running "pro and con" among the rich and famous and looking down her nose at the "poor pheasants." While this quality has been exaggerated, there is no question but that she is given to some of Washington's most extraordinary social remarks. "I *always* invite Senators," she says, "but I seldom play around with the Lower House." And, on one occasion, when the present Senator Monroney was running for re-election, she paid him her highest accolade. "I'm going to have you," she announced firmly, "even if you lose."

Small in size, but handsome in appearance, Mrs. Cafritz calls a dinner for twenty-two people an "intimate" affair, and, although such knowledgeable Society writers as Betty Beale and Hope Ridings Miller are inclined to take her, in one of her own Malaprops, "with a dose of salts," the fact remains that her Sunday party before the first Monday in October has marked, of late years, the all but official opening of the Washington "Season." Abroad she has hardly fared as well—as witness the story of a fancy dress ball in Venice when she arrived in a striking costume topped by two antennae on the top of her head. Everyone agreed she was wonderful but wanted to know who she was. "Don't you know," she said, "I'm Madame Curie." There was still doubt; whereupon Mrs. Cafritz explained further. "Madame Curie," she said, by now growing irritable, "you know, the inventor of radio." Very quietly but definitely, a guest explained. "Not radio, Mrs. Cafritz, radium."

To old-time Washingtonians, however, both Mrs. Mesta and Mrs. Cafritz pale before perhaps the most amazing arbiter-hostess in modern publi-social history—the late Evalyn Walsh McLean. With no less than three excellent claims to publi-ciety—the daughter of a highly publicized strike-it-richer, the wife of a newspaper owner, and the last private owner of the world-famed Hope Diamond— Evalyn Walsh McLean's life was a true-life version of the ancient and honorable legend of the West—in which the miner, upon striking it rich, suddenly throws down his pick and exclaims, "Thank God! Now my wife can be a lady!"

But the daughter of Tom Walsh, of Tipperary, Ireland, and Sowbelly Gulch, Colorado, had ideas of her own. "It's no fun to be a lady," she once declared. At times it was not, but one time young Evalyn enjoyed it hugely: on moving to Washington, her father gratified her first whim—to hire her a horse and carriage in which to ride to school. "I should be a liar," she later recalled in Father Struck It Rich, "if I tried to say I did not enjoy right down to the bottom of my soul, the 'ohs' and 'ahs' that came from the other girls." At the age of 12 she also took to drink, sneaking down-stairs and lapping up, from the dining-room cupboard, her father's *crème de menthe.*

Traveling to Paris—her father was, incredibly enough, one of the "National Commissioners" at the Paris Exposition—Evalyn gratified her growing thirst for "important people" by striking up a friendship with Chicago's Mrs. Potter Palmer. "She let me finger to my heart's content," she recalled, "her necklace of emeralds and diamonds, and seemed to understand the passion in my eyes as I looked at them." Later her father gave her a diamond of her own. Back in Washington she was packed off to boarding school at Dobbs Ferry, but, when homesickness set in, her father rushed to her assistance. "Finally father came to give me a Saturday of fun in New York. He asked me what I wanted and I said jewels." This time her father bought her a turquoise and pearl dog collar. Once again back at school, decked out in her collar she was called "vulgar" by one of the teachers and so ran away. Later she attempted to study for a while in Paris, but when she was about to marry an Italian prince her father once again stepped in, bought off the prince, and bought his daughter a Mercedes instead.

In Newport in the summer of 1908 Evalyn and her only brother, Vinson, were riding in an automobile when a blowout occurred and her brother was killed. She, herself, was badly injured. At the age of 15 she had first met the late Edward Beale ("Ned") McLean in the dancing class of his mother, the wife of publisher John R. McLean. It had been love at first sight for Ned, but Evalyn kept putting him off. Finally, having been engaged "dozens of times" and each time having broken it off, they were married suddenly in Colorado with Denver's Crawford Hill as best man. Then began what is undoubtedly the most incredible honeymoon in American social history—one which went all over the world and for which the two fathers vied against each other, each in the end putting up the sum of $100,000 for the "young people to enjoy themselves." In pre-war days such a sum was almost unspendable, but the couple managed to do it. "One day in Leipzig," Evalyn recalled, "we lost

patience with the fact that we had only one Mercedes and went overnight to Paris and bought an extra one." On the honeymoon, also,
Ned thoughtfully bought his bride her first famous diamond—the
Star of the East. Unfortunately this was the end of their $200,000;
they had to cable home for money to pay their last hotel bill.
Coming home, and as a fitting climax to the jaunt, they successfully
smuggled the diamond past the customs.

Soon Evalyn became, via Pierre Cartier and $154,000, the posses-
sor of the most famous diamond in the world—the blue, 44½-carat
Hope. She knew even then its reputation for bringing bad luck—it
had reputedly been owned by Marie Antoinette and by a Greek
broker who fell off a cliff—but she was confident she could break
the spell. In Washington, in her fabulous home, "Friendship," she
entertained on a scale which Washington had never seen before
or since. "Anyone might be invited to eat or drink," says Charles
Hurd, "as long as his name made the headlines." Mrs. McLean
herself rarely rose until 5 P. M., but, as she has described it, one
hardly would blame her:

> A mad place, truly!—with a monkey in my bathroom, a llama on
> the lawn, and our corridors shrill with the curses of our parrot
> (learned from a diplomat). In the stables when my children wished
> to play at being grownups they could find there midget horses and
> the coach, brightly painted, that had once belonged to General
> Tom Thumb.

For one who complained throughout her life of how "spoiled"
her husband had been, Mrs. McLean brought up her children in
remarkable fashion. There were four of them: Vinson, "Jock," Ned
Jr., and young Evalyn. Vinson was nine years older than Jock,
and one day Vinson's father conceived the idea that, since he had
had a Negro boy to play with when he was young, Vinson should
have one too. Mrs. McLean agreed. "We could not buy a colored
boy, of course," she noted, "although it was our habit to buy anything we wanted. But Ned made arrangements with the parents of a
little five-year-old named Julian Winbush to let him come and
live with us. They relinquished all control of him for ten years."

The experiment was not an unqualified success. Although to Pullman porters on the way to Palm Beach the little colored boy who, they thought, was being reared as a brother of the so-called "hundred-million-dollar baby," was "Aladdin, Sinbad and Ali Baba rolled into one," Vinson himself was none too pleased. "So far as he was concerned," Mrs. McLean wrote, "I would have done as well to have borrowed a playmate from the zoo."

In the end, although Mrs. McLean continued to minimize the ill-starred properties of her Hope Diamond—she even lent it to GI brides married at her home during World War II—the jinx would seem to have held. Her son Vinson was killed by an automobile, her daughter at age 20 married, in 1941, North Carolina's 57-year-old Senator Robert Reynolds and later died of an overdose of sleeping pills; and she herself died tragically. As for her husband, he eventually died in a mental institution after one of the most incredible celebrity lives ever lived. Alfred Friendly, of the Washington *Post*, writing to a potential biographer, has best summarized the exploits of a man which, as he puts it, "reached a new high, or low, in ingenious profligacy, inventive wildness, and general hell-raising of a sort that this enfeebled age, 30 to 40 years later, simply cannot conceive of, much less match":

> There was the item of the private train, with its whistle tied down, every time he left Washington for New York; the kidnapping of a Post reporter, who woke up, after being drugged, on a ship to Europe simply because McLean wanted trans-Atlantic company; the ten tarts standing nude on pedestals at McLean's garden parties; the stripping of his New Year's Eve guests and their running around the block naked to welcome the new year in; the mad affair with Marion Davies' sister that went on for months, if not years, all over Europe; the inevitable two bodyguards who wrote out orders for new hats to those barflies whose fedoras McLean liked to knock off with his cane; the last stages of his drunkenness, when he had to tie a bar towel around his wrist and make it into a pulley around his neck so that he could get his drinking hand up to his mouth; the coolness of Mrs. Harding because he urinated in the fireplace in the East Room (as well as down the leg of the Belgian Ambassador); the bottle of whiskey

delivered daily by a Post editorial writer from McLean's inexhaust-
ible cellars to his favorite pet seal, Col. George Harvey; the per-
jury in behalf of his friend, Albert Fall, to whom he said he had
lent $100,000 when, of course, Doheny had actually bribed Fall by
that amount; and so on and on.

The late Evalyn Walsh McLean, and her errant, second-generation
husband—who had been an only son—were far from the only
Publi-cietists to come out of nowhere in the era of what Mark
Sullivan has called "The Repeal of Reticence." During the 1920's
and 1930's, the columns, the tabloids and the Sunday supplements
made national figures out of the barest essentials—and, in some
cases, out of nothing at all. Indeed, half a dozen celebrated "Socialites"
were actually made up out of whole cloth—as if to prove that the
gossip truth, too, was no stranger to fiction. Cole Porter, a darling
of the columns himself, even made up an entire Family—the rich
Fitches—whose doings and undoings were faithfully reported from
Palm Beach to the Riviera. Maury Paul invented a Mme. Moira
Vincentie, the "pulchritudinous Irish-Argentine beauty" who never
wrote notes nor telephoned but carried on all her conversations by
telegraph and sat "in a pitch-black room for an hour a day," during
which period, he explained, she endeavored "to keep her mind
completely blank."

The rest of the country was not so fortunate. "Incessant publicity,"
complained Christopher Morley, "has turned the United States of
America into the United States of Amnesia." And nowhere, of
course, did this publicity show to better advantage than in the care
and breeding of "Socialites." Probably the best known of the era
was Mrs. Harrison Williams. Born Mona Strader in 1897, at "Fairland
Farms," Lexington, Kentucky, the daughter of a stableman, she met
and married, at the age of 18, a 37-year-old Milwaukean by the
name of Harry Schlesinger. The second generation of an iron and
coke Family and the owner of the stables in which Mona's father
worked, he thought she was "the prettiest thing I ever saw." They
were promptly married and had one son; the marriage, however,
lasted only five years, by which time Mona had met banker James

Irving Bush, once called the "handsomest man in America." In 1920 she was divorced from Schlesinger—she received $200,000 but gave up her son—and then became Mrs. Bush. This time there were no children, but again the marriage lasted only five years, and then there was another divorce. At this time, with no next marriage in immediate mind, Mona came to New York and with her "old Family" friend, Laura Curtis, opened a fashionable dress shop—a fitting career for one who was all her life a truly remarkable clothes-horse and for so many years the "world's best-dressed woman."

Young Miss Curtis had an elderly beau, some twenty-three years older than Mona, whose name was Harrison Williams. He was a utilities magnate and regarded as "the richest man in America." In any case, when Laura Curtis went to Paris to buy clothes, Mona agreed to look after him for her, and shortly after Miss Curtis' return, Mr. Williams and Mona—not Miss Curtis—were married. The affair, which in a later day would be closely paralleled by the Thelma Furness–Wallis Simpson exchange, caused a furor at the time, most New Yorkers were siding with Miss Curtis—or at least so siding until asked to dinner by Mrs. Williams.

One thing was certain. With this marriage Mrs. Williams was able to lead the life of a *grande dame*, something which was as far removed from her start in life as any case in social history. Her marble-halled house on 94th Street and Fifth Avenue became the central rendezvous of a group called "the only crowd in New York evenly divided between clever men and fashionable women." When this rendezvous failed, there were always four other houses in Long Island, Palm Beach, London and the Riviera. Even at formal dinner parties, Mr. Williams was rarely present, it being explained to guests that he was upstairs "busy with business," but few complained. As for Mrs. Williams, with her famous aquamarine eyes—Salvador Dali called them "the most beautiful eyes in the world"—and an ethereal quality which seemed far removed from the dictates of the world of fashion she symbolized, she had reached the pinnacle of success. She had a passion for what one friend called the three "n's"— "newness, neatness and niceness"—and if to Maury Paul her British accent was "phony," to Cecil Beaton, Mona Williams represented "the epitome of all that taste and luxury can bring to flower."

Mrs. Williams became one of the most highly publicized women in the world, but an almost equally highly publicized friend, Mrs. William Rhinelander Stewart, recalls at least one off-the-record conversation with her husband. "At that time," she says, "I believe the Nyzam of Hyderabad was the generally recognized criterion, but one day Mr. Williams told me that he believed he was richer. I think that he said he had just as many millions as he was old—and he was not young then. Anyway, I asked him why he went on working and why he didn't just stop and spend it the way his wife was doing. For a long time he looked very thoughtful and then he said, 'You know, I've never thought of that.'" Williams died in 1953 at the age of 80, after which his wife, who had never married a title, finally managed that also—with her marriage in 1955 to Count Edouard von Bismarck. For this offense, without so much as a kind word or an explanation, she was summarily removed from the *Social Register*.

However, even the success of Mrs. Williams paled before the climb—achieved without any claims to beauty—of the one and only Laura Corrigan, late of Cleveland, later of New York and latest of all of London. Variously called "America's Salon Queen" and "London's Social General," she was born Laura Mae Whitrock, in 1895, the daughter of a handyman in Waupaca, Wisconsin. In her teens she moved to Chicago and became a waitress, but she soon tired of this. Always ambitious and with a "come-hither" way about her, she walked into a Chicago newspaper office and talked her way into a job as a Society reporter. From that moment, her climb was rarely equaled in the history of Society, let alone that of Society reporters. First of all, however, she lost her job; then, saddened and down on her luck, she met the hotel doctor at the Hotel Blackstone, a man by the name of Duncan R. MacMartin. They were shortly married, and though Dr. MacMartin was not rich, he was soon persuaded by his wife to take his vacations at least among the Right People.

Mrs. MacMartin's life was changed permanently in 1913 by a party given by the late James Corrigan, son of Cleveland steelman "Captain" Corrigan, at his Dry Island home in the Thousand Islands. The MacMartins stayed at the party until dawn, and in afteryears Laura was wont to say that it was "love at first light," later also, she wrote a book entitled *The Dry Fable of a Dry Crowd at Dry Island*—one of her very few achievements—which was published privately. Young Corrigan had established quite a reputation for himself as a playboy and had just passed through a sensational breach of promise suit brought by a Pittsburgh girl. To him the matter of Laura's divorce from MacMartin and then her secret, "no scandal" marriage to him, was easily arranged. His wedding present to his bride was, however, no secret; it was a $15,000 Rolls-Royce, complete with a former chauffeur and footman of Jay Gould.

But when the Corrigans, Mr. and Mrs., descended on Cleveland, it was a different story. The Shaker Heights Set stayed away in droves from the Corrigans' Wickliffe estate—ironically called "Nagirroc," or Corrigan spelled backwards. Even business friends seemed to take their cue from Jimmy's mother, who frankly spoke of her son's marriage as a *mésalliance* and did not even ask her daughter-in-law to tea. At this juncture, too, the senior Corrigan died and left his steel company, not directly to his son but in trust—and with one of Mrs. Corrigan's mortal enemies, Price McKinney, as chief trustee.

Here Laura Corrigan showed the same resolution and spirit which would later enable her to come back for more after almost incredible social snubs and insults in New York and London. Traveling to New Jersey, she went to work on the heirs of the Corrigan Seniors' third partner, Stevenson Burke; after her persuasion, they agreed to sell their interest in the Corrigan-McKinney Company for $5,000,000. And, when Laura's husband told her he didn't have that much, she herself went out and, pawning her jewelry, begging, and borrowing from banks, managed to raise it. Finally, in 1925, she had the pleasure of having her husband walk into a stockholders' meeting which had been called to oust him and having him instead oust the ousters. A year later her rival, Price McKinney, entered the bathroom of his Cleveland mansion and shot himself. Then, in 1927, Laura's husband suffered a heart attack and dropped dead in the doorway of the Cleveland Athletic Club.

Now, with an income of some $800,000 a year in relatively taxless times, Laura Corrigan was ready for the big push. After the Mc-Kinney affair, literally all doors in Cleveland were barred to her, so she herself locked the doors of "Nagirroc" and set out to conquer New York. Here, although she lived in a hotel in the belief that she would have a better chance of meeting people than in a house or an apartment, she found the going hard. Still undaunted, she hired an "aristocratic lady" to sponsor her; once again failure dogged her. "The people she met," Maury Paul said sourly, "just weren't interested in her."

Again Laura Corrigan appeared downed. But, as so often in her life, it was darkest before the dawn. Suddenly giving up New York, she took off for London, and, as had been the case with so many American social careers from Pocahontas to Wallis Warfield, the success denied in this country came in full measure in England.* Just why this happened so often has baffled many social historians; it was perhaps the most sarcastically explained, in 1937, by *Fortune* magazine:

> The technique of climbing is much the same, except that the transatlantic method has recently been perfected by the discovery that British Society is much more quickly and directly purchasable by Americans (not by their own kind) than is New York. The reason is that the British cannot take seriously the fantastic idea that an American (or any other Colonial, including the Australian Bushman) could have a social position. They regard Americans as simple-hearted savages with a penchant for providing free lunch for their betters. So at the outset avoiding New York, our trans-atlantic climber opens a London house, begins giving big dinners for the proper people, and within a year is established as a London

* Pocahontas, daughter of Powhatan and savior of John Smith, was married in Jamestown in 1614 to the Englishman John Rolfe. Two years later, with her husband and several Indian maids, she sailed for England, where she was received, it is recorded, with the consideration due a princess. She was entertained by the Bishop of London "with festival, state and pompe" and was then presented to the King and Queen.

hostess. She can then invite her new friends to an American tour at her expense, loading them on the *Queen Mary*, the first class bulging with barons, earls protruding from the portholes, dukes squatting hopefully on the lifeboats, and the scuppers awash with mere knights, all of them warmly anticipatory of several months' free board, room and laundry. And as she leads *Burke's Peerage, Baronetage, and Knightage* down the gangplank the guide on this British safari can be sure that New York, which formerly snubbed her, will fall flatly and reverentially forward on their collective abdomens, and that henceforth all Café Society doors will be open to her, and she will be definitely in.

Laura Corrigan's career was close to a textbook example of this, except that being Laura she could not resist, at the time of her first return to America, a shipboard interview. "The trouble with many Americans who visit London," she said, "is that they come home elated over the fact that they have met Duchess So-and-so. The truth of the matter is that there are duchesses and duchesses." Then, explaining further to the American barbarians, she added, "I have two homes, one in London and one in Paris. At my English home everything is English. In my Paris home everything is French. At the London house nothing but English is spoken and in the Paris house nothing but French."

All this was certainly clear enough. One thing on which Laura Corrigan did not elaborate, however, was the way her career in London had started. Mayfair Society, engaged in making as much sport of her as had the Americans, started as a prank the rumor that Prince George was going to attend her very first party; the prank backfired when the Prince, hearing of the rumor, crossed up the pranksters by walking in on the party. At this, Laura was so overjoyed that she stood on her head—thereafter, accompanied by a roll of drums, this became a regular feature of her parties. Not only were her parties fun—with elaborate cabarets, lotteries and tombolas, as well as solid-gold prizes—but Laura herself was shrewd. She cultivated Princess Marina of Greece long before her marriage to the Duke of Kent, sent her a mink for a wedding present, and generally bet on them as the future social leaders. Events proved her correct. They so proved her also when she refused to "take up" her fellow climber, Wallis Warfield—a gesture which caused her to take a back seat during the short reign of Edward, but soon put her back on the inside track with the accession of George and Elizabeth. And, despite the various malapropisms which invariably accompanied stories of her, only once was she ever stopped for any answer at all. This occurred when at a luncheon the writer, George Moore, turned to her and remarked, apropos of nothing, "You know, Mrs. Corrigan, I always think that of all the sexual abnormalities, abstinence is by far the most revolting, don't you?"

During the war, although she remained a civilian, Laura nonetheless designed a uniform for herself—one far handsomer than the government issue—and proudly she wore it everywhere. Again, just when people were beginning to laugh her into oblivion, she turned about and did such excellent war work for France that even Maury Paul, on one of her returns, for the first time in his career, apologized publicly. "I predicted Laura Corrigan NEVER would make the social grade," he wrote. "I was wrong—and I hereby eat humble pie." Also, many years before her death, Laura took care to square matters with her home town. She organized a safari to Africa, one which, for pure comfort amid tropical rigors, has perhaps never been equaled. She took with her, in three airplanes, a newspaperman, a photographer, a movie cameraman, two secretaries, two maids, a doctor, a nurse, two cooks, three waiters, a hairdresser, a manicurist and a dressmaker. On this safari she scoured the Dark Continent for fourteen animals of varying degrees of rarity. These she did not shoot but captured them and, with infinite tact, sent them—along with a check for $5,000 for their food—back to the Cleveland Zoo.

No account of the rise and shine of celebrity in Society would be complete without a brief history of the American debutante. And once more it is necessary to return, briefly, to semantics. The word "debutante" is basically French, like so many other "English"-language words in our "American" Society. Furthermore, its origin was, of all things, in sports. It came from both bowling and billiards where *début*, as it was then written, meant "from the mark" or "from the goal." Since it was an expression used with *jouer* ("to play") understood, it was rather like our modern expression "on your mark," preceding, in other words, "get set." Indeed, translated literally "to play for the mark" or "goal," and allowing the substitution of a husband for the mark or goal, the word is still, in the sportive sense, going strong.

Gradually, in the early Seventeenth Century, the French verb *débuter*, was coined from the word meaning "to lead off," and then a noun was coined back again—*débutant* for a man and *débutante* for a woman—which meant someone who has led off with an original, or "lead off," stage appearance. And this, of course, set the backdrop; in a later day the word began to be used in the Society sense, for the "celebrity" debutante of today.

The modern history of the debutante is a progression—or perhaps we should say retrogression—from Gibson Girl to Glamour Girl, or from Irene Langhorne to Brenda Frazier. Properly, however, the history began as far back as 1870. In that year, New York's Archibald Gracie King persuaded old Charlie Delmonico—much to the latter's consternation—to allow him to hire Delmonico's largest room for a ball and supper for Mr. King's debutante daughter. Charlie Delmonico's concern was not only prophetic but also, in those days, proper. For the idea of presenting one's debutante daughter anywhere but "under one's own roof," as the saying went, was extremely shocking. The debut in those days was nothing more than the introduction or presentation, of one's daughter to one's friends—hence, cavalierly enough, to "Society."

And while the debutante of old was inclined to grumble about being "presented" to one's family friends—people she already knew —the fact remained that it had another significance. For with her debut the young lady was now permitted, properly chaperoned, of course, to go out with a young gentleman—something which before her debut would have been unthinkable.

To the grandmothers of the mid-Twentieth Century who remember such debuts the decision at Delmonico's was a point of no return. The die was cast, and there followed a steadily increasing emphasis of the public nature of the debut, and the loss of its private meaning, which was to culminate in the mass blowouts of the 1920's. Indeed, with the addition of the celebrity debutantes of the 1930's and 1940's, the roof which had once stood over one's debutante daughter would seem to have caved in completely. And the word itself perhaps came full cycle when New York's Miss Patricia Wagner, instead of having a coming-out party, persuaded the Hotel Pierre to permit her to have a "staying-in" party—one which included young people only, in old clothes, with no family present at all.

The "Smart Set," had, of course, during Prohibition gone from salon to saloon and from the Right Club to the Night Club. For these it was but a step, when it came to debutante parties, to go from home to hotel. Perhaps the landmark party here, for sheer, unadulterated elaborateness, was the party of Miss Helen Lee Eames Doherty, stepdaughter of Henry L. Doherty, gas and oil man, at the Mayflower Hotel in Washington, D.C., on the night after Christmas, 1926. On the eve of the debut, on Christmas Day, at a special dinner for twelve "intimate friends," Miss Doherty gave a dozen Ford cabriolet automobiles, complete with hunting scenes painted on their sides. She also gave an extra Ford to one "absent friend," the King of Spain.

But 1930 was a landmark date in another respect. Depression or no, this year marked the debuts of two of the most famous debutantes in the history of American Society. Their names were Doris Duke and Barbara Hutton—the Gold Dust twins who would from then on be known, seemingly forever, as the "Poor Little Rich Girls." Miss Duke's debut came first, during Tennis Week at Newport, but, because of the advanced age of her father, who was 56 when she was born, her own story went back almost a century.

Doris Duke's father, James Buchanan Duke, founder of Duke University, was by all odds one of the most extraordinary Family founders in social—which he certainly was not—history. Born in

1856 on a farm near Durham, North Carolina, he was brought up by his father, his mother having died when he was a baby. And when his father, Doris' grandfather, returned from the War Between the States, he was left with a single half-dollar and two blind mules; their farm had been totally ransacked by the invading Yankees except for one small quantity of leaf tobacco, which had been overlooked. This, young James, with his father and his brother, promptly pounded and packaged, and, labeling it "Pro Bono Publico," carried it on the backs of their blind mules to market.

From these humble beginnings came in 1890, by dint of James Buchanan Duke's incredible combination of ego and energy, gall and gumption, the giant American Tobacco Company—of which Duke became the first president. As self-made as his first tobacco, he gave the money to Duke University, then Trinity College, only on condition it change its name to Duke, and to this day on the Duke campus he lies recumbent in marble in the chapel; outside the chapel, surveying his work, he stands in bronze, cigar in hand. Once in New York he tried to make a deal in the house of the "second-generation" tobacco gentleman Pierre Lorillard, famed founder of Tuxedo Park. The deal was interrupted when a group of Lorillard's young friends burst into the conference and insisted on carrying off Lorillard for an evening of fun. After they had gone, Duke turned contemptuously to his lawyer. "Guess I'll have to go out," he said, "and buy me some friends."

Such a man had his troubles in the marriage line as well. He was married for the first time when he was 48 years old—to a 42-year-old New York divorcée named Mrs. William McCredy. But he got himself a divorce on the grounds of adultery the very next year, and to the end of his life he and his ex-wife were in constant legal battles. Three years after his divorce he tried marriage again—this time with Mrs. Nanaline Holt Inman, whose husband, of Atlanta's famous cotton Family, had died two years before. The second Mrs. Duke, mother of Doris, had been born in Macon, Georgia, and grew up something of a legendary belle. Her father, however, had died when she was in her teens, and her mother had been forced to take in boarders and at the same time make party dresses for more fortunate neighbors. According to John Winkler, Nanaline and her sister used to deliver the gowns and, in so doing, would try them on; in this way she developed a love of fine clothes and a distaste for poverty which did not leave her, even through her first marriage to Walter Inman, and throughout her second to one of the richest men in the country. On her daughter, Doris, born in 1912 in New York, she enforced a penny-pinching program which included having all of Doris' dresses made by a seamstress.

Doris' mother also had a penchant for Society, and when Doris was 10, persuaded her husband to buy her "Rough Point" at Newport, the former home of Frederick W. Vanderbilt. Her ambitions at Newport, however, were rather thwarted by the scandals attendant on the elopement of her son, Walker Patterson Inman, Doris' half brother, with the divorced wife of a song writer; their subsequent divorce case, even by Newport's generous standards, was extraordinary. Walker at one time accused his wife of having relations with three men—a vaudeville tenor, an international confidence man, and a bootlegger named Yip.

In this atmosphere, with an overindulgent father and a mother over whom she towered at the age of 10, "making them both self-conscious," Doris Duke attempted to grow up. Tall, slim, shy and solemn-faced, with honey-blonde hair and an overlarge chin—on which she later had an operation, "Dee-Dee," as she was called, was constantly torn between her father's Horatio Alger homilies—"Nothing makes people happier than luxury" and "How can you be happy if you're not busy"—and her mother's almost psychopathic poverty pleas, and, on the other hand, an almost incredible fortune. When she was 13 her father died and she inherited some $70,000,000, plus, for good measure, a Pullman car named "Doris."

At her debut, at age 18, three orchestras played for four hundred guests; later that year in London she was presented at Court. Sometimes called stingy, she was actually mortally afraid, having been trained by both mother and father, not to be an easy mark. "People wouldn't have money long," she said, "if they didn't ask how much things cost and then refuse to buy half of them." In 1934, four years after her coming-out, she married James H. R. Cromwell, the famous "Jimmie," son of Mrs. E. T. Stotesbury, of Philadelphia. He was sixteen years her senior and had been divorced from Delphine Dodge of the Detroit automobile Family. They met at Bar Harbor, where, said Jimmie, "it was love at first sight." In 1937 the couple moved to Hawaii, where they built their famous dream-house "Shangri-La"—a Moroccan-Persian mansion with two stone camels in the doorway and water channeled in Moorish style down flights of marble steps. When Cromwell was later made Minister to Canada, Doris accompanied him everywhere. Then in 1940 came tragedy—a baby girl was born prematurely and died twenty-four hours later. The couple separated that year, and the prolonged divorce proceedings, which lasted for three years, brought Doris Duke Cromwell into a limelight she had up to that time studiously tried to avoid.

During World War II she had her first job—for which she received $1 a year—helping American seamen via the United Seamen's Service. "I honestly believe," she said at the time, "I'm happier now than I've ever been in my life. I feel that I'm doing something worthwhile, earning the right to be friends with a lot of swell, interesting people that I've somehow missed before. I've discovered, I guess, that it's fun to work." After a brief spell doing newspaper work in the Balkans for the International News Service, in 1947 she became a fashion editor for *Harper's Bazaar*. That same year she fell total victim to the world of Publi-ciety in the person of Porfirio Rubirosa.

The year before in Rome she had met the already twice-married son-in-law of the Dominican dictator—one who was shortly to marry Barbara Hutton after her. "Rubi danced divinely," she said, while Rubirosa sighed politely, "Dee-Dee danced divinely too." In the marriage ceremony at the Dominican Consulate, there was a slight delay, as Miss Duke's law firm suddenly produced an iron-clad contract, protective of the Duke millions, for Rubi to sign. After several highballs he did sign, and then when Doris produced a large gold ring he seemed happy again, exclaiming, "Oh, boy." In turn he gave her a small, inexpensive band of rubies. The marriage lasted one year. In 1954 Miss Duke and jazz enthusiast Johnny Gomez bought "Falcon's Lair," the former Hollywood home of Rudolph Valentino. That same year, her aging mother broke a hip and went to New York's Doctors' Hospital. She liked it so well, in preference to her Fifth Avenue mansion and her Newport cottage, that she decided to close up those houses, dismissed her servants and stayed on at the hospital even after her hip was well. In the afternoons she was permitted to go driving and in the evenings she was permitted to have a few friends in for canasta. "I like it here," she said. "There is no servant problem and there are no worries or cares."

The story of Barbara Hutton, possibly the most famous heiress in the world, begins, appropriately enough, in Hollywood, where she was born in 1912. She was the daughter of Franklyn Laws Hutton, a stockbroker, and Edna Woolworth, who was one of three daughters of the founder of the great five-and-ten-cent store chain, Frank W. Woolworth. At 4 she saw her mother die, at 7 her grandfather —with whom she had spent much time—and at age 12 her grandmother. "My father was young and very busy," she has said. "He loved me, of course, but I was only an ordinary, rather stupid little girl and I couldn't be a real companion to a gay, brilliant young man, could I?" Of her mother she has spoken in perhaps even more revealing terms. "I hardly remember her," she said. "But I have missed her all my life."

Curiously, up to the time of his death her grandfather occupied much the same position in Barbara Hutton's life that Doris Duke's elderly father had in hers. And both men, originally farm boys and later incredibly successful, were not unlike—high in rugged, self-made qualities and fondness of homilies and low in culture and any kind of sensitive understanding. As a child Barbara Hutton played in her grandfather's Fifth Avenue house. Built in 1901, eleven years before she was born, the house had one amazing feature—a huge player organ, piped to all the rooms of the house and even, through hollow bedposts, to Woolworth's bed. When he was a child Woolworth had been tone deaf; he had been foiled in his attempts to play musical instruments, but he loved music and determined that his house would have it everywhere; conduits even led to the clothes closets. Furthermore, not content with the music alone, Woolworth had commissioned a Hungarian artist to paint portraits of Beethoven, Wagner, Liszt and Mendelssohn against allegorical backgrounds. "A guest," says Louise Tanner, "might have the strange experience of listening to *Die Walküre* to an accompaniment of lightning flashes and sound effects reminiscent of roulades of thunder, while out of the half-light there slowly materialized an ectoplasmic likeness of the composer."

Spending time with such a man in such a house—and a house in Glen Cove, Long Island, was similarly equipped—was hardly a normal beginning for Barbara's life. Woolworth himself was not normal, and his wife's mind had gone years earlier. Barbara's first party evenings consisted of a group composed of herself, Woolworth, his sick wife, his nurse and his wife's keeper. One "Grandpa Woolworth" trait she inherited—an almost unbelievable stubbornness. At the time of her grandmother's death she was left close to $30,000,000—with much much more to come. But at that same time her father remarried, to a Detroit divorcée named Irene Curley Bodie. Even at that age Barbara thought she knew what she wanted; in any case, she promptly refused to live with them. Her childhood was spent primarily visiting, particularly at the home of her uncle, Edward F. Hutton, of the brokerage firm, as well as at her aunts' homes, the James Donahues at Palm Beach and the Charles McCanns on Long Island. During these visits and between them her life was a succession of private schools, private bodyguards and private loneliness. "Though I had millions of dollars," she said, "I still had no home." At age 13 she took to writing poetry, and one of her poems was entitled simply "Why?"

> Why should some have all
> And others be without?
> Why should men pretend
> And women have to doubt?

Another poem she called "Question":

> Can it be all in vain;
> The hopes and sorrow;
> The laughter and tears;
> And dreams of tomorrow?

"All the unhappiness in my life," she once said, "has been caused by men, including my father." But she had almost equal trouble with girls. "They seemed to resent the fact that I had so much money," she says, "as though that gave me an unfair advantage over them in Society, or with men, or something." In any case, at 15 she met her first man, the 25-year-old Alexis Mdivani, who claimed to be a Prince in Russian Georgia, a place where there were no Princes. Later he and his brother were to become the famed "Marrying Mdivanis," but to Barbara he was her first love:

> He was so kind and so gentle. He listened to all my hurts and problems. When I tried to explain to him all my bewildered young thoughts, all the hurts and fears that were upon me, he didn't seem bored about it all, the way most older people did. He didn't dismiss my fears with a laugh the way other people did, and just told me that anybody who had as much money as I did shouldn't worry about anything.

In December, 1930, Barbara made her debut at a supper dance which cost $60,000, for which four orchestras played until dawn and for which silver birch trees, eucalyptus and Rudy Vallee were transported from California; the next year, as in the case of Doris Duke, she was presented at Court. At this time she also had her own private railroad car, outfitted for her personal use at a cost of $120,-000. In the nightclubs she was seen with several different men, but she was still dissatisfied:

> After a while I got the idea I wanted to get married. I was always so lonesome. I wanted a companion. Besides, I thought I would have more freedom if I was married. Before I was married, every time I went out with a man the papers printed it and everything was so complicated and embarrassing.

Her choice was still Mdivani, who in the meantime had married Newport's Louise Van Alen. In the hope of thwarting this match with Barbara, her father and stepmother sent her off on a world cruise. But Mdivani started off after her and, catching her in Bangkok, pressed his suit; he told her his first "Princess," Louise Van Alen, had already started divorce proceedings. They went on together to Paris where her father finally agreed to the match, despite the fact that Mdivani asked a $1,000,000 advance royalty. The wedding took place in 1933 in the Russian Cathedral in Paris with four Orthodox priests in attendance inside and outside a crowd of some four thousand people who finally overpowered the police and broke inside. It took Barbara twenty minutes to get from the church to her going-away limousine, at which time she told reporters, concerning Mdivani: "He's amusing, smart, interesting. All the American men I know are businessmen or want to be businessmen. Once they marry a girl, they wrap themselves up in a business again. It's going to be fun being a Princess."

Six months later Barbara came into $50,000,000 and this, in the depths of the depression, plus her marriage to a bogus foreign Prince, did not endear her to the $10-a-week Woolworth working girls back home. Once she begged her husband to drop the Prince. "We can be just as happy as Mr. and Mrs. Mdivani," she said. But in 1934, on the occasion of her twenty-second birthday party, she spent $10,000 to have a special orchestra flown from London to Paris. "We didn't think it fitting," Mdivani said, "to spend too much in these times."

Meanwhile, Barbara's private relations rapidly worsened. The Prince insisted on her going on a rigorous diet—something about which she had always been sensitive—and to please him she lost forty pounds in one year. Once, during a three-week period, she lived on black coffee only. Whatever she did, it didn't help, as the Prince, she admitted, cared more for the Society of his polo ponies than for her. Just before their divorce, she announced, "I didn't realize that the worst thing I could possibly do was to marry a titled foreigner. I didn't know Alexis had planned to marry me when I grew up—ever since he had first known me."

In 1935 Barbara divorced Mdivani at Reno, gave him another $2,000,000 and, within twenty-four hours, still in Reno, married Danish Count Kurt von Haugwitz-Reventlow. Seventeen years older than she, with a genuine title, money of his own and no interest in polo, to her he was everything. "I was young and impressionable," she said years later. "He was literally the handsomest person I'd ever happened to see. I couldn't take my eyes off him. Then we met and he looked at me and that was that." After their marriage there was also what had become the regular announcement. "Now at last I have found happiness," she said. "My search is ended. I know that this is safe and sure."

Following this, she renounced her U.S. citizenship—which, though explained by her lawyers as due to the complications of "dual nationality," nonetheless sat so badly on the American public back home that she decided to live in London. She spent $4,500,000 on the largest house in Regent Park—one which she later gave for the U.S. Embassy—and outfitted her footmen, much to London's amusement, in canary yellow and blue livery. At this time she had her only child, a son, Lance, by Caesarean operation—which once more wrecked her ever-precarious health. By 1937 this marriage, too, was coming apart at its gold seams. Again there was the inevitable statement:

> Poor Kurt, I feel sorry for him, in a way. He's still living in the time of the Czars. He used to wince when I'd speak to the servants. He thought it was beneath me—can you imagine? It was always, "I am the Count von Haugwitz-Reventlow," with Kurt. He never forgot it—until one day I said, "Who cares? Who cares about the Count von Haugwitz-Reventlow today? The world has come a long way from that sort of thing."

The world did care, however. The Count had warned her that if he didn't get $5,000,000 she would get "three years of hell with headlines," and Barbara received them. And their divorce did not become final until it was signed by King Christian himself in 1941. On her periodic returns to America, Barbara suffered more than ever. In 1939 pickets outside her Hotel Pierre suite bore signs saying, "We live on $16.50 a week. Could you?" and on entering a theatre she was mobbed by a crowd which screamed and clawed at her. "You rich bitch," one man shouted, "I'd like to throw acid in your face." Still incredibly naïve, Barbara couldn't understand it. "Why do they hate me?" she asked. "There are other girls as rich, richer, almost as rich. Why do they especially dislike me?"

The reason lay, of course, in the workings of Publi-ciety; there were, indeed, girls richer and almost as rich, but Barbara had had the Big Build-up and America was now ready, in its time-honored fashion, for the Big Come-down. The war, however, interrupted her attention, and by coming back to America to live in California with her son, Lance, she made her first step in the right direction by announcing, as she registered as an alien, that "The day I become an American citizen again will be the happiest day of my life." Sixteen months later she married Cary Grant—whereupon appeared the inevitable tag: "Cash and Cary." Although this marriage too was doomed to failure—"The servants had so many shifts to feed at mealtime," complained Grant wryly, "that Barbara and I were lucky to get a sandwich"—it was remarkable chiefly for the fact at divorce time that Grant did not ask for a penny. "We're still good friends," Barbara says of him, and he, typically, has never had a bad word to say about her.

In 1947, Barbara was back on her old track and chose, as her fourth husband, the Lithuanian Prince Igor Troubetzkoy. This time there was no statement of marital happiness and, after the marriage ended in 1951, Barbara snapped that her husband was "the meanest man in the world." In 1953 she married Porfirio Rubirosa, who had just divorced his third wife, Doris Duke. "I loved him the moment I met him," she said. They were married just before the end of the year 1953, despite the fact that Zsa Zsa Gabor kept issuing communiqués from her camp in Reno, where, she claimed—via publicist Russell Birdwell—she suffered from a black eye inflicted by Rubirosa. "I love George [Saunders]," she said, "Rubi loves me, Barbara loves Rubi, but who loves Barbara?" Barbara and Rubirosa were married at a macabre wedding conducted by the Dominican Consul General in his Park Avenue apartment. Throughout the ceremony Barbara alternately drank champagne and cried. Finally, after the contract was signed, she asked her bridegroom, "Aren't you going to kiss me now? The press has waited so long." But the press did not have to wait long for the divorce; after a Florida honeymoon trip in an 88-passenger plane, occupied by the newlyweds alone, the marriage lasted just seventy-two days. This time Barbara's statement was brief. "I feel as if I'd been hit over the head," she said. But Rubirosa, recalls Louise Tanner, had a longer statement:

> I was a bachelor and very happy between my divorce and marrying Barbara and I did not want to change. I fell in love with her. It was fine and it was fun. And then she said, "Let's get married." I said no, because I was afraid she would change. But she said, "I promise not to change." It was no good. She stays in bed and reads all day. It's a very boring life.

In 1955, Barbara married for the sixth time—to Baron Gottfried von Cramm, the former tennis ace who has never been admitted to the United States because of morals charges—although some feel these charges were framed by the Nazis. "Gottfried," says Barbara, "is the only one who has really wanted me to love him. I won't say my previous husbands thought only of my money, but it had a certain fascination for them."

In 1958, separated from von Cramm, Barbara made headlines with a possible husband No. 7, New York's Philip Van Rensselaer, at least twenty years her junior. "She gave me enormous sums of money," Van Rensselaer admitted. "She said I was a gentleman and I was meant to have lots of money. And anyway, she wasn't paying for me, she said, Grandpa Woolworth was." Van Rensselaer also reported that Barbara "didn't know the Right People from the Wrong People," and in fact, "didn't know people at all." As an example of her praising friends, he said, "Why, she thinks Jessie Donahue is a great lady!" Van Rensselaer also reported that he had caught Barbara's "phony foreign entourage" trying to get her in a deal whereby she would buy a spurious Picasso and then they would share the profits with the dealer. "I tried to tell her," he said, "but she didn't even want to hear about it. All she would say was 'I don't want to hear anything unpleasant.' One day I begged her to get up— she had been in bed for two months—and we went out. But she got sick and then we went home again. It was very boring, really. But I felt sorry for her."

Once the "Poor Little Rich Girls" had paved the way, the "Glamour Girl No. 1's" were soon to follow. Indeed, just as it somehow seemed significant that Barbara Hutton and Doris Duke had made their debuts in 1930—a year which marked not only the end of the boom but also the end of money as the sole common denominator of celebrity and/or Society—so it was significant that the Glamour Girls, the archetypes of the new Publi-ciety, should have made their appearance in the depression years. For, as money went downhill, both in fact and in prestige, so did publicity come to the fore.

First in the early 1930's came the Society Singers—girls like Eve (Mrs. Stuart) Symington, Adelaide Moffett, Sally Sears, Lois Elli-man, Audrey Gray, Jeannie Roberts and Suzie Mulligan. In a sense they provided a sort of opening number chorus for the Glamour Girls to follow. And in 1935, in fact, there was an actual chorus of six Society Singers at once on the Starlight Roof of the Waldorf— Gloria Braggiotta, Gwendolyn Fisk, Ruth Mager, Mrs. W. R. K. Taylor, Jr., and Mimi and Natalie Kountze.

In 1935, too, came a girl who was an almost "Glamour Girl No. 1"—the phrase was typically of Maury Paul coinage. Her name was Lucy Saunders, but she was known primarily to the few, rather than the many. Then in 1936 came another "almost"—the late Eleanor ("Cookie") Young. She became more widely known than Miss Saunders and with her began a long tradition of Glamour Girl tragedies. Described as an "exotic blossom" by Society writers, she had, like "Mimi" Baker and Brenda Frazier to follow, shoulder-length black hair, crimson lips and the so-called "white-face" look. She was the only child of the late self-made railroad baron, Robert R.

Young. Born in Texas, the son of a cowboy, Young made a notable latter-day career as a railroader, resorter and perennial host of the Duke and Duchess of Windsor. He was married to the sister of the artist, Georgia O'Keeffe. Young had a Napoleonic complex, carried on all his business from his Newport and Palm Beach houses and loved the limelight; his daughter, on whom he lavished virtually everything she wanted, liked it also.

A restless beauty, Cookie thrived on excitement and, like her father in his pursuit of the Windsors, she seemed to be pursuing something herself. Moving back and forth across the ocean, seeming to have so many homes, she actually had none at all. She made a glittering debut in 1936, in Newport, and by the next year was rumored engaged to half a dozen men, including a British title. Then in 1938 she eloped to Warrenton, Virginia, with Robert Ogden Bacon, Jr. Before a year was over, she was in Reno. The combination of too much money and too much publicity had once more taken its toll. After taking back her maiden name and being once more on the front page, Cookie made a last headline on June 2, 1941. At this time, she and a young Greek shipping heir, Nicholas Embiricos, who was a beginner pilot with only 136 flying hours to his credit, were in a plane owned by Embiricos' wife, from whom he was separated, when, in a thick fog, they plunged into the surf at Matunuck Beach, Rhode Island. Embiricos was killed instantly; so was Cookie's little dog, a Skye terrier. Cookie herself was still alive when the lifeguards pulled her from the water, but died forty minutes after reaching the hospital.*

The successor to Cookie Young for the year 1937, and the first nationally recognized Glamour Girl No. 1, was Gloria ("Mimi") Baker. She was the daughter of Mrs. Margaret Emerson, whose second husband was the late Alfred Gwynne Vanderbilt and whose third was Mimi's father, a former director of the U.S. Mint. A far different kind of girl from Miss Young, Miss Baker had the advantage

* The crash was attributed to "pilot failure." In February, 1958, Cookie's father, Robert R. Young, distraught over a so-called "Aunt Jane" (small stockholder) letter to his New York Central, killed himself with a shotgun in Palm Beach.

of having as a mother one of the best-loved women in American Society. Nonetheless, the blazing light of Publi-ciety took its toll early. At the age of 12 she was dismissed by her private tutor, who despaired of ever educating her but admitted that someday she would "stand the stag line on its ears." Mimi traveled back and forth from the Adirondacks to Long Island, to Palm Beach to Honolulu, and at 14 was as mature as the average young lady of 20. At 15, she was seen at nightclubs and gambling at Bradley's at Palm Beach; no doorman would have presumed to question her age. Her hair was shoulder-length and black but she differed from other Glamour Girls in pioneering the wearing of practically no lipstick. Nonetheless, at her debut at a Long Island supper dance for a thousand guests, all the Society writers concurred that she was "the most gorgeous gal" there.

But 1937 was not propitious for what people still liked to think of as Society. Shortly after Mimi's coming-out party the New York *Mirror* carried an editorial—one, curiously enough, written by Tex McCrary—that Miss Baker was "not fit to be the wife of a truck driver." This verdict was harsh, since Miss Baker not only had, in the words of her mother, "an instinctive something against Society" but was "the most democratic person, bar none, I've ever known." In any case, the year after her coming-out, Mimi became the second wife of Henry J. ("Bob") Topping, a young man who with his brother Dan would have some eleven wives between them—and this counting as only one Miss Arline Judge, whom both married. Miss Baker lasted with Topping until 1943—they had two children— when she divorced him and, becoming one of the very few Glamour Girls to break the tradition of tragedy, settled down to a happy marriage with Brigadier General Edward Alexander. Right at the start, however, she had no small help from her new husband. "Alex warned me," she said at the time, "that if I appeared in any expensive jewelry he would refuse to go through the ceremony." Nearly twenty years later Mrs. Alexander looked back with amazement on her early career. "The whole glamour thing," she said, "was the most ridiculous thing I've ever lived through—and I just barely did."

Actually, in 1937 Mimi Baker was not the only Glamour Girl. Another was Esme O'Brien, who first married Robert Sarnoff and then, after a divorce, John Henry Hammond—of a mining fortune, later turned to jazz authority.

In 1938 there were half a dozen Glamour Girls. One of these was the late Diana Barrymore, whose rebellion against Society included such curious remarks as "When I made my debut you had to have background and breeding to come out in Society." Although Mrs. Cornelius Vanderbilt gave the daughter of Michael Strange her blessing—"You are the living image of your mother, my dear"—it was strictly a case of the blind leading the blind. For Diana was nothing if not Publi-ciety—and so was Mrs. Vanderbilt. One thing, however, Diana's debut did do—it proved how the stage, as well as the original meaning of the word "debutante," had at last come into its own where Society was concerned. As for the career of Diana, this also carried to its conclusion the sad tradition of the debutante.

In 1938, too, came the best known of all Glamour Girls—Brenda Diana Duff Frazier. She was the personification of the "white-faced" look, which made an almost blinding contrast with the screaming red of her overpainted lips and fingernails. With her long black hair, which she was constantly either brushing or combing, she was rated more glamorous than any movie star except Garbo. Brenda was born in 1921, the daughter of Frank Duff Frazier, a "midwestern broker" —the town, in a last holdover from anti-Midwestern "Four Hundred" days, was rarely identified—and his wife, Brenda Williams-Taylor, daughter of the general manager of the Bank of Montreal. Also, and more importantly from what was left of the "social" point of view in Glamour Girls, she had a grandmother, Lady Williams-Taylor, who was the reigning dowager of Nassau. Despite all this, Brenda came from a broken home. When she was three her father, a loyal Yale man, went off to a Harvard-Yale football game and, it is recorded, "never came home, although Yale won." When she was five

her mother married again—to the late lawyer Frederick Watriss—
and later she was married a third time, to Henry Pierrepont Perry.
During all this period, indeed from the age of three to her father's
death when she was 12, young Brenda lived, like Gloria Vanderbilt,
in the center of a notorious back-and-forth custody case. Afterwards,
although Brenda's father's will contained a clause stating that if
Brenda chose to live with her mother his money was to go to Yale,
her mother was successful in breaking the will, and Brenda, at
age 21, came into some $4,000,000. Before that, at the age of 18,
she had already had one of the most extraordinary coming-out parties
in debutante history—briefly headlined by the New York *Daily
News* "Bow's A Wow." Somehow, as E. J. Kahn, Jr., recorded in
The New Yorker, the quote was fitting:

> The theoretical climax of any debutante's season is her own
> coming-out party. Brenda happened to have a cold at the time,
> and the tabloids reported this with all the gravity that might
> attend the last earthly hours of a dying king or queen. Brenda's
> ball at the Ritz, despite her indisposition, was a gala affair, dis-
> turbed only by uninvited cameramen. Mrs. Watriss, who had de-
> cided that on this one night at least Brenda should remain pic-
> torially unchronicled in the press, barred all photographers but Jay
> Te Winburn, who was commissioned to record the occasion for
> Brenda's future entertainment. This was an admirable idea, but
> Mrs. Watriss underestimated the resourcefulness of the *Daily News*,
> which dressed half a dozen of its most attractive young men in
> tailcoats and supplied them with a room in the Ritz. From there
> they drifted casually into the ballroom, armed with concealed
> candid cameras. One, who decided that the chances of taking his
> own shots without being observed would be slim, sneaked up be-
> hind Mr. Winburn and, every time that fast-working gentleman
> laid down an exposed plate to pick up a fresh one, slipped it under
> his coat. After a spell he strolled out and sent his collection to the
> *News*. Another stationed himself on the bandstand, disguised as a
> musician. While waiting for an opportunity to begin shooting,
> however, he was recognized by another jealous photographer, a
> Russian free-lancer, who had managed to get in, but without his
> camera. The Russian reported the presence of the *News* man to
> Brenda, who had him thrown out and then had the Russian thrown

out too. She just stared blankly at one *News* man who was perched in a box overlooking the dance floor, making faces at her to hold her attention. She took him for one of the thousand guests, many of whom she had never seen before.

During her year Brenda was at the beck and call of press agents from the Stork Club to Saskatchewan. Only once, it seems, did she stop and think. "I'm not a celebrity," she said, "I don't deserve all this. I haven't done anything at all. I'm just a debutante." Being "just a debutante," however, entailed some remarkable ramifications —including, as Louise Tanner recalls, her famous "Hayride down Broadway":

> It was sponsored by the Coq Rouge and Radio Station WOR. The proceeds were to go to the National Bureau of Blind Artists. Station WOR supplied a small wagon, a team of horses, some hay, and fifteen minutes of radio time. The Coq Rouge supplied the debutantes—including Brenda, who was attired in an ocelot coat, dark blue slacks, white shoes and socks. The group progressed down Broadway to the strains of "Turkey in the Straw"—regaling passers-by with cultured halloos, cries of "free drinks, free meals, free supper, free floor show," and "don't look so glum, the Depression's over." When they reached Times Square, a man gave an imitation of a hog caller. Brenda gave a carefully rehearsed squeal as a rubber mouse was produced from a handbag; and an announcer explained to the listening audience that Brenda was colorful.

Followers of Brenda's press clippings, which were Hollywood-size, expected her to marry cartoonist Peter Arno; instead, in 1941 she married the Kentucky football hero, John ("Shipwreck") Kelly. They bought a farm in East Norwich, Long Island, and attempted to settle down; in 1945 their only child, Brenda Victoria, was born. But five years later Mrs. Kelly's life seemed a sort of one-woman United Nations date bureau. In the summer of 1951 she was going out with four different men at once: America's Kelly (still her husband), England's Francis Williams, Russia's Vava Adlerberg, and Italy's Pietro Mele. Then, too, came the heavyweight fights—first a no-decision bout between Adlerberg and Mele in Rome, then an incredible free-for-all in her Park Avenue apartment between Mele and a sizable section of the East Side police force. By this time, Cholly Knickerbocker reported, Brenda needed "pills for slimming, pills for sleeping, pills almost for existing." In 1954 she had a nervous breakdown. The hospital reported that she had been on a starvation diet since her debutante days in order to live up to the public's conception of what a debutante should look like; she had to start all over again to be "taught to eat."

Finally, in 1956, she was divorced—Kelly suing her, at long last, for desertion. Then came a retreat to Cape Cod and, in 1957, marriage to a hyphenated relative, Chicago's Robert Chatfield-Taylor. Before this, however, and after her divorce from Kelly, Brenda had stated in no uncertain terms what she thought about the business of Society glamour. "Being the No. 1 Glamour Deb," she said, "is the worst thing that can happen to you. . . . It's all so superficial. It means nothing. . . . I wouldn't let it happen to my child at all."

One who not only did let it happen to her child but in fact encouraged her, with all the art of a legendary stage mother, was Cobina Wright, Sr. Her daughter, Cobina, Jr., making her debut the same year as Brenda, superseded her the next year as Glamour Deb No. 1. "Certainly in 1939," wrote her mother proudly, "Cobina, Jr. was the 'most' girl, most photographed, most publicized, most sought after."

Cobina's mother, too, had had her share of attention. Born Elaine Cobb in Oregon—she invented the "Cobina"—she was first married to writer Owen Johnson, and then, after a divorce, to New York broker William May Wright. From the beginning, however, the author of *I Never Grew Up* believed firmly in a lady's being seen:

> It has always been the fashion to say that one "loathes publicity," doesn't like one's picture in the paper, and doesn't wish to meet the press. Truthfully, I never minded in the least. In fact, I thought it was a lot of fun. Loving people, all and every kind, I liked sharing my parties with them via a full rotogravure of pictures of our guests in costume. I liked recognition and acclaim of my "talents" as a hostess just as much as I had liked applause and *bravas* when I sang. To read accounts of our doings was part of the game. I

have never been shy or self-conscious, and nothing about The Press ever bothered me, even before I became a newspaper woman myself.

Her daughter, Cobina, Jr., was born in 1921, and from the beginning was taught to move front and center. Indeed, it was hardly an exaggeration when later in her life a Hollywood publicity department would report that she had a specially built miniature automobile in which she was driven to the polo matches at Sands Point, Long Island, by a midget chauffeur. Despite this luxury, however, as well as her mother's public success as singer and hostess, there was private trouble at home. Airing everything, as was her wont, Cobina, Sr. wrote:

> My husband was capable of kissing the governess, being with his secretary in the home that had once been mine, romancing with my friend. No longer could I persuade myself to doubt. My handsome, elegant, gently fastidious husband . . . but why, why, why, why?

Then came the crash: the Wrights "awoke one morning millionaires and went to bed the same night penniless." But, typically, they gave a "last party," before they "joined the ranks of the *nouveaux pauvres.*" And even afterwards, although Cobina, Sr. and her husband were drifting "further and further apart" toward eventual divorce, she managed a trip to Europe and a brief romance of her daughter with Prince Philip. Although the latter was at that time, of course, not yet married to Elizabeth, when that event occurred Cobina, Sr., regarded it, in her inimitable way, as something of a comedown. Later mother and daughter moved to Hollywood and here, recalls Kyle Crichton, "Cobina, Sr., launched a campaign on behalf of Cobina, Jr., that for subtlety and finesse has not been surpassed since Grant's investment of Vicksburg." This campaign, too, failed: "Hollywood made up its mind about us," says Cobina, "before we came." And then in 1941 Cobina, Jr., met and married a corporal in the Army by the name of Palmer Beaudette, of Pontiac, Michigan. After their marriage, when visiting the Beaudettes at Christmas, Cobina, Sr., did her best to make a go of his family, but it was hard sledding. Her son-in-law seemed to her to enjoy drawing the contrast—"always to my disadvantage," she recalls—between "my own Café Society, my energetic, active way of life" and the "serene women of his family, their interests in their small social group, their symphony, their homes and their fireside."

Back in California, Cobina, Sr., learned the sad news that her 80-year-old mother was very ill. She went back to Oregon to see her, and her mother died. Returning to Hollywood, having lost husband, daughter and mother, she was desperately alone but, indefatigable as always, she determined to go to a party and selected from her "stack of mail" an invitation to cocktails from the late Atwater Kent:

> I put on a defiant red hat with a gay veil and a ridiculous plumed bird climbing up the side of it—and went.
> My host, the perfect gentleman . . . came forward to greet me "Cobina, my dear," he said, "so nice to see you. How are you?" "Atwater," I said, "my mother just died." "How charming," he replied sweetly, passing on to the next guest.
> A few minutes later he came to me again, a glass of sherry in his hands, and because we were very old friends and I wanted sympathy I told him once more. "Atwater," I said, "my mother just died." But my host's eye had just lighted on Greer Garson who hadn't gotten a drink yet. "Delighted to hear it," he said, dashing off. I went home.

With World War II the curtain rang down on the era of the Glamour Debutante. *Life* magazine picked as Glamour Girl No. 1 for 1939 no debutante but a screen star—Lana Turner. Then for the year 1940 it was the turn of Jinx Falkenburg—a young lady who at the age of two had been persuaded by her stage mother to have a full-page picture story in the New York *Sun* about her exploits as a "baby swimmer." But the wheel did not come really full cycle until the year 1941. In that year there were two Glamour Girl Debutantes No. 1: "Josie" Johnson and Gloria Vanderbilt—both of whom were the Glamour Debutantes all right, but neither of whom ever made a debut at all.

After the war there were occasional revivals of this strange world. The most extraordinary of all was the story of Joanne Connelley, the Glamour Debutante No. 1 for 1948. She was the daughter of a Fort Worth oil man whose wife later left him to marry M. S. Huntington Watts—a man whose Publi-ciety fame in turn rested on the fact that he had introduced to Society the red tuxedo vest. Joanne was spotted early by publicity man Ted Howard. He called her "an immature kid, right out of a private school, a normal, popular girl, with a million friends."

"One day," Howard told Robert Levin, "I saw this beautiful blonde having lunch with another girl at the Little Club. I began thinking this was the most beautiful girl I'd seen in the clubs in a long time and thought of the job I could do in making her into a new Brenda Frazier." Working together, Howard and Joanne's ambitious mother (who was shortly after divorced again) soon made a national figure out of a girl whose chief asset was, in their promotion, her figure. Over and over her name appeared in the columns, together with her pictures wearing as few clothes as possible. She became the "Golden Girl," but Howard invariably made sure she was also seen with the Right People and at the Right Time in the Right Places. At the Knickerbocker Ball of 1948, she was crowned, along with her friend Pamela Curran, one of the two "Queen Debs" of the year. Next came her picture on the cover of *Life* and finally, at age 18, came marriage to the 37-year-old former British golf champion Robert Sweeny. To the people who mentioned the age differential, Joanne's mother scoffed. "Eighteen is a wonderful age to marry," she said. "I was married young. Age doesn't make any difference. Look at the Duke and Duchess—she's a few years older than he is and they're a divine couple."

Joanne and Sweeny had two children, Sharon and Brenda. But Joanne, as ill-fitted to be a mother as she had been to be a Glamour Girl, was constantly worried about losing her figure. First came pills to kill her appetite, then barbiturates for nighttime and benzedrine for daytime. In 1953 she cabled from the Riviera for her mother; when her mother arrived, she found her daughter weighing ninety-five pounds and her marriage breaking up. Then came a suit brought by Sweeny, claiming his wife had been surprised by a hotel maid in a bedroom with Porfirio Rubirosa. Sweeny got the divorce—Joanne didn't contest it—and custody of the children.

Soon there was another man in the picture—Bolivian tin-plate heir Jaime Ortiz-Patino, another pillar of the International Set. The night before their wedding Joanne upbraided her mother. "You pushed me into this," she said. But later she was sorry. "After my breakup with Bobby," she said, "I'd have married anybody who made me feel I was important to him." Once, when a sentimental Frenchman gave her a bunch of violets, she broke down and cried.

Patino did not give his "Joey," as he called her, violets; instead he gave her $250,000 worth of jewelry, including a $100,000 wedding ring. Then came a 49-day honeymoon on the Island of Capri. On the 49th day, however, Joanne disappeared. She was found in a coma in a cheap hotel; she had swallowed forty sleeping pills. Jaime took her to Rome for treatment but she fled from him again. And in 1954 he, like her first husband, filed suit for divorce. He called her a "worthless woman who did everything for money." She, for the first time answering, called him a man who was not only cruel but who so abused her that she "lay down to die." The case dragged on for three years, during which time Joey, speaking no French or German, languished in lonely isolation in a Swiss villa. She had a heart attack induced by an overdose of reducing pills, then another, and finally a third. In July, 1957, at the age of 27, the Golden Girl, the Queen Deb of 1948, the last of the Glamour Girl No. 1's, was dead. Her body was brought back to New York and a friend arranged that her grave should be under a tree. "Joey," she explained, "couldn't bear the sun."

CHARLES DANA GIBSON

IV

SOCIAL SECURITY—*Clubs and Titles: From the*

Union Suit to the Windsor Knot

AT ABOUT ten o'clock on the evening of November 28, 1881, a distinguished French gentleman in New York by the name of Joseph Florimond, Duc de Loubat, left his room at the old Glenham Hotel and walked across Fifth Avenue to the Union Club. By the time the Duc de Loubat—or Count Loubat, as he preferred to be called—had left his club, less than an hour later, he had started something which was not only the *cause célèbre* of its own time but was probably the most famous single story in the history of American clubdom.

Count Loubat was not wealthy, had poor digestion, and was by his own admission an irritable man. Nonetheless, born in Paris, he was a Papal Count, a Knight of the Legion of Honor of France, and a bachelor; as such he was much in demand socially. Furthermore, he was a literary man and, from the "Four Hundred" point of view, in the least offensive and most housebroken way. Three years before the incident at the Union Club he had published a huge two-volume history entitled *The Medalic History of the United States of America;* this book included the story of every medal struck off by the United States government in its first hundred years.

If the Count was a man to be reckoned with, so too was his club, to which, on the payment of $1,000, he had recently been elected one of ten lifetime members. In 1881 the Union was *the* club of clubs; it was also the proud and so-called "mother" of New York's other clubs. The only club socially comparable to it, the New York Club, had some years before dissolved completely and all its members, 144 in number, had been taken into the Union. As for the Calumet, last to be founded before the Loubat affair, it was often called a "Junior Union Club," it having been formed as a waiting club by gay young blades impatiently sitting out a Union Club waiting list ten years long. Perhaps the most awe-inspiring demonstration of the Union's prestige and power of the era was when a Union Clubber by the name of Frederick deCourcy May had, in the course of an argument, the misfortune to kill a New York policeman. Fellow Union Clubbers promptly rallied round, hid Mr. May for a time in the club proper, then spirited him away to South America for a year until the unpleasantness blew over.

Exactly what happened in that hour on the fateful evening of November 28, 1881, will never be known. One thing is certain, however. Count Loubat engaged in conversation, in the time-honored black-leather-chair manner of clubs then and now, one Henry Turnbull. According to Mr. Turnbull, the conversation began with Count Loubat twitting Mr. Turnbull on being the father of a fine son. In response, Mr. Turnbull asked the Count why *he* didn't get married—to which, according to Mr. Turnbull, the Count replied, "Nobody would have me. I am not rich enough." Mr. Turnbull then asked the Count why he didn't marry a certain lady, naming a rich widow well known in the Society of the day. To this, the Count replied, still according to Mr. Turnbull, "Why should I marry her when I've been trying for ten years to ——— her daughter?"

Exactly what word or phrase the Count used never came out, not even in the subsequent court testimony in which Mr. Turnbull's version of the conversation invariably used the blank—a sharp and appealing contrast to a later era. In any case, Mr. Turnbull immediately turned on the Count and declared, "Any man who would make use of such language as that is a dirty, low blackguard and is not fit to be a member of any club and should not be admitted to any gentleman's house."

The Count's version of the affair, which was also given in subsequent testimony, varied somewhat from Mr. Turnbull's version. According to the Count, Mr. Turnbull had started by twitting the Count, not the Count by twitting Mr. Turnbull, and had said, "By the bye, Mrs. ——— says you are after Miss ———." "At this impertinence," declared the Count, "I lost my temper and made remarks which, although gross, could not be construed by any man as an insult to the lady in question." Furthermore, the Count claimed that Mr. Turnbull had not only said what he said he had said, but had also volunteered the gratuitous intelligence, "Nobody but a Frenchman could make such a remark!"

Unfortunately there were only two witnesses to the exchange and both were friends of Mr. Turnbull rather than of the Count. One later not only backed Mr. Turnbull but also admitted that, following the exchange, he had turned on the Count and said, "You and McAllister are always discussing everybody's social position." The other, who also backed Mr. Turnbull, later admitted he had literally backed it—in other words, his black-leather chair had its back to the conversation and he had not been able to hear it all.

As for the principals, they parted that evening only after Mr. Turnbull had sworn never to speak to Count Loubat again. He was unable to keep this promise, however, because upon meeting Loubat in a dark corridor of the club some evenings later, he said, on mistake, "How are you?" thinking the Count was somebody else. His nonspeaking vow hit another snag several days later when the Count saw him on Fifth Avenue. "Hello, Turnbull, have you cooled down yet?" asked the Count. "I am always cool," replied Mr. Turnbull, "except when the occasion warrants my being otherwise."

But Mr. Turnbull could not stay cool. When the Count shortly left on a trip to San Francisco, Mr. Turnbull denounced him, at a ball, as no gentleman. This was brought to the attention of the Count and so enraged him that he wrote Mr. Turnbull a letter denouncing him as a liar. Following this—the time was now May of 1882—Mr. Turnbull, on the advice of his Union Club friends, published a thousand copies of a circular, which was distributed to all members of the Union Club and stated that Count Loubat had no proof to support what Mr. Turnbull called "your unwarranted attack on my veracity."

By now the case, whether one of virginity or of veracity, was a national scandal. Members of the Union Club divided sharply into the so-called "Old Hens," who supported Mr. Turnbull, and the so-called "Young Roosters," who supported the Count. The Old Hens maintained that it was the Count who made the remark in the first place and hence was primarily responsible for disgracing the club; the Young Roosters, on the other hand, maintained that it was Mr. Turnbull who publicly aired the affair and hence was primarily responsible. The point in the Count's favor was that immediately on returning from San Francisco he went to the house of the lady in question and apologized, apparently to the satisfaction of both the lady and the daughter, for having said whatever it was he said he said.

In any case, all the leading figures of the day were asked to comment. Chauncey Depew, citing *Labouchère* v. *The London Beefsteak Club,* gave his opinion that the character of the Union Club was at stake, while Elihu Root declared that the lesson taught by the affair, from a club standpoint, was that the less members talked about such matters the better, and, taking the lesson to heart, said he had no opinion to offer. The most famous joke of the day was that of an elderly New Yorker saying to his young son, "My boy, I hope when you grow up and join that Union Club you will keep out of difficulty." William R. Travers, the stuttering wit who belonged to twenty-seven clubs, used the occasion for his most famous *bon mot*. On passing the Union Club, he was asked if all of the men who could be seen in their chairs from the street outside were actually habitués of the Club. "N-n-no," he replied, "s-s-some are s-s-sons of h-h-habitués."

The entire country thought that a duel was in the offing, and a Southern gentleman, who admitted to having fought "thirty or forty" duels and was apparently always consulted in such matters, delivered his opinion from that standpoint. In the Southerner's opinion, had Count Loubat made an insulting remark about a lady connected with Mr. Turnbull, then it would have been Mr. Turnbull's duty to challenge the Count. That not being the case, since Mr. Turnbull had no connection with the lady in question and had merely volunteered the remark about her as coming from a "blackguard," then Mr. Turnbull must be considered the aggressor and it was the Count's duty to challenge Mr. Turnbull.

Just how this should be done, the Southerner admitted, presented a problem, since a gentleman did not fight with anyone but a gentleman and this obviously presented the problem that Mr. Turnbull had declared that the Count was not one. "The line must be drawn somewhere," the Southerner declared. "In Germany they draw it with an apothecary. He can fight but a haberdasher cannot." The Southerner suggested that a friend of Count Loubat's who was an acknowledged gentleman should say to Mr. Turnbull that if Mr. Turnbull would not fight the Count then he must fight him. If Mr. Turnbull also refused this, however, then the Count could make one of two choices: publicly to slap Mr. Turnbull's face or post him in the newspapers as a coward. The Southerner firmly advised the latter. "There is no need," he said, "for blows or pulling of noses." He felt equally strongly on the matter of name-calling as duel inauguration; he said that one of his most successful affairs had been fought after he had merely called his opponent a thief. "It is essentially vulgar, this bandying of epithets," he concluded. "It is allowed in no code but the Irish and it is not to be encouraged there."

Nonetheless, encouraged by the Southerner, Count Loubat promptly journeyed to Virginia in an attempt to find a more equable dueling climate, and there awaited his adversary. But Mr. Turnbull did not follow him. For at this stage in the proceedings the president of the Union Club, aptly named William Constable, appointed a subcommittee of his club to determine "an exact statement of facts in relation to the difficulties existing between Messrs. J. F. Loubat and Henry Turnbull." On May 19 both parties were summoned, separately, before the subcommittee, and, following the subcommittee's report to the governing committee, the latter voted 18-4, on May 25, to expel Count Loubat from the Union Club.

Immediately Count Loubat took court action. Claiming his expulsion was irregular, he brought suit against Herman R. LeRoy, treasurer of the Union Club, and engaged in his defense the celebrated Joseph H. Choate. The Union Club, in turn, engaged James C. Carter, who ranked second only to Choate as the leading lawyer of his day. *Loubat* v. *LeRoy*—the Union Suit, as it came to be called—was tried at the end of the year 1884 before Judge Hooper C. Van Vorst, sitting in a special term of the Supreme Court of New York. The argument soon came down to a question of whether or not the subcommittee had been biased against Count Loubat and whether or not the governing committee, which had not had a full attendance at the time of the vote to expel, had any right to do so. The most famous individual feature of the trial was Choate's closing argument, which is still regarded as one of his most powerful speeches:

> Why, what is this man struggling for? Forced association with these gentlemen? No. They may never one of them speak to him again, if they see fit. Forced enjoyment of the pleasures of the clubhouse? Never. What is it then? Why, it is the greatest and most valuable, the dearest thing that any man can ask for. What is it? A stigma has been put upon him by a company of gentlemen

with whom he used to associate. It has followed him around the world. It meets him on the streets of New York when he is walking with his friends. It meets him on the Boulevards of Paris when every year he goes to visit his aged mother. It haunts him by night, and it follows him by day everywhere. No man can exaggerate the extent of the mischief and damage which he has suffered.

What does he say about it? Why, that it was inflicted upon him thoughtlessly, carelessly, by a committee of gentlemen in whose hands he had placed himself. Without hearing what he had to say in his defence, or whether he had anything to say, they heard his accusers, three of them. Those three made a charge against him which gentlemen might well consider whether it was ground for expulsion or not. And without informing him what it was, or what his accusers had said, without giving him a chance to show whether it was true, and to say what he had to say against it, they cast him out upon the world, and simultaneously they published upon the million wings of the press all over the world that he was no longer fit for the company of gentlemen.

Now, if there is a cause in which a man may worthily invoke the aid of the Court of Equity, if there is a subject on which a Court of Equity may worthily exercise its sublime power, it is exactly here and for this man. If he has been charged with offences which unfit him for the society of gentlemen, he wants it to be proved and found. He knows that he has not committed any such offences. He knows that no committee of gentlemen, hearing the whole case, can come to such a conclusion, and that the Governing Committee only came to it because they took the evidence behind his back. It is on these grounds, and for this great and sacred object that he appeals to your Honor, and I know that he will not appeal in vain.

Actually, Count Loubat did not "appeal in vain." Although he and Choate lost the case in Judge Van Vorst's court, they appealed and two years later, in 1886, at the General Term of the Supreme Court, Judge Noah Davis handed down a verdict in favor of Count Loubat. This was important, however, as far as the Count was personally concerned, only as a matter of principle. For, although reinstated in his club and living to 1927, to the age of 90, he never again passed through the Union Club door through which, five years before the Court's final verdict, he had passed almost every day of his life.

On the other hand, the importance of the Union Suit, in the matter of club legality, cannot be overestimated. The Union Club, as might be expected, in view of its eminence, had to learn the lesson twice. A few years after the Loubat suit the club, which had again had the temerity to urge a member to resign, promptly backtracked when the member engaged none other than ex-Judge Noah Davis, himself, to obtain an injunction. But other clubs have to this day taken stern cognizance of the lesson. One Harvard Club lawyer, for example, while declining the honor of being quoted by name, put the matter as follows: "To coin a phrase, you might say that the Union Suit proved for all time a member has a 'vested interest' in his club and cannot be irregularly expelled. For instance, at the Harvard Club, we never expel members. We just keep suspending them until they resign."

The history of American clubdom is actually a story of Social Security—with capital "S's." From the very beginning clubs were formed not primarily to get people in but rather to keep people out; thus, as early as 1747 we find, in the *Maryland Gazette*, under date of March 24, a letter signed by a "Gentleman of the East Shore," who was obviously part of a new club which admittedly had no very clear purpose except to avoid "an Omnium Gatherum who are neither capable of improving or being improved." He wished "to find means, furthermore, of ridding his group of a 'Medley of disagreeable Members.' "

The good gentleman wished to obtain the rules of "some good club," and actually even in those days he could have found many right in Carolina, which, according to Carl Bridenbaugh, "formed more private societies than any other American community"— among them a "Whisk Club," a "Smoaking Club," a "Beef-Steak Club," a "Fancy Society," and even a "Laughing Club." Baltimore's lordly Maryland Club, however, dates to the next century, having been formed in 1857, six years after Boston's famed Somerset and one year after San Francisco's surprisingly early Pacific Club—the latter, later the Pacific Union, owing its early date, it is recorded, to the "socially minded Peytons, Wards, Colemans and McAllisters who had arrived in the wake of the Forty-niners." In the ancient tradition, however, Baltimore's Maryland Club yielded to no other in austerity. For example, if Boston's Somerset could have at the turn of the century no less than half a hundred members who confidently listed their occupations as "gentlemen," as recently as the 1940's three gentlemen from Baltimore's Maryland Club—John W. S. Foster, Lawrence Bailliere, and the late Howell Parr—were entertaining a visiting Pittsburgh Steeler. After some time the Steeler asked Mr. Foster and Mr. Bailliere what they did for a living. "We don't do anything," they replied, "we just live." Finally the steelman put the question to Parr. "Me?" asked Parr. "Why, I'm in business with these boys."

Despite the eminence of New York's Union as the "mother of clubs," the honor of being the country's oldest club goes to Philadelphia for its famed Fish House, or "State in Schuylkill," as it was called when it was founded in 1732. And this was no idle name, for originally the Fish House was indeed a separate state and was so recognized by colonial governors. Ever since its founding the club has been primarily a cooking club, known for its beefsteak as well as its Fish House Punch, the recipe for which was a dark secret for some century and three quarters but then, in the 1900's, was for some unaccountable reason suddenly made public. The club itself, however, could never be accused of going public. In its first 228 years of existence, up to 1960, the Fish House had less than 400 members in all. Indeed by its rules there may be no more than 30 "Citizens," or members, at one time, all of whom gather twice a month during the summer. Although they gather before lunch, the main event of the meeting is dinner, which is cooked by the "Citizens" but served by the "Apprentices," all of whom aspire, in some cases rather despairingly, to full citizenship.*

* Frank Brookhouser gives the recipe of the Fish House Punch as follows: "Two bottles of rum, old and potent. A bottle of brandy, old and potent. Three quarters of a pound of sugar to each bottle. A wine glass of peach

Second in point of age to the Fish House is the Philadelphia Club, which, founded in 1830, antedates New York's Union by six years. Rated on a par with the Fish House and the Philadelphia Assembly, it has been called by Dixon Wecter "probably the most compact and inviolable little group of Aristocrats in America." Like New York's Union, it too had a *cause célèbre* in which the results were not unlike that of the Union Suit. This happened during the Civil War when a member, entering, declared, "This place reeks of copperheads." "A fellow member," recalls Wecter, "promptly knocked him down, was expelled, reinstated by court order, again expelled and again reinstated by Federal command; he then entered the club, ordered a drink, and handed in his resignation for ever."

Three college clubs also antedate New York's Union Club. One, the oldest continuously operating club of all, is Harvard's Hasty Pudding "Institute," dating back to 1770. Another is Harvard's Porcellian Club which, as we have already noted, dates back to 1791. And Yale's most famous "Senior Society," Skull and Bones, originally called the "Russell Trust Association," is also ahead of New York's Union, having been founded in 1832. No club has more legends than this—among them the pious belief that all members must leave the room if, outside of the Bones building itself, the club is ever mentioned. On one occasion, the Harvard *Lampoon*, knowing there was a joke about Skull and Bones in Harvard's Hasty Pudding show, hired a group of Negroes to sit in prominent positions all over the orchestra; the moment Skull and Bones was mentioned, they all got up and left the theatre. The cruelty of this was rather reversed when, some years ago, Yale's great Negro football player, Levi Jackson, was not only selected for Skull and Bones but also had the honor of being the "last man tapped" on Yale's "Tap Day." Jackson promptly proved himself fully cognizant of other ramifications of college club snobbery. "If my name had been Jackson Levi," he said, "I'd never have made it."

---

brandy to each bottle. Three quarters of a quart of lemon juice. The sugar (it has to be lump sugar) goes into the bowl first. The water is then poured in and the sugar is stirred into a syrup. After that the lemon juice is added. And finally the potent liquids. Here's a warning: It's dynamite."

But the general picture of what has happened to what was once the ultimate in the American male's social security can best be seen by the story of what has happened to the New York men's clubs. And this story, too, begins with the Union. It begins indeed in the 1930's, that same era which saw, on the one hand, so many obituaries for the word "gentleman" and, on the other, the rise and shine of celebrity and glamour Society.

In 1936 there occurred the one hundredth anniversary of New York's Union Club. From all parts of this country and even from abroad there arrived, from lesser clubs, congratulatory messages, impressive gifts, and particularly large offerings of floral tributes.

As so often happens in gentlemen's clubs, however, at the actual anniversary banquet, despite the dignity of the occasion, the severe speeches and the general sentimental atmosphere, there was a little overdrinking. And one member overdrank a little more than a little. Shortly before dessert he decided he had had enough, at least of the food, and disappeared. Furthermore, he did not reappear.

After the banquet some friends of his decided to conduct a search. The faithful doorman in the hooded hallporter's chair gave the news that no gentleman of that description had passed out, or rather passed him, and the friends redoubled their efforts. High and low they combed the missing member's favorite haunts—the bar, the lounge, the card room, the billiard room, the locker room, the steam room, etc. One even tried, on an off chance, the library. There, as usual, he saw only a seniority list of the Union's ten oldest living members and a huge sign reading SILENCE.

Finally, in one of the upstairs bedrooms, they found the gentleman. He was stretched out full length on a bed in his faultless white tie and tails, dead to this world.

To one of his friends this gave an idea. It was the work of but a moment to enlist support and soon all the man's friends had joined in. From all corners of the club they procured the floral tributes; these they piled in great profusion around, under and over the gentleman. Then they worked out, in shifts, a guard duty.

A couple of hours later the guard sounded the alarm. The gentleman had stirred. Quietly his friends filed into the room and took planned positions. They stood silent around the bed, hands clasped in front of them, heads decorously bowed, all either actually weeping or giving visible evidence of great grief.

The gentleman stirred once more, moaned something inaudible, then sniffed several times. Finally, gingerly, he opened his eyes. At once he shut them again, blinked a couple of times, and then reopened them, this time very quickly as if to take the sight by surprise. This time, hardly believing, he took in the beautiful flowers piled bank on bank, his loyal friends shaken with such obviously deep grief, and the dearly familiar bedroom of the club he loved so well. With a sigh he sank back and reshut his eyes. Before again resuming his sleep, however, he murmured one line which was not only clearly audible but also clearly happy: "I never knew it would be like this."

Today in the opinion of club old-timers it would have been better, from the standpoint of permanent happiness, had the gentleman actually passed on in that manner. For, during the intervening years, what has happened to the great city clubs of New York is one of the most extraordinary social changes of our times. Furthermore, this change is being duplicated, to a greater or lesser extent, in almost every other major city.

Years ago New York's Union and the Century, the Union League and the University, the Knickerbocker and the Racquet and Tennis, the Metropolitan and the Manhattan, the Brook and the Links, were legendary names. They were names known not only to New Yorkers but to people all over the country, from whom they drew, albeit sparingly, their nonresident members. The power and prestige, the pomp and circumstance of these clubs were awe-inspiring. A young man of Manhattan felt that his life was meaningless, if not actually broken, if he did not "have" a club—the expression "make" a club was always frowned upon—and such a young man, looking forward to being had, cheerfully sat out club waiting lists, in some cases— as we have noted—ten years long. No humorous magazine, and indeed no sightseeing bus tour, was complete without some reference to the mustached men in the black-leather chairs of the oak-paneled rooms overlooking Fifth Avenue.

Elsewhere around the country the pomp and circumstance was equally notable. Probably the most remarkable example of this was demonstrated at the Chicago Club during the Chicago Fire of 1871. First, recalls Emmett Dedmon, the members toasted their defiance of the destruction of their businesses with a champagne breakfast. Then, when the fire roared into the club itself, the members hastily filled their pockets with cigars and liquor bottles, picked up the red-satin sofas from the lobby and took them to the lake shore. "Here," he concludes, "they sat down and finished their meal."

Today, in New York at least, the change in the clubs, which in some ways seems comparable to a great fire, has passed the philosophical stage. "Bah," said the late Alexander Hamilton Rice, shortly before his death in 1954, "it's just a plain damn revolution." Rice at his peak belonged to forty-three societies and twenty-seven clubs, including the Automobile Clubs of both New York and Philadelphia; at the end of his life he was down to a baker's dozen. Rice's stern view was seconded by the Hon. Sumner Welles, former Undersecretary of State, who is now down to his last two clubs. "There is no such thing as club society any more," says Mr. Welles. "They can't even keep in the men they used to keep out." Bruce Barton, of "Martin, Barton and Fish" fame, concludes the case on a B.B.D.O. note. "Club life is dead," he says flatly. "The only reason I go to the University Club is to take a bath."

In the clubs themselves, if the old-timers will not discuss their own club they will, at the drop of a hatband, give you very good reasons for not joining any other club. "You wouldn't want the Knickerbocker," says a member of the Union. "If Nelson Rockefeller hadn't bought the place, there wouldn't be a club." A member of the Knickerbocker, in turn, warns against the Century. "You could go very wrong there," he says. "They're all over a hundred and it isn't even a club. That's why they call it the Century Association." A member of the Century continues with stern counsel against the Union League. "Look out for those boys," he says.

"They put a tag on everybody—I guess they have to. They never say they're dining with So-and-so. It's always So-and-so, president of Such-and-such, and then they both deduct each other from their income tax." A member of the Union League follows with a strong caution against the Metropolitan. "They take in anybody," he says. "They get some fellow who doesn't know the first thing about New York clubs and the first thing he knows he's in there, and then where is he?" A member of the Metropolitan proceeds with a critical view of the Manhattan. "It isn't even just everybody," he says. "It's everybody and his friends. Why, they even have two entirely different crowds. It's textile men at lunch and lawyers at dinner. They never even speak to each other."

A Manhattan member, obviously, has no use for the University. "They can talk about their library all they want. It's a rather crowded and not very exclusive hotel. Nobody knows who anybody is and half the time nobody's even heard of the college they're from. It's like a cemetery in there at night, and at lunchtime it's like Jones Beach." A member of the University has some fatherly advice about the Racquet and Tennis. "They do nothing but drink and gamble and talk about their rice pudding," he says. "Who wants to join a club on account of rice pudding?" A Racquet Clubber, of course, takes a short snort in the direction of the Links. "They're always telling you about their big-shot executives and how strong they are out of town. They have to be, I guess, because in New York nobody even knows where they are." A member of the Links concludes with a parting shot at the Brook. "They don't even know what time it is," he says. "I had to go over there a couple of months ago and tell them it was their fiftieth anniversary." And, finally, a member of the Brook brings the wheel full cycle by ending up again back at the Union. "I mean to say," he says, "I could take you up there for lunch, but there wouldn't be anyone there. It wouldn't be a good lunch, I mean to say, and it wouldn't be a bad lunch. I mean to say, it just wouldn't be anything."

This sort of defection is a great change from the Good Old Days. In those days the clubs had their differences, of course. The Century, for example, which dates from 1847, was formed in the belief that the Union was slighting intellectual eminence. "There's a club down on 43rd Street," said one Union Clubber, "that chooses its members mentally. Now isn't that a hell of a way to run a club?" The Union League, a Republican club dating from 1863, was formed in answer to the fact that the Confederate Secretary of State was allowed to resign from the Union Club, when, according to Union Leaguers, he should have been expelled; the Manhattan, originally a Democratic club, was formed a year later in answer to the answer. The Knicker-bocker (1871) was formed because its members felt the Union was taking in too many out-of-towners and wanted a club limited to men of Knickerbocker ancestry; the Metropolitan (1891) was formed because the elder J. P. Morgan could not get a friend of his into the Union and thereupon, in the Morgan manner, built his own club; and the Brook (1903) was formed because two young Union Clubbers had been expelled for having attempted, unsuccessfully, upon the bald head of the Union's most revered patriarch, to poach an egg.

But basically these were minor differences. The gentleman of the "Four Hundred" belonged to not one but many clubs and wore them like ribbons—actually wearing them, in fact, on neckties, hat-bands, vests, garters and suspenders. The elder Morgan forgot the difficulty about his friend and was soon again a member in good standing, not only of both the Union and the Metropolitan but also of every other major club. Even the errant Brook Club eggheads were soon reinstated in their mother club, and by the time of the Union's hundredth anniversary, it could boast that the presidents of no less than thirteen other clubs were all good Union men.

Even before, on Thanksgiving Day, 1920, the Union had given an extraordinary example of club solidarity. In the forenoon of that day the Club, which was located at Fifth Avenue and 51st Street across from St. Patrick's Cathedral, was flying, along with the American flag, the Union Jack of Great Britain; this latter was to commemorate the three hundredth anniversary of the landing of the Pilgrims. At this juncture some four thousand members of the

Cork Men's Benevolent and Protective Association hove into sight marching down Fifth Avenue. The loyal Irishmen were headed for a solemn requiem High Mass to be celebrated for the repose of the soul of Terence McSweeney, the late Lord Mayor of Cork who had starved himself to death in prison as a protest against Great Britain. Unfortunately, the sight of the hated Union Jack floating in the breeze outside the Union Club library was more than the Sein Feiners could bear. Although some of the marchers went on into the Cathedral, a group of half a hundred broke off and stormed into the club.

The Union Club doorman gave ground easily, but not so the rest of the members. Since it was Thanksgiving, most members were out of town, but the twenty or so who were there rose to the challenge; in fact they promptly took their stand on the great stairway determined, it is recorded, "to repel the invaders at all costs." Even the *New York City Telegraph* reported their bravery. "Some very dignified New Yorkers," it said, "set up a little Thermopylae." Fists flew, and there were bloody lips and bloody noses, and many eyes were blacked—but finally, due to the quick thinking of one member, who barricaded himself in a telephone booth and called the police, the rioters were repelled.

This was but a lull in the battle, however. Unknown to the Unioneers, the club manager had, during the fray, drawn in the offending flag. Learning of this afterwards, Arthur Weekes, chairman of the House Committee and chief of staff on the stairway, held a hasty consultation with a bruised and bleeding Union Club vice-president, J. Frederick Tams; promptly the manager was overruled and the Union Jack once more went out on the Union flagpole. This time the club refused to take it in for any reason—despite demands of the police, shouts of anger from a constantly increasing crowd, and even the well-reasoned pleas of Monsignor Lavelle, Rector of the Cathedral. And, after the Mass, when the Sein Feiners were filing out of the Cathedral, the Union's second battle began. This time a boy started it, by throwing a stone which smashed one of the large windows. Immediately the mob started throwing any and all missiles; every window in the club was smashed, and once again the Irishmen rushed to the breach. This time, though, the club was ready for them and, reinforced by police, held its ground. "As twilight came on," concludes the Union Club book, in its pardonably prideful prose, "the old clubhouse, with its window frames gaping like so many eyeless sockets, was left to nurse its wounds—but the flags, true to the principles of liberty for which our country was founded, still flew in the breeze."

Messages of congratulation from clubs all over the country poured in. Many referred, inevitably, to the fact that the Union would henceforward be forever known as "only a stone's throw from the Cathedral." There was one cable from a Union Club nonresident as far off as London. His name was Captain Lawrence Timpson, and to Telfair Minton, a member of the Union army whose eye had been blacked, his message was brief: "Oh, Say, Can You See?"

To understand the causes of the great club revolution, which began in the 1920's and raged unabated through the 1930's and on to the present day, it is necessary to look for a moment at club history. The American city clubs were patterned originally on the English idea of a gentlemen's club. Although they never carried this pattern to the extreme of the English club, where in the old days members wore their hats everywhere in the club except the dining room, the American gentleman found, like the Englishman, that his club, and not his home, was his real castle. Here he had the best of his well-bred friends, the most comfortable of his well-stuffed chairs, the best of food, drink and cigars from his well-stocked larders and cellars, the least irritating of reading material from a well-censored library, and the best of games from well-mannered losers. Here he could do what he pleased when he pleased where he pleased and with whom he pleased; here, and only here, did he find sanctuary and his four freedoms: freedom of speech against democracy, freedom of worship of aristocracy, freedom from want from tipping, and, above all, freedom from fear of women.

Actually, in the case of the last-named, he even found freedom from fear of the double standard of the day. It was to a gentleman's club, rather than his home, that the extra, or extras, among his lady friends wrote, and the tactful servant would always bring such a letter on a silver tray, butter side down; this was, of course, on the chance that the lady might be connected, in some fashion, with another member.

With such appeal it is small wonder that the clubs were, in the unpopular sense of course, popular. Ward McAllister himself blessed the movement. "Men whose personality is not remarkably brilliant and who, standing by themselves, would not be apt to arouse a great deal of enthusiasm among their associates on account of their intellectual capacity," he said, "very frequently counteract these drawbacks by joining a well-known club. Thus it will be seen that a club often lends a generous hand to persons who, without this assistance, might ever remain in obscurity."

Today this obscurity might be said to be on the other foot; certainly the four freedoms of the city clubs have gone with the wind. First came the competition for "family memberships" of the country clubs—of which "*The* Country Club," Boston's famed debutante launching pad, located in Brookline, is generally accorded "first" honors. After the country club came Prohibition. At first thought to be a boon to the clubs, with their secret bars and lockers, in the end it proved a bane. Clubmen found it easier to stop off at a speakeasy than risk arrest at their own club, and they thus went, as we have seen, from the Right Club to the Night Club.

And finally, of course, there came the depression. The first two club freedoms—anti democracy and pro aristocracy—seemed, in the political implications of that era, slightly to the right of Charlemagne. Even today it is a vital part of club tradition that Presidents like Herbert Hoover and Dwight Eisenhower are either honorary or actual life members of every major social club while a President like Harry Truman is neither an honorary nor an actual member of any.*

* "I am not a club man," Truman advised this writer, when we questioned him on the subject, then added, "which is perhaps fortunate, since I've had so many club snubs I can't even remember them individually." In this connection

Even Truman, however, as an object of snubs paled before Franklin D. Roosevelt. Perhaps the latter's most gentle rebuff came at the hands of the late Miss Edith Benjamin, a lady who founded New York's most select dancing class and numbered Franklin among her early pupils. In her later years, quietly but definitely, she always referred to him as "that Roosevelt boy with the nice smile whose name I never can remember, who was President for so long." On the other hand, some of F.D.R.'s club snubs were far from gentle. At the Harvard Club of New York, following his death, there was a running battle over whether or not his name should appear on the War Memorial, and even after it was finally decided that his name should appear, there was a considerable to-do about how prominent a position his portrait should have. Eventually it was removed from the main hall and placed, behind the buffet table, in the dining room.

At the Union Club there was a memorable membership committee meeting concerning the candidacy of another Roosevelt. In vain was one member reminded, ere he cast his black ball, that the Roosevelt under consideration was not directly related to Franklin—that he was an Oyster Bay Roosevelt, not a Hyde Park one. To the member it made no difference. "Goddam all Roosevelts," he said.

Not only did the depression usher in an era when assessments were added to dues, it also ushered in an era when the club waiting list became a grab bag. "The only reason I got into the Century in 1931," says lecturer and critic John Mason Brown modestly, "was because they thought I was John Nicholas Brown, the world's richest baby." Coupled with club poverty went an almost complete breakdown of club morality. In that era there was hardly a single club which did not complain of members' stealing. For fifteen years a member drove up to the University Club on Sunday morning in

it is perhaps significant to note that New York's only high-ranking Democratic club, the Manhattan, changed with remarkable rapidity from Democratic to Republican, and when Gordon Dean, former chairman of the Atomic Energy Commission, spoke in 1953 to the Union League Club, he was advised that he was the second registered Democrat who had addressed the club in ninety years. "I never did find out who the first one was," he says. "I think it was Robert E. Lee."

a chauffeur-driven automobile, sneaked in and surreptitiously made off with a Sunday paper; at the Union League there was a similar story. Even card-playing in many of the clubs became a problem—the all-time low in this regard being reached by the brief appearance of a sign on the Racquet Club bulletin board: MEMBERS ARE CAUTIONED NOT TO PLAY CARDS WITH MEMBERS. Almost equally poignant was the 1939 stunt of Maury Paul in publishing a chart, Social Register style, of the 1911-1939 dwindling of club memberships of Percy R. Pyne II, a man whom Paul rated the No. 1 clubman of the metropolitan Smart Set:

> PERCY R. PYNE, 2nd—Un.
>   Uv. R. Mg. Rh. Bg. Snc. T.
>   Ss. Ao. Gg. Au. Mb. Dt. P.
>   '03.
>   From the N.Y. *Social*
>   *Register*, 1911.

> PERCY R. PYNE, 2nd—Un.
>   K. Uv. R. Rh. Bg. Snc. Ss.
>   Ao. Gg. Mid. Ng. Pr. Mt. Ul.
>   Ny. Au. B. M. Mb. T. Dt. P. '03.
>   From the N.Y. *Social*
>   *Register*, 1917.

> PERCY R. PYNE, 2nd—Un.
>   K. Uv. R. Mb. Tf. T. Ss. Ln.
>   Mid. Ns. Gg. Pr. Wk. Uu. Ch.
>   Dt. B. Ct. Ny. Snc. Mb. Ul.
>   Mt. Ng. Mtw. Php. Rep. Trb.
>   P. '03.
>   From the N.Y. *Social*
>   *Register*, 1928.

> PERCY R. PYNE, 2nd—B. Un.
>   R. Mb. Ss. Ng. Pr. P. '03.
>   From the N.Y. *Social*
>   *Register*, 1938.

SOCIAL SECURITY 209

PERCY R. PYNE, 2nd—B. Ss.
Ng. P. '03.
From the N.Y. *Social
Register*, 1939.

Following the depression, of course, came two and a half wars, inflation, and, worst of all from the club point of view, a king-and-a-half sized servant problem. The whole tenor of club life depended upon service, and yet the problem of keeping servants and at the same time maintaining the precious third freedom—freedom from want due to tipping—became an almost impossible task. No club worthy of the name permits any gratuities to employees, except a regular Christmas contribution, any more than it permits members to pay cash for purchases, and yet a new generation of servants apparently arose who failed to understand what an honor it was to serve a club. The Century made a memorable *noblesse oblige* effort in this direction at the close of World War II when all the younger colored servants who had been in the Services were welcomed back into club service at a dinner; they were marched in, in uniform, while the entire club membership rose and sang "Mine Eyes Have Seen the Glory." But even this effort failed to stem the tide. "The only person you can call nowadays who will come quickly and cheerfully," recently opined New York, Florida, and Southampton clubman Newell Tilton, "is the undertaker."

Probably the club which has made the greatest efforts in the servant direction is New York's Brook Club. Named for Tennyson's poem, the club had definite ideas of what club service should be even before it was founded. In 1901 its first president, Thomas B. Clarke, lingering late in the Union Club one evening, was irritated by the crash of cutlery in the kitchen. "Gentlemen," he announced to his friends, "the impatient waiters, by these signs, are telling us that it is time for us to leave. One of these days we shall have a small club which shall provide its members with continuous service." Two years later the Brook was founded and, symbolizing the proud announcement that the club would be open twenty-four hours a day, Clarke tied the keys of the front door to a balloon and let them float skyward. Since that time also, as in better days at Boston's Somerset Club, members have never had to trouble to sign checks; instead they are trailed by a faithful servant who unobtrusively totes up their account. With the most attractive of all small club-houses as well as the most lavish of all accoutrements, the Brook's membership, numbering some 400 souls, is perhaps clubdom's richest from the point of view of inherited wealth. "It's full of the men," says Joseph Alsop, lion of Harvard's Porcellian, "who twenty-five years ago would have been called fashionable, but I'll be damned if I know what you'd call them today." Of late years Brook members have also had to keep a weather eye on one of the club's senior citizens, who, since all dine at one large table, regularly refuses to continue eating if anyone whom he dislikes sits down. When this happens, wherever the gentleman happens to be in his meal, he immediately gets up and goes across to the Brussels restaurant next door. "He's had a great many Brook Club soups," says George Plimpton, "but he's never yet gotten to the demitasse."

The troubles of New York's Brook over servant problems and increased costs, however, have been as nothing compared to those of the larger clubs. The Union Club's move uptown to its location opposite the Russian consulate—its fourth move—represented, to many old clubbers, the last straw. "I just think it's damned undigni-fied," barks George Palen Snow, "the way these clubs keep hopping around." The Metropolitan, in contrast, has never moved but now sincerely wishes it had, as of 1929, when the Hotel Pierre offered $5,000,000 for its Stanford White castle and stately drive-in turn-around. By the year 1934 it was close to the wall; in that year eighty-two members resigned and a notice was posted saying the club had experienced a deficit of $51,435. The notice also stated that it was hoped each member would try to recruit a new member, and that the board of governors were "receptive" to "suitable prop-ositions for a merger with another club of similar standing." Since that time, with a full roster of celebrities such as Douglas Mac-Arthur, Thomas J. Watson, Jr., the late Dale Carnegie, Conrad Hilton, Floyd Odlum, Spyros Skouras and Stavros Niarchos, the club has done better but, as one member said, as of 1958, "The Club will never be what it was in the old days. Today's members don't seem to have the time or the inclination to devote themselves to club life."

The Knickerbocker also had merger ideas and in 1954 came within a whisker of its eldest member of passing back into the Union, out of which, in better days, it had sprung. The club was saved at the last moment only by such stalwarts as the late Alexander Hamilton Rice, Sumner Welles and Winthrop Aldrich agreeing to have its bonded indebtedness settled at ten cents on the dollar—and also by a handsome gift on the part of Nelson Rockefeller. This latter amounted to his actually buying the club and yet permitting it to occupy the premises rent-free for ten years and for ten years after that if Rockefeller is still living. The irony of this, from the point of view of the age-old process of Celebrity to Society to Aristocracy is that, as comparatively recently as April 8, 1934, Maury Paul had written:

> The third generation of the Rockefellers have definitely "made the grade" in New York Society. The late John D. Rockefeller, Sr., founder of the family fortune, never was able to gain member-ship in any of Gotham's worthwhile clubs. His son and namesake, present head of the Rockefeller clan and interests, declined to place himself in the position where he might be subjected to the rebuffs administered to his father. But the grandsons and great-nephews have fared much better.*

Although clubman J. Carvel Lange, one of the foremost stock market prognosticators, maintains that club memberships nowadays "vary with the Dow Jones averages," the underlying fact of the great club revolution would seem to be that there is no genuine new generation to take the place of such time-tested veterans as Harold Vanderbilt, Winthrop Aldrich, the late Vincent Astor and Myron

---

* Paul is perhaps unduly stern here. John D. Rockefeller, Sr., did belong to the Union League Club. As for John D. Rockefeller, Jr., he was not a "club man" out of personal preference—or rather, out of personal advice received from his philanthropic mentor, Frederick T. Gates. "In this business [of philanthropy]," Gates told Rockefeller, "you have to lead the life of a recluse. Never make friends. Don't join clubs. Avoid knowing people intimately."

Taylor; all of these men belong or belonged to virtually every club except the S.P.C.A. and Boys Town. What should be the new generation has, in fact, many doubts on the score. "Honestly," says young Mrs. Alfred Gwynne Vanderbilt, "I don't know what clubs Alfred belongs to, and what's more I don't think he does either." R. Stuyvesant Pierrepont, Jr., who frankly classes such downtown clubs as India House, the Recess, the Lunch Club and the Downtown Association as "pigeon clubs," believes that now the pigeons, aided by expense accounts, have come home to roost uptown. "At the Metropolitan or the Union League or the University," he says, "you might do a $10,000 deal, but you'd use the Knickerbocker or the Union or the Racquet for $100,000 and then, for $1,000,000 you move on to the Brook or the Links." In the midst of such figures, ex-clubman Edgar Ward becomes philosophical. "The whole club thing nowadays," he says, "is sort of like English titles. To an American, they're still very impressive, but to an Englishman the Earl of Warwick isn't necessarily any more social than just plain Mister Charles Winn."

Men's clubs around the country vary from the St. Louis Racquet Club, founded in 1907, which has a hard-and-fast rule for membership that every member must be on a first-name basis with every other member, to the Houston Petroleum Club, which one recent Christmas spent $50,000 on decorations alone. One problem, which they all share, however, is the problem of getting the club to be used at dinnertime—and indeed getting it to be used at lunchtime on something other than a business basis. This is particularly difficult in such clubs as Pittsburgh's Duquesne Club, where U.S. Steel maintains a suite, the Chicago Club, where one officer estimated that 90 per cent of the checks received by his club were company checks, or the Cleveland Club, where the talk may occasionally concern whether or not the club should take down its prominent nude painting but soon gets back to more important matters—stocks, bonds, earnings, death and taxes. New York's comparatively brand-new Pinnacle Club is perhaps today's best example of what might

be called the "expensive account" clubs. A 675-member organization
located on top of the Socony-Mobil Building, it was founded by
such industrialists as Brewster Jennings, Charles Munson and Howard
Shepherd, and admission fees run to some $1,875. The feature of the
club, the idea of which was borrowed from Harvard's Porcellian, is
an enormous one-way mirror which permits occupants to look across
a hall through windows commanding a breath-taking view, at the
same time that other men, entering the dining room, can look at
themselves.

Business too, but without the view, is New York's Links Club,
at 36 East 62nd Street. Once, however, it was not, for it was formed
in 1921 "to promote and conserve throughout the U.S. the best
interests and true spirit of the game of golf." In those carefree
twenties days, also, no bills were kept at all; members, using the
club as much or as little as they wished, were all assessed equally
at the end of the year. From this came sharp reverse to a strict business basis, in both bills and membership. In 1958, for example, the
Links' nonresident membership was almost entirely business—a
Bechtel from San Francisco, a Pillsbury from Minneapolis, a Ford
from Detroit, a Field from Chicago, a Humphrey from Cleveland, a
Mellon from Pittsburgh, a Du Pont from Wilmington, a Pew from
Philadelphia, and a Cabot from Boston. These, along with a distinguished resident membership, live in relatively Spartan surroundings—the club has only two bedrooms—and indulge in excellent
meals, very informal bridge (where kibitzing is always encouraged),
and reading a scrapbook compiled by the perennial Link president,
Charles C. Auchincloss. This scrapbook contains not only sentimental homilies in prose—"The 'acid' test of whether a man is a
desirable member of a Club is whether, when you meet him in the
Club, you are glad to see him"—but also sentimental and laudatory
verses to members. One of these honoring U.S. Steel's Enders Mc-
Clumpha Voorhees, whose nickname is Van, will perhaps suffice:

Once again, let us drink to our Van,
A superlatively companionable man.

He can bid like a Blizzard,
Toss dice like a Wizard,
And can he shoot birdies? He can!
                                Our Van!

If such a club may seem slightly out of touch with the present, so too, at least at times, can its giant parent, the Racquet and Tennis Club at 370 Park Avenue. The Racquet has been a bastion against, among other things, business building; as of 1960 it was the last private building in a sea of office buildings in its area on Park. And, amid such difficult surroundings, its more than two thousand members still live by its original objective "to encourage all manly sports among its members." Actually such manliness boils down to all manner of racket games, both on the courts and on the card tables, on the part of its younger members; golfers like T. Suffern Tailer and Clark Benton and tennis players like Ogden Phipps and Alistair Martin happily combine with indoor gamesters like Barclay Cooke and Stuyvesant Wainwright, Jr. Although once in a while a member like the Duke of Windsor writes a book, an extraordinary number of Racquet Clubbers have no regular occupation beyond clipping coupons or perhaps fellow members. At the same time, while many sports at the club such as court tennis, an involved squash game, or "towie," a three-handed bridge game, are virtually unknown elsewhere, no sport or, for that matter, drink passes unnoticed, and the entire club recently applauded when Dwight F. Davis, Jr., was presented with the Knapp Cup for Outstanding Improvement in Bottle Pool. The same sort of enthusiasm greeted another Racquet Club man who one Easter Eve left the club clad only in a tablecloth and descended on Grand Central Terminal. There he was picked up by police, but not until the next morning, following a night in jail, would he relinquish his firm conviction that he was, as he vainly tried to explain, the Easter Bunny.

Probably the most interesting of New York clubs and easily the most distinguished, from both a *Who's Who* and a *Celebrity Register* point of view, is the Century Club—or the Century Association, as it is called. "The authors and the artists cannot stand apart from the practical world," the founders wrote in 1847. "The world of politics and economics and the price of pig iron has a heavy hand in fashioning the artist." In any case they decided to invite "amateurs of letters and fine arts to join them—amateurs," they said, "in the dictionary sense of those who love, are fond of or have a taste for a subject"—as well as a group of "gentlemen of any occupation provided their breadth of interest and qualities of moral and imagination make them sympathetic, stimulating and congenial companions in the society of authors and artists." This was a large order, club-dom being what it is, and has led through the years to some rebuttal. The late Francis Henry Taylor, director of the Metropolitan Museum, once looked at a Century Club art exhibit of one of the members. "Just how the hell bad an artist," he inquired, "does one have to be to get into this club?" On the other hand, the Century, because of its eminence, yields to no other club in austerity. Many years ago, for example, Philadelphia architect John Frederick Harbeson took a friend of his, General North, to the club; ever since that time he has himself invariably been addressed, by both members and staff, as "General Harbeson." Legion are Century stories of one of the "amateurs" sitting down to explain something to a fellow member—and then finding out afterward his companion was the world's leading authority on the subject. In this spirit Austin Strong once corrected Charles Evans Hughes on a point of law. Years later Ed Streeter, humorous author, shortly after his election complained to a fellow member that he didn't like it because he didn't know anybody. "You're not supposed to," he was told. "You have to work at being a Centurion."

The Century, like New York's Union, is a "mother of clubs" and also on a national scale—among its children being, in New York, the Lotos, the Players, the Lambs and the Coffee House, and elsewhere in the country the Tavern Clubs of both Boston and Chicago, the Cosmos in Washington, D.C., and the Cactus Club in Denver. Perhaps the most remarkable of these is San Francisco's Bohemian Club, which boasts a clubhouse on Nob Hill equipped with a 750-seat theatre as well as its own 2,800-acre "grove" outside the city. Here, each summer, some twelve hundred "Bohemians"—who are chosen, says one veteran, "for their talent, among other considerations"— gather for two weeks of high thinking and low drinking. This is accompanied by the club's own 70-piece symphony orchestra and invariably begins by an evening around a giant campfire in a ceremony under the redwoods called "The Cremation of Care."

If what has happened to the first three club freedoms is a stern story, what has happened to the fourth freedom—freedom from fear of women—is a positive nightmare. As far back as 1838 James Gordon Bennett had pondered editorially in the New York *Herald* as to whether or not he should accept his invitation to join the new Union Club. "What is the use of any social system in which women do not participate?" he asked. "In which their petticoat is not seen— where glossy ringlets cannot enter and make it Paradise?"

For a hundred years the laugh was on Mr. Bennett; the last laugh, however, has not been. Indeed, nothing seems more ironic from the point of view of the ladies' wing of the great club revolution than the Loubat case. Here was a man saved only by the New York Supreme Court from a fate apparently worse than death—all because he took a lady's name in vain in his club. Yet shortly after his death the ladies themselves, let alone their fair names, would roam the men's clubs almost at will. Even the New York Yacht Club, which, in happier days, permitted no gentlemen who did not own a yacht of a certain length, has come to permit ladies, after five and except Saturdays and Sundays, with no boat at all, while the Metropolitan Club allows ladies every day all day and even has full-fledged lady members who can do anything except spend the night. The two most active of today's clubs, the Regency and the River, the former a bridge club and the latter an East River tennis club, are now completely family clubs. "At the River we have very few what I call 'tea cozies,'" says Mrs. William Grace Holloway, Sr., "except me. But we're a very successful club for nowadays."

At the Union, as might be expected, the change is the most revolutionary. For a century no lady ever saw the inside of the club unless she was either a female employee or the wife of the club president. If the latter, she was permitted to visit the club once, on some morning when the club was empty, for the sole purpose of seeing her husband's portrait and where it was hung. Otherwise, literally for a hundred years, only one other lady had the honor.

This lady was the wife of an inveterate Union Club whist player. She went berserk one afternoon in the 1880's, pushed aside the doorman, ran up the stairs and burst into the card room, apparently intent on getting her husband out. Immediately there was a deathly silence, and what followed is best recalled by Reginald Townsend, at the time of writing the president of the Union Club's Distinguished Visitors Committee:

> The unfortunate member—whose wife was responsible for this unheard of breach of etiquette—retained his presence of mind. Gravely he introduced his wife to his fellow members at his table. Then he turned to her and courteously and politely asked her to be seated until the rubber was ended. When this had been accomplished he offered his arm to his wife, bowed gravely to the other members and left the club—never to set foot inside the clubhouse again.

Such a club did not give in to the new era without a struggle. All men's clubs have strict rules that the ladies who enjoy signing privileges, and hence may use the club without benefit of male escorts, must be in the immediate families of members. The Union's rules have been perhaps the strictest in this regard—but still not strict enough. The late Union Club wit, Albert Eugene Gallatin, arriving at his club one popular Thursday "maid's night out" and seeing the invasion of a stream of ladies, about some of whom he had doubts, could not resist a sly wink at the ancient doorman. "Do you mean to say," he joshed, "that the Union Club has come to a day when a man can bring his mistress to the club?" Along with the great club revolution, the doorman remembered the great club tradition. "You may, sir," he replied stiffly, "if the lady is the wife of one of the members."

Besides their fall to the feminine invaders, the great men's city clubs have been forced to witness, as insult added to injury, the extraordinary rise of the women's own clubs. In the past century—indeed, right up to the early 1890's—such a movement would have been unthinkable, but by the early part of the Twentieth Century there was a veritable deluge of women's clubs. Generally accorded first honors in what was in those days an extremely controversial field is Philadelphia's Acorn Club, which was founded in 1899 by Julia and Emily Biddle. Not long after came Boston's Chilton Club—which was not, however, founded without difficulty. Actually the club was an outgrowth of the old Mayflower Club, with which the young Boston women were dissatisfied and told Mayflower president Mrs. Barrett Wendell that they "wanted a club like the Acorn where they could play bridge, have cocktails and invite their fathers, husbands and sons." Whereupon one Boston lady, Miss Jane Mottey, it is recorded, rose up in wrath. "To think," she said, "that Boston women wanted a place where they could drink, gamble and have assignations with men!" At this, Florence Hall recalls, "Mrs. Wendell grew furious and told her to be quiet, but for some unknown reason, the then famous Baptist minister at Tremont Temple got hold of the story and preached a Sunday sermon on the wickedness of Boston Society women. Then the women were furious and wanted to sue him for libel, but, when told they would all have to appear in court, they decided instead they would just blackball any Baptist who applied for membership."

Even clubs, it seems, start out as innovations or, in a sense, celebrities, and go on through the process of first Society and then Aristocracy. This process could be seen not only in Boston and Philadelphia but also in Chicago and Denver, both of which soon had their Fortnightly Clubs—Chicago had a Friday Club as well—and all over the country there burgeoned often quaintly named but soon extremely aristocratic clubs which varied from New Orleans' famous Le Petit Salon to the Contentment Club of—where else?—Dedham, Massachusetts. Easily the most prominent, from a national point of view, was the Junior League—indeed, its history embodies, in itself, an era story of far-reaching proportions.

This story began in New York one evening in 1900 when Miss Mary Harriman, daughter of E. H. Harriman, returned from her debutante ball and, before retiring for the night, was moved to tears over the thought that the dozens upon dozens of bouquets that her beaux had given her would soon fade; also she felt that there were too many of them for her to enjoy alone. Still thinking these thoughts the next morning, she summoned her friends and took the flowers to various local hospitals. The girls then agreed to make this a regular practice, and led by Miss Harriman, who later became Mrs. Charles Cary Rumsey, some eighty debutantes were organized, under the title Junior League, into doing regular welfare work for a settlement house. The cult caught hold. "They were smart," says Countess Széchenyi, the former Gladys Vanderbilt, using the word in its social sense, "and they made it smart." In 1907 Boston debutantes copied the New Yorkers and in 1910 both Brooklyn and Portland, Oregon, started Leagues.*

In its early day the Junior League's idea of charity was often curious. A graduate of the Scranton, Pennsylvania, League recalls that her first job on transferring to a New England League consisted of going to the local museum, cutting pictures out of the *National Geographic* magazine and putting them into tin cake boxes marked with the names of various continents. No one ever told her why she was doing it. An inmate of an Ohio League remembers being assigned the task of finding the fathers of illegitimate children abandoned in a certain area. "I found only one," she declares, "and there was so much trouble about him that I was sorry I did."

Even more ludicrous, perhaps, were the League's provisional

---

* The idea of a Junior League in such a naturally democratic place as Brooklyn, third oldest though it is, has never been accepted in some quarters of the hierarchy. Some years ago the president of the Brooklyn League admitted to this writer that Flatbush debutantes have through the years grown extremely tired of the "So you're from that place!" approach at national conferences. "I don't know whether I should be telling you this," she whispered darkly, "but our girls get so self-conscious when they have to stand up and speak that we've decided to do something about it. I know other Leagues generally send their best welfare workers to those conferences, but lately we've been sending the best-looking girls we have. You ought to have seen one we sent to the last conference. She was a knockout!"

training courses which were supposed to give the young ladies some idea of social service. Never very intellectually taxing, they reached rock bottom when a unit of the New York League offered a curriculum consisting of ten lectures on Robert's Rules of Order, a field trip to a biscuit factory, and an examination which asked for an essay on the question: "What would you do if your unmarried maid suddenly told you she was pregnant?"

If in the 1920's the Junior League had reached the rock-bottom low charitably it also reached in the 1920's its all-time high socially. The peak was reached symbolically on May 8, 1929, when the first bit of mortar of the Manhattan clubhouse was laid with a silver trowel by the New York League president, Mrs. B. Tappen Fairchild; the edifice, which cost $1,200,000 to build, included half a hundred offices and bedrooms, a swimming pool and two squash courts, a hairdressing salon and a formal ballroom, a snack bar, and a cocktail bar, two dining rooms and a theatre-ticket agency. In dedicating the building Mrs. Fairchild compared the Junior League with the ancient order of the *schola*. This she defined as being made up of members of the leisure class who were responsible for the artistic and intellectual glories of their people. "Someone—father, mother, husband—" she said, "has provided us with our homes, our clothes, our education, and has released us from the necessity of doing those things for ourselves. We in our turn have the privilege of making a business of leisure, and in this leisure applying ourselves to the study of the needs of our community and of fitting ourselves to carry forward the future of all that is essential in the civic and economic advancement of our country and our generation."

Fired with these words, the New York League installed on the seventh floor of their building a beautifully glassed-in baby shelter in which the members intended to take care of poor children whose parents were ill or otherwise unable to attend them. Somewhere in the shuffle from squash court to swimming pool to theatre-ticket agency, however, the idea of taking care of the babies got lost. For years the cream of crop after crop of New York debutantes paid annual dues of $120, got their permanents, had their manicures—and bravely fought the depression by holding a Jubilee Ball, which was described by one columnist as the most refined riot of the 1930's— but their charitable endeavors were severely handicapped by their surroundings. Furthermore, since the New York League was by far the largest and by that time the parent of well over a hundred other Junior Leagues, the unhappy situation affected the entire organization.

After World War II, however, some 47,000 Junior Leaguers— age 18 to 39—engaged in what their officers called a period of soul-searching. In short order, at a famous meeting of the New York Junior League, under the leadership of Mrs. William S. Kilborne, it was decided to sell the New York clubhouse to the Catholic Archdiocese, which had offered $600,000 for it, and to move to smaller quarters. After that, from Seattle to Stamford, Connecticut, city editors of newspapers were visited by League publicity chairmen who first disarmed them with quotations from a League public relations pamphlet entitled "How to Get Off the Society Page" and then asked that stories of their baby clinic and volunteer bureaus, etc. be put in the general news columns and not on the social page.

The campaign continued with an effort to prove to the newspapers that the Junior League was not entirely composed of members like Mrs. John Jacob Astor in the New York League, Mrs. Pierre du Pont in the Wilmington League, and Mrs. Henry Ford in the Detroit League. The Junior League admitted that it had these ladies but also wanted the public to know that it had 46,997 other members too— as well as two presidents named Jones. Coupled with this went a new attitude toward all the various charitable endeavors—including the removing of girls who did not work—and a total de-emphasis of Society per se. How successful this movement has been varies, of course, from city to city, but in the 1950's it was notable that the New York Junior League's most prominent social event, its Mardi Gras Ball, not only chose as Queen its hardest worker rather than its outstanding socialite but also acquired its large television audience far less through its so-called "Society" than through its ability to entice into its orbit such celebrities as Raymond Massey, Henry

Fonda, Suzy Parker, Jinx Falkenburg, etc. This, along with the remarkable state of undress of some of the Junior League models, was far more conducive to a large audience than any aura still remaining from its once-formidable social reputation. In a word, the Junior League would seem to have been able to get "off the Society pages" all right—and onto the TV screen.

Hard on the heels of the Junior League came another Harriman-founded New York woman's club which was to receive much national prominence. This was New York's Colony Club, which was founded in 1903 by Mrs. J. Borden Harriman along with Mrs. Richard Irvin, Mrs. John Jacob Astor III and Mrs. W. S. Rainsford. Curiously enough, considering the later character of the club, the early Colony had many women who were coming to the fore in the arts and other vocations, such as Ethel Barrymore, Maude Adams, Elisabeth Marbury and Lady Mendl, the last-named being the decorator of the club. All of them were forced to take many slings and arrows about their adventurousness; as far off as Germany, a paper agonized for two columns over the club as "the swan-song of the American home and family" and prophesied for the nation at large "everlasting perdition." And Grover Cleveland himself spoke out in 1905, obviously in reference to the Colony, saying of woman in general, "Her best and safest club is her home."

Nearer to her own home, Mrs. Harriman's husband was doubtful. "Daisy," he told her, "I don't think you can make it pay." And over at the Princeton Club plans for a new clubhouse were put in abeyance on the theory that the Colony would soon fail and be for sale at a bargain price. But such was not to be the case. "Anne Morgan sent word that she was keen," recalls Mrs. Harriman, "especially if we included a running track in our plans," and soon there came that memorable night when "that valiant spirit Mrs. Perkins," who was "herself the mother of club presidents" (having several sons as heads of men's clubs), sailed into the Colony Club dining room. "I've waited for this evening all my life," she said. "I've just telephoned the boys, 'Don't wait dinner. I'm dining at my club.'"

Old-time Colonyites particularly enjoy chuckling over the early

fear of the men—a curious example of the day's double standard—
that their club would be nothing but a rendezvous for clandestine
letters. "They were jolly well right," the late Margaret Emerson
recalled. "Anyway, I know that's where I got mine." And again the
club wheel turned full cycle when the Colony boasted, within its
own membership, the so-called Sabbatical Club. Founded by the
irrepressible Ethel Barrymore, it was originally composed of just
seven ladies; seven times a year they met seven men—not their
husbands—for dinner at seven o'clock. Not until eleven o'clock were
their husbands allowed to call for them.

One of the most extraordinary success stories in club history has
been New York's Cosmopolitan Club. The founders—among them
Mrs. Ellwood Hendrick, Mrs. V. Everett Macy, Mrs. John Sherman
and Mrs. John D. Rockefeller, Jr.—started the club in 1911 as a
club for governesses. In those days governesses had no sitting rooms
—or, as a rule, even bedrooms—but slept in the same room as the
children, and the ladies were, in Mrs. Hendrick's words, "resolved
to improve their lot." Soon, however, the governesses fell by the
wayside and the ladies of the house took over, having an extremely
good time with their so-called "revels," at which no men were
allowed. The most memorable of these was a Persian fete at which
the members, dressed as astrologers, snake dancers, and Arabian
Nights characters, had such a grand time that the next morning they
woke up not only with hangovers but also with a high reputation
for being an amusing and desirable group. Dutch, Roman and other
"revels" followed, from which the club graduated first into a club
for those "engaged in or interested in the liberal arts or professions"
and later to include, along with members like Helen Keller, Anne
Morrow Lindbergh, Mrs. Richard Rodgers and Emily Kimbrough,
a large membership category which became the "attractive generals."
In recent years, to the misfortune of a large waiting list, this latter
has been so loosely applied that it has been filled to overflowing.*

* At the Colony no one, including a severe board of male advisors, has ever
been quite sure just what the qualifications for membership are; all agree,
however, that in addition to the usual proposing and seconding letters there is
a final so-called "Inquisition." This consists of the chairman of the Board of

If the whole club situation looks dark from the point of view of men clubbers, they can at least take heart, if not from the Cosmopolitan, from some recent goings on at the Colony. In the opinion of old-timers the club, like Society itself, is far from what it used to be. "They've spoiled it completely," says founder Mrs. Harriman, while Miss Jessie Fanshawe, New York's premier social secretary, seconds the motion. "Frankly it's stuffy," she says. "I've resigned twice." For some years the club had been rocked with dissension over how to overcome this stuffiness—one not entirely satisfactory suggestion was that a copy of the *Social Register*, which has for many years been chained to a table in the main room, be unchained. Also, whereas a few years ago, in order to find the men's coat room a male guest needed written directions, a compass and preferably a sandwich, the Colony is now, according to Mrs. Joseph H. Choate, Jr., "just letting men absolutely *everywhere*." Meanwhile, there have been other difficulties. Some years ago a member had to be suspended for drinking, and in 1954 the entire club was in a virtual state of siege because another member became so enamored of the place that she insisted on spending the night in the lounge. Then, too, the advanced-age bracket of the club membership has always presented something of a problem—as witness the advice given to Mrs. Thomas K. Finletter, wife of the Secretary for Air, who, about to deliver a talk to the club, had asked how long she should go on. "Talk," she was told sternly, "until you hear the canes rattle."

In recent years the ancient and honorable Colonyites have seemed to take out some of their own difficulties by carrying on a cold war with the up-and-coming Cosmopolitan—a curious state of affairs since quite a number of ladies belong to both clubs, the latter being called "ambi-clubsters" and including, among others, Mrs. John

---

Admissions and three lorgnette-type assistants. Candidates, facing this group, are never permitted to talk about the subject at hand but spend half an hour discussing the servant problem and kindred matters. Afterwards, if she passes, the candidate receives a handsome letter telling her so, together with a bill for initiation fee and a bill for a year's dues. If the candidate fails, she doesn't hear anything until she hears of someone who received such a letter who she knows faced the inquisition after she did. Then she knows she was blackballed.

Foster Dulles. Colonyite Miss Katharine Beach, for example, cannot forgive the fact that Cosmopolitanites insist on calling their club the "Cos." "Whoever heard," she asked sharply, "of a Harvard man saying he was going over to the Har?" The Cosmopolitans, for their part, return this scorn with interest. "Ha," says Miss Helen Howe. "They can't even say they are going over to the Colony. Nowadays everybody thinks they mean the Colony Restaurant."

Many male club philosophers believe that this sort of defection will ultimately result in the same kind of revolution that has overtaken their clubs. Whether or not this is true, there have already been unmistakable signs of change in the whole idea of both men's and women's clubs. One of these changes is in the matter of publicity. For, while clubs like New York's Union League have long been proud of their four prohibitions—"no women, no dogs, no Democrats, no reporters"—the fact remains that in their great days the clubs may not have had much publicity from the inside, but from the outside the publicity was the same as made Society in the first place. In this connection it is worthy of note not only that James Gordon Bennett was asked to be a founding member of the Union Club, but also that William Randolph Hearst, Sr., was a member all his life. It is true that there were occasional movements to have him expelled but nothing was ever done about it because of the Loubat case and also because, says one old-timer, "He never came around." In the 1860's Manton Marble, editor of the New York *World*, a popular man among the club members, was blackballed for no reason, apparently, except that he was a journalist, whereupon the man proposing him became so irritated that he announced he would blackball every candidate that came up until Marble was elected. After some months of seeing that the man meant what he said, the Union Club revoted on Marble and took him in. Today, in contrast, a man like Henry Luce is *persona grata* not only in the Union but in a variety of other clubs as well.

Judging by at least two actors, Robert Montgomery and Fred Astaire, it is apparent that actors too, long regarded socially as something out of the zoo, have come of club age. Montgomery joined not only the Racquet Club, but the Brook and Links as well, while Fred Astaire went a step further and in his movie *The Bandwagon* wore, as a private joke, his blue, green and yellow hatband of the Brook Club. Generally speaking, however, this country's major clubs, which might have been expected to provide leadership in the direction of a genuine Aristocracy, have instead proved that they have little conception of even the basic rudiments of the American social process. One reason for this is a simple one. The kind of men— and women—who would have some concept of the larger picture are much too busy to spend their time on club membership committees; indeed, even club presidents are usually second-generation, just-made-it types, whose own social security is more often than not on as narrow a base as their social outlook. The net result has been that never have clubs, as clubs, seemed more forbidding than to the younger generation of the 1960's.

The matter of the blanket anti-Semitism prevailing in so many clubs is an excellent example of this inhibition—the *cause célèbre* here being undoubtedly Eleanor Roosevelt's resignation from the Colony Club over the blackballing of Mrs. Henry Morgenthau. Unhappily few Christians seem to have the slightest conception, recognition or even curiosity about the Jewish Aristocracy, which is as firmly founded as the Christian and probably more forward-looking. The Harmonie Club, for example, of which the spelling alone indicates the German-Jewish Aristocracy, was not only the fourth oldest of all social clubs—founded in 1852, it was preceded only by the Union, the New York Yacht Club, and the Century—it was also the first club to admit ladies.

On the hopeful side, it is significant that New York's most successful social clubs of the 1960's—the Century, the Cosmopolitan, the River, and the Regency, as well as the socio-theatrical and literary clubs like the Lotos, the Players and the Coffee House—all have Jewish members. So, too, do the extraordinarily successful college clubs. Membership in these latter does not merely require previous attendance at a college, it also requires being proposed, seconded and voted on as in any other social club. Once minor-league citadels of sentimental snobbery, they have become easily the most desirable from the utilitarian point of view of all city clubs. The Yale Club, located across from Grand Central, is such a beehive that it is sometimes difficult to tell where the station leaves off and the club begins, and the Harvard Club's membership in 1960 exceeded seven thousand. All in all, lawyer John Reynolds, who resigned from the Union Club after World War II after twenty-two years of membership, has ever since belonged to just two clubs—the Century and the Harvard. "I want a club," he says, "where I can take a couple of friends without producing a birth certificate, a marriage license and a blood test."

Clubs being what they are, it is not likely that lawyer Reynolds will get his wish in all directions overnight, but it is perhaps significant that among his remaining clubs is the Harvard, which in 1958 without any fuss or fanfare elected a Negro member. So too, in 1959, did the Cosmopolitan Club. Their new member was Marian Anderson; the Harvard Club's was not even a celebrity. Obviously the time will come when many clubs will have many Negro members, and when that happens, in the vanguard, of course, will be not the Society clubs but the Aristocratic ones.*

If clubs have often been tried and found wanting in America's age-old quest for social security, even more perilous has been the search via titles. But, as we have seen, Americans have since the days of George Washington dearly loved titles. Omaha's Ak-Sar-Ben Ball is probably the most curious example of this. This ceremony, of which the name is Nebraska spelled backwards, is one in which, each October since 1896, Omaha's leading citizens have dressed themselves elaborately as princes and princesses, counts and countesses, and have gone to a ballroom to await the emergence, from behind golden curtains, of their new Queen. Their new King is invariably

---

* In this connection it is noteworthy that the most aristocratic of this country's private schools, Groton, was the first of the Eastern "St. Grottle-sexers" group to admit Negroes. Although many other private boys' schools, as well as girls' schools, have followed their example, by 1960 there were three Negroes in Groton and one already had graduated.

a substantial middle-aged citizen and together the pair become monarchs of the Graustarkian Kingdom of Quivera. In recent years as many as fifteen thousand people from all over the West have crowded in to see this ball.

More famous than Ak-Sar-Ben is the Veiled Prophet's Ball held in St. Louis every October since 1878. Here the Queen is not known to anyone except herself beforehand, and the Veiled Prophet's identity is not revealed even afterwards. Despite the public nature of the spectacle itself, the high point of the St. Louis social season comes the night before the parade, at the Kiel Auditorium, where the ever-secret Veiled Prophet holds his "Court of Love and Beauty." Queens must agree not to become engaged or married for a year and when, some years ago, one queen was discovered to be not only married but also pregnant, it was one of the greatest *cause célèbres* in St. Louis history. Nothing like it, however, has ever happened since, and the Veiled Prophet Ball is easily *the* event of the entire West.

Most famous of all the mass titular functions is, of course, New Orleans' famed Mardi Gras, which boasts the venerable date of 1699. In America's own Paris, the city which boasted the first apartment building, the first cocktail, and the first use of the word "Dixie," there is no question but that the combination of clubs and titles has always here reached its highest peak. Here too the keys to the oft-confusing riddles of the carnival are to be found in the men's clubs—for the "Krewe" Proteus, for example, overlaps with the membership of the Pickwick Club, Comus with the Boston Club, Momus with the Louisiana Club, and Mithras with the Stratford Club. Rex, the King of the Carnival, has for many years been a member of the Boston Club, which is perhaps New Orleans' most severe organization and derives its name not from the city but from the old card game. Rex himself was invented to celebrate the visit to New Orleans during the Mardi Gras of 1872 of His Imperial Highness, Alexis Alexandrovitch Romanov, brother of the heir to the Russian throne, who was at that time in pursuit of a musical comedy actress, Lydia Thompson; the song she sang in her musical comedy *Bluebeard* has become the Mardi Gras theme song:

If I ever cease to love
May the Grand Duke Alexis
Ride a Buffalo to Texas.
If I ever cease to love.

Unfortunately, Alexis' visit was not an unqualified success. He refused several prominent invitations and even transferred his affection from Lydia Thompson to another showgirl, but the final straw was that he refused to sit on the throne that New Orleanians had built especially for him. "But I thought," he said gently, "that this was a democratic country."

Mardi Gras balls vary in "exclusiveness," but in high favor in recent years have been the Ball of the Twelfth Night Revelers and that of the Atlanteans—indeed, the latter will not include in their court any girl who has been a member of any previous court. But no matter how seriously New Orleanians take their Mardi Gras— and this can hardly be exaggerated—they can sometimes be brought up short. There is, for example, the story of the aristocratic Creole lady who spent the better part of her day properly masking and costuming her three daughters and then turned at last to prepare her small son also. "But, Mother," he protested, "I don't want any mask or costume. I want to be just a plain American boy."

Mere "pretend" kings and queens are only a small part of the long procession of American girls who through the years have, aided and abetted by regally inclined mothers, entered into the ranks of the nobility by marriage. By 1900 one social historian estimated that no less than 500 of America's "400" have married foreign titles— which is certainly a fair percentage. But what might be called America's golden fleecing, when this country Marshall-planned her debutantes and England and various other countries put up their dukes, did not proceed without protest. Charles Dana Gibson, in cartoon after cartoon, savagely attacked the girl—and the mother of the girl—who married for title only. And in the *Anglomaniacs,* a novel by Mrs. Burton Harrison published in the 1890's, the father of a title-prone wife and debutante daughter finally exploded. "What man," he said, "wants to work his head off to lay up money and then see a fool and a profligate walk away with it and his daughter into the bargain, so that his grandchildren may have handles to their name and learn to despise America?" And at the same time the elder Henry Cabot Lodge sternly observed that the fathers were just as guilty as the social-climbing mothers. "Every pork-baron," he wrote, "will buy a European title because he comprehends that the title has a value as a trade-mark, and a trade-mark he understands."

Perhaps the most thorough research on the foreign-title craze was done some years ago by a distinguished professor of English history who made a canvass of England, county by county; there was scarcely a village or small community in which the vicar or the landlord did not remark to him, "There's a countrywoman of yours living hereabouts, the American wife of ———— who years ago brought him the money to mend his house." And, recorded the professor, if it was the landlord speaking, he would often add in a burst of confidence, "And they do say, sir, that she's had a bit of a hard life of it too." And, as recently as 1959, Lady Elizabeth Kinnaird, who signs her books Elizabeth Eliot, wrote a book entitled *Heiresses and Coronets*, in which the jacket featured a kind of titular tote-board, as follows:

AMERICAN HEIRESS	HER FORTUNE	MAN SHE MARRIED	HOW HE TREATED HER
Anna Gould	$15,000,000	Count Boni de Castellane	Spent her money on other women, abused and struck her.
Consuelo Vanderbilt	$15,000,000	Duke of Marlborough	Squandered her money.
Alice Heine	$10,000,000	Prince of Monaco	Excluded her from State Ceremonies.
Helen Morton	$ 6,000,000	Duc de Valeccay	Insulted her immediately after wedding, deserted her.
Alice Thaw	$ 5,000,000	Earl of Yarmouth	Extorted money from her at wedding, deserted her.

Ella Haggin	$ 5,000,000	Count Festeils De Toina	Took her among cannibals, left her with them.
Lilian May	$ 1,000,000	Lord Bagot	Stopped her from taking her child to church.
May Brady Stevens	$ 500,000	Major Hall	Did crochet work about the house.
May Travers	unknown	Lord Wentworth	Brought prize fighters home to dinner.

The title craze properly began in a city which was later to become world-renowned for it—Baltimore. Here in 1785 was born perhaps the most famous of all Baltimore belles, Betsy Patterson, who had long dark hair, hazel eyes, a soft skin and a pretty figure, and whose Irish immigrant father was, as of 1800, the second richest man in Baltimore. In 1803, when Betsy was 18, she was introduced at a party given in Baltimore to Jerome Bonaparte, the darkly handsome younger brother of Napoleon, who was on a tour of America. Within weeks the couple were married. Among Betsy's charms was her penchant for wearing an absolute minimum of clothing. One guest at her wedding declared that the bride's dress was so scanty that he could have put the whole thing in his wife's pocketbook. And when Betsy later descended on Washington several ladies there sent word that if she wished to meet them she must promise to have more clothes on. Unhappily, Napoleon took a similarly dark view of his brother's bride. He forced Jerome to desert his wife and, by that time, an infant son as well—and to make up for her he gave his brother the Kingdom of Westphalia and a bride, the daughter of the King of Württemberg.

Betsy was never allowed into France—in some ways the parallel with the Wallis Warfield story is extraordinary—but was given a handsome annuity by Napoleon and spent most the rest of her life wandering around Europe. When Napoleon died, Francis Beirne recalls, she made a point of praising Napoleon's genius despite the fact that "He hurled me back on what I hated most on earth, my Baltimore obscurity." In 1840, at the age of 55, she returned from Europe to live in a boardinghouse on Cathedral Street. Here she lived, poor and relatively friendless, until 1879 when, at the age of 94, she died. Shortly before her death, however, she confided her secret: "My ruling passions have been love, ambition, avarice. Love has fled, ambition has brought disappointment, but avarice remains."

The second outstanding title match of the Nineteenth Century was a happy one—that between Brooklyn-born Jennie Jerome and Lord Randolph Churchill, son of the Seventh Duke of Marlborough. This marriage, which took place in 1875, was remarkable on a number of counts. For one thing, Miss Jerome's husband was rich, handsome, and a remarkable man in every way. For another, the bride and groom violated all the ground rules for an "advantageous marriage" by loving each other to distraction. And, perhaps most remarkable of all, the match produced the outstanding figure in world history of the first half of the Twentieth Century—none other than Winston Churchill. Jennie's father, Leonard Jerome, was a lawyer, sportsman and diplomat, who shortly after Jennie's birth became the American Consul at Trieste. In 1873, while the Jeromes were vacationing in Cowes, a seaside English town, Jennie and Randolph met at a ball and danced the quadrille. Randolph, it is recorded, had "never been in love before and the force and volume of the tide swept him altogether off his feet." Although both sets of parents, in contrast to most transatlantic unions, objected bitterly to the match, their resistance was eventually overcome and the couple lived happily at Lord Randolph's magnificent ancestral "Blenheim." Lord Randolph became a Member of Parliament and died in 1895. The incredible Jennie, in 1900, married George Cornwallis West, who was the same age as her son, Winston. The couple were deeply happy for many years but Jennie, still unpredictable, divorced him in 1914.

One other happy story also warrants inclusion—the marriage of Mary Leiter, daughter of Levi Leiter, to George (later Lord) Curzon, who became Viceroy of India. A strikingly beautiful girl from Chicago—or Washington, D.C., as her family preferred to think of it—she entered the title-marrying game with her eyes wide open. She believed that as the wife of some genial nonentity she would lack the leverage necessary to make her money do a maximum of good in the world; on the other hand, she believed that as the wife of a man of high position she could leave her stamp on the times. And, whether that seemed a rationalization of her real wishes, the fact remains that she did indeed leave her stamp. Meeting Lord Curzon at a London dance in 1890, she set about making herself over into the sort of wife he would need for his career. In a courtship and engagement which lasted five years, rather typical of the times, she had time to master British politics and diplomatic history. By the time of her marriage to Curzon she had become a celebrated hostess. Significantly, the English gentry were more impressed by her person than by her fortune, and the marriage, which had in its origin certain cold and mechanical overtones, blossomed into a tender, passionate relationship. Curzon eventually became Viceroy of India and, as his Vicereine, Mary proved the most popular in history. Madame Jacques Balsan, herself, has written a memorable tribute to the lady who was in many ways America's most remarkable export:

> Mary Leiter was a compatriot of mine, and a dazzling beauty. I thought that she had shed her American characteristics more completely than I was to find myself able to do. Wholly absorbed in her husband's career, she had subordinated her personality to his to a degree I would have considered beyond an American woman's power of self-abnegation. I was moved by the great love they bore each other. Her admiration for her brilliant husband's conspicuous attainments, her strong partisanship, her sympathetic understanding of his faults, the humour with which she accepted the secondary role he assigned her, even in the domestic duties usually delegated to women, were altogether admirable.

Madame Balsan herself, as Consuelo Vanderbilt, was the leading figure in what still ranks as the most controversial title match in social history. At the age of 17, willowy and languishingly beautiful, she had fallen in love with the 30-year-old New York bachelor, Winthrop Rutherfurd, but her mother, Mrs. O. H. P. Belmont, the most domineering mother in the annals of the "Four Hundred," literally tore her daughter away from Rutherfurd. "She made me leave the country," her daughter testified before the Rota in 1926. "She intercepted all letters my sweetheart wrote and all of mine to him. She caused continuous scenes. She said I must obey. She said I knew very well I had no right to choose a husband, that I must take the man she had chosen."

The man her mother had chosen was none other than a ridiculous, haughty 24-year-old renegade who went by the name of the Ninth Duke of Marlborough. An official document dated on the couple's wedding day gave Marlborough $2,500,000 in stock of the Beech Creek Railway Company on which an annual payment of 4 per cent was guaranteed by the New York Central. Also on the wedding day Mrs. Belmont had a guard stationed outside her daughter's room and forbade anyone to speak to her or even to approach her. All in all, the marriage cost the Vanderbilt family over $10,000,000. In 1908, after she had borne him two children, Consuelo separated from her husband; the marriage was not annulled by the Rota, however, until 1926. Perhaps the most incredible thing about the whole affair was the fact that in the end Consuelo was reconciled with her mother.

New York and Chicago were not the only fertile fields for the title-fortune hunters. In Detroit half a hundred daughters of prominent families joined the trend, among them Clara Ward, daughter of the Eber Wards, who married Prince Chmay of Belgium, and was hailed as the most beautiful woman on the Continent. The Kaiser is said to have forbidden her picture to be displayed in Germany because her beauty was thought to be so disturbing. In San Francisco two daughters of Mrs. Abby Parrott married titles but almost alone of all the thousands who did so, they did not use their titles and insisted on being called simply "Madame." And in 1896, at the height of the hysteria, came a notable event in Newport—the marriage of Gertrude Vanderbilt to no title at all, but to Harry Payne Whitney. So remarkable was this that on the bridal morning at Newport's "Breakers" an orchestra leader by the name of Nathan Franco played not only the expected compositions by Wagner and Mendelssohn but also, in a burst of enthusiasm, struck up "The Star-Spangled Banner."

Asked about this, Franco was firm. "It is so rare," he said, "that an American girl marries one of her own countrymen that I thought the selection was decidedly in keeping with the occasion."

In 1936 came that most extraordinary of all title marriages, that of Wallis Warfield and the Duke of Windsor. This story, like our first title match, that of Betsy Patterson and Jerome Bonaparte, goes back to Baltimore. Wallis, or Bessie Wallis as she was christened, was born at the Baltimore summer resort of Blue Ridge Summit, Pennsylvania, on June 19, 1896. According to an elderly Baltimorean who knew her well, the first words of the future wife of the King of England were not "Ma-Ma"; they were "Me-Me." The same lady also distinctly recalls that, whereas other children were playing with dolls of more humble means, Wallis' first two dolls were named Mrs. Astor and Mrs. Vanderbilt. It is an American Society truism that the poor child of a poor family, one who is brought up by a mother constantly cooking goodies in the kitchen and generally satisfying her offspring's every last wish, is often far more spoiled than a child with the most luxurious upbringing, who is taught to toe the mark by stern governesses, tutors, etc. Wallis was no exception to this. Her father died when she was six months old and she was brought up by an attractive, witty mother, who was warm and loving and extremely interested in men—in fact, she rapidly married twice more. In between her marriages, businesses and other affairs, in the opinion of people who best knew the situation, the young mother obviously overcompensated when it came to her only child.

In fairness it should be said that Wallis was not from the wrong side of the tracks. Neither was she from the right side. Her mother's family, the Montagues, were of an old but unimpressive Virginia clan. Her father's family, the Warfields, had a certain amount of rather Yankee prominence in Maryland, having made their money after the unpleasantness of the 1860's. But Wallis' own father was on the wrong side of this; his job at the time of his death was that of a simple clerk. It is clear that for some years after his death Wallis' mother did take in boarders, and it is typical of Wallis that she not only is not proud of the fact—as someone from a more secure Southern Family would have been—but is actually ashamed of it and categorically denies it. However, such denials are meaningless—and on no less authority than Wallis' first camp mistress, Miss Charlotte Noland. "I have never known anyone," says Miss Noland, of Wallis, "who could so consistently for so many years so successfully evade the truth."

Carter Osburn, Wallis' first beau in Baltimore, frankly remembers both good and bad about her. On the one hand, she was fun to take out because she "matured early"; on the other hand, she was regarded by the boys as both a flirt and extremely expensive. When one boy wished to take her out, she made him take her in his father's car, then to the theatre and afterwards not for an ice-cream soda, which was what he had planned, but for a drink in the Baltimore Hotel dining room. Furthermore, once there, Wallis first looked around the room to see what drink was "fashionable" and then ordered that for both of them. She didn't touch hers and, when the waiter came, the boy did not have enough money to pay and suffered the embarrasment of being told it would be billed to his family. He never took Wallis out again.

Only one person, Baltimoreans agree, really stymied Wallis—her uncle, "Sol" Warfield, who controlled the family purse strings. From Wallis' personal point of view he was obviously a stern and rather difficult old bachelor; on Sol's side, Wallis equally obviously gave him a good many reasons to be stern. From the beginning Wallis was ambitious and wanted perhaps as much as anything in her early life to have a large coming-out party. Unfortunately, years of angling for this via Uncle Sol fell through when, because of World War I, he decided to call it off. From that time on Wallis was bitter about him and he, in turn, disliked her so much that in the end he left her out of his will.

Wallis always, Baltimoreans remember, fought to be "first." She was the first girl of her coming-out year to announce her engagement—about which she was inordinately proud. His name was Lieutenant Earl Winfield Spencer, Jr., and he was an aviator, which made him the personification of glamour and the "catch" of Wallis' set. But when Wallis went to meet his family and found he lived in Highland Park, Chicago, rather than Lake Forest, she was less pleased.

Not long after they were married Spencer was transferred to San Diego. Here, recalls Mrs. Emory Sands, Wallis rapidly expanded her social contacts at the expense of her husband—who, in Mrs. Sands' firm opinion, took to drink, not for the reasons Wallis has always said he did, but simply because of the exasperations occasioned by her flirtations with other men. Back home, separated from Spencer, Wallis spent some time in Washington, D.C., where she had what most people who know her believe to be the one genuine love affair of her life—with a South American diplomat—and, to Wallis' credit, the breakup of this affair seemed to have been one thing in her life which moved her very deeply.

After this came a trip to China and a reunion with her old friend, the late Herman Rogers, who in abdication days took her into his villa at Cannes and played such a large part in her life up to that time. The Wallis Windsor of the Café Court was something that the gentle aristocratic Rogers could never understand, however, and in his last years he did not see her at all. "In the old days," Rogers said, "she could be fun, but she was always the most selfish woman I've ever known in my life. There is one of her in every grade, in every school, in every country in the world—the kind who learns about the 'important people,' the people to play up to sooner than the others, and who always pleases the grownups but the children know her for what she is. Even men she didn't want, she didn't want anyone else to have either."

Still not divorced although she had been separated from Spencer for years, Wallis finally came home and got her decree. While visiting her friend Mary Kirk Raffray in New York she met Ernest Simpson and his wife. Simpson, who was half English, spent half his life in London and half in New York. According to Wallis, at the time she came into the picture the Simpsons were having marital difficulties. According to the first Mrs. Simpson, a gentle white-haired lady of the New England Parsons family, whose whole life, she says, was "ruined" by Wallis, this is a total falsehood. "From the moment I met her," she says, "I never liked her at all. I've never been around anybody like that. I've never seen anything like the cold, decayed Society around her. She moved in and helped herself to my house and my clothes and, finally, everything."

As for Mr. Simpson, in an interview with this writer in 1956, he said: "Wallis never had dignity nor proportion. She never could take even minor criticism. She needed a strong man with judgment. If she was hurt she would fly into a tantrum. She was wild when she was angry and there was no end to her hate or temper. I think the Duke has always been mortally afraid of her."

The career of the Duchess in England, or Wallis in Wonderland, is perhaps most memorably recalled in the diary of a prominent American lady who married a distinguished British title. Unique and uninhibited, she kept a diary throughout most of the abdication period, and in her characteristic manner wrote without fear, favor or hope of future reward:

JUNE 5TH, 1935
Dining at Chips & Honor's was fun—everyone in tiaras and on to the Derby Ball charity—It is Sheila Milbank's last "go" as chairman—she had been at it for 7 years—The Prince of Wales let her down by not attending as usual, and sent her 100 pounds for charity instead. Guess he was busy with his new "bit" Mrs. Simpson—it's all so funny as she was Thelma's best girl friend, and now she steals the Prince away from Thelma—Mrs. S. is a very déclassé American married to a fourth rate Englishman—the Prince is sinking lower and lower in his taste in women.

JUNE 8TH
At Portia's for weekend at Holwood—Prince George, Marina, Sheila Milbank and Seymour Berry make up our party. Prince George seems very restless—she is most attractive and sweet (with child). They simply loathe the Prince of Wales' attitude, the world in general and his "pushing" Mrs. Simpson about. . . . It was a pleasant weekend and I enjoyed the arguments. Wales refused point blank to go to the Court Balls unless Mrs. Simpson was given an invitation. That did make London's older crowd indignant. Wales made a statement several years ago that he hated and was

bored by the English nobility—& he certainly shows it—by cutting most of his old friends & "hanging out" with whatever friends happen to be his mistress's at the time.

MAR. 22ND, 1936

Lunch with Gordie Sutherland at Sutton—the Goldwyns & the newly married Douglas Fairbanks' also with us—Sylvia is a bit conscious of her triumph at landing "Doug." London is seething with gossip about the new King and his blatant exploiting of his Mistress Mrs. Ernest Simpson & her 8th rate husband always in tow.

Everyone seems to have a new disease "Simpsonitis" & "sucking up" to dear Wally is the thing to do. Emerald Cunard heads the list as the biggest horse's ass, then Duff Cooper—it really strikes me as being ludicrous, all this toadying it is all so temporary, one never knows when Mrs. S. will be "out" & some new horror "in"—the King is selfish & slip-shod in his very responsible position as the only important ruler of our times—& refuses to marry & seems to enjoy his influx of 3rd rate Americans & companions— as an American I resent the old traditions being done away with, & in their place, this cheap & undignified display of modern ruling. Most of the old retainers are being "sacked"—& a whole new régime in hand. A very rowdy weekend was held recently at Himly Hall, Lord Dudley's place, & the chosen consisted of Eric Dudley, Foxie Gwynne (American), Pat Jersey (recently estranged from her husband) & the King & Mrs. Simpson—my authentic reports of this party are terrific—it seems odd that a King could do such a thing—but then, I'm an American & narrow-minded about such things, especially where ruling royalty are concerned.

JULY 18TH

If I ever made a mistake in my life, I did when I said that "Queenie" Simpson would be "out" & a new one in—I'm afraid when a man reaches 42 (as our monarch is) & if he loves a plain woman his own age—it is a thing that will last—(also for the country). Mrs. Simpson is lucky & benefits where all the others have lost—She has over 100,000 pounds worth of jewels from him!! To say nothing of clothes & furs & things she never had before.

OCT. 3RD

Court circular printing Mrs. Simpson sojourn to Balmoral Castle & the King riding 50 miles to meet her—it's really got to be serious —the old greybeards & members of Parliament are in a dither over the approaching worries. Mrs. S. has had her divorce posted—& it was not allowed to be printed, other than a small announcement— she is free (or will be) & rumor has it our dear Monarch wishes to marry her—he has given her Queen Alexandra's jewels & the poor Queen is heart-broken over his many stupidities. The American Press are plastered with "Wally" new Queen of England—of course it couldn't happen—but it really has gone too far.

DEC. 7TH

Imagine Mrs. S. having to leave on short notice, for "parts unknown" but known to everyone—she has wended her way to Cannes midst abuse & sneers. But these "dignified" British papers namely the Rothermere & Beaverbrook press are beyond belief— boosting the King's cause & the . . . Mrs. S. Thank God, for a steady, reliable sensible Prime Minister, Mr. Baldwin—his job is tough—getting abuse from the press & now Winston Churchill has an opening to try & howl him down & poison the King's mind against him. In the meantime the King is at Fort Belvedere drinking like a spoiled boy . . . when so much is at stake.

DEC. 8TH

Every minute counts now—Baldwin motoring down to Fort Belvedere, spending hours with the Royal . . . (pardon my French) Members of the Royal family, visiting him, trying to persuade him to use his mentality—instead of pouting that he wants his "Wally"—it's too much. People, in fact the world is in a frenzy—& he bull-headedly wants to marry that . . . Mrs. S. You wouldn't believe anyone could go quite so mad—if he does abdicate, which is more than possible—well, . . .

DEC. 10TH

He has abdicated!
How nice for Perry Brownlow—having been sent as bodyguard, protector, secretary etc. to Mrs. S. in Cannes—he will be "out," like all the rest of that crew.

DEC. 11TH

Our X-King did his stuff on a radio farewell—I must say it left us all cold—so cheap & would-be-dramatic . . . "The woman I love" business was nauseating . . . (Mrs. S. made him add that) She has been at him on the phone from Cannes—still trying to run him—as she did, & made him the world's biggest goat & failure.
He sailed on a destroyer tonight.

OCT. 20TH, 1937

Eileen Sutherland's memorable ball for the new King & Queen, at which every royal household of every country was represented —a truly brilliant affair. . . . Queen Mary was the belle of the evening—so gracious & gay & remained 'till 2—the new King and Queen have taken a new lease on life—they were radiant with their success and happiness in knowing they are so beloved by all.

The 1930's saw many other title matches besides the Windsor debacle. Two of the most remarkable of these were on the part of one girl, Newport's Louise Van Alen, who in short order married two brother Prince Mdivanis. Although they were perhaps the most blatant heiress-hunters of the modern era, they met, in a sense, their match with Louise, who was second to none as a title-hunter. In 1931 she married Alexis Mdivani, who later, as we have seen, was to marry Barbara Hutton. Divorced from him, she next married his brother, Serge Mdivani. In 1936, within a month of each other, both Mdivanis were killed—Alexis in an automobile crash in Spain and Serge in a fall from a polo pony in a match at Delray Beach, Florida. Louise, at the time married to Serge for less than a month, was watching the game when the accident occurred.

Ranking close behind the Mdivanis was the remarkable career, in Palm Beach and other points social, of Count José Rex Holstein Dorelis, a count from a country (Rumania) which has no counts, but who was able to leave the resort of Palm Beach with two ex-Rumanian countesses. In this era also, even America's two "richest women in the world," the "Beauty Queens" Helena Rubinstein and Elizabeth Arden, both fell under the spell of the great title search. Miss Rubinstein married in 1937 Prince Artchil Gourielli-Tchkonia, while Miss Arden was married and divorced from Prince Michael Evlanoff.

On the international scene, two of the most famous title matches, in their different ways, were those of the late Lady Mendl and the late Lady Cunard. Of these, the career of Lady Mendl was, maritally, perhaps the most extraordinary. America's pioneer interior decorator, Elsie de Wolfe had been in love for many years with a man she had never married; when her lover died she suddenly decided, one day in

1926, to marry Sir Charles Mendl, at that time an attaché of the British Embassy in Paris. It was never a love match, and Lady Mendl never pretended that it was. "When one has passed the portals of middle age," she said, "one's greatest necessity is companionship. Charles and I had a deep affection for each other and mutual respect and admiration." In 1935 she wrote, apparently happily:

> The truth is that we are a contented and happy couple, carrying on together in much the same way as we did when we were single. We divide our time between our apartment in town and the Villa Trianon—our weekends are passed at Versailles, and the middle-week in Paris. Neither of us has changed very much, even though the times have changed.

The story of Emerald Cunard was a more typical one. Born Maud Burke in San Francisco, she achieved her social career, like Laura Corrigan, not in her own home town, or even in New York, where she also tried and failed, but in London, where so many Americans have found things, socially, so easy. Soon she was married to a rapidly aging but extremely rich member of Britain's fox-hunting set by the name of Sir Bache Cunard, of steamship fame, and from then until her death in 1948 she was a curiously influential figure. Unlike Lady Mendl, who even at the age of 80 was beautiful, Lady Cunard was never even pretty. Small in size, usually over-rouged and painted, with a large nose and pale yellow hair, she was, at best, extraordinary looking. Nor did she have genuine wit—she was too full of herself and her machinations for that. But she was extremely animated, and her conversation had a kind of non-stop quality which often became, almost despite its speaker, fascinating. Her dissatisfaction with her own name was typical. She had always detested the fact that it was spelled, since childhood, "Maud," without the final "e," and she determined to make up for this by giving herself a new name—one which she cherished—Emerald. A leading figure, as has been noted, in the "Windsor circle" during abdication days, she is perhaps best remembered in inner circles today for the fact that the present Queen Mother is supposed to have said, shortly after she became Queen, that she was afraid she and her husband would never be included in Lady Cunard's set. "You see," she said, "Emerald has so often said that Bertie and I are not fashionable."

In the mid-Twentieth Century, somehow it was extremely fitting, in the general picture of Society, that the crowning climax to the long history of America's title search should be delivered by an American movie star. The marriage of Philadelphia and Hollywood's Grace Kelly to Prince Rainier of Monaco was a landmark event in another way also, for it marked the all-time high in the power, prestige and all-around pushiness of the press.

No fewer than 1,600 reporters from all parts of the world—many more than had covered D-Day in Normandy—covered the marriage of America's "movie princess"; and from the day in the spring of 1956 when Miss Kelly boarded the *Constitution* to sail for Monaco, to the time when a fortnight later she escaped on her honeymoon on the Prince's yacht, she was not only headline news everywhere but was consistently badgered, bullied and inaccurately reported in almost every journal, and on almost every radio and television station, in the world. The license of what Martha Hodge has called the "free dumb press" reached almost unbelievable heights—particularly in the tiny principality of Monaco, where the Monagasque police force, consisting of only a handful of men, was totally unable to handle the ruthless and unfeeling newsmen and photographers. At one time an extremely courteous Monagasque policeman attempted to dissuade two American photographers from driving up to the Prince's palace; politely the policeman explained that the parking space was full there and that, instead, a bus system had been devised to take people up and down. The photographers, furious, simply backed their car off —and when, still polite, the policeman again tried to stop them, they literally ran him down; he was taken to the hospital.

Meanwhile, to all corners of the world sped "shipboard interviews" Miss Kelly had never given, totally fabricated stories of her money and the Prince's poverty, the definite impression that it was no love match—although anyone could see the couple were in love— and, above all, a completely distorted picture of the wedding itself— which was one of the most colorful and fascinating spectacles in modern social history. Just why Miss Kelly—who has since her wedding managed to give the lie to such treatment and has, indeed, become probably the only genuine ornament in America's whole "International Set" abroad—should have been singled out for such a morass of meanness is difficult to understand. It is, nonetheless, explainable. In the first place, she was rich, beautiful, young and, by Hollywood standards, "social"; to add to all this she was marrying a prince—which, to a press that dearly loves breaking down a "build-up," was simply too much to endure. In the second place, and almost equally important, there were no possibilities for individual interviews and preferential treatment for powerful columnists—to which the latter have long been accustomed—and hence they immediately took out their displeasure on the principal parties involved. Third and finally, Mrs. Kelly, the mother of the bride, got the whole thing off to a poor start by several naïve newspaper articles she had signed, which, though well-meaning and written for the benefit of her favorite charity, started with the incredible words, "My husband is a bricklayer and now my daughter is marrying a Prince."*

In view of such distortion, a few facts, not only about Miss Kelly and how she met her Prince Charming—and a charming man he is, to those who know him—might not be amiss. Also included should be the story of Grace's father, an extraordinary man in every way.

As for Grace herself, she grew up a shy girl, outshadowed not only by her father, a dominant mother, a rowing hero brother and two other sisters—one, as she says, the "funniest" and the other the "nicest"—but also by two famous uncles, vaudeville star Walt Kelly and Pulitzer playwright George Kelly. She met her Prince for the

---

* To this writer, on board the *Constitution*, Mrs. Kelly said: "I've never had time for 'Society.' We could have been members of the '400' if we'd wanted to, but we had other things to do. I asked the girls if they wanted to have a party to come out after they got out of school. They told me no, they'd find their own men. I remember Grace telling me most of the debutantes she had met gave her a pain." At the same time, Miss Kelly herself told this writer, "Nothing my mother has ever done embarrassed me so much as those articles. I don't blame the press. I got tired of reading about myself too. But I do blame some of the columnists. There's one whom I won't mention by name who has never, in all the times she has been writing about me, ever written a true word. I really don't know why, either. I've never said two words to her in my life."

first time on a side trip from location in the shooting of *To Catch a Thief*. They both, as she says, "thought nothing about it."

The next Christmas, however, when the Prince was in America, he came to a dinner at the home of the Russell Austins in Margate, New Jersey, close friends of the Kellys'. Grace came to dinner too, and three days later they were unofficially engaged. The official engagement awaited the visit of the Prince's private prelate, Father Tucker, to the home of Mr. Kelly.

John Brendan Kelly, who died in 1960, was one of the most remarkable men in Philadelphia history—and perhaps in the city's history the most personally popular. Although he was from the start extremely successful, he nonetheless had two keen disappointments in his life. The first was when he was disallowed from competing in England's Diamond Sculls on the theory that, as it was said, "A man who had worked with his hands should not compete against gentlemen." This disappointment was compensated by his son's later winning the Diamond Sculls. The second disappointment was not being elected Mayor of Philadelphia in 1935. Bucking the powerful Republican machine, he nonetheless polled the unbelievable total of 330,000 votes; the previous Democratic candidate had polled 31,000 votes.

Such a man was not overawed by Father Tucker's visitation. "I'm not impressed with royalty," Kelly told the prelate firmly, "I'm interested in the man." Satisfied on this score, he wanted to know the Prince's financial situation. Father Tucker began retailing this. "When he got to one million dollars," Kelly said, "I stopped him," but there was still a final question. "I've heard that this fellow," Kelly said, "has a mistress. There'll be none of that, or Grace will quit him."

On his death, Mr. Kelly left perhaps the most remarkable will in Family history. "For years," Kelly said, "I have been reading last wills and testaments, and I have never been able to understand any of them at one reading. Therefore, I will attempt to write my own will with the hope that it will be understandable and legal. Kids will be called 'kids' and not 'issue' and it will not be cluttered up with 'parties of the first part,' 'per stirpes,' 'perpetuities,' 'quasijudicial,' 'to wit,' and a lot of other terms that I am sure are only used to confuse those for whose benefit it was written."

After he had made the usual observation that he was drafting his will in a state of sound mind, he added, "Some lawyers will question this when they read my will; however, I have my opinion of some of them, so that makes it even."

Mr. Kelly cut off Prince Rainier and his other sons-in-law. "I don't want to give the impression that I am against sons-in-law," he wrote. "If they are the right type, they will provide for themselves and their families, and what I am able to give to my daughters will help pay the dress shop bills, which, if they continue as they have started out, under the able tutelage of their mother, will be quite considerable."

After disposing of various other bequests, including a hope that the family would never have to go to court over what he called the "spoils"—"for, to me, the all-time low in family affairs is a court fight"—Kelly proceeded to conclude his will with the same indomitable spirit that made him the remarkable gentleman he was:

> As for me, just shed a respectful tear if you think I merit it, but I am sure that you are all intelligent enough not to weep all over the place. I have watched a few emotional acts at graves, such as trying to jump into it, fainting, etc., but the thoroughbred grieves in the heart.
>
> Not that my passing should occasion any "scenes" for the simple reason that life owes me nothing. I have ranged far and wide, have really run the gamut of life. I have known great sorrow and great joy. I had more than my share of success.
>
> Up to this writing my wife and children have not given me any heartaches, but, on the contrary, have given me much happiness and a pardonable pride, and I want them to know I appreciate that.
>
> I worked hard in my early life, but I was well paid for that effort.
>
> In this document I can only give you things, but if I had the choice to give you worldly goods or character, I would give you character. The reason I say that is, with character, you will get worldly goods, because character is loyalty, honesty, ability, sportsmanship, and, I hope, a sense of humor.
>
> If I don't stop soon this will be as long as *Gone With the Wind.* So just remember, when I shove off for greener pastures or whatever it is on the other side of the curtain, that I do it unafraid, and, if you must know, a little curious.

PART TWO

FAMILY CIRCLE

How shall a man escape from his ancestors, or draw off from his veins the black drop which he drew from his father's or his mother's life? It often appears in a family, as if all the qualities of the progenitors were potted in several jars—some ruling quality in each son or daughter of the house,—and sometimes the unmixed temperament, the rank unmitigated elixir, the family vice, is drawn off in a separate individual, and the others are proportionately relieved.

—Emerson, *Conduct of Life: Fate*

O Damsel Dorothy! Dorothy Q!
Strange is the gift that I owe to you;—
What if, a hundred years ago,
Those close-shut lips had answered No,
When forth the tremulous question came
That cost the maiden her Norman name,
And under the folds that look so still
The bodice swelled with the bosom's thrill
Should I be I, or would it be
One-tenth another, to nine-tenths me?

—O. W. Holmes, *Dorothy Q*

i have often noticed that
ancestors never boast
of the descendants who boast
of ancestors i would
rather start a family
than finish one blood will tell but often
it tells too much

—Don Marquis, *a roach of the taverns*

(l. to r.) Countess Mercati, Forsythe Wicks, and the late Mrs. Cornelius Vanderbilt—*the* Mrs. Vanderbilt—with her famous headache band. (Max Haas)

Mrs. Crawford Hill of Denver, ruler of Denver's social seas. (De Lux—Denver *Post*)

The late Marion Devereux, press queen of the "Queen City" of Cincinnati. (AP—Cincinnati *Enquirer*)

The late F. Scott Fitzgerald and his daughter, Scottie, in 1928. (Culver)

A few years later, the late Jack Kelly swings his daughter Grace on the beach at Ocean City, N.J.

And, in 1956, Robert J. Kleberg, Jr., with his grand-niece, Ida Louise Clement, at his King Ranch at Kingsville, Texas. (Slim Aarons)

Lady Mendl holds court. (Jerome Zerbe)

And Elsa Maxwell has a ball. (l. to r.) Stripper Della Carroll, Reginald Gardiner, Elsa, Bert Lahr, Bea Lillie. (Jerome Zerbe)

The late Margaret Emerson here presents her debutante daughter, Glamour Girl No. 1 Gloria (Mimi) Baker. (Jerome Zerbe)

A generation later, Mrs. Emerson brings out a granddaughter, Lucille Vanderbilt. (Jerome Zerbe)

Lucius Beebe in white tie, the late Maury Paul (Cholly Knickerbocker No. 1) in black tie. (Max Haas)

Cobina Wright, Sr., and Cobina Wright, Jr. (Jerome Zerbe)

Mrs. Hamilton McKown Twombly, last grand-daughter of Commodore Vanderbilt. (Brown Brothers)

Mrs. Edith Rockefeller McCormick, who succeeded to Mrs. Potter Palmer's throne in Chicago, with Edwin Krenn. (Slim Aarons)

Mrs. Frederick Guest, the former Amy Phipps. (Slim Aarons)

Mrs. Henry B. Joy, late *grande dame* of Detroit, with proof positive that her fortune was *pre*-gasoline. (Detroit *Free Press*)

The Paley wedding; (l. to r. rear), Mr. and Mrs. Henry Cushing and three Cushing girls: Minnie, Babe and Betsey with their husbands, Vincent Astor, William Paley and John Hay Whitney; (front), Mrs. Harvey Cushing with, standing, the two Mortimer children by Mrs. Paley's first husband, and, sitting, two Roosevelt children by Mrs. Whitney's first husband, James Roosevelt, Sarah Delano and Kate. (Jerome Zerbe)

The late Mrs. Charles Dana Gibson (the original Gibson Girl), Mrs. Harvey Cushing, and one of her daughters, Minnie (Mrs. Vincent Astor, later Mrs. James Fosburgh). (Jerome Zerbe)

Brenda Diana Duff Frazier Kelly Chatfield-Taylor, most famous of all "Glamour Debutantes." (Slim Aarons)

Mrs. Harrison Williams, later Countess Bismarck, with her Dali portrait. (Jerome Zerbe)

Mrs. George Gould, wearing her $500,000 necklace. (Brown Brothers)

Washington's late Evalyn Walsh MacLean with the famed Hope diamond and Henry Luce. (Max Haas)

Mrs. Horace Dodge, one of the country's richest women, with Angier Biddle Duke and the Count de Motrico. (Slim Aarons)

Mr. and Mrs. Anthony J. Drexel Biddle, Jr., and his sister, Cordelia Biddle Duke Robertson. In foreground, a three-year-old cousin, Doris Duke. (Max Haas)

Photograph of a photograph of Cleveland, Ohio's (and England's) late Laura Corrigan in her personally designed World War II uniform, which she wore though a civilian. (Jerome Zerbe)

The Condé Nast dynasty: Condé Nast, Edna Woolman Chase, Margaret Case, Ilka Chase and Frank Crowninshield, editor of *Vanity Fair*. (Jerome Zerbe)

Above, left, Henry Ford, Sr., dances with Anne McDonnell, bride of his grandson Henry Ford II (Detroit *Free Press*), and right, the late Charles Francis Adams, fifth in the "royal" Boston Adams line, here at the wheel of the America's Cup yacht, *Yankee*. (AP—Boston *Herald*)

Washington's historic garden party (1939) for King George VI and Queen Elizabeth at the British Embassy, the first fete of its kind in this country. (l. to r.) Mrs. Cordell Hull, Queen Elizabeth and King George, Lady Lindsay, Sir Ronald Lindsay, Mrs. John Nance Garner, Vice-President Garner and Jim Farley. (Acme—*The Diplomat Magazine*)

Below, the last "Enchanted Evening" at the old Ritz before the tearing down of New York's Ritz-Carlton Hotel; (above) the dance contest is judged by Louis Bromfield, Adele Astaire (Mrs. Kingman Douglass, formerly Lady Cavendish), Irene Castle, William De Rham. (Jerome Zerbe)

Last meeting of the New York Junior League in the library, after decision to sell its lavish clubhouse to the Catholic Archdiocese for $600,000, symbolizing League's desire to get "off the Society pages." (Ivan Dmitri)

Even Pittsburgh strove for aristocratic simplicity. Here the early days of the Rolling Rock races; (l. to r.) Mrs. R. B. Mellon, Mrs. John J. Bissell, Richard King Mellon and Mrs. Lucius Robinson (later Mrs. Clement Gile). (Pittsburgh *Press*)

Two of the country's all-time greatest manners mentors: (above) Virginia's famed "Miss Charlotte" Noland with her third generation of girls at Foxcroft School at Middleburg (Slim Aarons), and (below) New England's late, great Endicott Peabody with his fourth generation of boys at Groton School, Groton, Mass. (Ivan Dmitri)

Dorothy Kilgallen and Sherman Billingsley at "Table 50" at the Stork Club.

Also at "Table 50," Mr. and Mrs. Franklin D. Roosevelt, Jr. (Ethel du Pont), Mr. and Mrs. Elliott Roosevelt (Faye Emerson).

Stuart Symington, Walter Winchell, Gen. Hoyt Vandenberg, Gen. Toohey Spaatz, Capt. and Mrs. John Eisenhower.

(Photos—Stork Club)

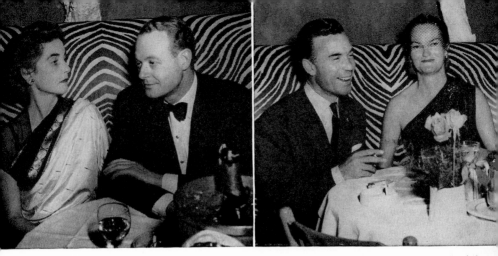

Two "Poor Little Rich Girls"—left, Barbara Hutton and her escort, Herbie Klotz; and, right, Doris Duke with Porfirio Rubirosa, at El Morocco. (Jerome Zerbe)

At a ball in Palm Beach: Dolly Hylan Heminway Fleischmann O'Brien, Charles Munn and ill-starred Glamour Girl Joanne Connelley Sweeny Ortiz-Patino, who, after two unsuccessful marriages, died of an overdose of pills. (Slim Aarons)

More night clubbing: left, the Duchess of Windsor and the late Charles Cushing; and, right, Mrs. Brooks Howe and the Duke of Windsor. (Stork Club)

The late Mrs. Byron Foy (Thelma Chrysler) and irrepressible "extra man" Harry Evans. (Slim Aarons)

Perle Mesta and Herbert May. (Max Haas)

CHARLES DANA GIBSON

V

NEW ENGLAND AND THE OLD SOUTH—

From Cabots, Lowells and Adamses to Byrds,

Randolphs and Lees

IN THE YEAR 1794 an Englishman named Hodgkinson wrote a book about this country which he signed, "By a Gentleman, Lately Returned from America." And among Mr. Hodgkinson's late returns was an observation concerning American Families. "I could not help smiling," he wrote, "at the American definition of *a man of family*. With them it signifies one who has got a wife and five or six children."

It is, of course, undeniable that Americans have often been rather more Family conscious in the immediate parental, rather than the long-term ancestral, sense. It is also undeniable that they have long used the word "Family" in remarkable combinations—from the "Family Bible" and the "Family Meeting" to the "Family Doctor" and even the "Family Wash." In the old days in the West, saloons had their "Family Entrance," for those who did not wish to enter through the bar, the South had its "Family Company" which consisted entirely of "kin," and all over the country the theatres had their "Family Circle," the latter meaning, though it was also called the upper gallery, the poorest seats in the house, far above the "Dress Circle" and even the balcony.

Nonetheless, in the years since Mr. Hodgkinson made his typically deprecating British remarks, this country has also done its unlevel best to redeem its definition of Family in the patriarchal, capital letter sense. By the early Nineteenth Century in Boston, for example, so great was the concern over ancestors and "men of Family" that the entire city was said to be suffering from a malaise known as "Grandfather on the Brain." And, in 1857, something over a century ago, Oliver Wendell Holmes, poet and doctor and father of the late Mr. Justice, issued a remarkable manifesto on the subject. Asked by an anxious Boston mother when her child's education should begin, Dr. Holmes replied, gently, "About a hundred years, Madam, before he was born." Then, in his famed *Autocrat of the Breakfast-Table*, he went further:

> What do I mean by a man of family?—O, I'll give you a general idea of what I mean. Let us give him a first-rate fit out, it costs us nothing.
>
> Four or five generations of gentlemen and gentlewomen; among them a member of His Majesty's Council for the Province, a Governor or so, one or two Doctors of Divinity, a member of Congress, not later than the time of top-boots with tassels.
>
> Family portraits. The member of the Council, by Smibert. The great merchant-uncle, by Copley, full length, sitting in his armchair, in a velvet cap and flowered robe, with a globe by him, to show the range of his commercial transactions, and letters with large red seals lying round, one directed conspicuously to The Honourable etc. etc. Great-grandmother, by the same artist;

brown satin, lace very fine, hands superlative; grand old lady, stiffish, but imposing. Her mother, artist unknown; flat, angular, hanging sleeves; parrot on fist. A pair of Stuarts . . .

Books, too, with the names of old college-students in them,— family names;—you will find them at the head of their respective classes in the days when students took rank on the catalogue from their parents' condition. . . .

Some family silver; a string of wedding and funeral rings; the arms of the family curiously blazoned; the same in worsted, by a maiden aunt. . . .

No, my friends, I go (always other things being equal) for the man who inherits family traditions and the cumulative humanities of at least four or five generations. Above all things, as a child, he should have tumbled about in a library. . . . I tell you he is at home wherever he smells the invigorating fragrance of Russia leather. No self-made man feels so . . .

One may, it is true, have all the antecedents I have spoken of, and yet be a boor or a shabby fellow. One may have none of them, and yet be fit for councils and courts. Then let them change places. Our social arrangement has this great beauty, that its strata shift up and down as they change specific gravity, without being clogged by layers of prescription. But I still insist on my democratic liberty of choice, and I go for the man with the gallery of family portraits against the one with the twenty-five cent daguerreotype, unless I find out that the latter is the better of the two.

Even before the good Dr. Holmes, as far back as 1839, a "German Nobleman," as he styled himself, by the name of Francis J. Grund came over to America and made a special study of the problem. "I have heard more talk about Aristocracy and family in the United States," he wrote, "than during my whole previous life in Europe."

Mr. Grund chose the Aristocracy of the Quakers in Philadelphia as America's finest—an Aristocracy which, he said, "consists not so much in wealth as in family":

They have more of the *à-plomb* of gentlemen. There is less motion and more dignity in their carriage, and you can see, from a hundred little circumstances, that the higher classes have an advantage of a generation over the ordinary run of Aristocrats in the United States.

Besides this, Mr. Grund had a few kind words for the South. "I prefer," he said, "the white-gloved democrat of the South, with his *aristocratic* bearing, to the ungloved Aristocrat of the North, with his republican humility, and his cravings after popularity and power." He also saw hope in the West. "Among the Western hunters and warriors," he wrote, "there are better materials for a future aristocracy than can be found in the Atlantic cities. They are, at least, owners of real estate, and possess the soil on which they play the lords." But for the North, and concerning American Aristocracy in general, Mr. Grund had nothing but the harshest of words—and prophecies:

> The *moveable*, moneyed Aristocracy of our times I consider as the greatest enemy of mankind, in comparison to which all the terrors of the feudal system are as nothing. The nobility of the middle ages offered to the people protection for vassalage, and set them the example of chivalry and valour. A mere moneyed aristocracy, on the contrary, enslaves the people without giving them an equivalent, introducing everywhere the most sordid principles of selfishness, to the exclusion of every noble and disinterested sentiment. A mere moneyed proponderance of one class of citizens over the other, does not form as historical a link between the present and the past; neither does it, like the masses, represent the interests of mankind in general. All its tendencies are downward, reducing a people gradually to a degree of moral degradation, from which perhaps they might have been saved by the presence of a powerful nobility of family.*

Just why certain American Families have risen rapidly into the "Family Circle," or upper gallery—first becoming "social" and then "Aristocratic"—while at the same time certain other Families, many equally well fortune-founded, and with even better continuation of distinction, have never so risen, remains something of a mystery. The late Dixon Wecter, for example, stated that it was primarily

---

* Despite Mr. Grund's fierce denunciation of America's Family Plan Aristocracy, he apparently liked things better in this country in person than he did in print. He shortly became an American citizen, a political leader of the German-Americans in Pennsylvania, an American consul at Antwerp, Bremen and Le Havre, and even chose to die in America—which he did, among his beloved "Philadelphia Aristocracy," in 1863.

due to the "personality" of the Founding Family father—and cites
as an example for his thesis the fact that the great wealth amassed by
the grandson of the Scotch shoemaker, the late Andrew Carnegie,
should have had little impact upon American Society, while an older
fortune, made by another Scot, Henry Burden, of Troy, New York,
had much impact. The fact remains, however, that in the first place,
Andrew Carnegie gave away most of his money and, in the second, that he had only one descendant, his daughter, Mrs. Roswell
Miller. On the other hand, the tight-fisted Henry Burden had two
sons, James A. Burden and I. Townsend Burden, and, besides, the
first of these had four sons and the second two sons—and, all in all,
an American "Four Hundred" dynasty was soon on its well-heeled
way.

The historian Wecter also came to the conclusion that wealth
accumulated through banking and brokerage has been "the sort most
easily to escape the odium of manufacture and trade," but here again
there are pitfalls. It is, of course, true that the day would come when
The Mrs. Astor would refuse to entertain a carpet manufacturer.
"Just because I buy my carpets from him," she complained, "that
is no reason why I should ask him to my house to *walk* on them."
But here Mrs. Astor was merely exhibiting the age-old process of
the rise from trade to anti-trade, and the fact remains, Wecter to
the contrary, that for every Morgan in the history of America's
Planned Familyhood, there has been at least one Marshall Field and,
for that matter, for every Gallatin, Jay or even a banking Biddle,
there have been at least two Astors and Vanderbilts—who were
nothing if not trade.

Other historians have gone even further and have given the impression that, American Society being what it is, a Family in the
American pantheon is, by and large, no better and no worse than
its social press agentry. Proponents of this thesis believe, for example, that it is highly doubtful if the Cabots of Boston would ever
have attained their lordly position in the firmament of Hub heaven
had not an anonymous "Western man," at a Harvard alumni dinner
in 1905, delivered a toast "To the Aristocracy of Harvard"—one

which was later refined, in 1910, by Dr. John Collins Bossidy, a Holy Cross man, to be recited, apparently for all time, as follows:

> And this is good old Boston,
> The home of the bean and the cod,
> Where the Lowells talk to the Cabots
> And the Cabots talk only to God.*

Press agentry and poetry to the contrary, however, the fact remains that the Proper Bostonian Families, including not only the Cabots and the Lowells but also Adamses, Saltonstalls and many others, had been making history not only on a local but on a national scale for at least two hundred years before anyone had ever thought of their conversing with the Deity. And if more than a hundred years ago, in 1846, a pamphlet entitled *Our First Men, A Calendar of Wealth, Fashion and Gentility* appeared with the statement that "It is no derogation, then, to the Boston aristocracy, that it rests upon money," few Proper Bostonians would have quarreled with it. "Money," said the pamphlet, "is something substantial. Everybody knows that and feels it. Birth is a mere idea which grows every day more and more intangible." That too the Proper Bostonian would have admitted. But a hundred years after the pamphlet he might also ask for something else to be set on the record—and that would have been the accomplishments of the outstanding Boston Families. For the plain fact of the matter is that a very small number of Families were able to produce an Aristocracy which, for accomplishment, was one unmatched by any British or for that matter any titled Aristocracy anywhere.

As recently as the span of 1949-1959, for example, there was a *Mayflower*-descended Robert Fiske Bradford, as Governor of Massachusetts, a Sinclair Weeks as the country's Secretary of Commerce, a Robert Cutler as special assistant to President Eisenhower, a Chris-

---

* Some years later, perhaps in self-defense, a Yale poet, F. S. Jones, proposed a toast to New Haven, under the title of "On the Democracy of Yale":

> Here's to the town of New Haven,
> The home of the Truth and the Light,
> Where God talks to Jones in the very same tones
> That He uses with Hadley and Dwight.

tian Herter who replaced the late John Foster Dulles as Secretary of State, a Henry Cabot Lodge as Ambassador to the United Nations, a John Davis Lodge as Governor of Connecticut and later Ambassador to Spain, a John Cabot as Ambassador to Brazil, a Robert Moors Cabot as perhaps the country's No. 1 Marshall Plan authority, a Leverett Saltonstall as U.S. Senator serving on such vital committees as Appropriations and Armed Forces, a William Gurdon Saltonstall serving as principal of Exeter Academy, one of the oldest and largest of private schools, a Charles Francis Adams serving as the head of Raytheon, one of the country's largest electronic concerns, and last but by no means least, a Pulitzer Prize poet by the name of Robert Traill Spence Lowell, Jr.*

If such eminence were rooted in trade, the answer seemed in practical America—which after all was itself, via Jamestown, trade-rooted—so be it. In New England, even the most prominent of the early-day Families, the Otises and Quincys, Faneuils and Boylstons, Hutchinsons and Gores, Royals and Vassalls, Dudleys and Pinchons —almost all of whom all but disappeared before the Nineteenth Century's mercantile Families—were themselves mercantile-founded, and if such Families as the Holmeses and the Winthrops survived, they did so not because of either earlier or later public distinction but because they became engulfed in the Nineteenth Century's Golden Age of First Family-founding. The Winthrops, in fact, secured their position not through Boston banking but through New York banking. Even the Saltonstalls for all their record in politics and public service, as symbolized by the mid-Twentieth Century's Lincoln-esque-looking Leverett, would not be the Family they are in this century had they not produced in the Nineteenth Century a man

* Such a listing is perhaps incomplete without the recent accomplishment of John Fitzgerald Kennedy, of Boston's illustrious Kennedys; indeed, this Family is almost a textbook example of the progression from Celebrity (Grandfather "Honey Fitz" Fitzgerald) to Society (Joseph P. Kennedy) to Aristocracy (the present generation). But even the list as it stands would still fail to impress certain Boston types, notably the lady who was asked if she didn't think that Robert Cutler had made quite a name for himself in Washington. "Well, I suppose he has," admitted the lady doubtfully. Then suddenly she added sternly, "But, after all, it's not Boston—it's just *national*."

who went after the job of Family-stabilizing in a determined manner. First he married a widow who had inherited not one but three
Boston fortunes—an Appleton fortune from her husband, a Silsbee
fortune from her father, and a Crowninshield fortune from her
mother—then he went out on his own and made a fourth fortune
as a mill man.

"Every real Boston Family," said Thomas Gold Appleton, "has a
sea captain in its background." In actuality, however, the wish has
often been founding father to the thought. For the mundane fact is,
for every genuine "clipper ship Family," such as the Perkinses, the
Forbeses and the Codmans, there are a dozen so-called "old Families"
among whom a senior partnership, if not, in deference to W. S.
Gilbert, a junior partnership, was, in reality, the only "ship" the
Family indeed "ever had seen." On the other hand, among the more
genuinely "old" Families from Nantucket or Salem, the Appleton
statement has accurate validity. Such Nantucket Families as the
Coffins, Macys, Folgers and Starbucks have incontestably salty backgrounds—albeit such intramural ones, matrimonially speaking, that
it has been said they have all been "stirred up in one big pudding
dish with a big spoon." In Salem not only the Peabodys, but also
the Derbys, Crowninshields and Pickerings, were ancient and honorable long before the Boston Families were honorable, let alone ancient. And even before them were the so-called "Old Planters"—
Families such as Balch, Palfrey, Woodbury and Conant, all of whom
were already settled in Salem when Governor Endecott landed
there in 1628.

To other countries, particularly England, it has always been something of a matter of mirth that America, as it most assuredly did,
"made up" its Family Aristocracy. However, even if this is one
more illustration of the fact that in a country where all men were
declared equal, most all men also tried to be as unequal as they could,
it is also, upon fair analysis, one more illustration that, speaking
generally, America so far has done a pretty fair job at it. Starting
with the Cabots, for example, whether one looks at them in their
own Family resort of "Cabotville" in North Haven, Maine—which

is the Cabot answer to the Boston all-Forbes resort of Naushon—
or whether one looks at them in the 1960 edition of *Who's Who*,
where there are some eleven present-day members of the Cabot
Family listed, they are undoubtedly Boston's and New England's
most extraordinary clan. Indeed, measured by total accomplishment
per family member, they are probably the most outstanding Family
in America. Yet as we have seen, the Cabots missed the *Mayflower*
by some five generations; they came, not from England at all but
from the Isle of Jersey, and they settled not in Boston but in Salem.

The Cabot Family, genealogists to the contrary, do not ascend to
the explorers John and Sebastian. Nor even, Family armorers to the
contrary, do they ascend to the French Chabot Family. They do
ascend, however, to three brothers who, from humble circumstances,
left the Isle of Jersey approximately in 1700 to seek their fortune
in America. The eldest, George Cabot, like so many Cabots since,
married well, taking to wife the daughter of a merchant and, according to tradition, building for his father-in-law the first brick house
in Salem. Unlike so many Cabots since, however, George failed in
business. On the other hand, the youngest brother, John, not only
did not fail in business, he became one of the leading Salem merchants. This same John sired thirteen children, of whom no less than
two of his sons and two of his daughters married Boston Higginsons
—at that time a far more prosperous Family than the Cabots were.

Such a high marital standard, as well as such an intramural one,
was by no means unusual among later Cabots and, along with over-
lapping generations, caused such genealogic confusion that according
to Mary C. Wheelright whose own mother was a Cabot, "It sometimes happened that a Cabot girl would be a great-aunt before she
was born." On the reverse of the Cabot marital coin, old Colonel
Lee, Nineteenth Century lion of Boston's famed Lee, Higginson &
Co., once declared that not only his Family, but the Lowells, the
Jacksons and the Higginsons as well, "came up from Newburyport
to Boston, social and kindly people inclined to make acquaintances
and mingle with the world pleasantly. . . . But they got some Cabot
wives to shut them up." From this it was only a step to a latter-day

definition, on the part of a Cabot historian himself. "A strange dynasty," he wrote, "with customs but no manners." This verdict is harsh. Charm may not be the Cabot Family's longest suit, but even the most forbidding of all latter-day Cabots, Godfrey Lowell Cabot himself, had, at the age of 99, a severe code which might have been styled mannerless by New York "social" standards, but code it was, nonetheless, something which in New York Society would seem to have disappeared altogether.

The late Havelock Ellis, in his *Study of British Genius*, demonstrated that in large families the talented one is usually either the oldest or the youngest. If so, the Cabot Family have long disproved the thesis. Throughout their generations the Cabots have shown not only talent but also, what is a good deal rarer, talent combined with hard work and this in at least some measure in almost every individual in every individual family. Although in the Eighteenth Century it was the custom, even among fairly prosperous families, to send only one son to college, this did not stop the Cabots. One Cabot who ran away from Harvard and shipped to sea as a cabin boy went on to become the country's first Secretary of the Navy; another Cabot established the country's first cotton mill at Beverly, Massachusetts. In their middle era there was a Cabot among the Brook Farmers and there was also a Cabot who was first president of the Society of Architects.

But it has been in later eras that the Cabots, in contrast to so many other Families, have really shone. Varying from Godfrey Lowell Cabot, pioneer of carbon black, to Charles Cabot, whose investigations of working conditions in cotton mills were responsible for a host of labor laws, this remarkable Family has also produced two brothers, the late Dr. Richard Cabot, one of the country's greatest medical reformers, and the late Dr. Hugh Cabot, a man of such world-wide eminence that there is, in Russia, a penicillin factory named for him. And finally, although the Cabots cannot match the Saltonstall record of ten unbroken generations at Harvard, even here they have been formidable. Starting with John Cabot, of the class of 1729, there have, as of the 1960's, been more than fifty Cabot descendants at Harvard. And it was perhaps the ablest of all present-day Cabots, Paul Cabot, present treasurer of Harvard, who was primarily responsible for the naming, in 1953, of the first non-New England president in 317 years of America's oldest corporation.

Meeting Nathan Marsh Pusey, formerly of Lawrence College in Appleton, Wisconsin, in the office of Thomas Lamont, of J. P. Morgan & Co., Cabot was so enthusiastic about the man that from that moment on, according to one associate, "it would have been impossible not to name him." For a Boston Cabot, famed in liberal chapter and verse as the very archetype of this country's conservatism, to prove the spearhead in nominating to the leadership of Harvard one who had already demonstrated a strong brand of intellectual and political liberalism would seem an anomaly—but only, of course, because the reforming and liberal streak in all Cabots has, like so many of their other streaks, long been played down by their own determined wish. Liberal doubting Thomases might also be interested in knowing how the informing of Dr. Pusey took place. The first call to Dr. Pusey was made by Roger Weed, Senior Harvard "Fellow." Later there was another call, from Paul Cabot—and, in the words of Dr. Pusey himself, "I never was sure until Paul Cabot called. I thought Weed's call might have been an initiation prank or something." But even after this one final call remained to be made. There was still a feeling among the Harvard "Corporation" that, although they were satisfied with Dr. Pusey's intellectual equipment and business acumen, they did not know much about him as a person—for all they knew he might be, as one of them now admits he feared at the time, "one of those real Midwestern fanatics—you know, a teetotaler or something." In any case, all such fears were allayed late one night by a telephone call to the home of Paul Cabot. "It was so late," recalls Cabot, "I didn't know whether to answer it or not, but my wife made me. She thought it might be an emergency. It was too. It was from Appleton, Wisconsin, and it was Tom Lamont. 'Paul,' he said, 'you can go back to bed now. But I just wanted you to know I've just had three old-fashioneds with the new President of Harvard.'"

Close on the heels of Cabots in present-day distinction, and surpassing them in past record, is the Lowell Family. A remarkable
combination of poets and dreamers, scientists, men of affairs and
jurists, the Lowells have included, besides the present Robert, the
late cigar-smoking Amy and James Russell Lowell, ambassador and
poet, a succession of Federal jurists which began with the "Old
Judge" John Lowell and continued, in direct descent, with his great-
grandson, great-great-grandson, and even great-great-great-grandson
—as well as the pioneer cotton merchant Francis Cabot Lowell,
the historian Edward Jackson Lowell, the architect Guy Lowell, the
astronomer Percival Lowell, and the clergyman Robert Traill Spence
Lowell. The latter, incidentally, a noted hymn writer and medical
missionary, was the first Lowell of the Family's first two hundred
years in America who both married a non-New England wife and
chose to live outside of New England.

Despite the wide range of family achievements, there has also
been present, in a surprising number of the members of this illustrious
Family, at least some talent in all the different fields in which the
others excelled. The very first Lowell to come to this country, for
example, Percivall Lowle, who emigrated to America from Somerset-
shire, England, in 1639, was a merchant who established a successful
business in Newbury, Massachusetts. Yet on the death of Governor
Winthrop, it was he who was nominated to compose the Governor's
funeral elegy—one which, if no threat to future poetic generations
which would include James Russell, Amy and Robert, was at least
a portent in that direction:

> Here you have Lowle's loyalty,
> Pen'd with his slender skill,
> And with it no good poetry,
> But certainly good Will.

Curiously enough, even the greatest of Lowell poets often demonstrated that the muse, alone, was not enough. "You know what a
deep distrust I have of the poetic temperament," James Russell Lowell once wrote in his *Letters*, "with its self deceptions, its real un-
realities, and its power of sometimes unblessed magic." And some

time later, the Ambassador to Great Britain wrote to his fellow Boston author Thomas Bailey Aldrich, "Think of me after I am gone on (for in the nature of things you will survive me) as one who had a friendly feeling for everything human. It is better to be a good fellow than a good poet."* As for Amy herself, Lowell poet laureate, despite her Elizabethan outspokenness and her Olympian unconventionality, she was a New England Lowell through and through when it came to love of home and hearth. Taken to Europe when she was eight years old, she suffered serious illness from the overstimulation of her mind, and though she traveled much in later life, the center of her young universe was reflected in her invariable childhood identification. "I am Amy Lowell," she used to say, "of Brookline, Massachusetts." Years later, in her sonnet, "The Fruit Garden Path," she best expressed her own family circle:

> Dear garden of my childhood, here my years
> Have run away like little grains of sand;
> The moments of my life, its hopes and fears
> Have all found utterance here, where now I stand;
> My eyes ache with the weight of unshed tears,
> You are my home, do you not understand?

Throughout the Nineteenth Century the Lowell Family was a dominant force in the life of New England, from a cultural as well as a mercantile point of view. There was, for example, the John Lowell, son of Francis Cabot Lowell and the man who founded the famed Lowell Institute, the lecture platform which stood as a foundation-stone in the cultural life of New England. His gift of $250,000 for the purpose was, with the exception of the Girard bequest in Philadelphia, the largest ever made up to that time—

* Thomas Bailey Aldrich had already learned another hard lesson on the subject of poetry. He once proudly exhibited to the Boston merchant for whom he was working a check for fifteeen dollars he had received from *Harper's*. The merchant fingered the check for some time, saw it was, though not from a Boston bank, a "perfectly good" New York bank, then asked Aldrich what it was for. Aldrich stated it was for a poem. "A *poem!*" the merchant roared, "a *poem!*" Once more he looked at the check, then handed it back to Aldrich. "Why," he asked slowly, "don't you send the damned fool one every day?"

1832—by any private individual for the endowment of a literary institution. And his will, in rather typical Lowell fashion, provided that each successive trustee of the Institute should be required to deposit in the archives of the Boston Athenaeum a slip of paper designating his successor, one who must be, according to the terms of the will, a male descendant of the testator's grandfather, Judge Lowell, "preferably one bearing the name of Lowell, if among them anyone has the necessary qualifications." The first of his successors was his son, John Amory Lowell, who obviously exhibited the necessary qualifications early in life. His graduation thesis bore the title "Whether Prosperity and Increase of Wealth have a Favorable Influence upon the Manners and Morals of the People."

Still another giant among Nineteenth Century Lowells was the extraordinary Charles Russell Lowell, Jr. The possessor of a brilliant mind, an incredibly voracious student, he graduated first in his class at college, then threw himself into the Ames Company's mills, "toiling terribly," as he himself admitted, but meanwhile, with the keenest developed social conscience of all Lowells, trying to instill among his fellow workers a desire of reading "solid books." "How the great men do stand out among the merely able, or the merely earnest men," he wrote home to his family, "Bacon and Goethe by the side of Henry Taylor and Carlyle, even Emerson and William Humboldt by the side of Phelps, Kingsley, etc. Rather discouraging to us modern people."

When the war came, he enlisted in the cavalry and as a young officer was asked to go home and raise in Boston a "regiment of gentlemen." Charles refused. "What do you mean 'gentlemen'?" he asked. Later, the assignment liberalized, he went home and raised his regiment. The next summer, in 1863, his best friend, Robert Gould Shaw, who had raised a regiment of Negro troops, was killed leading them in a charge on Fort Wagner. Soon after Lowell married Shaw's sister, and less than a year later, in September of 1864, commanding a full regiment of cavalry, by the word of Sheridan himself "the finest officer of cavalry on the Union side," he was shot at Cedar Creek. His arm broken, his lung collapsed, and unable to speak above a whisper, he nonetheless ordered his men to put him in the saddle and charged again. This time he was wounded again and, after an agonizing night, in which he first spent the remains of his strength on a fellow wounded Union officer and then sent the surgeon who might have saved him to care for Confederate wounded instead, he died. Paradoxically, at the exact time he was making his last charge, his commission to the rank of Brigadier General was being signed in Washington by Abraham Lincoln.*

Ferris Greenslet has best stated Lowell history's most fascinating "if" of the Family's most talented son:

> Well, just supposing the eye or trigger-finger of some unknown Southern soldier had been a little off on the afternoon of October 19, 1864. Brigadier General Charles Russell Lowell, soon to be promoted to Major General, and in command of all Sheridan's cavalry and doing better with it, would have come out of the war a popular hero. With his high social aims . . . his personal magnetism and gift of leadership, what could have kept him from leadership? Ben Butler's drooping eye might never have looked out over the governor's desk beneath the Golden Dome of Park Street. Lowell had not the advantage of birth in Ohio, but he was born of the best stock in Massachusetts. There were no grocery kings or coal barons to be his political backers, but some of the solidest and ablest financial interests in Boston and New York would have been behind him. It is not impossible that either Major McKinley or Colonel Hayes might never have been a tenant of the White House and that Massachusetts would have had a president midway between John Quincy Adams and Calvin Coolidge.

If Colonel Lowell was remarkable, no less so was his wife, who after the death of her husband and brother in the war devoted no less than forty years to social welfare work, among her enduring monuments being the Charity Organization Society of New York, and the Consumer's League. In 1911, through the generosity of the late William Rhinelander Stewart, a complete book was written of

* Just a month before, at Winchester, Colonel George S. Patton, of the Twenty-Second Virginia, in command of a brigade, was promoted to Brigadier General on the field, only to receive a mortal wound before the day was done. The Confederate Colonel was the grandfather of the late General George S. Patton, of World War II fame.

her work—one which contained the memorable poem, "A Woman of Sorrows" by Richard Watson Gilder:

> It was but yesterday she walked these streets,
> Making them holier. How many years
> With all her widowed love immeasurably
> She ministered unto the abused and stricken
> And all the oppressed and suffering of mankind—
> Herself forgetting, but never those in need;
> Her whole sweet soul lost in her loving work,
> Pondering the endless problem of the poor.

Measuring the Lowell Family by its alma mater, Harvard, is, as it was in the case of the Cabots, hazardous, and indeed is one more example of the ephemeral nature of a Family's social prominence— at least from a "First" point of view. For in the old days students at Harvard were actually ranked, on entering the Freshman class, not on the basis of their entering grades but on their families' social position. The first Lowell who entered, in the class of 1721, stood, of thirty-one students, at the very bottom of the list. Above him were such names as Hancock, Winslow, Wolcott and Sewall, and at the very top stood two students by the name of Foster Hutchinson and John Davenport. Yet over two centuries later it remained for the most distinguished of latter-day Lowells, the late Abbott Lawrence Lowell, president of Harvard, to speak out forthrightly on the ticklish present-day question of college for everyone. "The idea that going to college is one of the inherent rights of man," he said in a speech at Haverford College, "seems to have obtained a baseless foothold in the minds of many of our people." Lowell's speech was made in 1931, and he died in 1943; it is perhaps fortunate that he did not live to see the post-World War II college programs or the "study now-pay later" plans of the 1960's.

The Harvard president's generation of Lowells also included the astronomer Percival, a man who was not only a pioneer astronomer but the first reputable scientist to go so far as to say of his studies of the planet Mars, "That Mars is inhabited we have absolute proof." The entire last part of his life was spent at his observatory at Flagstaff, Arizona, where one of his associates described him as a man "buoyant with strength, ambition, love, sincerity, nobleness of purpose, in fact all that was highest in life." Of all latter-day Lowells, however, it remained for Harvard's Lawrence Lowell to make the most indelible impression on his generation. He was of course, as he himself well knew he would be, vilified for his part in the celebrated "Sacco-Vanzetti Case"—the execution, in 1927, of Nicola Sacco and Bartolomeo Vanzetti, the Italian "radicals" who were accused of the murder of a paymaster and his guard in South Braintree, Massachusetts, in 1920. Yet what many people who had harsh things to say of Boston's "First Family" man have forgotten is that Lowell was, together with Judge Robert T. Grant and President Stratton of Massachusetts Institute of Technology, brought into the case to review the findings of the Court by none other than such other "First Family" men, who first spoke out in favor of such a review, as the late Bishop William Lawrence and the late Dr. Richard Cabot. Such derogators of Mr. Lowell have also conveniently forgotten that it was none other than the "Yankee from Olympus," Mr. Justice Holmes himself, who refused to issue a writ of *habeas corpus* in the case. "I cannot say that I have a doubt," he wrote, "and therefore I must deny the stay." As for Lowell himself, though he never doubted the guilt of the accused, as Henry Yeomans found out from questioning him, yet neither did he ever question the right of anyone who had gone so far as to read all the evidence at the trial— which almost none of the critics did—to come to a different conclusion. And in 1936 he wrote the editor of the *New Republic*, who had questioned him on the subject, "If I could relive that part of my life with the knowledge that I have now, that I should suffer persecution for doing my duty as a citizen, I should nevertheless do it as I did before."

Certainly no one who has studied the character of Lowell would believe that he would ever have sent two men to the electric chair, no matter how radical, unless he had fully believed in their guilt. Lowell's liberal record as the country's outstanding educator of his era is secure. He was forever jumping to the defense of his own professors who were accused of "radicalism," and indeed his whole program at Harvard was designed to liberate Harvard education from his far more hidebound predecessor, Charles William Eliot, of "Five Foot Shelf" fame. Furthermore, externally cold as he was, Lowell was not only basically an extremely human person, he was also not without a sense of humor. On the personal side, for example, he would have no truck with such basic Proper Bostonian virtues as getting up at dawn. "People who get up early in the morning," he once said, "feel virtuous all morning and sleepy all afternoon." As for education itself, on one occasion a distinguished graduate accosted Lowell at a Commencement exercise in the 1930's. "I," he said proudly, "was Ought Six." For a moment Lowell was deep in thought, then he smiled. "Well," he said, "one thing you ought to remember is that in my judgment somewhere between the years of 1905 and 1907 Harvard education reached an all-time low." Among Lowell's own students, though many liked to joke about putting up a monument "at the place Lowell once spoke to a Freshman," the fact remains that in after years they never forgot what their president called his "Silver Rule" for entering Freshmen. "Do that which you would be glad to have done twenty years hence." One particular undergraduate, who had failed in a contest he had wanted desperately to win, never forgot Lowell's consolation. "My boy," he said, "life is a series of failures, but, added together, they make a tolerable whole."*

Even taking into account their ascent vocally to the Deity Himself, the Cabots and the Lowells must still take rank below what is certainly the most historic, if not aristocratic, of all American Families—the Adamses. Boston's so-called "royal" Family, the Adamses include not only two Presidents, John, the country's second President, and John Quincy, the country's sixth, but also two Signers of the Declaration, John and Sam, as well as three Ambassadors to

* There is a simple reason for Lawrence Lowell's generally poor "press." For twenty-five years he administered Harvard, a quarter of a century that, according to Louis Lyons, "marked the most tremendous development of publicity the world has yet seen"—without ever giving a newspaper interview.

Great Britain, John, John Quincy and Charles Francis I, all of whom in three succeeding generations represented their country at a time when British feeling was strongest against it. Besides these, there are also, in this incredible Family, two admitted giants of American literature and history, Henry Adams, the philosopher who wrote like a historian, and his brother Brooks, the historian who wrote like a philosopher. What makes the Adams story most extraordinary, however, is the fact that their distinction has continued to the present era. The late Henry Cabot Lodge, delivering in 1915 a "Memorial Address" on the subject of Charles Francis Adams II—who, though a curiously "Adamsy" combination of businessman and rebel, was by no means among the great Adamses—stated that it was impossible to find in all history, even in real royalty, four successive generations of equal intellectual distinction and public service:

> In some of the long royal dynasties instances of great ability are no doubt found, but they are as a rule isolated and the high position itself is inherited, not won. Among the Plantagenets even, the dynasty more productive of remarkable men than any other of modern times at least, the highest ability came at intervals and the union of ability and character only at very protracted intervals. The House of Orange-Nassau in William the Silent, his two sons and later his great-grandson, William III, presents a very famous case of inherited ability; but there again the great opportunity and the high position were a birthright.
>
> There have also been many instances of long descent where the same family has held through centuries the same titles and estates, but this means little because the titles and estates usually sustain their possessors instead of the possessors upholding and adding glory won by the hard-handed, hard-headed founder of the line. . . . We have, of course, the famous instance of the elder and the younger Pitt who both reached the zenith of power, but then came the end, as it did in the less conspicuous case of Lord Burleigh and the Earl of Salisbury, after whom the line waited two hundred and fifty years before it again shone forth in the high places.

"But in our American family," Lodge concluded, "with no adventitious aid of titles or estates, without the lucky chance which

Lord Thurlow described as 'the accident of an accident,'" the Adamses "rose to the highest pinnacle of public service and public distinction." And the late James Truslow Adams, historian of the Family—though he denied "royal" Adams connection himself—makes clear that wealth, which played such a formidable part in the rise and continued eminence of the Cabots and the Lowells, played a small part indeed in the history of the history-making Adamses:

> Many an American family has sprung from obscurity to promi-
> nence and then carried on its new sphere owing to inherited
> wealth. John Adams, however, had no such wealth to bequeath.
> That the family, instead of slipping back, maintained itself in its
> new phase was due to no inheritance of possessions, but to one
> of intellect and character. That sudden, mysterious something that
> had occurred in the family strain with John, that had made the
> sons of generations of village yeomen one of the half-dozen greatest
> men that America has yet produced, was to continue in his de-
> scendants. It is that which gives to the family its peculiar interest
> and significance, the continuance, once begun, of the combination
> of exceptional intellect with exceptional character.

Character was ever the watchword of Adamses—indeed, probably no other Family in America has ever had so much. In an Adams face, it has been said, one can always see three things—intellectual power, calm determination and, above all, iron will. And if the Cabots spoke to God, it was, in the words of the old Revolutionary cry, the "Adamses *and* God." But for all this, Adams distinction was slow a-borning. The first Adams came to America in 1636, but not for three generations did the Family even "make" Harvard, let alone become "royal," and, when it did, in the person of Joseph Adams, a farmer's son, he ranked socially at the very bottom of his Harvard class.

John Adams, first of the "royal" Adamses and the real Family founder, also was a farmer's son, albeit he was the grandson of the farmer's son who had become a minister—which in those days was the recognized avenue to social success. John's father, Deacon John Adams, also made the first successful marriage in Adams social history from a financial point of view. He chose Susanna Boylston, a relative of Thomas Boylston, of a family long since disappeared but at that time adjudged the richest man in provincial Massachusetts. Susanna's share was not considerable, but her son John also married well— after some difficulty in getting his bride's family to say yes—choosing the famed Abigail, daughter of the Reverend William Smith of Weymouth. Abigail's mother had been a Quincy—pronounced, of course, "Quinzy"—a name which in provincial New England was a high-ranking one indeed.

Actually two Adamses cropped up in the first royal generation of Adamses. Besides John there was his cousin Sam. The famed "Man of the Town Meeting" was not only the personage perhaps individually most important in starting the American Revolution but also the one who first called England—a line later credited to Napoleon —"a nation of shopkeepers." It was he who engineered the Boston Tea Party and it was he whose fanatical hatred of England supplied the popular foment which was as necessary to the successful War of Independence as the sagacity and character of its later and greater leaders. Although Sam's life after the irrevocable breach with England was anticlimactic and ended in years of "honorable poverty," this was, as his cousin John noted, typical of the man who was "too attentive to the public and not enough to himself and his Family."

In contrast, the life of John Adams could not have started out, politically, less prepossessingly. Indeed it began with his defense of the British captain who was tried for murder after the Boston Massacre. But this too was typical of an Adams who was to make his mark on his countrymen primarily in reverse. Over and over again in his life he undertook the course which was at the time unpopular but which his fellow leaders would later in their own conscience realize had been necessary. Later, as Minister to England, and even later, as President, he was often accused of being a monarchist, but as he wrote his friend, Dr. Rush, in 1790, "I am no friend to *hereditary limited* monarchy in America. This I know can never be admitted without an hereditary Senate to control it, and an hereditary

nobility or Senate in America I know to be unattainable and impractical." As James Truslow Adams has pointed out, however, if John
was no friend to monarchy, neither was he to democracy:

> There was not, and never had been, a single one of the Revolu-
> tionary leaders, not even the most radical of all, Sam Adams him-
> self, who believed in the people. What they believed in, with
> varying degrees of extension, was the people who had money,
> talents, or social position. John Adams, whose fundamental theory
> of government had been adopted in practically all the state con-
> stitutions and also in the Federal one, during his absence, was of
> the same mind. . . . With all his voluminous writings, he never
> gave his views any great precision of statement on this point, but
> he did always lay great stress on the three factors of birth, wealth
> and talents, which he claimed formed a natural aristocracy.

John was also, it should be said, severely influenced on the question
by his remarkable wife, Abigail. "The manners of women," he once
said, "are the surest criterion by which to determine whether a republican government is practicable in a nation or not." Judged by
Abigail they certainly were. The patrician Albert Gallatin called her
sneeringly "Her Majesty," but the remarkable author of *Letters*,
who wrote that "every American wife should herself know how to
order and regulate her family; how to govern her domestics, and
train up her children," was also able, among other things, to make a
"natural aristocrat" out of John, the farmer's son. Indeed, as early
as 1780, John Adams seemed to have had premonitions that he was
establishing a Family Aristocracy, for in a letter to his wife he wrote:

> I must study politics and war that my sons may have liberty to
> study mathematics and philosophy. My sons ought to study mathe-
> matics and Philosophy . . . in order to give their children a right
> to study painting, poetry, music, architecture, statuary, tapestry
> and porcelain.

This was an almost exact foretelling of the generation of Adamses
to come with Charles Francis and then Charles Francis' sons, Henry
and Brooks. Before them, though, in the second royal generation,
came the Adams of Adamses, John Quincy, who even as a young

man was called "Old Man Eloquent," whose own diary he himself called a "treasury of damnations," and who, though possessed of the highest IQ of all Americans in the Hall of Fame, was so controversial to the general populace that when he was elected President, he received practically his entire vote from New England and New York, getting only seven electoral votes from the remainder of the Union. Fiercely independent, even of his own party, his conscientiousness alone aroused fury in his opponents; at the age of 58, when President, he arose at five o'clock in the morning and read two chapters of the Bible before tackling the newspapers. Sentimental always concerning his mother, Abigail, at the age of 76 he broke down in sobs when one of her letters was read aloud in his presence. He himself married Louisa Catherine Johnson, a girl whose mother was English, whose father was American, and who had spent all her early life in France. Yet even this training was hardly enough to cope with a man who, as President, liked not only his morning Bible reading but also a pre-dawn hike of five miles, and later in the day a nude, hour-long swim in the Potomac, while rude onlookers "laughed at his bald head popping up and down in the water."

Ambassador to Russia, France and England, as well as President, John Quincy Adams returned from the White House virtually penniless, his real estate in both Boston and Quincy mortgaged to pay his debts. Almost immediately, however, he returned to the wars, and for eight successive Congresses—a period of seventeen years—he sat humbly in the House of Representatives which he had once addressed as President. The patrician Henry Clay sneered at him. "He was, beginning again," Clay said, "like a boy." Even Adams' own family could not believe it; his friends were amazed. Yet for all those years he did his duty as he saw it, "refusing," says Karl Schriftgiesser, "with tart asperity, to sacrifice his judgment to ministers, kings or people." Finally, at the age of 81, he suffered a stroke on the floor of the House as he strove to rise to answer his name in the roll call. "This is the last of earth," he said, dying. "I am content." But, with all his accomplishments, John Quincy Adams was, like his father, curiously conscious of Family-founding. In 1824, wandering among the tombstones in the Family burial plot, he had long thoughts on the subject—which, like all good Adamses, he recorded in his diary:

> Four generations, of whom very little more is known, than is recorded upon these stones. There are three succeeding generations of us now living. Pass another century, and we shall be mouldering in the same dust, or resolved in the same elements. Who then of our posterity shall visit this yard? And what shall be read engraved upon the stones? This is known only to the Creator of all. The record may be longer. May it be of blameless lives!

The record was indeed to be longer. The third Adams generation was carried forward in the almost equally able and far more diplomatic person of John Quincy's son, Charles Francis Adams I. As Ambassador to England during the Civil War, he won what has been called the most celebrated triumph in all American diplomatic history. The England to which he came in 1861 as Lincoln's emissary was already on the verge of war with the Union, and with its sympathies more and more with the Confederacy, it was only the ability of Adams—one which constantly managed to put his adversaries on the defensive—which over and over again stood between his country and war. A man of almost absolute self-control, he was, as his son Henry called him, "singular for mental poise—absence of self-assertion or self-consciousness—the faculty of standing apart without seeming aware that he was alone—a balance of mind and temper that neither challenged nor avoided notice, nor admitted question of superiority or inferiority, of jealousy, of personal motives, from any source, even under great pressure." And, in his *Education*, Henry gives the most enduring portrait of his father as the greatest anti-Anglophile:

> Almost alone among his Boston contemporaries, he was not English in feeling or in sympathies. Perhaps a hundred years of acute hostility to England had something to do with this family trait; but in his case it went further and became indifference to social distinction. Never once in forty years of intimacy did his son notice in him a trace of snobbishness. He was one of the ex-

ceedingly small number of Americans to whom an English duke or duchess seemed to be indifferent, and royalty itself nothing more than a slightly inconvenient presence. This was, it is true, rather the tone of English society in his time, but Americans were largely responsible for changing it, and Mr. Adams had every possible reason for affecting the manner of the courtier even if he did not feel the sentiment. Never did his son see him flatter or vilify, or show a sign of envy or jealousy; never a shade of vanity or self-conceit. Never a tone of arrogance! Never a gesture of pride!

By his marriage to the daughter of Peter Chardon Brooks, who died in 1849, leaving what was then regarded as the largest fortune in Boston—about $2,000,000—Charles Francis Adams I had, for the first time in eight generations, put the Adams Family on a firm financial footing. Never again would there be the spectacle of an Adams President virtually penniless. But, as wealth had, of all America's Family Dynasties, the least to do with the Adamses' rise, so it had little to do with the continuation of their eminence. In fact, in the fourth generation, which might be termed the "Rebel Generation" —though in fact all Adamses were rebellious in spirit—the Family came up not with just one man of eminence or even two, but no less than four.

The first of these, and the eldest, was John Quincy Adams II. A staunch supporter of Lincoln during the war, he was "unable to stomach" the Republican methods of postwar Reconstruction and in 1867 became the first Adams to ally himself with the Democratic party. For many years he was the leader of the Democratic party in his state, and in 1869 he confounded not only all of Boston but even all other Adamses by turning down the highest Proper Bostonian honors—the presidency of Harvard. Brooks Adams, the youngest son of Charles Francis, also rebelled early. Trained in law, he soon took to writing, and with his first book, *The Emancipation of Massachusetts*, caused a storm of protest because of its stern criticism of what had been up to that time the blind acceptance of ancestor-worship. Later, in his *Theory of Social Revolutions*, he went so far as to demonstrate the ineffectiveness of the capitalist class altogether—or at least when it came to the capitalist class running the government.

But even Brooks paled as a rebel beside his brother Charles Francis II. Rising to Colonel during the Civil War, he came out of the war to study and write on railroads, later becoming not only a successful businessman himself but also a leading figure in politics. Although he refused the nomination for Governor of Massachusetts when it was offered him in 1883, declining it on the grounds that a third candidate would make the defeat of General Butler less certain, he took an active part in business, only to become, by the time of his *Autobiography* (1916), one of the country's strongest critics of the growing plutocracy:

> Indeed, as I approach the end, I am more than a little puzzled to account for the instances I have seen of business success—money-getting. It comes from a rather low instinct. Certainly, so far as my observation goes, it is rarely met with in combination with the finer or more interesting traits of character. I have known, and known tolerably well, a good many "successful" men—"big" financially—men famous during the last half-century; and a less interesting crowd I do not care to encounter. Not one that I have ever known would I care to meet again, either in this world or the next.

The fourth and most famous of the four rebel brothers, Prince Royal of the fourth royal generation, was, of course, the great Henry Adams. The late Alexander Woollcott said Adams "always moved about the earth with something of the shrinking gait of a professional violet crossing the ballroom floor." Actually, such criticism, like so many of the late Mr. Woollcott's, is far more indicative of Woollcott's character than it is that of his subject. Adams himself would have been amused. "Everyone," he once said, "carries his own inch-rule of taste, and amuses himself by applying it, triumphantly, wherever he travels." Certainly if Adams had written only two books, *Mont-Saint-Michel and Chartres* and *The Education of Henry Adams,* the first "a Study of Thirteenth Century Unity" and the second "a Study of Twentieth-Century Multiplicity," his place in American letters would be a towering one. Besides these, however, must be set not only his other books but also his original and brilliant work in philosophy—a science which, Adams fashion, he defined as "unintelligible answers to insoluble problems."

"Down to 1850, and even later," Adams wrote in his *Education*, "New England society was still directed by the professions. Lawyers, physicians, professors, merchants, were classes, and acted not as individuals but as though they were clergymen and each profession was a church." In contrast, Adams himself was ever an individual. Even his Family was "rather an atmosphere than an influence." But, rebel though he was, he was no ne'er-do-well. Such a thing, in an Adams, was unthinkable—a fact which he himself frankly discussed:

> As far as outward bearing went, such a family of turbulent children, given free rein by their parents, or indifferent to check, should have come to more or less grief. Certainly no one was strong enough to control them, least of all their mother, the queen-bee of the hive, on whom nine-tenths of the burden fell, on whose strength they all depended, but whose children were much too self-willed and self-confident to take guidance from her, or from any one else, unless in the direction they fancied. Father and mother were about equally helpless. Almost every large family in those days produced at least one black sheep, and if this generation of Adamses escaped, it was as much a matter of surprise to them as to their neighbors. By some happy chance they grew up to be decent citizens, but Henry Adams, as a brand escaped from the burning, always looked back with astonishment at their luck. The fact seemed to prove that they were born, like birds, with a certain innate balance.

As a boy of ten, Henry Adams made his first visit to the Capital, to visit his Grandmother Adams and more or less incidentally to see President Zachary Taylor, all the while feeling, as he said in after years, "as though the White House belonged to the Adamses, never for a moment doubting that he himself would live there some day." Opposed to a life in Boston, he at first refused a teaching position at Harvard, because, he said, he knew "nothing of history, less about teaching, and too much about Harvard." Nonetheless, after some years abroad, during which he served with distinction as his Ambassador father's secretary, he did return to teach, and, said one of his students, the late Henry Cabot Lodge, he "founded and established the department of American History at Harvard, and what was still more important, he revolutionized the methods of teaching and studying history in the University." Elizabeth Stevenson recalls the comment of another student, Lindsay Swift:

> There was no closing of the eyes in slumber when Henry Adams was in command. All was wholly unacademic; no formality, no rigidity, no professorial pose, but you may be sure that there was never a suspicion of student roguishness or bad manners. We faced a well-disposed gentleman some twenty years older (not quite that much older, but perhaps he seemed so) than ourselves, whose every feature, every line of his body, his clothes, his bearing, his speech were well-bred to a degree. . . . He would make us laugh until we ached, but it was the laughter of a club and not a pothouse. . . . "One fact or a thousand—that makes no difference," he said on one occasion. Now and then he would walk up and down before his chair, always with his hands in his pockets, speaking with entire informality, as if talking to himself.

"The chief wonder of education," Adams said, "is that it does not ruin everybody concerned with it, teachers and taught." He himself labeled his teaching career a "failure." It was not, of course; he had at least taught his students his own dictum—"They know enough who know how to learn."

In 1872, Adams married Marian Hooper, of Boston's well-known Hooper Family. After his teaching, in 1877, he settled in Washington, first in the old yellow Corcoran mansion on Lafayette Square and later in a house of his own building. Here he found the happiest years of his life. His wife, descended on the one side from the Pilgrim Sturges Family, on the other from the Puritan Hoopers, was a woman of charm and intelligence who could not only lead dinner-table small talk but could stir her husband "into a spasm of work by reporting the number of candles George Bancroft consumed before breakfast." The Adams circle in Washington reached probably as high a peak of true "Society" as existed in any city. "One friend in a lifetime," Adams wrote, "is much, two are many; three are hardly possible." Adams had two—the witty and erudite Clarence King and the great John Hay, Lincoln's secretary and later

Secretary of State. At this period he even authored an anonymous satiric novel on Washington Society, *Democracy*. "The capacity of women to make unsuitable marriages," he wrote, "must be considered as the corner-stone of Society."

Then, on the night of December 6, 1885, his world collapsed. His wife, disconsolate over the death of her father, her nerves so taut they finally broke under a strain of melancholy, took an overdose of sleeping pills and died. For the last months Adams had taken her on trips and had tried to distract her from her melancholy, but he had failed. His grief was absolute. Until the funeral he stayed alone in the house with her, permitting no one to come in. Afterwards, he went off to Japan and the South Seas with his friend John La Farge.* There, visiting the Samoans, he found kinship. "They are tremendous aristocrats," he wrote. "Family is everything." Back in Washington again he commissioned Augustus Saint-Gaudens to sculpt a monument for his wife's grave in Rock Creek Park. Stanford White designed the granite setting, but Adams himself supplied the sketch for Saint-Gaudens to work from, jotting down under his sketch four cryptic lines only:

Adams
Buddha
Mental repose
Calm reflection in contrast with the violence or force in nature

Standing today in Rock Creek, the famed "Woman and Hood" is one of America's most extraordinary statuaries. "Infinite wisdom," said John Hay, "a past without beginning and a future without end; a repose, after limitless experience; a peace, to which nothing matters." Hay also wrote perhaps the finest tribute to Mrs. Adams. "Is it any consolation," he asked Henry in a letter in 1885, "to remember her as she was? That bright intrepid spirit, that keen, fine intellect, that lofty scorn of all that was mean, that social charm which

* Actually, no listing of the Great American Families would be complete without those intellectual Aristocrats—the La Farge and James Families. A similar Family of perhaps even more eminence in our modern day is the Van Doren Family.

made your house such a one as Washington never knew before, and made hundreds of people love her as much as they admired her?"

On the monument itself there are no words and no epitaph. Henry wished none. Many clergymen criticized the "despair" and even "atheism," while others, even in those days, found it "un-American." Henry himself would often come and sit, sometimes all day, oblivious to the tourists around him who asked what he considered "meaningless questions of meaning." "To the artist," he wrote, "meaning is indifferent." And, he added, "Every man is his own artist before a work of art." So closely did he draw what James Truslow Adams called the "veil of his grief" that in all the pages of his great *Education*, which was not written and published for years afterwards (1906), there is not one mention of his wife. In 1894 he was elected president of the American History Association, yet this honor and the fame which had come his way meant virtually nothing to him. After the war broke out in 1914, he wrote nothing, "judging that," says Carl Becker, "next to good humor silence was the chief mark of sense." After John Hay's death he lived out what he called his "posthumous existence" in Quincy. "My friends die daily," he wrote, and at 80, on March 27, 1918, he himself died—to be buried beside his wife under the monument in Rock Creek. At the time of his death the casualty lists from France were heavy, and even the Boston *Evening Transcript*, which, under ordinary circumstances in the case of a death of a First Family son, would have had a front-page article and an editorial, had only a stick of type. As for other papers, they wrote briefly that "Henry Adams, an historian," had died. Adams would have liked the irony. "I have written too much history," he once wrote, "to have faith in it, and if anyone doubts me, I am inclined to agree with him."

Henry Adams had no children, but in the fifth royal generation the Family was distinguished by the presence of the late Charles Francis Adams—actually the Third—who carried the Family to new heights in modern-day prestige. Proper Bostonian No. 1, former Mayor of Quincy, Secretary of the Navy, international yachtsman and America's Cup defender, he was also for thirty years treasurer of Harvard. And, as befitting a man who ranked as the country's

No. 1 businessman, his corporate directorships numbering close to a hundred, he had the privilege of escorting Harvard's endowment, during his treasurership, from $12,000,000 to over $120,000,000. As for his son, the present Charles Francis Adams started out, in the sixth royal generation, as a broker, but in the 1950's moved to higher things as president of Raytheon, one of the giants of New England's soon-to-be No. 1 industry, the electronics business. "My father," he says quietly, "never talked much about 'Family.' But the day I went to work he told me, 'I believe you have a reputation for honesty—God help you if you lose it.' That was all he said."

Such a story had an added poignancy when, in 1958, the story burst upon the country of the relationship between Governor Sherman Adams, Eisenhower's right-hand man and so-called "Abominable No-Man," and Boston industrialist Bernard Goldfine. From the latter, it was discovered, Adams had accepted free hotel rooms, a vicuña coat and an Oriental rug. Nationally and even internationally, of course, the story had all the elements of classic American drama, as well as irony—Adams symbolizing, at least up to that time, the incorruptible, umpteenth generation Yankee and Goldfine symbolizing, again up to the unpleasantness, the textbook Horatio Alger story on an immigrant scale. Locally in Boston, however, the story managed to have a rather happier ending, at least in one respect, than it had elsewhere. For almost immediately local Family historians were sent scurrying to their genealogies, and one sent to his erring son in Manhattan a letter bearing good news:

> The news about Adams is bad, Son, and Sherman is an Adams, it is true. But your Mother and I looked it up last night, and it is quite clear that Sherman is, after all, a *New Hampshire* Adams. There are very many of these, as I am sure you know, and they are only very distantly related to the Boston Adamses. Some of them have never even established any connection at all, and certainly in Boston nobody who knows anything about it at all would ever for a moment consider Sherman one of *the* Adamses.

Probably the most famous case of First Family heredity, one which has delighted eugenists above all others in the history of the country, is one which does not concern Cabots, Lowells or Adamses—it concerns, instead, the Family of Richard Edwards, erudite and able merchant of Hartford, Connecticut. In 1667 he married a woman from Massachusetts named Elizabeth Tuttle, one who was, it is recorded, a woman of "great beauty, strong will and extreme intellectual vigor, of mental grasp akin to rapacity." The lady also possessed, however, "an extraordinary deficiency of moral sense," and in 1691, on the grounds of his wife's "adultery and other immoralities," Edwards was divorced from her. Later one of her brothers murdered his own sister, and a sister murdered her own son.

Edwards and his wife had one son, Timothy Edwards, whose son in turn was none other than the great Jonathan Edwards, from whom descend a baker's dozen of college presidents, including three of Yale alone, as well as Aaron Burr, the American author Winston Churchill, and the founder of the Columbia Law School. Through the daughters of Edwards and his brilliant but erring wife descend many other extraordinarily eminent men—among them two Presidents of the United States, Grant and Cleveland, Robert Treat Paine and Chief Justice Morris Waite.

On the other hand, when Richard Edwards married again, this time choosing a woman named Mary Talcott, who, it is recorded, was "a mediocre woman, average in talent and character and ordinary in appearance," and proceeded to have five sons and a daughter by her, it is noteworthy that not a single one of their progeny "rose above mediocrity and their descendants gained no abiding reputation."

Charles Benedict Davenport, author of *Heredity in Relation to Eugenics,* offers another example of extraordinary Family inheritance —in this case respecting the Virginia and Kentucky Family Aristocracy, one which came about through the relationship with what he calls a "noble" Irish Family. "Nearly two centuries ago," he declares, "John Preston, of Londonderry, Irish born, though English bred, married the Irish girl, Elizabeth Patton, of Donegal, and to the wilderness of Virginia he took his wife and built their home, 'Spring Hall.' They had five children, and from them," Davenport declares, "have come the most conspicuous of those who bear the name of Preston, Brown, Smith, Carrington, Venable, Payne, Wickcliffe, Wooley, Breckinridge, Benton, Porter and many other names written high in history." Then quoting a manuscript which, he declares, was furnished by "a reliable genealogist," he proceeds:

> They were generally persons of great talent and thoroughly educated; of large brain and magnificent physique. The men were brave and gallant, the women accomplished and fascinating and incomparably beautiful. There was no aristocracy in America that did not eagerly open its veins for the infusion of this Irish blood; and the families of Washington and Randolph and Patrick Henry and Henry Clay and the Hamptons, Wickcliffes, Marshalls, Peytons, Cabells, Crittendens, and Ingersolls felt proud of their alliances with this noble Irish family.
>
> They were governors and senators and members of Congress, and presidents of colleges and eminent divines, and brave generals, from Virginia, Kentucky, Louisiana, Missouri, California, Ohio, New York, Indiana, and South Carolina. There were four governors of old Virginia. They were members of the cabinets of Jefferson and Taylor and Buchanan and Lincoln. They had major-generals and brigadier-generals by the dozen; members of the Senate and House of Representatives by the score; and gallant officers in the Army and Navy by the hundred . . . fifty of them at least the bravest of the brave, sixteen of them dying on the field of battle, and all of them, and more than I can enumerate, children of this one Irish immigrant from the county of Derry, whose relatives are still prominent in that part of Ireland, one of them was recently (1910) mayor of Belfast.

Surely, it is clear, the generation of Irish Aristocracy which would arise with the Kellys and Kennedys, Murrays and McDonnells and all the others, was far from the first in this country. Eugenist Davenport, however, points out one interesting fact concerning the progenies of New England's Elizabeth Tuttle vs. Virginia's Elizabeth Patton—this being that, whereas the New England Family of the former abounds with scholars and inventors, the Virginia Family of the latter abounds with statesmen and military men. This he attributes to the different traits of the New England settlers and the Virginia Cavalier-colonists. And, in conclusion, he finds that the original

Family Founder became a great progenitor "largely because of some fortunate circumstances of personal gift or excellent reputation that enables his offspring to marry into the 'best blood.' "

Blue blood or no, there is no question but that, with the Southern Families, as was the case with the New Englanders, trade very definitely rears its often none too handsome head where Family-founding was concerned. "Although family records were until of late less carefully preserved (in Virginia) than in New England," says Virginia historian John Fiske, "yet the registered facts abundantly prove that the leading families had precisely the same sort of origin as the leading families of New England. For the most part they were either country squires, or prosperous yeomen, or craftsmen from the numerous urban guilds." And Virginia's own *Magazine of History and Biography* declares that "if the talk of 'Virginia Cavaliers' indicates an idea that most of the Virginia gentry were descended from men of high rank, who had adhered to the King's side and afterwards migrated to Virginia, it is assuredly incorrect." The magazine concludes:

> As we have before urged, and as we believe all genealogists having any competent acquaintance with the subject will agree, but few "scions of great English houses" came to any of the colonies. Gloucester . . . has always been distinguished in Virginia as the residence of a large number of families of wealth, education and good birth; but in only a few instances are they descended from "great houses" even of the English gentry. The families of Wyatt, Peyton and Throckmorton are perhaps the only ones derived from English houses of historic note; but they were never, in Virginia, as eminent for large estates and political influence as others of the same country whose English ancestry is of much less distinction. Next, as known descendants of minor gentry, were the families of Page, Burwell, Lightfoot and Clayton. Other leading names of the county, nothing certain in regard to whose English ancestry is known, were Kemp, Lewis, Warner etc.

Thomas Wertenbaker, after much research on the subject, finally came up with two dozen genuine "Cavaliers." However, while all of these men were indeed prominent at the time of their emigration, their names were not the great "Family names" of the Aristocracy of Southern Families. On the other hand, there are statistics to prove that early Family founders outdid even New Englanders when it came to leaving fortunes. When, for example, Virginia's "King Robin" Carter, whose descendants were to number two Presidents, six Governors of Virginia and Robert E. Lee himself, died as far back as 1732, he left an estate of more than 300,000 acres of land, 1,000 slaves and over 10,000 pounds—a huge fortune for those days —as well as his own private church. In this, Christ Church in Lancaster County, he not only had his own family pew but he had designed a whole quarter of the building for the use of his tenants and servants; upon his death he also had the largest, richest and heaviest tombstone in the country. Unhappily, as something of an antidote for the eulogy delivered by the parson concerning the "King," a brief verse was anonymously scribbled on the tombstone in chalk:

> Here lies Robin, but not Robin Hood,
> Here lies Robin that never was good,
> Here lies Robin that God has forsaken,
> Here lies Robin the Devil has taken.

Equally trade-minded, if less controversial, were Virginia's Fairfaxes, Fitzhughs and Randolphs, or, for that matter, the later Cobbs from Georgia, the Aikens from South Carolina, or the extremely successful Joseph Davis, brother of Jefferson Davis, of Mississippi. And down in aristocratic Charleston, when Nathaniel Heyward died in 1851—from whose family descended the late Dubose Heyward of *Porgy and Bess* fame—he left no less than fourteen rice plantations, 2,057 slaves and a total estate of $2,000,000. Meanwhile, up in Maryland, families of prevailingly middle-class mercantile origin who graduated into the Aristocracy included such as the Tilghmans, the Burwells, the Lloyds, the Goldsboroughs, the Blakes, the Ridgelys and the Lowndeses.

This does not mean, however, that there was not "birth" as well as money to the Southern Aristocracy—there was, of course; in fact there was much more emphasis on birth than on money, and one observer, Felix de Beaujour, noted: "A Bostonian would seek his fortune in the bottom of hell, but a Virginian would not go four steps for it." Nonetheless, there was stern similarity between the Aristocracy of South and North, although the "landed" nature of the Southern Aristocrat enabled him to stay "planted" far longer than his up-and-down Northern counterpart. The better Southern Families, like the better New England Families, had a proud code. An Adams, for example, would have subscribed heartily to Robert E. Lee's dictum that "duty is the sublimest word in the English language." Farther back, Clifford Dowdey recalls in his story of one of Virginia's oldest and grandest plantations, Berkeley Hundred and the famous Harrison Family, that children were told from an early age not to take advantage of those in an inferior position. "Carry yourself so that everybody may respect you," one father wrote his children. "Be calm and obliging to all the servants, and when you speak, do it mildly, even to the poorest slave." The Planters also had at least as stern a devotion as the New Englanders when it came to their public duties. "Year in and year out," says Louis Wright, "one finds the Lees, the Corbins, the Fitzhughs, the Carters, the Ludwells, the Burwells and others of the ruling families carefully performing the duties of public offices, even those which offered little reward in material things." And yet Wright makes clear trade was ever-present:

> Some of the most enterprising and prominent families of colonial Virginia were descended from merchants and tradesmen. Thomas and Philip Ludwell, Nicholas Spencer, Thomas Stegg, William Byrd I, Robert Bolling, Richard Booker, Miles Cary, George Brent, John Chew, and many others who might be named, belonged to trading families distinguished for their industry and shrewdness. Most of them grew rich in Virginia and begot sons to add luster to their names. As planters, they utilized every opportunity to increase their wealth and improve their status. But their social ambitions, one should always remember, were subservient to their financial interests, and no Seventeenth or early Eighteenth Century

Virginian was so foolish as to despise trade. Conditions of life in the colony prevented the growth of towns and placed a monopoly of trade in the hands of the planters. For this blessing they thanked God, and violently resented a coasting schooner from New England that came up their rivers to traffic with their poorer neighbors, tenants, or slaves. The only trade the planters despised was the petty traffic of interlopers.

Carl Bridenbaugh, who has made a study of virtually all the Societies of the Colonial South, declares that the Family was "the one human institution common to and binding all ranks together." He also makes clear that stemming from this and intensified "by the condition of rural life" was the large number of intermarriages. "This," he concludes, "was naturally most discernible among patrician families, although eventually nearly every white person—and sometimes black—became kin to everyone else." Also, as not only Bridenbaugh but also a far earlier authority, Jonathan Boucher, noted, the Family left a permanent imprint in the sands of time. Reporting back to his English readers in *Reminiscences of an American Loyalist,* he declared:

> Certain districts came to be settled by certain families; and different places are there known and spoken of, not as here (in England), by any difference of dialect (for there is no dialect in all North America) but by their being inhabited by the Fitzhughs, the Randolphs, Washingtons, Carys, Grimeses, or Thorntons. This circumstance used to furnish me with a scope for many remarks, such as do not often occur here. The family character both of body and mind, may be traced thro' many generations: as for instance every Fitzhugh has bad eyes; every Thornton hears badly; Winslows and Lees talk well; Carters are proud and imperious; and Taliaferros mean and avaricious; and Fowkeses cruel.*

Probably the most remarkable Southern Family from the point of long-term eminence is Virginia's Byrd Family. Known in its most

---

* This writer recently received a communication from a professor at Johns Hopkins who declared that he was engaged in tracing hemophilia—a disease which occurs, for practical purposes, only in males but is transmitted through females. In one single Family, New England's highly pedigreed Appleton Family, the professor had been able to trace hemophilia for 350 years.

recent generation through the Senator, Harry, as well as for his late brother, Admiral Richard, the explorer, this generation also includes another brother, Thomas; thus the trio of Byrd brothers have been known, rather ironically in view of the social gravity of the Family, as "Tom, Dick and Harry."

Some years ago the three brothers repaired, after a day's hunting in Virginia, to a friend's house for dinner. The meal was remarkably good, and afterwards, during the after-dinner brandies, Senator Harry Byrd announced, in his self-possessed manner, that he wished to present his personal compliments to his friend's cook. The latter, a Negro, was promptly summoned, whereupon the Senator bon-homously thanked him, then asked what was his name. Replied the cook gently, "Byrd, sir." "Byrd?" asked the Senator, surprised. "How do you spell it?" "B-y-r-d," spelled the cook.

Before the astonished Senator could comment, his brother Tom entered the conversation. A retiring and modest member of the Byrd brother trio, he is not known publicly and prefers it that way, confining himself to his excellent apple farm. In any case, he too asked the cook to spell his name. "B-y-r-d," again spelled the cook. For a moment Tom said nothing, then, his eyes twinkling, he said, "You are an excellent cook, Byrd, and I want you to meet two very distinguished relatives of yours—Senator Byrd and Admiral Byrd." The introductions accomplished, Tom once more retired into the anonymity he prizes.

The late explorer, who died in 1957, was perhaps the most pompous of all Twentieth Century Byrds. Nonetheless, it should be remembered that if he was the man who most thoroughly epit-omized latter-day Byrd traits, he was also a man of lasting scientific accomplishment. And even he, in a more philosophical moment late in life, said, "A man doesn't begin to attain wisdom until he is no longer indispensable." Furthermore, although with the exception of Tom Byrd, Byrds have not been known for their humor, it was also the late explorer who said, "No woman has ever stepped on Little America, and we have found it to be the most silent and peaceful place in the world."

The first Byrd to step on Big America was William Byrd the Elder. Born in London in 1652, he was the oldest son of a London goldsmith who had married the daughter of a rich ship captain who traded to the Virginia Colony. The Family founder came to Virginia in his youth to live with his uncle, Captain Thomas Stegg, from whom he inherited rich properties near where the city of Richmond would one day stand. In 1673 he married the daughter of a Royalist refugee named Warham Horsmandel; they had four children, although only one son survived to carry the Family into the next generation. But one was enough, for William Byrd I was an extraordinary Family founder. "Tobacco planter, merchant, fur trader, slave dealer, importer, speculator, public official, Colonel of militia," says Thomas Wertenbaker, "he typified the spirit of the Seventeenth Century Virginia Aristocracy." He also, it might be said, like so many of the New Englanders, seems to have had a premonition of Family-founding. Even his three daughters were sent to school in England as "mere infants," and in 1685, when one of his daughters was only four years old, Byrd wrote his father-in-law in England his own slant on growing up in a slave Society. "My wife hath all this year urged me to send little Nutty (Ursula) home to you," he wrote, "to which I have at last condescended, and hope you will excuse the trouble. I must confess she could learn nothing good here in a great family of negroes."

As for his son, William Byrd the Younger, or William Byrd II, the elder Byrd first placed him under the tutelage of a famous English schoolmaster in England, then sent him to Holland, where, in the care of one of his mercantile correspondents, he would learn about business and trade. "Byrd had no intention," says Louis Wright, "of bringing up a son who would have the polish of a gentleman and yet lack the training needed to carry the burden of business that was a necessary concomitant of a great planter's life." And finally, on his death in 1704, the Family founder cut off his surviving daughters with a few hundred pounds and left all the rest of his great estate to his son.

In 1706 William Byrd II married the daughter of Daniel Parke, who had fought with Marlborough on the Continent and had brought the news of the victory at Blenheim to Queen Anne. "My wife and I quarrelled about her pulling her brows," he wrote in his diary in 1711, in time-honored husband style. "She threatened she would not go to Williamsburg if she might not pull them." The affair was concluded, however, far differently in those happy-husband days. "I refused," Byrd wrote briefly, "and got the better of her and maintained my authority."

The couple had four children, but only two daughters survived. One of these, however, Evelyn Byrd, became one of the greatest belles in Southern history. At sixteen she was presented to George II, who stared on her in amazement. "Are there many other as beautiful birds," he asked, "in the forests of America?" This play upon words evidently suggested to Sir Godfrey Keller the thought of painting Evelyn with a cardinal bird in the background. Hers was perhaps the greatest triumph of any American girl in London, before or since. Declares one Family biographer:

> Her hand was kissed by my Lords Oxford and Chesterfield; of whom sneering Harvey deigned to approve; who supped with Pope at his Twickenham villa, while yet the town was ringing with the success of his Odyssey; who was noticed by Beau Nash, the autocrat of Bath; who saw Cibber and Mrs. Oldfield play; who read Gulliver's Travels as they were first presented to the public by his reverence the dean of St. Patrick's, then resident in Dublin; who from the presence-chamber of unroyal royalty, through a Society reeking with wine and musk and snuff and scandal, passed back to her plantation home in the new country as unblemished as she came.

Nonetheless, the final story of Evelyn Byrd was the saddest of all the many many sad stories of Southern belles. She had fallen in love in London; the gentleman's name was Charles Mordaunt, handsome grandson and heir of Lord Peterborough. Unhappily, William Byrd and Lord Peterborough had a quarrel. Some say it was over cards, others over religion; still others hint at a darker reason. In any case, once fast friends, they became mortal enemies. Byrd refused to sanction the match and brought his daughter home to Westover. In the nine years that remained to Evelyn she never lacked for other admirers; her beauty was if anything enhanced by her suffering. But day by day, according to Family records, she literally pined away, and on the thirteenth day of November, 1737, at age 29, she died. In the aged Family record in Brandon, where her famous portrait hangs, there is a brief note—"Refusing all offers from other gentlemen, she died of a broken heart." At Westover, where she lived, for more than two centuries there have been stories of her ghost. "There are some who say," says Edith Tunis Sale, "they have felt the light touch of her exquisite fingers, others who have seen the white wraith hover near one of her favorite haunts; but there are none who fear the ghostly presence of the tender, lovely Evelyn, who asked of life the one thing it denied her." And, concludes Miss Sale, in *Old Time Belles and Cavaliers:*

> The lengthy inscription upon her heavy tomb is guarded jealously by mosses and lichens which screen the best they can the piteous words from idle gaze. This tiny bit of God's earth, sacred to the memory of one of His most beautiful human creations, is thickly carpeted with the periwinkle vine ever-green through dreary winter months in remembrance of her who sleeps beneath. . . . The days that Mistress Evelyn knew belonged to that unique and beautiful era when high-heeled dames coquetted with gold-laced cavaliers; to that delightful and remarkable period which produced minds and masters, belles and beauties in whom vanity was blended with bravery with such wonderful results that the American people are what they are today. Hers was a time of filial obedience, which made it an age of tyranny and selfish parents. More than all, it was a day of pretty love stories, sometimes of pathetic disappointments and broken hearts, yet never has there been such a picturesque age, never will be again such famous belles, and never will life be so unique and well worth living as when Evelyn Byrd was the toast of two worlds.

The first Mrs. Byrd II died in 1724, and Byrd took as his second wife the daughter of an English gentleman of Kensington. By her he had three daughters and a son, William Byrd III. The latter became the heir of Westover, but, says William Meade, soon engaged in "all the prodigalities and dissipations to which young men of rank and fashion are addicted." Finally he dissipated his property as well as himself, turned Tory during the Revolution, and eventually committed suicide.

In coming to grief in its third generation the Byrd Family failed the hurdle which has plagued so many families outside of America's Family Circle. The general pattern has been, or so this writer has found, that the first generation, the man who makes the money and founds the Family, is inclined to be tough and hard, rough and ready, with a self-made, often small-town wife, at his side. But even allowing for the fact that both may be inclined to be boorish and more takers than givers, the fact remains that, generally speaking, both have been, in their limited ways, pretty able citizens. When the second generation comes along, however—the generation that spends the money—here the son, given everything on a silver platter which the first generation had to work for, is inclined to be soft, spoiled and selfish; his wife, chosen from the upper ranks which the first generation finally reached, can either be as bad, or, as sometimes happens, the saving factor in the situation. In any case, the third generation is the crucial one. Here the Family either nobly proves its staying power and its ability to hold its place in the Aristocracy or it fails miserably and falls back again to oblivion. In the words of Virginian John Stuart Bryan, "Many men can make a fortune but very few can build a Family."

Although the Byrds did indeed fail in their third generation, the fact that they did not run through the usual second-generation miseries is generally regarded by Family historians as being primarily responsible for their managing, despite the weakness of the third generation, to establish themselves firmly in the upper echelon of Families—one which has continued, both in direct lines and in collateral ones, to the present day.

Actually, in their second generation the Byrds produced, in William Byrd II, one of the outstanding planter Aristocrats in the country's history. Despite the miseries of his daughter Evelyn, and indeed the fate of his son, William III, the second generation came up with an extraordinary man indeed. "Explorer, churchman, *bon vivant*, linguist, scientist," says Marshall Fishwick, "William Byrd II saw and thought as much as any American who died before the Revolution." While Governor Spotswood railed against "the haughtiness of a Carter, the hypocrisy of a Blair, the malice of a Byrd," Byrd led the fight in the Virginia Council for what, on a local scale, would later be an almost exact parallel between the States' Rights and Federal issues. In his own lifetime, as one of the Commissioners of the dividing line between Virginia and North Carolina, Byrd proved himself a pioneer surveyor and geographer, not only of the South but of the West as well. A man who had as much hunger for success as his father—rare indeed in any second-generation story— he increased his estate from 23,231 acres at his father's death to 179,440 acres at his own. Yet he was far from primarily a material man. All his life he maintained a tremendous correspondence with his English friends, writing letters which were both erudite and witty, and his library of 3,600 volumes was the largest of any in the South and was equaled in the North only by that of his New England contemporary, Cotton Mather. And if his diary indicates he made good use of his books, it also indicates he did not spare himself a good time. One entry indeed, from 1709, is not only a lasting picture of a planter's lighter side—one which is, curiously, not so different from a Puritan's—but also contrasts rather sadly with the life of his poor daughter, Evelyn:

> I rose at 6 o'clock and read a chapter in Hebrew and some Greek in Lucian. I said my prayers and ate milk for breakfast, and settled some accounts, and then went to court where we made an end of the business. We went to dinner about 4 o'clock and I ate boiled beef again. In the evening I went to Dr. B-r-t's, where my wife came this afternoon. Here I found Mrs. Chriswell, my sister Custis, and other ladies. We sat and talked till about 11 o'clock, and then retired to our chambers. I played at (r-m) with Mrs. Chriswell and kissed her on the bed till she was angry and my wife was also uneasy about it, and cried as soon as the company was gone. I neglected to say my prayers, which I should not have done, because I ought to beg pardon for the lust I had for another man's wife. However, I had good health, good thoughts, and good humor, thanks be to God Almighty.

Far outranking the Byrds in past distinction and one of the all-time greats of Southern Families are the Randolphs of Virginia. Although the name still has an aura about it—in keeping with its once-proud position as the No. 1 "F" in F.F.V.—the fact remains that few Randolphs have been nationally prominent in recent times. In the 1960 *Who's Who*, for example, not a single one of the nine Randolphs listed was born in Virginia, had addresses in the Old Dominion or, for that matter, had direct descent to "royal" line. And, as almost a final indignity, the most prominent of living Randolphs, as of the 1960's, was Jennings Randolph, United States Senator from—of all places, from the F.F.V. point of view—*West Virginia*. The Twentieth Century, it is true, has seen several locally well-known Randolphs, including Harrison Randolph, president of the College of Charleston, Norfolk's late Bishop Randolph, railway president Epes Randolph, lawyer Hollins Randolph, civil engineer Isham Randolph, and a well-known doctor, William Mann Randolph, as well as pianist Harold Randolph, ophthalmologist Robert Lee Randolph, and author Sarah Nicholas Randolph. But none of these has been able to add lasting luster to a name which in the Eighteenth and Nineteenth Centuries ranked in the North as well as in the South as one of America's greatest Families.

Although certain Randolphs have derived armorial comforts from the Scottish clans of Randolph, the evidence supporting such claims is thin. On the other hand, there is better support for their claim of descent from Pocahontas and her English husband, John Rolfe. In any case, one thing is certain. The American Family founder, "well connected or not," was as much a merchant and trader, and indeed a self-made story, as any to come out of New England or the West. Arriving in Virginia in 1673, well after the early troubles and "starving time," he was able to take advantage of the disturbances culminating in Bacon's Rebellion—in fact he secured one of Bacon's confiscated estates—and received lands which from the days of John Smith had been known as "Turkey Island." Married to the daughter of Henry Royall Isham, of the neighboring plantation, "Bermuda Hundred," he went on to acquire vast tracts of land

and establish all seven of his sons on plantations of his own. H. J. Eckenrode, historian of the Randolphs, describes him as a "Colonial Horatio Alger hero." "He did not start out blacking boots," he says, "but he did make his beginning by building barns." And, summing up, he says:

> William Randolph was essentially of the predatory type—such men nearly always succeed in a new country. In later times he would perhaps have been a lumber magnate or a captain of industry. His great hawk nose indicated that he looked on mankind as his prey and knew how to make the most of his opportunities, which were unusually good near the end of the seventeenth century. A poor emigrant, he established the leading family of colonial Virginia, one of the noted families in America. An economic and political strategist, he planted his sons along the James River in situations by which they individually profited and furthered the prestige and power of the family. There were few stronger or more prescient men in colonial America than William Randolph of Turkey Island. His was a classic story of colonial success. He began life without an acre and before he died he owned 10,000 acres. The prototype of the nineteenth-century millionaire, he was able to profit by the opportunity that colonial unrest made for him.

Not the least of William Randolph's accomplishments was the size of the Family he established. His children, named, as was the custom, together with their plantations, were William II, of Turkey Island, Thomas of Tuckahoe, Isham of Dungeness, Richard of Curles, Henry of Chatsworth, Sir John of Tazewell Hall, Edward of Bremo, and Mary and Elizabeth. From these he had the extraordinary number of thirty-seven grandchildren, a number which, considering the fact that a baby had about a fifty-fifty chance of living in those days, was almost incredible. In any case, more than one historian has emphasized the fact that Randolph blood flowed in the veins of nearly all the Virginia immortals, including John Marshall and Robert E. Lee. As for Thomas Jefferson, he was more than half a Randolph. His father, Peter Jefferson, who was himself a Randolph connection, had married Jane Randolph, daughter of Isham Randolph of Dungeness, and Jefferson's daughter, Martha, would later marry her own cousin, Thomas Mann Randolph I, Governor of Virginia. The marriage of cousins was a common occurrence among Randolphs. So too were early marriages, and it was not considered unusual when Randolph relative John Marshall married a bride of fourteen. But Thomas Jefferson's influence on, and influence by, the Randolph Family is an unusual part of Randolph Family history. "The transmission of estates from generation to generation," Jefferson wrote, "to men who bore the same name, had the effect of raising up a distinct class of families, who, possessing by law the privilege of perpetuating their wealth, formed by these means a sort of patrician order, distinguished by the grandeur and luxury of their establishments." Yet Jefferson, who was to deal such a blow to primogeniture, brought his own daughter up with an aristocratic philosophy which seems to have fitted her admirably for marriage into the South's leading aristocratic Family. She was also brought up almost incredibly well disciplined, as witness the following letter Jefferson wrote to her when, at age 11, she was attending boarding school in Philadelphia:

> With respect to the distribution of your time, the following is what I should approve: From 8 to 10, practise music. From 10 to 1, dance one day and draw another. From 1 to 2, draw on the day you dance and write a letter next day. From 3 to 4, read French. From 4 to 5, exercise yourself in music. From 5 till bed-time read English, write, &c. . . . Inform me what books you read, what tunes you learn, and inclose me your best copy of every lesson in drawing. . . . Take care that you never spell a word wrong. . . . It produces great praise to a lady to spell well.

The best known of the sons of William I of Turkey Island, a man who was to carry the name forward to new heights in the difficult second generation, was Sir John Randolph of Tazewell Hall. Although he died at the age of 43, he was easily the country's outstanding lawyer of the first half of the Eighteenth Century. Educated at the then new College of William and Mary, he went to England and was admitted to study law in Gray's Inn in 1715 as "John Randolph of Virginia, gent."—which is proof positive that even in the Eighteenth Century the Mother Nation recognized that her American Colonies could make a gentleman in, if not one generation, then at least in two. Later John was to return to England when he was chosen by the Virginia Assembly to present its grievances over tobacco to the King. At this time, despite his querulous mission, he was so widely admired for both his legal and diplomatic skill that he was, in 1732, knighted—a rare accomplishment indeed for a Colonial anywhere.

Also, although Sir John died in the prime of his life, the Randolph Family did not suffer the usual trials and tribulations of third-gen-erationdom. Indeed Sir John's son, Peyton Randolph, not only fol-lowed his father in almost all of the latter's offices but also became, in the decade preceding the Revolution, the presiding officer of virtually every important Revolutionary assemblage in the Virginia Colony. Married to the daughter of Colonel Benjamin Harrison— her brother later became President Harrison—it was Peyton who established the precedent of Randolphs holding political office almost by the fact of their being Randolphs; unlike so many of the others, however, he was not only able but popular as well. Thomas Jefferson himself lauded him. "None was," he said after his death, "ever more beloved or respected by his friends." This, despite Jefferson's Randolph Family ties, was high praise indeed, for not only were Randolphs rapidly developing their well-known family traits of hauteur, irascibility and scorn of the opinions of others, they also, generally speaking, stood foursquare against the Jeffer-sonian ideal of anti-primogeniture in particular and pro-democracy in general. But it should be borne in mind that Randolphs could not be easily type-cast. Peyton Randolph, for example, who once shouted that he would give five hundred guineas—an incredible sum in those days—for one vote against the "homespun demagogue" Patrick Henry, later not only joined Henry but also chairmaned the first intercolonial committee to keep the patriots in one Colony informed of what was happening in the others. Says Eckenrode, memorably describing this group:

What a wonderful committee it was! We see them conferring, eager and perhaps anxious, uncertain of the outcome of their effort to knit the colonies together in resistance to the British government. There were: Randolph, tall and powerful and red-faced, a veritable ox of a man; Nicholas, thin and philosophical-looking, with a high forehead; Cary, slender and debonair and fierce-eyed, a real revolutionary (he was to threaten to stab Henry if he became a dictator); Richard Henry Lee, hatchet-faced, with the black eyes all Lees have; Patrick Henry with his actor's mobile face, now wearing a better coat, no longer a rustic; Jefferson, tall and slender, with his ugly red hair and his long face, his prominent nose and his jutting chin; Carr, calm and elegant—soon to die and to be lamented by Jefferson for all his days; Harrison and Digges, rather commonplace-looking gentlemen. A group of men setting upon a great task and accomplishing it.

Even in such company one finds a Randolph as leader. However, if Peyton Randolph was perhaps the prime example of a Randolph as Patriot, Sir John's second son, another John, was a prime example of a Randolph as Tory. Like his father and elder brother, he started out in the usual "Randolph" offices and became a King's attorney. But when the Revolution came, he threw in his lot with the King's side and fled, with his wife and two beautiful daughters, to England. Although during the Revolution he drew up a plan of conciliation with America—one which he proposed, unsuccessfully, to the British ministry—he died as he had lived, a Loyalist, relenting only so far as to urge his daughter, just before he died, to bring his body back to Virginia for burial. The wish his daughter faithfully carried out.

This John Randolph's son, the great Edmund Randolph, never accompanied his family to England. Instead, from the beginning of strong patriotic sympathies, he stayed in America and was brought up in the family of his uncle, Peyton Randolph, who had no children of his own. At the age of 23 he became the youngest member of the Virginia Convention which adopted the first constitution of the States. An extraordinary man in every way, he was such a successful lawyer that clients, it is recorded, "beset him on the way from his office to the courthouse with their papers in one hand

and their guineas in the other." Perhaps the most personally charming of all Randolphs, he also married a charming wife, Betsy Nicholas, daughter of Robert Carter Nicholas, and of her he wrote, in high Randolphian style:

> She won me by the best of all graces, cheerfulness, good sense and benevolence. I do not recollect that I reflected much upon that range of qualities which I afterward found to be constituents of nuptial happiness; but Providence seemed to be kinder to me than my most deliberate judgment could have been.

Not the least remarkable thing about this remarkable man was that he was, all his life, an unalterable opponent of slavery. A relatively poor man, he also inherited, on his uncle's death, a large debt —one which he would have been able to pay off had he been willing to sell his uncle's slaves. Unwilling, however, to do so, he was, in a sense, trapped by them. "Virginians of that period," says Eckenrode, "were eaten out of house and home by darkies of every age and condition, some of them a hundred years old. Slaves sometimes ran away from masters and masters sometimes ran away from slaves."

As Governor of Virginia, Edmund Randolph played an important part in getting Virginia to ratify the Constitution and afterwards served with distinction as Washington's Attorney General. When he became his country's Secretary of State, however, his position was a difficult one, since the people, as well as their government, were sharply divided in their opinions and affections in respect to both Great Britain and France—and not always in the same direction. Randolph, opposed by both Jefferson and Hamilton, did his best to act as a buffer between all parties, but finally, after charges brought by the French Minister Fauchet, that Randolph had improperly divulged secrets about his own government, he resigned. He was later forced to pay an immense debt to the government, which, it was alleged, he had improperly incurred. Although his friends rallied and totally denied the charge, Randolph in the end paid every penny. In his latter years he rose to eminence once more—albeit to typically controversial eminence—as senior counsel for Aaron

Burr in the famous treason trial. Here his brilliance and erudition flowered once more, and Randolph's defense of Burr not only resulted in a "not proved" verdict, it is also still studied as a master-piece of legal defense. Shortly afterward he died, succumbing to what was the so-called Randolph "Family disease"—paralysis.

There were many other distinguished Randolphs in the Nine-teenth Century—in the Family's fifth, sixth and even seventh gen-erations. One of these was Edmund's grandson, another Edmund Randolph, who went out to San Francisco during the Gold Rush and afterwards became, it is recorded, "more powerful in invective than any other lawyer among his contemporaries." Another was Thomas Mann Randolph, who married Jefferson's daughter, Martha, and lived with Jefferson at Monticello. Like Jefferson, Randolph was a free thinker and once said he considered theology "a depart-ment of the imagination." He had ten children, ranging from the eldest, Thomas Jefferson Randolph, later handler of Jefferson's financial affairs, to the youngest, George Wythe Randolph, Secre-tary of War under the Confederacy. And, if the latter failed in that thankless task—primarily due to Jefferson Davis' continual meddling —the fact remains he was no Southern sunshine patriot. Among other things, he read a Latin or Greek author in the original every morn-ing before breakfast.

The most brilliant of all Randolphs—albeit also the most unstable —was the great John Randolph of Roanoke. Descended from what has been called the "weak strain" in the Family, he was the great-grandson of William I of Turkey Island, the grandson of Richard of Curles, and the son of John Randolph and Frances Bland; he was also the great-great-grandson of Pocahontas. But the "Curles" planta-tion of his grandfather had given way to a plantation named "Bizarre" by the time of John of Roanoke's birth in 1773. And the plantation was, as it turned out, well named. John of Roanoke's father died young, and in the custom of the times, his mother mar-ried soon again, this time choosing St. George Tucker, thus allying the Randolphs with that elderly and distinguished Bermuda Family. By him, she had several children, and the Tuckers were to carry on their distinction, particularly in the Episcopalian ministry, into the Twentieth Century.

Not so the Randolphs—and particularly not so in this Randolph line. For, with the death of John of Roanoke's father, John's older brother Richard became master of Bizarre. A nervous, introverted young man, he married, at the age of 20, his cousin Judith, daughter of Thomas Mann Randolph, when she was only 16. Again, in the custom of the times, Judith's sister, Nancy, came to live with them. And then Nancy, not Judith, became pregnant. The tragedy was played out at a plantation near Bizarre, named Glenlyvar, which was owned by Randolph Harrison, where Richard, Judith and Nancy all went together on a visit. Here, on a dark and stormy night in October, 1792, Nancy either underwent a primitive abortion operation or else gave birth to a child which was later found to be dead. In any case, in the greatest scandal in Randolph Family history, Richard and Nancy went on trial together for murder.

No trial in Virginia history was more of a *cause célèbre* than this. So almost unbelievably upper-case was the influence involved that not one but two lawyers were engaged for the defense—their names were Patrick Henry and John Marshall. The key witness turned out to be none other than the wife, Judith, who bravely fought to uphold what in those days was a very definite thing—Family honor—and declared that the only untoward event which had occurred the fateful night was that her sister Nancy had had one of her "hysterical attacks," for which she had taken laudanum. John Roanoke also testified for his brother and sister-in-law, although he had long believed that Nancy was engaged to his other brother Theodoric. In any case, Richard and Nancy were acquitted.

The aftermath of the trial was in many ways as extraordinary as the trial itself. Nancy, the principal, recovered completely and later went on to marry, still in her twenties, the distinguished 60-year-old Gouverneur Morris of New York; their life was an apparently happy one. On the other hand, Richard of Bizarre never recovered. Broken completely by the trial, he died within four years. Theodoric also died young. Judith lived for many years, but always in the shadow of the shame. And as for John of Roanoke, he was left with a bitterness not only toward Nancy but, it seems, toward the world in general. He removed to his plantation at Roanoke and, though once engaged to a girl named Maria Ward, who later married the son of Edmund Randolph in his stead, never married. There were, in fact, no more Randolph children at all from this line; the so-called "weak strain" was over.

But John Randolph of Roanoke left a stronger mark on his country than many a man with ten children. "I am an aristocrat," he said proudly. "I love liberty. I hate equality." Even as a boy, despite the kindly efforts of his long-suffering stepfather, St. George Tucker, he was distrustful, arrogant and difficult. "A tall, gawky-looking, flaxen-haired stripling," one contemporary described him, "with a complexion of a good parchment color, beardless chin, and as much assumed self-confidence as any two-footed animal I ever saw." His passion, however, as a young man, was four-footed animals, and as a distance-racing rider he was, despite his early-evidenced delicate health, extraordinary; he once rode non-stop from Charleston to Savannah. A voracious reader, even as a child his casual speech was interwoven with dozens of classical references. As a phrasemaker, he was soon without an equal—and, for that matter, so quick was his tongue he was also soon without a friend. In his youth he barely avoided a half-dozen duels—and not because he backed out, for he was a crack shot. Later in life, he fought a famous duel with his bitter enemy Henry Clay.

There was never a duel like it in the history of dueling. The weapons chosen were pistols; the distance, the mortal one of ten paces only. But on the morning of the duel Randolph appeared with his lean, now rapidly emaciating body wrapped in an enormous cape—one which he carried as widespread as possible. "It constituted such a vast circumference," said *Harper's Magazine*, "that the locality of the Senator was at least a matter of vague conjecture." Before the signal to fire, Randolph's pistol went off. Clay generously declared it was an accident. Once again they squared off. This time both fired, but neither was hit. Once more the signal was given. This time Randolph pointed his pistol skyward and said, firing, "I do not fire at you, Mr. Clay." Clay, however, did fire at his opponent —in fact, he hit the object, then rushed forward toward his opponent in consternation, shouting "Are you hurt?" Whereupon, Randolph parted the vast folds of his cape and appeared utterly uninjured, except to exclaim in his piercing voice, "Mr. Clay, you owe me a coat—you owe me a coat." Clay, it is recorded, then pointed at his opponent's heart. "Mr. Randolph," he said, "I thank God I am not deeper in your debt."

As a politician Randolph, who served not only in the Virginia legislature, but also in the Congress and later the Senate, was an anomaly even in his own day. First he was pro-Jefferson, then vitriolically anti-Jefferson. First he was pro-French Revolution, then bitterly opposed to all things French and devoted to all things English—in fact he became probably the best friend England ever had in the American Congress. Against slavery, privately and on principle, he was nonetheless for it publicly and practically when it involved his beloved issue—States' Rights. A champion of Lost Causes, he also showed an almost uncanny prescience concerning the South's future miseries. And, for all his eccentricities, he had, in the entire history of the country, no peer as an orator. Even the "Godlike Dan'l" Webster, so praised in the North and another bitter enemy of his, paled before him. Furthermore, Randolph held people with none of the time-honored equipment of the great orators. His voice was thin, almost piping, his looks eccentric and feminine, his health, indeed his lung capacity itself, poor. But even his enemies who disagreed with everything he said, even people who came only for the purpose of scoffing and jeering, were invariably spellbound before he had concluded his first sentence. His "draw" was extraordinary; even in the backwoods districts a speech of his was tantamount to a declared holiday of people from every walk of life. "His eyes," said one observer, "were brilliant beyond description. Though he was as much excited as a speaker could well be, yet he did not betray his emotion by any quivering of lip, tremor of a nerve, or hurry of a word." Hugh Blair Grigsby, who was himself a member of

the Virginia Convention, years later caught best the power which
Randolph exerted, not only in Virginia, but later in Washington:

> He inspired terror to a degree that, even at this distance of time,
> seems inexplicable. He was feared alike by East and West, by
> friend and foe. The arrows from his quiver, if not dipped in poison,
> were pointed and barbed, rarely missed the mark, and as seldom
> failed to make a rankling wound. He seemed to paralyze alike the
> mind and body of his victim. What made his attack more vexatious,
> every sarcasm took effect amid the plaudits of his audience. He
> called himself, on one occasion, a tomahawker and scalper, and
> true to the race, from which he sprung, he never explained away
> or took back anything; and, as he knew the private as well as
> public history of every prominent member, it was impossible for
> his opponents to foresee from what quarter, and on whom his
> attacks would fall. He also had political accounts of long standing
> to settle with sundry individuals, and none could tell when the
> day of reckoning would arrive. And, when it did come, it was a
> stern and fearful one. What unnerved his opponents was a con-
> viction of his invulnerability, apparent or real; for, unconnected
> as he was by any social relation, and ready to fall back on a
> colossal fortune, he was not on equal terms with men who were
> struggling to acquire a competency, and whose hearts were bound
> by all the endearing ties of domestic love.

The reference to Randolph's fortune is exaggerated; far from
"colossal," his fortune was a modest one. Nonetheless, the idea of
his invulnerability is indeed accurate. Curiously, Randolph's wit-
ticisms were of such a personal nature and so appropriate to the
occasion that he has not gone down in history as a wit—indeed
rarely is he found at all in books of quotation. This is a pity, for wit
he was, as witness his characterization of Clay: "So brilliant, yet so
corrupt, like rotten mackerel by moonlight, he shines and stinks."
Or, for another example, take his statement on the appointment of
Richard Rush as Secretary of War: "Never was ability so much
below mediocrity so well rewarded; no, not even when Caligula's
horse was made Consul." Once on the floor of the House, in the
midst of one of his harangues, he was three times interrupted by a
Representative Beecher of Ohio who would shout, "Previous ques-

tion, Mr. Speaker! Previous question, Mr. Speaker!" At first Randolph ignored him completely, then some time later he began. "Mr. Speaker," he said, "in the Netherlands, a man of small capacity, with bits of wood and leather, will, in a few moments, construct a toy, that, with the pressure of the finger and thumb, will cry, 'Cuckoo! Cuckoo!' With less ingenuity, and with inferior materials, the people of Ohio have made a toy that will, without much pressure, cry, 'Previous question, Mr. Speaker! Previous question, Mr. Speaker!'"

One of John Randolph's best-remembered speeches was the one in which he took, as usual, the unpopular side, from the people's point of view, of a proposal to pay Congressmen, instead of $6 a day, the sum of $1,500 a year. Randolph began by seeming to take the people's side—in fact he personally, he said, was in favor of not paying Congressmen at all, since they were, after all, supposed to be gentlemen. Unfortunately, his argument ran, they were apparently not gentlemen, and therefore he supposed that they should get about as much an hour as a man got for sawing wood—which was all the new bill proposed. Well remembered too is his reply to one of Webster's early speeches. "Asking one of the States to surrender part of her sovereignty," he said, "is like asking a lady to surrender part of her chastity." Less well remembered is the rage which led Webster, on another occasion, to accuse him of impotency. "I would not attempt to vie with the honorable gentleman from Massachusetts," retorted Randolph, "in a field where every nigger is his peer and every billy-goat his master."

In the end, his frail body racked by years of disease, he nevertheless still spoke regularly, and even from a wheel chair the effect was overpowering. Also he maintained, to the bitter end, his biting correspondence. One of the last of his letters, dated the year of his death, is addressed to Jacob Harvey:

> The springs of life are worn out. Indeed in the abject state of the public mind, there is nothing worth living for. It is a merciful dispensation of Providence that death can release the captive from the clutches of the tyrant. . . . I could not have believed that the

people would so soon have shown themselves unfit for free government. I leave to General Jackson, and the Hartford men, and the ultra Federalists and Tories, and the office-holders and office-seekers, *their triumph over the liberties of the country. They will stand damned to everlasting fame.*

Only one thing, at the actual end, worried Randolph—where he would be buried. "I would not die in Washington," he declared, "be eulogized by men I despise and buried in the Congressional Burying Ground. The idea of lying by the side of ———! Ah, that adds a new horror to death." Actually he died in Philadelphia and was buried in Roanoke, but not, as is the custom, with his face to the east. Instead, in accordance with his last wish, he was buried with his face to the west. This, it was long rumored by local residents in Roanoke, was so that, even in death, he could "keep an eye on Henry Clay." And when, in 1779, Randolph's body was exhumed by John Randolph Bryan and his son, Joseph Bryan, for reburial in Richmond's Hollywood Cemetery, the rumor was found to be correct. John Randolph of Roanoke had indeed been buried with his face to the west.

Despite the Randolph rank in the generally recognized "F.F.V." hierarchy, it must take second place to one other—the Lee Family. Indeed so extraordinary is the Lee Family for past eminence that it still reigns supreme in this regard among all American Families save only the Adamses. "I know of no country," said George Washington, "that can produce a family, all distinguished as clever men, as the Lees." And yet Washington said that in 1777 when the greatest of all Lees had not yet even been born. And two years later John Adams also paid tribute to the greatest of all Southern Families. "The Family of Lee," he said, "has more merit in it than any other Family."*

* There is also a noted Boston Family of Lees, no relation to the far more distinguished Southern Family, but nonetheless of no little New England eminence and the Family from which descends, among others, the firm of Lee, Higginson & Co. A "clipper-ship" Family, the founder, Captain Joseph Lee, went to sea in 1658, at the age of 13, later making a fortune and getting himself one of the "Cabot wives" of "shut them up" fame. Colonel Henry Lee was one of the most formidable members of this clan, originator of banking's "safety

The first Lee to come to this country was Richard Lee who, arriving in 1640, shortly became the right-hand man of Sir William Berkeley. Described as a man of "good stature, comely visage, an enterprising genius, a sound head, vigorous spirit and generous nature," he set in more ways than one the pattern which was to culminate so many generations later with the leader of the Confederacy. Married to a woman who bore him eight children—one whose maiden name, to the misery of Family genealogists, has been lost to posterity—he became by the time of his death the greatest landowner of his generation. Later when the country was opened to the West, other larger landowners like Carters and Byrds, Fairfaxes and Fitzhughs would out-acre the Lees, but in 1664 no Virginian equaled his 13,000 acres of rich tobacco soil. A man of two countries, he crossed and recrossed the Atlantic almost as often as modern captains of industry. He chose, nonetheless, to come back to die at his beloved "Cobb's Hall."

As in the case of the Byrd children, the four sons of the Lee Family founder were educated in England. The first died young, another married and lived the rest of his life in England. Still a third, Harold Lee, educated in America, married the granddaughter of Isaac Allerton, richest of *Mayflower* passengers, and produced a Lee line of his own, known as the "Ditchley line" from the name of their plantation on the Chesapeake. The son who was to prove the able heir apparent, however, was Richard II. A scholarly, bookish, rather melancholy man, he "played the part," says Burton Hendrick, "of a General Monk, firmly settling a Virginia dynasty on the throne." Whereas his father had married an "unknown," he set the high

---

vaults" and serving regularly as chief marshal at Harvard Commencements. One of those he escorted was President Cleveland, who, meeting the Colonel years afterward, said, "Oh, yes—you were the person who bossed me around so at Cambridge." A distinguished latter-day Lee citizen was the late Joseph Lee (1862-1932), known as the "Father of American Playgrounds." Extraordinarily liberal in the cause of philanthropy, he once considered giving up all his property and visited Count Tolstoi in Russia to discuss the question. Tolstoi, however, discouraged him and he returned to devote his life to social legislation. When Harvard conferred upon him in 1926 an LL.D., Lee felt it appropriate. "I have devoted a large part of my life," he said, "to 'doctoring laws.'"

marital standard which most future Lees would follow by marrying a Corbin, of a family which were extensive landowners in England for some fourteen generations. Furthermore, he also had four sons.

The fourth of these was the founder of the most famous line of Lees—the so-called "Stratford line." His name was Thomas Lee, and, as the fourth son, he was not sent to England to study and received only a small inheritance from his father. Nonetheless, this oversight merely served—something so many other Family founders might well have noted—to put the young man on his mettle. "Pride, ambition, aggressiveness, determination—these qualities," says Hendrick, "manifested in an unassisted conquest of ancient learning, were the ones that made Thomas Lee the foremost Virginian of his day." And his self-education was apparently no small factor in his ability to win an extraordinary wife. Her name was Hannah Harrison Ludwell, daughter of a descendant of a Family which, though it became extinct with the Revolution, is one which appears in colonial Virginia history even more frequently than that of Lee.

Hannah and Thomas were an extraordinary couple; their love of each other was combined with deep religion and decision of character, and, it is recorded, "dislike of cheap ostentation." They had eleven children, and they both died within a few months of each other in 1750. Hannah, however, died first, and Thomas, drawing his will just a month afterward, was torn by filial devotion to his mother and his love of his wife. "I desire that I may be buried," he wrote, "between my Late Dearest Wife and my honoured Mother, and that the bricks on the side next to my wife may be moved, and my Coffin placed as near hers as possible, without moving it or disturbing the remains of mother."

The terms of the will were strictly followed, and to this day, over two centuries later, in Burnt House Fields, the three graves lie exactly as Thomas had wished. In his lifetime Thomas had risen to be the "President of Virginia." He had also, however, organized the Ohio Company and is generally recognized as being the first American not only to realize the importance of the Great West but also to visualize the Colonies' someday becoming an independent nation running from sea to sea. To his own descendants, though, his crowning achievement was the founding of the Stratford line of Lees and, for that matter, building Stratford itself. One of his grandsons, Thomas Lee Shippen, has recorded the effect of the Great Hall and its portraits:

> Stratford, whose delightful shades formed the comfort and retirement of my wise and philosophical grandfather, with what mixture of awe and pious gratification did I explore and admire your beauties! What a delightful occupation did it afford me, sitting on one of the sofas of the great Hall, to trace the family resemblance in the portraits of all my dear mother's forefathers, her father and mother, her grandfather and grandmother, and so on upward for four generations. There is something truly noble in my grandfather's picture. He is dressed in a large wig, flowing over his shoulders [probably his official wig as President of the Council] and in a loose gown of crimson satin, richly ornamented. But it is his physiognomy that strikes you with emotion. A blend of goodness and greatness; a sweet yet penetrating eye, a finely marked set of features and a heavenly countenance, such as I have almost never seen. Do not think me extravagant; my feelings were certainly so when I dwelt with rapture on the portraits of Stratford and felt so strong an inclination to kneel to that of my grandfather—it was with difficulty that my uncles, who accompanied me, could persuade me to leave the hall.

In their fourth generation in general, and in their second generation of the Stratford line in particular, the Lees produced—the offspring of the remarkable Thomas and his equally remarkable wife Hannah—the most talented group of brothers in American history. At one time, when five of the six brothers were in politics, there were no less than seven Lees in the government in Williamsburg. All four of the older brothers had been granted, by the terms of their father's will, in the custom of the times, landed estates of their own. The two younger brothers, however, were left to make their own way, the father's will adjuring the older brothers to rear the younger "religiously and virtuously, and if necessary, bind them to any profession or trade, so that they may learn to get their living honestly."

These two brothers, William and Arthur, respectively, went to

London, William to learn the tobacco business, Arthur to be a doctor. In 1773, however, William was elected Sheriff of London and two years later was chosen an Alderman—the only American who had ever held that office. Arthur's career was, if anything, even more remarkable. A few days after landing, he had become a close friend of Dr. Johnson, a man about whom, however, he had some doubts. "The too assiduous cultivation of his mind," he wrote home, "seems to have caused a very great neglect of his body." Arthur himself was not to linger long in medicine. Soon he, like William, was deep in politics. An able writer and, like his brother, as aristocratic as his English friends, he was torn as the Revolution approached. "The first wish of my heart," he wrote, "is that America may be free; the second is that we may forever be united to England." Considering the centuries to come, it was high prophecy. And there were even more prophetic tidings contained in his letter, in 1772, to his friend Sam Adams in Boston:

> To one who adores liberty and the noble virtues of which it is the parent, there is some consolation in seeing, while we lament the fate of British liberty, the rise of that of America. Yes, my friend, like a young Phoenix she will rise full plumed and glorious from the mother's ashes. The number who are daily emigrating from this country, and the multitude that in any public calamity will resort to us, must in a little time lay the most permanent foundation of populousness and power. America, in her turn, will be the imperial mistress of the world.

And, in his latter days, disillusioned as he was with his own failures in France and in other political arenas, Arthur Lee would also seem to have foretold an era when his own country would not hesitate to put forward, into positions of high office, Roosevelts and Harrimans, Kennedys and Rockefellers:

> The science of government is no trifling matter. It requires education and experience, it requires the habit of great worlds and great men, it requires the leisure which independent fortune gives and the elevation of mind which birth and rank impart. Without these you might as well attempt to make Sèvres china

out of common earth as statesmen and politicians out of men bred and born in the sordid occurrences of common life.

Of the four older Stratford brothers, only the eldest, Philip Ludwell Lee, failed to make his mark on the generation. A lonely figure, isolated from his brothers, although affectionate and charming with his own family, he died at the age of 49, on the eve of the Revolution, still loyal to King and Crown. The second brother, Thomas Ludwell, was, in contrast, perhaps the most popular of all the brothers. Like them, he made his way as an American Aristocrat with no difficulty in London. He studied law at the Inner Temple, then returned to Virginia to serve in the House of Burgesses. Later he became a member of the Mississippi Company, a signer of the Westmoreland Resolutions, and took an active part in getting Virginia to pass its first resolution for independence. Francis Lightfoot Lee also was a firm patriot, and, in person, a paragon of virtue even among Lees. Described as "genial, smiling, humorous, handsome and lovable," he was the "Atticus" of the Virginia Burgesses—one perhaps best remembered for his dictum, "What damned dirty work is this politics!"*

But if Francis Lightfoot was "Atticus," his brother Richard Henry Lee, greatest of all the brothers, was "Cicero." "A masterful man," John Adams described him, "tall and spare." Another hearing him speak called him "the harmonious Richard Henry Lee." Often called the "Aristocrat of Aristocrats"—a phrase that crops up frequently in any discussion of Lees—he nonetheless steered from the beginning a democratic course, and it was he who first introduced the resolution on July 2, 1776, which established American independence—the phrasing incorporated two days later in Jefferson's Declaration was in many places the same as his. And, as far back as 1764, it was he who drew up the first two petitions of the House of Burgesses, addressed to England's House of Lords and to the King himself—whom Lee called "the Author of our Miseries."

Even more remarkable perhaps was the fact that Richard Henry Lee was the first Southerner to speak out forcefully against slavery.

---

* He suffered a tragic end; in the terrible winter of 1796-97, his house could not be kept warm and he and his wife died of the cold.

First freeing his own slaves, he next spoke out against "that iniquitous and disgraceful traffic." More than a hundred years before the War Between the States, it was his voice, in 1759, which carried the dire prophecy: "And well am I persuaded, Sir, that the importation of slaves into this colony has been, and will be attended, with effects dangerous, both to our political and moral interests." Lee, unlike so many lesser men who grow less and less democratic as they grow older, grew, if anything, more and more so. Later, when the Constitution was laid before Congress, in his famous *Letters of the Federal Farmer* he opposed it not because of its encroachment on States' Rights but for the opposite reason—that it was, as he called it, the attempt of "aristocratical men" to transfer the governmental power "from the many to the few." But if Lee was against the Aristocrats of his own class, he was even more strongly against the "little insurgents, the men in debt, who want no law, and who want a share of the property of others." And finally he was again the first of all Southerners to speak out in behalf of the people in between, the Middle Class—the men, he called them, "of middling property, not in debt on the one hand, and men, on the other content with republican governments and not aiming at immense fortunes, office and power."

No record of the Stratford Lees would be complete without reference to the distaff side of this remarkable Family. In particular the charming daughters of Richard Henry Lee, Hannah, Nancy and Molly, made the Lee home at Westmoreland a memorable picture of plantation life in the late Eighteenth Century—a picture which is fortunately preserved in the *Journal of a Young Lady of Virginia* written by Richard Henry's niece, Lucinda Lee, daughter of Thomas Ludwell. "About sunset," she writes, "Nancy, Milly and myself took a walk in the garden. We were mighty busy cutting thistles to try our sweethearts, when Mr. Washington caught us, and you can't conceive how he plagued us—chased us all over the garden and was quite impertinent." Again "Mr. Washington" appears in another memorable scene:

I must tell you of our frolic after we went into our room. We took it into our heads to want to eat; well, we had a large dish of bacon and beaf; after that a bowl of sago cream, and, after that, an apply pye. While we were eating the apply pye in bed—God bless you! making a great noise—in came Mr. Washington, dressed in Hannah's short gown and petticoat, and seazed me and kissed me twenty times, in spite of all the resistance I could make; and then Cousin Molly. Hannah soon followed, dressed in his coat. They joined us in eating the apply pye and then went out.

With the Revolution another Lee line—the so-called "Leesylvania Lees"—came front and center. The founder of this line was Henry Lee, sixth son of Richard Lee II and younger brother of Thomas, founder of the "Stratford Lees." After the first Henry came Henry II, and although he served in the government in Williamsburg, it was not until the third generation that the Family flowered in the person of "Light Horse" Harry Lee, the great Revolutionary cavalry leader, as well as his brothers, Charles, U.S. Attorney General, under both Washington and John Adams, and Richard Bland, Congressman, Federalist and one of the men responsible, against much opposition from the North, for the establishment of the new Federal capital on the Potomac.

Here again, eugenists delight to point out, the Leesylvania Lees did not emerge from obscurity until a distinguished mother appeared —in the person of Lucy Grymes, Henry II's wife. This same argument is also used to prove that the Stratford Lees did not move into prominence until the marriage of Thomas and Hannah Harrison Ludwell. In any case, Miss Grymes was a remarkable woman; even as a young girl, tradition and Washington Irving have it, George Washington, as a bashful boy of fifteen, wrote halting poetry to her. But Light Horse Harry's marital career also provides an interesting case for the eugenists. He married twice, first his Stratford cousin, Matilda Lee, by whom he had four children, only two of whom survived.* His second wife was Ann Hill Carter, of Shirley, great-

* Of these the only son, Henry, last Master of Stratford, was responsible for the worst scandal in Lee Family history. He was married to the daughter of Daniel McCarty of Westmoreland and when her sister came to live with them, he seduced her. Worse still, from the point of view of the future of

granddaughter of Virginia's first "King" Carter, and it is doubtful if, in the long history of stalwart Southern ladies, there was a more extraordinary one than she. Unhappily by the time she was married to her dashing cavalry officer his dashing days were over. He had been not only an heroic officer but also Governor of his State; now he was heavily in debt and in the twilight of his career. Indeed after the Revolution he came to national attention only once, when he delivered the funeral oration on Washington's death and spoke the famous lines, "First in War, first in Peace and first in the Hearts of his Countrymen."

Light Horse Harry himself was by this time far from first in peace and indeed far from being first in the hearts of his countrymen. His wife, who had tried to be a good stepmother to his erring son by his first marriage, now found that she also had to see her own husband go to debtor's prison. In jail he tried to write his way out of debt, but a book of his war experiences failed. Finally released, he had one brief moment of old glory when, in Baltimore in 1812, he defended the offices of Alexander Hanson, editor of the *Federal Republican*, against an anti-Federalist mob and, heroic as always when action was concerned, was badly wounded. Afterward, however, he deserted his family—which by this time numbered four children—and wandered off to the West Indies. Six years later, trying desperately to reach Virginia before he died, he landed at Cumberland Island and died at the house of the daughter of his old General, Nathanael Greene. Even in his last misery, though, he found time to write his wife Ann Carter's oldest son at Harvard—a last letter which is not only notable for its Latin phrases, typical of Lee Family erudition, but also, considering his own sad life, a poignant farewell indeed:

Stratford, he robbed her. As his wife's sister, she was his "ward," and as her guardian, he had unwisely used her inheritance—a crime which was responsible for her creditors, in the end, seizing Stratford. "Black Horse Harry," as he was called, was still enough of a man of ability and political influence to be employed by Andrew Jackson to write his speeches and to receive, himself, twelve electoral votes for Vice-President. He died in poverty in Paris in 1837.

My dear Carter, what is happiness? *Hoc opus, hic labor est.*
Peace of mind based on piety to Almighty God, unconscious
innocence of conduct, with good-will to man; health of body,
health of mind, with prosperity in our vocation, a sweet, affectionate wife; *mens sana in corpore sano;* children devoted to truth,
honour, right and utility, with love and respect to their parents;
and faithful and warm-hearted friends, in a country politically and
religiously free—this is my definition.

Meanwhile, back at the Lee plantation, which would also soon be
foreclosed, Light Horse Harry's wife, a frail woman, small in height
and wan in coloring, led a life that seemed to go from bad to worse.
Her husband was first a prisoner, then severely wounded, then lost
altogether, and finally dead; her house, once the center of gaiety and
affection as well as politics and history, grew every day shabbier,
lonelier and even colder. Only by carrying a charcoal brazier from
room to room could she even create an illusion of warmth in what
she called "our poor old dwelling." And, despite the difficulties with
her husband and the raising, singlehanded, of her children, there
were even greater miseries ahead. Her oldest son, her father, her
sister all died within one year; her own health failed. Once, after
seeing her husband for the last time, she went six months without
leaving her house. "I may with much truth be said to live," she
wrote, " 'the world forgetting, by the world forgot.' " Yet the world
did not forget. For the fifth of Ann Carter Lee's children, one she
had not wanted and whom she had named for two of her brothers—
whose very names reminded her of happier times—was Robert
Edward Lee, greatest of all Lees, of all Southerners and, in character at least, perhaps of all Americans.

VI

NEW YORK, PHILADELPHIA AND POINTS

WEST—*From Roosevelts, Du Ponts and Biddles to*

Ryans, Mellons and Phippses

IN 1900, at the height of New York's "400" days, Miss Margherita Arlina Hamm, in the introduction to a large and expansive volume entitled *Famous Families of New York*, made the large, expansive and ungrammatical statement that "nearly every one of the names are eloquent in their own right." She states, for example, that Van Cortlandt "tells by its Dutch form of having come from the Netherlands and by its etymology of having pertained to that part of Russia in the Baltic which in the Middle Ages belonged to the Order of the Teutonic Knights." A little later, over another name, she becomes positively lyrical. "The noble name of Hoffman," she writes, "so organic a timber in the ship of state, tells of the Dutch period, far off Scandinavia, and back of that some Germano-Norse invasion into Scandinavia from the southern coast of the Baltic."

Family pride and Miss Hamm to the contrary, however, the meanings of Family names are rarely so eloquent. Elsdon D. Smith, for example, in his *Dictionary of American Family Names*, points out that the name Van Cortlandt means nothing more or less than a person who came from Cortlandt, a local district of Holland. As for Hoffman, the name means simply one who worked a farm—it could even mean, indeed, a farm or manor servant. And, in actual point of fact, it might be added, the first Hoffman to come to this country was a humble saddler.

A few Family names, it is true, have relatively interesting derivations, such as Biddle, which comes from bell-ringer or town crier, or Rockefeller, which means dweller in, or near, the rye field. But more, and by far the majority of our most prominent names, do not even descend as colorfully as the Rothschilds, a name which derives from the red shield swung before their door in Frankfurt. Although Crowninshields were, as might be guessed, dwellers at the sign of crown and shield, they too are exceptions. An Adams, for instance, means simply a son of Adam, an Astor is a descendant of a child born at Easter. Most of our names are, generically speaking, almost embarrassingly ineloquent. A Guest is, simply, a guest, a Gardner—or Gardiner—a gardener, a Fish a fisherman. A Harriman is a servant (man) to Harry (or Henry), the "home ruler." And, if Appletons once lived near a place where apples grew, Du Ponts once lived, of course, near a bridge, Van Dykes near a dike, Roosevelts near a rose field, and Lees near a meadow or lea. Even Whitneys were place-named—for Hwita's Island, or White Island in Herefordshire. As for the Lowells, they dwelled "at the sign of the little wolf." And finally, in view of what happened to the Stuyvesant Family, it is not without irony that they came from a place, Stuyvesant, in Zeeland, which means "quicksand."

Although occasionally an American Family name will have outstanding characteristics—Morgan, for instance, means "great" or "bright," Aldrich means "noble" or "ruler," and Curtis means one endowed with "court-like or elegant manners"—it is certainly unwise to push even this investigation too far. A Byrd, for example, is "one with bird-like characteristics" and a Cabot, their accomplishments to the contrary, is "one with a small head." But if Cabot heads are small, the Kennedys, for all their handsomeness, come from a Family name meaning "one with an ugly head." As for the Kellys, the name stands for "contention," and proceeding to Straus, one finds, unhappily, "one with ostrich-like characteristics." All in all, if a Vanderbilt, as Family historians delight in pointing out, means "a dweller at, or near, the heap or mound," it should be borne in mind that the place, not the name, is high, and that one is actually better off, in the final analysis, with something as simple as Gould, or "gold," or, for that matter, Eisenhower—a hewer, obviously, of iron.

Regardless of the meaning of their names, however, certain New York Families are as steeped in antiquity as their illustrious confrères in New England and the South. Although, generally speaking, their erudition and culture were lower than New England and well below the South, they too had a planter—or rather patroon—aristocracy. And, Washington Irving to the contrary, old New York under the Dutch was, in the extraordinary story of America's made-up Aristocracy, by no means an entirely laughable matter.

The first of the great Dutch patroonships was Rensselaerwyck. Including some 700,000 acres—an enormous tract—on the west bank of the Hudson, it was bought in 1630 for Kiliaen Van Rensselaer for "certain quantities of duffels, axes, knives, and wampum"—which ranked it, assuredly, second only to Manhattan as a shrewd deal. Kiliaen himself never came to this country at all, but he was a rich Amsterdam merchant—in fact the leader in the guild of merchant princes of his day. He was also an able man, carefully selecting as colonists to people his land farmers who had to meet four requirements—they should be strong, healthy, intelligent and married. So successful was his colony that Rensselaerwyck was a thriving concern until the middle of the Nineteenth Century, the last of the great patroons being Stephen Van Rensselaer, eighth in direct line from the original Kiliaen. Heir to the estate at the age of five, he later served in Congress and cast the deciding vote for John Quincy Adams for President, explaining that, upon taking his seat, being still in doubt how to vote, he had bowed his head in prayer and, on opening his eyes, had seen at his feet a ballot bearing Adams' name. In 1824 he established the country's pioneer scientific school, Rensselaer Polytechnic Institute, and though it was said of him he was a "genuine Aristocrat," yet he was always ready to meet the "new Democracy" halfway. Lenient to a fault, he was loved by his people for his "simple tastes, democratic behavior and genial manners."

Along the Hudson too were English manors—in order, Livingston Manor ceded to Robert Livingston in 1686, Pelham Manor to Thomas Pell in 1687, Philipsborough to Frederick Philipse (pronounced "Philip-see") in 1693, Morrisania to Lewis Morris and Cortlandt Manor to Stephanus Van Cortlandt in 1697, and Scarsdale to Caleb Heathcote in 1701. These manorial English Families, together with their Dutch predecessors and the Schuylers of Albany, comprised New York's most ancient Aristocracy, and of these Families the two which most resembled the landed gentry of England were the Livingstons and the Morrises. Of old Judge Robert Livingston the story is told that in 1765 he had a family party in Clermont with his son, his son-in-law Montgomery and his grandson Robert. "It is intolerable," said the head of the House of Livingston, "that a continent like America should be governed by a little island three thousand miles away. America must and will be independent. My son, you will not live to see it. Montgomery, you may. Robert, you will." The prophecy was fulfilled. The judge's son did indeed die before Independence was achieved, his son-in-law Montgomery was killed at the siege of Quebec, while his grandson Robert became one of the leaders of the new Republic.

As for the Morris Family, "For two centuries," says Family historian Margherita Hamm proudly, "they have been identified with great estates on the one side and public affairs on the other. Few of their long roll ever touched trade—and only a minority ever cared for the professions." Among this clan, from whom New York's able Newbold Morris descends, probably the most aristocratic was old Colonel Lewis Morris. The first "Lord of the Manor" of Morrisania, he was the son of a merchant himself and was therefore anti-trade in the extreme. "As New England excepting some Families," he wrote, "was ye scum of ye old, so the greatest part of the English in the Province (New York) was ye scum of ye New."

Lewis' grandson, hardly surprisingly, was the last "Lord of the Manor" before its breakup by the law against entail. Nonetheless, he was a signer of the Declaration of Independence, as also was his half brother, the famed Gouverneur Morris, who first feared the Revolution as the "domination of a riotous mob," then took the Patriots' side and even suffered the loss of a leg in the Cause—albeit it was caused by a carriage accident suffered while he was a member of the Continental Congress. Years later, as Minister to France, during the riots of the French Revolution, his carriage was attacked by a howling mob with cries of "Aristocrat!" Thrusting the stump of his leg out the window, Morris shouted, "An Aristocrat! Yes— who lost his limb in the cause of American liberty!" Whereupon, it is recorded, he was cheered to the echo and drove off unmolested, later, in 1809, at the age of 60 to marry Nancy Randolph, principal in the famous Randolph *cause célèbre*. Scandal or not, however, it was not only a happy marriage, it also united one of Virginia's most aristocratic clans with the one New York Family which could at least claim a large measure of freedom from trade. This was, how- ever, the exception to the rule of trade-rootedness among New York Families. "Outside the pale of Morrisania," says Dixon Wecter, "trade claimed all the prosperous Families of Eighteenth Century New York." And, turning for his evidence to the stern *Memorial History of New York*, written by the late trade-aristocrat Anson Phelps Stokes, he continues:

> The Bayards, Van Cortlandts, Roosevelts, Livingstons, Schuylers, and Rhinelanders were the sugar-refining business. The Rhine- landers also imported crockery, while the Schuylers sold mer- chandise from Europe and India. Barclays, Rutgers and Lispenards

were brewers. General traders and shippers were Verplancks, Whites, Murrays, Baches and Franklins, while Beekmans, Van Zandts, Clarksons, Setons and Buchanans were importers or dealers in dry-goods. The Goelets and the Brevoorts were ironmongers and the Schermerhorns were ship-chandlers. The Gouverneurs traded with the West Indies, and the Keteltas family operated warehouses. Gerard and Nicholas De Peyster were merchants. James Alexander, of the family of Lord Stirling, ancestor of the Duers, had a thrifty wife who eked out the income by running a small shop. In the files of New York newspapers at the close of this and the beginning of the next century one finds humble advertisements bearing names long since divorced from the squalor of trade: Peter Goelet from his shop in Hanover Square offers the public saddles, hardware, pewter spoons, hair trunks, "and a consignment of playing cards"; Isaac Roosevelt advertises "loaf, lump and strained sugar and sugar-house treacle"; plain Jacob Astor in Queen Street calls attention to guitars, fifes, and pianofortes; similar solicitations appear from Archibald Gracie, Abraham Brevoort, Leonard Kip and others.

There is, of course, irony in the fact that there would come a day, as we have already noted, when these Families would look down upon trade. For example, of Nineteeth Century New York, one finds the same historian commenting: "While some of the old families, like the dull but canny De Peysters, the proud and retiring Livingstons, the colorful Van Cortlandts, the practical and unimaginative Schuylers, and the proverbially parsimonious Winthrops, were clipping coupons, living upon a fraction of their incomes, and snubbing the new millionaires of shipping and railroads, other ancient families were slipping slowly but perceptibly, like the kind and friendly Beekmans and the charming but indolent Van Rensselaers, who since the first patroon have never gained any money except by marriage."

This may be a little harsh, particularly as of the 1960's, on two busy and unmarried present-day Van Rensselaers in the New York social scene—Charles, a kindly assistant Society editor, and Philip, a witty man-about-Barbara Hutton. Generally speaking, however, the statement is accurate and is certainly one more example of the age-old rise-and-fall process of both Society and Aristocracy in America. At least one New York Family, however, deserves special mention as a Family Aristocracy of remarkable duration. This is the Bowne Family—pronounced as "Brown" but without the "r." John Bowne, the American ancestor, built the oldest private dwelling in America, in Flushing, in 1661, and later defied the ban placed by Governor Stuyvesant on that "abominable sect"—the Quakers. When solitary confinement in a dungeon on a diet of bread and water failed, Bowne was transported as an example to others, but, sent to Holland, made such an earnest plea for tolerance and liberty of conscience that he was set free and returned to America. After about three hundred years in the Bowne family, the house was dedicated by the government in 1945 as a national shrine to religious freedom. The late Frederick Bowne was the last of the name to own the house. His grandson, Martin, ninth generation, was a Marine Corps jet pilot.

Any number of ancient and honorable Families might be chosen to illustrate the extraordinary early-day link between New England and New York. Among these, ranging from the Aldriches, Alsops and Auchinclosses to the Warrens, Wendells and Whites, particularly notable are the Fishes, the Rogerses and the Wetmores, all three of whose American ancestors arrived in Boston in 1635 on the appropriately named ship *Increase*. Although rarely have individuals in these three Families played leading roles in "Society," exceptions would include, among the Fishes, the late Mrs. Stuyvesant and the present Hamilton of "Martin, Barton and Fish" fame, the Wetmore sisters of Newport, and the late Herman Rogers of the Riviera. Nonetheless, all of these Families have for more than three hundred years been extraordinarily public-spirited citizens—an example, in another century, being Judge Seth Wetmore, who served for 48 successive terms between 1738 and 1771 as deputy to the General Court of the Connecticut Colony.

An even closer New England-New York link is the case of the Morgan Family. New York's great J. P. Morgan, for example, attended English High School as a boy in Boston in the class of 1854. His son-in-law, Herbert Satterlee, best records how New York's latter-day first citizen encountered the basic homogeneity then prevalent in the American population:

It is interesting to note that there is not a boy among the seventy-two who entered with Pierpont whose name betokens that he was of other than New England stock, and in those days that meant English ancestry. There is not an Irish, German, Italian or any other than an English surname on the roster, unless it is Delano, and the Delanos had been in this country about as long as any other family. With a school made up of boys like these, the atmosphere was the old God-fearing, law-abiding New England spirit. But they were young progressives as was proved by the after lives of many of them—Pierpont included.

Mention of the Delanos and, even more, of progressivism, brings up also the matter of what is, in many ways, the most interesting of all New York Families—the Roosevelts. First in length of continued prominence of all Manhattan clans, their antiquity has often been obscured by their sharp division in modern times into two branches, the Hyde Park, or Franklin D. Roosevelts, and the Oyster Bay, or Theodore Roosevelts—which Frank Sullivan called, during F.D.R.'s heyday, the "Out of Season" Roosevelts. On one thing, however, both branches agree, and that is that the name is pronounced as in "rose" and not to rhyme with "goose." Actually, both branches of the Family go back to the year 1644, their pioneer immigrant being a Dutchman named Klaes Martensen Van Rosenvelt (also spelled Claes Martenszen). In contrast to the severity of pride in descent exhibited by most American Families, both Presidents Theodore and Franklin D. Roosevelt went to the opposite extreme. Theodore, for example, spoke of both branches' common ancestor as being "very common," and Franklin D. Roosevelt emphasized the point by noting that when his original ancestor died, his wife and children were left to be cared for by others. "Remember," the late President once said, "remember always, that all of us, and you and I especially, are descended from immigrants and revolutionists."

For four generations the Roosevelts confined themselves to agriculture, trading and the management of real estate, albeit also establishing something of a record—one which has continued to the present day—of having large families. In the fifth generation, however, there were four relatively well-known citizens, including Jacobus II, afterwards known as James I, a hardware merchant and the first rich member of the Family, his brother Nicholas, a pioneer steamboat inventor, Captain John J. Roosevelt, a reckless but fairly brilliant soldier, and finally Isaac, who was known as "Isaac the Patriot" from his firm espousal of the Revolutionary cause and who became the Family's first politician. Married to a member of the Hoffman Family, Isaac was the first Roosevelt politician to sit in the New York Senate. Before that, however, he had not only built the city's first sugar refinery but had also become the second president of New York's first bank. Although Isaac's generation was still a perilous one for children—of his eight children, five died in their early youth— he was in the sense of establishing the Family the real Family founder. He was, however, distinctly in the Hyde Park branch, although his son, James II, was the actual founder of this branch, since he sold his Harlem property and moved up the Hudson to the present Hyde Park.

Had James II not sold his property farther down the river, his-- torians have speculated, he might have left the Hyde Park branch as rich as the Astors, with whom the Family became maritally allied when James Roosevelt Roosevelt, Franklin D.'s father's son by his first wife, married Helen Astor, aunt of the late Vincent Astor. But if the Hyde Park branch was not as rich as the Oyster Bay branch, it was ancestrally more impeccable. For Franklin D.'s father's second wife, and Franklin D.'s mother, was the beautiful Sarah Delano, whose ancestry, says Karl Schriftgiesser, historian of Roosevelts, "stretches back into Colonial history and includes such distinguished names as Cushman, Allerton and Lyman. . . . The fact is Franklin's line is more distinguished than Theodore's."

There is, however, still a third line of Roosevelts—the so-called "Pelham branch," as they used to be known. Established by Elbert, born in 1767, of the sixth generation, this branch descends through various distinguished citizens of Westchester County, one of whom, the late Henry L. Roosevelt, was an Assistant Secretary of the Navy, a post which has been held by no less than five Roosevelts, the others being Theodore, Franklin, Theodore, Jr., Theodore Douglas Robinson. Of these three branches, two at least were united when Eleanor, of the Theodore branch—she was the daughter of Elliott, brother of President Theodore—married Franklin, of the Hyde Park branch. But there had been several other cousin marriages in the Family before that—in fact, by 1931 and the time of Franklin D.'s son Jimmy, the relationships in the Family had become so intramural that *Fortune* magazine declared that Jimmy was "his own sixth cousin once removed"—a relationship that, when the insurance and divorce difficulties of Jimmy were at their height, many other Roosevelts would have been glad to remove even further. *Fortune* also declared, as of 1931:

> There is, of course, no laying down a specific description that will precisely fit every member of so large a clan. Yet one can describe "a Roosevelt" and be fairly sure that three out of four epithets hit the mark. In the first place a Roosevelt is likable: the people who have to do with him become his friends and grow warmly attached to him. He has a great deal of energy and vitality—there is not a Roosevelt whose biography isn't full of things that he has done and places he has been. He is, in the language of psychology, an extrovert (very nearly the exact opposite of an Adams). You will seldom find him occupied over matters of pure intellect: he has practical concerns. He is probably a merchant (in more recent times an engineer) or a banker, possibly a politician. His avidity for knowledge is really an avidity for experience—you will not find him in one of the learned professions. He is sympathetic and is apt to be aggressive. The same qualities which determine his profession determine his amusements: he likes the out of doors, he likes the spice of danger, he likes to hunt game, and he is almost certainly skipper of a sailboat. What is more, he is well-to-do because his family has a high average of business competence.

Despite this similarity, close to unique among American Families, there were many extraordinary individuals in the Family's long and distinguished past. One of these, in the Nineteenth Century, was James Henry Roosevelt, a man who a century earlier than the late

Franklin D., and also in the prime of his life, was stricken with polio. A brilliant student, he had just graduated from Columbia Law School and started practice when the illness occurred. Although he was to be a lifelong invalid and had to discontinue his law, he nonetheless turned to business and, conducting his affairs almost entirely from his bedroom, built up a fortune of over a million dollars— which made him the richest Roosevelt of his day—almost all of which he left to found Roosevelt Hospital. Not the least extraordinary thing about this extraordinary man's career was the fact that, shortly before his illness struck, he had become engaged to a remarkable young lady of the Boardman Family. Although, due to his illness, they never married, neither did either of them ever marry anybody else. They remained the closest of friends throughout their lives and, when Roosevelt died at the age of 63, he left her an annuity, the only sizable part of his will not devoted to charity, and made her executrix of his will.

Another extraordinary Nineteenth Century Roosevelt was Hilborne Lewis Roosevelt. His life span was but 37 years, but in that brief time and in a day when the line between "gentleman" and "mechanic" was strictly drawn, he nonetheless determined over all his Family's objections to become a mechanic in the making of organs. He became a pioneer in the field, built the first electric-action organ in the country and by the time of his death had a thriving business in both church and home organs with factories in Philadelphia and Baltimore as well as New York. Still a third remarkable past-century member of the Family was Robert Barnwell Roosevelt. Christened Robert "Barnhill," he later changed it and adopted the name Barnwell, of another distinguished family. First and foremost a political reformer, lawyer and member of Congress, active in the exposure of New York's "Tweed Ring," he was also a pioneer conservationist and the author of numerous books which had an important influence in awakening people to proper fish and game laws —later to be so ignored by his nephew and nephew's children in enthusiasm for the slaughter of big game in Africa and elsewhere.

There was also, prophetically enough, second-generation trouble in the Robert Barnwell Roosevelt family. Robert Barnwell Roosevelt had two sons, John Ellis and Robert Barnwell, Jr. Both built large places near their father's home on Long Island and, never friendly, fenced themselves off from each other. Both sons married twice and both marriages of each ended unhappily. By John Ellis' first marriage to Nannie Vance, he had two daughters, one of whom married, in Roosevelt fashion, her second cousin, Philip Roosevelt, and the other married Fairman Dick, who was killed riding to hounds with the Meadowbrook Hunt. John Ellis' second wife, the former wife of a Navy paymaster, was 25 years his junior and was also the younger sister of his brother's second wife. They were shortly divorced, and the case reached high tabloid sensationalism when the younger brother testified against his older brother on the subject of the language he had heard his brother use to his wife. Later, as Karl Schriftgiesser records, Robert Jr.'s only son "was killed when he fell in front of a bus early one grey morning in New York."

A generation before these troubles, however, the elder Robert Barnwell's brother, Theodore I, father of the President, also was an extraordinary man. He married Martha Bullock, whose great-grandfather had been the first President of the Provincial Congress of Georgia, and who was, in the words of her son Theodore II, "a sweet, gracious, beautiful Southern woman." Theodore II also affectionately described his father, primarily a banker but also active in political reform and a wide variety of philanthropies:

He combined strength and courage with gentleness, tenderness and great unselfishness. He would not tolerate in us children selfishness or cruelty, idleness, cowardice or untruthfulness. As we grew older he made us understand that the same standard of clean living was demanded for the boys as for the girls; that what was wrong in a woman could not be right in a man. With great love and patience, and the most understanding sympathy and consideration, he combined insistence on discipline. He never physically punished me but once, but he was the only man of whom I was ever really afraid. I do not mean that it was a wrong fear, for he was entirely just, and we children adored him.

Theodore II, the President, remains of course, even to Franklin D. partisans, the most endearing of all Roosevelts. An asthmatic weakling as a boy, by dint of sheer will power he made himself a strong physical specimen. At first, out of college, he did not know what to do—not long later he wrote his sister Anna, Mrs. William Cowles, of the "dull" life of his fellow classmates. He described them as "fellows of excellent family and faultless breeding, with a fine old country-place, four-in-hands, tandems, a yacht, and so on; but, oh, the decorous hopelessness of their lives!" Starting a literary and history-writing career which he was to continue off and on throughout his active life, he nonetheless also early dreaded the possibility that he might be forced to enlist among "these small men who do most of the historic teaching in the colleges"—a remark which was hardly calculated to lead to high academic recognition. In 1886 he ran for Mayor of New York and finished third behind Abram S. Hewitt and Henry George. Twelve years later, as Assistant Secretary of the Navy, he waited until Secretary Long was out of Washington and then cabled Admiral Dewey a message which all but started the Spanish War.

After San Juan Hill, he was invincible, and with his brilliantly uniformed "Rough Riders" grouped around him, there has probably been no such awe-inspiring candidate on the American political dais before or since. In one of his first speeches as candidate for Governor on his return, he grinned at the crowd for a long period, then finally spoke. "It's bully to be back," he said, "really bully." Nominated for Vice-President in Philadelphia in 1900, with no negative vote but his own, he took office as President on the assassination of McKinley in 1901. As President, he was nothing if not colorful. Three years after taking office, for example, nearing 50 years in age, he wrote his son Kermit, under date of March 5, 1904, of his efforts to "keep fit":

> I am wrestling with two Japanese wrestlers three times a week. I am not the age or the build one would think to be whirled lightly over an opponent's head and batted down on a mattress without damage. But they are so skillful that I have not been hurt at all. My

throat is a little sore, because once when one of them had a strangle hold, I also got hold of his windpipe and thought I could perhaps choke him off before he could choke me. However, he got ahead.

The President's first wife was Alice Hathaway Lee, of Boston's Lee Family. She died tragically in 1884 after the birth of their only child, the remarkable Alice Roosevelt Longworth. Since Roosevelt's mother died almost simultaneously, there was, in the fashion of the times, a double funeral. Two years later, in 1886, Theodore married, in London, Edith Carow; at the time, asked to name his father's occupation, he wrote unhesitatingly "Gentleman." The present Alice, however, his daughter by his first wife, would have scoffed. "Hell's bells," she told this author in 1960, "the Roosevelts aren't Aristocrats at all in the sense of the word that I use it. As a matter of fact, I like the word 'patrician' better but the Roosevelt Family aren't that either. It's nonsense. The Roosevelts were Dutch peasants who achieved burgherhood by making respectable marriages—which few of them, I might add, have done since."

On this score Mrs. Longworth would seem to be on firm ground —at least in any discussion of the Franklin D.-Eleanor Family. Indeed, an extraordinary contrast presents itself between the President Theodore boys and the President Franklin D. boys. There were four in each case. Of Theodore's sons, all served with almost unbelievable distinction in the First World War. Quentin, the youngest, a flyer, was shot down and killed behind the German lines, Theodore, Jr., was gassed and shot through the leg, and Archie was so badly wounded—he suffered a paralyzed arm—he had to be invalided out. Only Kermit fought through the war without being wounded—and he had enlisted in the British Army before America even got into the war. In World War II, Theodore, Jr., died heroically in harness after begging to go ashore in the invasion of Normandy, Archie was distinguished for bravery in the Pacific, and Kermit died on a mission to Alaska. All of these sons were married only once, all had distinguished careers and all were, generally and individually speaking, ornaments to their whole generation. In contrast, the four sons of Franklin D.—or at least three of them—have been some distance from ornaments to their generation. In the entire history of the White House, says J. J. Perling, historian of Presidents' sons, "no other sons whose fathers occupied the White House have aroused so much curiosity, comment, or criticism; every episode in their careers has kindled nationwide interest—their marriages, their money-making, their medals, their dividends, their divorces, their dogs." And, of their shortcomings, he concludes:

That Franklin Delano Roosevelt was a devoted father, there can be no question; but between him and his sons there did not exist that comradeship and constant intimacy which characterized the relationship between earlier Presidents and their sons—particularly, the Adamses, Martin Van Buren, Rutherford Hayes, and Theodore Roosevelt. This can be explained only in part by the fact that the thirty-second President for a long period of time was unable physically to engage in the activities of his sons; the cause lay also in the individualistic personalities of the sons themselves who, undeterred by the father and with seeming indifference regarding the effect of their activities upon his political fortunes, pursued their several, independent ways. Thus, when the friends of Franklin Roosevelt were risking their own political futures in seeking a third term for the President, one of his sons actually was advocating the candidacy of a rival; when a prominent industrialist and an influential publisher were using all their resources to end the career of the Presidential father, a son married the daughter of one, and a second obtained employment from the other.*

The story of the Roosevelt boys and their marriages—one of which was Franklin D. Jr.'s marriage to Ethel du Pont—brings us next to a consideration, in Wilmington, of the greatest industrial Family in American history. The story of this Family is steeped in more romance—as befitting its French origin—than any other. According to Family history, the first two Du Pont brothers to come

* J. J. Perling, in contrast, recalls a story of Theodore Roosevelt, Jr., who, when Governor of Puerto Rico, used the same old college try as his father—one which, in the matter of language, was not always successful. For example, he made a speech in Spanish in which, referring to one-horse vehicles, he used the literal equivalent for the words "drawn by single horses" and proceeded to tell his startled Spanish audience about "wagons pulled by *unmarried* horses."

to America, Victor Marie and Eleuthère Irénée, were once made by
their father to stand over their mother's grave in France and swear
to be forever united. After they had done so, their father, the first
Pierre du Pont, blessed them. "May each generation of your descendants," he said, "strive unceasingly to make the next generation
better than his own." From this Pierre, too, came the famous Family
dictum: "No privilege exists that is not inseparably bound to a
duty."*

The first Pierre du Pont, who lived at Bois des Fossés, not far
from Nemours from which the company received its name, was
granted a coat of arms by the King of France in 1783. He chose
ostrich plumes supported by a lion and an eagle—a design which, in
view of the tradition of public reticence of the Family, as well as
its underlying private strength, would seem to have been prophetic
indeed. Pierre's oldest son, Victor Marie, was actually the first to
come to America. He was a handsome, six-foot-three, amiable and
rather lighthearted man, who was described by his future wife, a
young lady named Gabrielle Joséphine de la Fite de Pelleport, as
having "a very charming ease." In any case, he came to this country
as attaché to the first French Legation. Later he also served as French
consul in Charleston, South Carolina, then regarded as the country's
most desirable post, and Philadelphia. He had two children, Amélie
and Charles Irénée, neither of whom, nor their descendants, was to
figure largely in the affairs of the company.

Victor's younger brother, Eleuthère Irénée, was the real American Family founder. Not as handsome as his brother, but a remark-
able-looking man just the same, and far more energetic, he had been
an indifferent student but had already made something of a name
for himself in France, both as a chemist in a powder laboratory and
as a sensitive romanticist. In 1791, at age 20, determined to marry a

* The Family in France is spelled as one word with, of course, a capital
"D." Although certain members of the Family still spell it this way, when the
name crossed to America it began being spelled as two words—the "du" with
a small "d" when preceded by a first name. As for the accent, the Du Pont
Family in America prefer the accent over the second syllable. The company,
however, is generally accented over the first syllable. The Duponts of France,
however, do not accent either syllable.

girl, Sophia Madelaine Dalmas, 16, whose family his father thought was beneath them, he showed something of his future mettle by prevailing not only over his father but also over another suitor, with whom he fought two duels. Eight years later the whole Family, including Pierre, Victor, Victor's wife and two children and Irénée, his wife and by this time three children, set sail for America. After a 91-day voyage of almost incredible hardship, they landed, appropriately enough, at Newport, Rhode Island. The date was appropriate too—New Year's Day, 1800. But no Family ever had a more curious first day in America, as William Dutton, Du Pont historian, records:

> Newport . . . was in the grip of one of its worst New England winters. The ship had been given up for lost and nobody met them. Half frozen and nearly starved, the party set out to find warmth and something to eat. At the nearest lone house nobody answered Du Pont *père*, although he both knocked and shouted. Finally he peered in a window to see a table loaded with food and set for a meal. A fire crackled in the open hearth. It was too much. Du Pont tried the door, found it unlatched, and let his famished followers in to feast.
>
> There was some excellent wine, new logs ready for the fire, and they cleaned the table. Still there was no sign of the owner, who evidently had gone with his family to church. They held a conference. Du Pont *père* cheerfully agreed that they may have committed a felony, so he fined himself one gold coin and left it at the head of the ravished table.

The Family had originally planned to organize a land company to exploit land in the valley of the James in western Virginia. A chance hunt with a Colonel Toussard, however, was responsible for a change to a more promising undertaking. Running out of powder, Irénée stopped and bought some more to finish out the day's shoot. Later, impressed with its poor quality and high price, he determined to make a study of powder-making in America and, with his plans for a plant in mind, had an audience with President Jefferson. Jefferson was in favor of the idea but wanted the plant located near Washington. Irénée, however, decided after investigation that, so records Broadus Mitchell, "the country, the people, the location are all worthless." Instead he purchased the 95-acre farm of one Jacob Broom on the Brandywine River, four miles from Wilmington. Settling his family in a log cabin, he set about building powder mills. One of his first innovations was to build, rather than one large mill, several small mills some distance apart; the country's first powder mill, one which, curiously, had been located at the age-old aristocratic stronghold of Milton, Massachusetts, had been completely demolished by an explosion in 1744.

In the beginning, "E. I. du Pont de Nemours," as the company was named, was capitalized at $36,000. "Citizen du Pont," or Irénée, was named "Director" at a salary of $1,800 a year "and one-third of the profits or losses, should there be any"—an unusual agreement indeed. At first, again setting a precedent, this time for future family reticence, Irénée refused all advertising, desiring no part of what he called "the public attention in my establishment" and also "all that savors of self-praise and bragging—a method that seems to me more harmful than useful in any kind of business." An incredibly hard worker, he nonetheless suffered many disappointments and reversals, both in business—his struggle with debt was a difficult one—and in his personal life. His father died, after an all-night session fighting the company's first fatal fire, and in the terrible explosion of 1818 his wife received an injury from which she never recovered. The last years of her life he nursed her constantly, and during her last few months he refused, despite all pressures from business, to go out of the range of her voice. Finally his beloved "double brother" Victor, whom he dearly loved despite the fact that he was his opposite in "tastes, temperaments and talents," also died. In his own last years he found solace only in work, but on his death in 1834 on a business trip to Philadelphia, the Delaware State *Journal* recorded a moving tribute to one of America's most un-robber baron industrial Family founders. "The anxiety of our citizens until the morning steamboat arrived from Philadelphia was intense," the paper said. "Crowds assembled on the wharf to learn the event; and when the fatal intelligence was announced of the loss of one so esteemed and so loved, each seemed to feel it a blow inflicted upon himself."

The first Irénée left three sons, Alfred Victor, Henry and Alexis. "At the age of twelve," says Dutton, "Alfred knew every piece of machinery in the mills, every step in the processing of powder and its ingredients, every workman by his name." And, three years after his father's death, at the age of 39, Alfred Victor drew up a partnership agreement, one unique in business annals and one which was to last the company for sixty-two years and indeed to last longer than that in its pattern for Family-founding. John K. Winkler best records it:

> It was a peculiar form of partnership. . . . There were no officers, no president, secretary or treasurer. In correspondence the partners were referred to merely as "Our Alfred du Pont," "our Henry du Pont," etc. By virtue of seniority and rigid family discipline, Alfred became the senior partner. His position was very much like the Old Man of ancient tribes. He wrote and signed all letters and his decisions were unhesitatingly accepted as final by his brothers.
> All property was communal. Even the farmlands that now comprised several hundred acres, running far back into the rolling country on both borders of the Creek, were owned jointly. As each partner married, the company built a house for him, exacting no rent. They did not even own private carriages or horses. If a trip to Wilmington or elsewhere was necessary, a message to the company stable eventually produced a mount or a horse and buggy.
> The partners drew no salaries, each being credited on the books with a proportionate share of the profits. Sums for personal needs were drawn as required from the cash box. A single clerk combined the functions of bookkeeper and cashier.

Those were indeed the good old days. And to go with them, the company came up, in its second generation, with a real "Old School" merchant and a West Pointer to boot. His name was Henry du Pont, to whom Alfred Victor relinquished the titleless position as head of the company in 1850. Married to Louise Gerhard, Henry ran the company, as well as the Family, with a rule of iron. First he would figure out how good he could make his powder and still break even; then he would see his production manager whose only real pay would come from profits and say, grimly, "If you want profits, salvage them out of costs." For forty years he kept his desk and chair in the same position, wearing out the floorboards but refusing to have them replaced. Each night he also wore out three candles. Refusing a stenographer or a "newfangled" typing machine, he personally wrote by hand every business letter—over 6,000 a year. Early in Henry's tenure, Alexis, the third partner, was fatally wounded in an explosion.* There were twenty-four children of the three brothers, but in accordance with the dynastic principle which the company was already following, Lammot, second son of Alfred Victor, was chosen to succeed to the triumvirate—he was rated the most promising of all the twenty-four, not to mention the offspring of Irénée's daughters or the grandchildren of Victor, with whom he also competed.

The principle of getting rid of Family deadwood—who have always been first tried and then, if found wanting, have been pensioned off—has continued to this day. "I can look you right in the eye," says the present Henry B. du Pont, great-great-grandson of the founder, as of the 1960's, "and tell you that there is darn little nepotism in the Du Pont company today." Another Du Pont, the present secretary, Pierre du Pont III, puts the matter of present-day

* This occurred in 1857, and Alexis du Pont was blown thirty feet in the air. Landing, he leaped back into the powder mill to try to fight the explosion. The building, however, blew up in his face, and, terribly mangled, he was carried home. Although in agony, he said that he wished to say good-by to his workmen as well as his family, and "a procession of grimy men, in overalls and boots," it is recorded, "passed into the darkened bedroom and silently pressed the hand of the dying man." Through the years, the relationship between Du Pont workers and the Du Pont Family—all of whom are called by the workers by their first names, and by no means always prefixed with a "Mr."—have been remarkable. On New Year's Day, 1900, for example, the Du Pont Family celebrated, at a dinner for approximately a hundred members of the Family, the one hundredth anniversary of the landing of their ancestors in America. Two years later, when a new generation of the Family took over, the employees of the firm presented a resolution: "Resolved, That we the employees of the firm in 1902, wish to record the fact that we appreciate the kindness shown to us by the present officers and members of the Du Pont Family . . . and as we have loved and been faithful to their fathers we mean to do the same for the present generation."

working Du Ponts equally bluntly. "I don't have to work," he says. "I work because I think I can help the company." Twenty years ago Marquis James phrased it more objectively but withal admiringly:

> Down the generations, it is almost uncanny the brains that Du Pont has been able to pluck from its own family tree. A Du Pont by birth not being available, one by marriage was usually on hand with the qualifications required. . . . Since the first generation in America, marriages with young men who could be of use in the firm have kept the family vital, and consanguinate marriages have kept it tightly knit. Rigorously edited down to bare names and dates printed in type smaller than that on this page [about the same as this], the Du Pont genealogy chart from 1800 to 1936 fills a sheet 36 by 38 inches. It is as crisscrossed by matings of cousins as that of a European reigning house.

At one time, under old Henry, there were so many cousin marriages that they were forbidden on pain of being removed from the company hierarchy entirely. This cousin marriage, however—one of the few Du Pont failings—has been difficult to control. Eugene du Pont, for example, who succeeded old Henry, was married to a cousin himself, and when he retired William du Pont, who had had the temerity to divorce his wife, was not only divorced from a cousin but also later married one. In the company's fifth generation there was a whole rash of cousin marriages. On the other hand, there have also been marriages outside the pale, of which the company has strongly disapproved. When Henry's nephew, Lammot, in 1865 married Mary Belin, who was one quarter Jewish, many Du Ponts felt that their marriage would be one of these and that old Henry would join the anti-faction. Instead, old Henry appeared to find high satisfaction in his nephew's choice of a wife whose grandfather, Augustus Belin, had been employed by Du Pont in the earliest days of the business. On New Year's Day, 1866, the brief *cause célèbre* was settled when Henry's "modest rig," it is recorded, "halted at Lammot's house and he left a gift for the bride." The marriage turned out to be an extremely happy one, and Mary Belin and Lammot proceeded to have five sons, including all three most recent Du Pont presidents of the company, Pierre (1915-1919), Irénée (1919-1926) and Lammot (1926-1940).

Curiously enough, so great a hold has the company had on the more able members of the Family that few Du Ponts have ever made notable careers outside the company. Among these, however, should be included, in the Nineteenth Century, Samuel Francis du Pont. A tall and strikingly handsome man, with the cleft in his chin which is a Du Pont Family trademark, he married Sophie Madeleine du Pont, daughter of the founder of the company, but instead of a career in the company, chose instead to be a naval officer. He had a remarkable career in the Mexican War and afterwards, in 1849, served as a member of the Board appointed by the Navy to consider a "course of study appropriate to a Naval Academy." The report of this board provided a Naval Academy comparable to the Military Academy at West Point, and Du Pont was appointed its first Superintendent. In 1860, on the outbreak of the Civil War, he was commandant of the Philadelphia Navy Yard and he was shortly, as Commodore, given control of all naval operations on the coast south of the boundary between the Carolinas. His first important victory consisted in forcing the surrender of the Confederacy's two forts at Port Royal—one of the few times in our history that forts have surrendered to ships. Later he attempted and failed—with seven monitors, an ironclad and an armored gunboat—to reduce Fort Sumter and capture Charleston, after which he was subjected to what is generally regarded as shabby treatment by the Navy Department. Washington's Du Pont Circle is, however, named in his honor.

Another Du Pont officer, albeit one who later joined the company, was Henry Algernon du Pont. A Captain of Horse Artillery, and known for his gracious, courtly manners, he was brevetted Major for gallant services at Opequon and Fisher's Creek and received the Congressional Medal of Honor for extraordinary gallantry at Cedar Creek. He ended the war as Colonel and is best remembered for his refusal to obey orders and shell undefended historic buildings in Lexington, Virginia, during the sack of the Valley of Virginia by

General Hunter in 1864. In 1889 he inherited the most remarkable of all the many remarkable Du Pont homes, "Wintherthur," in Christiana Hundred, New Castle County, Delaware. This historic home, now one of the country's most extraordinary museums, had been originally built by the first Du Pont "in law," James Bidermann, who married one of the daughters of the original Irénée and who named it for the city in Switzerland where his family had lived. Bidermann's son, in turn, had sold the estate to Henry du Pont, the Colonel's father. On the Colonel's death in 1926, the estate passed to his son Henry Francis du Pont, the last private owner. The latter Du Pont lived in it through 1950, though he had long planned it as a museum "to help show modern Americans how earlier Americans had lived."

In many respects the most individualistic Du Pont in the Family history since the first Irénée was Alfred Irénée. The eldest son of the eldest son of the founder of the company, he saw both his parents die when he was 13 and immediately showed his mettle by resolving that his orphaned brothers and sisters—five of them, the oldest 17— would not be broken up as a family and parceled out to other Du Pont families. When the elders of the Family came to get them, led by Alfred Victor, their "Uncle Fred," they found themselves denied admittance to "Swamp Hall"—as Alfred Irénée's father had humorously named his home. Instead, they were met by the five youngsters, led by Alfred, all of whom were armed, one with a bow and arrow, another with an ax and Alfred himself with a 12-gauge shotgun. After an embarrassing pause, Uncle Fred asked for a parley —which Alfred granted, and then, allowing his older sister Annie to speak for them, they stated the case for running their own home. They were granted their request to keep their young family intact.

Twenty-five years later, at the most crucial moment of Du Pont history, Alfred was to show the same kind of determination in keeping the Du Pont company intact. It happened in 1902, when, after Eugene du Pont's death, the elders of the Family were in favor of selling out to their largest competitor, the Laflin and Rand company. At a board meeting Alfred himself first made the motion, which was immediately passed, that the company should be sold to the highest bidder. Then, after the motion, he said quietly, "I'll buy the company—for $12,000,000," a sum which Laflin and Rand were bidding and which he had raised by bringing two of his cousins, T. Coleman du Pont and Pierre du Pont, into the picture. Afterwards, asked how he knew the company to be worth $12,000,000 when he had not even had access to the books, he replied, "By the character of the sellers"—a remark which was later repeated on the witness stand by the present Pierre, patriarch of the modern company, and which deserves to take its place in business annals along with Morgan's statement that he wouldn't lend money to a man he didn't trust "on all the bonds in Christendom."

They were an extraordinary triumvirate, these famous "Three Cousins," as they were called. "They were like race horses," John K. Winkler describes them, "waiting for the springing of the barrier—Alfred, lanky, careless in dress and manner; Coleman, a mountainous individual with the build of a heavyweight boxer; Pierre, small, slender, neatly garbed." But all, of course, had the "tell-tale cleft in the chin." Not long after they had taken over the company, in the most extraordinary turnabout in business history, Alfred, T. Coleman and Pierre bought, for a cash outlay of only $4,000, the very company, Laflin and Rand, which shortly before had offered $12,000,000 to buy them. Alfred, however, for all his early family and later business solidarity, was unable to keep his own personal life intact. First married to a First Family Boston girl by the name of Bessie Gardner, he later caused consternation in elder Du Pont ranks by divorcing her, after four children, and marrying his cousin Alicia Bradford. The daughter of a stern Circuit Court judge, she had, about the time she first met Alfred, fallen in love with a man named George Amory Maddox. When her father objected to the match, Alfred saw to it that she was able to get married over her father's objections, then promptly fell in love with her himself. In what a later generation would consider a time-honored manner, he brought his seven-year-old son to see her. "How would you like to have me for a mother?" Mrs. Maddox asked. "Why, Cousin Alice,"

338   WHO KILLED SOCIETY?

replied the boy in amazement, "I wouldn't like it at all."

Later, when both Alfred and Alice were divorced, they were married, but the Du Pont Family felt very much as the boy had. In contrast to old Henry's day, they did not come to call. In fact, not long after this T. Coleman and Alfred were totally estranged, and it was Du Pont vs. Du Pont in the law courts. In the end, Pierre sided with T. Coleman and Alfred's days with the company were numbered. His marriage too was a short one. His wife had two children die in infancy, then died tragically herself in 1920. Afterwards, he married another, an early childhood sweetheart, Miss Jessie Ball of Ball's Neck, Virginia, a lady who did much to reunite him with his family.* Unlike most Du Ponts, who are rarely quoted on any subject and not known for leaving behind bits of philosophy, Alfred Irénée at least left the Family one maxim—which, in view of his own life, was not without irony. "Never form a habit," he once told his young cousin, "good or bad. There is no such thing as a good habit. All habits impair will, initiative and free agency."

Altogether, in the Twentieth Century the Du Ponts would seem to have given a good account of themselves—and this despite close to constant harassment on the part of the United States government which, in more than three wars, on short and usually totally unprepared notice, they have been forced to save. The year 1940 was something of a landmark in Family history, for in that year, after the reigns of the "Three Brothers," Pierre, Irénée and Lammot—at least one of whom, Irénée, announced that he was stepping down at the age of 49 because "I'm slowing up"—the company had for the first time a president, Walter Carpenter, who was unrelated to the Family. In 1948, however, the company went back to the Family, at least by marriage, and chose as president Crawford Greenewalt, husband of the daughter of Irénée.

The late Maury Paul, the first Cholly Knickerbocker, once stated

* In 1932, along with other loyal Virginians, Jessie Ball du Pont took an active part in the restoration of the Lees' Stratford Hall, and even opened her own home, "Nemours," to the public to raise money for the purpose—probably the first time one of the country's marble palaces was ever used to further the cause of an ancient aristocratic homestead.

that he was "fascinated" by the fact that the Du Ponts were unable to "crash" New York Society. A more ridiculous statement could hardly be imagined, as any Du Pont who has wanted to crash what passes for "Society" in New York or anywhere else has had no trouble in so doing. They have, however, generally speaking, preferred to go their own aristocratic ways without the help of such as the late Mr. Paul. As of the 1960's, there were over 1,600 Du Ponts, and an average of about 100 were being born each year. In 1955 the Family as a whole was perhaps best summed up by James Warner Bellah in *Holiday* magazine:

> I have known several Du Ponts. One ranks high among the world's most charming hostesses—an incisive mind denying the moated walls of great wealth and living eternally in the reality of the world. One is an insufferable travesty of Chaucer's Eglentyne, eternally prefacing a complete absence of any sound opinion with "As a Dewopawn" [Du Pont]. One is a victim of sadistic family possessiveness to a point of shuddering almost visibly at the sound of the name. And one, with an excellent war record behind him, works hard at the family trade as his forebears did before him. Some are known intimately and as well in Wilmington as any run-of-the-mill neighbors in any small town. Some are towering swells, only heard from in distant places. Some people in Wilmington whisper the name in awed reverence. One prominent Wilmingtonian who bore it as a middle name never even used the initials. . . . Some Delaware Du Ponts live with imposing formality. Some answer their own doorbells. Some dwell in a hundred rooms. Some in three and a kitchenette. At least one has committed suicide. One held the Congressional Medal of Honor. One enclosed his 300 acres of home park with a ten-foot wall topped with jagged inset glass to "keep all the skunks in Delaware out"—as he put it—"most of them named Du Pont." Two were United States senators. One has been married four times (you must be married five times to be an *officer* of that club). . . . One built the Equitable Building in New York. One tried to sue half the female population of Wilmington for libel. One is a ranking tennis champion. One married an Irish barmaid between boats at Queenstown—and never came home.*

* The latter story seems to have an almost permanent place in Du Pont Family history. Actually, the Du Pont here was Alfred's younger brother,

Moving from Wilmington to Philadelphia, one encounters a city with aristocratic traditions second to none, save Charleston. Here Family-founding fathers date more often than not to the Eighteenth Century, and almost invariably not later than the Nineteenth. With a Family Aristocracy which has long been proud of its close associations with the South—the Chews of both Virginia and Philadelphia are an example of this link—Philadelphia has almost as many romantic aristocratic stories as the South itself. Furthermore, no "Northern" city ever boasted a fuller complement of belles to go with the romantic stories—among them being at least three Revolutionary belles, all of whose lives were star-crossed. First was Peggy Shippen, devoted wife of Benedict Arnold, who was so highly regarded by the Patriots that, after Arnold's treason had become known, Washington himself commissioned a bearer to "go to Mrs. Arnold and tell her that though my duty required no means should be neglected to arrest General Arnold, I have great pleasure in acquainting her that he is now safe on board a British vessel." The second Philadelphia belle was Peggy Chew, who was beloved by the ill-fated Major André and all her life, though she married Baltimore's distinguished John Eager Howard, who afterwards became Governor of his State, carried with her the drawings and poems and other mementoes of her first love. "What is life, in short," she

---

Maurice, an earlier stalwart of his young "Swamp Hall" army. Maurice did indeed meet Miss Margery May Fitz-Gerald in Queenstown, but he did not marry her until a later trip. And she was descended from a proud Irish family which had run out of money; not a barmaid at all, she was working in a hotel office. Nonetheless, the newspapers, as is their time-honored wont with such "Society" doings, had a field day with such headlines as "Beauty and Virtue Her Only Dowry." Marquis James recalls that such attention had, by the time of Maurice and Margery's return, all of "Wilmington on the *qui vive* and the Du Pont clan in a lather." But the outcome, James records, was happy:

"Tart of tongue, good-looking and witty, Margery captivated The Swamp household. Alfred and Bessie turned their hands to the work of pacification and a few of the Du Pont women called on their new in-law. They liked her. The calls were returned and the family ruckus subsided considerably. Nevertheless, Maurice declined invitations to enter the company—at the bottom, as his brother had done. . . . So after a few months he and Margery resumed their travels, sojourning where fancy struck them, an occupation at which they have been destined to spend a good part of their lives."

once wrote, "but one continued scene of pain and pleasure varied and chequered with black spots like the chess-board, only to set the fairer ones in a purer light?"

Third and by no means least of the great Philadelphia belles was Anne Willing, who was married at sixteen to William Bingham, not only Philadelphia's but also the country's richest man. Although she lived to the age of 37 only, she left an indelible impression upon both sides of the Atlantic, in France as well as England, and thus has fair claims on the honor of being the first member of the International Set—at a time when, happily, the phrase was unknown. Rufus Wilmot Griswold best describes her:

> Her beauty was splendid. Her figure, which was somewhat above the middle size, was well made. Her carriage was light and elegant, while ever marked by dignity and air. Her manners were a gift. Sprightly, easy, winning, are terms which describe the manners of many women, but while truly describing hers, they would describe them imperfectly, unless they gave the idea that they won from all who knew her a special measure of personal interest and relation. Receiving neither service nor the promise of it, every one who left her yet felt personally flattered and obliged.

Miss Willing's husband was remarkable also. Conscious of his wealth, he seems to have been conscious of his own Family-founding as well. When, shortly after the French Revolution, Louis Philippe asked for the hand of one of his daughters in marriage, Bingham promptly refused. "Should you ever be restored to your hereditary position," the Senator told the Duke, "you will be too great a match for her. If not, she is too great a match for you."

Another Philadelphia Family story of a later era—it dates to 1858 —is told of Mrs. Roberts Vaux, wife of the patrician Quaker merchant, who was most concerned with news which was brought to her that her son Richard, at that time Secretary of the American Legation in London, had danced with Queen Victoria. Like the great Queen herself on another occasion, Mrs. Vaux was not amused. "I hope my Richard," she said, "will not marry out of Meeting."

Along with such stories of old Philadelphia belongs a poem, dating to the middle of the Eighteenth Century, written by a Mrs. Mc-Ilvaine:

> Judge Allen drove a coach and four
> Of handsome dappled grays,
> Shippens, Penns, Pembertons, and Morrises,
> Powels, Cadwaladers, and Norrises
> Drove only pairs of blacks and bays.

Actually, like most social doggerels, the verse leaves something to be desired, except as indication of the mercantile base of even Colonial Philadelphia. For Judge Allen, of a Presbyterian Family from Dungannon, Ireland, was not only the first Grand Master of Freemasons, Mayor of Philadelphia and brother-in-law of the Governor, he was also the man who, out of his own purse and, it is recorded, "despite labor troubles," financed Independence Hall. As for the "Carriage Trade" in general, Scharf and Wescott, in their *History of Philadelphia*, present stern evidence that the term in Philadelphia was a most definite one. A list of the eighty-four Families "with private equipages" was published just before the Revolution and was probably the country's first Celebrity Register. This list has been preserved to this day, and listed as "Coach" owners—loftiest of "Carriage" status-seekers—were eight Families, among them those of Benjamin Chew, Thomas Willing, John Cadwalader and Joseph Pemberton.

John W. Jordan, in *Colonial Families of Philadelphia*, declares that the three leading Philadelphia Family founders in the early Eighteenth Century were Israel Pemberton, Isaac Norris and Anthony Morris—no relation, incidentally, to the New York Morrises, or, for that matter, the Robert Morris who financed the American Revolution. The latter, whose parentage was unknown, rose in the office of the Willings, shipping merchants, to his later position—one of such eminence that he was offered and declined the position of Secretary of the Treasury in Washington's Cabinet —only to end his days, after three and a half years in a debtors' prison, as Philadelphia's most forgotten man. Of his five sons, two died before the father—which also did not abet the future Family.

In contrast to this sad story, Anthony Morris, progenitor of Philadelphia's eminent Morrises of both yesterday and today, was a brewer, a man who married four times and fathered, not only a future Family, but an immediate one of fifteen children.

William Penn, himself founder of Pennsylvania, was the son of a British Admiral, but his grandfather had been a merchant of Rotterdam. Expelled from Christ Church College, Oxford, for his nonconformist principles, he came to Pennsylvania via New Jersey, but his "Holy Experiment" in Pennsylvania resulted from a King's grant in payment for a debt owed by the King to his father. Penn was easily one of America's greatest men. His descendants, however, contrasted unfavorably with him, and though he had given Philadelphia its name as the "Quaker City," it was Thomas Lloyd who, says Frederick B. Tolles, historian of Quaker merchants, was "in a real sense the patriarch and progenitor of the Philadelphia Quaker aristocracy." One of the few genuine patricians to be converted to Quakerism, the descendant of an ancient Welsh family, he came to Penn's Colony in 1682, bringing "a Family Coat of Arms with fifteen quarterings." However, soon not only the Lloyds but also the entire "inner circle" of Shippens, Wynnes, Pembertons, Penningtons, etc., were in trade—and all well before the Revolution. But, declares E. Digby Baltzell in his *Philadelphia Gentlemen*, the last twenty-five years of the Eighteenth Century were the real Golden Age of Philadelphia's Family-founding:

> Many of the inner circle of Proper Philadelphians in the middle of the twentieth century, men who dominate the Philadelphia Club, the First City Troop, and the ancient Assembly Balls, as well as the banks, had prominent ancestors during the Revolutionary period. Rare is the First Family in Philadelphia, whose members have ever again contributed so much to the nation, or to the world. In the last part of the eighteenth century, in sharp contrast to the twentieth, the members of the city's upper class were also leaders of a national elite. . . . Wharton, Morris, Cadwalader, Biddle, Ingersoll, Coxe, McKean, Hopkinson, Chew, Willing, Rush, and White families played prominent roles during the Revolution and the founding of the new republic. The seeds of revolution and

independence, for example, were sown by the Stamp Act of 1765. Among the leading Philadelphia merchants who signed the "non-Importation Resolution," protesting this symbol of British imperialism, were Thomas Willing; Thomas, Charles, and John Wharton; Anthony, Israel, Isaac, Cadwalader, and Samuel Morris; Thomas, John and Lambert Cadwalader; Owen and Clement Biddle; Israel and James Pemberton; Charles Coxe; John and Benjamin Chew; George Meade; Daniel and John Wister; William Rush; and Thomas and James Penrose.

An extraordinary number of Philadelphia Families show surprising continuity of profession through the generations. In the Pemberton Family there were three generations of merchant-philanthropists; in the Whartons, four generations of statesmen-lawyers, and, among the Ingersolls, no less than five generations of lawyers. The Drexel Family, founded by, of all people, a charming Austrian portrait painter who started in Louisville, Kentucky, and then moved to Philadelphia, was soon to boast four generations of investment bankers. The second of these, Anthony J. Drexel, graciously "took in" as a partner in 1871 none other than the late J. P. Morgan the Elder. After Drexel's death, Morgan returned the favor and "took in" the late E. T. Stotesbury, who with his late wife was to cut such a large swath in the Society of the Twenties.

Through the years, also, the "Philadelphia doctor" has been almost as famous as the "Philadelphia lawyer." There have been several doctor dynasties, the most prominent in recent times being the Pepper Family. This Family was founded by Henry Pepper. Hailing from Strassburg, Germany, and alias Johan Heinrich Pfeffer, he was, like the first Morris, a brewer. On the other hand, an extraordinary number of Philadelphia Families were actually founded by doctors. Two of these deserve special mention. First is the Rush Family, which included among its future sons the first American sculptor, William Rush (1756-1833), and yet was also a Family of enough stability and staying power to produce, as recently as the 1940's, a Chairman of the Board of the Insurance Company of North America.

The founder of the Rush Family was Dr. Benjamin Rush. The son of a gunsmith who died when he was but five years old, he graduated from Princeton at the age of 15, and though his later political career was ill-fated by his indirect association with the "Conway Cabal" against Washington, yet he was a pioneer psychologist and also the first medical man in the history of the country to achieve a general literary reputation. He had thirteen children, of which nine, including two able sons, James and Richard, carried the Family to new distinction in its second generation. James Rush, like his father, was a physician and psychologist while Richard Rush had a political career unique in American history. He held high office under no less than four Presidents: Attorney General under Madison, Secretary of State, Secretary of the Treasury and Ambassador to Great Britain under Monroe, Secretary of the Treasury under John Quincy Adams, and Minister to France under Polk.

Perhaps the most aristocratic of all Philadelphia Families was also founded by a doctor. His name was Dr. Thomas Cadwalader who, in 1683, married the daughter of New Jersey's rich landowner, Thomas Lambert. Dr. Cadwalader was also, however, distinguished in his own right. He performed the country's earliest recorded autopsy and was the first doctor regularly to employ inoculation against smallpox. In 1731 he was also associated with Benjamin Franklin in the founding of the Philadelphia Library. Even more extraordinary was the fact that, in 1760, Dr. Cadwalader's courtly manners—a family trait of Cadwaladers—were responsible for saving his life. A deranged Philadelphia soldier named John Bruleman, who had, so he thought, "lost his character," decided to commit suicide, but lacking the will to do so, he determined to commit murder instead and then hang for it. One evening he took his musket and walked down the street resolved to shoot the first person he met. That person, however, turned out to be Dr. Cadwalader, who, records Struthers Burt, "spoke to him so courteously and doffed his hat so politely that Bruleman did not have the heart to kill him." Later that evening, however, Bruleman entered the Centre Tavern, saw Captain Scull playing billiards, and mortally wounded him. And not long after, he was, as he had wished, hanged.

In the second generation Dr. Cadwalader's two sons, John and Lambert, not only went into business together but also carried the Family to new distinction in the Revolution. Although they were born and lived most of their lives in Trenton, New Jersey, John Cadwalader organized the famed Philadelphia "Greens"—the "Silk Stocking" company, as it was at first sneeringly called—which under his colonelcy performed heroically. He also took up personally for Washington in the matter of the Conway Cabal and challenged General Conway to a duel. The latter was severely wounded and his "cabal" virtually ended. Lambert also was a Colonel in the war and was captured in the defense of Fort Washington. Although both the Nineteenth and Twentieth Centuries were to see many distinguished Cadwaladers, it is the Eighteenth Century's Lambert who still stands as the epitome, not of the Philadelphia lawyer or doctor, but as the Philadelphia gentleman. Of him, a friend wrote:

> To the good breeding, courtesy and elegance of the gentleman, he united the advantages of early education and the acquisition of an enlarged and cultivated understanding, regulated by classical taste and improved by habits of general reading. Few were so happily gifted with the power of pleasing and the disposition to be pleased.

Surpassing the Cadwaladers in long-term distinction and ranking only slightly below them in Philadelphia's iron-clad hereditary hierarchy is the Biddle Family. The American ancestor of this Family was one William Biddle, a shoemaker in Cromwell's army who came to America in 1681. The fact that he was in Cromwell's army, however, is of more than passing interest, for no American Family has a prouder record of fighting service for their country—one which continued to the days of the late Anthony J. Drexel Biddle who, in World War II, at the age of 63, in the hot sun of Quantico, taught jujitsu to picked men of the U.S. Marine Corps.

The first William Biddle purchased some land from William Penn and established himself as one of the proprietors in West New Jersey. His grandson, William Biddle of the third generation, was, however, the real Family founder. He moved to Pennsylvania and married well—a habit of Biddles to the present day—choosing Mary Scull, daughter of Nicholas Scull, of a Family at that time far more distinguished than the Biddles. From that time on, the Family grew rapidly, in both quantity and quality. A hundred years later, in 1860, according to a well-worn story, when the Prince of Wales visited Philadelphia he was pointed out so many Biddles that he could not resist asking, "Pray, what is a Biddle?" Philadelphia has never been sure, but it has at the same time been justly proud of its most interesting Family.

There were half a dozen distinguished Biddles in the Revolution, among them Clement Biddle who, even before the Revolution and notwithstanding his Quaker training, formed a military corps for the protection of a party of friendly Indians who had sought refuge in the Quaker City from a mob which had cruelly massacred a band of unoffending Conestoga Indians in the interior town of Lancaster. Later both Clement Biddle and his brother Owen had distinguished Revolutionary careers, Clement in particular rendering important service as Commissary General of Forage under General Greene and actually staving off a total famine at Valley Forge. There was also a naval officer, James Biddle, who served bravely in the War against Tripoli—he was a prisoner for nineteen months under terrifying conditions—in the War of 1812 and again, at an advanced age, in the Mexican War.

But the most remarkable of all Biddle soldiers or sailors was the first Nicholas Biddle. The sixth son of the William Biddle who had first moved to Philadelphia and his wife Mary Scull, young Nicholas was, in the tradition of the Boston clipper merchants, "bred to the sea." At the age of 13 he made his first voyage, and at the age of 15, while on a voyage to the West Indies, he with two others, chosen by lot—presumably because of starvation problems—were left for two months on an uninhabited island. In 1770, still before his majority, he entered the service of the British Navy and sailed with Lord Nelson. When the Revolution broke out, he returned to America and was given command of a little brig named, curiously, the *Andrea Doria*. With her, on his very first voyage, he won so many merchantmen prizes that when he put back to port he had only five of his original crew; the rest were all in charge of the ships he had taken, and he ran the *Doria* with five men and a skeleton crew composed of trusted volunteers among his prisoners. In 1778, however, on his last voyage, he was in charge of the *Randolph*, of 32 guns, and in order to save the rest of his fleet was forced to attack the British *Yarmouth*, of 64 guns. Mortally wounded early, he "ordered a chair," it is recorded, "placed on the quarter deck and continued to direct the battle." In the end his *Randolph* was blown up completely, and 310 of her 315 men, including Biddle, perished, but the very fact of her utter destruction, at a time when she was so close to her opponent, damaged the *Yarmouth* enough so that the rest of Biddle's fleet escaped. J. F. Cooper in his *History of the Navy* records a moving tribute to the most heroic of the fighting Biddles:

> His death occurred at the early age of twenty-seven, and he died unmarried, though engaged at the time to a lady in Charleston. There is little question that Nicholas Biddle would have risen to high rank and great consideration, had his life been spared. Ardent, ambitious, fearless, intelligent, and persevering, he had all the qualities of a great naval captain, and, though possessing some local family influence perhaps, he rose to the station he filled at so early an age, by personal merit. For so short a career, scarcely any other had been so brilliant . . . he had ever been successful until the fatal moment when he so gloriously fell.

Ironically enough, in view of the fact that a sizable number of latter-day Biddles have been known as fairly heavy drinkers, Nicholas Biddle I, on the testimony of his brother Charles, "never drank a quart of liquor in his life." In any case, the most remarkable of all Biddles also was named Nicholas. Author, scholar, statesman and financier, he was the son of Charles Biddle, a Vice-President of Pennsylvania under the Constitution of 1776, and Hannah Shepard, who came from the aristocratic little town of Beaufort, North Carolina. So extraordinary a student was this Nicholas that he had received all his credits to graduate from the University of Pennsylvania at the age of 13, but he was not permitted his degree because of his age. After graduate work at the College of New Jersey at Princeton, he was, at 18, entrusted with spoliation claims arising out of the Louisiana Purchase. Back home he practiced law, served in Pennsylvania's House of Representatives, and wrote the definitive story of Lewis and Clark's expedition. Married to Jane Craig of the famed "Andalusia" homestead on the Delaware, he entered the State Senate and was later called upon by President Monroe to serve as one of the five government directors of the Bank of the United States. In 1839 he retired to "Andalusia," which became the scene, says the *Dictionary of American Biography*, with mild irony, "of an intellectual and social life which was not then common in the United States":

> Distinguished European exiles were often his guests, and records of their conversations on great events abroad were preserved by him. His interest and aid in all branches of internal development did not diminish his love for classic Greece and her freedom. His active mind not only determined the character of education in Girard College, of whose board he was president, but its architecture. Both the college and the Bank of the United States, as well as his remodelled seat at "Andalusia," followed classic Greek lines. His later papers and addresses were notable for their peculiarly modern tone, one of them advocating shorter hours and higher wages for workmen as sound economical truth. With his death at the age of fifty-eight, there passed a great gentleman and scholar.

In the Nineteenth Century two of Philadelphia's greatest Families were founded by sons of bricklayers—a fact which, in view of the career of the late John B. Kelly, father of Princess Grace, shows nothing if not tradition. One was Peter A. B. Widener, who started work as a butcher boy in his brother's meat shop and during the Civil War secured a contract from the government to supply with mutton all its troops located within a radius of ten miles of Philadelphia. With some $40,000 in profits from this, he entered the streetcar business with his partner, William L. Elkins, and became one of the country's foremost traction magnates. The other son of a bricklayer was none other than John Wanamaker himself. Incredibly poor, he started as an errand boy for a publishing firm at $1.25 a week, and despite such ill-health that before he was twenty he was forced to take an extensive rest, he went on to become the "Prince of Merchants." Although "Pious John," as he was also called, did not originate the one-price system—he himself always credited it to A. T. Stewart—he carried the system further than Stewart ever had, and he did originate his famed "Money Back." Other Gilded Age merchants included the controversial Thomas Dolan, first president of Philadelphia's Manufacturer's Club, and the great department store founders, Justus Strawbridge and Isaac Clothier. But, concludes E. Digby Baltzell, after a long study of their Families, "None of these men has produced . . . descendants who have established themselves in the city as outstanding lawyers, physicians, statesmen or intellectuals."

The Penrose Family are one of Philadelphia's most interesting clans. Beginning with the Eighteenth Century shipbuilder, Bartholomew, they moved on with the Nineteenth Century lawyer, Charles Bingham Penrose, and on into the Twentieth with the famous brothers, Boies and Spencer. The latter shocked his older brother by moving west, fresh out of Harvard, to seek his fortune in Colorado. Soon he was wiring his brother for $1,500 to go into a mining deal—long before, incidentally, his Colorado Springs and Broadmoor days. Boies Penrose promptly telegraphed him $150 for train fare home and warned him against the deal. Years later "Spec," as he was called, returned to Philadelphia and dumped on his brother's desk $75,000 in gold coins. Boies looked at the money in amazement, then reminded his brother he had sent him only $150. "That's why," replied Spec, "I'm only giving you $75,000. If you'd sent the $1,500 I asked for, I'd be giving you three quarters of a million."

The younger Penrose was not the only Philadelphian who went afield. Like the Bostonian merchants, the Philadelphians were responsible for the development of industry in many other cities. A Philadelphia merchant, for example, William Walters, joined with two Boston men, George Peabody and Enoch Pratt, as well as native

Maryland Johns Hopkins, who was also a Quaker, though not a Philadelphian, in becoming the "Big Four" of Baltimore's Nineteenth Century merchant princes. Philadelphia also bequeathed to Baltimore one of the latter city's long-standing First Families in the person of Enoch and Mary Levering, who moved there in 1773—at which time Baltimore was still a small city indeed, with less than 10,000 inhabitants. Baltimore's athletic Families of Riggses and Poes, however, were not Philadelphia products, no more so were such Families as the Fishers, the Bartons, the Duers, or, for that matter, the Moales, Howards, Carters, Buchanans, Gilmors, McKims, McLanes and Perines.*

Baltimore historian Francis Beirne has noted that so great is the tendency of Baltimore's old and large Families to "run to the distaff side" that their surnames have today been all but lost. Judge Gary's family, for example, included no less than seven daughters, all attractive, and all Baltimore expected great things of matches with the Symingtons, who had no less than seven sons and lived conveniently across the way. Curiously enough, however, although all the Gary girls married, there was not so much as a single marriage with a Symington. Despite these difficulties, Baltimore as a city is second to none in Family consciousness, and Dorseys, Stewarts and Kinsolvings are accorded the same sort of First Family honors as Cabots, Lowells or Adamses in Boston or Biddles, Cadwaladers and Cassatts in Philadelphia. Indeed, Baltimore goes a step further than either of those cities in keeping up the quaint old custom of adding the first initial

* A Riggs was early associated with George Peabody. However, the "athletic" designation of Riggses and Poes refers to the fact that in the 1880's and 1890's there were eight well-known Riggs brothers and six well-known Poe brothers in Baltimore. All starred for Princeton's football teams, and two Poes, John Prentiss and Edgar Allan, were chosen for Walter Camp's "All-time All-Americans." To this day in Baltimore, the poet, who was the grandson of David Poe, Washington's deputy Commissary General during the Revolution, is often referred to as the "other" Ethan Allan. Born in Boston, he came to Baltimore via Richmond to seek out his relatives, and, at the age of 26, married his cousin, Virginia Clemm, at that time a girl only 13 years old. He returned to Richmond and traveled widely but came back to Baltimore to die in 1847. Two other aristocratic Baltimore literary lights, members of the socio-literary Delphian Club, were Francis Scott Key, author of "The Star-Spangled Banner," and John Howard Payne, author of "Home, Sweet Home."

of one's father's name to one's own. Thus the late John Fife Symington was known as John Symington of W. (or son of William) to
distinguish himself from a cousin who also bore the name of John.
Other Baltimoreans who have followed this custom are, according
to Beirne, John Eager Howard of B., John E. Hurst of W., Lawrason
Riggs of J., John Merryman of J., John Ridgely of H., and J. William Middendorf of H.

Baltimore also shares the distinction, along with New Orleans, St.
Louis and San Francisco, of having a proud and aristocratic Catholic
Society. There were, from the beginning, four Catholic cities in
North America; of these, two, St. Louis and New Orleans, were of
French origin, a third, San Francisco, was of Spanish origin, while
Baltimore alone was of English origin. The first Lord Baltimore,
George Calvert, the man who laid the foundation for one of the most
successful governments in the American Colonies, had embraced
Catholicism early in the Seventeenth Century; both he and the city
were named for a small fishing village on the south coast of Ireland,
in the "parish nearest America." One of American Catholicism's
most spectacular Families, the Thomas Fortune Ryans, started on
their road to fame in Baltimore. Although the Family founder,
Thomas Fortune Ryan, himself was born on a small farm in Nelson
County, Virginia, and was left orphaned and penniless at 14, at 17
he made his way to Baltimore. Here he "walked the streets" until he
was hired as messenger boy in the dry-goods commission house of
John S. Barry.

But young Ryan had not had a mother with a middle name of
Fortune for nothing. Moving to New York, but still with the aid of
Barry, whose daughter, Ida, in the Horatio Alger tradition, he married, he became a partner in a firm of his own—Lee, Ryan and
Warren—and in 1874 he had his own seat on the Stock Exchange. A
man of no little charm—the Achilles' heel of so many Ryans since—
he was tall, thin, lanky and loose-limbed. He was also, however,
shrewd—with people as well as with figures. Getting to know such
people as William C. Whitney and Peter A. B. Widener, his affairs
were soon a tangled, but vastly successful, web of railroads and street

railroads, lighting systems and coal companies, all of which were later expanded to tobacco, life insurance and even the Belgian Congo diamond fields. The latter Ryan had been asked to reorganize by none other than King Leopold himself, a job to which he addressed himself with his usual energy, acumen and, eventually, profit to himself. One of the most amazing men in the history of American finance, he was aware of the power of publicity—he had early hired Lemuel Quigg, one of the country's first publicity agents—but he was also, paradoxically, called by Whitney "adroit, suave and noiseless."

In his latter years, living on a grand scale—a third of a block beside his Fifth Avenue home was devoted to statuary—he was also, with his wife, philanthropically inclined where the Catholic Church was concerned, giving it some $20,000,000. In 1907 Mrs. Ryan was made, by Pope Pius X, a Countess of the Holy Roman Empire. Mrs. Ryan was an invalid in the last years of her life, and though there were many stories of the difficulties of their life, nonetheless, Ryan, a staunch Catholic, would not countenance divorce. Then in 1917, on the death of his wife, he married again, at the age of 66, and only twelve days after his wife's death. Her name was Mary T. Nicoll; a sister of the late De Lancey Nicoll and a member of a Family which had been prominent in New York for two centuries, she had been married twice before—to James Brown Lord and Cornelius C. Cuyler. This rapid remarriage did not please any of Ryan's sons, although only one of them, the eldest, Allan, spoke out. "It is," he said at the time, "one of the most disrespectful, disgraceful and indecent things I've ever heard of."

These words were probably the most expensive ever uttered by any scion of any American Family. In 1928, when Thomas Fortune Ryan died, leaving an estate of $135,000,000, Allan Ryan was left two black pearl shirt studs. The rest of the estate was divided into fifty-four parts—twelve each to Ryan's widow and his two surviving sons, John Barry and Clendenin, eight for Allan's six children, and five for the children of Ryan's deceased sons, William Kane and Joseph.* In

* Joseph's children were Joseph, Jr., and Elinor. Joseph and his wife, Nannie Morse, of Washington, D.C., were separated, however, by the time of Joseph's

this same will Ryan left no money to charity "for the reason that in my lifetime I have contributed largely to religious, charitable and educational causes." He did, however, add a stern proviso to the effect that if any of his bequests were questioned, the heirs who complained would lose their shares. Shortly after the will, John Barry and Clendenin made an agreement with their disinherited brother, Allan, that he would receive $50,000 a year for life.

No American Family had more second-generation troubles in all directions than the Ryans. With many sons of the Family founder, they were, like the Goulds, with whom they are often compared, almost a textbook example of Family disintegration via drink, multiple marriage and other attendant vagaries at least partially attributable to money and publicity. Allan Ryan, before his disinheritance, had already gone bankrupt after an unsuccessful "corner" of Stutz motorcar stocks—one which got him expelled from the Stock Exchange and caused losses amounting to $32,000,000. Then, in 1922, he had a court battle with the late George Maxwell, president of the American Society of Composers, Authors and Publishers, over the affections of his wife, the former Sally Tack, of Philadelphia. The Ryans were divorced in 1925 and that same year he married a Montreal girl, Irene McKenna. In 1933, Ryan was sued for $100,000 by his housemaid, on whom, it was alleged, he had forced his attentions.

The third generation of this eldest-son branch which had the least money—due to their father's disinheritance—suffered the least from the many difficulties which beset the other branches. Of the six children, Allan, Jr., and Fortune Peter, made excellent careers for themselves with the Royal Typewriter Company, and Allan has also distinguished himself in the raising of Black Angus cattle. Another son, Theodore, a gentleman farmer of Connecticut, is also a well-known Black Angus man as well as prominent in Connecticut politics. There were also two girls, Sally and Miriam, as well as still another son, Barry, who not only owned race horses but also distinguished

---

death in 1921. In his will Joseph left his wife $100 and his estate to an actress named Lucille Whiteford. Joseph, Jr., owner of Mont Tremblant, Canadian ski resort, died under circumstances suspicious of suicide.

himself as a trainer of them—in fact considers himself, and is recognized as, a professional trainer. There were also, however, many multiple marriages here too, Allan, Jr., taking the prize in this regard, having been married no less than four times and all to distinguished "Society" figures—Janet Newbold (also the famed Mrs. William Rhinelander Stewart), Eleanor Barry, Priscilla St. George and Grace Amory.

The second son of the second generation, John Barry, Sr., was a poet and dreamer who published verse under the name of Barrie Vail and generally managed to spend as much money as he was able to get his hands on. Married to Nan Morgan, he had an incredible number of children, some fifteen in all, of whom ten lived—Adele, Virginia, Nina, John Barry, Jr., Dorothy, Natalie, Thomas Fortune, Basil, Donald and William. Of these, the girls made generally successful marriages, one of them, Nina, marrying Philip Carroll, direct descendant of Charles Carroll of Carrollton. On the other hand, they too were not immune from Ryan scrapes, Adele in 1930 becoming involved in a $500,000 breach-of-promise suit. As for the boys, while John Barry, Jr., William and Donald were dazzlingly handsome as young men, strong and excellent at sports, they had some difficulty in growing up, and Basil, at least, once distinguished himself by driving a car through Stamford, Connecticut, throwing rocks in all the store windows and ending by driving his car up the courthouse steps and as far into the court as he could go—a gesture that made his apprehension considerably easier than it might otherwise have been but also made the episode rather more expensive.

As for the late Thomas Fortune II, he first married the Pittsburgh divorcée, Margaret Moorhead Rea, then, after a divorce from her, married still another divorcée, Mayme Cook Masters, of Sheridan, Wyoming. He died in 1955, his greatest difficulty in life apparently having been, as one member of the Family expressed it, that "he just couldn't seem to keep off the front page." The most socially prominent of this generation, John Barry, Jr., after a career of reporting, settled down to a marriage with Margaret Kahn, daughter of Otto, and one of the most cultured and cultivated figures on the whole New York-London-Paris axis. Their children, in the fourth Ryan generation from the original Thomas Fortune or the third generation of the second son of Thomas, are Virginia Fortune, who in 1949 married Lord David Ogilvy, eldest son of the Earl of Airlie, and John Barry Ryan III, who on his mother's side, via Kahn, represents the fourth generation in the Family to work for Kuhn, Loeb & Company and is married to Dorinda Dixon; the latter in 1959 was one of America's ten best-dressed women.

None of the Ryan Family difficulties can compare, for stark tragic drama, with the fortunes of the third son's branch of the Family—the Clendenin Ryans. An early partner in his brother Allan's ill-fated Stock Exchange firm of Allan A. Ryan & Bro., Clendenin had married well and had four children, Caroline, Clendenin Jr., George and Richard, when in 1923 he was sued for $500 "room rent" by a showgirl. Then, in 1939, in the library of the five-story graystone mansion in Manhattan which had been the Ryan Family home since the days of Thomas Fortune, he put his head into a gas fireplace and committed suicide. Incredibly enough, eighteen years later, in 1957, in the same house, his son, also named Clendenin and also a man with four children, also committed suicide.

Moving west to Pittsburgh, one is confronted with Family-founding with a vengeance—albeit it is all Family-founding of the Nineteenth Century variety. "Probably no community in the world," says W. A. Powers, "since the days of the great merchant princes of Venice and Florence, has ever produced such sudden and such vast personal fortunes as did Pittsburgh in the latter half of the Nineteenth Century. . . . Wherever the aristocracy of Pittsburgh moved —and there wasn't a millionaire who wasn't a member of the aristocracy—they built huge mansions, furnished them in the elaborate taste of the times, and lived and entertained on a lavish scale." And yet Pittsburgh's self-made "steelers" were not themselves the great Family founders. Andrew Carnegie had arrived during the depression of 1848; his first job, with the Blackston Cotton Mills, netted him $1.20 a week. But, as we have seen, he left only one daughter

and gave away most of his fortune. Another Pittsburgh pioneer, old
Henry Oliver, of "Oliver luck" fame, was a former messenger boy
with Carnegie and later rose with him. Although he reached close
to the pinnacle of steeldom, he too failed to found a Family.

Curiously, probably the oldest Family name in Pittsburgh in the
Family-founding sense—Scaife—is one of the few Family names,
which, despite the antiquity of their riches, is not known to the rest
of the country. A Scaife married a Mellon and there is today more
than one Scaife high up in the Mellons' Gulf Oil Company—but
the fact remains that a Scaife was manufacturing japanned trays before the War of 1812 at a time when Mellons were unheard of and
Pittsburgh itself was a mere pup; much later came "Wm. B. Scaife &
Co., Iron Mongers." As for many of the other top steelers in the very
forge of America's industrial might, the self-made angle has been
exaggerated by most historians. Henry Frick, for example, second
only to Carnegie among the great steelers, started out working in his
uncle's store for literally no money except his board and the privilege
of sleeping at night upon the counter. Nonetheless, he came from an
old Swiss Family and was the fourth generation in America on both
sides of his family. And the motivating force of his young life was
to be as rich as his grandfather Overholt, a man who operated a successful distillery and had relatively successful Mennonite forebears.
Frick left a son and daughter but, like Carnegie, no dynasty. Neither
did George Westinghouse, who had only one son and, though he
founded an industrial empire, failed to found a Family. Refusing
Mellon aid in the crash of 1890—at that time he was aided by August
Belmont—the great inventor succumbed in 1908 when, in the words
of Harvey O'Connor, "the bankers took over his enterprises and
gave the old man a nominal position from which he resigned in
disgust."*

Two Pittsburgh Families who have made the transition from Ridge
Avenue to Sewickley and finally to Ligonier—pronounced "ligo-

---

* The present dominating "family" in Westinghouse is that of the able
Mark Cresap and his wife. However, Cresap, like so many of today's inheritors
of Family enterprises, came through the management consultant route. He was
born in Chicago.

near"—and the Rolling Rock Hunt Club, not to mention the down-town Duquesne—pronounced "doo-cane"—are the Joneses and the Heinzes. The first Jones, whose name was Benjamin Franklin Jones, was born in Claysville, the son of Jacob Aik Jones. At 19 he left New Brighton Academy to go to work, in the great Pittsburgh tradition, without salary; not so many years later he teamed up with James Laughlin to found Jones and Laughlin. Described as "genial and companionable," rare for a Pittsburgh Family founder, he left four children and on his death, in 1903, was called by *Iron Age* "the most highly respected man in the iron trade." Henry John Heinz, like so many other Family founders, was the son of a bricklayer. He too started in bricklaying but in 1869 founded a partnership to sell grated horseradish. Married to a girl of Irish descent, he had five children and was an active "Sunday-schooler," although "through accident rather than through any change of doctrinal opinion," it is recorded, "he became a member successively of the Lutheran, the Methodist Episcopal, the Methodist Protestant and the Presbyterian Churches." In 1896 he coined his world-famous slogan—"57 Varieties." "I well knew," he said, "that my factories were making many more than that, but 57 was to me the best number—the most magic sounding."

The greatest of all Pittsburgh Families—one which was already a Family of millionaires when Carnegie was working as a bobbin boy in a cotton mill—was, of course, the Mellon Family. The dynasty began with Thomas Mellon, a farmer's boy who was born in 1837 in a town which might have been named by Horatio Alger, Jr., himself—Poverty Point. At the age of nine, with 99 cents in his pocket, young Tom Mellon was on his way to make his fortune. "Going to Pittsburgh, eh?" said a passing farmer friend. "Well, you'll see more in one day than at Poverty Point in a lifetime." Mellon went to Western University, read law and later became a judge; not until he retired as a judge, in 1870, did he start the banking venture which would leave his sons and grandsons in control of one of the greatest financial empires in the history of the country. Although among his distinctions was the fact that he was the first person to extend credit to Carnegie, as well as the man who lent Henry Frick his first $10,000, nothing in Judge Mellon's life was as typical as his courtship—indeed, no future Family founder in American history ever went about the choice of a wife so carefully. First he made a list of all eligible young women, ignoring all physical attributes. A wife, he wrote, should be "for a helpmate, not for display." Then, before he even had any girl in mind, he decided to eliminate what he called the "shy, coy, evasive methods in use" and wrote out instead, according to Harvey O'Connor, a four-point program:

> Agreement that both parties are candidates for matrimony; agreement that each is acceptable to the other *prima facie*, subject to rejection on further acquaintance; no love to be excited or admitted on either side until each party is fully satisfied with the nature, disposition and character of the other; each to be bound to the other by honor and etiquette, in case the relation is declined on either side, to entertain no ill feeling in consequence, and never to divulge any information whatever obtained during such preliminary stage.

Finally he chose Sarah Jane Negley, whose family's farmhouse he had admired on his trip to Pittsburgh as a boy of nine. Miss Negley was, he wrote, "quiet, pleasant and self-possessed . . . the surroundings were favorable, neither too coarse nor too fine. . . . There was no love making and little or no love beforehand so far as I was concerned. . . . When I proposed if I had been rejected I would have left neither sad nor depressed nor greatly disappointed, only annoyed at the loss of time."

"Such was the courtship," concludes O'Connor, "of the parents of the Lord of Aluminum and Oil and Steel, Secretary of the Treasury, and Ambassador to the Court of St. James." And even the loss of two daughters in early childhood was, in the opinion of this incredible Family founder, a minor matter:

> Females may be brought up in all the comfort and enjoyment which tender care and wealth can confer to be launched on a hard and unfeeling world. Whilst celibacy is the safest, it has its drawbacks; and marriage is a fearful risk. Apart from the pains and anxious cares of maternity, the chances are so great of obtaining a husband who may turn out to be heartless and cruel, or a

drunkard and spendthrift, and the consequences so tremendous, that daughters who die young need not be greatly lamented.

Besides Andrew, Judge Mellon had four other sons, and all were brought up with a strictness that would put to shame the most proper of Boston's best. Young Mellons were warned, their father's letters make clear, not only against other boys and girls but against Society in general:

> Make no friends until you know their private moral character. Make no friends—that is companions—of theatre-going, party-going or young men who talk of the pleasure of company and the like. . . . I have never warned you enough against female company keeping. I know nothing which so unfits a young man for manly, serious studies and business, and it is worse than useless. My good uncle Thomas ruined his whole family by encouraging them to mingle in good society for the purpose of polishing their manners, as he called it. It is proper to treat female company, when necessarily thrown into it, with proper, manly politeness, but what character is more odious to males and females than a *ladies' man?* What business has he hanging around girls that he cannot or has no intention of marrying?

When the Civil War came, Judge Mellon was firm in his counsel to his boys that it was only "greenhorns" who enlisted:

> You can learn nothing useful in the army. . . . Here there is no credit attached to going. All now stay if they can and go if they must. Those who are able to pay for substitutes, do so, and no discredit attaches. In time you will come to understand and believe that a man may be a patriot without risking his own life or sacrificing his health. There are plenty of other lives less valuable or others ready to serve for the love of serving.

The contrast between the Lowells of New England and the Lees of the South with the Mellons of Pittsburgh is a strong one—but, to their credit, the Mellon boys did not all take their father's advice. As for Mellon himself, in his last years he took, in the Family-founding tradition, a coat of arms. "The name Mellon," he wrote in explanation, "is so ancient as to be prehistoric."

Writing his own life for a biographical reference book, he was,

Mellon-fashion, brief: "Became wealthy," he wrote, "from invest-ments." On February 3, 1908, on the day of his 95th birthday, Judge Mellon's descendants gathered in the old mansion on Negley Avenue, and on that day he died.

As far back as 1882, Judge Mellon had transferred the ownership of "T. Mellon & Sons, Bankers" to his fourth son—the one who, he foresaw, had the best business brains in the Family. His name, of course, was Andrew Mellon, and, taking over at the age of 27, he amply proved, through two new eras of Mellon Family-founding, aluminum and oil, his father's foresight. But on the personal side the life of Andrew Mellon was not a happy one. Lacking magnetism, with his cold blue eyes and tight little lips masked by a mustache, he was further embittered by an unhappy love affair in his youth; at the age of 25 his fiancée contracted tuberculosis and died a year later. Then, for twenty years, until he was 45, Mellon lived in his father's home—only to fall in love, at that time, with the young, beautiful, high-spirited Nora McMullen. She was the granddaughter of Dub-lin's famed brewer Peter Guinness, of a Family which has played a large part in the Twentieth Century's International Set. They were married in 1900, and soon there were two children, Paul and Ailsa, later Mrs. David Bruce. But, as she was later to say in her divorce statement, the high-spirited Irish girl, twenty-five years younger than her husband, soon wearied of her life in Pittsburgh:

> My first great disillusionment came when I learned that his people were not of his people at all. I had dreamed of another Hertford-shire, with Hertfordshire lads and lassies; I had arrived in a strange land with strange people, strangers in the strange land. "They are foreign, Huns and Slavs, and such as that, and you can't do anything with them," I was told about the people whose affection I had dreamed of winning for my children. It was not only men. There were women and children, too, all toilers in my husband's vineyard; but none of them given the laborer's recognition, toiling and working on the estate and adding to its wealth but not recognized as a part of it. The whole community was as cold and hard as the steel it made, and chilled the heart to the core. . . . Nights that I spent in my baby boy's bedroom,

nursing these thoughts of his future, my husband, locked in his study, nursed his dollars, millions of dollars, maddening dollars, nursed larger and bigger at the cost of priceless sleep, irretrievable health and happiness. Always new plans, bigger plans for new dollars, bigger dollars, dollars that robbed him and his family of the time he could have devoted far more profitably to a mere, "Thank God, we are living."

Such a picture of the Pittsburgh of the 1900's contrasts sharply with the Pittsburgh of the 1960's—now, as elsewhere in the country where Labor and Capital are concerned, the shoe is on the other foot. Also, even in its own day, the quotation should be read in the light of Mrs. Mellon's personal bitterness at the time. In those days, where Mellons were concerned, the Pittsburgh papers were like the Wilmington papers where Du Ponts were concerned. People in either city who wanted to read about either Family read the Philadelphia papers. During the Mellon divorce, what they read were stories of the so-called "Mellon" amendment to the Pennsylvania State divorce law, making it possible to hear divorce evidence in private—what was called "the law making it easy for rich men to get rid of their wives." But even then the fault was not all on Andrew Mellon's side, as is perhaps indicated by the goings on in the Guinness Family since. In any case, Mellon did get his divorce, his wife went back to her native Ireland, and from that time on, Mellon, always a reticent man, became so publicity-shy that he became a legend. Up until the time he was being considered for Secretary of the Treasury in 1921 —at a time when he was 66 years old—his name, let alone his picture, had never appeared in the *New York Times,* and even Pittsburgh itself was hardly aware of his existence. Yet he was the officer of dozens of corporations, director of half a hundred more, worth somewhere between one billion and two billion dollars and, altogether, second only to John D. Rockefeller in power, wealth and influence in the whole country.

Serving as Secretary of the Treasury under three Presidents, the longest tenure in history, Andrew Mellon became, if anything, even more of a legend. As Harvey O'Connor tells the story, at a Cabinet meeting under Harding, when the possible scrapping of a $12,000,000 government war plant was under consideration, Mellon was asked for his opinion. "I had a similar case recently in one of my own plants," he said. "The amount involved was the same. I scrapped mine." Some time later the question of the Chicago Eastern Railway arose. "Now we've got him," Harding whispered to Daugherty. "Surely he wasn't in on this." Then to Mellon he said, "I don't suppose, Mr. Mellon, that you were interested in the Chicago Eastern Railway, were you?" "Oh, yes," replied Mr. Mellon, "we had a million or a million and a half of their bonds."

Under Coolidge, it is recorded, "The President and Mr. Mellon conversed almost entirely in pauses." Later President Hoover, who preferred Undersecretary Ogden Mills for his Treasury post, prevailed upon Mellon to accept the ambassadorship to Great Britain. Here, with his daughter Ailsa, wife of the son of Maryland's Senator Bruce, as his hostess, Mellon offered "a pleasing hospitality"—not the least of which was an advance look at a portion of the art collection which was soon to become the National Gallery of Art in Washington. Allan Nevins perhaps best summed up the most famous of all Mellons. "His veiled and reticent personality," he says, "cloaked an essentially, simple, thoughtful and just nature. With the misfortune of excessive wealth he coped as conscientiously and efficiently as his training and traditions permitted."

As a young man Paul, the son of Andrew, felt far closer to his mother than his father; he spoke often of his father's "ice-water smile" and described himself as "more McMullen than Mellon." After Choate and Yale, however, and a brief attempt at literary and publishing pursuits, he settled down to Mellon interests and his famous Rockaby Stables. During the 1957 visit of Queen Elizabeth II, he gave the one private lunch for her—at his Oak Spring Farm near Upperville, Virginia. But the titular head of the Mellon Family empire, ever since 1934, has been the son of the late Andrew's brother Richard—Richard King Mellon. He had been carefully picked for the post by both his uncle and his father. When he was 17, for example, his father told him he had deposited $5,000 to his name in a checking account. Five years later, he had not touched the money. "Anticipating," says Homer Shannon, "that some day his father would call for an accounting of how he had spent it, he simply left it where it was so there would be no explaining to do." Graduating from Princeton—he had already been to Culver Military Academy— young Richard began as a messenger boy in the Mellon National Bank. In 1936 he married Constance Prosser, the widowed daughter of Seward Prosser, then Board Chairman of the Bankers Trust Company. Their first heir was a two-month-old boy whom they adopted; their family soon consisted, however, of four children, Richard, Cassandra, Constance and Seward. Richard King is far from publicity-shy, and it is some jump from the late Andrew, in this regard, to him. If the uncle's name, at least up until Andrew's appointment as Secretary of the Treasury, rarely appeared in print, the day seldom goes by when his nephew's does not appear several times— and most often, in Pittsburgh at least, on the front pages. Nonetheless, Richard King Mellon is a hard worker; he is personally credited with being primarily responsible for the reconstruction, unsmogging and general renaissance of his city.

Second only to the Mellons of the great Families to come out of Pittsburgh is the Phipps Family. The first Phipps in America spelled his name Phips and settled in Pemaquid, Maine, in 1649; later one of his sons, as the first royal Governor of Massachusetts, recovered some sunken Spanish sea treasure in the sum of £300,000—an event for which he was knighted and which will be of no surprise to those knowing this close-fisted, hard-working, publicity-shy yet incredibly successful Family of today. Unhappily, few present-day Phippses have been able to establish satisfactory genealogical connections with the royal Phips. For all practical purposes—which the Phippses are nothing if not—the real Phipps Family founder was Henry Phipps, the son of an emigrant from England, who was born in Philadelphia in 1839. In 1845 he and his family moved to Allegheny City, Pennsylvania, where the elder Phipps became a master shoemaker. Beside them lived a family named Carnegie, and when Carnegie's mother began binding shoes for Phipps' father for $4 a week, a bond was established in more ways than one; Carnegie's own grandfather had been a master shoemaker.

Soon Henry Phipps ranked along with Frick as one of Carnegie's top men. Called the perfect "inside man," crafty and, like so many Phippses since, incredibly close-mouthed, of him it was said that he knew better than any man "how to keep a check in the air." It was also typical of Phipps' contribution to the steel business that he was responsible for the profitable utilization of more waste products than any other man. In the end Carnegie's "silent partner" was to have even more money than Carnegie and a dynasty as well; married to Anne Childs Shaffer, the daughter of a Pittsburgh manufacturer, he had three sons and two daughters. At the same time, his philanthropies, not only in Pittsburgh but also in Baltimore and New York, were numerous. He lived to the age of 91, dying in 1930 at his home, "Bonnie Blink," in Great Neck, Long Island. By this time, in the time-honored mutations of the American aristocratic process, no less than four of the grandsons of the son of a shoemaker were recognized, out on Long Island's proud Meadow Brook, as four of the country's leading polo players—Hubert and Michael Phipps and Raymond and Winston Guest.*

By mid-Twentieth Century, however, the Phipps Family, in its latter generations, was known for far more than polo. Through its own Family corporation, Bessemer Industries, it held what is undoubtedly the largest amount of Eastern real estate controlled by any American Family. Indeed, Phippses have a large proportion of the entire Eastern shore all the way from Long Island to Florida. And out in the West there are Phippses also. Lawrence C. Phipps, for example, retired from Pittsburgh at 39, went west to Colorado and, becoming active in politics, served two terms as the country's richest

* When, in 1947, Boston's controversial debutante, Lucy ("Cee-Zee") Cochrane, a former Ziegfeld Follies showgirl, married Winston Guest, the Guest-Phipps Family took steps to buy a revealing portrait of Cee-Zee which was painted by Diego Rivera and which reposed in a bar in Mexico City. At first the bar refused—they liked the picture. Finally, however, when the Family prevailed upon them to accept a substitute, they agreed to part with it. The substitute was an also revealing portrait of Linda Christian. Shortly after this affair, Cee-Zee was elected one of America's ten best-dressed women.

Senator. His son, Lawrence C. Phipps, Jr., was, as of the 1960's, Master of Foxhounds of one of the most unusual hunts in the world —the Arapahoe. Meeting at Highland Ranch, on the Phipps estate, the Phipps hounds hunt, not fox, but coyote.

Probably the most popularly famous—or rather infamous—of all Pittsburgh Families is the Thaw Family, and this, of course, because of the late Pittsburgh "idler," Harry K. Thaw, who, on the night of June 25, 1906, in the roof garden theatre of Madison Square Garden, shot and killed the great architect Stanford White. Although the murder occurred over the Pittsburgh chorus girl, Evelyn Nesbit, all of the country's Family dynasties were in a way concerned, since White himself came from one of the oldest New England-New York dynasties. His American ancestor was a selectman in Cambridge, Massachusetts, in 1635; his great-grandfather was an Episcopal clergyman; his grandfather was a New York shipping merchant; and his father was a lawyer and man of letters who was one of the founders of the New York *World* and the writer of weekly letters to the London *Spectator*, which he signed "A Yankee." The architect himself had designed not only the building in which he met his end, but also a host of other landmarks of the "Four Hundred" era, including, besides private houses, the Century Club, the Metropolitan Club, the Washington Arch, and the present Random House building. At 52, it is quite clear from the trial transcript, the late Mr. White's morals were not of the best; they were, however, generally speaking, no worse and no better than the morals of the Four Hundred in general. They were, in short, a product of the recognized double standard of the day.

The morals of the late Mr. Thaw, on the other hand, were something else again. Like so many other Pittsburgh Families, the founder of the Thaw Family was the son of a Philadelphian who had moved to Pittsburgh as early as 1804. The Family founder himself, William Thaw, at 16 traveled through the Ohio Valley on horseback, making collections for the Bank of the United States. Thereafter, transportation improvement became his passion in life, and before his death in 1889 he had made $10,000,000 in transportation companies. He left ten children, five by each of two wives, the second of whom,

Mary Sibbet Copley of Pittsburgh, the mother of Harry K., he had married when he was 50 and she was a younger woman.

Thaw was brought up by an aging father and a doting, idiotically "Family proud" mother. While examples of second-generation difficulties vary from William Randolph Hearst, Sr., to Tommy Manville, one thing is certain, the late Harry K. Thaw was the all-time low. A sadistic pervert who became insanely jealous over the fact that someone else had once been intimate with a girl—one with whom, before they were married, he had traveled all over the world and with whom he enjoyed an almost incredibly unnatural relationship—he was defended by his equally incredible mother, who had already spent half of her fortune bailing him out of previous unsavory escapades. She not only hired the late Delphin M. Delmas, the so-called "Napoleon of the Pacific Slope," as a lawyer to defend her boy but also bribed dozens of witnesses, including a battery of alienists, to say that he was insane. Generally speaking, during the trial this defense did far better than District Attorney Jerome, who was over and over again stymied by the curiously barefaced, back-and-forth testimony of Miss Nesbit. In any case, the first trial resulted in a hung jury; the second, a year later, won for Thaw a verdict of "Not guilty because of insanity at the time of the act."

After the trial Thaw was remanded to an asylum, where he spent a few years only, then escaped to Canada. Back in the States, he was adjudged sane, first by a Federal Court in New Hampshire and then, in 1915, by a New York jury. Among other things established by these lunacy hearings was the fact that as a "Professor," Thaw had often rented rooms in a disorderly house and spent his time giving "stage training" to girls by whipping them. Once freed by judgment of the court, Thaw divorced Evelyn Nesbit—who was meanwhile making a good thing out of her fame by playing in nightclubs—and the next year, 1917, was indicted for horsewhipping a teen-age boy. Once more remanded to an asylum, he was once more, in 1924, freed. He died in Miami in 1924. All in all, the result of the whole affair was far more shattering on the Pittsburgh Family in its final effect than if Thaw had been, at the first trial, convicted of murder in the first degree.

VII

MIDWEST, SOUTHWEST AND FAR WEST—

From Rockefellers, McCormicks and Fields to Big Fours and Little Fours

MOVING FROM Pittsburgh to Cleveland, one runs squarely into the Family saga which affected more other Families, in the Family-founding sense, than any other—the Rockefellers. What Morgan was to Family-founding in the East, both by marriage and by making his famous "partners," Rockefeller was to Cleveland and later New York; if such Families as Nicholses and Pennoyers, Lloyd-Smiths and Merle-Smiths, were Morgan-rooted, John D. Rockefeller and Standard Oil spread like a warm blanket over a baker's dozen of American Families—among them the Andrewses, the Harknesses,

368

the Flaglers, the Archbolds, the H. H. Rogerses, the Paynes, the Bostwicks, the Stillmans and the Pratts. Indeed, to take just one instance, the Pratt Family, Ferdinand Lundberg as far back as 1937 counted no less than twenty-one individual Pratt families all affected to a greater or lesser degree by Standard Oil.* In such a Family as a whole, the relationships were by the mid-Twentieth Century almost unbelievably complicated—as witness the story of Sherman Pratt being asked some time ago if Helen Pratt was any relation of his. "Yes," he replied, "she's 25, I'm 26." Since Pratt was obviously not referring to age, the reply rather baffled the questioner. "You see," explained Sherman, "the Family's gotten so complicated it's like a library—we use the Dewey decimal system."*

Perhaps the most interesting of the "Rockefeller Families"—and certainly the most important from the point of view of contribution to their country—is the Harkness Family. The American ancestor of this Family was, like Carnegie, a Scotsman. In 1840 his descendant, Stephen Harkness, originally a harness maker, and the real Family founder, moved west to Ohio. Then, in 1866, at that time the owner of a distillery in Republic, Ohio, he lent John D. Rockefeller $70,000; that one loan not only made the Harknesses as a whole one of America's richest Families, it has also made every succeeding generation of individual Harknesses rich. The great philanthropy of the Family, however, occurred right in the second generation with Stephen's son, the late Edward Stephen Harkness.

Born in Cleveland in 1874, Harkness married Mary Stillman, of the famous banking Family, in 1904. They had no children and he literally devoted his life to good works. As the Rockefellers themselves were the country's greatest "institutional" philanthropists, so

* Lundberg lists, as of 1937, Mr. and Mrs. Frederic Bayley Pratt, Mrs. Charles M. Pratt, Mr. and Mrs. Harold Irving Pratt, Jr., former Congresswoman Ruth Baker Pratt, Mr. and Mrs. John T. Pratt, Mr. and Mrs. Samuel Croft Register II, Mr. and Mrs. Richardson Pratt, Mr. and Mrs. Theodore Pratt, Mrs. George Dupont Pratt, Mr. and Mrs. George D. Pratt, Jr., Mr. and Mrs. James Ramsey Hunt, Mr. and Mrs. Richard Stockton Emmett, Mrs. Pratt McLane, Mr. and Mrs. David R. Wilmerding, Mr. and Mrs. Herbert L. Pratt, Jr., Mr. and Mrs. Charles Pratt, Sherman Pratt, Mr. and Mrs. Elliott Pratt, Mr. and Mrs. James Jackson, Jr., Mr. and Mrs. Robert H. Thayer, Mr. and Mrs. Edwin H. P. Pratt, and about thirty children.

Edward Harkness was perhaps the outstanding personal philanthropist. Although he was responsible for such charities as the Commonwealth Fund, which gave attention to child health and child guidance all over the world, he is perhaps best remembered for his Columbia-Presbyterian Medical Center and his gifts of Harvard and Yale's "House" Plans. In connection with the latter gift, it is curious to note that the "Houses" were originally offered to Yale, which college Harkness had attended; but when Yale was slow to accept, Harvard's Lawrence Lowell was not. Thereafter, Yale followed suit. A patient, kindly man, shy and modest—a family trait of Harknesses—Edward Harkness had a memorable view of the so-called "value" of a dollar. "A dollar misspent," he once said, "is a dollar lost, and we must not forget that some man's work made the dollar." He personally gave away well over a hundred million dollars.

As for the Rockefellers themselves, no Family in American history ever went through a greater change in respect to their public regard. Nor has this change been confined to the general public. Only a generation ago, for example, Mrs. David Lion Gardiner, dowager empress of New York's proud Gardiner Family, was informed that her young grandson, Robert David Lion Gardiner, was about to go out and play with the Rockefeller children. Mrs. Gardiner forbade it. "No Gardiner will ever play," she said, "with the grandchild of a gangster." And among his fellow oilmen Rockefeller's name has remained extremely controversial. In 1957, for example, the late E. DeGolyer, dean of the country's oilmen, explained to this writer why he had never been able to complete his projected history of the oil business. "I never could decide," he said, "whether John D. Rockefeller was the greatest oil man who ever lived, or a goddam lying pirate who made a monkey out of the whole capitalistic system."

One thing is certain. Whether due to the efforts of the late great publicist, Ivy Lee, to the character of the late John D. Rockefeller, Jr., or to that of his wife, or perhaps even due to a misunderstanding to begin with, the fact remains that the Rockefellers in their third generation since the Family founder have proved themselves extremely highly regarded citizens indeed. The five brothers, individually characterized by John Watson, as "shy" John, "outgoing" Nelson, "venturesome" Laurance, "maverick" Winthrop and "dogged" David, have also with the possible exception of "maverick" Winthrop made large contributions to the change in public attitude. Indeed, today the Family has, in retrospect, almost the character of a Morality Play. Thus Nelson becomes Everyman, John D. Rockefeller, Sr., Worldly Goods with overtones of Gluttony, and John D. Rockefeller, Jr., a composite of Good Deeds and Charity.

The Rockefeller Family saga was, however, something of a Morality Play long before the present brothers Rockefeller. The American ancestor of the Family was Johann Peter Rockefeller, a miller who migrated to America from Sagendorf, Germany, in 1722. Settling in Somerville, New Jersey, he became a farmer and a Father, one of his ten children being a John Rockefeller who married his cousin Christina Rockefeller. John and Christina, in turn, produced a son Godfrey, "a thriftless, shiftless fellow," it is recorded, "fond of his tipple"—one who may certainly fill the character, in the Morality Play, of Sloth. Furthermore, Godfrey, having married Lucy Avery, of Great Barrington, Massachusetts, also produced another Sloth—the incredible William Avery Rockefeller, the improbable father of John D. himself. Known as "Big Bill," he actually went further than Sloth—in fact, he was extremely close to the Morality Play idea of the good-natured Devil who emits hints and glints of Lechery and Fleshly Desire.

A large handsome man whose source of income was long kept secret from his family and friends, he described himself as a traveling salesman but was actually a "herbal doctor" selling quack cancer cures at $25 per treatment—a fairish fee in those days, even for a lifesaving cure. Between trips on the road, Big Bill, an apparently irresistible ladies' man, courted and finally eloped with Eliza Davison, daughter of a hard-fisted, well-to-do Richford, New York, farmer. The latter understandably took the blackest possible view of the marriage. But Big Bill and Eliza nonetheless settled on a 60-acre farm outside Richford. They had six children: Lucy, John Davison—

born July 8, 1839—William, Mary Ann, and twins (Francis and Frank); their rearing was mainly Eliza's privilege and problem, since her husband was forever on the road plying his trade.*

For biographers who see the grown man primarily as childhood experiences writ large, John D. Rockefeller's early days on the farm are a regular treasure trove of traumatic experiences. Actually, while he worked his fingers to the bone doing odd jobs for small change, and while the family was forced to live on credit when his father was off on prolonged trips, his life was not all hard scrabble. Just when the storekeepers would start muttering about cutting off credit, father Bill would come booming into town exuding charm and scattering five-dollar gold pieces. And all would temporarily be well. However, the family experienced other types of stress and strain. Rumors circulated that Big Bill was a horse thief, a skirt-chaser, and an all-around dastard. These tales may well have been fabricated by his disgruntled father-in-law or by his rivals in business and romance. The fact remains, however, that in July, 1849, when Big Bill's son, John D., was going on six and the family was living in Moravia, New York, Big Bill was indicted on a charge of impairing the morals of his family's hired girl. Whatever the truth of the charges, Big Bill avoided court action by hastily settling his family in Owego, New York, which was in another jurisdiction. Later they moved to Strongville, Ohio, near Cleveland. Unquestionably, it was the rocklike integrity of Eliza Davison Rockefeller which prevented the ignominy and financial deprivation attendant

* Of this "Family-founding generation," the future career of Frank, John D.'s brother, is a curious one. He was the only Rockefeller to serve in the Civil War, and was twice wounded. Afterward, in 1870, he married Helen Scofield and had four children, two of whom died young. Never a good businessman and incurably jealous of his brother, he split with him completely in 1900 and went west. The breakup was so bitter that he even had the bodies of his two children removed from the Cleveland family tomb. Settling in Belvidere, Kansas, he bought some land and announced, "I am not Frank Rockefeller, brother of John D. I am Frank Rockefeller Stockman"—a statement that seems to find a future corollary in the latter-day statements of Winthrop Rockefeller, of "Winrock," Arkansas. Of Frank Rockefeller's two surviving children, one, a daughter, left Belvidere and went to Montana. Here all traces of her—even to her own family—were lost.

on these events from shattering her family completely. Eliza Davison was also herself a stern disciplinarian. Once, John D. recalled in his *Random Reminiscences*, he was being whipped by his mother for "some unfortunate doings" in the village school. In the middle of his punishment he protested his innocence. "Never mind," said his mother grimly, "we have started in on this whipping, and we may as well proceed. It will do for the next time."

As a young boy, John D. attended high school and business school in Cleveland. Always a shrewd bargainer, interested in all manner of swaps and minor business transactions, he called his shots cannily after graduating from business school in 1855. He chose as his first employers a large firm of commission merchants, because he wanted a broad view of the business scene. "I did not guess what it would be," he said later, "but I was after something big." In any case, having learned the ropes as an assistant bookkeeper, with a starting salary of $3.50 a week, he joined forces with Maurice Clark in setting up a brokerage firm handling farm products and sundry manufactured items. Within a few years their little company, riding the updraft of the Civil War and still some time before Rockefeller's entry into oil, was a burgeoning and highly respected member of Cleveland's business community.

In 1864 Rockefeller married Laura Celestia Spelman, the daughter of a Cleveland businessman of Massachusetts birth. Already of understandable bent in the direction of piety and rectitude—due to the reaction from his errant father—Rockefeller was now maritally allied with a Family which had been, for generations, temperance pioneers; the combined character of Mr. and Mrs. Rockefeller, Sr., was undoubtedly responsible for the fact that for two generations, from John D. through John D., Jr., no drink was ever served in the Rockefeller homes.

The late John D. Rockefeller, Jr., the couple's only son, was born in Cleveland in 1874. Of his money, the man who was to give away more than any other man in the nation's history once said, "I was born into it. There was nothing I could do about it. It was there, like air or food or any other element. The only question with wealth is what you do with it. It can be used for evil purposes or it can be an instrumentality for constructive social living." In any case, in the opinion of his sons, the brothers Rockefeller, the greatest single influence on John D., Jr., was not Ivy Lee or Frederick T. Gates or any other people who are so often credited with changing the Family, but his wife. Indeed, it is she who is credited by all who knew her as being primarily responsible for turning not only her husband but the entire Family inside out. And it was, all agree, no easy task. Her husband was at first an introverted, mother-dominated boy; later he was more father-influenced and, despite the change in his father, still basically tight-fisted when it came to money. But all this was changed by the late Abby Aldrich Rockefeller.

Born in 1874, the daughter of the distinguished Senator Nelson Aldrich and the sister of banker and future Ambassador Winthrop Aldrich, she was never beautiful but seems to have been born with such an innate happiness and generosity that, in the words of one admirer, "it shone on her exactly like beauty." They met in Providence, where Rockefeller was attending Brown University. Up to that time the shy scion, conforming to his family's idea on avoiding all temptations, had never liked dancing; after dancing with Abby, however, he decided that he did like it after all. Theirs was, in a sense, a graham-cracker romance—he kept a supply in his left coat pocket and Abby, according to her biographer, Mary Ellen Chase, "developed a way of impulsively helping herself from his pocket, a companionable gesture which gave him not a little conscious delight."

The next step, of course, was for John, like all suitors of his day, to ask the consent of the bride's father. The appointment took place on Senator Aldrich's yacht. The Senator "listened dutifully," Raymond Fosdick records, "while the nervous suitor made his request and then proceeded to detail his financial status." The thought of the richest scion in the history of the world having to "detail his financial status" is assuredly an intriguing one. In any case, after due deliberation and a lengthy engagement, as again was the wise custom of the day, they were married. The bride was 27. "I am so grateful," she later wrote one of her sons, "that I didn't marry the man who asked me when I was 18, or even the later ones."

As a wedding present John gave her money. Some time later he asked her what she had done with it. She informed him she no longer had it. "You see," she said pointedly, "I gave it away." Early in their honeymoon he told her he thought it would be wise if she formed the habit of keeping an expense account. Her reply was instantaneous. "I won't," she said. Years later she even did the impossible—she persuaded her husband to go to the theatre. They went to the play *Harvey*. Afterwards, she wrote one of her sons:

> Your father enjoyed it, but he asked me if it proved anything. I told him it proved the importance of having pleasant people in the world. Though the principal character was a drunkard, he was so very delightful that you had the feeling all the time that perhaps to be pleasant and amusing might be more important than to be sober and disagreeable.

The lessons were not lost—as was proved by the incredible gifts that were increasingly forthcoming to the world at large. But Abby Aldrich kept up her teaching—just in case. On her sixtieth birthday, in 1934, she determined to give herself an "orgy of telephoning"— to all of her children away from home. When the first of the month came, her husband took her to task. "My dear," he said, "these telephone bills are getting a bit out of hand." Abby's reply was a question. "John," she asked, "has it never occurred to you that you always think *your* telephoning a necessity and *mine* an extravagance?" Her own generosity, on a personal as well as a larger scale, was almost incredible. Once, passing through Grand Central Station, she saw a woman who looked very sad. She went over to the stranger, comforted her and, as it turned out, befriended her for life. During World War II she took it into her head to send a Christmas present to every single soldier in one of her sons' regiments. "But, Mother," he wrote back, horrified, "be reasonable. Do you know how many men are in a regiment?" At once she replied. "No, I don't," she said, "and I don't care but I don't want a single man not to have some remembrance." That Christmas, despite her son's efforts to keep it "reasonable," she sent over nine thousand anonymous gifts.

All her life she taught her children consideration for others, sympathy for those who were lonely and, above all, attention to older people. "Old people like to be made a part of things," she said. "Don't forget to go out of your way to make them feel wanted and at home." In her own last illness she wrote one of her sons that she had a "wonderful" new doctor. "He's very skillful," she wrote, "but I love him mostly because he doesn't bother me much." Mary Ellen Chase best concludes the story of a truly remarkable *grande dame* at the age of 74:

> On Sunday afternoon, before she drove back to New York with her son David, she insisted upon putting on a new dress and hat. "I've got to wear something entirely new," she said, "for I've never been so happy in all my life!" She held her newest grandchild on her lap all the way home; and, once there, still overflowing with the joy of her return, she went to see a son's new home, his rugs which she wanted to pass judgment on, his new walls and pictures. Nor would she be deterred from visiting her most recent daughter-in-law, whom she had not been able to welcome, except by letter, since her marriage. She could not bear the day to end, she told her husband; and before she went to bed, she telephoned to her sister Lucy in Providence to say that, with her family about her, she had had the most wonderful time in all her seventy-four years.
>
> It was a day of fulfillment and her last on this earth. She died early the next morning, the 5th of April, 1948.

Because of the prominence of the John, John D., Jr., and the brothers Rockefeller "main" line, several other branches of this Family have all but been lost in the shuffle—which is exactly the way most of them, who have moved into the American Aristocracy as rapidly as any American Family, would prefer it. The majority of the "Other Rockefellers" stem from John D.'s brother, William, and since he preceded John D. in coming east—he came as early as 1867 to represent his brother—they are also known as the "Eastern Rockefellers." William Rockefeller had married Almira Geraldine

Goodsell in 1854. A throwback to his father, Big Bill, William was a jovial man who loved good living, had small interest in piety or philanthropy and was very much a member of, in fact perhaps the leader of, the so-called "Standard Oil gang"—which also intimately included H. H. Rogers and William Rockefeller's particular friend, James Stillman. Nonetheless, he was also, and again like his father, a man of more personal charm than the original John D., and therefore it is not surprising that a large number of "Eastern" or even "Greenwich" Rockefellers—for they have lived in Greenwich, Connecticut, for three generations—have also inherited this charm.

William had four children who survived him—William G., Emma, Percy and Ethel, who later changed her name to Geraldine. Emma married Dr. David Hunter McAlpin, while Geraldine married Marcellus Huntly Dodge, grandson of the founder of the Remington Arms Company. As for William G. and Percy, both of them married daughters of their father's friend, James Stillman, William G. marrying Elsie Stillman and Percy marrying Isabel Stillman. Thus, of the four boys and one girl of William G. (Almira, William Avery, Godfrey, James and John) and the four girls and one boy of Percy (Avery, Isabel, Winifred, Faith and Gladys), all ten of them grew up in Greenwich as double first cousins.

There were, of course, differences in this branch of the Rockefellers, stemming from the different personalities of Elsie Stillman, a gregarious, charming woman who held her head high despite her husband's drinking, and Isabel, who was a direct and forthright woman and more of a homebody. Generally speaking, however, both branches, stemming from their founder William, were a far gayer group than the Cleveland Rockefellers—which included John D. Rockefeller, Jr., and his sisters Alta (later Mrs. Ezra Parmalee Prentice), Bessie (later Mrs. Charles Augustus Strong) and Edith (later Mrs. Harold Fowler McCormick). John D. Rockefeller, Jr., years later spoke of the contrast in recalling his strange childhood in Cleveland:

> We children didn't have what those children had and we used to notice the difference. They had a gay kind of social life, with

many parties which we used to wish we could have. Our social life, looking at it from today's standards, was cramped. It centered on the church. We didn't have in Cleveland a social life that other children had. We didn't go to school and when children visited at Forest Hill they were apt to be the friends of Father and Mother. Everything centered around the home and the church and there was nothing else. Our prime interest in the Sunday school centered around the orchestra because we all played instruments, myself and my sisters. It was a sort of social group by itself. Otherwise we had no childhood friends, no school friends.

There were also, however, similar characteristics in both the "main line" and the "other branch." In personal characteristics the William Rockefellers too ran to large noses and large mouths. They too were almost invariably shy, none too well co-ordinated when it came to athletics and, if not mavericks and heavy drinkers—and there were several of these—were also industrious in work and deferential to other people in their social life. The late Percy, for example, who died in 1934, had not only a genial, sweet and outgoing personality, but also had, along with it, a penchant for making money—and on either a rising or a falling market. When his father, William, died in 1922 at the age of 81, he not only left a will of close to $200,000,000, but also left one which was the largest ever recorded, which stretched down to the fourth generation. The Payne Whitney estate of $178,000,000 stopped at the third generation, as did the Thomas Fortune Ryan estate of $135,000,000. But William Rockefeller, who curiously for a Rockefeller left no charitable bequests at all, devised an extraordinary will setting up four trust funds, one for each of his children, allowing them the income only and directing that the principal be divided, after their deaths, among their children equally. Although he made an exception in the case of his favorite son, Percy, leaving him three-quarters of his trust fund outright, he was obviously determined to maintain intact the family fortune as long as the law allowed—"through two lives in being," that is, through a second and a third generation, with distribution in the fourth generation. Commenting editorially on this will in 1937, the New York *Journal American* noted:

William Rockefeller, extending his patriarchal beneficence unto the fourth generation, has endowed his country with some fifty prospective millionaires in their own right—all but two of whom had not yet entered this world when he left it and nearly half of whom are still unborn.

Nothing quite like this is likely ever to happen again. Inheritance taxes took only one-fourth of William Rockefeller's estate. Today they would take three-fourths of an estate that size, and the rates are more likely to be raised than lowered. So there probably will not be another such dynastic transmission of wealth.

There is irony in the fact that, despite this "dynastic transmission" and its lack of charitable bequests, the William Rockefeller branch has, generally speaking, been able to hold on to its wealth with considerably less success than the main Rockefeller line. The latter, despite the immensity of their charities and their public endeavors, have also in the brothers Rockefeller generation managed to come up with remarkable investments in electronics (Itek, Laboratory for Electronics, etc.) which have been hugely profitable. On the other hand, the William Rockefeller branch has not only been less successful with their money but have also been broken up by a host of divorces—the most widely publicized being the divorce by Florence Lincoln of William Avery Rockefeller. There have also been a number of bizarre and un-Rockefeller happenings in this branch. One girl married a man forty years older than she; another startled the Vassar College campus by having her aviator boy friend drop love letters from the sky. Meanwhile, when more typically Rockefeller Spartan vigilance was exercised, it was often overdone. One Rockefeller fourth-generation boy was disinherited for failure to meet his father's boat upon returning from Europe; another received so little allowance at Yale that he was forced to work as a night telephone operator.

At the same time, it should be remembered that the great American Morality Play to the contrary, there have also been bizarre and un-Rockefeller happenings right in the main line—indeed one of John D.'s own sons-in-law, Chicago's Ezra Parmalee Prentice, finally washed his hands of human heredity entirely and wrote a book on the heredity of cattle. One of the John D. Rockefeller, Sr., grand-daughters, Margaret Rockefeller Strong, married the controversial ballet producer, the Marquis de Cuevas, and even John D. Rockefeller, Jr.'s oldest child, Abby, sister of the brothers, has had three marriages, to David Milton, the late Dr. Irving Pardee, and finally to the extroverted Austrian, Jean Mauzé. As for John D. Jr.'s maverick son, Winthrop, his $5,500,000 adventure with the ubiquitous "Bobo," née Jievute Paulekiute, was the tabloid sensation of the early 1950's; since Bobo was a coal miner's daughter, the affair has been called history's most expensive conversion from anthracite to oil. As for Bobo herself, she commented, in reference to her first husband, Proper Bostonian Richard Sears, Jr., "I was surprised to find the Rockefellers included in the *Social Register*—the Sears Family considered them merchants."

Actually, the most bizarre and un-Rockefeller offshoot of all the branches was also located right in the main line—the second oldest daughter of John D., Sr.; her name was Edith. In her youth blond, with a mass of ringlets above her high forehead, she had gray eyes and a demure smile and was unobtrusive in manner and studious in mien. Bicycle riding was her favorite sport, and her principal debutante activity was teaching a Sunday-school class. All of this changed, however, when, on the afternoon of November 26, 1895, she married Harold Fowler McCormick, a second-generation—and in fact very second-generation—son of Chicago's "Reaper King," Cyrus Hall McCormick. Young McCormick, just out of Princeton, first represented the Harvester Company at Council Bluffs, Iowa; then in 1896 he and his bride moved to Chicago—to a huge graystone mansion at 1000 Lake Shore Drive. Not since the days of Mrs. Potter Palmer I had the Windy City seen anything like the late Edith Rockefeller McCormick, and it is highly unlikely they will ever see anything like her again.

Mrs. McCormick started her queen-beeing slowly. In short order, however, the McCormicks had four children, John Rockefeller, who died at five of scarlet fever, Fowler, Muriel and Mathilde. But for her favorite daughter, Muriel, Mrs. McCormick soon moved into high gear. Taking over the ballroom of her mother-in-law, she transformed it into a French kindergarten, for which she engaged a staff of expert French teachers, who studiously conducted all activities, both games and conversation, in French.* This kindergarten, however, soon proved only the first step in a career of remarkably upper-case living. Mrs. McCormick's jewels were unrivaled; they included a $2,000,000 rope of pearls, a million-dollar emerald necklace, which included 1,657 small diamonds, as well as another necklace believed to be made in part of Russian crown jewels. All of these she displayed in all their candlepower particularly at opera openings; indeed, here her appearance was almost mandatory, for so great was the desire to see her that the mere announcement she would attend almost invariably assured a full house. Her hobbies included psychoanalysis; she studied for years in Switzerland under Jung and became proficient enough to take on a hundred patients of her own—including, she announced proudly, herself. She maintained, indeed, that she had cured herself of tuberculosis on three different occasions. On the other hand, when a woman approached her and said, "Oh, Mrs. McCormick, I would adore having you give me some lessons in psychoanalysis," Mrs. McCormick spoke sharply. "I could do nothing for you," she said, "and you could do nothing for me." A curious combination of pomp and circumstance, on the one hand, and an almost pathetic simplicity, on the other, Mrs. McCormick was best described in the former category by Emmett Dedmon:

> Mrs. McCormick carried out her social program in a regal manner; no queen or ruler of a court could have been more rigid in attention to protocol. Even her children, when they were grown, could see her only by appointment. . . . Four men were required to serve a luncheon for two. Her large household staff included a first and second butler, two parlor maids, a coachman, footman, houseman and six detectives. Her personal maid had a

---

* Among the Chicago girls who passed through the country's most remarkable kindergarten were Helen Isham, Bertha Honoré, Janet Fairbank, Carol Elting, Felicia Gizycka, Teresa Higginson, Lydia Hibbard, Marjorie King, Mary Meeker, Ginny Carpenter, Anna Wren, and Jane and Betty Scriven.

helper, a sewing woman, who in turn had an assistant, described as a mending woman. . . . Mrs. McCormick allowed herself to speak to only two servants—the chief steward and her personal secretary. Through these she ruled her entire household. When she called for her carriage (and later for a car) the coachman was given detailed instructions for the trip before he left the house. He was never addressed directly during the trip; the time at which he was to return for his passenger was set before he left, eliminating the need for Mrs. McCormick to speak to him.

The only exception Mrs. McCormick made to her "gracious living" was for her opera dinners. Her guests were invited for seven o'clock and at five minutes to seven she stood in the drawing room to receive them; at five minutes after seven, everyone sat down to dinner, and those who were late simply missed whatever courses had gone before. No liquor, not even wine, was ever served in her house, and a five-course dinner was literally clocked—for Mrs. McCormick had a gold clock in front of her—in exactly thirty-five minutes. Almost invariably Mrs. McCormick would begin a conversation by asking the gentleman on her right, "What has been interesting you lately?" When it was time to "turn the table," guests would equally invariably hear her address exactly the same question to the gentleman on her left. Among her own interests were walking (she invariably took the same walk, carrying the same muff, every day), animals (she established a zoo and was particularly fond of giraffes), travel ("For a non-traveler," said the Chicago *Daily News* gently, "she had the most remarkable knowledge of the world, gained principally through going to the movies regularly"), astrology (she celebrated her own Christmas "by the stars" on December 15), philosophy ("My object in the world," she once said, "is to think new thoughts"), reincarnation (she believed that in her previous existence on earth she was Ankn-es-en-pa-Aten, the child wife of Tutankhamen), and song writing (having had too much of hymns in her childhood, she detested them and instead turned to writing love songs, at least six of which, including "Love," "Between," "Thou," and "It is Spoken," were published).

Unhappily, Mrs. McCormick's own love life was not a happy one.

After twenty-odd years—in more ways than one—of marriage, her husband became enamored of the Polish opera singer Ganna Walska, and though the latter was at the time already married to her second husband and later married another before she finally agreed to marry him, Mr. and Mrs. McCormick were eventually divorced. Later he courted Miss Walska by sending to her château in Versailles, on her birthday, one of every kind of machine produced by International Harvester—of which he was, curiously, treasurer. When she arose on her birthday she saw "to my great surprise . . . a whole regiment of robot soldiers." Then, in 1922, at the age of 50, just before his marriage to Miss Walska, Mr. McCormick entered Wesley Memorial Hospital for a secret operation by the famed Dr. Lespinasse, author of the statement that "a man is as old as his glands." The operation entailed the transplanting of a younger man's glands into Mr. McCormick, and since the younger man was reputed to have been a blacksmith, following the operation, no Chicago Society drawing room was complete without the none too kind verse:

> Under the spreading chestnut tree,
> The village smithy stands;
> The smith a gloomy man is he;
> McCormick has his glands.

Apparently the operation made little impression on Miss Walska, who later wrote that she "could not even imagine the possibility of his preferring to seek further for a gross and limited pleasure rather than being satisfied with the divine companionship of the spiritual love she was willing to share with him." In any case, in 1931 they separated and were later divorced, after which McCormick married in 1938, just three years before his death, Adah Wilson. Incredibly enough, by that time he was chairman of the board of International Harvester.

Meanwhile, back at the mansion, Edith Rockefeller had not been idle. On one of her rare trips abroad—she spent the last twenty years of her life without ever leaving her home for a night—she brought back with her the son of a well-known Austrian artist named Edwin

Krenn. From that time on Krenn became her constant companion. Although Chicago Society disapproved of him—even to one who defended him, he was "small and blond, with pudgy, dimpled fingers" and "reminded me of a newly hatched duckling"—but all agreed his relations with his employer were not only proper but extremely stately. Living across from her, in an apartment at the Drake, he would dutifully appear each day at one o'clock bringing a nosegay of her favorite flowers, and in the afternoons and evenings, in a Rolls-Royce, accompanied by at least one and sometimes two detectives, they would go to as many as three movies a day. One New Year's Eve, Mrs. McCormick reversed things and had a party at the Drake Hotel. "The room was full of balloons," Arthur Meeker recalls. "There was Edith, stiff as a poker, gravely batting them back and forth across our table, because that was expected of her." Meeker also memorably recalls Edith Rockefeller's last days, in 1932, when she was only sixty:

> Her end was a sad one. Owing to unwise real estate speculations, on which she'd embarked with Krenn—principally, I suppose, to give him something to do—she lost enormous sums of money at a time she could ill afford it, when the stock market crash had set values tumbling all over the country. I've never understood how such a colossal fortune could vanish so quickly and completely; one would have guessed her share of the Rockefeller millions to be hedged by sufficient parental restrictions to remain safe. But ultimately it seems there was nothing left. Her brother, John D. Rockefeller, Jr., assumed her debts and brought as much order as he could out of the financial mess. Towards the close of her life she was obliged to leave her house for a suite at the Drake, where she died of a painful and lingering disease. This she had attempted to cure, in accordance with her individual views, by strictly psychiatric methods, which she finally confessed had proved a failure. Poor woman! her last days must have been full of rue; her eyes, my mother said—when the latter called to say good-bye before leaving for the summer, and they both knew it meant good-bye for good—were like a frightened child's.

The Harold McCormick-Edith Rockefeller children too, it seems, inherited their parents' penchant for the offbeat. Just a year before his mother's death, their son, Fowler, married one of the most highly publicized divorcées of the 1920's, Anne ("Fifi") Stillman, who was not only much older than he but had also been part of a divorce with her husband, James Stillman, in which there were charges on the one side that he was keeping a Follies girl and, on the other, that she had seen a good deal of an Indian guide in the Canadian backwoods. As for the McCormicks' youngest daughter, Mathilde, she had already created a large scandal of her own by marrying, at the age of 17, a 47-year-old Swiss riding master. Finally, daughter Muriel led the most controversial life of all. Her first marriage was a "spiritual" one with the ghost of Lieutenant G. Alexander McKinlock, Jr., only son of her friend and Chicago and Palm Beach's *grande dame*, Mrs. McKinlock; the young officer had been killed during World War I and Muriel had never even met him. For a while she appeared in a few plays on the Chicago stage under the name Naranna Micor, then in the early 1930's she chartered and served as president of the Palm Beach Playhouse. Her "second" marriage was to Elisha Dyer Hubbard, who described himself as a "gentleman farmer" and died in 1936. When World War II came she started her career as chairman of the Palm Beach Chapter of the British-American Ambulance Corps. Later she joined the WAC and rose from private to technical sergeant. After the war she adopted a male sergeant—in fact, on her death in 1959, she left no less than four adopted children, including John Rockefeller Hubbard, Harold Fowler McCormick II, Elisha Dyer Hubbard, Jr., and Anna Joan Dyer Hubbard.

Chicago's McCormick Family should not be assessed only in terms of its erring second-generation son, Harold Fowler McCormick I. Actually the McCormicks are one of America's most interesting Families if for no other reason than because they were established, in the Family-founding sense, by an inventor, Cyrus Hall McCormick. The American ancestor of the Family was Thomas McCormick, a weaver who emigrated from Ulster in 1734 and settled first in Lancaster County and later Cumberland County, Pennsylvania.

The father of Cyrus also was an inventor. His name was Robert McCormick and, since the Family had by that time moved from Pennsylvania to Virginia, he was born and died at his farm, "Walnut Grove," in Rockbridge County, Virginia. In 1808 he married Mary Ann Hall, also of Scotch-Irish descent, and in 1834 he produced a threshing machine—one which served as the inspiration for his son's famed "McCormick Reaper," which was developed a year later. Far from the first to secure a reaper patent—Cyrus McCormick was in fact the forty-seventh to do so—he nonetheless produced the only one capable of being improved to its final success. No "parlor inventor," he, like his father, was a farmer, but when the Virginia farmers declared, on seeing demonstrations of his reaper, that they were running farms and "not circuses," the young inventor decided to try riper fields. At one time, in 1839, when the panic of 1837 hit the more remote regions of Virginia, Cyrus' fortunes were at their low—and, in his hour of debt and defeat, a man who came to collect a bill for $71 was offered instead a quarter interest in the reaper. He refused; instead, he came back with the sheriff to try to collect "real money"—had he made the deal he would, a score of years later, have been one of the richest men in the country.

That was the only chance anyone ever had to get the better of Cyrus McCormick. In many respects the most unusual of all Family founders, he was not only an inventor but an inventor who was determined that he would not suffer the fate of most inventors. Eli Whitney, inventor of the cotton gin—no relation to *the* Whitneys —failed to found a Family. Robert Fulton, inventor of the steamboat, died at 50, "plagued and plundered," it is recalled, by imitators. Even Goodyear, who gave the world rubber, died in poverty and neglect. But not so Cyrus McCormick. Without money, without credit and without customers, he still persevered.*

* The most unusual of all this country's inventors was undoubtedly Isaac Merrit Singer, of the sewing machine fortune. Born in Pittstown, New York, the son of a millwright, he left home at 12 and for forty years was an unskilled laborer. Then, one day in Boston in 1851, when he was at work in a machine shop, a Lerow and Blodgett sewing machine was brought in for repairs, and Singer, always mechanically adept, was called upon to help fix it. Within twelve hours he had made a rough sketch of a better machine—and eleven days

McCormick resolved to go west and in 1847 he struck up an acquaintance with the "first citizen" of what was at that time "an insignificant lakeport." The "first citizen" was William B. Ogden, the "insignificant lakeport" was Chicago. From the first, Ogden was impressed with McCormick, who was, indeed, as impressive a figure of a man as any Family founder, save possibly Commodore Vanderbilt. With his massive head, broad shoulders and piercing eyes, he soon persuaded Ogden to lend him money—later he paid Ogden back double and owned his first factory outright. Along with his "drivin' ways," he was also an indefatigable worker. "He was so strong," says Herbert Casson, "so dominating, so ready to crash through obstacles by sheer bulk of will power, that smaller men could never quite subdue a feeling of alarm." Besides this terrifying quality, McCormick also, it is recalled, "labored hard to be correct in matters that appeared trifling to others." He invariably carried, for example, a dictionary; also, when an associate would submit a telegram to him, he always drew circles around the superfluous words. "His mind," Casson said, "was too ponderous an engine to do good service in a light conversation. If a subject did not interest him, he had nothing to say." Yet McCormick was no ordinary robber baron. "I have throughout my life," he once said, "been opposed to all measures which tend to raise one class of American people upon the ruin of others."

"He was in reality," concludes Casson, "a great dynamo of sentiment." In any case, not until 1858, when he was close to 50, did he marry. At that time, however, he chose a remarkable woman, Nancy (Nettie) Fowler of Jefferson County, New York, a woman of keen perception and rare charm, who bore him seven children. On one

---

later had built one. In patent trouble with Elias Howe, Jr., he sought out the New York law firm of Jordan and Clark, and was referred to Edward Clark. Within the year Singer and Clark were equal partners and the Clark Family was on its way to "First Familydom." One of the reasons the Singer Family fell by the wayside was, ironically, the family instability of Singer. In all he had twenty-five children, of whom eight were legitimate. The most famous of them was the illegitimate Paris Singer, traveling companion of Isadora Duncan and the man who with Addison Mizner was responsible for the renaissance of Palm Beach.

occasion, when his $2,000,000 factory burned to the ground in the great Chicago Fire of 1871, Nettie, in New York, came west and met him at the station. McCormick was in a half-burned overcoat, exhausted after spending all night in a vain effort to fight the fire. For once he was beaten; he would go east and retire on his investments. But Nettie would not hear of it, and in a moment changed McCormick's mood. "The workers cheered," it is recorded, "and the work of rebuilding was begun even before the ashes were cold."

On another occasion, with no help from Nettie, McCormick showed his stubborn side. Leaving with his family and his trunks for Chicago from New York, a baggage agent charged him $8.70 for excess weight. McCormick immediately took his family off the train and ordered his trunks off; too late, his trunks rode to Chicago and were burned in still another fire. McCormick promptly sued the railroad for $7,193. He won the case—in fact he won and won, but the case kept being appealed and appealed. Finally, by the time of the last appeal, before the United States Supreme Court, all the witnesses but McCormick and his wife were dead. Once more McCormick won, and at last, after a 20-year fight, the richest man in the country received his money. He lived to be 75. At the very end, he spoke to his wife. "Nettie," he said, "life *is* a battle." Afterwards, in a death stupor, he said two more words, both the same—"Work, work!" Afterwards, one of his workers told Ernest Poole that "in spite of his temper and drivin' ways," McCormick was "the grandest old feller ever lived." Said the worker:

> He knew how to get spirit into his men. At Blue Island we worked from seven A.M. to five-thirty, with half an hour for lunch; and when there was a rush of orders, it would often be midnight for us. I don't mean we had to stay unless we wanted, but most of us did—not only because we got overtime pay but because he could make us feel like that—because he was one of us, understand? No white-collar boss but right out on the job, workin' hard with his sleeves rolled up on some new gadget that had gone wrong. He knew machines like his own mother. While he was livin' we had one boss—and if anything went wrong, you could go right to him and get it fixed up. In these new days of big

companies, you have a dozen bosses—and where are you? With Old Cy we knew. When he died there were mourners in our crowd, for now we had lost him, and we knew we'd never have a boss like him again.

Two brothers helped Cyrus McCormick with his reaper. One was Leander McCormick, who, although he later split with his brother, was on his own a man of many parts, an art collector and donor of the observatory of the University of Virginia. Another was William S. McCormick, who, when the War Between the States came, was still Virginian enough to wear a Confederate uniform, although he did not fight. In the second generation there were seven children of Cyrus and Nettie: Cyrus Hall, Jr., Mary Virginia, Robert Fowler, Anita, Alice, Harold Fowler, and Stanley. Of these the most controversial and widely publicized was, as we have seen, Harold Fowler; the ablest was the late Cyrus Jr. A serious, reserved man, in sharp contrast to his brother, he knew enough about the business to exhibit the reaper all alone in England at the age of 18, and at 25, on his father's death, became president of the company—the largest manufactory of its kind in the world. In 1902, with William Deering and other leaders of the industry, he was primarily responsible for engaging J. P. Morgan to underwrite the International Harvester Company, of which he became president. He was married twice, first to Harriet Hammond, daughter of a sea captain of Haverhill, Massachusetts, by whom he had three children, and second to Alice Marie Hoit, daughter of an early Chicago merchant and his secretary for many years. He died in 1936.

In the second generation of the Family founder's brothers, among the sons of Leander was Robert Hall McCormick, who was an art collector and also socially famed as the man who introduced coaching to the West. Among William S.'s sons was Robert Sanderson McCormick, who married Katharine Medill, daughter of the editor of the Chicago *Tribune*. His career was, in fact, to have a large influence on the whole Midwest, inasmuch as one of his sons was the late Senator Medill McCormick, whose wife was Ruth Hanna, daughter of Mark; the other was the late giant of the *Tribune*, "Colonel" Robert R. McCormick himself.

Robert Sanderson McCormick was a diplomat; he became not only the first American Ambassador to Austria-Hungary, but also Ambassador to Russia, during the Russo-Japanese War. But it was his very first assignment, as Secretary to the Legation in London under Minister Robert T. Lincoln, which was to leave such future Anglophobic scars on his sons—particularly young Robert, the future Colonel. In preparatory school at Lansdowne, says John Tebbel, McCormick was intensely unhappy:

> In Chicago, he had been a McCormick, with all the privilege and position the name carried with it. In English Society, particularly rigid English school Society, he was an outsider who did not and could never belong. Young Robert acquired an upper-class English accent, an English attitude toward dress and behavior and a profound distaste for everything English.

Later the future Colonel of the *Tribune* went to Groton; afterwards he became "a standard Groton product aggravated by loneliness and the traditions peculiar to his family." Soon, however, this Family, maritally allied with the Medills and Pattersons, was to become one of the country's most powerful publishing dynasties—one which at its height had the late Colonel publishing the *Tribune* in Chicago, the late Captain "Joe" Patterson publishing the *Daily News* in New York, the late Eleanor ("Cissy") Patterson publishing the *Times-Herald* in Washington, and the present Alicia (Mrs. Harry Guggenheim) publishing *Newsday* on Long Island. John Tebbel, in *An American Dynasty*, saw in the case of Patterson, as he had with McCormick, that Groton was the basic cause of his social distress—a verdict in the expression of which he would seem overly severe on the school. In any case, of Patterson he says:

> Like McCormick, he got off to the wrong kind of start. Born into a rich family, living on Chicago's fashionable North Side, he seemed at first to be destined inevitably for the kind of conventional rich man's life that his socially conscious mother had mapped out for him. He was sent to private schools in Chicago and France, and in 1890 found himself at Groton.

McCormick began his rebellion against the world at private school in England. Patterson opened his at Groton, where he underwent the same kind of cruel teasing. McCormick was teased because he came to Groton with the accent he had acquired in England; Patterson suffered because he came to the school with a typical Midwestern accent, rendered incongruous by his English blazer. All in all, Patterson had a rough time at Groton and came to have a healthy loathing for most of the young snobs who went there.

In 1954 the late Cissy Patterson, in an article on her niece, Alicia, took time out to speak with pungent humor of herself. "The trouble with me," she said, "is that I am a vindictive old shanty-Irish bitch." McCormick, whom Cissy called "that old Bourbon, my cousin Bertie," never spoke as frankly of himself but went his cousin even better when it came to his pet hates. "To hell with the Marshall plan!" he once exploded. "It's really a snob plan." And through his stormy, albeit mightily successful career, McCormick spearheaded American isolationism and was utterly convinced that England was the root of all American evil. "The British Aristocracy," he maintained, "continues to direct the foreign policy of the United States and thereby rules the world. . . . Ancestry [there] is more important than accomplishment." To this writer, meeting him in Palm Beach, the Colonel started in, apropos of nothing, on the Boston aristocracy. "It's even worse than the British," he said. "It's—it's—well, it's no better than New York's and the Roosevelts!"

McCormick's first marriage was in 1915 to Annie de Houle Irwin, who had been previously married to his second cousin, Edward Shield Adams. For many years, up to the marriage, they had all been close friends and her divorce from Adams was a messy one— following which, curiously enough, in view of McCormick's Anglophobia, they were married in London. The first Mrs. McCormick died in 1939, after which the Colonel remained a widower for five years. He then married Maryland Mathison, of Baltimore, who also divorced her first husband, Henry Hooper—in this case after twenty-one years of marriage—to marry him. At the wedding, Captain Patterson gave the bride away, Chauncey McCormick was best man, and Mrs. Chauncey McCormick was matron of honor. The latter was soon after, by a rival paper, the Chicago *Daily News*, "elected" Queen of Chicago Society. "After all," Athlyn Deshais, Society editor of the *News*, explained, "she was a Deering, you know. She's farm implement on both sides."

The late Dixon Wecter called Chicago "the paradise of parvenus." This statement is rash. In the first place, if Chicago's Family fortunes were trade-rooted so, as we have seen, were the Eastern, Southern, and indeed all the other great Families of this country. Secondly, if Chicago's great Families were founded the way the other American Families were, it is hardly their fault that they came later—so, too, did their city. And thirdly and finally, the fact remains that, all things considered, if Chicago's great Families have not held up notably better than other American Families, neither have they held up notably worse. A list of Chicago *grandes dames* in the late 1950's would at least have been possible; in New York it would have been virtually impossible.*

And even Wecter, after some stern words first, has some solace for the Midwestern Families which were once the butt of all Eastern jokes:

> The great meat-packer who founded the Swift fortune compelled his wife and sons to take turns at keeping books, as a measure of economy and discipline. Thrifty, sluggish, bourgeois, with a gloomy vein of Teutonic pessimism, the Swifts have added little to the social gaiety of Chicago—though an element of fashionable Bohemia entered their doors with the marriage of Charles Swift to the noted German *lieder* singer, Claire Dux. Armours and Cudahys have produced both hard-working business men and

* Such a list would have included Mrs. Chauncey McCormick (farm implements), Mrs. Robert R. McCormick (publishing), Mrs. John T. McCutcheon (widow of the late great *Tribune* cartoonist), Mrs. Patrick A. Valentine (meat packing), Mrs. John Rockefeller Prentice (oil), Mrs. Edward A. Cudahy (meat packing), Mrs. Loyal Davis (wife of the surgeon), Mrs. Edward L. Ryerson (steel), Mrs. Howard Linn (investments), Mrs. James Ward Thorne (merchandising), Mrs. Jacob Baur (carbonics), Mrs. Charles Garfield King (brokerage), Mrs. Alfred P. Shaw (architecture), Mrs. Robert E. Wood (merchandising), Mrs. Laurance H. Armour (meat packing), Mrs. Clive Runnells (Pullman Company), Mrs. Walter B. Wolf (law) and Mrs. William McCormick Blair (farm implements and investments).

sporting sons, but no preeminent leaders of Society. Indeed the meat-packing families of the Middle West have suffered unduly from that mysterious malady which stamps a family with an indelible trademark, like one of their own admirable hams. Just as Society finds it difficult to dissociate Dorrances from Campbell's Soup, Manvilles from asbestos and tar, Brokaws from ready-made clothes, Hartfords from the A. & P., and Mr. Frazier Jelke from butterine. Perhaps the wisest course has been followed by Mr. and Mrs. Robert Woods Bliss of Washington, who, it is reported, at one time ordered the advertising of Castoria to cease in the District of Columbia under the theory—as their less fortunate social rivals phrased it—that ignorance is bliss. It may be solace for these families to reflect that grandfathers of those who profess to sneer at trade-names were in their good time ironmongers, watchmakers, and chandlers.

Second only to the McCormicks as a Family dynasty in Chicago are the Marshall Fields—originally of course, from the famous store. But the Fields were not alone in rising from the remarkable store which once itself rose from the ashes of Chicago's fire. There were other Families too, notably the Potter Palmers and the Levi Leiters, not to mention the Shedds. Indeed, it is highly unlikely if any other one merchandising emporium in the country ever gave rise to so many distinguished figures in American Society.*

The founder of Marshall Field's store was the first Potter Palmer. Born in 1826 in Albany County, New York, he was a Quaker and a self-made man even by self-made standards—his education never

* Fred Harvey, of the famed Western Harvey restaurants and Family, once clerked in the basement of Marshall Field's. So too did one of London's top merchants, the late Henry Gordon Selfridge, who, in his Marshall Field days, was known as "Mile-a-minute Harry." Other well-known American Families which have stemmed from other stores are the Macys (originally the Nantucket Family), later the Strauses, the Gimbels (the first Adam Gimbel founded his first store in 1842 in Vincennes, Indiana), the Woolworths (Frank Woolworth of Rodman, New York, opened his first successful store in 1879 in Lancaster, Pennsylvania), the Hartfords (the original George Huntington Hartford came from Augusta, Maine), as well as the Riches of Atlanta (here there were four brother-founders), the Rosenwalds of Sears, Roebuck (Julius Rosenwald succeeded Alvah Curtis Roebuck), the Filenes of Boston, the Kaufmanns of Pittsburgh, the Halles of Cleveland, the Marcuses of Dallas, and the Mays of California (originally of Leadville, Colorado).

went beyond elementary school. He arrived in Chicago in 1852 and opened a dry-goods store on Lake Street. Although he was to retire in twenty-five years, in that time he not only built his store to incredible proportions but also was the first merchant ever to permit his customers to inspect their merchandise in their own homes; they were also permitted to exchange merchandise, not only for other merchandise but also, if they wished, for cash. Potter Palmer is best known in social annals for his wife—a lady who became, in short order, the greatest hostess in Chicago history. Potter saw her for the first time, records Ishbel Ross, when he was 36 and "Chicago's richest bachelor but a lonely man" and she was only 13, "moving with grace against a backdrop of ancestral French furniture in her father's house in Chicago." Although she was a "mere schoolgirl" and wore "a simple white muslin dress and black lace mitts," Palmer watched her all evening and years later told his son, Honoré, that he had decided that night to make her his bride. Her name was Bertha Honoré; she was one of the famous "Kentucky belles" from Louisville, and her sister was later to marry the son of Ulysses S. Grant. Her father, Henry Honoré, had been a leading citizen of Louisville who later moved to Chicago. By the time Potter and Bertha were married, when she was 21, his mammoth "Palmer House" was ready for her; he gave her the hotel for a wedding present. In the great fire that year he lost ninety-five buildings but when he was discouraged and ready to give up, Mrs. Potter Palmer was, as Mrs. Cyrus McCormick had been, equal to the occasion. "Mr. Palmer," she said (she invariably addressed him as "Mr." even when they were alone), "it is the duty of every Chicagoan to stay here and help rebuild this stricken city."

From that time on, Mr. Palmer not only did as he was told, but also saw his wife make her own "Palmer Castle"—her incredible turreted Rhenish castle, designed by Henry Ives Cobb—the social center of both her city and, for a time at least, the whole country. And, according to Ernest Poole, Palmer never regretted it:

"He loaded her with jewelry," I was told by a woman friend, "and he loved to see her wear his gifts. I remember his saying proudly: 'There she stands with two hundred thousand dollars on her.' When they went abroad, he slept with her diamond tiara under his pillow. Some people said that back at home he got so jealous he would lock her in. But I never believed it—first, because she kept clear of all the romantic little affairs; and second, because she ruled the roost. Though he loved his small room up in the tower, when she commanded, he would come down. Late one evening at a ball, I found him on a sofa in one of the quieter rooms; and when I asked if he were tired, he gave me a weary little smile. 'No, but my feet hurt,' he said. I could always start him talking by asking questions about his wife. He simply adored her. His pride rose to a climax in the Columbian Exposition, when she served as president of the Board of Lady Managers; and his feelings were cut to the quick when the Infanta Eulalie of Spain came to Chicago and snubbed Mrs. Palmer because she was only an innkeeper's wife. In his will he left her most of his money, without any conditions attached; and when the point was made to him by his lawyer that she might marry again, he answered: 'If she does, he'll need the money.'"

Mrs. Potter Palmer did not marry again. She died in Sarasota, Florida, in 1918, after which, says Wecter, "chronic illness and increasing reticence have kept the Palmers from their old social domination of Chicago." Actually, however, Potter Palmer, Jr., president of Chicago's Art Institute, lived to 1943, and, married to Pauline Kohlsaat, had four children, Potter Palmer III (he married Boston's Rose Saltonstall Movius and was later divorced), Betha (later Mrs. Oakleigh Thorne), Gordon Palmer, and Pauline (later Mrs. Arthur W. Wood). The family of the other son, Honoré, consisted of two sons, Honoré, Jr., and Potter D'Orsay Palmer. The latter, in the third generation, was the best example of the family's disintegration. He was married four times—to a 16-year-old farm girl, to an Argentine "heiress," to a New York "society girl," and, in 1938, to a roadhouse waitress, who, asked if she truly loved him, replied, "Sure, I'm his wife, ain't I?" At the time of Potter D'Orsay's death in 1939, she was suing him for $300,000 separate maintenance; his death occurred, ironically enough, following a fist fight at a stag picnic.

No more successful at long-term Family-founding than the Potter

Palmers was the Family founded by Potter Palmer's first partner, Levi Ziegler Leiter. A colorful little man himself, a former clerk in a village store who soon rose to be credit manager, he married an even more colorful woman, Mary Theresa Carver, daughter of a Chicago merchant. Mrs. Leiter, though a woman of some erudition —in fact, a schoolteacher—was later to become, in both Chicago and New York, perhaps the most famous Mrs. Malaprop in the history of American Society. She was once, she maintained, in very "seduced circumstances," later she had a house full of "statutes," as well as "spinal staircases" and "sexual bookcases." When her husband was dressed for a fancy-dress ball, she claimed he was going "in the garbage of a monk." And, on another occasion, complaining at dinner of the rats in her house, she turned to her dinner partner and said graciously, "and, my dear, I suppose that even in your little house you are troubled by mice."*

After Leiter left Marshall Field's he moved his family to Washington, D.C., and, to Chicago's wrath, rarely mentioned having originally come from Chicago. The Leiters had four children, including three daughters, all of whom married in or near the British peerage —Mary to Lord Curzon, Nancy to Major Colin Campbell, a relation of the Duke of Argyll, and Margaret to Lord Suffolk. The youngest, and only boy, Joseph Leiter was educated at St. Paul's and Harvard and began his career as a speculator with a million dollars in cash which his father gave him. In the winter of 1897-98 he tried to "corner" wheat, but the corner failed, and his father, who stood behind him, lost $9,750,000. Joseph Leiter married Juliette Williams of Washington; they had three sons and an adopted

* Two latter-day challengers for Mrs. Leiter's throne were Mrs. Jay Paley, aunt of William Paley, who used to speak of her "photogenic memory" and keeping up her "sphinx-like figure," and Mrs. Adeline Loeb, wife of Carl Loeb. When the latter's son got into a fight with another man at the Century Country Club, his mother complained. "But, Mother," explained her son, "he called me a son of a bitch." Replied Mrs. Loeb questioningly, "But he doesn't even know me." On another occasion, she was told the modern story of the time when Oscar Levant's ex-wife married Arthur Loew, and Oscar, on their wedding night, facetiously called him to ask what was playing at Loew's State. Told the story, Mrs. Loeb asked blandly, "Well, what was?"

daughter, but only one son, Thomas, survived Joseph on his death in 1932. As for the elder Leiter, whose estate on his death in 1904 was valued at $25,000,000, he had, some years before his demise, been disturbed by the robbery of the body of New York merchant A. T. Stewart and resolved that no such evil would befall him in the future. His will ordered the construction of the country's most formidable tomb. In a grave which includes 4,000 square feet of ground, his body lies embedded, in Washington's Rock Creek Cemetery, in a solid mass of steel and concrete.

Far more successful in Family-founding than either the Potter Palmers or the Levi Leiters, and indeed second only to the McCormicks in the Chicago hierarchy are the Marshall Field Marshall Fields themselves. The American ancestor of the Family was Zachariah Field who came to Dorchester, Massachusetts, about 1629. The real Family founder, however, born in 1834 in Conway, Massachusetts, of farming parents, was Marshall Field I. He started his career clerking for five years in a dry-goods store at Pittsfield, Massachusetts. A blond, handsome young man, he had good manners but did not appear extraordinarily qualified for success. However, when he was offered a partnership in the business, he refused it with what to the proprietor was the amazing intelligence that someday he would run a store which "will have doors worth more than this place." Going west, the young man took a job in Chicago's wholesale dry-goods firm of Cooley, Wadsworth & Company. The first year his salary was $400; out of this, by dint of sleeping on the counter and other economies, he managed to save $200.

"Cold-souled and courtly," Ernest Poole described Field, but also spoke of his "soft voice and charming manners." One of Field's partners was brief: "His business was his passion." Nonetheless, one evening at a friend's party, Field met Nannie Douglas Scott, the 23-year-old daughter of an Ironton, Ohio, ironmonger who was visiting in Chicago. A delicately pretty girl, she had attended Miss William's School for Young Ladies in Troy, New York. John Tebbel best tells the story of the one time in his life when Field forgot business:

Field sat in a corner and looked shy, but Nannie drew him out and inspired him to attentive conversation. Perhaps she sensed his future greatness; more likely it was sheer romance, for Nannie Scott remained a romanticist until the day she died. At any rate she made it plain to young Mr. Field that she liked him and the lonely New England boy responded to her evident affection. This was an emotion almost unknown to him. In that moment it took so great a hold on his sense that it led him to the one completely impulsive, unplanned act of his life, one he lived to regret. For the remainder of Nannie's visit he mooned about, like any other stricken youth, and then on the last day, when he realized that nothing whatever except glances and words had passed between them, and that she was leaving on the train, perhaps forever, he hurried to the station in a panicky state. As the train pulled out he yielded once—just that once—to impulse and jumped aboard. Miss Scott was flustered by his sudden reappearance, but not so flustered that she was unable to accept when Field proposed to her as the train moved through the yards.

After his marriage, Field returned to his real passion. He had already come into contact with Levi Leiter, and, when Potter Palmer wished to retire in 1865, he offered the store to Field and Leiter. They took over in 1867 and, a score of years later, Field managed to push Leiter out. His method was characteristic. "Mr. Leiter," he said, "I feel that it is time that we part, and my proposition to you is this. I'll name a figure to cover a half interest here and at which either one of us may buy or sell the business. I'll give the first choice to you—to buy or sell." Leiter agreed and Field named the figure. It was so low that, though Leiter immediately decided to buy, he asked for twenty-four hours to consider, as Field knew he would. During that twenty-four hours, as Field also foresaw, all the key employees told Leiter they would not stay with him; thus when Leiter returned in twenty-four hours, he had no other course than to sell—and at Field's figure.

From that time on, the "merchant of merchants" bought out other future partners with equal ease; he also equally successfully bought his merchandise. Instead of waiting, as his competitors did, for consumer demand for merchandise, Field bought first, anticipating the demand and if none came, he created it—whereupon his competitors would have to pay increased wholesale prices. Meanwhile, he kept his own scale of living reasonable. "No frills," he told Richard Hunt, who designed his house, and, driving from Prairie Avenue, he would habitually have his carriage stop a block before the store and walk the rest of the way; it was bad taste, he felt, to drive to the door behind his "high steppers." His success was immense. By 1905 he was the largest individual taxpayer in the United States and, even among his confrères of the Chicago Club, he became a legend.*

When it came to publicity and newspaper interviews, Field was a sphinx. Only once in his entire life did he make a public address— and that was at the dedication of the library which he had given to his home town of Conway. When tragedy struck him in the form of the mysterious suicide of his only son, Marshall, Jr., he became enraged at the photographers who each day snapped him on the way to his dying son's bedside. "Who are you?" he would ask, marching on them, brandishing his cane. "Why do you do these things? What sort of men are you? What do you think of yourselves?" For such a man to have both a grandson and a great-grandson high up in the newspaper business was a strange irony indeed. But even before the tragedy of his neurotically "second-generation" son, Field's own personal life had not been a happy one. His wife, described by Tebbel as "a romantic girl whose dreams ended at the altar," bore him two children, Marshall, Jr., and Ethel, and though she gave one memorable party for them—her famed "Mikado Ball" of 1886 for children and adults—she soon spent increasing time abroad, and as

---

* Among his particular associates were two other Family founders, the remarkable "P.D." Armour and the curious George Pullman. The latter was a particularly tough customer—even matched against a cityful of them. Once a gushing admirer approached Mr. Pullman and asked him if in his early days he had ever dreamed of his vast company "with its palaces on wheels scurrying over the face of the earth." Replied Pullman gruffly, "No, I did not. If I had dreamed them, I'd be dreaming still!" On another occasion, during the building of his 3,500-acre model mill town for his employees on Lake Calumet, the architect, a man named Beaman, came to him and proposed he be allowed to have it named after him. Pullman had a different idea. "I'll tell you what we'll do," he said, "we'll take the last half of your name and first half of mine—and call it Pullman."

her children married, Marshall to Albertine Huck, daughter of a Chicago brewer, and Ethel to Arthur Tree, they too preferred life in England. In 1896 Mrs. Field died in Nice.

Soon it was bruited about Chicago that Field was in love with his neighbor on Calumet Avenue—the beautiful Mrs. Arthur Caton, wife of Chicago's distinguished lawyer and clubman. In 1904 Caton died suddenly, his wife was left a widow at 50, and Field at 71 promptly married her. But even this happiness was destined to be a short one. Scarcely two months later came his son's death—which occurred in the Field mansion—and scarcely two months after that he himself was dead. His will was 22,000 words long; characteristically, it was the most comprehensive and airtight one ever recorded by the court. The bulk of the large fortune was left in trust for his grandchildren, Henry and Marshall III; they were not, however, to come into full possession of the estate until thirty-nine years after Field's death, and in fact were not to get even their income except in installments. Marshall III, for example, was to receive $450,000 at 25, at 30, at 35, and at 40, while Henry, his brother, was to get $200,000 at 20, at 30, at 35 and at 40. As for their sister Gwendolin, she was to have a $1,000,000 trust fund, but until she was 18 the income was to be "reinvested for accumulation," at which time she should get half of it; then at 25 she was to get three-quarters of it, and the total at 40. If she died without children, the fund would revert to the estate; otherwise she could pass it on to her children.

Field, not noted for philanthropy in his early years—"It is very easy," he once said, when criticized for this, "to give away other people's money"—did leave $8,000,000 to the Field Museum and another $100,000 to asylums and hospitals. But these were only a small part of an estate which was to make his descendants enormously rich. Most of these descendants, as we have seen, had already removed themselves to England. Right after the funeral of her husband, for example, Mrs. Marshall Field, Jr., had gone to England permanently, and after her father-in-law's death, in 1908, she married Captain Maldwin Drummond of the British Army and scion of a banking Family. Ethel, the elder Field's only surviving child, also remained in England. She had three children by Tree: Lambert, who died in childhood, Gladys, and Arthur Ronald. Later, like so many Fields, she was divorced, and remarried to a British naval officer, Admiral David Beatty.

At the age of 12, sickly and shy, Marshall Field III, growing up in England, with his three-fifth interest in $130,000,000, was described as "the richest boy in the world." Unlike McCormick and Patterson, however, he liked England. He attended Eton and Cambridge, restored his health with athletics, became a handsome young man and led a gay social life. In 1914, returning to America on the *Lusitania*, fortunately a year before she was sunk, he fell in love with Evelyn Marshall, who was a New Yorker but whom he had already met in London. They were married in 1915 by a Catholic Bishop—both Field's parents, but not his grandparents, were of that church. In 1917 he showed his mettle by enlisting in the Army as a private. After the war he went into investment banking, and settled down in "Caumsett," a Long Island showplace which boasted everything from indoor tennis to seaplaning, and from a hundred registered Guernseys to three Abyssinian jackasses. Here, with eighty-five servants to look after him, grew up his first three children: Marshall IV, Barbara and Bettine; both of the girls later married doctors.

In the thirties Field's life began to change. In 1930 came his first divorce, and his wife, who first received a settlement of a million dollars a year, then married Diego Suarez and bought an estate near enough to Field's "so that the children could divide their time between parents." Field too married again, this time choosing an English girl, Audrey Coats, widow of Captain Dudley Coats, and a goddaughter of Edward VII. An active sportswoman, she and Field went hunting and yachting all over the world; then, in 1934, came his second divorce. Afterwards, and after undergoing analysis by the late, highly publicized Dr. Gregory Zilboorg, Field next married, in 1936, Ruth Pruyn Phipps, ex-wife of the reticent and rich Ogden Phipps. They had two children, Phyllis and Fiona, and with his most congenial wife, he was now ready, with Zilboorg's urging, to turn to an entirely new career—the publishing business. On meeting Ralph Ingersoll, he became interested in the newspaper *PM* and bought $200,000 worth of its stock; later he bought out the other stockholders, including John Hay Whitney, for 20 cents on the dollar. Meanwhile, before the demise of *PM*, he entered the lists against the Chicago *Tribune* with the Chicago *Sun*.

If the *PM* fight had been bitter and made Field's name synonymous with "do-gooding" in its most criticized, left-wing sense, it was as nothing compared to the difficulties with the *Sun*. Not the least of its difficulties was the fact that it first saw the light of day just three days before Pearl Harbor and at one time in 1942 the late Colonel McCormick in his *Tribune* even went so far as to attack Field:

> Field is of age to volunteer. He cried for war before it came. Now that it has come, he lets men like MacNider and O'Hare do the fighting while he skulks in his clubs, night and otherwise. No one would suggest that he is indispensable to *PM*, or to anything else. The term to fit to him and to all the herd of hysterical effeminates is coward.

"This was the same Field," says Tebbel, "who enlisted as a private in the first World War, while McCormick went in as an officer on Pershing's staff." Yet Field did not "reply in kind." Indeed, one of the reasons for the ultimate success of his battle to secure a foothold in Chicago's journalistic jungle was the fact that Field proved himself the gentleman and McCormick otherwise. In 1947 he bought the Chicago *Times* to add to his *Sun*, and by the time of his death, in 1956, even his most controversial public statement had its apologist. This statement ran as follows: "I happen to have a great deal of money; I don't know what is going to happen to it and I don't give a damn." Although later explained as having been said in context of a speech in which Field maintained he would never encourage fascism in the hope of keeping his fortune, the statement even provoked the retiring John D. Rockefeller, Jr., into a rare quote: "I don't care what happens to Marshall Field's money, but I do care what happens to mine."

In any case, one who does "give a damn" is Marshal Field III's son, Marshall IV, or Marshall Field, Jr. Along with several other Family scions—among them being Ogden and Whitelaw Reid, Jr., of the New York *Herald Tribune*, Philip Graham, son-in-law of Eugene Meyer, of the Washington *Post*, and Henry Ford II—Field came into a position of enormous responsibility before the age of 40. A curious cross between his great-grandfather and his father, he has been accused by liberals as being too conservative and by conservatives as being too liberal; in any case he is both modest and able and also the first Field in three generations to make money. After a distinguished World War II career in the Navy, he married first Joanne Bass, daughter of the former Governor of New Hampshire, by whom he had two children, another Marshall and Joanne; after a divorce he married, in 1950, Katherine Woodruff, daughter of a Joliet banker, with whom, despite protestations of living a "middle class" life, he shares one of Chicago's most active "farms" in Libertyville. His wife is one of Chicago's most exciting leaders, and they have three children, Frederick, Katherine and Barbara. In 1956 the Field Family came full cycle in one way when young Marshall supported Dwight Eisenhower; it came full cycle in another way when, in 1959, after Field's purchase of the Chicago *Daily News*, he received a wire from Mrs. Robert R. McCormick, widow of the Colonel. "Congratulations," the wire said, "you have now succeeded the Colonel as first publisher of Chicago."

Second only to Pittsburgh as an industrial Family-founding city is Detroit. But nothing is more infuriating to Detroit's "First Family" Aristocracy than, in the words of social historian John L. Oliver, "the several unenlightened who appear to believe that the city sprang full-blown from the assembly lines along with the Model T." Indeed, even the automobile Families join with more elderly Detroiters in pointing with pride to the paragraphs devoted to Detroit in Harriet Martineau's famed *Society in America*. As far back as 1839, Miss Martineau, the ubiquitous English visitor, unstintingly praised the city:

The Society of Detroit is very choice; and, as it has continued so since the old colonial days, through the territorial days, there is every reason to think that it will become, under its new dignities, a more and more desirable place of residence.*

"We don't know exactly to whom La Martineau alluded," says Oliver, chronologically tracing Detroit's Family history, "but as the names of Newberry, Joy, Buhl, Alger, Barbour, Lothrop and Hinchman begin to appear, our ears prick up and things begin to look more familiar." Detroit, which in the Eighteenth Century had found its social status largely determined from military rank, had in the Nineteenth Century its landowners, its merchant princes, its shipping tycoons and its lumber kings. The Newberrys were perhaps its outstanding Nineteenth Century Family. Oliver and Walter Loomis Newberry, who were born in New York and Connecticut, respectively, opened a dry-goods business in Detroit as far back as 1826; the store sold everything from oxbows to hairpins. Later, however, the brothers branched out still further, Oliver primarily into shipping and Walter into land investments; they were among the richest citizens in the country. They were also colorful. Oliver, in particular, became known through his shipping as the "Admiral of the Lakes" and, a man who scorned paper work, he deposited all the papers needed for each day's business in his hat.

Neither Oliver nor his brother left any direct descendants. Oliver never married, and though Walter Loomis Newberry married and had four children, two sons died in infancy and his two daughters died unmarried. His chief legacy to the future was in fact his gift of $2,100,000 for the founding of the Newberry Library in Chicago. Nonetheless, the Family did continue, carrying on in the next generation in the able person of the nephew of Oliver and Walter Loomis, John Stoughton Newberry. The latter graduated from the

* This was unstinting praise indeed. Only a few pages before, writing of the Society of Montgomery, Alabama, Miss Martineau had said:

"I suppose there must be such pioneers; but the result is a Society which it is a punishment to its best members to live in. There is pedantry in those who read; prejudice in those who do not; coxcombry among the young gentlemen; bad manners among the young ladies; and an absence of all reference to the higher, the real objects of life."

University of Michigan in 1847, then studied law; afterwards, with his partner, James McMillan, he formed the firm of "Newberry and McMillan, capitalists." By the time of his death in 1887 he was a director in almost every industry in Detroit.

John Stoughton Newberry married twice; in 1855 he married Harriet Newell Robinson, who died in 1856 leaving one son, and in 1859 he married Helen Parmalee Handy, daughter of the Truman Parmalee Handys of Cleveland. They had three children, Truman, John and Helen, and as far back as 1876 the family started spending their summers at Grosse Pointe—"not the first to do so," says John L. Oliver, still sternly beating the antiquity drum, "but certainly among the most illustrious and durable."

On the score of durability there can be little question—particularly when one considers the career of the late Helen Newberry, who later became Mrs. Henry B. Joy. From her early days in the late 1880's to her death in 1958, at the age of 88, she reigned supreme in Detroit Society, far outranking in *grande dame* status all the newer "motor people." "Her death ended an era," said the Detroit *Free Press* in 1958. "It was an era that began in the warm glow of gaslight and terminated in the awful glare of nuclear explosion. . . . She was the City's friend, benefactor, conscience."

A tiny, white-haired lady who at the time of her death belonged to no less than eighty-three civic societies and who had been every single summer for fifty-nine years to Watch Hill, Rhode Island, Mrs. Joy was a fixture not only at the Grosse Pointe Memorial Church—"I can't enjoy church," she used to say, "until I get my gloves off"—but also all over Detroit. For forty-four years, as proof positive of the fact that her Family was pre-automobile, she had carefully driven, never exceeding ten miles an hour, her 1914 navy-blue car—an electric-powered brougham. "I am very respectful of the age of my little car," she said at the 1957 automobile show. "I have to treat it very carefully because it is very difficult to get parts."

But even Mrs. Joy became, willy-nilly, at least for a time a part of Detroit's gasoline Society—an event which happened early in the 1900's when her husband and her brother, Truman Newberry, as well as several other prominent businessmen, bought the Packard Automobile Company and moved it to Detroit from Warren, Ohio. By that time Detroit's motor Families—all of whom were primarily Twentieth Century in origin—were already rising to power: the Fords, Charles B. King, Ransom E. Olds (his was the first car in the city), David Dunbar Buick, the brothers Dodge, John and Horace (who rose from struggling bicycle mechanics to a business which in 1925 was sold for $146,000,000), as well as Henry Leland, James Couzens, William Durant, Walter P. Chrysler, Charles Kettering, William Knudsen, the Briggses, and the six brothers Fisher. Together with such allied Families as the Firestones—the latter entered the charmed circle when Harvey Firestone, who had five sons to carry on, became a summer-camp as well as business friend of Henry Ford—this group was soon on its way to the highest Society life Detroit had ever known, or in all probability ever will know. Among its numerous peaks was the 1936 debut of the then-current Dodge heiress, Frances, who threw not only Detroit but most of Michigan into a turmoil by wearing at her coming-out party a black orchid. "Botanists confessed themselves somewhat nonplussed," it is recorded, "until it was revealed that the hue had been achieved by the painter's art."

Not only among the motor fortunes of Detroit but also throughout the West there were, by the mid-Twentieth Century, hundreds of distinguished Families in their third generation since their "trade" Family-founding. Even in such a relatively new business as the oil business, one finds several instances of four generations. The oldest Family in this regard is the Tulsa, Oklahoma, Law Family, which in the person of young T. N. Law, Jr., represents the fourth generation since his great-grandfather, William Barnsdall, drilled the country's second oil well after the Drake Well in 1859; in the person of the T. N. Law, Jr., children, who presumably also will enter the Family business, there will be a fifth generation. Denver, Colorado, also is a surprisingly "old Family" city; in the banking fraternity alone there have been three generations of John Evanses and three generations of John Clark Mitchells to join the other "elders" of Denver Society such as the Kountzes, the Boettchers, the Chappels, the Cranmers and the Hills. Of particular social eminence among the latter ranks Mrs. Crawford Hill, of whom it was said, even in depression days:

> Louise still waves the magic wand
> That rules the social sea;
> The smarties wait for her command
> And follow her with glee.

Of all this country's Western Families with Nineteenth Century Family-founding roots, however, none is more remarkable than the Texas King-Kleberg Family of King Ranch fame. Certainly no American Family founder ever got started earlier on the business of Family-founding than the fabled "Captain" King himself. Born in 1824 in the unlikely spot of New York City, of unknown and desperately poor Irish parentage, he was at the age of nine signed away by his family and apprenticed out to a jeweler to learn the trade. Instead of teaching him the trade, however, the jeweler's family soon put him to work as a hired boy about the house, sweeping, cleaning and, to his final wrath, minding a baby. At the age of 11 he ran off and stowed away on a ship bound for Mobile. For four days he lived like a mouse in a hole; but when, due to his hunger, he was discovered by the captain, he showed no signs of fright. Indeed, the captain was mightily impressed with the square-jawed courageous 11-year-old and gave him the run of his ship. Before he was 15 he was a river boat captain, although one of his employers, Captain Holland, sent him back north to Connecticut to school. Here he rather reluctantly studied for eight months— his only book learning in his entire life. He fought in the Seminole and Mexican Wars, became a friend of Robert E. Lee and, with Captain Mifflin Kenedy, began buying land. He met his wife when, docking a river boat, he swore heartily at the bad "parking" of another—and looking up met the flashing eyes of 22-year-old Henrietta Chamberlain, who, though a Presbyterian minister's daughter, was not above answering him back. Together they were a remarkable pair; their early days were, as Tom Lea ably recalls, fraught with pioneer-life dangers:

> On an evening, probably late in 1856, when the Kings were making camp by the side of the road, a lone Mexican appeared from the brush and asked permission to join camp for the night. King gave permission and sent him out for wood. As the captain bent over lighting twigs to start a fire, his wife was tending the baby. . . . Henrietta King looked up, suddenly frightened in the dusk, and called out, "Captain *King! Behind* you!" With the twist of a veteran riverfront brawler, King swept back both his powerful hands and grabbed tight—to an arm holding a knife. He jerked, swinging the whole weight of his assailant overhead, slamming him to the ground with the knife arm twisted helpless. In that time and in that place most men would have killed the would-be assassin. King only told him—with emphasis not hard to imagine— to get out and stay out.

On his off-ranch trips, King established a pattern for Texan behavior. Once, dining in a hotel in New Orleans, one of his guests was served a tough piece of meat. When neither the waiters nor the headwaiter would do anything about it, King got up, went across the street to another restaurant and ordered a meal sent over. When the hotel waiters, seeing the new waiters arrive, refused to clear the old dishes, King grabbed the tablecloth and sent dishes, food and all to the floor. "Now serve that," he said to the hotel waiters, pointing to the new meal—and this time the waiters served. At the same time, he ran his own ranch in enlightened fashion. Once, early one morning, his *vaqueros* came around to the main house and announced that they wished to live life the way the boss did, and just sit in the house. Immediately King invited them all in, got chairs for them and proceeded to sit until noon. By that time the *vaqueros* were heartily sick of the life of ease and ready to go to work.

In 1885, dying of stomach cancer at the age of 61, King eased the pain with drink. Although his doctor warned him he was shortening his life, he refused to stop until the doctor brought him a message from his wife; she always hated his drinking. "Tell him with

At the Greenbrier Hotel, a group of New York hostesses at large, 1950. (l. to r.) Mrs. John Floyd of Texas, Mrs. Harold Talbott (in front), Mrs. Screven Duke (behind), Mrs. Allan A. Ryan, Jr., Mrs. Winston Guest, Viscountess Duncannon (front), Mrs. Eric Eweson (behind), Mrs. Thomas R. Blake of Houston, the late Robert R. Young, Mrs. Morton Downey (front), Brenda Frazier, Mrs. Tuck Guest (standing), Mrs. Edward McLean, Mrs. Ronald Balcom, Mrs. William Randolph Hearst, Jr. (front), and Mrs. Warren Johnson. (Jerome Zerbe)

In a museum framework, a group of San Francisco hostesses, 1953. (l. to r.) Mrs. Charles de Limur, Mrs. Ferdinand Stent, Mrs. Robert Folger Miller, Mrs. William Wallace Mein, Jr., Countess Marc de Tristan, Mrs. Edwin M. Wilson, Mrs. Christian de Guigné, Mrs. Paul Miller, Mrs. Abbott Robertson, Jr. (Slim Aarons)

Baltimore's Symphony Ball. (l. to r., front), Mrs. Gentry C. Waldo, Mrs. Charles Stedman Garland, Mrs. Allen W. Morton, Mrs. Iredell W. Iglehart, Mrs. John R. Montgomery; (rear) Mr. Waldo, Mr. Garland, Mr. Eugene Williams, Mr. Montgomery and Mr. Morton. (Baltimore Sunpapers)

And Charleston has a "Society for the Preservation of Spirituals"—descendants of old plantation families. (l. to r., foreground) Loulie Jenkins Stoney, May Hutson Dawson, Josephine Parker; (second row) Katherine Jenkins Hutson, Augustine T. Smythe, Julia Ravenel Dougherty, Mary Ridgway Smythe, Panchita Hayward Grimball; (third row) John Foucheraud Grimke, Randy Parker, Harry Colcock Hutson, Jr., John Arthur Siegling, Francis Dougherty; (rear) John M. Harlbeck.

St. Louis' Veiled Prophet Ball. The identity of the "V.P." is always a secret. The queen must promise not to become engaged during her year's reign. One queen, however, was not only engaged but pregnant. Here the 1958 queen, Miss Carolyn Lee Niedringhaus, with her bouquet of 500 rare orchids. (St. Louis *Post-Dispatch*)

The queen in San Antonio selected by the "Order of the Alamo"—San Antonio's men's club. Here Miss Linda Nixon (1951) in front of the original Alamo. (Slim Aarons)

W. Stewart Woodfill, arbiter-owner of the Grand Hotel, keeps a lonely vigil watching for the arrival of Queen Elizabeth II through the Straits of Mackinac.

The late Francis Higginson Cabot at Murray Bay, Canada. (Slim Aarons)

Paul Cabot, Treasurer of Harvard, and Ralph Lowell, banker, on Boston's State Street. (Herb Kratovil—*Business Week*)

Three *grandes dames:* Above right, Mrs. Allan Forbes of Boston in the oriel of her Beacon Street house (Slim Aarons). Below right, Miss Mary Wing Tebo of New Orleans, here pouring sherry in the famous ceremony of Le Petit Salon, ladies' club (Slim Aarons). Below left, the late Mrs. "Spec" Penrose, Colorado Springs, benefactress of Pike's Peak region (Denver *Post*).

Mrs. William De Rham, wife of New York's late dancing master, instructs William Randolph Hearst III. (Slim Aarons)

Robert David Lion Gardiner (foreground), of Gardiner's Island (the only Charles I grant in America), gives a dinner in his New York apartment. Eleventh generation from the original Lion (1639), Gardiner still possesses "decapitation" rights on his island. (Slim Aarons)

San Francisco's Mrs. James Flood with her daughter Judith, granddaughter of James C. Flood of Comstock Lode fame. (San Francisco *Examiner*)

Ambrose Clark, king of steeple-chasers. (Slim Aarons)

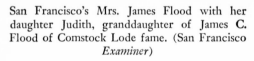

Alfred Gwynne Vanderbilt II. (Slim Aarons)

Mr. and Mrs. Benjamin R. Kittredge picnic in their Cypress Gardens outside Charleston with a friend. (Slim Aarons)

The Thanksgiving Hunt, Middleburg, Va., 1959; (l. to r.) Mrs. C. Oliver Iselin, Jr., Donald MacKenzie, Newell J. Ward, Jr., and (back to camera) Henry Loomis. (Allen-Middleburg)

Mrs. Gordon Prince at the Myopia Hunt Club on Boston's North Shore. The club was so-named because of the nearsightedness of its original members. (Slim Aarons)

The best of America goes abroad as well as the International Set. (l. to r.) Elizabeth Jackson (Viscountess Cowdray), ex-Ambassador Lewis W. Douglas of Arizona, Mrs. Milton Arnold of Middleburg, Va., and Mr. and Mrs. Paul Warburg of New York in Oudenarde, Belgium.

In the library of the celebrated "Texan who could read"—the late oilman E. DeGolyer of Dallas—with his daughter Mrs. George McGhee, ex-Secretary of State Dean Acheson (right) and Mr. McGhee. (Denny Hayes—Dallas *Times Herald*)

Washington scene: Above, left, Mrs. Marjorie Post Close Hutton Davies May and Mr. May; right, Mrs. Morris (Gwen) Cafritz and "Tony" Biddle; below, left, Mrs. Robert Woods Bliss and the Countess of Motrico; right, Mrs. Robert R. McCormick, on the right, with Mrs. Joan Ashton. (Carlo Maggi—*The Diplomat Magazine*)

Oilman Robert F. Windfohr brings out his daughter Anne with 80,000 twinkle lights, three orchestras and 1,000 guests at the Ridglea Country Club, Fort Worth, Texas, 1959.

In contrast, a "mass" debut in aristocratic and more frugal Boston. Here the 1958 Debutante Cotillion in the main ballroom of the Copley Plaza—seldom called the Sheraton Plaza. (Slim Aarons)

Three photographers from Chicago papers arrive to cover Windy City's Beau Nash Ball and, of course, the next step was to take pictures of each other.

The Denver Symphony Debutante Ball in Brown Palace Hotel lobby. Young ladies who were once presented to their families' friends are now presented to the public's television. (Denver *Post*)

The Younger Set: At Round Hill, Jamaica, above, Mr. and Mrs. Robert Sarnoff (Felicia Warburg); right, Mr. and Mrs. Henry Ford (Anne McDonnell) (photo, Marguerite Allen). Below, left, Mr. and Mrs. Marshall Field, Jr. (Katherine Woodruff), at a benefit; right, Mr. and Mrs. Sidney Lumet (Gloria Vanderbilt) at an opening. (Max Haas)

Ends of the Line: above, Cornelius Vanderbilt VI—as of 1960, he had been married seven times; below, John Jacob Astor VI—in 1958 he applied to the New York Supreme Court to find out to whom he was married. (Max Haas)

Mrs. William Woodward, Sr., New York *grande dame*, and Mrs. Gustave Rainville (Millie O'Connell Tansill), charity ball dynamo, pictured at the Belmont track. (Slim Aarons)

Tulsa, Oklahoma's first "Cinderella Ball," 1956; Mrs. Frank Grant McClintock (later Mrs. Horace Schmidlapp) greets Miss Lily Pons. (Lee Gillette—Tulsa *Tribune*)

New York's annual Belmont Ball; (clockwise) Thomas E. Murray, Jr., Mrs. Cord Meyer, Jr., Alfred Gwynne Vanderbilt II, Mrs. John Slocum (in rear), Brenda Frazier (behind her), Cornelius Vanderbilt Whitney, Gerald Gordon, the late Mrs. Byron Foy, and Serge Obolensky; (foreground) Clyde Roche, Tex McCrary (in plaids). (Slim Aarons)

April in Paris Ball: Upper left, photographer wants just the right shot of English movie actress Sabrina; right, Mrs. Winston and two other unidentified Guests; lower left, Elsa Maxwell, feuding with Duchess of Windsor, produces Marilyn Monroe instead, and, right, Mr. and Mrs. Edward Fisher. (Max Haas)

a smile," she said, "I need him a while longer." With that, still a man of incredible strength, he rose half-dead from his bed, left the hospital and went to his wife. And never again did he touch a drop of liquor. Tom Lea recalls the final estimate of one of America's most colorful Family founders—one which was given sixty-seven years after King's death by his old trail driver, Walter Billingsley. "He was a rough man," said Billingsley, "but he was a good man. I never knew a rougher man, nor a better man."

At the time of King's death the King Ranch had a population of 100,000 cattle, 20,000 sheep, 10,000 horses, close to a thousand people and an acreage of half a million. It was even then the largest privately owned land empire in the world. And it has remained so. Thus King's career from age 11 to 61 ranks second only to Commodore Vanderbilt's as the most remarkable individual success story in American Family-founding history. King and his wife had five children: Nettie, who married Major E. B. Atwood "against the captain's will" and was later estranged from her parents; Ella, who married Louis Welton of St. Louis and San Antonio; Alice, who married Robert Justus Kleberg III; Richard, Jr., who married Pearl Ashbrook of St. Louis; and Lee. The King girls attended Mrs. Cuthbert's Seminary in St. Louis; here they were brought up to be "young ladies" despite the difficulties attendant on their father's visits, in which he always appeared loaded with gifts. As for the King boys, both Richard, Jr., and Lee attended Centre College. Lee was studious and quiet, but not so was the "rollicking" Richard who, in high second-generation style, came to college with both a carriage and his own manservant. He cut a large swath both at the college and in town, but later settled down; at the time of his death in 1925, one paper wrote: "There is probably no other man in South Texas who held the regard of his fellow man more than Mr. King."

Captain King's wife survived all her children except her daughter Alice. Dressed in mourning for forty years, she lived on and on. "As her age advanced beyond ninety," says Tom Lea, "the frail figure in widow's black seemed invested with the stateliness of a lone survivor from a former chapter of history." Finally, in 1925, she died; at her funeral "gray-haired bankers from Manhattan rubbed shoulders with leather-faced brush choppers from the lonely *callos* of El Sauz." And the service was, Lea records, itself memorable:

> When the casket was lowered into the earth there was a stir at the edge of the crowd where the bare-headed horsemen stood. They mounted to their saddles. They came reining forward in single file, unbidden and uncommanded save by their hearts, to canter with a centaur dash once around the open grave, their hats down at side salute to Henrietta King. Then her vaqueros rode away in the silence, towards the herds they had watched for her and would go on watching.

Actually on King's death the second generation of both family and ranch passed for all practical purposes to the capable shoulders of son-in-law Robert Justus Kleberg III, husband of King's daughter Alice. A second-generation German, and a lawyer by training, he ran the ranch as if he had been born to it, and by the time of the birth of the present owner, his son Robert J. Kleberg IV, the debts had been paid off and further expansion begun. This expansion has proceeded apace in the Twentieth Century; in 1960 the ranch was double its size on King's death, with its operations extending not only from the Nueces to the Rio Grande, but also to Pennsylvania, Kentucky and, through partnerships, to Cuba, Brazil and even Australia. Under the Klebergs have come the King's famed new breed of Santa Gertrudis cattle, a famed racing stable, and large and rich oil production. The cattle were named after Robert Justice Kleberg III's daughter, Alice Gertrudis (later Mrs. Tom East); in 1944, one of the most beloved figures in ranch history, she died, and two years later the ranch lost another beloved senior member, the colorful bachelor, "Caesar" Kleberg. In 1950 Richard Kleberg, for thirteen years a Texas Congressman, joined his brother in ranch management and in 1953 the ranch celebrated its centennial—just 100 years from Captain King's first purchase of land. It was typical of the present management that the celebration was neither a big parade, a pageant nor a "blow-out"; it was instead devoted to an exchange of ideas between a group of practicing ranchmen and a group of authorities who ranged from geneticists, nutritionists, botanists and climatologists to members of the faculties of nineteen colleges in America and abroad. In 1960 Robert Kleberg, asked by this writer if there would be a King Ranch in 2060, said quietly, "Yes—if there's a world. But it will be a mechanized ranch and it won't be the same." Mrs. Kleberg was more doubtful. "It all depends," she said, "on the young people—not only on the King but all over the country, whether they care enough about the individual and individual responsibility."

Moving from Texas to Arizona, one finds the dominant Families the so-called "Pioneer Families"—not the actual pioneers, of course, but the Families who founded businesses in the latter part of the Nineteenth Century or the early part of the Twentieth. "If these Families had enough money to keep up with the new ones," says Joan Ganz, whose grandfather founded a bank, "they kept up— otherwise they were lost in the shuffle." Among the Families who have kept up strongly are the Goldwaters, from the store of the same name, and the Brophys, banks and cattle. Nonetheless, the "shuffle" of Eastern money and name, particularly into the Paradise Valley and Scottsdale, was not to be denied, and by the mid-Twentieth Century the Bartons and Bentons, the Rubicams and the Chisholms, the Clarence Budington Kellands, the Westbrook Peglers, and the Henry Luces were among the leading Family lights in the nation's youngest state; so too was the late Frank Lloyd Wright.

At the same time it should be noted that there have always been Boston overtones to Arizona—just as there are Boston overtones to Santa Barbara and other "Proper" Western outposts. The town of Prescott, Arizona, for example, first territorial capital, was named for none other than Boston's great First Family historian, William Hickling Prescott. Even Tombstone, Arizona, most famous of all Western towns as "the town too tough to die," was not without Boston aid in its early days. None other than Endicott Peabody, late of Groton School, started his career as a young preacher there.

During his very first sermon a gunman stood up in the back of the church and told young Mr. Peabody to sit down. Mr. Peabody, six-foot-three and never afraid of a soul, living or dead, gazed at the gunman for some moments in silence, then said quietly that he would indeed sit down but only after he had finished his sermon—after that, he said, he would be happy to see the man directly behind the church. They met there afterwards and, with one punch, Mr. Peabody knocked the gunman out.

Some idea of the newness of Arizona may be gathered from the fact that the state capital of Phoenix was founded and developed within the span of one lifetime—that of Mrs. Adeline Gray, who, arriving in 1868, was the first permanent white woman settler in the area; she died in 1936. Probably the most distinguished of all Arizona Families with Nineteenth Century roots, however, is the Douglas Family. The Family was founded by the late James Douglas. Born in 1837, the son of a Quebec surgeon, he never became an American citizen but made such a name for himself in the American mining business that he was called "the dean of the mining and metallurgical professions" and the town of Douglas, Arizona, was named for him. Spare and Scottish-looking, he was not only widely loved but also established the Douglas Family tradition of being more than "just businessmen." In his youth he was a licensed preacher—later he served as a professor of chemistry in Canada and still later as professor of history at Cambridge, England. He was also Chancellor of Queen's University, Quebec.

James Douglas married, curiously, another Douglas, although no relation; she was the daughter of a Captain Walter Douglas. The couple lived in their last years in a large mansion at the ancient Dutch patroonship of Spuyten Duyvil, New York—a mansion where the Queen Mother stayed during her visit to America after their death. The Douglases had two sons, James Stuart and Walter. Both carried on the family tradition with a wide variety of other interests as well as their mining, engineering and banking pursuits. The late Walter Douglas, who died in 1946, married Edith Margaret Bell and had five children, Elizabeth, Katherine, Naomi, Walter and

Robert Bell; the late James Stuart Douglas, who died in 1949, married Josephine Leah Williams and had two children, James and Lewis.

Lewis Douglas was born in the mining town of Bisbee, Arizona, in 1894. From Amherst he went to World War I, where he was gassed in the Argonne offensive. Back to Amherst again, he became a history teacher, then went to his father's Arizona mines; he became a day laborer and finally went to Congress. After brief service as Director of the Budget under Franklin D. Roosevelt, he split from the latter as far back as 1934. Through the years since he has moved back and forth between Big Business (principally the insurance business) and Education (he served as vice-chancellor of McGill University). He has also grown increasingly conservative through the years but still considers himself a Democrat. In 1947, with his wife, Peggy Zinsser, and children (James Stuart, Lewis, Jr., and Sharman), he moved to England to become Truman's Ambassador there. Here in difficult postwar days he proved himself one of America's ablest and most popular ambassadors in history. His daughter's friendship with Princess Margaret was widely publicized. Less well known but no less definite was the rapport existing between the rest of the Royal Family and the rest of the Douglases. The patch over Douglas' left eye was the result of a fly-fishing accident; when Douglas' great friend, the late E. DeGolyer of Dallas, also lost the sight of one eye, Douglas sent him a cheerful telegram, welcoming him into the "Cyclops" Society and reminding him that the one-eyed people were, in ancient Greece, a race of giants.

Another nationally distinguished "Western" Family with Nineteenth Century roots is the Reid Family. Here the Family founder was Whitelaw Reid, who was born the same year as the Douglas Family founder—1837. Although his grandfather and American ancestor came to America from Ireland, Reid was of Scotch descent on both sides of his family. He was born in Xenia, Ohio, and his father was a humble farmer. Early exhibiting a scholarly and literary bent, Whitelaw managed to be sent by his family to Miami University; afterwards he became editor of the weekly Xenia *News*. It was a

long jump from there to becoming Horace Greeley's managing
editor and later owner of the New York *Tribune*, but Whitelaw
Reid made it largely through the distinction of his Civil War correspondence for the Cincinnati *Gazette*. In any case, by the age of
35 he was head of what was recognized as the most powerful newspaper in the country. Here, according to Allan Nevins, he "often
worked eighteen hours a day and had a bedroom fitted up in the
Tribune Tower."

In 1881, Reid married Elizabeth Mills, daughter of Darius Ogden
Mills, thus allying his wealth with one of the country's leading San
Francisco fortunes.* They had two children. A lifelong Republican,
Reid was the nominee for Vice-President in 1892 with President
Harrison. When Cleveland was elected, he regarded it as an "ap-
palling calamity." In 1905 he was chosen by Roosevelt to be Am-
bassador to England, where he died in 1912. His wife, a lifelong
philanthropist who helped Dr. Trudeau found his sanatorium at
Saranac Lake and who was chairman of the Red Cross in London
during World War I, lived until 1931.

Whitelaw's son, the late Ogden Reid, took over the *Tribune* on
his father's death in 1912. The year before, he had married Helen
Rogers of Wisconsin; they had three children, Elisabeth, who died,
Whitelaw and Ogden (or "Brownie") Reid. When the elder Reid
died in 1947, his son Whitelaw became editor of the *Tribune* and
was regarded, along with Henry Ford II and Marshall Field IV, as
one of the country's very foremost fair-haired young men. In 1955,
however, Whitelaw was succeeded by his brother Ogden, and in
1958, John Hay Whitney gained control of the paper which had
been in Reid Family hands since 1872. Afterwards, Ogden Reid

* Mills' grandson, Ogden Livingston Mills, was Secretary of the Treasury
under Hoover. In 1936, despite the fact that he was then the dominant figure
in the Republican party, he was passed over for President in favor of Alf
Landon, much as the late Robert Taft was passed over in favor of Dwight
Eisenhower. Mills was married twice, first to the daughter of Mrs. W. K.
Vanderbilt and second, after a divorce, to Mrs. Dorothy Fell, daughter of
Philip Randolph of Philadelphia. Both his wives were active in Aristocratic
rather than Society circles but were not averse to the latter as well. Mills had
no children.

was named Ambassador to Israel. Married to Mary Louise Stewart, he has three children. Whitelaw has two children; he and his wife, Joan Brandon, were divorced in 1959.

A second "Western" and mining publishing Family which was to have wide influence on the entire field of Society is, of course, the Hearst Family. Often thought of today as a Family founded by the elder William Randolph Hearst, and based on a fortune derived from his newspapers and magazines, the Family was—and in fact as of 1960 was—primarily based on mining. And the Family founder was not the late William Randolph, but his father, Senator George Hearst. Of English-Scotch stock, he was the son of William G. Hearst, a South Carolina farmer and cattleman who moved to Franklin County, Missouri, in 1808. Married to Elizabeth Collins, of Georgia, he had two children; one was a girl who died unmarried, the other was George Hearst. Born in 1820, at 26 George inherited, on his father's death, his father's farm. In 1850 he abandoned it, however, left Missouri altogether and crossed the Plains on foot beside an ox-wagon. Arriving in California, he turned to mining. Not notably successful until 1859, at that time he made some finds in western Nevada. In 1866 and again in 1874-1875 he suffered large reverses; at the latter time he even gave up his house in San Francisco.

The next year his fortunes changed. With his able partner, James Ben Ali Haggin, at Lead, South Dakota, he brought in the Homestake, greatest and richest of all Western Hemisphere gold producers, and for the remaining fifteen years of his life he was one of the richest men in the world. In 1880 he acquired the San Francisco *Examiner*, and, after being defeated for the Senate by Leland Stanford in 1885, was later appointed to that body. Called by himself, as well as by other people, "the silent man of the Senate," he was nonetheless in person a large, hearty, handsome man with deep-set eyes and a bush miner's beard. His "emphatic honesty" was perhaps his outstanding trait and, according to John Winkler, by no means an easy judge, he was "almost worshipped by rich and poor alike. . . .

The day the news of his death reached San Francisco there was scarcely one in the Sunshine Club who did not openly weep." His death occurred in 1891, by which time his estate included, outside of his mining interests, some 2,000,000 acres in California, including 450,000 acres south of San Francisco, a large interest in a 250,000-acre cattle ranch in New Mexico, 25,000 acres near Phoenix, Arizona, as well as over a million acres in Mexico.

Not the least of George Hearst's assets was his wife. Her name was Phoebe Apperson, and she came from a Family of landowning Virginians; her father was the richest farmer in Franklin County. Small in size but erect and graceful, she was remarkable for her rare combination of wit and tact. Before her marriage to Hearst in 1862, she had taught in public schools, and after her husband had made his Homestake strike, she had not only the character but also the intelligence to cope with the responsibility of such a fortune. From that time on she devoted her life to charities, not only in San Francisco but also in Utah, South Dakota and Montana mining communities, where she established both libraries and kindergartens. In Washington she founded the National Cathedral School for girls and was president of the Columbia Free Kindergarten. In later years she took particular interest in the University of California at Berkeley, where her benefactions, notably for women students, were almost innumerable.

George and Phoebe Hearst had only one child—William Randolph Hearst. Born in 1863, he early gave evidence that he was indeed "second generation," very much an only child and, in character, far below either of his remarkable parents. After grammar school he was sent to St. Paul's School in Concord, New Hampshire, to prepare for Harvard. "Neither Willie nor St. Paul's liked the arrangement," says Stewart Holbrook, "and he left to study at home under tutors." Entering Harvard with the class of 1886, he proceeded to live one of the most flamboyant rich-boy existences in the history of the country's richest college. First he was suspended for a "spectacular demonstration" celebrating the election of Grover Cleveland —he had hired brass bands and fireworks for the occasion—and then, after being taken back in again, he was finally expelled for sending to each of his professors a gift; this gift, with each of their pictures on it, was a chamber pot.

Between such displays, he had managed one achievement—he had been a successful business manager of the humorous publication, the Harvard *Lampoon*. Leaving Cambridge, he spent a year "drifting around" in New York, then went west and badgered his father into giving him the least successful of all the Senator's many enterprises—the *Examiner*. One day the elder Hearst made one of his infrequent visits to the *Examiner* and waited in his son's office until noon. Whereupon the Senator, in whose eyes his erring son could do nothing wrong, congratulated him. "That's right, son," he said. "Never waste time getting to work early. Let the other fellow do that. You come down about noon and beat him out of what he's made in the morning."

Most of the rest of the son's life would seem to have been spent in beating a lot of people out of a lot of things—from headlines to the most extraordinarily heterogeneous collection of art ever assembled in this country. Nonetheless, in his first eight years on the *Examiner* young Hearst quadrupled the paper's circulation and, after the death of his father, prepared to enter the New York newspaper field. First, though, he paid a call on his mother; he warned her it would take a lot of money to do what he proposed to do —beat Pulitzer. "Without the slightest hesitation," says Winkler, "Mrs. Hearst offered to advance any money her Will wished." In short order Hearst negotiated a deal with John R. McLean to buy the New York *Morning Journal* for $180,000. Hardly was the ink dry on the deal when a check arrived from his mother; the amount was $7,500,000.

One of the ways Hearst built his papers, and one which was to have more influence on the country's growing radicalism than he ever knew, was his oft-expressed thesis, "Only the rich man is interesting." Another was his admitted credo: "It's what you leave out of a newspaper that keeps the dullness from it. The more you leave out, the brighter the paper becomes." Perhaps the most famous of his dicta was his wire to the painter, Frederic Remington, whom, after the sinking of the *Maine*, he had sent to Cuba to paint war scenes. Remington wired that he wanted to come home because there was no war. "Please remain," wired back Hearst. "You furnish the pictures. I'll furnish the war." On the credit side of the ledger, it should be said that the American newspaper business in general and American Society in particular, would never be, after Hearst, the same as it was when he found it, and at least a few of the changes, including the "star system" among reporters, had its merits. On the credit side also, it should be said that, although Hearst carried his antivivisection campaign to ridiculous limits, he was all his life a good friend to animals.

Among the many sayings of Hearst which were not without irony in view of his own life, perhaps the most extraordinary was his statement: "Blondes come high—Old Masters last longer." In 1903, at the age of 40, he married Millicent Willson, one of the two famed "dancing sister" daughters of George Willson, the 1890's vaudeville dancer. Early interested in philanthropy, Mrs. Hearst liked to help young women get a start on the stage and fifteen years after their marriage was ironically responsible for lending a helping hand to a girl then appearing in the Ziegfeld *Follies*. The girl's name was Marion Davies, née Cecilia Douras, and from the time that he met her—he was 55 and she was 21—Hearst and Miss Davies were inseparable. Not content with pushing her career in the movies, via such of his "friends" as the late Louis B. Mayer, Hearst also ordered all his critics to praise her. That the latter task was not always an easy one is evidenced by the judgment of one non-Hearst critic. "Miss Davies," he wrote, after seeing one of her lesser epics, "has two expressions—joy and indigestion."

Although Hearst's marriage was publicly maintained, he and Miss Davies lived together from almost the moment when he first met her, and his incredible castle of San Simeon—now a state park— was to the bitter end a private affair. Finally America's most widely known and least publicized triangle played itself out in a macabre ending on a morning in 1951 when Hearst died in Miss Davies' house in Beverly Hills; not long before he had borrowed a million dollars from her. For the last few days Miss Davies maintained a constant vigil at his bedside. However, after the last night's vigil, she was persuaded to take sedatives and get some sleep. Thus the morning Hearst died she had the misfortune to be still sleeping heavily. Within an hour the top Hearst executives had the body and all Hearst's belongings removed from the house and by the time Miss Davies woke everything was gone. "For thirty-two years I had him," she said wistfully, "and they leave me with his empty room." She was not even informed of funeral plans and did not attend the funeral when it took place. Later she was even induced to relinquish her rights—expressly ordered in Hearst's will—as sole voting power in the Hearst Corporation. "I don't like the idea of a fight," she said. "I'm not the fighting type." The same year she married Horace Brown, an ex-Hollywood stunt man.

From such a background it would be remarkable enough if the Hearst Family still existed in its third generation, let alone showed signs of accomplishment. To its credit, it has. Although because of the character of the press they represent, as well as their own predilection for publicity—even in their own papers—it would be difficult to make a case for the Hearst sons having entered the American Aristocracy, still it can be stated that the sons have, generally speaking, improved upon their father. And this was accomplished with small aid from the latter. The boys were, with depressing regularity, in and out of various schools, and when Mrs. Hearst became concerned, Hearst wrote her admitting that "they do not take kindly to education." At the same time he added, "Anyway, a certain kind of good mind does resist education." Whether or not the Hearst boys had such minds, the fact remains that, despite a large number of divorces and one particularly sad life—that of the late John Hearst—at least four of the sons, George, born 1904, William Randolph, born 1908, and the twins, David and Randolph, born 1915, were by the mid-Twentieth Century well settled down. All four were working in the newspaper business, and William Randolph, Jr., was the proud possessor of a Pulitzer prize. On a larger scale, he was also primarily responsible for his papers' growing up—particularly with respect to his support for the United Nations and other matters for which his late father had nothing but scorn. "There is no such thing," young Hearst said, upon taking over the mantle, "as isolation any more."

The Hearst Family was by no means the most remarkable family to come out of San Francisco—indeed, that remarkable city is not only recognized as the most Family-conscious of all America's Western cities but also the favorite "Family" city of more Americans, Eastern, Western and Southern, than any other. From the beginning San Francisco had a proud Society—in fact San Francisco's Spanish Families are among America's few Families which are genuinely steeped in antiquity. As far back as 1793, a Spaniard named Juan Bernal was the richest man in the Presidio; he owned 23 head of cattle and 246 sheep. At that time, too, one of the proudest of all San Francisco's Spanish Families, one still famous in the Twentieth Century, the Peralta Family, was just getting started. In 1793 their two brother Family founders, Luis and Pedro, had just two head of stock each; the day would come when their herds would cover the seven hills of San Francisco and the Coast Range down to Santa Cruz. But the day would also come when at least one branch of this Family, the Domingo Peraltas, would fall upon evil days. Julia Cooley Altrocchi best tells the memorable story of the last days of their ranch:

> This had been an unusually happy ranch home for many years. But now that the widow and her sons and daughters had been left unprotected, the property had gradually drifted out of their hands into the clever clutch of the Yankee. The new possessors were due to come riding in at any minute. The horses of the Peralta family were waiting outside, several of them packed with the last belongings. As the mother of the family stood on the veranda, looking for the last time into the old home, she chanced to drop a remark about how much she had cherished the hardwood living-room floors which she and her mother before her had polished daily to a queen's-coach brightness. One of her sons,

already astride his horse, hearing his mother's remark, immediately drove his mount up the steps and into the living room, and back and forth, with gouge-hooved frenzied patterns over the polished wood, turning it into a ridged barnlike floor.

"The Yankees shall not have our *home!* But they may have our *stable!*" he cried.

Of the coast city's American Families, the most fabled nationally are, of course, the "Big Four"—the Crockers, the Hopkinses, the Huntingtons and the Stanfords. Of these the Crockers easily rank first. The Family founder was a blacksmith apprentice. Born one of five brothers in 1822, the son of Isaac Crocker, an unsuccessful merchant of Troy, New York, and his wife, a farmer's daughter, Charles Crocker grew into a large, powerful man who weighed some 250 pounds. "I never had a nursery period," he once said of his boyhood. "It was my habit to work day and night." At the age of 10 he was earning, and saving, his first money; at the age of 12 he had quit school. In 1836, at 14, he worked in a sawmill in Mishawaka, Indiana; his father had failed in business in Troy and the family had moved there. When the Gold Rush came, Charles went west with his two younger brothers, Clark and Henry—a third brother, Edwin B., soon followed—and, after an unsuccessful effort at mining, he opened a small but soon very successful store in Sacramento. In 1854, in the Horatio Alger tradition, he returned to Mishawaka and married Mary Ann Deming, the boss's daughter; her father had been the owner of the sawmill.

In 1860, Crocker became associated with the other members of the Big Four in the building of the Central Pacific. Incredibly enough, although he had no education, knew nothing of engineering or railroading, he not only became the actual construction boss of the work, but also did an excellent job at it. He paid the laborers himself, riding into the midst of them on horseback and tossing coins into their outstretched palms, gold from his right saddlebag, silver from his left. The Central Pacific was completed in 1869, and in 1871 Crocker was made president of the Southern Pacific. "I was naturally a leader," he often said, neither conceitedly nor offhandedly but utterly matter-of-factly. In 1876 he built his famous mansion which boasted a 76-foot tower, 12,500 feet of floor space and a fully equipped theatre; the cost, together with furnishings and his art collection, was $2,300,000. Located a block west of his partners, Hopkins and Stanford, on Nob Hill, Crocker's property gradually extended until he owned the whole block except for a small lot owned by the local undertaker. The latter refused to sell despite increasingly higher offers; finally Crocker, in fury, completely surrounded the undertaker's dwelling with a 40-foot wall.

The "spite fence" was not, however, typical of Crocker. A plain man, he lived, considering his era and money, plainly. After establishing a resort hotel at Del Monte, he moved on to New York and bought and furnished a mansion there. But he was never happy in New York and here, ironically, in a fall from a carriage in 1886, he suffered the injuries from which, two years later, he died. His fortune was estimated at $40,000,000. The very next year Mrs. Crocker also died. Called the "courtly Mrs. Crocker," the lady from Indiana was widely known for her Boys and Girls Aid Society and her Old People's Home; in contrast to her husband, she was the soul of hospitality as well as generosity and is still remembered today as second only to Mrs. George Hearst in the annals of San Francisco's "first generation" Society.

Of the Crocker brothers who had gone west with Charles, or followed him, only the eldest, the late Edwin B., of Sacramento, had any formal education, and he died relatively young. Later his daughter, Aimée, married Prince Galitzin and led a spicy life which she retailed to the public in a book, *And I'd Do It Again*. Charles and Mary Ann Crocker, however, had three sons and a daughter, all of whom soon carried on the Family name, if not to new national distinction, at least to solid local entrenchment. Notable among these was the late Colonel Charles Frederick Crocker, who financed several scientific expeditions and served as a trustee of the University of California. More socially eminent was the late William H. Crocker, who married the former Ethel Sperry and entertained J. P. Morgan himself when the latter went west for his famous

Episcopal Church convention in 1901. Even after his father's house was burned in the fire, the William H. Crocker balls and *fêtes champêtres* at their "New Place" in Burlingame were highlights of the era's partygoing; Crocker was also president of the Crocker First National Bank for forty-three years. As for Mrs. Crocker, she not only boasted a chain of mammoth emeralds but followed in her mother-in-law's footsteps when it come to charitable endeavors. During World War I she adopted the entire French village of Vitrimont, which the Germans had destroyed, and completely restored it to its former estate; her sole concession to a newer day was the addition of modern plumbing. In 1934 she and her husband gave for the last time their annual New Year's servants' party; at this the Crocker butler acted as host, the guests were servants from all over the Bay area, and Mr. and Mrs. Crocker appeared at exactly midnight to give "greetings."

In the Crocker third generation, the Family leader was the late Charles Templeton Crocker—he was the "Colonel"—who with his wife, the former Hélène Irwin, took first place in the city as "host-to-nobility" and also managed other activities varying from writing an opera to financing half a dozen expeditions of William Beebe. Also notable in this generation was another Crocker bank president, W. W. Crocker—he was the son of William H.—and his wife, the former Ruth Hobart; in the 1940's they gave perhaps San Francisco's most memorable debut for their daughter, Diana, great-granddaughter of the original Charles. All in all, although the Family has by no means the resources it had in happier days—the Charles Templeton Crocker "Uplands" mansion together with its "original Spanish grant" has now passed from the Family, and the Henry J. Crocker estate at Cloverdale is now the "Covered Wagon Dude Ranch"—the fact remains that the Crockers have, generally speaking, fared far better than the majority of comparable Eastern Families. And few American Families have moved so rapidly and surely from Society to Aristocracy. "Men and women of the Crocker Family," says Julia Altrocchi, "have all been of fine strong caliber. The stock has stood as firm as a forge, as rail steel, as the granite of the Crocker Bank and the St. Francis Hotel." Such a tribute in latter generations is rare indeed in the history of American Familydom, and surely the original Crocker, blacksmith, railroad builder, banker and hotelman, could have asked for nothing more.

Less happily ended is the story of the second of the Big Four—the Hopkins Family. Born in Henderson, New York, in 1813, the Family founder, Mark Hopkins, was at 15 a clerk in a New York village store. He came to California via a succession of partnerships —the final one being with Crocker, Huntington and Stanford— and tall, bent and lean, he was soon known as "Uncle Mark." Not only the eldest of the Big Four, he was also the least pioneering; he was about equally careful of his cash, his calories and his conversation. He spoke with a lisp, and he neither smoked nor drank. In 1854, at 41, he rather dubiously took the step of marrying; he chose, rather typically, his cousin, Mary Sherwood. A pretty girl, much younger than he and far more cultured, she grew steadily more restless. They had no children; in contrast to the others, they owned at first no mansion, instead they lived in a rented cottage. Hopkins soon had his millions but he was so careful that he would go out of his way on the street to pick up a nail or a scrap of metal.

The first step in Mrs. Hopkins' fight against restlessness was to persuade her husband to adopt a son, Timothy Nolan. He was the son of a New Englander who had come west and worked as a dockhand to accumulate money for the rest of his family to follow him; the father had fallen into the Bay and drowned the day his family left for the West. To Timothy Nolan fell the job of looking after his mother and his sister; a third child had died on the voyage. Timothy came to work in the Hopkins home, and Mrs. Hopkins took a liking to him. Her husband agreed to the adoption. The second step in Mrs. Hopkins' fight was to persuade her husband to allow her to build a mansion, in the manner of his partners. Finally he agreed to buy a lot on Nob Hill, but as his wife went ahead with her vast plans, the mere thought of spending so much money all but killed him. In any case, before the house was completed, he died at 64, on a Southern Pacific train bound for Arizona. His wife thoughtfully provided him with a rose-colored mausoleum in Sacramento.

His widow, by now close to 50, kept on with her own building. Finally, her Nob Hill mansion was completed and far outshone in splendor even the Crocker and Stanford residences. But the willfulness of Mrs. Hopkins had not been wholly successful. "The Mark Hopkins house," said Gertrude Atherton, "looked as if several architects had been employed and they had fought one another to a finish."

After her husband's death, Mrs. Hopkins placed her affairs in the hands of Timothy Nolan Hopkins. Later, in New York, Timothy married May Crittenden, Mrs. Hopkins' niece, and when the couple returned to San Francisco, Mrs. Hopkins gave them one of the most memorable receptions in the history of the city; afterwards she bought them their own mansion, the former Milton Latham home, "Sherwood Hall." But Timothy did not handle all Mrs. Hopkins' affairs. She moved to New York and not only started a new wave of building—including a Fifth Avenue mansion, a $2,500,000 castle in Great Barrington, and a house on Block Island—but she also took it into her head to marry, at the age of 73, a 46-year-old decorator by the name of Edward Searles. This estranged her not only from San Francisco Society but also from Timothy, and by the time of her death she was totally estranged from him. In her will she cut off Timothy entirely and left her entire estate, over $30,000,000, to Searles. There was not a single provision for relatives, family friends, servants or charity, and this despite the fact that her husband had a brother, Moses Hopkins, and she herself had still another niece, Mrs. Mark Severance.

The shock felt in San Francisco at the outrageous will finally induced Timothy to contest it. Halfway through the trial in Salem, Massachusetts, in which Searles admitted he married Mrs. Hopkins "for love *and* money," the trial was suddenly called off, and Timothy received a $10,000,000 out-of-court settlement. Later, to his credit, Edward Searles made reparation to San Francisco by giving the Nob Hill mansion to the city. But even as late as 1931 people claiming to be heirs and even natural children of Mark Hopkins kept turning up in San Francisco courts, although none of them ever received any money; the latter had, in fact, been long since distributed by the probate court. As for Hopkins' home, it became the first home of the San Francisco Art School and later in the postwar building boom, the site of the famous hotel—named for the man who would, of course, have thoroughly disapproved of such extravagance.

The third Family of the Big Four was the Huntington Family. In late years Collis Potter Huntington, the Family founder, was wont to say that he started in life and business with advantages; he had *not* had a liberal education and he had *not* had money. Such a statement was typical of the self-made credo of the Big Four. Huntington's father was a tinker; Collis was the fifth of nine children born in Harwinton, Connecticut, in 1821. At 14, his formal schooling ended and he was supporting himself by working for a neighbor for $7 a month and board. The next year he went to New York and, beginning as a peddler of watches, soon established with his brother, Solon, a successful store in Oneonta, New York.

Physically a large man, like all the Big Four save Hopkins, Huntington weighed well over 200 pounds and his strength was legendary; at the age of 70 he was to remember only one illness in his life, and that a brief scrap with dysentery. Traveling west via schooner to Sacramento, he stopped on the way to do some trading in Panama, which necessitated frequent trips from coast to coast across a thick jungle. "It was only twenty-four miles," Huntington later recalled, "so I walked it." He had no stomach, however, for mining; one day's work at it convinced him that he wanted to be a miners' supplier. In 1860 he was approached by the promoter Theodore Judah concerning railroad communication to the East; he eagerly embraced the scheme and soon joined with the other members of the Big Four.

The chief financier of the group, Huntington was less popular than either Crocker or Hopkins—indeed, more than one commentator, assessing his character, turned to piscatorial imagery. "No more soul than a shark," said Arthur McEwen, while Huntington's lifelong enemy, the *Examiner*, called him "ruthless as a crocodile." One thing was certain; he was the dominant figure of the Big Four, and he was also so dominant in his home life that for years the general public did not know whether he was married or not. Actually, at 23 he had married Elizabeth T. Stoddard of Litchfield, Connecticut, who made him what he wished—an utterly self-effacing wife. They had no children but, as in the case of Hopkins, adopted one—Clara Prentice, daughter of Mrs. Huntington's deceased sister. In 1889 she made a widely publicized marriage to Prince Hatzfeldt of Germany—a nuptial which was later to cost her father several million dollars.

In 1884, however, his wife died, and only a few months after, at 63, he married again, this time choosing an attractive widow, Mrs. Arabella Duval Worsham (Yarrington) of Alabama. Again there were no children but again there was an adoption—in this case a young man, Archer Huntington, a son of Mrs. Huntington's first marriage. The second Mrs. Huntington, however, soon proved herself a very different Mrs. Huntington from the first. Almost immediately she took steps to disprove her husband's proud boast that he never spent more than $200 a year on "personal adornment"; she got him to the opera and even took him to the Paris Exposition. But it was not an unqualified success. French reporters asked him to comment on the Eiffel Tower, then the pride of France. "American engineers," said Huntington briefly, "could build one a mile high if they wanted to. Besides, what's the use of it?"

Huntington had also begun to have a growing distaste for California. It was, he maintained, a "climate for weaklings." Mrs. Huntington, however, liked California—in fact, she liked to have houses virtually everywhere, and soon there were half a dozen Huntington houses, in California, New York and even the Adirondacks; in San Francisco she purchased the famed David Colton house. In 1885, increasingly dissatisfied at home and in his business, Huntington openly broke with Stanford—the first breach in the Big Four armor. In fact, by exhibiting proof that Stanford had been elected to the Senate at the expense of his (Huntington's) personal friend, A. A. Sargent, he soon blackmailed Stanford into resigning as president of the Southern Pacific. He remained a fighter to the end. The year before his death at the age of 80 at Raquette Lake in the Adirondacks, the man who had never liked newspapers anyway read a report of an elderly man in Connecticut who said he had once beaten Huntington in a school fight. For once Huntington freely gave an interview. "No boy in school ever licked me," he said, "or ever could! I could wipe up the floor with half the boys in school all together!" Promptly his old enemy, the *Examiner,* suggested the two fight all over again, and although it is recorded that Huntington was sorely tempted—particularly when the paper pointed out that the public would pay well to see the match—the fight never came off because of Huntington's death.

In the second Huntington generation the mantle of the Family descended not on the adopted Archer, but on the great library builder, Henry E. Huntington. He was the son of Collis Huntington's elder brother, Solon, with whom he had started the store in Oneonta. Born the year his uncle arrived in California, young Henry early became a clerk in a store, then, as his uncle rose, he too rose rapidly in railroading. A tall, handsome man, severe in appearance and reserved in manner, he was once asked for the secret of business success; he said grimly that there was no secret except to be well prepared and be "on the job all the time." Henry Huntington was as good as his word. Although on his uncle's death he sold the Southern Pacific to E. H. Harriman, he was soon a man to be reckoned with on his own. Devoting himself to real estate, he looked southward toward growing Los Angeles. In short order he had tens of thousands of acres of city and country property and became the greatest single landowner in Southern California.

Even Huntington's marital career was, in a sense, single-minded and in any case unparalleled for its intramural scope. His first wife was Mary Alice Prentice, the sister of his uncle's adopted daughter. He was divorced from her in 1906 and seven years later, at a time when both were in their sixties, he married his uncle's widow. With the bulk of a $70,000,000 fortune to build from, not to mention his own successes, he spent the last fifteen years of his life in the building of his famed library and art gallery. To this end he devoted not only the traditional Huntington drive but also a taste which was far more cultivated than his uncle could have imagined. He also devoted some $30,000,000. To disappointed fellow collectors who complained of the "brute force of money," he had a stock answer. "I am an old man," he would say. "I haven't much time." In any case, in 1919, eight years before his death, he placed his library and art gallery, substantially endowed, in trust for the public. The institution has taken rank as probably the greatest single private treasure house in the world of the art and literature of the English-speaking peoples.

The fourth and biggest of the Big Four was Leland Stanford—at his peak he weighed 268 pounds. Of all of them, however, he was the most susceptible to flattery, the most publicity-conscious, the least able, and, ironically, the least self-made. Born in 1824 in Watervliet, New York, he was the son of Josiah Stanford, a farmer of some means. There were seven sons and a daughter, and although young Leland went to school only to the age of 12, he was taught at home for three years after that, and, when he evinced a desire to study law, his father gave him a law library. Stanford began his practice in 1848 in Port Washington, Wisconsin. Two years later he married Jane Lathrop, the daughter of an Albany merchant. In that same year Stanford's office had a fire, and his law library was burned; not too successful a lawyer anyway, he decided to go west to Sacramento where his brothers had already started a wholesale house. Not for several years did his wife join him—something which occasioned much gossip in Albany and left Mrs. Stanford with a lifelong distaste for her aristocratic home town.

Once in California, Stanford devoted himself to politics, and although he ran for a number of offices, including that of Governor in 1859 against Milton Latham, he was invariably beaten by sizable majorities. Nonetheless, it was characteristic of him that he kept on trying, and finally, in 1861, at a time when the Democratic party was split, he ran on the Republican ticket and won. Oscar Lewis best describes the age-old picture not only of politics in general but of the Stanford type in particular:

> Stanford's low-geared thinking, the painful slowness with which he translated his thoughts into words, was the opposite of a handicap. It did much to make him a success in politics. Extemporaneous speaking was of course beyond him; campaign speeches and every sort of public address had to be written in advance. Brief remarks were memorized and recited; those of any length were read, not from notes, but from complete manuscripts. This method gave him twofold advantage over more agile adversaries. For one thing, during his entire political life he never made a statement that had not been considered in advance, whereas most of his opponents could be depended on to extemporize themselves into trouble at least once during a campaign. But the chief value of his handicap lay in another direction. It was the spectacle of this big, earnest man on the platform, stolidly reading his speech line for line, page by page, that won the votes of his listeners. Here obviously was no speechmaker intent on swaying the electors by the sinister force of eloquence. The speaker was uninspired and he must therefore be sincere; he was dull and hence very probably profound; and of course only thoroughly honest politicians make thoroughly bad speeches.*

It was as Governor of the State that Stanford first became, incredibly enough, allied with the Big Four—in fact, still as Governor

---

* Lewis also tells the story of a visiting Englishman who had the dubious honor of dining alone with Stanford. While dinner was difficult, however, it was nothing compared to the after-dinner period. "For the next half hour," the visitor wrote, "we talked. That is, I talked and Mr. Stanford sat silent. I do not say that he listened, for that I had no means of knowing. He merely sat, regarding me not impolitely but with a face from which all expression had been erased. He may have heard every word I uttered or he may have heard nothing. I began by feeling that I must be boring him, then by wondering if I had perhaps given him cause for grave offense. Next, it occurred to me that he might be sleepy; finally I became certain that he was ill." Afterwards, Lewis records, the visitor got up, Stanford accompanied him to the door, shook his hand affably and remarked how much he had enjoyed their "chat."

he became president of the railroad. "Stanford had no scruples," says Stuart Daggett "about taking official action as Governor when his private interests as railroad president were engaged, or he overcame such as may have occurred to him." Nonetheless he was not re-nominated and he held no other office until he was elected to the Senate in 1885, a position where he was even more out of place. "He had little talent for sustained thought on difficult problems of a general sort," says Daggett, "and his reading in economics seems to have confused rather than to have clarified his mind." Indeed, only once in his life did Stanford make a memorable quote; this occurred during his fight with Huntington when Huntington called him a "damned old fool," and Stanford, stung to the quick, replied that he trusted Huntington only so far as he could "throw Trinity Church up Mount Shasta."

Meanwhile, with his ambitious wife and money pouring in, Stanford was building house after house, each one more splendid than the last, first in Sacramento, then on Nob Hill, and finally at Palo Alto. Here his trotters became world-famous and his farm the center of horse breeding in the entire West. Here too, Elinor Cogswell recalls, to settle an argument over the position of a horse's feet while trotting, photographer Eadweard Muybridge made the "instantaneous" pictures which were credited with leading to the first movies.

In 1868, after eighteen childless years, Stanford and his wife had their first and only child, Leland Stanford, Jr. The Stanfords were inordinately proud of their son and from the very beginning treated him like a royal heir apparent. Bertha Berner, however, recalls the very first time the heir was apparent:

> When the baby was only a few weeks old, Mr. Stanford asked Mrs. Stanford to arrange a dinner party for a group of their particular friends. It was a large party, and when they were seated the waiter brought in a large silver platter with a cover and placed it in the center of the table. Mrs. Stanford was very much surprised, for she had planned nothing of the sort, and also she had not seen the platter before. Then Mr. Stanford arose and said, "My friends, I wish to introduce my son to you." When the cover of the silver dish was lifted, the baby was discovered lying

on blossoms. He was carried around the table and shown to each guest. He was smiling, and went through his introduction very nicely.

Despite the predilection of his parents to spoil him, young Stanford was a remarkable child and not only gave evidence of a promising career but also of both charm and mentality far outranking his parents'. Unhappily his health was not robust. His parents had taken him on one of the Grand Tours in the fashion of the day. At 14, in Italy, he suffered an attack of typhoid fever. Taken quickly to Florence, desperate measures were tried, including "a periodical wrapping of the patient in sheets dipped in ice-water." Finally in 1884, a week before his sixteenth birthday, he died. According to legend the grief-stricken father immediately turned to his wife, saying, "The children of California shall be our children" —and there and then decreed the creation of a university "To the Memory of Leland Stanford, Jr., and the Glory of God." According to another legend, the Stanfords were told to create the university by God Himself—at a séance in New York conducted by the famous spiritualist, Maud Lord Drake.

In any case, the idea of the creation of Stanford was by no means unanimously popular. A Western newspaper pointed to the fact that the University of California at Berkeley was only forty miles away from Palo Alto and had never had an enrollment of more than three hundred. And, as might be expected, an Eastern newspaper was even more severe. "There is about as much need," it said, "for a new university in California as for an asylum of decayed sea captains in Switzerland." Nonetheless, plans proceeded apace. David Starr Jordan, suggested to Stanford by Cornell's great Andrew Dickson White, was chosen first president, and on October 1, 1891, the first student was assigned to a room in Encina Hall; his name was Herbert Hoover. Two years later, however, disaster struck. Stanford died, and it was soon apparent that his estate, never in good order since his battle with Huntington, was not equal to the task of maintaining the university. For a time professors' contracts named a salary and added "or as much of it as shall be available."

Here Mrs. Stanford, to her credit, leaped into the breach. For so many years a behind-the-scenes figure, she now emerged as a dynamo. Taking her private railroad car from one end of the country to the other—her car was carried free as a courtesy by all major roads—she begged, borrowed and cajoled money from any and all sources. She even journeyed to England to Queen Victoria's Jubilee in a desperate but unsuccessful attempt to sell her jewels to the Queen. Meanwhile, she herself practiced stringent economies, and by dint of these, plus selling her houses and jewels, as well as many gifts and a favorable Supreme Court decision on her battle with Huntington, she did indeed save the university. In the end, shortly before her own death, in 1905, she even paid a call on Mr. Huntington. "Mr. Huntington," she said, "I have come to make my peace with you." The latter, records Lewis, took both her hands, had her sit down, mopped his brow and ejaculated, "Well, I declare."

Nor, in the end, were the Stanfords' only children to be the children of California in general. The many brothers of Leland Stanford had children which carried the Family forward, and one of Leland's younger brothers, Thomas Welton Stanford, who had almost as much ability to make money as Leland, gave the university in 1917 the Thomas Welton Stanford Art Gallery as well as a Chair of Psychic Research. He himself, however, sailed for Australia in the 1920's and was so seasick he never returned to this country.

Contemporary with the Big Four was another San Francisco Family of a prominence comparable with any in the city—the Spreckels. The Family founders were Claus and Bernard Spreckles, two brothers who were born in the 1820's in Hanover, Germany. Claus came to Charleston, South Carolina, in 1846 and found employment in a grocery store, and, typically, he soon bought the business. In Charleston he also married Anna Christina Mangel, by whom he proceeded to have no less than thirteen children. Meanwhile his brother Bernard, who had settled in San Francisco, induced him to come there; in 1863 they founded the Bay Sugar Refining Company. Getting their raw materials from Hawaii, they were soon recognized, both nationally and internationally, as "Sugar Kings." In 1899, however, the Family, by now under the leadership of Claus alone, underwent a feud—one of the most famous in Family annals—in which two of Claus' sons, Rudolph and Charles Augustus, succeeded in defeating their father and two other brothers, Adolph and John Diedrich. Eventually, in 1905, the Family had a reconciliation and by 1908, on Claus' death, the Family was thoroughly reunited behind some $15,000,000 (which Claus left) as well as the Spreckels Building, the city's first skyscraper. Although Rudolph became active manager of the company, it was John Diedrich Spreckels, pioneer developer and philanthropist of San Diego, who was perhaps the most distinguished of the second generation. He died in Coronado in 1926, leaving four children. Other Spreckels families were by the mid-Twentieth Century scattered from California to Hawaii—all in either their third or fourth generations of refinement.

Refinement was not such an easy matter, however, when it came to San Francisco's second Big Four, that remarkable quartet of Irish "Silver Kings," from the Comstock Lode—Mackay, Fair, Flood and O'Brien. From its discovery in 1859 to its decline in 1879, the Comstock at Virginia City, Nevada, was the most valuable single pocket of ore ever found, and from its mines came more than $500,000,000. Besides the Big Four, millionaires were also made of Adolph Sutro, William Sharon and William Ralston. Ralston in particular had one of the most extraordinary up-and-down stories in San Francisco's up-and-down social history. The son of a saw-mill owner, born in Wellsville, Ohio, he clerked on a Mississippi River boat and came to San Francisco in 1854. Ten years later, with Darius Ogden Mills, he founded the Bank of California. From this he went on to build the Grand Hotel, the Palace, the California Theatre and a dozen other buildings that made him, along with his $4,000,000 from the Comstock, the First Citizen of his city. Then, in 1875, his bank failed, and it soon transpired that his affairs were hopelessly tangled in a web of debts and phony bonanzas. Ralston had a wife and four children, but the day the directors of his bank asked for his resignation he gave it immediately; then that afternoon walked down to the Bay, as was his custom, and went for a swim. That afternoon, however, San Francisco's First Citizen swam out to sea until he drowned.

Two of the Comstock's Big Four had been partners before. Their names were James C. Flood and William S. O'Brien, and they had run a bar and restaurant known as the Auction Lunch Rooms. Flood had mixed drinks and O'Brien had achieved a measure of fame as a chowder mixer. They took mining tips over their respective bars, however, and with the Comstock were soon multimillionaires. O'Brien early dropped out of the quartet, but Flood kept going, and the bartender and erstwhile "poor gamin of the New York streets," as Dixon Wecter called him, not only founded a Family but also became, into the bargain, one of San Francisco's best-known housebuilders. His was the last "blockbuster" brownstone to go up on Nob Hill—but he had built it sturdily and it was one of the few buildings to survive the Earthquake, later to become the proud home of the Pacific Union Club. Flood had also built another "residence"—a palatial country house at Menlo Park—"a miracle," Lucius Beebe called it, "of turrets, gables and gingerbread." Another wag dubbed it "Flood's Wedding Cake."*

The Flood Family also boasted one of San Francisco's most famous belles—Jennie Flood. A raven-haired girl with a flashing smile, in the summer of 1879 she was courted by no less a beau than Ulysses S. Grant, Jr., and it was shortly bruited about the city that her father had bought the couple a château at Newport. When young Grant returned after a trip east, however, he delayed so long in reaching the Flood home, "dallying along the way with Dora [Miller] and other adorables," that Jennie broke the engagement. Later she was also courted by Lord Beaumont, but this too

* So elaborately furnished were these houses at this time that John Sloane, the carpet manufacturer of New York, was forced to send representatives to San Francisco; they were kept so busy that Sloane's has been an important fixture in San Francisco ever since.

was discontinued. Actually she never married, albeit remaining "a prominent and beloved figure in the social and civic and charitable life of her city."

In the second generation also, the James L. Floods were active in their social life. Their house—later to become the city's school of the Order of the Sacred Heart—was the scene of many of San Francisco's most lavish latter-day parties, the most famous of which was their 1938 "Original Costume Ball" for their son, Jimmie. It resembled, records Julia Altrocchi, "the fabulous old balls of *autres temps*":

> The great pillared entrance hall had been transformed into a garden of azaleas and blossoming fruit trees. The costumes represented both old and current "characters." Mrs. Flood wore an old-fashioned crinoline of magenta silk. Her son, Jimmie, acted the part of Pop-Eye the Sailor Man. Mrs. Harold McKinnon was "charming in the wedding gown of her grandmother." . . . "One of the loveliest costumes of the evening was that of Mrs. Willard Somers who went as the ark. Her pale blue gown was painted with animals two by two and her ark hat had a dove of peace in front and Noah's three brothers in the back." Charles Theriot, as a newsboy, "distributed a one-page edition of the *Chronicle*" describing "floods" in the city, and specifically Jimmie Flood and his yacht, Dorade, which had just won the San Pedro to Honolulu race in 1936. The prize for the most amusing couple was awarded to Mrs. George A. Pope, Jr., as "a Floradora girl in pale pink over a chemise and over that an old-fashioned black satin laced corset" and to her partner Tallant Tubbs, as "a second baseman of the Seals." First prize for women went to Mrs. Sheldon Cooper, who arduously represented the framed picture of the Dauphin, and first men's prize to Dick Magee who "entered the ballroom as a muleteer—with a live mule."

Of all the Comstock Big Four, the saddest story was undoubtedly that of the Fair Family. The founder, James Gordon Fair, later known as "Slippery Jim," was born near Belfast, Ireland, in 1831. He came to Chicago at the age of 12, and at the age of 18 was on his way to California. Before he was 30 he had a mill on the Washoe in Nevada and later was chiefly responsible in ousting San Franciscans from controlling Nevada development—which he later took into his own hands through the Bank of Nevada. In 1881, after his Comstock strike, he was, like other Comstock millionaires—among them Jones, Sharon and Stewart—elected by the Nevada legislature to the United States Senate. "He made no impression on the Senate," says Frederic Logan Paxson, "save to advertise it as a haunt of millionaires, and he rarely took part in its debates. . . . But the gaudiness and irregularity of his life and the social ambitions of his family, to which his wealth allowed full gratification, attracted much attention for two decades."

In 1861 Fair had married Theresa Rooney, by whom he had four children; when he was divorced from her, his wife retained custody of both the girls, Theresa ("Tessie") and Virginia ("Birdie") as well as one of the sons, Charles, while he retained custody of the other son, James. Shortly thereafter James committed suicide. And, following this, Charles made a youthful marriage which so enraged his father that he disinherited him; before they could be reconciled the son and his wife were killed in a motor accident. Of the two daughters, Tessie later married Hermann Oelrichs in one of San Francisco's largest weddings—to which her father was not invited —and went on from there to become one of the great dowager dynamos of Newport. In her last days she was insane. As for Birdie, she had a difficult marriage with the late W. K. Vanderbilt. Fair himself lived out his last years alone in San Francisco's Lick House. By the time of his death in 1894 he was estranged from every member of his family and most of his former friends; his affairs, both business and personal, were so far beyond repair that in his will he left $50 each to "any widows or children" who might after his death prove themselves so.

The story of the last and greatest of the Comstockers, John William Mackay, contrasts as sharply with the Fair story as did the personalities of the two Family founders. Mackay, most popular of all the Big Four, was a tall, slender, well-knit man with gentle manners and a generous personality. And he was, if anything, even more self-made than they; he was born in Dublin, Ireland, in 1831 of desperately poor Irish parentage. Emigrating to America in 1840, he was first apprenticed in the office of the New York shipbuilder, William H. Webb. Although he distinguished himself there, he was determined to go west. In his early days he worked as a $4 a day pick-and-shovel man; instead of taking all his pay in cash, however, he always insisted, on whatever the job, that he receive some of his pay in stock in the company. After he made his first large strike, in the Mother Lode, he remarked that when he made $200,000 he was going to retire, that "the man who wanted more than that was a fool." Later, owning two-fifths of the richest mine on earth, he was to revise his judgment, but then he did indeed retire, at least to other fields.

In 1867, already many times a millionaire, he felt sorry for a young widow named Louise Hungerford Bryant. She was the daughter of a barber, had been born in New York, and after going west had been left virtually penniless in Virginia City at her doctor husband's death. Mackay, always generous, arranged to get up a subscription to help her; then, taking her the money, promptly fell in love with her. Asking her to marry him, he told her to make up her mind on the basis of him as a person and not what he repre-sented. "Circumstances in the mining business," he warned her, "change quickly." But even if he lost every dollar he owned, he told her, he could still "dig a living with his bare hands." He vowed, too, that he would always protect her—with his fists if need be.

The young widow's answer to the handsome young miner in the open shirt was favorable. A few months later, in the parlor of Jim Fair's cottage in Virginia City, they became man and wife. Their life together was one of the most remarkable in American social his-tory—through all the dazzling splendor of their life on two con-tinents they remained genuinely and wholeheartedly devoted to each other. In 1874 they moved to San Francisco and two years later went east to become the toast of New York, Paris and London. Even the Prince of Wales was impressed. "The most unassuming American I have ever met," he called Mackay. At the same time, for all the "top-of-the-heap living," as Mackay called his wife's life, he once admitted, entering a poker game at the Washoe Club, that he had lost something too. "I don't care whether I win or lose," he said. "And when you can't enjoy winning at poker, there's no fun left in anything."

Mackay did find future "fun," however. In 1883 he founded the Commercial Cable Company and for the next two years won the attention and admiration of the business world by his struggle to break the Gould cable and telegraph monopoly. And, against seemingly hopeless odds, he won. Modest enough twice to refuse nomination to the Senate—in sharp contrast to his Comstock partners—in 1891, when he was 60, came his chance to make good on the boast he had made his wife a quarter of a century before. A series of scurrilous articles began appearing in the newspapers, in both England and America, about his wife—how she had been first a washerwoman, then lower than that, and how her little daughter had begged with a tin cup. Mackay vowed to track down the instigator of the articles, a man named Bonynge, and finally in the office of the president of the Bank of Nevada he saw him. Mackay let himself in through the back door and came straight for Bonynge. "I struck out with my right," Mackay later reported, "and hit him in the left eye. Then I hit him again. . . . I'm not so handy with my fists as I used to be twenty-five years ago on the Comstock, but I have a little fight in me yet, and will allow no man to malign me or mine."

Mackay had made good his promise to his wife. Furthermore, he had no more trouble with the newspapers. In 1895, however, he was again called upon to show his courage, when he was the victim of a cowardly attempt at assassination on the part of a disgruntled speculator. As for Mackay's charities, they were on a scale commensurate with his character. Says Lucius Beebe:

> The whole tally of Mackay's charities will never be known to anyone. Almost in their entirety, and that was in the millions, they were contributed to causes he considered worthy on condition that they should be absolutely anonymous. Such institutional benevolences as the Church of St. Mary's in the Mountains in Virginia

City and the Mackay School of Mines at Reno could not well be hidden, but there were quite literally loans to oldtime friends on the Comstock and donations to worthy beneficiaries running into the millions. It was because of this patrician disregard for expenditures in what he considered to be commendable channels that at Mackay's death in 1902 his business manager was able to tell the reporters: "I don't suppose he knew within twenty millions what he was worth."

In the second generation the Mackay Family consisted of Mackay's two sons, William and Clarence, as well as his two stepdaughters, Ada and Eva. Both of these, much to their father's displeasure, married foreign titles; only one marriage was successful. The greatest blow which was to befall Mr. and Mrs. Mackay, however, was the death of their son, Willie, at 25. Riding a racehorse on his own race track in France, Willie had the misfortune to have his horse startled by a shot; the horse, at full gallop, shied and at the far turn of the course Willie went over the fence head first into a tree. His skull was crushed. As for their second son, Clarence Mackay, in 1898 he married the aristocratic Katherine Alexander Duer and settled down at "Harbor Point," Long Island. Here in 1924 he and his wife gave a memorable private dinner and ball in honor of the visiting Prince of Wales. In spite of the lavishness of the house, its art collection and its furnishings, the Prince expressed interest in only one object—a small copy of the Gutzon Borglum statue of John Mackay—the "unassuming" man another and greater Prince of Wales had so much admired.

The elder Mrs. Mackay lived on to 1928. In the third Mackay generation, the Family continued in the persons of three children of Clarence and Katherine—John William Mackay, Katherine and Ellin. In 1925 Ellin wrote an article for *The New Yorker* magazine which heralded the new "Café Society": "Why we go to Cabarets." Shortly afterwards, she followed it with an even more personally prophetic article entitled, "The Declining Function":

> The belle has disappeared, and, to some extent, the eligible young man has vanished with her. Young men are still eligible;

still watched by greedy parental eyes; undoubtedly they are as determinedly elusive as ever. But the game has lost its savor; there is no longer the same breathless interest in which young lady will be fortunate enough to secure for herself the particular matrimonial prize that is at large. . . . Modern girls are conscious of the importance of their own identity, and they marry whom they choose, satisfied to satisfy themselves. They are not so keenly aware, as were their parents, of the vast difference between a brilliant match and a *mésalliance*.

The year after this article, in 1926, Ellin Mackay married a young song writer named Irving Berlin—a decision which caused consternation in the by then "aristocratic" Mackay Family. Shortly afterwards, Ellin's "second generation" father, the one who so opposed the match, himself divorced Katherine Duer and in 1931 married the concert soprano Anna Case.

VIII

FULL CYCLE—*From Jewish Grand Dukes Back to*

Astors, Vanderbilts and Whitneys and the Last of the

Firsts

NO ACCOUNT of the great Family dynasties of America would be complete without reference to the Jewish Families. For the simple fact is that no Families in America have more genuine claims to Aristocracy than they have, particularly the Sephardic Families, notably the Baruchs and Cardozos. Almost equally firmly Family-founded, however, are the German Jewish Families, notably ᵗhe Strauses, the Warburgs, the Lehmans, the Schiffs, the Loebs, the Morgenthaus, the Ochses, the Sulzbergers, the Seligmans, the Goldmans, the Sachses, the Bernheimers and the Blumenthals. This group has, in fact, been dubbed by Jews as well as Christians the

"Jewish Grand Dukes." Stern in regard to aristocratic standards and values and with strong aversion to publicity, they are rarely written about—which is exactly what they prefer. They are also extremely self-contained and intramural when it comes to marriage—the present Nathan Straus, for example, was once told by another "Duke" that they were related nine different ways. By mid-Twentieth Century, however, this marital intimacy was, along with most other Family Aristocracies, breaking down. A half century ago, when Alva Bernheimer married Bernard Gimbel, it was regarded as a remarkable "out of the crowd" marriage; in contrast, when fifty years later R. Peter Straus married Ellen Sulzberger, they were, in a new generation, regarded as almost the only ones who had married "in the crowd."*

Most of the German-Jewish Families came over to this country after the Revolution of 1848, and an extraordinary number of them have family roots in Cincinnati. In that city, by the mid-Nineteenth Century, the Jewish community was already a going and growing concern; the founder was Joseph Jonas, a watchmaker who came from England as early as 1817. Before the 1848 revolution, too, as Alvin Harkow records, had come a number of Dutch Jews—LeJeunes, De Jongs and Workums, among others. Here too the first Reformed congregation was organized in 1839 under Dr. Isaac Meyer Wise, who had come to Cincinnati from Albany. His descendant, Isidor Wise, has accurately stated the case for the city as the first Jewish homeland in the New World:

* Examples of the earlier marriages are legion. Paul Warburg, for example, originator of the Federal Reserve System, married Nina J. Loeb, daughter of Solomon Loeb, of Kuhn, Loeb & Company, while Felix Warburg, humanitarian and social worker, married Frieda Schiff, daughter of Jacob Schiff. The Schiffs, incidentally, are members of a Family which can trace its line through men of affairs and scholars of distinction back to 1370. Later, in all of these Families, there were notable marriages with Gentiles, among them being the marriage of John Schiff with Edith Baker, of the banking family, Gerald Warburg to Natica Nast, of the publishing dynasty. As for the daughters of the late Otto Kahn, they became Mrs. John Marriott and Mrs. John Barry Ryan, Jr. Kahn himself, once called "the fly-leaf between the Old and New Testament," lived on a scale paralleling that of the Stotesburys and the Kents, and on one occasion his grandeur overwhelmed a Mrs. Malaprop who, greeting him, gushed, "I know your father, the Aga, and your dear brother, the Alv."

Cincinnati is the pioneer city of the West; so far as the Jews are concerned, she is the pioneer city of the world. To the long-suffering children of Israel, she is indeed the "Queen City," and so will ever remain, though she lose her commercial preeminence ten times over . . . How many of her children, scattered through the new and vast territory beyond the Mississippi, may cry with the Maccabees, "If ever I forget thee . . . may my right hand be withered."

San Francisco, too, which before the days of the forty-niners had only a thousand souls in all, was soon to have a sizable Jewish population—one occasioned by the coincidence of the revolutions abroad with the Gold Rush in America. One of the first to come was the six-foot-seven grain king, Isaac Friedlander, of Oldenburg, Germany, who in 1835, at the age of 11, had settled in South Carolina and grew up "as ardent a Southerner as if the blood of a Thornton or a Crittenden ran in his veins." Arriving in San Francisco in 1849, he and his family, including three beautiful daughters, were soon a vital part of the community, and a young Englishman, visiting the city in 1860, was amazed by his massive dignity, polish and erudition.

Actually, anti-Semitism as it is modernly known—albeit happily ever lessening—in the upper echelons of Society was a relatively minor matter before the Civil War. According to Morris Schappes, in his *Documentary History of the United States*, up until that time the Jews occupied a "secure, stable and untrammeled place in American society"—and, adds John Higham, "Throughout the antebellum period Jews continued to enjoy almost complete social acceptance and freedom." In the War of 1812, Uriah Phillips Levy, a fifth-generation American, who had started his career as a cabin boy, rose to the highest rank then given in the U.S. Navy—Commodore. In the Mexican War a Jewish physician, Dr. David Camden DeLeon, jumped into the breach at Chapultepec when all the American officers had been killed or wounded and, without military training, took command and snatched victory from defeat; in so doing he earned the title of the "Fighting Doctor" and later became Surgeon General of the Confederacy. In the Civil War Jewish officers as well as men took prominent part on both sides; on the Confederate side, the Quartermaster General was Jewish, as indeed was the Secretary of War himself, later Secretary of State, Judah P. Benjamin.

In the Nineteenth Century, and up until far into the Twentieth, Jews belonged to the most fashionable city clubs in Richmond. New Orleans, too, was a particular ornament of American tolerance; in 1872 a Jewish businessman, Louis Salomon, was the first King of the first Mardi Gras. Such facts contrast sharply with the all-inclusive upper-echelon anti-Semitism of a later day. As for the latter, its senselessness is perhaps best illustrated by John Higham in his study of three American medium-sized cities, all of which took form at about the same time—Minneapolis, St. Paul and San Francisco:

> By 1920, the Jews of Minneapolis lay under a singularly complete ostracism. It was perhaps the only city in the land that shut out Jews from the service clubs (Rotary, Kiwanis, and Lions), to say nothing of the local realty board and the numerous civic welfare boards. Across the River, the twin city of St. Paul behaved somewhat more decently. Jews could at least belong to the local service clubs and the Automobile Club. San Francisco presented the other extreme. There acceptance of Jews extended very widely in elite social organizations, civic activities and even residential patterns. Thus discrimination has been strong in Minneapolis, moderate in St. Paul, and weak in San Francisco, as in the whole South. Yet all three cities had concentrated Jewish districts produced by recent immigration, and the ratio of Jews to the total population in 1930 was highest in San Francisco (6.5 per cent) and lowest in Minneapolis (3.5 per cent).

This kind of discrimination was in modern times illustrated by the story usually attributed to Barry Goldwater, who, starting to play golf, was told that the course was restricted. "But I'm only half Jewish," he said. "Can't I play nine holes?" Probably the most famous incident of discrimination in social history occurred in 1877 at A. T. Stewart's Grand Union Hotel in Saratoga Springs. For many years the distinguished Jewish banker, Joseph Seligman, had been

446 WHO KILLED SOCIETY?

coming to the resort and spending the entire summer with his family at the Grand Union. This particular summer, however, there had been a change of managers and Seligman was summarily told that there was a new policy and that no "Israelites" would be permitted. At first Seligman could not believe it; when he realized it was true, however, he simply left the resort and went back to New York. However, so great was the furor created by the incident that it became a *cause célèbre;* it resulted in a Jewish boycott of A. T. Stewart's New York department store which was so severe that it, in turn, resulted in the store's being sold to John Wanamaker.

Not the least of the many ironies of anti-Semitism is the fact that the Gould Family, which have long been regarded as Jewish despite their protestations to the contrary, are now regarded by most reliable authorities as not being so. On the other hand, the Belmonts, who have long been regarded as non-Jewish, were definitely of Jewish origin. Dixon Wecter stated the case of the "social acceptance" of the Belmonts sternly:

> Since the first August Belmont set foot in America, no member of that Family has ever married a Jewess, but invariably a Gentile of social standing. In this way, plus an exchange of the synagogue for Episcopal communion, a constant association with non-Jews, and the adaptability of Nature which has given Belmonts scarcely any Semitic cast of feature except in their patriarchal age, a complete break with their Old World background has been successfully effected. In social acceptance no later Jewish Family can compare with them.

These lines were written in 1936 and might well be challenged as of the 1960's—at a time when the Belmont Family is, in national prominence at least, hardly more than a memory. But one thing is certain. The first August Belmont, who arrived in this country as early as 1837, did as much to found a Family in one generation as anyone before or since. Born in 1816, in the Rhenish Palatinate, the son of Simon and Fredericka (Elsaas) Belmont, he first went to work at the age of 13, without pay, in the office of the Rothschilds. Moved by his employers first to Naples and then to Havana,

Cuba, he came to the United States at the age of 21 during the panic of 1837; despite the panic, he promptly rented a small office on Wall Street and established, practically without capital, August Belmont & Company. Backed by the Rothschilds, he was within three years one of the country's leading bankers. Like many future Belmonts, however, he was quick of temper, and in 1841 he fought a duel "over a subject too trite to be mentioned" with Edward Heyward of South Carolina; his honor satisfied, he carried a wound in his thigh the rest of his life.

Under medium height and on the stoutish side, with iron-gray side whiskers, round Germanic features and keen dark eyes, Belmont added to his rapidly growing prestige by marrying, in 1849, Caroline Slidell Perry, daughter of Commodore Perry, who "opened" Japan to the Western nations. Soon he had an enormous mansion on Fifth Avenue, an unequalled collection of paintings and porcelains and, being a lover of horse and horse racing, one of the finest stables in America. He was also Minister to Austria and later The Hague. More remarkable, however, was the fact that he became, in one generation, president of the American Jockey Club and a founder of the Manhattan Club. With it all, he did not lose perspective. "I prefer to leave to my children," he wrote in 1860, "instead of the gilded prospects of New York merchant princes, the more enviable title of American citizen, and as long as God spares my life I shall not falter in my efforts to procure them that heritage."

August Belmont lived until 1890. In the second generation he left three sons, Perry, August, Jr., and Oliver Hazard Perry, to carry the Family forward. All were not particularly remarkable men themselves, but two at least, August and Oliver Hazard Perry, had, in the great Belmont tradition, remarkable wives. Perry, the eldest, married Jessie Robbins; she died relatively early and Perry spent the remaining years of his life as Newport's No. 1 *bon vivant* and clubman. He lived to be 97 years old, dying in 1947. In 1924, however, he authored one book with a notably prophetic title, *National Isolation—an Illusion*. As for Oliver Hazard Perry, his first wife was Sarah Swan Whitney; his second, whom he married in 1896, was none other than Alva Smith, one of Newport's Great Triumvirate, former wife of William K. Vanderbilt and mother of Consuelo, later Duchess of Marlborough. Marrying Belmont at the age of 46— she was five years older than he—she led him a merry chase through Good Works, Suffragette Meetings, etc., until finally the strain told—on him, not on her. He died in 1908 but his wife lived on to die in 1933 in Paris at the age of 80. The second remarkable wife was the second wife of August Belmont, Jr. He had first been married to Elizabeth Hamilton Morgan.* On her death, in 1898, he married the celebrated actress, Eleanor Robson, founder of the Metropolitan Opera Guild and one of the country's outstanding charitable workers, who in 1957 wrote a remarkable book, *The Fabric of Memory*, in which she feelingly described the change from the life of the theatre to "Society":

> In retrospect, the past seems not one existence with a continuous flow of years and events that follow each other in logical sequence, but a life periodically dividing into entirely separate compartments. Change of surroundings, interests, pursuits, have made it actually seem like different incarnations.

In contrast to the Belmonts, the Goulds throughout their social history have long been made the scapegoats of all parvenus. Not long ago, for example, James Farley recalled to this writer taking a drive with the late Mrs. Vanderbilt and passing the Gould mansion, which was then being torn down. He remarked innocuously that it was too bad to see the old landmarks go. Replied Mrs. Vanderbilt sharply, "*We* never knew the Goulds."

If Mrs. Vanderbilt did not know the Goulds, she could hardly have failed to know *of* them—indeed, with the exception of the Vanderbilts, they have been perhaps the most highly publicized Family in the history of American Society. They have, however,

---

* By his first wife, like the first August Belmont, this August had three sons, another August, Raymond and Morgan. The latter August married Alice Wall de Goicouria, whose son is the present August (as of the 1960's). This August married, in 1931, Elizabeth Lee Saltonstall, by whom he had four children— Alice Lee, August, John and Priscilla. In 1946 he married Louise Victor Winston.

moved with some difficulty into the American Aristocracy. And the reasons for this are not primarily the question of their often-alleged Jewish "blood"—rather, the reasons are to be found in the flamboyant, publicity-loving, difficult personalities of so many members of the Family. The Family founder himself, Jay Gould, a small, vain, cold-blooded, unscrupulous man who, while admittedly brilliant with figures, was by the time of his death virtually friendless— a circumstance which would have bothered him not at all, since all his life he was as suspicious of personal friendships as he was of business partnerships. His sole hobby, which he characteristically liked to do by himself, was gardening.

Born in 1836 in Roxbury, New York, he was the son of a farmer who also kept a grocery store; the American ancestor of the Family was Nathan Gold (also spelled Gould) of Bury St. Edmunds, England, who emigrated to Milford, Connecticut, in 1647. Jay had only a village school education; afterwards, however, he supplemented this by making it a practice to rise at three o'clock every morning and read. At the age of 16, clerking in a neighbor's store, he overheard his employer telling a customer that he had his eye on a piece of land near Albany which he hoped to buy and then sell for a large profit; by the time he went to buy the property it was owned by his employee. A surveyor between the ages of 18 and 20, Gould also found time, at 21, to write a book on the history of Delaware County and the Border Wars. His first large business deal was made with a New York politician named Zadock Pratt; with him he opened a tannery in Pennsylvania, then bought him out with the aid of Charles Leupp. Later, under suspicious circumstances concerning Gould's part of the transaction, Leupp committed suicide.*

* Some idea of Gould's unpopularity even as a young man may be gained from the story of his first yachting trip. This took place on the yacht of the Cruger Family, of Cruger-on-the-Hudson, who had invited him because they felt sorry for him but soon became so incensed with his behavior that they determined to play a practical joke on him. Gould insisted that the yachting trip be cut short so he could catch a train. The Crugers took him toward the train, then purposely ran the yacht aground by letting the centerboard down. Gould, who knew nothing of sailing, was told that if he wanted to catch his

On one of his early trips to New York, Gould was befriended by a grocery merchant named Miller who took him to his house to board. Here Gould met and later married the merchant's daughter, Helen Day Miller. In contrast to the general feeling about her husband, Mrs. Gould was highly respected and regarded as an exemplary wife and mother. The Goulds had six children—Helen, George, Edwin, Howard, Anna and Frank Jay. While Gould concentrated on business, the rearing of his children was left in the apparently all too tender hands of his wife. Although Gould concentrated on railroads, owning as many as a dozen at a time, he also briefly owned (from 1879 to 1883) the New York *World*, as well as New York's elevated railways and the Western Union Telegraph Company. At the time of his death, which occurred at the relatively early age of 57 from tuberculosis, his estate was valued at $82,000,000; there were also, however, lands in Louisiana which were later sold for $12,000,000.

Mrs. Gould lived only a few years longer than her husband, and despite the eldest daughter, Helen, who endeavored to raise the youngest child, Frank Jay Gould, the Gould Family in their second generation afford textbooks examples of the deterioration of an American Family—one which reached its climax when the younger sons sued the elder, over a period of eleven years, for $50,000,000, the largest piece of private litigation in the history of the courts. In this second generation all the children, save Helen, were spoiled and led lavish Society lives almost entirely concerned with their Fifth Avenue mansions, their country places, their clubs—though none admitted their father, all welcomed the sons—their marriages, divorces, extramarital affairs, and their sports. All of these provided staple Society page fare for newspaper readers for several decades;

---

train he would have to swim for it. Whereupon, Henry Clews recalled, Gould took off his suit and dressed only in "aggressively scarlet undergarments" and holding his suit over his head, waded and swam ashore. Then, while waiting passengers laughed and ladies "hid their blushes behind parasols and fans," Gould scrambled out only to have the Cruger yacht promptly "up centerboard" and come in to within ten feet of him. Here, it is recorded, they not only waved good-by but advised "a warm mustard bath when he got home."

the Gould yachts alone were more written about than the American Navy, and they were, in fact, a small navy by themselves, including George's magnificent *Atalanta*, Howard's *Invincible* and *Niagara* —the latter at that time the largest yacht ever built in America— Anna's *Valhalla*, and Frank Jay's *Helenita*.

"Of all the Gould children," says W. A. Powers, "only Edwin and Helen can be said to have had normal marriages, and even Helen, who became Mrs. Finley Shepard, in her late forties achieved a certain amount of uniqueness by adopting four orphans, one of whom was found on the steps of St. Patrick's Cathedral." There was irony in this, as indeed there was in all the Goulds' mismarriages, since Jay Gould's will specifically prohibited his inheritance going to adopted children or to any children who were the result of a marriage to which all the other brothers and sisters had not given their consent.

Even Mrs. Shepard, who cared more for her "pet charities" than she did for Society, lived on a lavish scale; her "Lyndhurst" up the Hudson boasted not only a swimming pool but a lifeguard also. As for the charities, these included a "crusade against Mormonism" and an attempt to stop Mohammedanism by having several hundred thousand Bibles printed and distributed all over the Middle East. In her own home, however, as her daughter-in-law Celeste Andrews Seton recalled, economy was her watchword where her orphan children's allowances were concerned. Each child received 50 cents a month, which had to be itemized down to the last penny; of this, each week, 5 cents was to go to the Sunday-school collection and 5 cents to the church collection. The child was thus left to spend, as he pleased, 10 cents a month.

From the outset higher education was, with any of the Gould children, regarded as a lost cause. Even George, trained to take over the Family fortunes, never went to college. He took over on his father's death, at which time he was 28, and for a time appeared to be doing well. Soon, however, his interests conflicted with those of Harriman, and a second-generation Gould was no match for a first-generation Harriman; by the time of World War I he had managed to lose control of every single one of his father's railroads. Nonetheless, during this time, with a cavalier disregard for what was Gould money in general and what was George Gould money in particular, he lived in one of the country's most magnificent private residences, "Georgian Court," in Lakewood, New Jersey. As far back as 1886, six years before his father's death, he had married, his choice falling on Edith Kingdon, an actress whom he met by throwing his card over the footlights at one of her opening night performances. In the winter of 1913-14, however, he met another actress, Guinevere Jeanne Sinclair, and although he did not marry her until after the death of his wife, in 1922, he acknowledged three of her children—born 1915, 1916, and 1922—as his own.*

Of all the Gould second-generation marriages, the most publicized were those of the second daughter, Anna, who twice made title matches—first to Count Paul Ernest Boniface de Castellane and second to his first cousin, the Duc de Talleyrand-Périgord. Of the other brothers, although Edwin married only once, to Sarah Cantine, and stayed at home, both Howard and his younger brother, Jay, became expatriots and pioneered, in their separate ways, the future International Set. Howard first married actress Katherine Clemmons, then later accused her of infidelities and named no less a corespondent than Buffalo Bill. Meanwhile, the youngest son, the late Frank Jay Gould, who died in 1956, led the most extraordinary life of all.

First married to the 18-year-old Helen Kelly, who at that age became mistress of a 40-room mansion and supervisor of a staff of twenty—as well as the possessor of one of the country's most fabulous diamond collections—he early showed what kind of life he intended to lead by joining twenty-seven clubs and even building his own block-long private riding hall on 57th Street. By 1909, however,

* By Edith Kingdon, Gould had five children—Kingdon, Marjorie, Jay, George Jay Jr., and Vivian. Of these the late Kingdon became relatively distinguished in his own right. He married Annunziati Lucci, by whom he had three children—Sylvia, Edith, and Kingdon, Jr. Frank Jay Gould had two daughters by his first wife, Helen and Dorothy, while also prominent in the Gould third generation was the late Frank Miller Gould, son of Edwin. He married twice, first to Florence Bacon, by whom he had two children, Marianne and Edwin Jay, and second to Helen Canan.

Gould was paying court to two more girls, both actresses and one of them also named Kelly—Bessie de Voie and Edith Kelly. Then, when he was finally divorced from his first wife, it was on grounds of misconduct with two other girls. Then, in 1913, after marrying Edith Kelly in Scotland, Gould settled on the Riviera. Here he not only pioneered that area as a summer resort but also left local inhabitants with something to think about in the winter too. Eventually divorced by Edith Kelly, he married, for the third time, Florence La Case, the San Francisco-born daughter of a French newspaper editor. In 1916, Frank Jay Gould began his suit against his brother, George, for mismanagement of the estate—one which, although George was dismissed as executor in 1919, was to continue long after George's death, at which time it continued against George's successor as executor, Edwin. Finally, in 1927, Helen, Anna, Howard and Frank Jay received $50,000,000, minus some $4,000,000 in legal fees. Meanwhile, Frank Jay's second wife had learned her litigation through the Family. From 1918 to 1929 she sued Frank Jay Gould a total of thirteen times. All in all, from the time of World War I to 1960—when a Gould wife was in the process of suing *Town and Country* for its story on Frank Jay Gould—there was scarcely a single year in which at least one member of the Gould Family was not engaged in a highly publicized lawsuit.

More interesting than the Gould story, because of the far-reaching nature of both their fortune and their philanthropies, are the Guggenheims. The Family founder, Meyer Guggenheim, like so many other Jews, came to America in 1847. He had been born in Langnau, Switzerland, in 1828. With his elderly father, Simon, he came to America at nineteen, meeting and courting on the long voyage his future wife, Barbara Myers. He settled in Philadelphia and started his career by selling shoe polish on the streets; his first business coup, the technique of which he was to apply many times in later endeavors, led him to manufacture the shoe polish himself and hire other peddlers to sell it for him. Moving from shoe polish to the lace business—he imported the laces from his home town—he soon had a large business which he handled together with the largest and most extraordinary army of sons ever boasted by any Family founder. Out of eleven children, eight were boys; the total second-generation Family included Isaac, Daniel, Murry, Solomon, Jeannette, Benjamin, Robert (a twin of Simon who died at 11), Simon, William, Rose and Cora.

One of Meyer Guggenheim's partners in his lace business, a man named Graham, in 1873 came to him with a proposition to go into the mining business in Leadville, Colorado. At first Meyer sent his son, Benjamin, to investigate; when Benjamin reported the mines full of water, however, Meyer, still believing there might be something there, went himself—thus recalling the famous dictum of August Belmont II: "If you want a thing done, go; if you don't, send." Arriving in Leadville, the "little man from Philadelphia," as he was called, with his "whiskers parted in the middle," presented a strange picture among the rough-and-ready Westerners. But he soon proved himself a match for any of them. And, with his decision to buy two mines, the A.Y. and the Minnie, the cornerstone of the Guggenheim mining fortune was laid.

Soon, convinced that the road to certain riches lay not in the mining but in the refining and smelter end of the business, Meyer bought first the Globe Smelter and then sent a son to Monterrey to build the second Guggenheim smelter in Mexico. Then in 1893, when the great American Smelting and Refining Company was organized, Guggenheim refused to be a part of it unless he could control it; the Trust went ahead without him, and for many years Guggenheim and his sons fought almost alone against every other smelting operation controlled by the Trust. In the end, however, victory was theirs, as the Trust capitulated to them in 1901, paying the Guggenheims no less than $45,000,000 in stock. With the purchase of $6,000,000 more on the open market, the Guggenheims had control of the company.

The Family founder died, at 78, in Palm Beach in 1905. By the time of his death, however, his dynasty was secure. Up to the end he ruled his family with an iron hand; every Friday night his sons and their wives, and later their children, came to his house to be told, in no uncertain terms, what was what in their family affairs. After his wife died, however, he refused to live with any of them. "No two generations," he told Daniel, "should ever live for long under the same roof." When his own children were young, in his Philadelphia days, he had personally routed them out of bed at six to practice musical instruments in the basement; any son who failed to attend the "orchestra rehearsals" was whipped—for the elder Guggenheim believed in corporal punishment.

The second Guggenheim generation was particularly remarkable for the fact that the sons, too, showed great ability; Daniel, in particular, became head of the company after his father's death, and, although he had never had more than a high school education, was soon responsible for running a world-wide operation, developing tin mines in Bolivia, gold mines in Alaska, diamond fields in Africa, copper mines and nitrate fields in Chile, and rubber plantations in the Belgian Congo. With all this, he was a pioneer in liberal labor relations and the prime mover in many Guggenheim philanthropies. The second generation also was remarkable for the fact that all the children were not only married in their faith, but also to extremely distinguished Family names in the faith—Isaac to Carrie Sonneborn, Daniel to Florence Schloss, Murry to Leonie Bernheim, Solomon to Irene Rothschild, Jeannette to Albert Gerstle, Benjamin to Fleurette Seligman, Simon to Olga Hirsch, Rose to Albert Loeb and Cora to Louis Rothschild.

In the entire generation there was only one divorce, and this occurred when the youngest son, William, married in 1900 a divorcée, Grace Brown Herbert—a girl whom the Family considered unsuitable. Promptly he was told by the Family that he must either divorce her or be disowned. Eventually the case went to court, and, with William acceding to their demands, he and Grace were divorced.* The late Benjamin Guggenheim also split with the rest

* He later married a friend of his sisters, Aimée Lillian Steinberger, by whom he had one son, William, Jr. In 1933 he wrote his autobiography, *William Guggenheim*, by "Gatenby Williams," a pen name, "in collaboration with Charles Monroe Heath"; the book, a glowing account of his life and work, was published by his own publishing firm.

of the Family—primarily over the question of taking "outsiders such as the Whitneys" into the company enterprises—and had already ventured into an unsuccessful independent business when he was drowned on the *Titanic* in 1912. Although in this generation William had the only divorce, several of the Guggenheim brothers were identifiable members of the "double standard" of the day, and Benjamin was perhaps most notable in this regard, having a succession of well-known mistresses including the Marquise de Cerutti. Even on the *Titanic* he was registered with a "Mrs. Guggenheim" —a young blonde singer, who was saved—although his wife was back in New York. Benjamin had three daughters, Benita, who married Edward B. Mayer, Marguerite,* who married Eugene Vaile, and Barbara, who married first Sigmund Kempner, then after a divorce, Milton Waldman, and finally, after another divorce, Denys King Farlow-Nettleton. All these girls had difficult times, but Barbara's was the most tragic in all the Guggenheim history. Married while still in college, she never recovered from either her father's "double life" or his *Titanic* death. When her first husband, who lived in England and wrote books, asked for a divorce, she returned to New York with her two sons, one four and the other an infant, went to a relative's apartment, and, a few minutes later, the bodies of both her children were found dead on the pavement sixteen stories below. After two separate investigations, the deaths were pronounced accidental.

"Totaled," says Harvey O'Connor, "the ten Guggenheim brothers and sisters had twenty-four children, ten sons and fourteen daughters, averaging a trifle under two and one-half children, as compared with Meyer's wife's magnificent accomplishment (eleven children)." And in this third generation, adds Karl Schriftgiesser, "it has been said that the record for divorces established by the Guggenheims has never been equalled by any other rich and prominent American Family." Whether this is true or not, the fact remains that the

---

* Marguerite is, of course, better known as Peggy Guggenheim, whose Palazzo on the Grand Canal in Venice is an internationally famous gathering place for *avant garde* art and artists; her published autobiography is of such an intimate nature that private efforts have been made to suppress it.

Guggenheim third generation was a vast change from the second; it was notable not alone for its multiple marriages but also for the prevalence of Gentile marriages. Taking the sons of Daniel alone, the late Robert and the present Harry, each had three marriages, Robert to Grace Bernheimer, Margaret Weyler and Elizabeth Eaton, and Harry to Helen Rosenberg, Caroline Morton and the present Alicia Patterson, a publisher with him of *Newsday*. As for Harold Loeb and Edwin Loeb, the sons of Albert Loeb and Rose Guggenheim —after his death she had the only divorce, except William's, in the first generation—they too had six marriages between them. And, if the "double standard" had become, as in so many Families, the "divorce standard," it was at least better expressed. "It's the Puritan in us," Harold Loeb once said. "We marry the girls."

There was another difficulty too in carrying the Guggenheim Family forward—that was the preponderance of daughters to sons in the third generation. Three of the second-generation brothers, Isaac, Solomon and Benjamin, had no sons at all, and William's son died, although he left a son. Simon had two sons, John Simon and George Denver, but both died young before marrying, and Murry's son, Edmond, who married twice, left only a daughter. Indeed the only sons in all the Guggenheim fourth generation were Robert, Jr., son of Daniel's late son Robert, and William, Jr., son of the late William. Although Robert, Jr., had another brother, Daniel II, he too died young before marrying.

Perhaps the most remarkable thing about the Guggenheim Family as a whole is that the brothers of the second generation established not just many foundations but actually imaginative foundations— born from the imaginations of the men themselves. Among these are the Murry and Leonie Guggenheim Foundation for dentistry for school children, the Solomon R. Guggenheim Foundation, famed for its modern art collection and its novel Frank Lloyd Wright Museum, and the John Simon Guggenheim Foundation for Fellowships. The basic principle for choice of Fellows is as Simon planned it: "No infant prodigies or old men who have already done their jobs, but young, able, inspired men who have demonstrated promise." There is also the free-wheeling Daniel and Florence Guggenheim Foundation, established by Daniel in 1924, "to promote through charitable and benevolent activities the well-being of mankind throughout the world." The Foundation has lent its support to the establishment of an experimental laboratory for cardiac surgery and other medical projects, subsidizes free band concerts in New York, and has undertaken an active role in the promotion of pioneering projects in aeronautics and space flight.*

Although most limbs of the Guggenheim tree established by Meyer have dried up and died with the sap drained off by too much money, a branch of the Daniel family is still in vigorous new growth. Daniel had two sons and a daughter, Robert (deceased), Harry and Gladys. Gladys, with great executive ability, prominent and active in political and philanthropic circles, has had a constructive life never faced with scandal. She married Roger W. Straus, son of the first U.S. Secretary of Commerce. Roger, now deceased, entered the Guggenheim business sphere and became president of one of their leading enterprises, the American Smelting and Refining Company; he was also a Regent of the State of New York. Gladys and Roger had two sons and a daughter. The younger son, Roger, Jr., on his own initiative built a progressive and respected publishing establishment. The older son, Oscar, served as vice-president of the American Smelting and Refining Company until he joined the Family firm of Guggenheim Brothers to head their mining exploration enterprises.

Harry Guggenheim has three daughters, of which Joan, the oldest, enlisted in the WAC in World War II and reached the rank of Major; now associated with the decorating firm of Dorothy Draper, she is married to Albert Van de Maele, a former Belgian utility executive and an able member of the firm of Guggenheim Brothers. Harry himself has taken over the chief responsibilities of the Family in this generation, being senior partner of the mining and metallurgi-

---

* The Daniel Guggenheim Fund for the Promotion of Aeronautics was established by Daniel in 1926 at a time when aviation in the United States was inconsequential. The Fund was one of the principal early factors in establishing the science of aeronautics and the aviation industry in the United States in first place in the world.

cal firm of Guggenheim Brothers, Chairman of the Board of Anglo-Lautaro Nitrate Corporation, former Ambassador to Cuba, naval aviator in two World Wars, author and newspaper publisher. Indeed, in the person of this third-generation Guggenheim, on whom the mantle of the original Meyer would seem to have descended, the Family story would seem to have, in contrast to that of so many American Families, a happy ending. In any case, in 1955, at the age of 65 and in the hope that the Family tradition would carry on, Harry Guggenheim wrote to his daughter Nancy, the mother of his two grandsons, as follows:

> I have reached the time of life when it is wise that I prepare for the future, either with or without the help of my children. I have always hoped that my children and grandchildren would carry on the best traditions of the Family to the best of their abilities. . . . I believe there is a responsibility to use inherited wealth for the progress of man and not for mere self-gratification, which I am sure does not lead to a happy life. I also believe that every individual has the right and duty to follow a career in which he feels a great urge and inspiration. Very few in their youth feel this need and less have the will as well as the wish to sacrifice everything for success. . . . I think that children must be encouraged, inspired and directed, or they will take what seems a rosy path of least resistance.

A Family of sterner mettle than the Guggenheims, and, in fact, foremost among the inner circle of the "Grand Dukes," is the Straus Family. Now in its fourth generation at New York's famous Macy's, the Family was founded by Lazarus Straus, who came to this country in 1849 from Rhenish Bavaria. Landing in the South, virtually penniless, he made his way on foot to Talbotton, Georgia. Here he prospered enough in the crockery business to be joined, in 1854, by his wife and four children—Isidor, Hermine, Nathan and Oscar. The mother of these remarkable boys, all of whom were educated in a log-cabin school, was also named Straus, being a first cousin of her husband. Loyal to the South throughout the War Between the States, the Family moved north in 1865 and started the crockery business of L. Straus & Son—later adding an "s" to the sign, because, although

Nathan had joined his older brother, Isidor, they could not afford a wholly new sign. Of the brothers, Isidor, known as "that crazy Confederate who wants to pay his bills"—from the fact that he regularly hunted up his creditors—had the banker's mind, his brother Nathan, who originated among other things the depositors' account system, was the innovator and the man who took the chances. In any case, together they made a powerful team. In 1873 they sold Macy's on the idea of taking in crockery—which, since it then combined hardware with software, thus became in reality the first department store. In 1888 Isidor and Nathan Straus became Macy partners and in 1896 they became sole owners of the store.

The third brother, Oscar, was the only brother who finished school, let alone college; he graduated from Columbia in 1871 and received his law degree in 1873. Although he too became a Macy partner as early as 1881, he soon turned to diplomacy, being Minister to Turkey under both Democratic President Cleveland and Republican President McKinley. Under Theodore Roosevelt he became Secretary of Commerce and Labor, and after another term as Minister to Turkey he ran for Governor on the Progressive ticket; so great was his personal popularity that, though the party lost, he ran not only ahead of his ticket but also of Roosevelt. Married to Sarah Lavanburg, he had two daughters and a son and was founder and first president of the American Jewish Historical Society.

Nathan Straus, never a man of great wealth, was one of the outstanding philanthropists of his time. In the depression of 1892-1893 he contributed 1,500,000 buckets of coal for 5 cents each, and the next winter issued over 2,000,000 5-cent tickets for coal, food, or lodging, having previously established lodging houses to provide bed and breakfast for that sum. Besides these efforts, in 1892 he began his milk campaign, establishing at his own expense milk deposits in thirty-six cities. Fighting ignorance and political corruption all the way, he was responsible for compulsory pasteurization in almost all of the cities; ultimately he was also mainly responsible for more than halving the then-prevailing death rate for children under five. Married to Lina Gutherz, he had two sons and a daughter and lived to the age of 83. In 1930, awarded a medal by the National Institute of Social Sciences, he was called by the late Robert Taft "a great Jew and the greatest Christian of us all."

Isidor too was known for his civic as well as philanthropic activities. His father was friend and adviser of President Cleveland and twice declined the nomination for Mayor of New York. Isidor founded the Educational Alliance, forerunner of the Settlement House. He was married to Ida Blun, a woman of both charm and generosity, and with her was on the ill-fated *Titanic*. Since his wife refused to take to the lifeboat without him, and since he refused to get into a boat as long as there was a single woman left on board, they bravely went down together. Their son, Percy Straus, father of Ralph, Percy, Jr., and Donald, succeeded his father as Chairman of the Board at Macy's. Easily one of the country's outstanding Families measured by any criterion, it is indeed curious to find, in the 1950's, one fourth-generation Straus living in Houston, Texas, who changed his name to Seldon. "The name Straus," he was quoted as saying, "was a hindrance to me in my scientific pursuits."

The Strauses were by no means the only Family to reach national prominence via the South. So did the Lehmans; in fact the firm of Lehman Brothers, which dates to 1850, was originally of Montgomery, Alabama. The Family founder, Meyer Lehman, was the son of a Bavarian cattle merchant; he emigrated at the age of 20 from his birthplace at Rimpar, a suburb of Würzburg, to Montgomery. There he joined two older brothers in a grocery business. The firm evolved from groceries to cotton merchants and then after the War Between the States moved its headquarters to New York and expanded into investments and commercial banking. Meyer Lehman married Babbette Newgass and had three sons—Arthur, who became head of the banking firm; Irving, who became Judge of the New York Court of Appeals; and Herbert, who became Governor of New York and U.S. Senator.

Another extremely prominent Jewish Family from the South was the Ochs Family—one which reached New York by way of Chattanooga, Tennessee. Julius Ochs, father of the late Adolph Ochs, of *New York Times* fame, was originally apprenticed by an older brother to a bookbinder at Frankfort. Dissatisfied with his lot, he walked 600 miles to Bremen and from there, in 1845, he embarked for New York. He made his way to Chattanooga to join a brother and two sisters who had emigrated earlier. Moving to Nashville and later to Knoxville, he married a brilliant and forceful woman named Bertha Levy; he too was a cultured man but highly impractical.

In Julius' eldest son, Adolph, the virtues of the parents combined. Born in 1858, an undersized urchin, he went to work at age 11 sweeping out the office of the Knoxville *Chronicle* for 25 cents a day. He swept well, however, and with $250 bought what later amounted to control of the Chattanooga *Times*. In 1883 he married the daughter of Rabbi Isaac Wise of Cincinnati. In 1896 he was told by a reporter that the *New York Times* was for sale—at that time it had a circulation of 9,000 and was losing $1,000 a day—and with a borrowed $75,000 he bought it. Almost ruined by the war with Spain, during which the *Times* could not afford foreign correspondents, he was advised to raise the price from 3 to 5 cents; instead, he lowered it to 1 cent. From that time on the *Times* prospered—in fact so much so that, after World War I, New York members of the Ochs Family could not fail to derive some comfort from the fact that Chattanooga members of the Family, who had changed their name during the war to Oakes, decided to become Ochses again. In some cases, notably that of George Washington Ochs-Oakes, they kept both names.

When Ochs died in 1935, he was succeeded by his son-in-law, Arthur Hays Sulzberger; the latter's son-in-law, Orvil E. Dryfoos, in turn succeeded him. If the sons-in-law also rise at the *Times*, however, the paper, even as of the 1960's, remains Ochs' creation. It was he who coined the slogan, "All the news that's fit to print," and it was he who, when his daughter, Mrs. Sulzberger, became at an early age idealistic and humanitarian—and therefore somewhat summary in her opinions—gently but firmly insisted that she commit to memory a passage from Benjamin Franklin's *Poor Richard:*

> I made it a rule to forbear all direct contradictions to the senti-
> ments of others and all positive assertions of my own. I even

forbid myself . . . the use of every word or expression in the language that imported a fix'd opinion, such as *certainly, undoubtedly,* etc., and I adopted instead of them, *I conceive, I apprehend,* or *I imagine* a thing to be so and so; or *it appears to me at present.* . . . And this mode, which I at first put on with some violence to natural inclination, became at length so easy, and so habitual to me, that perhaps for these fifty years past no one has ever heard a dogmatical expression escape me.

Along with the remarkable publishing dynasty stories of McCormicks and Fields, Hearsts and Ochses, surely belongs the most remarkable of all of them—the story of the Pulitzer Family, of Pulitzer Prize and St. Louis *Post-Dispatch* fame. The name is pronounced, as Mrs. Joseph Pulitzer III sharply phrases it, "Pull-it-sir." The Family is of Magyar descent; Pulitzer's mother was a Roman Catholic. No Family founder in all American social history, however, ever had quite such a start in this country as Joseph Pulitzer I. Born in Mako, Hungary, in 1847, he left home at 17 and made his way to France, where he attempted to enlist in the British forces in India. Rejected for his poor physique and defective eyesight—he had previously met rebuffs from the French Foreign Legion—he fell in with an agent seeking recruits for the Union Army in America. On the boat he found out that the agent expected to collect a bounty for each recruit; just before the boat docked at Boston, he dropped over the side, thus becoming literally an immigrant who swam to this country.

In any case, he collected his own bounty and, after service in the war, was within twenty-five years the owner of two St. Louis newspapers. These he combined into the great *Post-Dispatch*. Then, in 1883, he bought from Jay Gould, for the sum of $346,000, the New York *World*. On acquiring this paper, Pulitzer at once announced its credo—that it would oppose the "aristocracy of money," but that it wished to become the organ of America's "true aristocracy," which he defined as the "aristocracy of labor"—something which, three-quarters of a century later, in a rather different way than Pulitzer might have expected, would indeed seem to have come about. Pulitzer was married to Kate Davis, a cousin once removed from Jefferson Davis, and was survived by three sons, Ralph, Joseph, Jr., and Herbert, and two daughters.* The late Ralph Pulitzer succeeded his father as publisher of the *World*. In 1911, however, the year before the elder Pulitzer's death, Ralph wrote a little-known but remarkable book entitled *New York Society on Parade*. In this he began by comparing, to its lasting disfavor, New York Society with European:

> Instead, indeed, of having an aristocracy whose caste is beyond question and beyond change and whose mutual hospitalities constitute Society, New York has an "Aristocracy" whose elevation is largely artificial, whose membership is largely arbitrary, and whose existence vitally depends upon those activities which are known as social functions . . . while in Europe the pleasures of Society are among the prerogatives of rank, in New York the pleasure of "rank" is the inducement to Society.

Not content with his general denunciation, Pulitzer then proceeded to parade his New York Society through at least three of its "functions"—The Dinner, The Opera, and The Dance. His Dinner in particular was perhaps as clever a satiric picture of the Society of the "Four Hundred" as was ever written:

> As the guests enter the house the ladies are ushered into one cloak-room and the men into another. The men go through the simple operation of taking off their overcoats and hats and getting a check by which to reclaim them. They are also handed a little stiff envelope containing a card which each man draws forth as gingerly as he would the fifth card to four of a suit. They then issue from their cloak-room, and each of them who accompanies

* The present publisher and noted art collector Joseph Pulitzer III, married to Louise Vauclain of the Baldwin Locomotive Family (they have a son, Joseph Pulitzer IV), is the son of the late Joseph, Jr. (1885-1955). The latter became publisher on the death of his father and was married twice, first to Elinor Wickham, by whom he had, besides Joseph III, two daughters, Kate Davis Pulitzer (Mrs. Elwood R. Quesada, wife of the administrator of the Federal Aviation Agency) and Elinor Pulitzer (Mrs. Louis H. Hempelmann, wife of the scientist). His second marriage was to Elizabeth Edgar, by whom he had Michael Edgar Pulitzer, who in 1960 joined the *Post-Dispatch* from the Louisville *Courier-Journal*. Ralph Pulitzer, who died in 1939, married twice, first to Frederica Vanderbilt Webb, by whom he had two sons, Ralph, Jr., and Seward Webb, and, after a divorce, to the famed historian Margaret Leech.

a lady stands, a monument of expectant patience, gazing wistfully at the door behind which the mysteries are taking place on whose accomplishment he waits. When the object of his patience finally radiates his view he follows her, generally up an imposing sweep of stairs, intently scrutinizing the edge of her train upon which Nemesis is hounding him to place his foot. Near the head of the staircase they find the hostess surrounded by a bevy of Beau Brummels. As they approach, the most distinguished-looking of these, stepping forward, enunciates their names in tones of great volume and distinctness, and the mistress of the house welcomes them with that indelible smile which hostesses share exclusively with coiffeurs' models and with Christian martyrs.

The first fifteen minutes of any dinner, we are told, is best. "Dowager or débutante, captain of industry or floor-broker, while they still hunger, are to that extent sincere." There is even a mellow period:

The ugly financier may drop a valuable hint on market tendencies if the beautiful young matron is sympathetic enough. The bright young Westerner may get the entrée to the fat old lady's drawing-room if he is amusing enough. The rising architect may get his plans accepted by the irascible-looking man if he can sufficiently interest the latter's daughter in the aesthetic possibilities of tenement-houses. The effeminate youth may be taken for years older than he is if he can talk cynically enough to the horsy-looking girl. The wistful débutante may catch the point of the risqué story, which her left-hand neighbor is telling the mournful lady on his farther side, if she can listen acutely enough with one ear while bending the other pensively to the remarks of the eloquent young rector on her right.

Finally the eating, at least, is over:

Meanwhile the dinner has run its course, and, beneath the babel of tripping tongues, a curious suspense makes itself felt. It is the telepathic manoeuvres of the hostess marshalling her feminine forces to rise and leave the stricken field for the tedious respite of the drawing-room. At this moment it would be of melancholy interest to know how many conversations cut short by this exodus have been of sufficient interest to cause in the conversers any disappointment at the interruption, or any intention to pursue the subject at the next opportunity.

We will, however, never know. For the ladies have repaired to the drawing room and the gentlemen to the library. Here the host is "apt to be momentarily embarrassed by one or more among his guests who, with misguided politeness, do not content themselves with admiring the masters on the walls, but ask him their names, and even the subject of their portraits." Fortunately, the "man talk" quickly turns to safer channels—"The Street." Meanwhile, the ladies too, of course, have been hard at what passes for their conversation:

> Those of them who have only just met converse with courteous caution, choosing as their text such trivial and non-committal subjects as the latest matinée to which they have both been, and which ones of their most creditable acquaintances they saw there; how delightful the dance was night before last. . . .
> Those who know one another somewhat better say charming things about one another's fascinating little children, and ask one another questions about the nationality of their nurses and the nature of their nourishments.
> Those whose acquaintance is verging on friendship talk clothes. . . . They inform one another of the latest dressmaker in Paris to whom respectable women are just beginning to go. They give one another addresses in Paris where they say one can get such pretty things so ridiculously cheap; but they do not give one another the addresses where they actually do get such pretty things ridiculously cheap. Those they keep sacredly to themselves for fear of spoiling the shop with too much custom.
> Those who are intimate friends, besides talking children and clothes, seal the bonds of this intimacy by plunging sorrowfully into the gloom of the servant question.

And now the moment has come when the host has said, "Shall we join the ladies?" And, albeit reluctantly, the men follow him in to where the women seem to present an "apparently impregnable solidarity." But fortunately it is soon broken up into "scattered couples and quartets":

> Now will come the supreme test of the evening's higher success. . . . Now they sit face to face, mind to mind, with neither food,

nor cooking, nor dress, nor stocks to serve as distractions and allies to their conversation. They sit in the regions of pure thought. Will their minds, groping toward one another along a tenuous bridge of words, meet and find companionship in mutuality of mental interest? Will their tastes in common soar from oysters to authors, from artichokes to architecture, from canvas-backs to composers, from peas to poetry? Or will their minds, like babies walking without furniture, toddle toward one another, meet in dizzy contact, and, having fallen painfully to earth, crawl sniffling piteously back to their respective nurseries?

No one will ever know. For at this moment when Opportunity stands smiling inscrutably with hands behind her, holding in either palm success or failure, there comes a strident twanging, and through the door at one end of the drawing-room march negro minstrels, fortune-tellers, mind-readers, provided to amuse the guests so that they need not face the ordeal of interesting one another.

Except, of course, for those who have decided to forgo the entertainment and have repaired, or escaped, to the bridge tables. Here people who have millions are in Seventh Heaven if they can win a few dollars. And thus, at long last, the evening comes to an end.

So the night runs on: Society is held together by the centripetal force of clowns, on the one hand, and competitive acquisitiveness, on the other. When, after a few hours more, both of these have served their purpose and preserved to the evening's entertainment its promised halo of success, the guests file past the hostess, appreciating with courteous monotony the hours of delight she has vouchsafed them.

They stream down the monumental stairs and quickly don their coats and wraps. The footman at the door calls their grooms, their chauffeurs, or their coachmen, and as the vehicles draw up their owners walk carelessly out of the artificial radiance of the threshold into the natural blackness of the night. But some few who have suffered from the brilliant obscurity within sigh their relief at the re-enlightenment that awaits them in the darkness.

To conclude the Family Circle, there remain the three dominant Families, on a national scale, in the entire history of American Society —the Astors, Vanderbilts and Whitneys, or, as they are irreverently

lumped together, the "Astorbilts." Of these, the Astors are the eldest
—indeed, as recently as 1936, the late Maury Paul (Cholly Knickerbocker No. 1) declared that "there can be no question about Astor
being the foremost social cognomen in the U.S.A. today."

In our today, as of the 1960's, only a short generation later, there
could be a good deal of question about it. This is not to say that as
of that time the once-vaunted "Astor Estate"—of late years in the
hands of the British branch of the family—was in danger of going to
the wall. Nor is it to say that there were not, particularly in England,
still prominent and busy Astors, such as John Jacob Astor V, publisher of the (London) *Times,* or, on the distaff side, the peerless
Lady Astor. It is to say, however, that, whereas fifty years ago, in
1908, a financial prophet predicted that the Astor fortune would
snowball until it reached, by the year 2000, exactly $80,000,000,000,
actually the prophet was not only wrong, he was, judged at the
halfway mark, almost totally wrong. For if the Astors had, by
1908, well disproved the old American adage of "shirtsleeves to shirtsleeves in three generations," they had also, as of 1958, rather well
proved that by six generations an American Family is about ready to
start all over again. Indeed, as a glance at the Astor listings in a New
York telephone book of the 1960's would demonstrate, the Astors
have become close to a textbook example of the fact that First
Families, born of commerce—which then, as we have seen, grow up
to snub people "in trade"—are fated in the end, as a sort of First
Family Gresham's Law, to wind up with their name being used for
trade only.

Still, giving the Astors their due, the original John Jacob Astor
founded not only the greatest real estate fortune in the world but
also an American Family which has made and kept more money,
and for a longer length of time, than any other in American history.
Originally a Spanish Family—spelled Astorga—they emigrated to
Germany in the Eighteenth Century and dropped the extra "ga."
The Family founder, John Jacob Astor (also by then spelled
"Ashdor"), was the son of a poor butcher and was born in 1763 in
Waldorf, near Heidelberg, Germany. He left home at the age of 17

with enough schooling to read and cipher but barely enough to write anything but a wretched scrawl—a deficiency which, along with his heavy German accent, he never overcame. In any case, with a few coins in his pocket he started afoot for the Rhine and on his way is said, in true Horatio Alger tradition, to have sat down and made three resolutions: to be honest, to be industrious, and not to gamble. Whether or not he actually did this, the fact remains that he arrived in this country, at age 20, with $25 in cash and seven flutes.

The explanation of Astor's flutes is that he had already spent three years working for his older brother, George, who was in London selling musical instruments. Tiring of this, he next headed for another older brother, who was a butcher in America and using the name of Heinrich Ashdoor. Arriving off Baltimore in January, 1784, Astor and his fellow passengers found that the Chesapeake was covered with ice. Not only could the ship proceed no further, but also there was actual danger of her being broken up, and the captain had assembled the passengers on deck ready to take to the lifeboats. All were dressed in their roughest clothing except Astor, who wore his Sunday suit. "What are you all dressed up for?" the captain asked, sarcastically. "If ve are saved," replied Astor, "I haf my Sunday suit on. If ve are drowned, it von't make no difference vot kind of clothes I haf on."

Actually some passengers were soon able to land over the ice, but Astor, whose ticket promised him food until the ship docked, did not leave the boat until she was able, in March, to enter Baltimore harbor. And he used the time to become better acquainted with some fellow passengers who were members of the Hudson's Bay Company and engaged in the fur business. By the time he reached New York and met his brother, Heinrich, he found that the latter had not only a thriving butcher business in the Bowery, but also a pretty immigrant wife. ("Dolly iss der pink of der Powery," he used to say.) Neither, however, appealed to John Jacob. Instead, he promptly entered the fur business and also chose for his wife Sarah Todd, daughter of the Widow Todd, at whose boardinghouse he stayed.

Miss Todd not only made him a capital wife but also brought him, literally, his first capital—$300 in cash. She brought him besides a clear head for business, and since she was a distant, though relatively impoverished, member of the once-powerful Brevoort Family, she also marked a distinct rise in the world for him. She was a curious combination of pride and reserve, ambition and shyness, and Astors today, it is said, still trace these family characteristics to her. In any case, John Jacob's rise from then on was rapid. In 1790 he was, by the old directories, listed as a "fur trader." In 1794 he was a "furrier" and in 1796 a "fur merchant." Already buying real estate, he was by 1800, at age 37, one of America's front-ranking merchants, and, not long after, through the American Fur Company, its first monopolist.

He was, however, not yet a Society figure. He lived for twenty-five years at 223 Broadway, later the site of the old Astor House, which he built as his descendants were to build the Waldorf-Astoria; but even after moving to a larger house, his plain dress, miserly habits and uncouth manners forbade his presence in what was then called "Upper Tendom." Albert Gallatin, former Secretary of the Treasury, refused in later years to manage his estates because "he dined here last night and ate his ice cream and peas with a knife." And Gallatin's son found him, in 1820, still beyond the pale:

> Really Mr. Astor is dreadful. . . . He came to *déjeuner* today; we were simply *en famille*, he sitting next to Frances [Gallatin's sister]. He actually wiped his fingers on the sleeves of her fresh white spencer [jacket].

Nonetheless, by 1835 Astor was the richest man in the New World, and if he could not have a Gallatin, *père* or *fils*, to manage his estate, he could at least employ no less an author than Washington Irving to hack-write the story of "Astoria"—the first permanent settlement, along the lower Columbia, in the Northwest. Astor could also, on occasion, jest in a dry way. When a charity seeker, to whom he had given a pittance, protested that his son had given much more, Astor was firm. "My son can afford it," he said. "He has a rich father."*

* The same story reappears, as a second-generation yarn, in almost every Family of wealth. It was told when George Baker's son bought himself a huge yacht.

In John Jacob's last years, his sole concern was founding the House of Astor—the first "House" in the Family sense in America. He and Sarah had eight children, three of whom died young, and three were daughters. One of these eloped with Colonel Walter Langdon during the War of 1812, another married first Adrian Bentzon, Governor of the Virgin Islands, and later an Englishman named Rev. John Bristed, both of whom left her, and the third made the country's first "title" marriage—to a Count Vincent Rumpff of Switzerland—and then died. Of Astor's two sons, the elder, John Jacob Astor, Jr., was incapacitated by a fall in childhood and mentally incompetent for the rest of his life. The other son, William Backhouse Astor—middle-named for a merchant who had befriended his father—at first led a dilettante life abroad but finally settled down and married Margaret Rebecca Armstrong, of the Revolutionary Armstrongs and the pre-Revolutionary Livingstons. Astor was delighted. "Villiam vill never *make* any money," he once said, "but he vill keep what he has."

Just to be on the safe side, however, old John Jacob dictated a marriage settlement which was to become a model for subsequent Astor generations. By this, for a sum princely to the Armstrongs but nothing to the Astors, the bride surrendered her dower rights to the Astor fortune if anything happened to her husband. By such a maneuver old John Jacob sought to outwit the New World laws against primogeniture and entail. Even he, however, could not foresee future taxes, future wars, future divorces, or, for that matter, future Astors themselves.

Late in life John Jacob suffered from such severe stomach trouble that his doctor ordered him, as a means of having his digestion stimulated, to be tossed in a blanket every day. At the same time the only food he could take was milk from the breast of a wet nurse. Even then, however, at 85, he still knew his rent-rolls by heart and heard a report on them every day. Nonetheless, the great librarian Joseph Green Cogswell, his "train-bearer and prime minister," never gave up pestering him about leaving a library to New York, and finally in a rare burst of generosity Astor agreed to leave $400,000 for such a purpose in his will.

In his will also, however, he left a final joke. His faithful secretary,

Fitz-Greene Halleck, had once railed against the futility of his master's trying to make more money. "Mr. Astor," he said, "of what use is all this money to you? I would be content to live on a couple of hundred a year for the rest of my life, if I was only sure of it." When the final will was read, there, without any comment, along with bequests like $18,000,000, was the sum of $200 a year for Halleck.

In the second generation, William Backhouse became, on the death of his father in 1848, the richest man in the country. "A tall, heavy-built man," Matthew Hale Smith describes him, "with a decided German look, a countenance blank, eyes small and contracted, a look sluggish and unimpassioned, unimpressible in his feelings, taciturn and unsocial." To make a Society figure out of such a man took no small doing, but the "landlord of New York," as the second Astor was known, not only managed to double his father's wealth but also, with the aid of his Armstrong wife, to make sizable social advances. Also, in spite of his methodical ways—up to four days before his death, at the age of 83, he walked to work and arrived at his office every morning at nine—he was also a more benevolent man than his father. For one thing, he raised his father's secretary's annuity from $200 to $1,500; for another, he gave $50,000 to St. Luke's Hospital and made the Astor Library his particular care. But his will left only $500,000 to charity—exactly the same amount his father had left—and this, despite the fact that the estate had doubled in value— from $40,000,000 to $80,000,000. It is not surprising that newspapers took umbrage at the size of his benefactions and recalled the story of a poor preacher and former classmate of Astor's at Heidelberg who had come to call one day. For a long time Astor did not even acknowledge his existence, then finally he looked up. "Can I do anything for you?" he asked. For some time the preacher looked at him, then quietly stood up. "No, sir," he said, and left.

By his will Astor's two daughters, Laura, who had married Franklin H. Delano and thus established an Astor-Roosevelt relationship, and Alida, who had married John Carey, received approximately a millon dollars each. Meanwhile, his youngest son, known as the "queer one"—there being many of these in Astor history—received only $30,000. (Originally he was to have received $350,000, but his marriage to a "peasant" in Dutchess County so displeased his father that he was reduced by a codicil in the latter's will.) As for his daughter, Emily, who had married into the Chanler Family and died young, he left her daughter, Margaret Astor Ward Chanler, $700,000. All the rest of the estate he left in equal proportion to his remaining two sons, John Jacob Astor III and William Backhouse Astor, Jr.— with the exception that John Jacob Astor III, as the designated new Head of the House of Astor, would also receive a large proportion of Astor real estate.

In the Astor third generation, however, there arose a challenge to the planned parental order of succession—and this challenge was nothing less than the wife of William Backhouse, the most famous lady in the history of Society. Her name was Caroline Webster Schermerhorn, of a Dutch ship-chandler Family far older than the Astors. Never a pretty woman but with rapidly increasing majesty— she liked to wear a dazzling diamond tiara over her black pompadour and an equally dazzling diamond stomacher—she had from the time of her marriage, in 1853, known exactly what she wanted, and what Caroline Schermerhorn wanted she had a way of getting. First she made her husband drop his middle name, which she detested, and then she herself dropped his first name and became *The* Mrs. Astor. By all odds this was the more important step.

It was, as a matter of fact, against all odds also. For, in the third Astor generation, her husband was frankly referred to, even in the Family, as the "first of the decadent Astors." In contrast, his brother, John Jacob III, was called the "first of the aristocratic Astors." Furthermore, John Jacob III also had married a lady of extremely prominent Family, Miss Charlotte Gibbs, of South Carolina. If she had wanted to use the same tactics as her sister-in-law, there is no question that she could have had the title. Then, too, there was still a third Mrs. Astor, and, for that matter, another Mrs. William Astor. She was Mrs. William Waldorf Astor, the former Mary Dahlgren Paul, wife of the son of John Jacob III. Fortunately for *The* Mrs.

Astor, this lady, described by *Town Topics* as a "typical Philadelphia woman," was above such social climbing; in any case, in 1882 she and her husband went to Italy, her husband having been appointed Minister to that country by President Arthur. By the time of their return, when William Waldorf Astor definitely wished the title for his wife, it was too late. Nonetheless, this Astor insisted for a time in the late 1880's that his wife use the title, and thus Fifth Avenue and Newport were treated by the spectacle of two Mrs. William Astors, living side by side, both of whom insisted on being addressed in person, and having their mail addressed, simply as "Mrs. Astor."

Everything seemed to go wrong for William Waldorf Astor. He built the Waldorf; his brother built the Astoria beside it. He even tried, twice, to run for Congress. But a multimillionaire First Family man running for Congress in the late Nineteenth Century was something very different from a Rockefeller or Harriman, or even a Kennedy, running in the mid-Twentieth Century. Even in New York's so-called "Silk Stocking" district, the man who beat him campaigned with the simple speech, "We have no landlord aristocracy here, thank God!" Finally Astor, in high dudgeon over two Mrs. Astors, two hotels and two election defeats, determined in 1890 to leave the country altogether. "America," he said, "is not a fit place for a gentleman to live." And, he added for good measure, "Politics is closed to a man who will not seek votes in the Irish slums; it isn't easy to see why people of independent means remain here." Two years after arriving in London, still inordinately sensitive about what people were saying about him back home, he perpetrated one of the greatest hoaxes in Family history by causing a false report of his death to go to America. Although several American papers wrote favorably on the subject—on him, not the fact of his death—Astor could take little comfort from the New York *Tribune's* obituary: "The death of William Waldorf Astor, though not an event of great and lasting significance either in the world of action or the world of thought, will be generally deplored."

The death of his wife in 1894 released the one restraining hand on Astor and he now was free to do entirely as he pleased. First he bought newspapers and periodicals; the first of these was the *Pall Mall Observer*, a paper "by gentlemen for gentlemen" which he promptly transformed from Liberal to Conservative. After this came the weekly *Pall Mall Budget* and then the monthly *Pall Mall Magazine;* years later he also bought the Sunday *Observer*. Then too came houses: first Cliveden, then Hever Castle, then Western House, Sorrento, and finally even a $1,500,000 building for the Astor Estate —a house, in a sense, to house other houses. Always eccentric socially, he became increasingly so. When a distinguished British naval captain, Sir Berkeley Milne, came to a concert at his house, having been brought by the lady, who had been invited by Astor, with whom he happened to be dining, Astor met him at the door and summarily told him to leave. The next day he published in his paper: "We are desired to make known that the presence of Captain Sir Berkeley Milne of the Naval and Military Club, Piccadilly, at Mr. Astor's concert last Thursday evening, was uninvited."

Actually this action caused something of a rift in the friendship between Astor and the Prince of Wales, whose Carleton Club had admitted Astor to membership, and Astor was later asked by the Carleton Club to apologize to Captain Milne. Generally speaking, however, the Prince of Wales, as well as most of the rest of the British Aristocracy—who have, since time immemorial, regarded American Society as consisting of Astors and Vanderbilts only— were notably inclined to overlook Astor's boorish behavior. In 1916 he was, incredibly, made a peer, with the title of Baron Astor of Hever Castle and the next year a viscount. He died—this time actually—in 1919, leaving three children to carry on in the next English Astor generation: Waldorf, John Jacob V, and Pauline— who had married, much to Astor's consternation, a commoner, Colonel Herbert Spender-Clay.

In the second English Astor generation, William Waldorf, who was never too close to his father and heartily disliked being a "Lord," chose for his wife someone who caused his father double consternation; she was not only not a member of the British peerage but she was also an American—and a divorcée to boot. Her name, of course, was Nancy Langhorne, one of the most remarkable women ever to grace the English scene. One of five beautiful and highly publicized sisters—in a day when publicity was extremely rare—she was the daughter of Chiswell Dabney Langhorne. Variously a hotel handyman, an auctioneer, a tobacco man, and finally a railway contractor, Langhorne had married a girl named Nancy Keene, a 16-year-old Virginia girl of Irish extraction. By her he had no less than eleven children. He was something of a professional Southerner, but despite his penchant for chewing as well as raising tobacco, he had both charm and a certain amount of luck and was somehow able to bring up his large family. Born in 1879, at 17 Nancy attended a New York finishing school, where her social life was largely under the direction of her older sister, who had married Charles Dana Gibson. At 20 Nancy married Robert Gould Shaw, of the noted Boston Family, but honeymooning at Hot Springs, after only a week, writes Maurice Collis, in his book, "she became aware of some sort of incompatibility." The incompatibility soon led to Shaw's drinking and then, apparently, to "other women," and in 1903 Nancy, who by this time had one son, Bobbie, was divorced. Asked by her father in 1904 if she didn't want a "season's hunting" in England, she went abroad and stayed on, setting up housekeeping on her own—which for a single woman caused a good deal of attention. In 1905 she went over again, and this time, on the boat, met her future husband. A shy man, he was called, like most Astors, "the richest man in the world."

Collis has called the years from 1906 to 1919 Lady Astor's "formative years." During this period, she not only became one of England's leading hostesses but also had five children: another William Waldorf, Phyllis, David, Michael, and John Jacob VII. In 1919, however, after the death of her father-in-law and the elevation of her husband to the House of Lords, she decided to run for the House of Commons. She was already famous for her *bon mots*. On meeting King Edward VII, who asked her to play cards, she said, "Why, I don't even know the difference between a king and a knave." Nonetheless, it was as a campaigner that her wit really came to the fore. One man shouted, "*I* will never vote for you!" She quickly shouted back,

"Thank heaven for that!" In a farming district a farmer sarcastically asked, "Say, missus, how many toes are there on a pig's foot?" Replied Nancy, "Take off your boot, man, and count for yourself." With these flashes came an over-all teasing that the voters loved. Once she took a crying baby in her arms; the child stopped crying as he played with her necklace. "You see," she said, "the way to keep your children happy is to let 'em play with a rope of pearls." And, concluding one speech, she said, "And now, my dears, I'm going back to one of my beautiful palaces to sit down in my tiara and do nothing and when I roll out in my car I will splash you all with mud and look the other way."

From 1920 all the way to 1945, this amazing woman retained her seat in Parliament, and even the slings and arrows which came her way as the leader of the so-called "Cliveden Set," which was accused of prewar Hitler appeasement, had little effect on her popularity. After the war she described herself as an "extinct volcano" and once, in a reflective moment, she said, "My vigor, vitality and cheek repel me—I am the kind of woman I would run from." Still, by her eightieth birthday she was at last philosophical. "Years ago," she said, "I thought old age would be dreadful because I should not be able to do things I would want to do. Now I find there is nothing I want to do after all."

The second son of the founding father of the English Astors was John Jacob Astor V. Like the English Astors in general—and in contrast to the American Astors—he was a remarkable, public-spirited man. He went first to Eton and Oxford and then served an aideship to the Viceroy of India. A Major in World War I, he was twice badly wounded, at Ypres and again at Cambrai; during the war he married Lady Violet Mary Elliot Nairne, daughter of the Earl of Minto and widow of an officer who had been killed at Ypres. An unsuccessful candidate for Parliament in 1920, in 1922 he bought for $7,000,000 the *Times*. Although he, as well as his brother and sister-in-law, was affected by the resentment against the Cliveden Set, he personally made many notable efforts in the direction of Anglo-American good will, among them being the collection of the names, for a memorial of some 28,000 Americans who either died in Britain or on service in British bases during World War II. As for the irrepressible Lady Astor, she said, in one of her numerous quotes on the subject, "I'm not asking for England and America to like each other, but they must work together."

Even as early as 1935 they were doing so, for in that year, as Harvey O'Connor records, the British Parliament boasted no less than five Astors: Waldorf in the Lords; Nancy in Commons for Plymouth; her son, Bill (William Waldorf Astor II) in Commons for East Fulham; Lord Willoughby de Eresby, his brother-in-law, in Commons for Rutland; and John Jacob V in Commons for Dover. In addition, Ronald Tree, who had married a niece of Nancy's, also was seated in Commons.

Meanwhile, the American branch of the Astor Family was having its difficulties. In *The* Mrs. Astor's lifetime—she lived until 1908—the Family as well as the Four Hundred in general remained under control. Mrs. Astor saw no evil, heard no evil, and above all, spoke no evil. Gossips could speak of the fact that her husband had gay parties on his yacht and ask her where she was, but Mrs. Astor simply rose above it. "I have never even set foot on his yacht," she said. "Dreadful confession for a wife, is it not? But I am such a poor sailor."

But *The* Mrs. Astor's children were, in the fourth Astor generation, soon demonstrating once more the First Family axiom that too much money and too many marriages can quickly bring about adverse effects. Mrs. Astor's eldest child was her daughter Emily. When Emily expressed the wish to marry James J. Van Alen, Mrs. Astor was not pleased. As for Mrs. Astor's husband, he was something more than not pleased. "Damned," he said, "if I want my family mixed in with the Van Alens." When this intelligence was communicated to young Van Alen's father, General Van Alen, he promptly challenged the elder Astor to a duel. Both chose up weapons and seconds, who consulted code books; then, after a series of notes, the elder Astor "himself consulted the code book," it is recorded, "and decided Van Alen had no right to satisfaction." Eventually he apologized, there was no duel and, in 1876, Emily and Van Alen were married.

The Astors' second daughter, in her turn, married James Roosevelt Roosevelt, thus making the second Astor-Roosevelt alliance, while the youngest daughter, Caroline, married Orme Wilson, Jr., of the famed "marrying Wilsons." The marital career of Mrs. Astor's "other" daughter, Charlotte, was, however, the beginning of real trouble. After a brilliant début, she married James Coleman Drayton, of Philadelphia and South Carolina, and then proceeded to have four children. At this juncture there broke the greatest scandal in Astor history. From a series of published letters it became apparent that Charlotte had gone astray—and with no less a gentleman than Hallett Alsop Borrowe, clubman and a vice-president of Equitable Life. There was, unfortunately, all too much proof, since Borrowe had even committed the heinous crime of selling Charlotte's incriminating letters to the newspapers. For weeks New York waited breathlessly to see if, again, there might be an Astor-caused duel. And indeed Drayton kept challenging Borrowe, and Borrowe kept accepting challenges—once they even crossed the Atlantic on the same ship—but still, when the chips were down, they avoided each other and once more there was no duel. In the end Charlotte was rather anticlimactically granted a divorce on the grounds of desertion resulting from "cruel suspicion as to her marital fidelity." She later married George Haig.

If all this was not enough to bring down Mrs. Astor's jet-black dyed hair with sorrow to the grave, there was finally the matter of the marital career of her son, John Jacob Astor IV. In 1891 he had married perhaps the outstanding beauty of the whole Four Hundred, Ava Willing—later Lady Ribblesdale—of Philadelphia, and the very next year, at 28, on the death of his father, he became the youngest head of the House of Astor in history. A reticent, brooding man, he was an inventor of sorts; among his contributions were a bicycle brake and a strange device to pick up dust from roads—the latter an outgrowth of one of his two chief hobbies, automobiling. He also enjoyed yachting and the Spanish War, coming out of the latter a Colonel and for the first time in his life feeling useful. None-theless, he had always taken both the Astor Estate duties and Four Hundred parties about equally in stride, and when, in 1910, he and Ava got a remarkably well-hushed-up divorce in New City, New York, the Four Hundred were stunned. They were even more stunned when that "Season," the 46-year-old "Colonel" Astor, as he was now called, "received" at his home at 840 Fifth Avenue, along with an 18-year-old girl named Madeleine Force; the latter was, said one reporter, "a member of an old Brooklyn family." Few of the Four Hundred, however, accepted the invitation to meet the young lady, and when, the following season, Colonel Astor and Miss Force were married, there were so many repercussions that, the season after that, they decided to go abroad. By the time they were ready to come back and try again it was the spring of 1912, and the ship on which they sailed was the *Titanic*. Madeleine, five months pregnant with John Jacob Astor VI, was saved, but Astor was last seen on the boat deck trying to kick in the door of the kennel where his dog was kept. Asked by a bystander, a barber, if he wanted a lifejacket, Astor refused it. "I am not going to jump," he said. He was not drowned but was killed, it is recorded, "by a falling object." When his body was recovered, he was found to have $2,500 in his pockets.

An era was, to all intents and purposes, also hit by a falling object. With the death of John Jacob Astor IV, the American House was already a house divided. By the terms of Astor's divorce from Ava Willing, he received custody of their son, Vincent, but Mrs. Astor received custody of their daughter, Alice. Both of these children, as well as John Jacob Astor VI, were to marry at least three times: Alice to Serge Obolensky, to Raimund von Hofmannsthal, to Philip Harding, and then to Bartholomew Playdell-Bouverie; Vin-cent, first to Helen Dinsmore Huntington, second to Mary Cushing (later Mrs. James Fosburgh), and third to Mary Brooke Russell Marshall; John Jacob, first to Ellen ("Tuckie") French, second to Gertrude ("Trudie") Gretsch, and third to Dolores ("Dolly") Full-man. Finally, in 1958, young John Jacob's affairs, marital and otherwise, had become so complicated that he applied to the New York State Supreme Court to find out to whom he was wed.

Vincent, or "V.A.," as he was called, was brought up strictly. To teach him the value of money, at St. George's School he was placed on an allowance of 50 cents a month, 35 cents if his marks or his conduct were poor. He went to Harvard and grew up to the height of six feet four inches—already, even before the sinking of the *Titanic*, a taciturn, shy man with a difficult personality. Six months before his twenty-first birthday, he inherited $70,000,000 of his father's $87,000,000 estate, of which about $63,000,000 was in real estate. He never went back to Harvard. He did, however, join forty-two clubs and also turned manfully, albeit rather doggedly, to the management of his real estate.

"Every dollar," Vincent said in one of his rare speeches, "is a soldier to do your bidding." When his "Cousin Franklin" and the New Deal came in, Astor was an early supporter of his and often lent his vast yacht *Nourmahal* to the President for cruises. When Astor's friend, Raymond Moley, became disenchanted, however, so did Astor; largely to provide his friend an outlet, he founded the magazine *Today*, which in 1937 merged into *Newsweek*, with Astor becoming the majority stockholder. Meanwhile, through his various wives and other troubles, he became increasingly moody and was particularly difficult in the early morning. When visiting in Jamaica's Sunset Lodge, he became incensed over a trifling matter one early morning and rang up the owner, Mrs. Carmen Pringle, on the telephone. "After all," he said crossly, "you own the place." Mrs. Pringle said nothing and promptly fixed the difficulty, but the next time she came to New York she stopped at the Astors' hotel, the St. Regis. She, too, was troubled by something, which happened early in the morning, and took the occasion to call Astor long-distance at his home in Rhinebeck, New York. Astor was incensed. "But why?" asked Mrs. Pringle gently. "After all, you own the place."

In his latter years Astor was also increasingly depressed over the activities of his stepbrother, with whom he had long been on long-distance terms. Young "Jackaster," as he was familiarly called, evidently had on occasion, between his wives and various troubles, ideas about working. Seldom, however, did they come to fruition. "I have found," he said in one of his memorable quotes, "that work interferes with pleasure." Once, though, during the depression, young John Jacob did try working—in a downtown brokerage office. But it was to no avail. "I didn't finish until five o'clock," he said, "and by the time I got uptown it was six. And then I had to get up early the next morning."

Altogether, the American Astor Family in its fifth generation would have made the original John Jacob turn in his grave. He would also have so turned only a short time before Vincent Astor's death, in 1958, when the latter was forced to sell his interest in Astor Plaza—on Park Avenue and 53rd Street—to the First National City Bank. Vincent had been unable to raise financing for its development, but John Jacob would never have sold. Where land was concerned, he had two mottoes. One was "Buy und hold. Let udders improve." The other, or "udder," was even simpler. "Don't sell nuddings." Once asked if, at times, this wouldn't make a man short of cash, he replied, "A man who hass a million dollars is as vell off as if he ver rich."

The same sentiment was put in a rather different way by John Jacob Astor VI when he wearily confided to a young lady that he was sick and tired of the public thinking he was so rich. "Everybody thinks," he said sadly, "that I have $90,000,000. Actually I only have $33,000,000."

The second Family in the great triumvirate of American First Familyland is, of course, the Vanderbilt Family. The American ancestor of the Vanderbilts was a man named Jan Aertsen van der Bilt, a Dutch farmer who came over to the New World from the village of Bilt, near Utrecht, and settled in the neighborhood of Brooklyn about 1650. About 1715 the Family moved to New Dorp, Staten Island. For four generations they were, as we have seen, "miserably poor squatters." Then all of a sudden, as it were, and out of nowhere, as it seemed, the fourth generation became the all-time all-American success story, the original Horatio Alger and the crowning glory of the age-old saga of the self-made. His name, of course, was Cornelius Vanderbilt.

Just why this happened disturbs pious believers in the all-powerful workings of heredity. However, they can take some satisfaction in the knowledge that the girl whom Cornelius' father had married, a woman named Phebe Hand, was vastly superior, both in distinction of ancestry and in constructive ambition for her children, to anybody with whom the Family had, up to that time, allied itself.

When the fourth of her nine children tired, at age 17, of farm chores and wanted to run away from his father—although in those days labor was due one's parents until one was 21—instead of scolding him, she made him a bargain. She would advance him $100 to buy a periauger, a two-masted, flat-bottomed sailing scow, if in the one month left before his 18th birthday he could plow, harrow and plant with corn an eight-acre lot. The boy promptly made a deal with every other young boy he could round up; if they would help him, he would give them sailboat rides. Late in his life, in a rare philosophic mood, he recalled the incident. "I didn't feel as much real satisfaction," he said, "when I made two million in that Harlem corner as I did on that bright May morning sixty years before, when I stepped into my own periauger, hoisted my own sail, and put my own hand on my own tiller."

One thing is certain. From that bright May morning on, his was the greatest success story not only in America but perhaps in the entire history of business the world over. Indeed, just seventy years after he had received his first $100 from his mother—which was advanced, not given—he was worth, in steamships, railroads and hard cash, $100,000,000, and this in a day when such a sum would be worth, by today's money, in the billions. Asked how he did it, he replied, "Never tell nobody what yer goin' ter do 'til yer do it," and, "Don't never buy nothing you don't want or sell nothing you ain't got."

Even at the age of 16, over six feet tall, blue-eyed and flaxen-haired, Vanderbilt was not only more man than boy, but a giant of a man at that, in physique, courage and energy, if not in education, imagination and character. People set their watches, it was said, on the arrivals and departures of his ferryboat. Once, trying to beat another boat by singlehanded poling, he slipped, and the poling oar all but crushed his chest; he bore the scar for life. Again, in the War of 1812, in which he characteristically fought a war of his own against rival transports, an officer in the Army, unjustly working for another ferryman, came on board and ordered him to stop his boat. When Vanderbilt refused, the officer drew his sword. Vanderbilt rushed him, fists against the sword, and promptly floored the officer with a right to the jaw.

Such a man had little time for girls. Profane, tobacco-chewing and generally uncouth, he made as little impression on the few girls he did meet—passengers on his ferryboats—as he himself was later to make on the Mesdames Astor or the Knickerbocker Families. When it came time for marrying—which he chose to do at age 19 against his parents' wishes—he chose his first cousin, a girl he had known since her barefoot days. A plain, hard-working, good-natured girl named Sophia Johnson, she had hardly more schooling than he, and, in her early teens, was doing housework for a more prosperous neighbor. They were married one evening after his work, and the next morning he was on the dock as usual at six o'clock waiting for passengers.

In the following years, the "Commodore," as he was at first mockingly called, moved from sail to steam and finally to railroads. In 1829 he sold his Staten Island house and moved to New York and made a characteristic frontal attack on the Society of the day. It was, however, doomed to failure. Although his name was linked in civic affairs with such merchants as Astor, Peter Cooper, Moses Taylor and Peter Goelet, the ladies of the old Knickerbocker Families found his tobacco-chewing too much for their carpets and his servant-pinching too much for their dinner parties, and, much to their relief, as well as to the relief of his wife, he soon returned to Staten Island to build another mansion—which he called Bellona

Hall. In 1844 he was, surprisingly enough, elected to the then eight-year-old Union Club. Recognition of his status as one of the most successful shipping and railroad men in the world pleased Vanderbilt, but at the same time his diversions at the club were limited to whist playing. One day he returned from a visit to the club with his son-in-law. "I have just seen the funniest thing," he told his wife, "Horace Clark and three grown-up men playing cards for nothing."

In 1846 he was back again for another assault on Manhattan, this time with a town house at 1 Washington Place. This time he tried without his wife, whom, in one of the shabbiest episodes of his career, he had committed to an insane asylum. During this period he also added a new diversion to his whist playing—driving a handsome pair of trotters. At the same time, to dramatize his success, he determined to put up a monument in Central Park—which would not only be the tallest monument in the city, but also one erected to the "joint glory" of Commodore Vanderbilt (first) and George Washington (second). Once more, however, he was saved by the only person who had ever been able to do anything with him—his mother, who was by that time in her eighties. She persuaded him to give up the idea of the statue and take his wife back from the asylum.

On his own again in 1853, the Commodore decided that if he couldn't impress Society at home, he would at least impress it abroad. First he pointedly resigned from the Union Club, and then he announced that he would, at age 59, take the first vacation of his life. And to do this, he said, he would build the most magnificent private yacht that had ever been seen; in it he proposed to cruise all over the Western world. As usual he was as good as his boast. His *North Star*, costing half a million dollars—an incredible sum for those days—ushered in, in style, the Golden Days of the Private Yacht. Over 270 feet in length and 2,300 tons in weight, she had a ballroom running half the length of her deck, and every one of her saloons was furnished either in rosewood upholstered in green plush or in a Commodore Vanderbilt idea of the period of Louis XIV; her dining room was decorated in ligneous marble adorned with medallions of Washington, Franklin, Webster and Clay (but no Vanderbilt). For this cruise the Commodore buried the hatchet with his family, taking all of them with him, even his in-laws. He also took along a minister, the Rev. J. O. Choules, for grace and evening prayers. "There never was any disagreement," the Rev. Mr. Choules reported. "The Commodore did the swearing and I did the praying."

Once again, however, the Commodore was not an unqualified success. The leader of the American colony in London, the banker George Peabody, entertained him, but London Society and the American Ambassador remained aloof. In Paris also he was cavalierly treated by Napoleon III—in fact, during the entire voyage, the only royal personage he was able to entice on board was the Grand Duke Constantine of, of all places, Russia, and the Grand Duke's sole request was, prophetically enough, that his naval officers be allowed to make sketches of the yacht. As for the Eastern Mediterranean countries, these were highly suspicious that Vanderbilt was some kind of revolutionist. "They were relieved," says Wheaton Lane, "when they decided he was only a mad American."

Yet, strangely enough, he had something to offer. After the death of his wife and mother, he became involved with spiritualists like Victoria Woodhull and Tennessee Claflin. But later, married again to a gentle, 30-year-old Alabama girl with the odd name of Miss Frank Armstrong Crawford, he began to mellow and was finally, in 1873, persuaded to give $500,000 to Central University at Nashville—which afterwards became Vanderbilt University. "Folks may say," he thundered, "that I don't care about education, but it ain't true. I've been to England and seen them lords and other fellows, and I knew that I had twice as much brains as they had maybe, and yet I had to keep still for fear I'd expose myself, damn it."

Somehow it was touching—in the same curious way that so, too, was the scene at his deathbed when the doctor prescribed, for his $100,000,000 patient, the richest man in the world, a glass of champagne every morning. "Champagne!" growled Vanderbilt with almost his last breath, "*every* morning. Damn it, I tell you, Doc, I can't afford it. Won't sody water do?"

The Commodore and his wife, Sophia, had thirteen children, nine of whom—a keen source of irritation to him—were daughters. Of the Commodore's sons, one died young, and his youngest and favorite child, George Washington Vanderbilt, died in service in the Civil War. As for his second son, just as John Jacob Astor had one son who was hopelessly insane all his life, so too did Cornelius Vanderbilt have one who all his life was both physically and mentally unwell. The only son who was not named for a President, he was called Cornelius Jeremiah, was the first, but by no means the last, of Vanderbilt black sheep. An epileptic, and gambler and ne'er-do-well besides, the Commodore first had him put in a sanitarium and then, when he had improved, let him out; but when the boy struck out on his own and went west, that was too much for Vanderbilt. He had him arrested, brought back home and banished to Hartford, Connecticut. From that time on he gave him $200 a week. As for his eldest son, William Henry Vanderbilt, who was named for William Henry Harrison and was obviously the one who would eventually succeed the Commodore, he was in his early days a severe or, as his father put it, a "damn" disappointment. Indeed, his father often described him, even in his presence, as "blatherskite," "beetlehead" and "sucker."

When his son married, at age 19, Marie Louisa Kissam, who was a young lady of refinement and "good family"—her father was a Brooklyn clergyman—the Commodore was enraged. He, too, had married at that age, but he regarded his son as much too weak and unstable to do the same. When William's health become poor, it was the final straw; his father also banished him, to a farm on Staten Island. One day the farm needed fertilizer, and William proposed to his father that he buy the manure from his father's horsecar stables at the Harlem Railroad. He offered $4 a load and the Commodore promptly accepted, thinking his son had made another sucker deal. The next day he came upon William on the dock ready to start for Staten Island with his scow filled with manure. "How many loads have you got there?" the Commodore asked, smiling in satisfaction. "One, Father," replied William without change of expression, "one scow load."

From that time on his father's attitude toward William changed for the better. Furthermore, since Cornelius Jeremiah had no children and all present-day Vanderbilts are descended, in the male line, from William Henry, they owe their well-being, in a sense, to that one scow load. For the Old Commodore, who at his death was to cut off all nine of his daughters with but $4,000,000 together—at the same time leaving William $90,000,000—might well have cut off William too, had the son not finally proved himself.

Ironically enough, it was the long-suffering, gentle, open-minded and relatively liberal William, who is remembered today for only one line—one which, ironically enough, the Vanderbilts themselves maintain he never said—"The public be damned." It happened, they say, when a newspaperman, attempting to get an interview which William did not want to give, said, "Mr. Vanderbilt, your public demands an interview." This, William's children claim, made their father laugh. "Oh," he said, "my public be damned."

There is quite a difference, of course, between this and the usual version of the story. But somehow one can picture the Old Commodore being once more, where his children were concerned, downright disappointed. He should not have been, for William Henry was one of the most remarkable second-generation scions in Family history. Already 56 years old when his father died—and to die himself eight years later—he managed, in that incredibly short time, to more than double the $90,000,000 he inherited. As moderate a man as his father was immoderate, he even ate sparingly, going weeks at a time without eating meat, never using tobacco, and dressing in plain black. He was strange-looking, wearing drooping "Piccadilly" whiskers, but he was also, as old-timers have recalled, an inspiring sight as he drove his famous trotters, "Maud S" and "Aldine."

Furthermore, with eight children himself, William treated his brother and sisters handsomely. The Commodore had left the weak Cornelius Jeremiah with only the interest on $200,000; William promptly upped the trust to a million. He also gave each of his sisters, out of his own fortune, a present of $500,000. In 1875, after dinner and seated in his library in the midst of a heated argument with

Robert Garrett over the rights of the Baltimore & Ohio Railroad to enter New York, he suddenly dropped dead. In his will, besides taking handsome care of four sons and a daughter, he left a half million to Vanderbilt University, a half million to the College of Physicians and Surgeons, $100,000 to the Metropolitan Museum, and $50,000 to the Home for Intemperate Men.

Fifty years ago the famous Wall Street broker Henry Clews declared that the young Vanderbilts who had succeeded to the estate of their father—Cornelius II, William Kissam, Frederick, and George Washington II—proved "how fast human evolution under favorable circumstances progresses in this country." "In other countries," Clews said, "it takes many generations to develop such men as the present Vanderbilts. In this country three generations in this instance have produced some of the best examples of nature's nobility, which is superior in every respect to the vainglorious production which emanates from the succession of a hundred earls in England, or even a greater number of barons, princes, and kings on the continent of Europe." Not content with this effusion, Clews, who was himself the son of an English potter and had become "more American than an American," called the young Vanderbilts "splendid specimens of nature's noblemen," and added that the "parchment nobility" of England and the Continent made "a sorry showing" when compared with the Vanderbilts.

Besides his four "nature's noblemen," William Henry Vanderbilt had produced four daughters—Margaret Louisa, who married Elliott F. Shepard; Emily Thorn, who married William D. Sloane and, after Sloane's death, Henry White; Florence Adèle, who married Hamilton McKown Twombly; and Eliza Osgood, who married William Seward Webb. Of these daughters Florence Adèle (Mrs. Twombly) reigned, as we have noted, as *grande dame* of the Family. All four daughters fared well under their father's will, each receiving an elegant house on Fifth Avenue in the vicinity of the father's mansion, and $10,000,000 worth of securities.

The sons, of course, fared even better. The two oldest sons,

Cornelius II and William Kissam, received some $60,000,000 each and the two youngest, Frederick and George Washington, got about $20,000,000 each. Not having been given homes, all four set about building them. Cornelius built at Newport "The Breakers," the country's largest resort cottage; William Kissam put up three magnificent homes; Frederick acquired a 600-acre estate at Hyde Park; and George Washington II erected "Biltmore," the country's most elaborate estate ever, near Asheville, North Carolina. Although the four may not have been up to the extravagant praises of Mr. Clews, they were extremely able third-generation men. Cornelius II, for example, became the railroad magnate of the Family and contributed various paintings—among them Rosa Bonheur's "The Horse Fair"—to New York's Metropolitan Museum. As for William Kissam, he was, according to Frank Crowninshield, "the greatest supporter of sport, opera, yachting, racing, art, architecture, coaching, and the theater in American social annals."

Frederick Vanderbilt died in 1938 at the age of 82. By that time he had served fifty-six years on the Board of the "Nickel Plate" railroad and sixty-one years on the Board of the New York Central. The only one of the brothers with a college education, he devoted his money and spare time to science and, at the same time, managed by shrewd investments to die the richest of all the brothers. Some idea of his wealth may be garnered from the fact that he kept one checking account which had in it, for long periods of time, as much as $3,000,000. The fourth brother, George Washington Vanderbilt, was an explorer, stock breeder, and pioneer in scientific forestry.

One striking thing about the four brothers was that marital instability—the Achilles' heel of later generations of Vanderbilts—did not afflict them acutely. True, Frederick married a girl who was not only a divorcée, but also a first cousin; the bride, Louise Anthony Torrance, had been divorced from Alfred Torrance, the son of William Henry Vanderbilt's sister. However, the union was a happy one, as was that of George Washington II, who married Edith Stuyvesant Dresser. William Kissam, however, was not so fortunate. He married Alva Smith, but the couple were later divorced—the first in a long succession of Vanderbilt divorces. He later married Anne Harriman Sands Rutherford. But, unhappy though William Kissam's first marriage was, it was also a milestone in the Family's history. For, with the advent of Alva Smith, daughter of a Mobile, Alabama, cotton planter, the Vanderbilts' social deficiencies were overcome once and for all. As was the case with so many other social leaders in the history of American Society, Alva was out to prove something; she wanted to prove not only that she was as good as the Vanderbilts—she never tired of explaining that her mother was a Desha of Kentucky—but also that the Vanderbilts were just as good as the Astors. This took some doing, since Alva, who later married O. H. P. Belmont, was not destined to be a Vanderbilt for long. Her key maneuver came when she announced plans for what is still generally regarded as the most elaborate dress ball in the annals of American Society. A few days before the ball— which was held on March 6, 1883—Alva heard that young Miss Caroline Astor, daughter of *The* Mrs. Astor, was busy organizing and rehearsing a "Star Quadrille" to put on at the ball. Mrs. Vanderbilt promptly sent word via a mutual enemy that she was sorry Mrs. Astor's daughter was putting herself to so much trouble, since, inasmuch as Mrs. Astor had never paid a call on her, it would be simply impossible—indeed, out of the question—for her to invite Mrs. Astor's daughter to the ball. *The* Mrs. Astor fretted and fumed, but there was nothing she could do but summon her carriage, drive to Mrs. Vanderbilt's home, and leave her card; and in answer to this capitulation Mrs. Vanderbilt dispatched young Miss Caroline's invitation. The die was cast. The mountain had come to Mahomet, and the Vanderbilts were for the first time a real "First."

Though they were now in "Society," the Vanderbilts still did not ascend easily into the upper reaches of the American Aristocracy. Celebrities they continued to be, and in fact give promise of always being; they were also, generally speaking, men and women of far greater charm than their contemporaries. The Vanderbilt eyes were famous—their Oriental look was likewise a trade-mark. But, despite these attributes, as well as a certain indefinite flair and dash, the workings of too much money and publicity and too little character and stability were, with certain notable exceptions, inexorable. By the fourth generation the Family showed at least some signs of wear and tear, as well as some outstanding citizens.

Frederick Vanderbilt, the one who married a cousin, had no children. George Washington II had only one child, Cornelia, who married the Hon. John Francis Amherst Cecil. In the William Kissam and Cornelius II branches there were, however, troubles which continued into the fifth generation. Although one son of William Kissam, Harold Stirling Vanderbilt, Cup racer and inventor of contract bridge, held the line at one marriage—to Gertrude Conaway— and led an able, aristocratic life, his marriage was without issue. Meanwhile his sister Consuelo, later Mme. Jacques Balsan, had been literally forced, as we have seen, to marry the Ninth Duke of Marlborough; unhappy though this first marriage was, it produced two children, John, the Marquis of Blandford, and Lord Ivor Charles Spencer Churchill. Mme. Balsan herself is one of the finest examples of the Vanderbilts as outstanding American Aristocrats.

The third child of William Kissam was the energetic and famous "Willie K." who in 1904 sponsored the first official race for motorcars in America, a 284-mile contest over country roads on Long Island. Frank Crowninshield gave this errant Vanderbilt full credit for popularizing the sport into an industry:

> It was very largely because of his interest in motoring, and that of other fashionable men of the day (David Bishop, Peter Cooper Hewitt, Albert Bostwick, Foxhall Keene, Joseph L. Breese, John Jacob Astor, Albert R. Shattuck, H. Rogers Winthrop, Lloyd Warren, etc.), that automobiles were, at the beginning (1) tolerated, (2) encouraged and improved, and (3) finally accepted everywhere and made the average American's way of life.

"Willie K." married Virginia ("Birdie") Fair, and later, after a divorce, married Rose Warburton. A carefree man, Willie K. was traveling in leisurely fashion aboard his $2,500,000 yacht late in 1941 when his faithful valet Jenkinson knocked on his cabin door one morning, bringing coffee and the stock-market quotations. "Central had hit 25," Willie K. wrote in his diary. "It was time to go home." Willie's branch of the Vanderbilts was characteristically complicated in its marital affairs. His daughter Muriel married first Frederick Church, second Henry Phelps, and third Dr. John Payson Adams, while his daughter Consuelo II, married first Earl E. T. Smith, second Henry Gassaway Davis III, third William John Warburton, and fourth N. Clarkson Earl, Jr. Indeed, by the time Willie K.'s stepdaughter, Rosie Warburton, in the succeeding generation, married Dr. William Gaynor and then Hugh Chisholm, it was becoming impossible to tell the Vanderbilts from anyone else—except that, as exemplified in Rosie's case, in each succeeding divorce and remarriage a scandal of major proportions was often involved.

In the Cornelius II branch, too, things had already begun to slide, although this was not at first so readily apparent. Cornelius II and Alice Gwynne had seven children: William Henry II, Alice Gwynne, Cornelius III, Gertrude, Alfred Gwynne I, Reginald, and Gladys. William Henry died at 21 of typhoid fever, while he was at Yale; Alice Gwynne also died without issue. As for the third son, Cornelius III, he incurred his father's displeasure by marrying Grace Wilson, of the famed "marrying Wilsons." Grace was the daughter of Richard T. Wilson, of Loudon, Tennessee, who had started on the road to fortune by selling blankets to the Confederate Army; he lived to see one daughter married to Ogden Goelet, of the New York real estate family, and his son married to Carrie Astor, daughter of The Mrs. Astor. Grace, who had been born in New York, had so obviously set her cap for a Vanderbilt that the displeasure of her father-in-law, and his eventual slighting of her in his will, was understandable. Nonetheless, in a story which closely parallels that of her aunt, née Alva Smith, Grace did manage to claw her way into the position of being The Mrs. Vanderbilt. Her son, the present Cornelius Vanderbilt, Jr., has written that his mother never entered a nightclub, never granted an interview; such statements have, however, been taken with a grain of salt by all who knew her and, for that matter, by the Vanderbilt Family itself. For example, when asked whether *The* Mrs. Vanderbilt liked publicity, the late Margaret Emerson (her sister-in-law by marriage) exclaimed, "Publicity? Grace invented it!" Some indication of how much more seriously the public took *The* Mrs. Vanderbilt than did the Vanderbilts themselves is given by Margaret Emerson Vanderbilt's son, the present Alfred Gwynne: "Honestly," he says, "I can't ever remember meeting her. I must have, of course, at some big family things and stuff, but I can't remember it."*

Perhaps the most typical *The* Mrs. Vanderbilt story—it is a favorite among the Vanderbilt clan—concerns the time on the Riviera when she complained to the maître d' about the table where she had been seated. She pointed out the one she preferred to have, but the maître d' expressed regret that she could not have it: the table was reserved for a prince. "Then," said Mrs. Vanderbilt, pointing to another table, "I will have that one over there." Once again the maître d' disappointed her—the table was being held for an English duchess. Whereupon in a voice clearly audible to a nearby table of Englishmen Mrs. Vanderbilt complained, "It is only here in France that I am treated this way. In England I take a rank something like that of the Princess of Wales." This was too much for one Englishman. "Oh?" he said. "Then who is your queen?"

An equally eye-opening story is told by an American, Eugene Reynal: "One day I went to dinner at Mrs. Vanderbilt's and I'll never forget it. It was literally impossible to have a conversation with her. She was *without* conversation. So, during the lull, I looked down the table and I suddenly realized that the name of

* Even Cornelius, Jr., in another of his memoirs of his mother, admits her predilection for publicity. "All her life," he says, "even when she was being maligned, Mother adored the limelight." Mrs. Vanderbilt's own letters indicate perhaps even better how incredibly egocentric she was. One example will suffice: "As soon as the King entered he looked around the house and again spied us out. He then pointed me out to some other royalties . . . and he said how charming I was. And they all said I had the most beautiful jewels in the house that night. This same lady in waiting said the King of England had told them before this that at Naples I had looked so lovely at the opera! Is it not kind of him to recommend me to the Italian King and Queen?"

every one there began with an 'R.' We were all obviously her secretary's 'R' list. But as I looked closer I didn't feel too badly. At least we did spill over a bit. There were a couple of 'S's.' "

For such a woman to be taken so seriously for so many years, not only by the columns and the tabloid press but also by visiting royalty and celebrities, is certainly something of a comment on the downhill slide of Society in general.

However, in some contrast to his wife, Cornelius Vanderbilt III —or "General" Vanderbilt, as he was sometimes called, from the fact that he had been a General in World War I—took little interest in Society and was a hard worker. He had left school at 16 to take a clerkship in a bank, and even after he became the head of the House of Vanderbilt he seemed to take a sort of refuge from his wife by arriving at work each morning at his desk in the Grand Central Building before a single clerk appeared. Among his business ventures was the construction of the Hotel Vanderbilt. Along with the General—far different from *The* Mrs. Vanderbilt—also belongs Gertrude, the fourth child of Cornelius Vanderbilt. She was the sculptress who married Harry Payne Whitney and was one of the greatest women in First Family history.

The fifth child of Cornelius II was Alfred Gwynne Vanderbilt I. After his father's break with Cornelius III over his marriage to Grace Wilson, Alfred I became head of the House of Vanderbilt; at his father's death he inherited some $42,000,000, of which he promptly and voluntarily gave $6,000,000 to the disinherited Cornelius. Perhaps the most charming of all the Vanderbilts, he led what passed in those days for a life of stardom. Later the movie stars would take over, but in those days the young Vanderbilts reigned alone. And if this life was fast horses, fast automobiles, fast yachts, and—at least some said—fast women, Vanderbilt was indeed quite a sight to see as he drove his famous drags, "Viking" and "Venture," along Fifth Avenue or along the Brighton road. Wayne Andrews recalls the time when Vanderbilt and insurance heir James Hazen Hyde undertook, in October of 1901, to tool a drag at top speed between New York and Philadelphia; in addition to seventy-eight horses, the youthful capitalists required a retinue made up of a carriage expert, a photographer, and a valet. They made Philadelphia in nine hours, twenty-five minutes, and after stopping for six minutes, were back in New York in another ten hours, ten minutes.

Like later movie stars also, young Vanderbilts were often divorced. Alfred's divorce from his first wife, Elsie French, was a rather messy one, costing him $10,000,000 and appearance at a trial wherein witnesses associated his name with a former St. Louis belle, Agnes O'Brien Ruiz, wife of the Cuban attaché in Washington. Afterwards Mrs. Ruiz committed suicide. But the show went on, and in 1911 Alfred Gwynne married the late Margaret Emerson McKim, a remarkable woman with whom he was idyllically happy; in the short life that remained to them together they were probably the most sought-after couple of their time. Then, in 1915, Alfred sailed for England on the ill-fated *Lusitania*, which was struck amidships by two German torpedoes and sunk with a loss of 1,198 persons. After the first explosion Alfred, who could not swim, gave his life belt to a lady and directed his valet, Ronald Denyer, to "save all the kiddies you can, boy." Unfortunately, both master and valet were drowned. A survivor recalled his last glimpse of Vanderbilt: "He stood there, the personification of sportsmanlike coolness. In my eyes he was the figure of a gentleman waiting for a train."

The sixth child of Cornelius II was Reginald, the famed "Reggie." Another darling of the rotogravures and gossip columns, he was considerably less attractive than his brother but led an almost equally spectacular life. His life was devoted to gambling, drinking, and automobiling. In the last-named pursuit he caused a great deal of comment by taking along his bull terrier, its legs enclosed in leather leggings, its back covered by a leather coat, and its eyes shielded by goggles. Reggie's first wife was Cathleen Neilson, his second Gloria Morgan, of the much-publicized Morgan twins. He announced his engagement to Gloria in rather typical fashion by giving a dinner to which he invited just one guest—Maury Paul. The couple were married in 1923, and by 1925 Reggie's doctor was advising Gloria Morgan Vanderbilt that her husband's drinking must be cut out. "That," she later wrote, "was like a sentence of almost complete annihilation. It is difficult to break the habit of a lifetime." Under such a verdict the only solution was to keep Reggie away from America and his old set for as long as possible. That his wife was not altogether successful in doing so is evidenced by the fact that, a few months after getting the doctor's report, Reggie died at Newport.

The seventh, and last, child of Cornelius was Gladys, the least publicized and by the same token perhaps the most aristocratic Vanderbilt of her generation. A gentle, dignified woman, she was married in 1908 to Count Lâszló Széchényi, whose father had been a diplomatic representative of the Austro-Hungarian court. From 1921 to 1923 the Count was, himself, the Hungarian Minister to Washington. He died in 1938, leaving five daughters: Cornelia, Gladys, Alice, Sylvia and Nadine. His widow is the present owner of the last large Vanderbilt mansion, the "Breakers" at Newport, and leases it, for $1 a year, to the Newport Preservation Society; she herself maintains rooms on the top floor. From this vantage point, as she watches the public troop in for $1.50 a head, to "view the remains," as she calls it, she has had an unusual opportunity to see firsthand the Decline and Fall of the Social Empire. "I guess when all is said and done," she says, "the people who should have set the standard, didn't."

In 1952, three-quarters of a century after her grandfather had been accused of saying "the public be damned," Gladys Vanderbilt could have been discovered taking, under an assumed name, a Dale Carnegie course on How to Win Friends and Influence People.

The fifth generation of Vanderbilts includes such well-known citizens as the three sons of Alfred Gwynne I: the oldest is William Henry Vanderbilt, the former Governor of Rhode Island, born of Alfred's first marriage, to Elsie French; the other sons, born of his second wife, are Alfred Gwynne II, horseman and guiding spirit of the World Veterans Association, and George, explorer and big-game hunter. The present generation also includes painter and actress Gloria Vanderbilt, daughter of Reginald and Gloria, and journalist Cornelius ("Neely") Vanderbilt, Jr. In this generation multiple marriage has shown up in startling proportions. Even the modest and retiring Grace Vanderbilt—who is quite a different person from her mother, *The* Mrs. Vanderbilt—has been married twice: first to Henry Gassaway Davis III, who also married her cousin, Consuelo, and second to Robert L. Stevens. Governor William Henry Vanderbilt also has been married twice, first to Emily Davies—who married and divorced twice more, then committed suicide—and then to Anne Colby, of West Orange, New Jersey. His brother George has been married to Lucille Parsons and Anita Howard; both marriages ended in divorce.

Young Gloria Vanderbilt has, of course, had three much-publicized marriages. Of her first, to actor's agent Pat Di Cicco, she said afterward, "I am proud to be Mrs. Di Cicco. I was never proud of being a Vanderbilt." Her next marriage, at 20, was to maestro Leopold Stokowski, 63, who was the veteran not only of two marriages but of a well-publicized tour of the world with Greta Garbo. Her third husband is the talented TV and movie director Sidney Lumet.

The otherwise serious-minded Alfred Gwynne II also has been married three times: to Manuela Hudson, niece of Charles Howard; to Jeanne Murray of the prominent Murray family; and to Jean Harvey, of the Harvey restaurant family. But perhaps the best symbol of the end of the Vanderbilt line is Cornelius, Jr., a man whose career has included attendance at seven schools, working on nine newspapers, writing seven novels and nine nonfiction books, and marrying seven wives (including Rachel Littleton, Mary Weir Logan, Helen Varner Anderson, Feliza Loraine Pablos, Patricia Wallace, and Anne Bernadette Needham). "All in all," he wrote in 1958, "these years—getting close to sixty—have been happy ones. I can't say, however, that I think my parents had very happy lives. For one thing, their marriage, achieved in the face of such difficulties, deteriorated seriously over the years. I saw it happening and I asked them why they didn't get a divorce. 'People in our position do not get divorces,' my father said."

The third member Family of the Great Triumvirate and the one which, after the Astors and Vanderbilts, has received most attention the country over, is the Whitney Family. Some time ago, in perusing a Family Genealogy of the Bolton-Payne-Whitney Families, this writer came upon the following quotation under Whitney:

> The origin and early career of this illustrious Family are practically synonymous with the very history of England from the Norman Conquest to the colonization of America. Whenever, during that long stretch of near seven hundred years, a particularly grave crisis arose—one demanding the utmost in physical prowess, mental alertness and moral courage—a Whitney was always on hand, able to cope with the situation and eager to defend, with his life if need be, his King, his Country, and his God.

Surely Family pride could go no further. But this genealogy did. It went on to declare that through two intermarriages Thomas Whitney, father of John Whitney, the American ancestor, "could claim blood relationship to royalty from William the Conqueror to Edward I." The genealogy then concluded:

> It is indeed fortunate that authentic and satisfactory data on the origin of this great Family has been preserved, and that, with the exception of some gaps for three or four generations prior to 1242, a direct line can be traced from the Norman Conquest to the present.

After such a mouthful, one has the urge to recommend for inclusion among those "gaps" a few chapters from the life of such a present-day Whitney as Cornelius Vanderbilt, or "Sonny," who married in 1958 not only for the fourth time but also some time before his third wife knew anything about it—or, for that matter, before his third divorce had been recognized by New York State. One might also include such a latter-day Whitney as Richard, late president of the Stock Exchange, who in 1938 went to Sing Sing Prison for defrauding not only the public and the State but also the treasury of the New York Yacht Club.

The fact remains, however, that there are actually few Families in America, let alone New York, which have more distinguished ancestry than the Whitneys and which have produced, along with the seemingly inevitable quota of black sheep, a higher percentage of able citizens. And even the ones which have been something less than this, notably Richard Whitney, seem at their worst to have had redeeming traits. Richard Whitney, for example, was not only a model prisoner at Sing Sing but also led a constructive life, on a private scale, once he was out.

The first Whitney to come to America was indeed, as the genealogy had it, a man named John Whitney; his wife, ironically in view of the publicity accorded the latter-day Eleanor Searle, third wife of Cornelius Vanderbilt Whitney, was also named Elinor. They arrived in 1630, and the boat which they took was the *Arbella*, the famed "second boat" after the *Mayflower*—one which also included such distinguished New England forebears as Sir Richard Saltonstall and John Winthrop. Up to the real Family founder, however, the Nineteenth Century's William Collins Whitney, all the Whitneys were New Englanders; probably the most distinguished of the earlier ones, General Josiah Whitney, who fought in the French and Indian Wars, was a delegate to the Constitutional Convention and also served in the Continental Army. A later Whitney was the extremely distinguished Eli Whitney, inventor of the cotton gin, who, despite his eminence, was unable to found the Family in the lasting sense and, indeed, was so harassed by a precarious business life that he could not even enjoy, it is recorded, "a normal domestic life until middle age." His biographer, Denison Olmsted, has characterized him favorably:

> Whitney was considerably above the ordinary average, of a dignified carriage, and of an open, manly and agreeable countenance. . . . His sense of honor was high and his feelings of resentment and indignation occasionally strong. . . . The most remarkable trait of his character was his perseverance, very remarkable because it is so common to find men of great powers of mechanical invention deficient in this quality.

Even William Collins Whitney, to whom all present-day Whitneys owe their fortune—and who is familiarly called "Old W.C."—was born in New England, in Conway, Massachusetts, in 1841. Educated

at both Yale and Harvard—the latter at the law school—he came to
New York in 1864, which is surely tardy, even for a "First" Family
founder. Once there, however, he lost no time in making his fortune.
Tall, suave and distinguished-looking, like so many latter-day
Whitneys, and as magnetic in his talk as he was mysterious in his
financial operations, he was a sharp contrast to the rough Astor
and Vanderbilt Family founders. Nonetheless, he was equally successful. Indeed, together with Thomas Fortune Ryan and Peter A.
B. Widener, he all but cornered New York's street railway system
and is credited with having made, in less than a decade, the sum of
$40,000,000.*

Whitney not only made money, he also married it. In 1869 he
married Flora Payne, of Cleveland, daughter of Ohio Senator Henry
B. Payne and a sister of Colonel Oliver Payne, the future treasurer
of the Standard Oil Company. Despite this, Whitney remained a
staunch Democrat—as indeed he did, despite his rapidly increasing
fortune, to the end of his life—and served as Secretary of the Navy
during President Cleveland's first administration. Here he did an
able job. When he took over, the Navy was at perhaps its lowest
point in American history. "In March, 1885," Whitney declared,
"the United States had no vessel of war which could have kept the
seas for one week as against any first-rate naval power." Fighting
dishonest contractors, Whitney not only built up an effective Department but also inaugurated the Naval War College at Newport.
He and his wife were also more than a match for Washington's
social wars. They took a large house, remodeled the ballroom, and
gave as elaborate parties as any up to the days of Evalyn Walsh
McLean. Mrs. Whitney became a close friend of Mrs. Cleveland
and to her fell the honor of denying the malicious charges circulated about Cleveland's treatment of his wife.

* Not the least remarkable thing about Whitney's fortune—as well as that
of the Ryans, Wideners and others—was that it was made on street railways
riding far fewer customers than in the Twentieth Century and at only 5 cents
at the most, and often even less, per ride. In the mid-Twentieth Century, with
most of the country's street railway and bus systems municipally owned, almost
all of them are not only not making any fortune but are actually losing money—
riding many more people and at 15 cents a ride.

Despite their success, the Whitneys did not remain in Washington for another term. As Whitney had first made his fortune and then left it to go into public service, so he now left public service and decided to devote the remainder of his days to Society, horses and houses. Where Society was concerned he was relatively gullible —being conned into thousands of dollars of "loans" to the black-mailing Colonel Mann of *Town Topics*—but he also set a pattern for the social democracy of later Whitneys when he found much pleasure in attending the famous Sunday afternoon parties given by Elizabeth Marbury and Elsie de Wolfe, later Lady Mendl. These were held in Washington Irving's old house on Irving Place. "You never know who you're going to meet at Bessie's and Elsie's," Whitney once said, "but you can always be sure you are going to have a good time." On the other hand, the pleasure was not always mutual. When he proposed to the artist, John La Farge, that he become La Farge's patron, La Farge was indignant. "It makes me think," he retorted, "of the elephant who adopted the family of a heartless hen, and to take care of the chickens, sat on them."

Whitney also pioneered in his inevitably successful, but at the same time, equally inevitably heavy-handed way, the horsy tradition of the Family. Originally he started this not out of any special love for horses or racing but out of rivalry with his fellow Wall Streeter, James R. Keene, who was at that time having great success at the tracks. Knowing nothing about the game, Whitney went about it the way he would have gone about any other business—he hired expert trainers, bought the best horses, and also engaged the services of the best jockey of the day, Tod Sloan. In short order, not only were Whitney's horses winning races, but "Toad" Sloan—as the jockey's father, an Indiana barber, called him—began calling himself James Todhunter Sloan.

When it came to houses and entertaining, Whitney put even the vaunted Four Hundred to shame. Purchasing the old Robert L. Stuart mansion at 871 Fifth Avenue, he turned it, in four years, into one of New York's most elaborate private residences. Bronze gates came from the Palazzo Doria in Rome, ballroom, banquet hall and drawing room came, respectively, from a castle in Bordeaux, a palace in Genoa, and a palazzo in Rome. One corridor came from a French monastery, everywhere were stained-glass windows taken from cathedrals, and one Flemish tapestry alone cost $100,000. As for the dining-room rug, on which ancient Persians had knelt in prayer, this was regarded as priceless. In this house, on the evening of January 5, 1901, Whitney gave a debutante ball in honor of his niece, Miss Helen Barney, which is generally regarded as having ushered in the Twentieth Century version of the Age of Extravagance—one which was to culminate so abruptly in 1929.

And yet this house was only one of ten which Whitney owned. At the time of his death, in 1904, he owned some 36,000 acres of homes in no less than five States—including two houses on Long Island, two in the Berkshires, two in the Adirondacks, not to mention "Blue Grass Farm" in Kentucky, "Stony Ford Farm" in Goshen, New York, and down in Aiken, South Carolina, a house, a farm, a race course, and 2,000 acres of hunting land. He also, of course, owned a shooting box in England, and there he succeeded in marrying one of his daughters into the English nobility. Indeed, only six days after Consuelo Vanderbilt became the Duchess of Marlborough in 1895, Pauline Whitney married Sir Almeric Hugh Paget, Baron of Queensborough. Unlike Consuelo's marriage, Pauline's did not end in divorce—in fact, it lasted until her unhappy death in 1916. But some idea of what her life with her British husband was like may be garnered from the fact that shortly after her death Lord Queensborough came back to marry another American wife with money—this time, in his sixties, choosing the 30-year-old daughter of the W. Starr Millers.

Whitney's other daughter, Dorothy, married first Willard Straight, and later Leonard K. Elmhirst. Whitney also had two sons, one of whom he named Harry Payne and the other—as he was sometimes called—"just plain" Payne. This was undoubtedly pleasing enough to Whitney's wife's family, but, since both Harry Payne and Payne *and* their wives were, in the next generation, to become extremely prominent, it has plagued, so far, at least three generations of newspapermen and Society reporters. This confusion was compounded in the immediate Whitney family when, in the famous family schism—after the death of W.C.'s first wife and his curious second marriage to a Mrs. Edith Sibyl May Randolph—his sons split their allegiance, Harry Payne siding with his father and stepmother and Payne with his mother. Thus, at the time of his father's death, Payne, who was alienated from his father, received only a tenth of his father's fortune, while Harry Payne received some $22,000,000 (Whitney had himself spent close to half of what he once had). On the other hand, Harry Payne had alienated Colonel Oliver Payne, bachelor brother of the first Mrs. Whitney. Thus, when that even richer man died, it was the time for Harry Payne to be cut off with only a few millions and Payne to receive the bulk of the fortune— $32,000,000.

Both Whitney sons, Harry Payne and "plain" Payne, married, within a few years of each other, two of the most ancestrally prominent young women in America. Harry Payne's bride was no less a personage than Gertrude Vanderbilt, daughter of Cornelius Vanderbilt II, and great-granddaughter of the Old Commodore, while Payne's bride was Helen Hay, daughter of John Hay, historian, diplomat and Secretary of State under Presidents McKinley and Theodore Roosevelt and, before that, private secretary of Abraham Lincoln. And, just to make the Harry Payne-Payne confusion more confusing, *Mr.* Harry Payne and *Mrs.* Payne were devoted to horses, while *Mrs.* Harry Payne was not, and *Mr.* Payne, though he also owned a stable, only mildly so.

Even confused, however, both Whitneys are probably as outstanding examples of what might be called the axiom, "Watch out for the second generation," did not, in the case of one First Family, at least, hold true. Harry Payne was both a ten-goal polo player and a director of the Metropolitan Opera; Payne, who played tennis up to and including the day he died, was a trustee of the Public Library and the Metropolitan Museum. Furthermore, both were able financiers, extremely popular with a large cross section of people, and considering their wealth and position, relatively retiring. As for their wives, they were at least some of these things, and some more besides. Although Mrs. Payne Whitney's first love was literature— she published some eight volumes of poetry as well as half a dozen children's books—she later took to racing with an enthusiasm which dwarfed her literary endeavors. Her famed Greentree Stables soon topped even that of her brother-in-law and, at her death in 1944, she was recognized as the Queen of American racing and the lady who had done most to preserve, through a grossly commercial era, the fact that the "Sport of Kings" was still a sport.

If Mrs. Payne Whitney was the First Lady of the American Turf, her sister-in-law, Mrs. Harry Payne Whitney, or Gertrude Vanderbilt, was the First Lady of American Art. Early in her career she set out to disprove the theory that American millionaires never bought anything but European Old Masters and, far from being a mere patron of the arts, became not only the founder of the famed Whitney Museum but in her own right one of America's greatest sculptors. As her great-grandfather had carved out, on the grand scale, his commercial empire, so she threw herself into the sculpture of subjects, as one critic put it, "lofty in spirit and heroic in scale." Among the most famous of these were the 70-foot "Columbus" at Palos, Spain, a 7-foot "Peter Stuyvesant" in Stuyvesant Park and her colossal "Buffalo Bill" in Cody, Wyoming, at the entrance of Yellowstone Park. For the latter she used a cow pony as a model, but the newspapers of the day immediately translated this into one of her husband's polo ponies—a misstatement which disturbed the local Indians far more than it did her. "In art," she once said, "man has always found the comfort and joy, relaxation and aspiration which help to take away heartbreak."

Then, in 1934, in the most extraordinary court case in First Family history, Mrs. Whitney won custody of her niece, the then ten-year-old Gloria Vanderbilt, from Gloria's mother, Gloria Morgan Vanderbilt. Mrs. Whitney's victory was complete. Not only did young Gloria, on Mrs. Whitney's behalf, testify against her own mother, but in the end the court said that Gloria Morgan had provided a life for the child that was "in every way unfit, destructive of health and neglectful of her moral, spiritual and mental education."

The first of the two Whitney brothers to die was Payne, who died in 1927, leaving a gross estate of $194,328,514—in those carefree tax days a net of $178,893,655. Altogether it was the largest estate ever appraised in the country up to that time, ranking far ahead of the $107,052,494 of Mrs. Stephen V. Harkness, the $87,217,691 of John Jacob Astor, or the $78,149,024 of J. P. Morgan. Furthermore, since the stock market was steadily booming upward between the time of death and the time of distribution of the estate, perhaps the most extraordinary fact of the inheritance was that the three Whitney grandchildren, Daniel, Sandra, and Payne Whitney Payson—daughters of Jock's sister, Joan, married to Charles Shipman Payson— were, at age, three, two and one, respectively, becoming $10,000 richer every hour. "Assuming," said one Sunday supplement, relating the story, "it has taken you ten minutes to read these words, the Whitney heirs have grown $1,666.67 richer since you first glanced at the page."

Exactly opposite circumstances prevailed on the death of Harry Payne Whitney, who had the misfortune to die in October, 1930. In the two years between date of death and date of distribution, his estate, in stocks at least, had shrunk from $47,000,000 to $40,000,000. He was survived by Mrs. Whitney, who died in 1942, as well as by his three children: Cornelius Vanderbilt ("Sonny") Whitney, Mrs. G. MacCulloch Miller, and Mrs. Barklie McKee Henry.

The third generation of Whitneys since W.C. in the Payne branch consists of the present John Hay, or "Jock," Whitney and his sister, Joan Payson. A sports enthusiast from the time she was young— "When I was small," Joan recalls, "children were allowed at the track"—she and her brother were brought up very differently from other New York royal heirs apparent. "We used to feel sorry for our Newport cousins," she says. "We had a wonderful time. We dressed in overalls all the time. We were the other side of snobs." Joan's brother, who was born in Ellsworth, Maine, in 1904 and made his first money picking blueberries on his family's place for a penny a hundred, saw his first schooling at Miss Chapin's School for Young

Ladies. "It was all right," he says. "At that time they admitted boys, too." Moving on to St. Bernard's and Groton, he got over a severe stammer—a strict nurse put a stop to that—and then remembers being asked by a French teacher at Groton when he was going to "stand up to my responsibilities." Before going to Yale, where, large and husky, he stroked the junior varsity crew, Whitney recalls another piece of advice on the question of responsibilities:

> When I was about to go to college, my father and I had a talk. He told me that his father, who was a rich man, had given him about half the allowance other boys of his age group received. My grandfather did this in order to teach my father the value of money and to make sure he didn't throw his weight around. The result, as my father described it, was that he could never do his share. My father told me that he was going to give me more than the other boys got, because he wanted me to do more than my share. Then he said, "The test is going to be whether any of your friends know you are doing more than your share. The first time I learn that they know you are doing more, I'll cut your allowance."

After college and a year at Oxford, Whitney entered the brokerage business, and although some of his investments turned out spectacularly, notably Freeport Sulphur, others did not, notably a heavyweight boxer and the American rights to an African hybrid tree which was supposed to corner the hemp market. One of the "Golden Boys" of the twenties and thirties, he was famous not only for the horses he owned as racers but also for his own polo playing; he captained the famous "Greentree Team" which starred Tommy Hitchcock. A familiar figure in the rotogravures and nightclubs, he was also concerned with the theatre, investing in both the giant hit *Life with Father* and the giant failure *Jumbo*, as well as with Hollywood, where he was a heavy investor in both Technicolor and *Gone With the Wind*. In 1930, in one of the country's most spectacular weddings, with the late Robert Benchley as best man, Whitney married Philadelphia's Mary Elizabeth Artemis—the famed horsewoman "Liz." Divorced, he married in 1942 Betsey Cushing, who was divorced from James Roosevelt. During the war, serving as an Air

Force Major, he was captured by the Germans, but eighteen days later, locked in a railway boxcar with forty-one prisoners, Whitney and ten others chose to make a break for it as the train went through a tunnel. They escaped, although thirty prisoners had deemed the risk too great. Becoming Ambassador to Great Britain in 1956, Whitney has also taken care of his post-ambassadorial career with the purchase, in 1958, from the Reid Family, of the New York *Herald Tribune*.

Whitney, who has no children of his own, adopted his wife's two daughters by James Roosevelt, Sara Delano and Kate, although both of them kept the name of their father. In 1953, Sara Delano married Anthony di Bonaventura, the son of a New York barber—a marriage which delighted the Sunday supplements and was, typically, annoying to Whitney only to the extent that the press played upon the barber angle. Whitney himself, who has been called by his rival newspaper, the *New York Times*, "The Amiable Aristocrat," has refused to be listed in the *Social Register*, which he calls a "travesty of democracy" with "absurd notions of who is and who isn't socially acceptable."

As for the third generation of Whitneys in the Harry Payne branch of the Family, this is, in the male line, in the tender mercies of Cornelius Vanderbilt, or "Sonny," Whitney. He is five years older than his cousin Jock. He was born in Roslyn, Long Island, in 1899 and went to Groton and Yale (1910) where he was not tapped for a Senior Society because of publicity attendant on the beginnings of his career as a playboy. (He had been sued for breach of promise by a former Ziegfeld Follies dancer, who not only lost the suit but also costs of $131.) In the years after college, Whitney might be said to have had six separate careers. The first of these was mining, where his industry led to his rapid advancement and eventual presidency of the Hudson Bay Mining Company. The second career was aviation, in which he started the Colonial Airways, which led eventually to his becoming—at least up until he had a split with Juan Trippe—the president of Pan American. Third was his racing career, where he not only raced his stable but also became, like his cousin, a polo player. Whitney's fourth career was politics. In contrast to his brother's branch of the Family—Republican—his branch has remained, like his grandfather, Democratic and, in the Truman Administration, Whitney served first as Assistant Secretary of the Air Force and later as Undersecretary of Commerce. Whitney's fifth career has been motion pictures—a career which began in the 1930's with his interest in *Gone With the Wind* and went into high gear in the 1950's with his own productions (*The Searchers, The Missouri Traveler,* etc.).

Sonny's sixth and by no means final career has been as playboy. He married first, in 1923, his neighbor, Marie Norton, later Mrs. Averell Harriman. Divorced in 1929, he next married, in 1931, Gwladys ("Gee") Crosby Hopkins, a horsewoman from Stratford, Pennsylvania. Divorced again in 1939, he married for the third time in 1941, this time choosing Eleanor Searle, of Plymouth, Ohio, a concert and church singer who, at the time, was soloist for Broadway's Temple Israel's services. In 1958 Whitney was divorced for the third time in a particularly messy action after which, within a few hours, he married for the fourth time, Mrs. Mary Lou Hosford, of Phoenix, Arizona, a star in his *Missouri Traveler.* The first that Mrs. Whitney No. 3 knew of Mrs. Whitney No. 4 was via a press conference held by Whitney in which he said that she was "married to the telephone, a social career and a love of luxury." The State of New York, as well as Mrs. Whitney No. 3, however, was interested in Mrs. Whitney No. 4, when it became apparent that a New York court had banned his Nevada action. As time went by, however, the fourth marriage seemed as established as the others, and since Whitney has children by each of his previous marriages and Mrs. Hosford has four children of her own, before Whitney, the Harry Payne Whitney line in a sense—but not much—went on.

Undoubtedly the most final event in American First Family history was the passing, in New York City, in 1953, of Augustus Van Horne Stuyvesant, Jr., last direct descendant of "Pegleg" Peter Stuyvesant, last Dutch Governor of New Amsterdam and, above all, last of the line of nine unbroken generations of New York's oldest and proudest First Families. A handful of people attended the funeral, and only one remained—Mr. Stuyvesant's butler, Ernest Vernon—in the pouring rain, down in the churchyard of St. Mark's-in-the-Bouwerie, while the massive bronze door, inscribed "Peter Stuyvesant—His Vault," enclosing the bodies of more than eighty Stuyvesants, was temporarily sealed.

A few days later this vault was sealed forever. Since there were no more direct descendants of Peter Stuyvesant, this was, indeed, as it should have been. But never in First Family history had anything seemed so final, and, had Mr. Stuyvesant had his way, the passing would have been even more so. For his will provided, among other things, that all family mementoes—miniatures, portraits, letters and personal records—should be destroyed. Mr. Stuyvesant had done this, it was later discovered, because he once attended a country auction near Newport and became extremely upset when he saw a bundle of old family mementoes sold for a dollar. Fortunately, however, through the good work of the New York Historical Society, this provision in Mr. Stuyvesant's will was broken, and later the Society put on a remarkable exhibition of Stuyvesant portraits. Here among Gerard Stuyvesants and Gerardus Stuyvesants, Peter Stuyvesants and even Petrus Stuyvesants, there was also, of all things, a pseudo Stuyvesant. This portrait, which hung for half a century in the main hall of Augustus Van Horne Stuyvesant, Sr.—who was under the impression that it was a portrait of the mother of Governor Peter Stuyvesant—turned out to be, on investigation, of all people, Anne of Austria, Dowager Queen of France!

But in a way it was fitting that, if the Stuyvesants had to have among their Family portraits an impostor, the impostor should have been genuinely royal. For New York's First Families have been distinguished for many traits—the Jays, for example, for moral heroism, the Astors for commercial genius, the Schuylers for statesmanship, and the Van Rensselaers for organizing eminence—but the Stuyvesants have, most assuredly, been the most distinguished for their regal behavior.

Governor Peter's regal behavior and general highhandedness are, of course, a matter of history—although he had traits too of not only bravery but also gentleness and, at times, even generosity. And during his rule there ruled with him not only his wife, the former Judith Bayard, but also his sister who, formerly married to his wife's brother, was early widowed. Together the two ladies, Mrs. Stuyvesant, who was a Bayard, and Mrs. Bayard, who was a Stuyvesant, set a high standard not only for all future Stuyvesants but for all future Knickerbockers. Peter left two sons and, by the time of New York's Colonial period, the Family was going strong, both financially and socially. Indeed, even a pear tree which Peter Stuyvesant brought from Holland in 1647, and planted at the corner of Thirteenth Street and Third Avenue, lived and bore fruit until 1867.

At about the same time as the pear tree gave up, however, so too did the Stuyvesant Family begin to show unmistakable signs of doing likewise. Indeed, by the sixth generation they were described, by one historian of the era, as "a generation of scholarly, well-to-do men, who devoted themselves to their estates, to study and to social relations, but who took little part in the great world of affairs." In the seventh generation, on the maternal side, came a great physicist and astronomer, Lewis Morris Rutherford, but with this exception, as well as a few collateral exceptions like the great Mrs. Stuyvesant Fish, *enfant terrible* of the Four Hundred, the Stuyvesants became, by the eighth generation, not only New York's but the whole country's best example of a Family going not forward but backward.

The peak of this unhappy state of affairs was reached, in the ninth and last generation, with Augustus Van Horne Stuyvesant, Jr. For eighty-three years Mr. Stuyvesant lived what is undoubtedly the most retiring life ever lived in the entire history of American Society. If his vault in after-life has one bronze door, the entrance to his six-story Fifth Avenue château had three, and here, for a quarter of a century, since the death of his younger sister, Anne, Mr. Stuyvesant, who never married, lived so completely alone that, though there were ten servants, he often went days at a time without one of them ever seeing him. During these days his food was left by his butler in his fourth-floor sitting room, and Mr. Stuyvesant would come out, eat and go back again to his bedroom. His bathroom had solid-gold fixtures.

Once he was in the hospital for a period of thirteen weeks, at another time for a period of eleven weeks. During both those times, except for his physician and his nurse, he never saw a single relative, friend or caller of any sort. Once, when Bishop Manning asked if Mr. Stuyvesant would see him, Mr. Stuyvesant sent word through his butler that the Bishop "could come if he didn't have anything else to do." The message was relayed, and the Bishop never came.

But Mr. Stuyvesant was no recluse in the ordinary sense of the word. In happier days he had been in Newport and had entertained, and been entertained, by what to him were the "new ones," like the Vanderbilts and the Whitneys. All his life he speculated in real estate, at which he was a stern match for any Astor or Goelet or others of newer real estate fortunes. Even in his last years he made some extraordinarily shrewd deals.

Every day, all by himself, at exactly noon, Mr. Stuyvesant would take a walk. His tall, stiff-collared, black-suited, white-mustached figure was easily recognizable; so was his quaint old-fashioned mannerism of holding one hand behind his back. Despite a severe speech defect which made him sound as if he were talking baby talk, he was unfailingly courteous and polite, even to complete strangers. Nor was he without his own peculiar brand of humor. When questioned one day about the Stuyvesant Rutherfurd family changing their name to Rutherfurd Stuyvesant, he almost smiled. "I fail to see why they would wish to do so," he said. "Peter Stuyvesant was a bounder." But to the lawyers through whom he conducted his real estate ventures, he was stern indeed. "He was of the generation," says one, "who believed that lawyers were servants."

Several times a week his chauffeur would drive him down to St. Mark's in the afternoon and he would spend hours wandering about in the churchyard. Once, questioned on this habit, he said, "I feel at home here." At another time a girl from Brooklyn approached him and asked him why a good-looking rich man like he was had never got himself married. "My child," he replied patiently, "I've never had the kind of nerve which made you ask that." In the Stuyvesant Family pew at St. James, fellow parishioners noticed that a strange woman kept barging into his pew before he got there. She did this for several years, but Mr. Stuyvesant never once asked her to leave or complained to the ushers; nor, on the other hand, did he ever speak to her.

Mr. Stuyvesant's closest cousin, Miss Margaret Steward, believes that he was by all odds the most self-sufficient man she ever knew. "He never had a friend," she says, "and he didn't believe in giving presents. He never answered a letter or returned a visit or a telephone call. I don't think he ever went out to a meal in his life and no one who didn't invite himself ever ate with him. I invited myself to call once a month or so for thirty years and I don't honestly know whether he ever enjoyed my visits or not. I never understood him at all, but I was never bored either."

Mr. Stuyvesant's butler, a 70-year-old Englishman named Ernest Vernon, probably knew him best. He entered his employment in 1920 and never took a vacation in thirty-three years. "We were perfect strangers," Vernon says. "No one ever passed the time of day with Mr. Stuyvesant. When Hoover, or some Presidents he liked, would be on the radio, I'd tell him and he'd listen but he never said anything about it. In 1937, before Miss Anne's death, we went to Europe once to buy something for the Stuyvesant Memorial in the Cathedral. I don't say we burned the place up but I lived the same as he. It stays with me, that trip. They cleaned his shoes and they cleaned mine."

Probably the most exciting event in Mr. Stuyvesant's life occurred in 1951 when, in his dressing gown, he was preparing for bed and suddenly noticed his door handle slowly turning. He retreated through his bedroom, his gold-fixtured bathroom, and through another bedroom and bathroom. Then, since there was nowhere else to go, he faced the inevitable and opened the door. There, directly in front of him, were two huge men, shoulder to shoulder, dressed in black with drawn revolvers. Mr. Stuyvesant looked at them for a moment, then asked politely, "What do you wish?"

In a moment the situation was cleared. They were two men from the Holmes Protective Agency. The Stuyvesant servants, taking advantage of the fact that he never rang a bell, had left the house all together, the last one inadvertently setting off the burglar alarm. An acquaintance of Mr. Stuyvesant's asked him what the Holmes men thought of it all—of one of the richest men in New York, over eighty years old and by this time quite deaf and almost blind, all alone in his vast mansion, wearing only a dressing gown. "They seemed very disappointed," Mr. Stuyvesant said, "that there had not been a murder."

Mr. Stuyvesant's will directed that almost his entire fortune, estimated at $10,000,000, go to St. Luke's Hospital to build a clinic for the poor on New York's lower East Side, on the exact site of Pegleg Peter's original farm. To his butler, Vernon, who was the only one who stood in the rain at the churchyard, he left $2,000. By Mr. Stuyvesant's standards, which never changed in a world that passed him by, Vernon was not a poor man.

"He was a just man," Vernon says, "but he was not kind."

PART THREE

THE PEOPLE'S CASE

I was early taught to work as well as play,
My life has been one long, happy holiday;
Full of work and full of play—
I dropped the worry on the way—
And God was good to me every day.
>   —John D. Rockefeller, Sr. (Poem written
>   by him on his 88th birthday)

With no uncertainty of fate
    He brushed aside the angel throne,
And strode through the emblazoned gate
    Into the Heaven of the Strong.
>   —G. S. Viereck. (Poem on the death of
>   J. P. Morgan the Elder)

"I don't recall your name, but your manners are familiar."
>   —Oliver Herford, to a back-slapping
>   person who approached him at the
>   Players with a confident "You re-
>   member me?"

"Tut, tut, child!" said the Duchess. "Everything's got a moral, if you
    can only find it."
>   —Lewis Carroll, *Alice's Adventures in Wonderland*

CHARLES DANA GIBSON

IX

MONEY, MANNERS AND MORALS

IN THE MATTER of "The People's Case," as the district attorney would conclude his presentation of the evidence to the grand jury, there remains the question of whether or not a "true bill" against Society—in other words, a proper indictment—should be found. And if, from our Family Circle case histories, disintegration seems to occur with depressing frequency in the second, third and fourth generations of so many Families, it should also be made clear that there are some extremely flourishing Families in the fifth, sixth and even seventh generations. And discouraging as may seem, generally speaking, the stories of the Astors and the Vanderbilts, the Ryans and the Goulds, the Guggenheims and the Potter Palmers, the Woolworths and the Dukes, it should also be made clear that balanced against these should be placed the records of the Rockefellers and the Du Ponts, the Cabots and the Lowells, the Adamses and the Byrds, the Crockers and the Fields, the Mellons and the Douglases, the Strauses and the Lehmans. All in all, if the conclusion is not entirely a happy ending, neither is it a Stuyvesant finish—and in the final analysis it would seem that America's made-up Family Aristocracy has nothing to be ashamed of in comparison with more genuine titled Aristocracies abroad.

Indeed, brought down to specifics, it would certainly appear that America could produce, even by the curious workings of the process of Celebrity to Society to Aristocracy, in three generations an aristocratic gentleman who would be the equal in every respect of, let us say, a thirty-generation English specimen. Matching for example America's Nelson Rockefeller against England's Duke of Bedford, one has to go along with Mr. Rockefeller—even under the Marquis of Queensberry rules.

On the other hand, it is equally clear from the record that, starting in the 1930's, with the obituary of the very word "gentle-man," with the rise of Publi-ciety, with the Glamour Debutante No. 1's and the Poor Little Rich Girls, and perhaps above all with the change from the root basis of money, one is faced with a kind of all-embracing breakdown—which may be handled in our three specific categories: money, manners and morals.

There is no doubt that the distribution of money has had one of the most pronounced effects on the social picture. In the opinion of today's Old Guard from one end of the country to the other, people just do not have money any more in the sense of the kind of "spending money" of the old days. And in this the Old Guard would seem to be eminently correct. Henry Ford II, it is true, was able to give in 1959 a $100,000 debutante party for his daughter Charlotte—one which included, in a Middle Ages décor at the Detroit Country Club, 1,200 guests varying from the Gary Coopers to Lord Charles Spencer-Churchill. The fact, however, that this party was called the "Party of the Century" was in itself a curious, if inaccurate, commentary—and for more reasons than one. In the first place it was some indication that young Henry, with his socially conscious McDonnell wife, has none of the inhibitions, where Society is concerned, of his late grandfather or, for that matter, his able, hard-working father, the late Edsel.*

In the second place, the commentary was some indication also that young Henry and his wife do not have the same kind of aristocratic inhibitions which would prevent, say, a Thomas J. Watson, Jr., or, for that matter, a Rockefeller, from giving such a Publi-ciety affair. And in the third and final place it was, coming right down to dollars and cents, some indication of the monetary low state of social high life today. For, compared to the good old days, the Ford party was scarcely more than a cook-out.

Compare it, for example, to Mrs. Stuyvesant Fish's famous "Monkey Dinner"—one given for a monkey attired in full dress and billed as the Prince del Drago—or, for that matter, to the infamous "Dog's Dinner"—for canines only. Other examples of outlandish extravagance of those days are legion. Chicago's C. K. G. Billings, whose father left him control of a gas company, was merely emulating what he thought the Four Hundred were doing when he moved to New York and at Sherry's gave his "Horseback Dinner." Albert Stevens Crockett recalls the event in *Peacocks on Parade*:

> The choicest mounts from Billings' stable were taken to Sherry's rear entrance and carried by elevators upstairs to the big ballroom on the fourth floor, which had been completely disguised as a woodland garden, with trees and shrubs apparently growing, and the floor sodded. In the centre was a great manger, where the bluebloods of the equine world were hitched, their part being to stand and contentedly chew sweet hay. Overhead, an effect of clear blue sky had been achieved, with twinkling stars and a harvest moon, and real birds twittered in the shrubbery. Waiters were dressed as grooms, in scarlet coats and white breeches. Over each horse was slung a table, securely anchored to the animal's flanks, and from its shoulders dangled two saddle-bags, stuffed with ice-buckets of

---

* On one of the very few occasions when the late Henry Ford, Sr., ever bothered with Society, he visited the E. T. Stotesburys at their 145-room, 14-elevator "White Marsh" home in Philadelphia. "The Stotesburys are charming," Ford said afterward. "It's a great experience to see how the rich live."

champagne. The guests came in riding costume. Each mounted the charger assigned to him, and in his saddle ate a bewildering array of courses, cooled with sips through long, nippled rubber tubes that led to the champagne bottles in the saddle-bags.

This was the era when Mr. and Mrs. Bradley Martin of Troy, New York, journeyed to Manhattan and after what was reported as "the slow growth of an imaginary hyphen" became *The* Bradley-Martins, married their 16-year-old daughter to Lord Craven and then decided, during the depression winter of 1896-97, to give as "an impetus to trade" a ball at the old Waldorf. Unhappily it was such a fiasco that even the host's brother, Frederick Townsend Martin, was moved to record that "the power of wealth" and "vulgarity" was "everywhere." Afterward the Bradley-Martins moved permanently to England. Expatriated too was James Hazen Hyde for his ball, also at Sherry's. Here the ballroom was transformed into a reproduction of the Hall of Mirrors at Versailles, and the ball, which cost $200,000, led to the investigation of Mr. Hyde's Equitable Life Assurance company. It was also the era of a bachelor dinner given by the nephew of P. T. Barnum, Herbert Barnum Seely, where girls danced, it was alleged, "in the altogether." This was followed by James L. Breeze's "Jack Horner Pie" dinner for twelve, honoring Diamond Jim Brady; in this case the pie enclosed a girl similarly unclad who, after being "reeled in" by Brady via a ribbon, was soon joined—in order that the other guests might not be disappointed—by altogether eleven other girls.

At the same time, long before the late Evalyn Walsh McLean had ever been heard of, Mrs. George Westinghouse descended on Washington and gave a dinner for a hundred at which, unostentatiously—and she obviously thought tastefully—enclosed in every napkin was a crisp hundred-dollar bill. And in 1906, Philadelphia, of all cities, ushered in the era of the debut deluxe when James Paul, one with whom Maury had difficulty establishing a connection, gave his famous "Butterfly Ball" for his daughter, Mary Astor Paul. Some 10,000 exotic butterflies from Brazil were concealed in a decorative bag hung close to the ceiling; at a prearranged time at the ball the bag was to be broken and the butterflies released throughout the ballroom. Unhappily, the heat of the ballroom was intense; the bag released its captives, all right, but no one who was there ever forgot the gruesome effect of the rain of some 9,997 dead butterflies. Three years later George Jay Gould spent $200,000 in 1909 dollars for the coming-out of his daughter Marjory, later Mrs. Drexel; the floral bill alone covered, Jack Thompson recalls, 5,500 lilies of the valley, 1,500 orchids, 15,000 white roses and, as an added touch, "every American Beauty rose in the East." But Thompson records that even more luxurious than this was the ball Mrs. W. Watt Sherman gave for her daughter Mildred, later Lady Camoys; again the place was Sherry's, and the crowning glory of the party was a huge swan which floated among 1,200 guests, then suddenly exploded to shoot some 10,000 pink roses into the air.

During the 1920's, from Palm Beach to New York's Ritz to Long Island and Newport, each debut seemed to be more elaborate than the one before. In price per minute the high point was reached by Otto Kahn, who paid Enrico Caruso $10,000 to sing two songs at his daughter's party. More memorable however was the party given by the Norman Whitehouses for their daughter Alice at Newport; at this, warships of the U.S. Navy were brought into line and, as a favor to the hostess, kept their searchlights playing on the party, thus providing spectacular lighting all night long. With World War II, as old Newporters recall, "it all stopped at once," but one last *noblesse oblige* party occurred in 1955 when the late prince of party givers, Alexander Hamilton Rice, gave himself, in three shifts, an 80th birthday party for all those who he said "had made his life happy and agreeable." The first shift consisted of the Newport tradespeople; the second, the servants of his friends; and, third and finally, his friends themselves.

Certainly this sort of spirit would seem to be gone with the east wind. At the same time, it should be remembered that all do not agree with a favorite argument of the Old Guard that *no one* has any money. Indeed, with a twenty-five-year booming stock market and the greatest prosperity the world has ever seen, this is so difficult to prove that occasionally one wonders if what has "spoiled" or even "ruined," in the Old Guard's words, the Old Guard's World is not so much the fact that too few people have money as that too many do. A place like Palm Beach becomes, to the Old Guard, either "spoiled" or "ruined," it seems, for the simple reason that too many people can now afford it, and hence the old settlers scatter to regroup at Hobe Sound, Fishers Island or Round Hill, Jamaica. Or, in the younger-generation words of Mrs. John Heminway, of Watch Hill, Rhode Island, "Nowadays it's so chic to be unchic it's almost chi chi."

"Nobody we know," says Philadelphia's Mrs. Atwater Kent, "has money any more." Yet Mrs. Kent, who yesterday "lived the way everybody did," is philosophical enough to admit that her "everybody" was yesterday's few. In the same way, when New York's Laurance Rockefeller says, "We just don't have money the way people used to have it," he is using, he admits, not the editorial "we," but the personal. And if his grandfather disproved in his own case Andrew Carnegie's dictum that "the man who dies rich dies disgraced," the present generation of Rockefellers would seem to have proved that an *embarras de richesse*, as the French say, can, properly handled, be far less an embarrassment than an ornament.

In contrast, there is the sad story of the late Hetty Green, who at the age of 66 acquired a mongrel dog by the name of Cupid Dewey. In her last years she lavished most of her remaining affection on Cupid Dewey, and since he was a rather difficult dog someone once remarked to her that he did not seem worth it. "He loves me," replied Hetty, "and he doesn't know how rich I am."

"To be poor is poor enough," said the late Henry Ives Cobb, "and to be poor and talk poor is even poorer. But to be rich and talk poor is indeed poor." Under that judgment most of today's social stalwarts would be found guilty in the third degree. On the other hand, when a veritable host of yesterday's Society and today's Aristocracy join in the lament, "We're the New Poor, you know—there's just as much a New Poor as there's a New Rich," they are speaking, if poorly, the hard truth. Not for them are the million-dollar-a-week incomes of Texas, or the world of the Goulandrises and Coumantauroses, the Lykiardopoloses and the Zouillas—all names which appear, with increasing frequency, in Society columns and which have led at least one *grande dame* to murmur, sadly, "It's *all* Greek to me." Even the famous Scott Fitzgerald–Ernest Hemingway colloquy of the Twenties—when Fitzgerald said, "The Rich are different from you and me," and Hemingway answered, "Yes, they have more money"—now seems strangely dated because, in the opinion of the Rich today, they don't.*

To sum up the question—which might be called the survival of the richest—we turn to Louis Lorillard, co-founder with his estranged wife, Elaine, of Newport's famed Jazz Festival and great-great-grandson of Pierre Lorillard, of the snuff and tobacco empire— the man on whose death, in 1843, the word "millionaire" was first coined. "In the old days," says Louis, "they passed money from generation to generation like a good after-dinner liqueur. Now it's more like a hot potato. A lot of people have it, sure, in oil and in stocks, and in tankers and Black Angus and even in expense accounts. But it's not the uncommon denominator it once was. People just don't look up to it the way they used to. Even with the people who may have more than anybody had in the old days it means a good deal less—and not only to other people but to them too."

One of the reasons, of course, that this money means a good deal less is that it can buy a good deal less, and, in particular, a good deal less labor. Thus today's "servant problem"—long Society's favorite topic of conversation—is actually almost as strong an argument for the fact that Society has been levelled as is the problem of money

* Even the $800,000-a-year salary of the late Eugene Grace, who died in 1960 after being for years the country's highest-salaried man, was comparatively meaningless. One lady in Pittsburgh, however, assured this writer that he was, really, the "last" of the millionaires. "I always felt like standing up when he came into the room," she said, "as if he were the Pope or something." According to Alfred Strelsin, one of the most successful of today's millionaires, today nobody could become a Rockefeller, a Morgan, a Carnegie or a Frick. On the other hand, "Almost anybody," he modestly feels, "could become a 'new' millionaire. Look what you've got going for you," he says. "There is a thing called the stock market—and a multiplication table times earnings that the old-timers never would have believed."

itself. The number of people who have had at least some trouble in this regard includes, apparently, everybody—even the servants themselves. For while there are, according to all employment agency figures, more people today who can afford servants—even at 1960's prices—than there ever were in the old days, there are also fewer people who want to be servants—and this despite the fact that no other group in our economy has had conditions improve to such an extent. In December, 1932, for example, *Fortune* magazine noted the following:

> You can have your garden taken care of in Los Angeles for $1 a week. You can get a dignified couple to run your Commonwealth Avenue house in Boston for $80 a month. A shuffle-footed but affable Negro will fry your chicken and do your washing for $8 a month in Virginia. Anywhere in the North you will find fairly well trained girls only too glad to work at $5 a week, and less trained but willing girls anxious to do any form of housework in return for their room and board. These are general conditions, not isolated instances.

"His Lordship," said the late Sir James M. Barrie, "may compel us to be equal upstairs, but there will never be equality in the servants' hall." The late Sir James may well have been correct—lower-echelon snobbery being what it is—but what he failed to foresee, for this country at least, was the passing of the servants' hall altogether. The servant, it would seem, has, consciously or not, challenged the whole social structure of which he was, for so long, the permanent prop. Let us take just two examples. One is the story of Mrs. William G. Holloway of Long Island, wife of the former chairman of the board of W. R. Grace & Co. She has, in the past twenty-five years, been in the kitchen of her 25-acre "Foxland" just once—and that was some years ago when an accident occurred and the roof caved in. During this era she once had a kitchen maid who worked for her for seven years without ever seeing her. In contrast, her daughter-in-law, Mrs. William G. Holloway, Jr., wife of an oil man, had, in her Fifth Avenue apartment, one at a time, an average of twenty cooks a year, for five years—"and," adds the ex-Mrs. Holloway, now Mrs. Denniston Slater, "I knew them all intimately." The second story concerns the small but vigilant little aristocratic outpost of Tryon, North Carolina, and involves the mother of the noted wit of Tryon, Clifton Murphy. A crisis had occurred in the Murphy domicile, and news was brought to Mrs. Murphy which indicated that her married butler had compromised an unmarried upstairs maid. Mrs. Murphy dismissed the messenger. "It is quite impossible," she said. "This may be the Twentieth Century, and the revolution may be here. But one thing we still have left—servants do not commit adultery."

One thing the Rich apparently do not have left is the line with which we left John Jacob Astor I: "A man who has a million dollars is as well off as if he were rich." Regarded in its time as a philosophic jest, it has come back with a vengeance for mid-Twentieth Century millionaires, for it would take half a hundred of today's millions to live the way the man who followed Astor's advice could have lived in his day on his one. Haunting today too is one of the most famous Rich Man's stories—the one told of the miser who is warned that his children will spend everything he has saved and replies, "I know all about that, but I'll be satisfied if they get half as much happiness out of spending my money as I've had saving it." In contrast, today's millionaires' sons, ranging from Wall Street to Hollywood, have had to learn the hard way not only the high cost of loving but also the truth of Thoreau's maxim: "A man is rich in proportion to the number of things he can afford to let alone."*

Take, for a millionaire example, the story of Richard Lounsbery, one of our original Society complainants, grandson of the founder —along with George Hearst—of the Homestake Mine, and a man so sensitive he can detect, by mere pronunciation, anyone putting an extra "r" in his name. One of the country's largest stock owners, and perhaps the country's most successful personal manager of an inherited estate—he is a millionaire several times over in insurance

---

* Many of today's millionaire sons indeed *have* to let things alone—for the simple reason that even in their parents' houses the things are not theirs. Practically everything in sight in these houses is, because of the tax deductions involved, earmarked not for their children, but for museums.

stocks alone—Lounsbery becomes particularly incensed when anyone suggests he pay his taxes and his other expenses with his dividends. "My dividends!" he groans. "I might as well stuff them down the toilet!" However, if the mere mention of taxable income makes Lounsbery sad, it has also won him a name as the "Last of the Small Spenders."

In the old days Lounsbery gave several memorable balls, but he wouldn't think of such a thing today. "I wouldn't any more think of giving an old-fashioned ball in New York today," he says, "than I would in Moscow. And there's no difference between the Republicans and the Democrats, either. The Republicans are Socialists, and the Democrats are Communists—that's all."

In his more philosophical moments, however, Lounsbery admits that the old Astor "million dollars . . . as if he were rich" line has indeed come back to haunt. A man who has a million dollars today, Lounsbery points out, would be lucky to be able to have an income of $40,000 a year before taxes, and after taxes something like $20,000. "And a man who lives on $20,000 a year in New York today," he says, "lives like a peon. There are more millionaires in New York today rattling around in shirtsleeves in their apartments eating out of the icebox than there are what we used to call—in the days when you could still find them—servants."

One of Lounsbery's few pleasures is reading stock market pages and matching his efforts against such a worthy antagonist as Alfred P. Sloan and his four million shares of General Motors. One day during the recent recession Lounsbery's stocks had held up well, but General Motors was off 2½. Lounsbery arrived at the Harvard Club in high spirits. "Well," he said, "I see Alfred lost ten million." Then a few moments later he was philosophical again. "Hell," he said, "none of it means a damn thing any more. It's just a game. The Government plays with the market like a child with a toy. We're all dead every April 15."

On the way home in a taxicab Lounsbery continued the discussion, and when he got out and gave the driver a twenty-cent tip, the driver, whose ears had been filled with upper-bracket discussion, first looked askance, then raised a ruckus. Finally Lounsbery was able to calm him down, and pointed to his tip, still in the driver's hand. "Do you know," he asked, "what that tip is to a man in the 90 per cent bracket? That's two dollars, man. If you don't want your twenty cents, I do want my two dollars." Then and only then did the man feel—for reasons perhaps even Lounsbery didn't suspect —that he was lucky to get a tip at all.

Not long ago James Hazen Hyde, back in this country, invited Lounsbery, six weeks ahead, to lunch with him at the Union Club. "Six weeks," says Lounsbery, recalling the event. "It was wonderfully old-fashioned. Nobody does things like that any more. And do you know what I did? I thought of that damn lunch every day. I thought of it every damned day for six weeks. Then, on the day of it, damned if I thought of it and I forgot it."

Somehow it is curiously significant that the luncheon of the late Mr. Hyde and the forgetful Mr. Lounsbery—one which in the good old days would have been a social event of high gravity—never came off at all. Indeed the whole root basis of their social position would, in New York at least, seem to have vanished. As Lounsbery himself admits, the axes of power—"and the battle-axes too," he adds—have shifted from money to publicity. Where once the key celebrity—in other words, representing the most power and prestige —one could have enticed to a dinner party would have been the elder J. P. Morgan, it is now a William Paley of C.B.S., a David Sarnoff of N.B.C., or a Luce, a Cowles, a Howard, a Hearst or any other large chain newspaper or television station owner. Indeed, from a look at the chief social groups anywhere—from the groups around Mrs. William Randolph Hearst, Sr., in New York to those surrounding Mrs. Norman "Buffie" Chandler, owner of the Los Angeles *Times* in Los Angeles, not to mention the McCormicks and the Fields in Chicago, and all the other way stations in between —it becomes immediately apparent that what was once barely the Fourth Estate has become what passes for today's First Estate.

Certainly the day has long passed when publisher James Gordon Bennett could say, "American Society consists of the people who don't invite me to their parties." Perhaps the watershed story of this change was the famous colloquy, recalled by Ishbel Ross, of the granddaughter of Horace Greeley and *the* Mrs. Astor. Waiting downstairs in Mrs. Astor's house, she was refused an appointment to see her; Mrs. Astor however sent down a $2 bill with the message, "You work for a living and you've been put to some trouble in coming here." Giving back the money to the maid, the granddaughter of Horace Greeley promptly sent back her own message. "Tell Mrs. Astor," she said, "that she not only forgets who I am, but she forgets who she is. Give her back her money with my compliments and tell her that when John Jacob Astor was skinning rabbits, my grandfather was getting out the *Tribune* and was one of the foremost citizens of New York."

Today society editors, gossip columnists and reporters find no necessity to use the "background" which Miss Greeley found so necessary to emphasize. Today indeed the same journalists who a generation ago received their guest lists—if they got them at all—via spies or at the back door now receive invitations to dinner and in many cases have the hostess send the car for them. Nor is this confined to publicity-conscious New York; in fact there is not a society editor in a single major city who has failed to note the change.

Just when all this began is again something of a moot point, but at least some date it with the beginning of Society signing testimonials. If so, the opening date here was the endorsement on the part of Mrs. James Brown Potter, written on Tuxedo Park stationery, of Harriet Hubbard Ayer's cold cream. But Mrs. Potter, who was born Cora Urquhart, in New Orleans, might have been forgiven; before her marriage she became the first Society figure to go on the stage and there, presumably, learned such sinful behavior. In 1923, however, two advertising agencies, William Esty and J. Walter Thompson, went all out for "Society names," and, as usually happens when advertising agencies go all out for something, they got them. Esty signed up, for Hardman pianos, Mrs. Oliver Harriman and the Duchess de Richelieu of Baltimore, and two months later Thompson corralled, for Pond's cold cream, not only Mrs. Oliver Harriman again, but also Mrs. August Belmont and even Washington's Mrs. Longworth herself.

Later, the dam burst completely when Esty, on behalf of Camels, signed a country-wide spread of social names including Mrs. John Gardner Coolidge II, Mrs. Hamilton Fish, Jr., Mrs. James Russell Lowell, Mrs. Adrian Iselin II, Mrs. Powell M. Cabot, Mrs. Potter d'Orsay Palmer, Mrs. Thomas M. Carnegie, Jr., Miss Anne Douglass Gould and Miss Mary Byrd. These were followed by such later endorsers as Mrs. Anthony Drexel Biddle, Mrs. J. Borden Harriman, Mrs. T. Markoe Robertson, Mrs. Langdon Post, Mrs. William Wetmore and Mrs. Rodman Wanamaker. By 1954, however, Society had obviously worn out its welcome in the field. In that year an "immediate release" from Endorsements, Inc., the largest organization in the field, revealed a list of the one hundred and eleven "most wanted" names for testimonials. Of these, the only Vanderbilt was the irrepressible Amy, and indeed the only names which could have been definitely classed under the head of Society were those of Mrs. Byron Foy and the Duke and Duchess of Windsor.*

Back before the turn of the century, when the late Hattie Carnegie, whose real name was not that of course, came to this country, she took the name of Carnegie because, she said, "It was the most important name in the country." One hesitates to think what name might be chosen by a similar arrival today. But one thing is certain; it would be a celebrity name, and the money would be a secondary consideration. If a celebrity has money, and most of them do, so much the better, but the power and influence, pomp and circumstance, that the monetary name once inspired have lost out to the

---

* As of the 1960's, the list, according to Jules Alberti, President of Endorsements, Inc., would not include a single Society name. Mrs. Foy had died, he pointed out, and as for the Duke and Duchess of Windsor, he felt they could no longer be counted in the "most wanted" class because of what he gently called their "commercialism." Alberti, who may be said to have contributed much to the Decline and Fall of Society via testimonials in general, feels that if he has done so it would be just retribution. His first job, as a boy of 15, was playing in an orchestra in Mrs. Potter Palmer's Chicago ballroom. "In those days," he recalls, "the Potter Palmers kept their musicians behind their potted palms. We were the opposite of children—we were to be heard but not seen."

"name" name—one which will undoubtedly be, as we have seen, in the next generation, a "Society" name.

A name like Bing Crosby's is particularly interesting in this regard. Judging by its second-generation difficulties—i.e., the Crosby boys —it is going to be a particularly difficult one in transition to Society and Aristocracy. But Mr. Crosby himself, in reference to his daughter by his second wife, was already looking forward to the transition when, in the October, 1960, *Ladies' Home Journal*, he wrote:

> Even though I'd probably give it a lot of thought before I plunged, I wouldn't be against shooting a bundle on something like a coming-out party for her. I've never been against things like that as long as parents could afford them, because of their importance to the main participant. Debuts are like honeymoons. A girl may look ahead to hers for only a few years, but she'll look back on it forever.

The warfare between Society and Aristocracy is, as we have seen, a stern one. But it is as nothing compared to the warfare of Celebrity and Aristocracy. Back in the 1890's, when the William H. Crockers gave a mere "breakfast" in their San Francisco home for Sarah Bernhardt, it was too much for the San Francisco *Argonaut*, which promptly editorialized:

> Better that the walls of unchiseled granite which uphold the luxurious Nob Hill mansion where Bernhardt was breakfasted, should be nicked for cinerary urns and be converted into a columbarium for the preservation of the ashes of dead domestic virtues than that its threshold should have been polluted by the crossing of this artist. . . . If we have not the courage to criticize the faults of the higher class that styles itself "best" when it violates the rules of its order and imperils the good name of our city, then we shall have earned for our journal an undeserved name for courage!

In Chicago, the conflict was apparent throughout the years when the aristocratic Arthur Meeker, Sr., shepherded two whole generations of visitors, including the Prince of Wales and Queen Marie of Rumania, through Chicago's stockyards. Only once, his son recalls, did he fail to show instant courtesy at his office at Armour and Company. On that morning, he suddenly snapped to his secretary, "Who the hell are Mr. and Mrs. Rudolph Valentino?" And, records his son, "he really didn't know." In the 1920's, the same conflict was apparent when the great celebrity of the era, Scott Fitzgerald, descended on a tea party outside Paris of Edith Wharton and a few of her aristocratic friends. Fitzgerald was, as Arthur Mizener recalls in *The Far Side of Paradise*, determined not to let them awe him:

> "Mrs. Wharton," Fitzgerald demanded, "do you know what's the matter with you?"
>
> "No, Mr. Fitzgerald, I've often wondered about that. What is it?"
>
> "You don't know anything about life," Fitzgerald roared, and then—determined to shock and impress them—"Why, when my wife and I first came to Paris, we took a room in a bordello! And we lived there for two weeks!"
>
> After a moment he realized that, instead of being horrified, Mrs. Wharton and her guests were looking at him with sincere and quite unfeigned interest. The bombshell had fizzled; he had lied outrageously, shocked himself, and succeeded only in bringing his audience to an alert and friendly attention. After a moment's pause Mrs. Wharton, seeming to realize from his expression how baffled Fitzgerald was, tried to help him.
>
> "But Mr. Fitzgerald," she said, "you haven't told us what they did in the bordello."
>
> At this Fitzgerald fled, making his way back to Paris, where he was to meet Zelda, as best he could. At first when Zelda asked him how it had gone he assured her that it had been a great success, they had liked him, he had bowled them over. But gradually the truth came out, until—after several drinks—Fitzgerald put his head on his arms and began to pound the table with his fists.
>
> "They beat me," he said. "They beat me! They beat me! They *beat* me!"

Also in Paris a striking demonstration of the warfare of celebrity and Aristocracy occurred in 1927 when Mrs. Denniston Lyon was visiting Ambassador Herrick at the time of Lindbergh's flight. Invited to dinner to meet him, she was horrified to learn, just preceding the dinner, certain details of the historic flight—which, in her characteristic manner, she could not wait to tell a later arrival.

"Why, do you know," she said, "that young man flew the Atlantic without a suitcase? Why, he didn't even have a dinner jacket!" Fortunately for Mrs. Lyon's peace of mind, Lindbergh was able to be fitted out with a butler's dinner jacket. Later on the same trip, however, Mrs. Lyon met another celebrity who told her he had had hard times in his youth. "We did too," commiserated Mrs. Lyon. "When my husband and I were first married, we had to do without many things. We had to do all our entertaining at home. Fortunately we had our own ballroom."

The 1930's were the heyday for the warfare with celebrities. During this period a visitor to the home of Dr. and Mrs. Thomas Hepburn in Hartford, Connecticut, was impressed with reading a particularly pleasant, almost society-page kind of write-up of Dr. Hepburn's daughter Katharine—a lady who at that time had an extremely unfavorable press elsewhere in the country; she was being labeled "Box-Office Poison" and was violently criticized for wearing slacks, opening her fan mail on the streets of Hollywood, etc. The contrast was so striking that the visitor could not resist questioning Dr. Hepburn, a surgeon who specializes in what is politely known as the "old man's operation." Dr. Hepburn's explanation was brief. "I have operated on half of the newspaper publishers in this city," he said grimly, "and I confidently expect to operate on the other half."

About the same time, also in New England, actress Estelle Winwood attended a tea party for the cast of a show in which she was appearing. "You know," she heard her hostess say, "*they're* really very nice." Miss Winwood smiled at her. "And you know," she said, "*we* are no more *they* than you are." In 1939, a strong demonstration of aristocratic strength against celebrities occurred when five young gentlemen of Virginia abducted Society columnist Igor Cassini from the Warrenton Country Club. Luring the columnist outside, from a dance which was in progress, they took him to a lonely road ten miles away, stripped him of his clothes and tarred and feathered him.

Later Cassini was able to identify three of his five assailants—

they had upbraided him during his ride about certain items in his columns—and the three were brought to trial. They were found guilty of assault and battery, fined small amounts and given suspended jail sentences. Among those who defended Cassini was Maury Paul, the man he was to succeed in New York as Cholly Knickerbocker No. 2. "Until you find a bomb every night in your car," Paul wrote, "until you be chased from every club, and are the fear of every hostess, you will not be a newspaperman."

Another curious example of the warfare of celebrity and Aristocracy occurred in Mount Kisco, New York, after World War II. Here Billy Rose had bought a 135-acre estate complete with greenhouses. One day a group of Mount Kisco children, tempted by what seemed to them acres of greenhouse glass, started throwing rocks. This resulted in considerable destruction, and afterward the parents of the children came to see Rose. They told him they were very sorry and would of course punish the children and wished to pay for the damage. Rose, however, had another idea; he told them he wished to talk to the children alone. Accordingly, the children were rounded up and sent to Rose's house. "I want you to know," Rose said, "that many of your fathers came by their places out here easily. I came by mine the hard way. Now as one ex-rock thrower to another, I want to cop a plea with you. I'm just a run-of-the-million guy. But I'd like to stay out here among you fox-hunters if it's all right with you. That's always been my idea of what America is. What do you say?"

The children not only saw Rose's point, but also agreed, Rose recalls, to see that no one else damaged his property during his stay in Mount Kisco. By the 1960's the man who once said, "It's tough to be five-three in a five-nine world," was providing, despite the almost unbelievable ups and downs of his private life, one of the most curious examples of an attempt to change from celebrity to Aristocracy. In his 93rd Street Manhattan house, formerly the home of the Baker son-in-law, William Goadby Loew, Rose has one of the country's most extraordinary collections of paintings and sculpture and furniture—not to mention an upstairs barber chair and his own stock ticker machine. But when *Life* magazine in 1958 wished to run a fourteen-page spread on Rose and his house, he refused. "I have outgrown that sort of thing," he said with some pathos. "I am trying to be a gentleman." In a somewhat similar vein, but with a reverse twist, is the story of Ben Sonnenberg, the country's leading publicist, who now lives in Mrs. Stuyvesant Fish's old mansion on Gramercy Park. Sonnenberg had decided to have a man-to-man talk with his son, who, at least to his eyes at that time, was leaning toward a ne'er-do-well life of Bohemianism, writing poetry, etc. He pointed around his enormous house—to the brass, the portraits, the autographs, the tapestries, and the *objets d'art*. "You know, son," he said, "*I* didn't *start* with all this." The son was unimpressed. "Well," he said, "*I* did."

Contrary to the general feeling around the country, however, New York is by no means yet totally overrun by celebrities. In 1958, for example, when the late Aly Khan was named Ambassador Extraordinary and Plenipotentiary, Permanent Representative of Pakistan to the United Nations, he found those powers unavailing when it came to buying an apartment in New York's River House; although his bid of $100,000 to buy a vacant apartment in that aristocratic dwelling was $20,000 higher than the next person's, Khan was turned down and the next person was accepted. And, on the other hand, there are occasions when celebrities, traveling around the country, find a curious rapport. The theater's Miss Dorothy Gish, for example, on a visit to Middleburg, Virginia, found clear evidence of this. "The horsey set and theater people are very much alike," she said. "They talk horses and we talk theater." In contrast, when St. Louis's Mrs. Allen Terwater West was asked if people in St. Louis talk about people like Arlene Francis and Jack Paar, she shook her head vigorously. "Of course not," she said. "We talk about each other."

But it remained for Boston, as indeed it should have, to provide the textbook story of the warfare of celebrity and Aristocracy. The story concerns the sale of their Brush Hill Road home by Mr. and Mrs. N. Penrose Hallowell. One more in a long line of old Boston Family houses to see the change to a new day, the house was sold, after some deliberation, to none other than Mr. Howard Johnson, of roadside restaurant fame. Mrs. Hallowell, a gentle person, thought it would be nice for the Hallowells to have some personal contact with the Johnsons in the course of the signing of the papers. At first, not knowing quite how to do this— she could not, of course, invite the Johnsons to a meal since she didn't know them—she decided at length to have them to tea. Since tea has always been perhaps the most democratic of all Boston institutions, it looked like the perfect solution; in Boston, you can ask almost anyone to tea.

Mr. Johnson arrived, bringing with him young Master Howard Johnson, Jr., at that time a young gentleman not quite ten. Everything went extremely smoothly. Mrs. Hallowell poured the tea from her customary position on the sofa, Mr. Hallowell sat in his old chair by the fire, the Johnsons, father and son, sat across the room, and the papers were signed and the tea, English muffins and S. S. Pierce marmalade satisfactorily consumed. Suddenly, however, a wave of sentiment overcame Mrs. Hallowell. She looked around the room at everything she loved—the portraits, the tapestries, and the books—and then she looked back at Mr. Johnson. "Oh, Mr. Johnson," she sighed. "I do hope that you and Mrs. Johnson will be as happy here in all the years to come as Mr. Hallowell and I have been in all the years that have passed."

There was a silence. Furthermore, it was soon apparent that it was a silence which was not going to be broken by Mr. Howard Johnson, Sr. Finally, however, it was broken by Master Howard Johnson, Jr. "There isn't any Mrs. Johnson," he said, obviously trying to be helpful. "One's dead and one's divorced. But Daddy's got a girl friend." He had said the latter in such a hopeful spirit that everyone was by now stunned. And there was another silence—this time an ear-splitting one. In many another Society, the breaking point might have been reached, but not in Boston Society. Boston Society has a way of coming through in the pinches—and now, surely, the pinch was on.

Out of the old Hallowell chair by the fire jumped Mr. Hallowell. Without a word he drew himself up, strode briskly across the room and smote Mr. Johnson, Sr., a smart blow on the back. Then, for the first time, he spoke.

"Bully for you, Johnson," he said.

Turning, as so many of our examples seem to lead us, to the subject of manners, we find that an extraordinary change resulting from the root basis of Society moving from money to publicity or from Family name to "name" name. Whether this is due to the general hardness of the world of Publi-ciety, or to a steady break-down ever since World War I, the fact remains that manners in the mid-Twentieth Century are probably at their lowest ebb since the early days of the Barbarian invasions of ancient Rome. Talk to any old-timer of today, whether Aristocrat, Socialite or celebrity, and he or she will tell you that in his or her own lifetime has come an almost steady retrogression in this regard. To old-time New Yorkers manners are, like so many other things, a casualty of the Twentieth Century, and not a few of them remember the days when there were even definite rules for "cutting." Let us take, for example, a chapter entitled "The Gentle Art of Cutting" from an old etiquette book entitled *Habits of Good Society*. Published in 1863, it reads today like something from prehistoric times—indeed to most moderns even the word "cutting" would be unfamiliar:

> There are some definite rules for cutting. Let the miserable culprit not be tortured to death, or broken in the social wheel, like a Damiens, however treasonable his offense. Never on any account, allow him to speak to you, and then staring him in the face, exclaim, "Sir, I do not know you!" or, as some people, trying to make rudeness elegant, would say, "Sir, I have not the honor of your acquaintance;" nor behead him with the fixed stare; but rather let him see that you have noticed his approach, and then turn your head away. If he is thick-skinned or daring enough to come up to you after that, bow to him stiffly and pass on. . . . Perhaps it should be added that a superior should never cut his inferior in rank; he

has many other ways of annihilating him. Certainly it must be laid down that people holding temporary official relations must waive their private animosities, and that two doctors, for instance, however much opposed to one another, should never introduce the cut over the bed of a patient.

For some five centuries probably the foremost holders of the line on manners were dancing masters, and one of the difficulties of the Twentieth Century seems to be that there have been, throughout the country, few men able to maintain the tradition established by such legendary Nineteenth Century figures as Allen Dodworth of New York and Lorenzo Papanti of Boston. Indeed, throughout most of this century the dancing master's craft has fallen, largely by default, to women teachers, and although some of these, notably Boston's ageless Miss Souther, have carved remarkable careers for themselves, still they themselves would be the first to admit that the job is primarily a male one.

The outstanding exception to this sad story was the career of the late William De Rham of New York. A man to the manners born— "De Rhams are De Rhams," he was fond of saying—he was an old-fashioned umpire of a modern dancing empire extending from Long Island to Palm Beach, with particular emphasis on Newport, where he grew up, Southampton, New York, Connecticut, New Jersey, and Philadelphia. Teaching some fourteen hundred grandchildren a year of what was once the Four Hundred—a group ranging in age from four to fourteen—he had under his wing, until his death in 1957, two generations of Astors and Whitneys, Fords and Chryslers, Paleys and Sarnoffs, Hearsts and MacArthurs, Gerrys and Goelets, Graces and Phippses, Loebs and Lehmans, Wideners and Wanamakers, Van Alens and Van Beurens. Indeed, De Rham all but cornered the Eastern Society dance market in much the same manner as his Wall Street uncle, the late Steven Whitney, once cornered mid-Western wheat. More importantly, unlike most dancing masters in the great tradition, who have apparently always had trouble in cornering boys and have usually offered them all kinds of inducements, De Rham never offered anything but blows, swears and fears. At a typical class one might hear him talk to his boys as follows:

"Dammit, you're a gentleman, not a hoodlum. I don't make you wear gloves but I want you to wear soap. You say 'Sir' to your elders and you stand up when you are spoken to—don't your schools teach you *anything*? I want your hair brushed and your trousers creased and I don't want to see a single shirt that was put on yesterday doing business today. I want dark neckties and dark socks and, if you can't keep your socks up any other way, I want garters. In the old days gentlemen carried little bags with their pumps in them. I don't ask you to do that but I want your shoes polished sometime between your last football game and here. I want your hands out of your pockets and nothing in them except a clean white folded handkerchief in your handkerchief pocket. I don't want any sprawling. The first thing you are going to learn to do is sit. You sit still and you sit straight and you sit up. None of you can sit any more because none of you have decent family meals—you just run into some kitchenette in some modern ranch house and run out again. I want you to choose a girl, offer her your right arm and march into the ballroom and stop with your heels together. Unfortunately none of you are ever spanked any more but I think you may have a rough idea where your derrière is— well, you don't poke it out. You bow from the waist. You shake hands with Mrs. De Rham and you give your whole name—your Christian name and your surname—and you do it in a clear voice. Then you take your girl to her seat and, if there is a seat, you sit beside her. And you don't leave her until she gets another partner or gets married."

Once Mr. De Rham was through with his boys, he next turned on his girls. Some of them might have intuitively thought that, because they were girls, they were going to be more gently treated than the boys. If so, they had another intuition coming:

"I don't want you girls to snatch and pull at the boys. You'll get a boy all right—we've gone to a lot of trouble to get them for you —but you might as well learn right now that you don't get one by grabbing. The kind of one you get by grabbing you don't want anyway. But I don't want you hanging back and pretending you're shy either. Being shy is just being conceited. You think everyone is looking at you and thinking about you. Well, they're not. It's just your own silly self-importance which your silly self-important families have given you. I want you to put your arms at your sides and not stand around hugging yourselves—you can wait for the boys to do that. And you cross your ankles in the ballroom and not your knees the way your mothers do at home. Girls have no more dancing ability than boys have—in fact most of them have less. They just like to show off their dresses more. I want you smiling from the minute you come into the ballroom until you go out, and when you've come in I don't want you to think you've made a curtsey when you've just banged your back toe on the floor. I want a long slow graceful curtsey, and I don't want to see the sole of your foot. A girl never shows the sole of her foot in the ballroom. And I don't want you to refuse a boy when he asks you to dance. There are only two reasons for refusing a boy a dance; one is that you don't know him and the other you're not old enough to know. If the boy is too small, that's just too bad. Girls grow faster than boys and you'll have to be patient—which, as you probably don't hear any more, is a virtue. When you get up to dance you surrender to the boy. You go backward gracefully and you don't clump back like a dray horse. And don't go home bawling to your mother that I said you looked like a horse. I didn't say anything about your looks—you all look alike nowadays and you all wear your hair the same way, and if you're ever going to get a boy you're never going to do it by your looks so you better learn to dance. All I said was you *danced* like a horse. Now look over the boy's left shoulder and don't look anywhere else. And finally, I don't want to see a single girl leading a single step. If the boy's out of step, it's your job to be out of step with him. Leading is bossing and boys don't like being bossed any more than your fathers do although your mothers have been doing it for generations and that's why so many of you have stepfathers and stepmothers."

At this point in the proceedings, the parents of the children in Mr. De Rham's classes were very likely to be squirming uncomfortably in the seats they took on the side of the hall. Mr. De Rham, who disliked squirming in any form, had, however, been waiting for this, and almost invariably then wheeled on them:

"In the old days children were told they should be seen and not heard. Well, nowadays the only thing *never* seen and *never* heard are you parents. You send your children to me to be taught manners. Well, they won't have any better manners than you have. In the first place, may I inquire who invited you into this ballroom? Since there are not enough chairs for both you and the children, I did not invite you, and since I happen to know that your children don't like your looking at them, I very much doubt that they did. I'll tell you why—you're in here because you "get a kick" out of seeing your little darlings dance. Well, as I have been trying to teach your little darlings, you don't go to a private party to get anything, particularly a kick. You either contribute or you get out. In the second place, if you do go to a party, even uninvited, to watch it, I should think you would have the courtesy to dress as the party is dressed. In the third and last place, may I say that I have often been criticized by you parents for singling out the children when they are making mistakes. This time I wish to make it clear that I am not singling out any of you. I am talking to you all together. Since you have brought your children to me to give them the bringing up you brought them up without, I would like to do it, from here on, in this brief hour, without any further distractions from you."

Considering the fact that the parents the late Mr. De Rham was addressing were some of the most influential men and women in America—and they not only took it but came back for more— it is obvious that Mr. De Rham was something very special indeed in a mannerless world. And it is, of course, only one of Mr. De Rham's one-steps from manners to morals. Indeed, the matter of manners and morals—and there would seem to be plenty the matter with them in our modern world—can almost be taken together from the standpoint of "standards" or customs. For, as Wilfred Funk has noted, the paternal ancestor of our word "morals" is the Latin *mores*, or customs. And, whether taken together or separately, the fact is that American Society morality, as of the mid-Twentieth Century, has reached very close to the stage of amorality—or no morals at all.

Surely from our Family Circle case histories it is apparent that the old double standard is now a standard which might well be described—as indeed it can be—as no standard at all. Where in the old days divorce was the exception, in the new days it is, in Society at least, the rule. The chances are that the debutante can look forward to an average of at least two and very often three husbands. And rare indeed is the male social animal who does not go through what might be called change of wife. In New York particularly the world of Publi-ciety is a marital jungle. The world of the Aly Khans, Rita Hayworths, Linda Christians—not to mention the "world's richest man," J. Paul Getty—challenges the very institution of marriage. Even the theater world, easily the most attractive of the various worlds of international Society, is suspect on this score. "It's a very poor world," says Janet Stewart, "to find a husband in." Mrs. Stewart, who as Mrs. William Rhinelander Stewart was one of the charter members of Café Society, lived through this world from its beginnings. And, though she realizes that the old days too, judging from what she heard, had their moral lapses, still it was, in her opinion, a "Boy Scout world" compared to the world of today. As for New York's Alice Topping, she feels that the world of celebrity has a great deal to do with the breakdown. "People in public relations," she says gently, "seem to have an awful lot of trouble with private relations."

One of our original grand jury of *grandes dames*, Mrs. Nicholas Longworth, the famed "Princess Alice" of the White House in turn-of-the-century days, believes that the biggest change of all in her lifetime has been the change in manners and morals. Mrs. Longworth's own mother died when she was born, and she was brought up by a stepmother. Yet, writing of that situation a generation ago, she says, "If this seemed to be a state of affairs that needed working out for the sake of all concerned, what must it have been for the children of families complicated by divorce?" Today, speaking of modern morals as compared with those of yesterday, Mrs. Longworth says that people have no idea what mountains were made of molehills in those days. "When I danced the 'hootchy kootchy' on Grace Vanderbilt's roof at Newport," she says, "you would have thought the world was coming to an end."

One world actually did come to an end—the world of *Town*

Topics, forerunner of today's gossip columns. Edited by the up-to-that-time redoubtable Colonel William D'Alton Mann, a man of highly suspect reputation where blackmail was concerned, *Town Topics* published in 1904 the following paragraph:

> From wearing costly lingerie to indulging in fancy dances for the edification of men was only a step. And then came a second step—indulging freely in stimulants. . . . Flying all around Newport without a chaperone was another thing that greatly concerned Mother Grundy. There may have been no reason for the old lady making such a fuss about it, but if the young woman knew some of the tales that are told at the clubs in Newport she would be more careful in the future about what she does and how she does it.

That one paragraph, which did not even mention Miss Roosevelt by name, nonetheless occasioned in its day a social and journalistic *cause célèbre*—one which resulted in the final breaking of the power of *Town Topics*. Read today, it hardly seems possible that such a thing could have happened, from what to our modern jaded eyes seems so innocent. But such was indeed the case—and a short half century later *Publishers' Weekly* would gently complain that young girls were now writing books which in the old days they wouldn't have been allowed to read. In any case, one who firmly agrees with Mrs. Longworth, and a recognized authority on "young girls," "the old days" and, indeed, the whole question of manners and morals, is Miss Charlotte Noland of Foxcroft School. "Miss Charlotte," as she was officially called on her honorary degree citation by Columbia University in 1959, has for three generations commanded perhaps the foremost of America's private girls' schools. And, among other distinctions, she was one of the very few "private persons" whom Queen Elizabeth II on her last visit to this country not only saw, but, more important, had expressed a wish to see.

Located in Middleburg, Virginia, Foxcroft is rooted in American history—its center brick house once belonged to a cousin of George Washington's—yet it is even more rooted in the personality of Miss Charlotte. And Miss Charlotte, a vigorous, charming 78, is herself not only well rooted—she represents the seventh generation of her family to live on her property—but also a firm believer in the fact that rootlessness is at the bottom of much of today's difficulty.

But if Foxcroft is rooted in American history and Miss Charlotte, it is even more rooted in Miss Charlotte's "ideals and traditions"— or, as the Foxcroft girls call them, Miss Charlotte's "idits." And it is these very "idits" Miss Charlotte told us she now believes are being challenged. Foxcroft's ideals and traditions, like America's own ideals and traditions, of course, concern many other matters besides manners and morals. But manners and morals, and particularly the latter, are a very important part of them. And Miss Charlotte, who founded her school in 1914—a year she now believes represented in many ways the high tide of manners and morals—now also believes that the present era represents, so far, the low tide. "Morals," she says firmly, "have dropped at least 75 per cent." Kinsey to the contrary, percentage in as indefinite a science as morals would seem a perilous business, but Miss Charlotte has three generations of the daughters of America's most prominent families to go by, and she knows whereof she speaks. She is, of course, well aware, and indeed at first hand, of the vast changes which have taken place in respect to the position of women.

Her own sister was the first girl to go to college in Virginia— "My grandmother wouldn't speak to her for months," she says— and right in her own school of Foxcroft, in its first graduating year, not a single girl went to college; in 1960, 95 per cent of her graduating class was college-bound. For another change, Miss Charlotte remembers that as a child she had an uncle who was divorced. For literally years, she recalls, her mother wouldn't even let her see him, let alone have any contact with him. "When I finally did get to see him all those years later," she says, "I was terribly disappointed. I had expected a real devil-looking person. But he looked just like anybody else. He didn't even have horns." Out of twelve girls in Foxcroft's first year, just one had divorced parents; in 1960 more than half did. Where it will all end, Miss Charlotte refuses to predict. But she feels it is high time people realize how quickly, in a sense, it all came about. "In the old days," she remembers, "there were only three things a Southern lady could do—she could play the piano, she could make preserves, or she could raise chickens. I have never thought there was anything so very ladylike about raising chickens," Miss Charlotte adds with a smile, "but I declare, it was at least as good as what they do nowadays—which is raise the dickens."

Miss Charlotte has thought long and hard about the reasons for our current moral dilemma, and she cites a wide range of factors —from stress (of the times) to dress ("girls going around in front of men with no clothes on worth mentioning"). But she also blames a larger matter, a word she comes right out with—"guts." "It's a good old English word," she says, "and people, both old and young, both men and women, just don't have as much of it as they used to —particularly when it comes to self-control in resisting temptation."

Miss Charlotte also takes to task what she calls the modern "fetish" for having everything out in the open—"as if that in itself were a virtue." "It's not at all," she says, "it's just the opposite. There's entirely too much talk about sex, and at the same time there's no real public opinion about it. Public opinion used to be a very powerful thing—a real force for making you do what was right even if you didn't have the 'guts' or 'gumption'—that's another good word, too—to do it by yourself."

All in all, from the money, manners and morals standpoint, if from no other, Society would indeed seem to have been destroyed, dispatched and done in. Before concluding the people's case, however, one last irony remains. Since it was, after all, a Society homicide, we have, from the standpoint of reality, precious little hope of ever bringing the murderer or murderers to the bar of justice. For the record of the police, where Society homicide is concerned, is hardly one to inspire confidence that they would be up to the task of pressing the case to its final conclusion in the much larger matter of the murder of Society in general.

Since 1920, indeed, there have been no fewer than seven major Society murders—and in all those seven not a single murderer has ever been tried, let alone convicted, for the slaying. And the one Society murderer who was actually tried—Harry K. Thaw for the murder of Stanford White—was, as we have seen, let off in as shabby a miscarriage of justice as was ever perpetrated by the American courts.

As we have said, the first of the seven occurred in 1920. In that year, on the morning of June 11, Joseph Elwell, bridge player, playboy, philanderer and so-called "darling of Society," was found dead by his housekeeper in his Park Avenue apartment. He was seated in a chair, dressed in his dressing gown, his bald head without his habitual toupée, a bullet hole between his eyes. Elwell was married, but his wife, unable to tolerate his philandering, had left him, together with their son, never to return. A friend of the late playboy Walter Lewisohn—whose own playboy career was reputed to cost him $1,000,000 a year—Elwell had the night before attended a "divorce party," celebrating a divorce of one of his girl friends from her husband. No gun was found, and the police never even arrested a single suspect.

The second unsolved murder occurred in 1932. In that year 20-year-old Zachary Smith Reynolds, of the ill-starred tobacco Family and brother of the three-times-divorced Richard J. Reynolds, Jr., was shot on the sleeping porch of "Reynolds," his North Carolina home. A strange, brooding, introverted youth, he had at 18 met and married the 20-year-old daughter of Joseph Cannon, of the towel empire.

A year after this marriage, in 1930, Reynolds had met torch singer Libby Holman and, though still married to Anne Cannon, nonetheless asked her to marry him. In 1931 Anne got a divorce in Reno and Reynolds did marry Miss Holman—a match which lasted until a night in July when, during a party, at one o'clock in the morning a shot rang out and Libby screamed, "Smith's killed himself!" Two other guests, "Ab" Walker and actress Blanche Yurka, were still at the party; the other guests were gone. Together with Libby, they drove Reynolds to the hospital, where four hours later he died.

A suicide verdict was given, although Smith was left-handed and yet had obviously been shot through the right temple. Some idea of the vigor with which the police pressed their investigation is evidenced by the fact that not until their third search of the premises did they find the murder weapon, a .32 caliber Mauser automatic, although it was right on the sleeping porch.

At subsequent testimony, Libby stated that she couldn't remember anything that happened that night or even that day, or, for that matter, the night of the day before that. Shortly after this unintelligence, the District Attorney, rather reluctantly it seems, indicted Libby for murder with Walker as accessory. Like so many other Society homicides, however, the case never came to trial, since in November Richard N. Reynolds, Smith's uncle and the titular head of the Family, wrote solicitor Carlisle Higgins that the Family would be "relieved" if the charges were "dropped." And, in the pattern of Publi-ciety murders, they promptly were.*

The third prominent unsolved killing, occurring in 1933, took the life of John R. Fell, a grandson of Philadelphia's Anthony Drexel. Like Smith Reynolds, a rebel without a *cause célèbre*, Fell had married when he was 19 Dorothy Randolph, a lady who, on divorcing him, went on to marry Ogden Mills. Fell next married Mildred Santrey, a Follies girl. "She was ideal as a sweetheart," he said, "but as a wife, Mildred seemed to be only interested in spending money." Divorced again, he met his third wife, Ohio-born Martha Enderton, who came to New York first as a chorus girl and later opened a dress shop. A poised, beautiful girl, she seemed to have no immediate desire to marry the hard-drinking, soft-living Mr. Fell, but a year after they met she gave in.

To celebrate his third wedding, Fell decided to take a trip

* Seven months after the shooting Libby gave birth to Reynolds' son, Christopher Reynolds. Seven years later she married Actor Ralph Holmes, and in 1945, a month after they had separated, he was found dead in his apartment. An empty bottle of sleeping pills was found nearby, and police listed it as an "accidental death." Then in 1950, Libby's son, Christopher, at that time 17 and attempting to scale Mt. Whitney, was killed in a fall.

around the world. And, after traversing Persia and India, the Fells liked Java so much they decided to stay for a while. On February 23 they planned to dine in their hotel suite. When the meal came, however, Fell was—according to his wife, who disliked mentioning his drinking—in no mood to eat, and his plate fell to the floor. When she went to the kitchen for a rag, she returned, she said, to find her husband on the floor, writhing in agony, with a carving knife in his chest. Almost immediately afterward he became unconscious. Mrs. Fell first pulled the knife out of his chest and then rushed out to get help. But while she was gone, Fell evidently regained consciousness, for when a badly frightened native came in, he told him, according to the native, "It's my fault. . . . I did it. . . . I got up to get a drink. . . . I had the knife in my hand. . . . I stumbled and fell on it." Certainly it was one of the most explicit suicide statements on record, but considering Fell's condition, one very difficult to believe. And once more police got nowhere—not even as to why Fell had a carving knife to begin with, when there was no carving to be done. And once more also, in the familiar pattern, the Drexel Family were happy to have the investigation quashed.

The fourth and most famous of the unsolved cases, in 1943, was the brutal bludgeoning to death, and blow-torch burning, of Nassau's 69-year-old Sir Harry Oakes, the multi-millionaire gold miner. Sir Harry, an American who became a British subject, bought his title and moved to Nassau to avoid taxes. He had made his first strike by being thrown off a train in Canada when he had no money and discovering, close to the place where he was thrown off, his Lake Shore Gold Mines. A brutal, degenerate man, he was spending the dark and stormy night on which he met his death with his friend Harold Christie, who was visiting Oakes at his Nassau home "Windborne."

In the Oakes case there was, remarkably enough, a trial. Oakes' son-in-law Alfred de Marigny, then married to Sir Harry's daughter Nancy, was tried for the murder, but, largely through the efforts of the late Raymond Schindler, was freed. No paragon, de Marigny had been married three times and, among other things, was exonerated largely because Schindler was able to establish the fact that he had spent the night with somebody else's wife. Nonetheless, though he later divorced Nancy, and had at the time many reasons for wanting to kill Sir Harry—who detested him as a fortune hunter—Schindler proved the case against him was primarily a trumped-up one. Schindler also demonstrated that the Nassau police force, all the way up to high government officials, had handled the case in an amateurish, totally inept manner and, blocking Schindler at every turn, never allowed him to proceed with an investigation which to his own dying day he believed could have solved the murder. Even now the Oakes murder is easily the most hushed up of all of Society's unsolved killings. And whoever attempts an investigation almost immediately runs afoul not only of Christie and the so-called "Bay Street crowd" but also a large section of the colored population, many of whom had extremely good reasons for wanting to kill Sir Harry also. To add to the mystery, one reporter, years after the crime, believed to be on the trail of a breakthrough, was found dead under extremely suspicious circumstances.

The fifth famous unsolved killing occurred in 1943 on a beach in Hollywood—the victim this time being Gaspar Bacon, Jr., scion of a well-known Boston family and the son of a Lieutenant Governor of Massachusetts. A handsome, talented youth, he was at college theatrically inclined and had starred in Harvard's Hasty Pudding shows, playing girls' parts. He was, however, married—to singer Greta Keller—and although she was not involved, murder most certainly was, since Bacon was stabbed in the back, apparently after a run down the beach. Once again, the family, back in Boston, had no desire for an investigation.

Sixth of the murders was the 1949 killing of Grenville "Beans" Baker, grandson of the so-called "Sphinx of Wall Street" George F. Baker and son of Mrs. George F. Baker, Jr. Like Reynolds and Fell, he was a rebellious young man, but, unlike them, he was widely liked. At the time he met his death, he was separated from Mexican movie starlet Alicia Grajales Corral, and that night he had been drinking in a tavern in Tallahassee, Florida, near his family's famed "Horse-shoe" plantation. Baker's companions on this particular occasion were a tavern owner named Floyd Whiddon, Mrs. Whiddon, and a divorced waitress named Thelma Griffin, to whom Whiddon had introduced him. After the drinking with such Al Capp–sounding characters, Baker returned to his plantation, then started out again, this time riding in a jeep with Mrs. Griffin and attempting to lead the Whiddons in their car out to the main gate through the intricate network of the estate.

At this juncture, Whiddon passed Baker, whereupon Baker, to attract Whiddon's attention, fired a shot from a pistol—one which, curiously enough, he apparently kept in the pocket of Mrs. Griffin's hunting jacket. Seconds later, Mrs. Griffin testified, Baker lost control of the car, the jeep hit an embankment, and both were thrown out. When Mrs. Griffin got up, she said, Baker lay sprawled on the road, moaning. Mrs. Griffin first ran to where Whiddon was waiting—he had stopped his car—and then all three returned to watch Baker die. Later they went to advise Mrs. Baker and the servants of the tragedy. This time, too, there was no real investigation, in deference to family wishes—and this despite the fact that a tenant farmer living nearby testified he heard first not one shot but two shots, then saw a figure pass in front of the car's lights, later saw the lights go off, and then heard a third shot.

The seventh killing was the shooting, in November, 1955, of William Woodward, Jr., by his wife, the former Ann Eden Crowell. Ironically, the evening of the fatal shooting the Woodwards dined at the Locust Valley, Long Island, home of Mrs. George F. Baker; that evening she gave a party in honor of the Duchess of Windsor. The Woodwards were a typical Publi-ciety couple. Woodward, owner of the famous horse "Nashua," was of a Four Hundred background out of Groton and Harvard; his wife, four years older than he, was out of Pittsburg, Kansas, via soap opera, modeling and big game hunting. They met and married in 1943 when he was a Navy ensign just out of college and she was an actress. They had two sons, but even judged by the loose standards prevailing in their Society, their marriage was a tenuous one; their public scenes had given grim indication of what their private life must have been.

In any case, on the night of the Baker party they had driven home through a storm and, tense over the matter of a "prowler" in the neighborhood, had become upset. Some indication of the state of their mentality may be gathered from the fact that the previous night they had left a glass of milk out with sleeping pills in it, apparently in hopes that the prowler would drink it and fall asleep, and thus be easier to shoot. Both seemed to want to shoot him themselves, and both retired to their separate bedrooms, each with a double-barreled shotgun.

Mrs. Woodward claimed she had gone to sleep with her gun in easy reach. Awakened by the barking of her dog, she crossed to the doorway and fired blindly into the darkness separating her room from her husband's. At that moment Woodward, apparently advancing toward his door, was hit in the head by one slug of the shotgun and instantly killed. Afterward, the Nassau County grand jury, on hearing Mrs. Woodward, declared the shooting accidental.

In the Woodward case, in view of the fact there were two Woodward sons—then ages 11 and 7—the pressure to have the case against Mrs. Woodward dropped as speedily as possible was highly understandable. But none of the unsolved killings illustrates better than this one the incredible state of Publi-ciety today—the world of "an I for an I," of feuds and fashions and photographs and gossip columns and sleeping pills and separate bedrooms. Relations between the sexes are so complicated that the only way you can tell if members of the set are "going together" is if they're married. Then, almost certainly, they are not.

However, if outsiders were so naïve as to believe that the Wood ward killing would put a damper on the activities of Publi-ciety, even for a few days, they were sorely mistaken. Activities did not even slow down, and as always—for that is the main reason for the activities—they were widely covered in the press. Sunday, the day of the shooting, Mrs. Lyon Slater gave a large luncheon in honor of the Duchess of Windsor. Tuesday, the night before the funeral of William Woodward, Michael Butler, described in the gossip columns as the Duchess' "latest favorite," gave a dinner. Wednesday, the day of the funeral, Mrs. Harold Brooks gave still another dinner. Meanwhile, of course, almost all of Publi-ciety—though not the Winston Guests and the "Laddie" Sanfords, who refused the parties— found they barely had time to dress for the funeral. For along with the special luncheons and dinners there were, of course, the regular luncheons at the Colony and the nightclubbing at El Morocco. "They seemed to treat the whole thing," said an awed onlooker, "like a rather successful floor show."

Many commentators on the Woodward killing played hard on the Cinderella angle—the fact that Ann Eden Crowell was the daughter of a Midwestern streetcar conductor, J. C. Crowell. To Publi-ciety, however, there was nothing extraordinary about this. One young lady was reminded of the old joke about the colored boys found at night in the chicken coop by the sheriff. "Ain't nobody here but us Cinderellas," she said. "You're Cinderella unless you're a Doris Duke or a Barbara Hutton. Then you're a Poor Little Rich Girl."

Again, in a strange way, this young lady was correct. In Publi-ciety there are half a dozen girls from small communities in Ohio alone, and the number of men who draw their wives from the small towns of the South and West—particularly from among the many girls who, like Ann Woodward, have used modeling or stage careers as an entrée to Publi-ciety—is almost endless.

The final grim fact, from the point of view of both money and morals, is that so many of these wives, upon entering the life of Publi-ciety, leave their parents totally behind them. Certainly no comment on the whole Woodward case contained more pathos than that of Mr. J. C. Crowell, the streetcar conductor, who first read with little concern of the killing of William Woodward, Jr., by Ann Eden Woodward. Later, when he learned who Ann Eden Woodward was, he could not believe it.

"I always thought," he said, "Eve Arden, the television actress, was my daughter."

ACKNOWLEDGMENTS AND INDEX

The author wishes to thank his editor-in-chief, Martha Hodge Amory, who has partnered every step, for seven long years, from idea to index. He wishes too to thank his publisher, Cass Canfield, for courtly candor and fiscal fortitude; his agent, Carol Brandt, for calm collection and cool confidence; his lawyer, Arnold Weissberger, for literate legality and eloquent arbitration; his manuscript editor, Beulah Hagen, for indomitable poise in deadline duress; and last but not least, his typist, Gwen Alden Williams, for virtuosity of both patience and skill. Warm personal thanks and high admiration for so many pictures are also due Slim Aarons and his wife Rita, as well as Ted Patrick, Harry Sions and the staff of *Holiday* magazine, and no less of same to that lion of the lens, Jerry Zerbe, and the staff of *Town and Country*. Then too the book could not have been completed without the cooperation and assistance of Hallowell Bowser and the staff of the *Saturday Review*, John G. Stewart and the staff of the *New York Times Magazine*, Hope Ridings Miller and the staff of *The Diplomat*, and Harriet Lundgaard and the staff of *Celebrity Register*. Besides these should be mentioned the late Dr. Arthur Adams and the staff of the New England Historic and Genealogical Society, Arthur Maynard and Frances Finley of the New York Genealogical and Biographical Society, Helen Ruskell and Sylvia Hilton of the New York Society Library, and Rufus Osgood of the library of the Harvard Club of New York; thanks too to Charles Scribner, Jr., and the staff of the *Dictionary of American Biography*. Apart from all these, signal service above and beyond the call of even remotely direct duty has been rendered by Marguerite Allen of Robert F. Warner Inc., Penelope Coker, James Copp, Emmett Dedmon, Athlyn Deshais, James A. Maxwell, Eleanor Arnett Nash, John L. Oliver, Eleanor Palmer, Stanton Peckham and Mrs. Margaret Ruhl.

The author also wishes to acknowledge his gratitude to the authors and publishers of the following works for the use of quotations, all of which are also credited in the text itself.

Adams, Henry. *Education of Henry Adams*. Massachusetts Historical Society. 1918.
Adams, James Truslow. *The Adams Family*. Literary Guild. 1930.
Altrocchi, Julia Cooley. *The Spectacular San Franciscans*. Dutton. 1949.
Andrews, Wayne. *The Vanderbilt Legend*. Harcourt, Brace. 1941.
Balsan, Consuelo Vanderbilt. *The Glitter and the Gold*. Harper. 1952.
Baltzell, E. Digby. *Philadelphia Gentlemen*. Free Press. 1958.
Beirne, Francis F. *The Amiable Baltimoreans*. Dutton. 1951.
Bridenbaugh, Carl. *Myths and Realities*. Louisiana State University Press. 1952.
Brown, Eve. *Champagne Cholly*. Dutton. 1947.
Bruce, William Cabell. *John Randolph of Roanoke*. Putnam's. 1922.
Cassin, Herbert N. *Cyrus Hall McCormick*. McClurg. 1909.
Chase, Mary Ellen. *Abby Aldrich Rockefeller*. Macmillan. 1950.
Collis, Maurice. *Nancy Astor*. Dutton. 1960.
Crawford, Mary Caroline. *Famous Families of Massachusetts*. Little, Brown. 1930.
Crockett, Albert Stevens. *Peacocks on Parade*. Sears. 1931.
Crowninshield, Francis W. *Manners for the Metropolis*. Appleton. 1908.
Davenport, Charles Benedict. *Heredity in Relation to Eugenics*. Holt. 1911.
Dedmon, Emmett. *Fabulous Chicago*. Random. 1953.
De Wolfe, Elsie. *After All*. Heinemann. 1935.
Dutton, William S. *Du Pont*. Scribner. 1942.
Eckenrode, H. J. *The Randolphs*. Bobbs Merrill. 1946.
Fishwick, Marshall W. *Virginia: A New Look at the Old Dominion*. Harper. 1959.
Fosdick, Raymond B. *John D. Rockefeller Jr*. Harper. 1956.
Greenslet, Ferris. *The Lowells and Their Seven Worlds*. Houghton Mifflin. 1946.
Grund, Francis J. *Aristocracy in America*. Harper. 1959.
Hamm, Margherita Arlina. *Famous Families of New York*. Putnam. 1901.
Harlow, Alvin F. *The Serene Cincinnatians*. Dutton. 1930.
Hendrick, Burton J. *The Lees of Virginia*. Little, Brown. 1935.
Hurd, Charles. *Washington Cavalcade*. Dutton. 1948.
James, Marquis. *Alfred I. Du Pont*. Bobbs Merrill. 1941.
Lea, Tom. *The King Ranch*. Little, Brown. 1957.
Lewis, Oscar. *The Big Four*. Knopf. 1938.
McLean, Evalyn Walsh. *Father Struck It Rich*. Little, Brown. 1936.
Meeker, Arthur. *Chicago with Love*. Knopf. 1958.
Mizener, Arthur. *The Far Side of Paradise*. Houghton Mifflin. 1949.
O'Connor, Harvey. *The Astors*. Knopf. 1941.
———. *The Guggenheims*. Covici-Friede. 1937.
———. *Mellon's Millions*. John Day. 1933.
Perling, J. J. *Presidents' Sons*. Odyssey. 1947.
Poole, Ernest. *Giants Gone*. McGraw-Hill. 1943.
Pulitzer, Ralph. *New York Society on Parade*. Harper. 1910.
Ravenel, Mrs. St. Julien. *Charleston: The Place and The People*. Macmillan. 1925.
Ross, Ishbel. *Silhouette in Diamonds*. Harper. 1960.
Sale, Edith Tunis. *Old Time Belles and Cavaliers*. Lippincott. 1912.

Satterlee, Herbert L. *J. Pierpont Morgan.* Macmillan. 1959.
Schriftgiesser, Karl. *The Amazing Roosevelt Family.* Funk. 1942.
——. *Families.* Howell, Soskin. 1940.
Sedgwick, Henry Dwight. *In Praise of Gentlemen.* Little, Brown. 1935.
Smith, Elsdon C. *Dictionary of American Family Names.* Harper. 1956.
Stevenson, Elizabeth. *Henry Adams.* Macmillan. 1955.
Tallant, Robert. *The Romantic New Orleanians.* Dutton. 1953.
Tanner, Louise. *Here Today.* Crowell. 1959.
Tebbel, John. *An American Dynasty.* Doubleday. 1947.
——. *The Marshall Fields.* Dutton. 1947.
——. *The Life and Good Times of William Randolph Hearst.* Dutton. 1952.
Townsend, Reginald T. *Mother of Clubs.* Union Club. 1936.
Vanderbilt, Cornelius, Jr. *Queen of the Golden Age.* McGraw-Hill. 1956.
Wecter, Dixon. *The Saga of American Society.* Scribner. 1937.
Wertenbaker, T. J. *The First Americans.* Macmillan. 1927.
——. *The Shaping of Colonial Virginia.* Russell and Russells. 1910.
Wharton, Edith. *A Backward Glance.* Appleton-Century. 1934.
Winkler, John K. *The Du Pont Dynasty.* Reynal and Hitchcock. 1935.
——. *Tobacco Tycoon.* Random. 1942.
——. *W. R. Hearst.* Simon & Schuster. 1928.
Wright, Cobina. *I Never Grew Up.* Prentice Hall. 1952.
Wright, Louis B. *The First Gentlemen of Virginia.* Huntington Library. 1940.

Abbett, E. Marie, 140
Abridged Compendium of American Genealogy, 96
Acorn Club, 218
Adams (family), 42, 47, 53, 100-101, 254, 266 ff., 284, 304, 315, 351, 518
  Arthur, 100 ff.
  Brooks, 267, 270, 273, 274
  Charles Francis, 255, 267, 270, 272, 273
  Charles Francis II, 267, 274
  Charles Francis III, 278-279
  Charles Francis IV, 279
  Deacon John, 268-269
    Mrs. Susanna Boyleston, 269
  Edward Shield, 391
  Henry, 267, 270, 272 ff.
    Mrs. Marian Hooper, 267, 277
  James Truslow, 43, 268, 270, 278
  John, 31, 63, 64, 75, 266, 267, 268, 269-270, 304, 309, 311, 328
    Mrs. Abigail Smith, 269, 270, 271

Adams (family)—*Cont.*
  John Payson, 493
    Mrs. Muriel Vanderbilt Church Phelps, 493
  John Quincy, 263, 266, 267, 270-272, 317, 328, 345
    Mrs. Louisa Catherine Johnson, 271
  John Quincy II, 273
  Joseph, 268
  Maude, 222
  Sam, 266, 269, 308
  Sherman, 279
Addams, Jane, 51
Adlerberg, Vava, 183
After All, 21
Age of Innocence, The, 26
Aiken, S. C., 503
Aiken (family), 283
Ak-Sar-Ben Ball, 227-228
Albany, N. Y., 317, 429, 443, 449
Albemarle, Va., 86
Albert of Belgium, 108

Albert Edward, 116 *n.*
Alberti, Jules, 529 *n.*
Aldrich (family), 316, 320
  Abby, 42, 374
  Nelson, 374
  Thomas Bailey, 261
  Winthrop, 140, 211, 374
    Mrs., 140
Alexander, Mrs. Charles B., 132
Alexander, Edward, 180
  Mrs., 180-181
Alexander, James, 319
Alexandra of England, 240
Alfonso of Spain, 167
Alger (family), 48, 404
Allen, Judge, 342
Allerton, Isaac, 305
Alsop (family), 115, 320
  Joseph, 210
Alston, Washington, 90
Altrocchi, Julia Cooley, 420, 423-424,
  436
Ambassador Hotel, 55
American Armoury and Blue Book, 96
American Dynasty, An, 390
American Jockey Club, 447
American Quarterly Review, 113
*American Queen and Town Topics,
  The*, 124
American Scene, The, 24
Americans of Royal Descent, 99
Amory, Grace, 255
"Andalusia," 349
Anderson, Helen Varner, 498
Anderson, Marian, 227
And I'd Do It Again, 422
André, Major, 340
Andrea Doria, 347-348
Andrews (family), 368
  Charles M., 41
  Wayne, 495
Anglomaniacs, 229
"Anglo-Saxon Society Woman, The,"
  58
Anheuser (family), 48
Anne of England, 288
Apperson (family), 416
  Phoebe, 416
Appleton (family), 105, 256, 285 *n.*, 315
  Thomas Gold, 256

Appleton (family)—*Cont.*
  William Sumner, Jr., 104
Appleton, Wisc., 259
April in Paris Ball, 19, 56
Arbella, 41, 500
Archbold (family), 369
Arden, Elizabeth, 53, 241
Arden, Eve, 551
Argyll, Duke of, 396
Armour (family), 392-393
  Mrs. Laurence H., 392 *n.*
  "P. D.," 399 *n.*
Armstrong-Jones, Antony, 17
Armstrong, Margaret Rebecca, 471
Arno, Peter, 183
Arnold, Benedict, 340
  Mrs. Peggy Shippen, 340
Artemis, Mary Elizabeth, 507
Arthur, Chester A., 474
Arwood, E. B., 409
Ashbrook, Pearl, 409
Ashburn, Frank, 85
Ashdor, Heinrich, 469; *see also* Astor
Aspegren, Mrs. John, 132
Assembly Balls, 343
Association for the Preservation of
  Virginia Antiquities, 71
Astaire, Adele, 135
  Fred, 225-226
Astor (family), 25, 47, 49, 87, 100-
    101, 134, 253, 315, 322, 467 *ff.*,
    484, 491, 499, 501, 510, 512, 537
  Alice, 480
  Alida, 472
  Caroline, 479, 491
  Carrie, 493
  Charlotte, 479
  David, 476
  Dolly, 469
  Emily, 473, 478-479
  George, 469
  Helen, 322
  Jacob, 319
  John Jacob I, 50, 113, 120, 143, 468-
    472, 487, 492, 506, 525, 528
    Mrs. Sarah Todd, 24, 98, 221,
    469-470, 471
  John Jacob II, 471
  John Jacob III, 142, 473
    Mrs. Charlotte Gibbs, 222, 473

Astor (family)—*Cont.*
John Jacob IV "Colonel," 479-480
Mrs. Ava Willing, 489, 490
Mrs. Madeleine Force, 490
John Jacob V, 468, 475, 477-478
Mrs. Violet Mary Elliot Nairne, 477
John Jacob VI, 18, 480, 481-482
Mrs. Ellen French, 480
Mrs. Gertrude Gretch, 480
Mrs. Dolores Fullman, 480
John Jacob VII, 476
Laura, 472
Michael, 476
Pauline, 475
Phyllis, 476
Vincent, 211, 322, 480-482
Mrs. Helen Dinsmore Huntington, 135, 480
Mrs. Mary Cushing, 480
Mrs. Mary Brook Russell Marshall, 480
William, 120
Mrs., 22, 24
William Backhouse, 471, 472
Mrs. Margaret Rebecca Armstrong, 471, 472
William Backhouse, Jr., 473
Mrs. Caroline Webster Schermerhorn, *The*, 11, 107, 108, 114, 118, 120, 121, 253, 473-474, 478, 491, 528
William Waldorf I, 473-475
Mrs. Mary Dahlgren Paul, 473-474
William Waldorf II, 475-476
Mrs. Nancy Langhorne Shaw, Lady, 15, 87, 111, 153, 468, 475-477, 478
William Waldorf III, 476, 478
"Astorbilts," 468
Astor House, 470
Astoria Hotel, 474
Atalanta, 451
Atherton, Gertrude, 425
Atlanta, Ga., 49, 125
Attridge, Mrs. John J. (Margaret Roche), 126, 127
Auchincloss (family), 320
Charles C., 213

Austin, Russell, 245
Mrs., 245
Autocrat of the Breakfast Table, 250-251
Avery, Lucy, 371
Ayer, Harriet Hubbard, 528
Aztec Club, 70

Bache, Jules, 135
Babbitt, Irving, 77
Backward Glance, A, 121
Bacon, Florence, 452 *n.*
Gaspar, Jr., 548
Mrs. Greta Keller, 548
Mrs. Robert Low, 151
Robert Ogden, Jr., 179
Mrs. Eleanor Young, 179
Bagot, Lord, 231
Bailliere, Lawrence, 197
Baker, Edith, 443 *n.*
George, 470 *n.*
George F., 42, 84-85, 548
George F., Jr., 548
Mrs., 548
George F. III, 85
Gloria "Mimi," 10, 178, 179-181
Grenville "Beans," 548-549
Mrs. Alicia Grajales Corral, 548, 549
Margaret Emerson Vanderbilt, 179-180
Balch (family), 256
Baldwin, Stanley, 240
Balfour, Lord, 108
Ball, Jessie, 338
Ball of the Atlanteans, 229
Ball of the Twelfth Night Revelers, 229
Ballot, Jeanne, 138
Balsan, Jacques, 492
Mme. Consuelo Vanderbilt Marlborough, 233-234, 492
Baltimore, Md., 37, 52, 62, 100, 121, 123, 126, 147-148, 196, 197, 231, 235, 236, 312, 324, 352, 365, 469, 528
Baltimore, Lord, 352
Baltimore Cotillon, 90
Baltimore Hotel, 236
Baltimore *News,* 148

Baltimore *Sun*, 148
Baltusrol and Pacific Railroad, 5, 124
Baltusrol Golf Club, 5, 124
Baltzell, E. Digby, 343, 350
Bancroft, George, 28, 276
Bandwagon, The, 226
Barber Cox, 58
Barclay (family), 318-319
Barbour (family), 404
Bar Harbor, 170
Barnard, Reginald, 150
Barney, Helen, 503
Barnsdall, William, 406
Barnum, P. T., 520
Barrie, James M., 524
Barry, Edward C., 4, 5
   Mrs. Bertha Eastmond, 3 *ff.*, 125, 127
Barry, Eleanor, 355
   Ida, 352
   John S., 352
Barrymore, Diana, 181
   Ethel, 36, 222, 223
Bartlett, John, 64
Barton (family), 351, 411
   Bruce, 201
Baruch (family), 442
   Bernard, 129
   Sailing, 129
Bass, Joanne, 403
Baur, Mrs. Jacob, 392 *n.*
Baxter, Billy, 139
Bayard (family), 318
   Judith, 511
   Mrs. Stuyvesant, 511
Beach, Katharine, 225
Beale, Betty, 155
Beaton, Cecil, 161
Beatty, David, 401
Beaudette, Palmer, 185-186
   Mrs. Cobina Wright, Jr., 185-186
Beaujour, Felix de, 284
Beaumont, Lord, 435
Bechtel (family), 213
Becker, Carl, 278
Bedford, Duke of, 518
Beebe, Lucius, 133, 135-136, 435, 439-440
Beebe, William, 423
Beecher, Rep., 302-303
"Beechwood," 107

Beekman (family), 46-47, 319
   Charles Keller, 7, 125, 127
Beirne, Francis, 37, 231, 351, 352
Belin, Augustus, 334
   Mary, 334
Bell, Edith Margaret, 412
Bellah, James Warner, 339
"Bellona Hall," 484-485
Belmont (family), 49, 446
   Alice Lee, 448 *n.*
   August, 132, 357, 446-447
      Mrs., 529
   August, Jr., 447, 448, 454
      Mrs. Elizabeth Hamilton Morgan, 448
      Mrs. Eleanor Robson, 448
   August III, 448 *n.*
   August IV, 448 *n.*
      Mrs. Elizabeth Lee Saltonstall, 448 *n.*
      Mrs. Louise Victor Winston, 448 *n.*
   August V, 448 *n.*
   Fredericka, 446
   John, 448 *n.*
   Morgan, 448 *n.*
      Mrs., 132
   O. H. P. (Oliver Hazard Perry), 447-448
      Mrs. Sarah Swan Whitney, 447
      Mrs. Alva Smith Vanderbilt, 11-12, 24, 134, 233-234, 447-448, 491
   Perry, 447
   Priscilla, 448 *n.*
   Raymond, 448 *n.*
   Simon, 446
Benchley, Robert, 138, 507
Benedict, Gamble, 19
Benjamin, Edith, 207
Benjamin, Judah P., 445
Bennett, James Gordon, 216, 225, 527
Benton, Clark, 214
Bentzon, Adrian, 471
Berkeley, William, 305
"Berkeley Hundred," 63, 284
Berlin, Irving, 441
"Bermuda Hundred," 292
Bernal, Juan, 420
Bernardsville, N. J., 52
Berner, Bertha, 431-432

Bernhard, Karl, 30
Bernhardt, Sarah, 530
Bernheim, Leonie, 455
Bernheimer (family), 442
    Alva, 443
    Grace, 457
Berry, Seymour, 238
Best, E. M., 99
"Between," 382
Beverly, Mass., 258
Beverly Hills, 112, 419
Biddle (family), 13, 47, 100-101, 131,
    253, 315, 343, 346-349, 351
    Anthony J. Drexel, 346
    Mrs., 529
    Charles, 348
    Mrs. Hannah Shepard, 348
    Clement, 344, 347
    Mrs. Craig, 132
    Emily, 218
    James, 347
    Julia, 218
    Laura, 134
    Mrs. Livingston, 52
    Nicholas, 347-348
    Nicholas II, 348-349
    Mrs. Jane Craig, 340
    Owen, 344, 347
    William, 346
    William II, 346-347
    Mrs. Mary Scull, 347
Bidermann, James, 336
Billings, C. K. G., 519
Billings, Josh, 46, 81-82
Billingsley, Sherman, 16, 18
Billingsley, Walter, 409
"Biltmore," 490
Bingham, William, 60, 341
    Mrs. Anne Willing, 341
Birdwell, Russell, 176
Bishop, David, 492
Bismarck, Count Edward von, 161
    Countess Mona Strader Schlesinger
        Bush Williams, 161
"Bizarre," 298
Black, Charles Alden, 130
    Mrs. Shirley Temple, 130
Black, William, 9
Blackwell, Earl, 143
Blackwood's Magazine, 58

Blair, William, Jr., 16
Blair, Mrs. William McCormick,
    392 n.
Blake (family), 283
Bland, Frances, 298
"Blenheim," 232
Bliss, Robert Woods, 393
    Mrs., 151, 393
Block Island, 425
Bluebeard, 228
"Blue Grass Farm," 503
Blumenthal (family), 442
Blun, Ida, 461
Boardman (family), 324
Bodie, Irene Curley, 172
Boettcher (family), 407
Bohemian Club, 215-216
Boissevain, G. Louis, 132
Bolling, Robert, 284
Bolton (family), 48
Bonaparte, Jerome, 231, 235
    Mrs. Betsey Patterson, 21-22, 132,
        231-232
Bond, Christina, 93
Bookman, 136
Boothe, Clare, 20, 138
Bonheur, Rosa, 490
"Bonnie Blink," 365
Booker, Richard, 284
Borden, Lizzie, 148
Borrowe, Hallett Alsop, 479
Bossidy, John Collins, 254
Boston, 9, 11, 12, 15, 23, 31, 37, 41, 42,
    47, 51, 53, 61, 62, 74, 76, 85, 123,
    126, 127, 135, 136, 138, 196, 197,
    206, 210, 213, 215, 218, 253, 254,
    255, 256, 257, 261, 263, 271, 273,
    275, 276, 277, 278, 279, 308, 320,
    327, 337, 411, 463, 524, 534-535,
    537, 548
Boston Club, 228
Boston Evening Transcript, 278
Boston Herald, 127
Bostwick (family), 369
    Albert, 492
Boucher, Jonathan, 285
Bourne, Whitney, 130
Bowen (family), 105
Bowers, Claude, 63

Bowne (family), 320
  Frederick, 320
  John, 320
Boylston (family), 255
  Susanna, 269
  Thomas, 269
Bradford (family), 103
  Alicia, 337
  Robert Fiske, 254
  William, 42
Bradford, N. Y., 117
Bradley-Martin (family), 520
Brady, Diamond Jim, 520
Brady, Mrs. Nicholas F., 132
Braggiotta, Gloria, 178
Brandon, Joan, 414
Brayton, Alice, 51
"Breakers," 234, 490, 497
Breckinridge (family), 281
Breese, Joseph L., 492
Breeze, James L., 520
Breitung, Mrs. Edward N., 132
Brent, George, 284
Brevoort (family), 319, 470
  Abraham, 319
Bridenbaugh, Carl, 196, 285
Briggs (family), 406
Bristed, John, 471
Brokaw, Clare (Clare Booth), 138
Bromfield, Louis, 153
Brook Club, 200, 202, 209-210, 212, 226
Brookhouser, Frank, 197 n.
Brookline, Mass., 206, 261
Brooks, Mrs. Howard, 108, 551
Brooks, Peter Chardon, 273
Broom, Jacob, 331
Brophy (family), 411
Brougham, Lord, 63
Brousseau, Mrs. Alfred J., 69
Brown, Eve, 108, 133, 135
Brown, Mrs. Gardner, 132
Brown, Horace, 419
  Mrs. Marion Davies, 419
Brown, Isaac Hull, 115-118
Brown, John Mason, 109-110, 207
Brown, John Nicholas, 207
Browning, Charles H., 99
Brownlow, Perry, 240
"Brown's Brigade," 117

Bruce, Mrs. David (Ailsa Mellon), 361, 363
Bruleman, John, 345
Bryan, John Randolph, 304
  John Stuart, 290
  Joseph, 304
Bryant, James McKinley, 140-141
Bryant, Louise Hungerford, 438
Bryson, Lyman, 144
Buchanan (family), 319, 351
  James, 281
  Mrs. Wiley, 151
Buffalo Bill, 452 n.
Buhl (family), 404
Buick, David Dunbar, 406
Bullock, James, 75 n.
Bullock, Martha, 325
Burden, Arthur Scott, 134
  Mrs. Chester, 12
  Henry, 253
  I. Townsend, 253
  James A., 253
  Mrs. William Proudfit, 132
Burr, Aaron, 115, 280, 297-298
Burke, Stevenson, 162
Burnham, Sarah, 125
Burt, Struthers, 345
Burwell (family), 282, 283, 284
Busche (family), 48
Bush, James Irving, 159-160
  Mrs. Mona Strader Schlesinger, 159-160
Butler, Ben, 263
Butler, General, 274
Butler, Michael, 551
Butler, Nicholas Murray, 77, 111
"Butterfly Ball," 520-521
Byrd (family), 44, 285 ff., 305, 316, 518
  Evelyn, 288-289, 290, 291
  Harry, 286
  Mary, 529
  Richard E., 286
  Thomas, 286
  Ursula, 287
  William, 44, 284, 287
  William II, 287-291
    Mrs., 287-288, 289
  William III, 289-290
Byron, Lord, 57

Cabanne (family), 48
Cabell (family), 281
Cabot (family), 23, 47, 101, 213, 253,
    254, 256-257, 258-259, 264, 266,
    268, 316, 351, 518
  Charles, 258
  George, 257
  Godfrey Lowell, 15, 258
  Hugh, 258
  John, 255, 257, 259
  Paul, 259
  Mrs. Powell M., 529
  Richard, 258, 265
  Robert Moors, 255
  Sebastian, 257
Cactus Club, 215
Cadwalader (family), 13, 47, 100-101,
    115, 342, 343, 351
  John, 79, 342, 344, 346
  Lambert, 344, 346
  Thomas, 344, 345-346
Café Society, 17, 20, 107-108, 121, 131,
    132-133, 135, 140-141, 143, 164,
    186, 440, 541
Café Society Register, 140
"Cafeteria Society," 152
Cafritz, Morris, 154
  Mrs. Gwendolyn Detre de Surnay
    "Gwen," 18, 151, 154-155
Callas, Maria, 147
Calumet Club, 123, 124, 190
Calvert, George, 352
Cambridge, Mass., 366
Camoys, Lady Mildred Sherman, 521
Camp, Walter, 351 n.
Campbell, Colin, 396
Canan, Helen, 452 n.
Candler (family), 49
Cannon, Anne, 545
  Joseph, 545
Cantine, Sarah, 452
Capp, Al, 142
Cardozo (family), 442
Carey, John, 472
Carleton Club, 475
Carnegie (family), 364-365
  Andrew, 46, 84, 129, 253, 356-357,
    358, 522
Carnegie, Dale, 210
Carnegie, Hattie, 529

Carnegie, Mrs. Thomas H., Jr., 529
Carol of Rumania, 140
Carow, Edith, 327
Carpenter, Ginny, 381 n.
Carpenter, Walter, 338
"Carriage Trade," 342
Carrington (family), 281
Carroll, Charles of C., 63, 355
Carroll, Philip, 355
Carroll, Mrs. Royal Phelps, 98
Carter (family), 44, 284, 285, 291,
    305, 351
  Ann Hill, 311-312, 313
  James C., 194
  "King Robin," 283, 312
Cartier, Pierre, 157
Caruso, Enrico, 521
Carver, Mary Theresa, 396
Cary (family), 44, 285
  Miles, 284
Case (family), 48
  Anna, 441
  Harry, 12
  Margaret, 51
Casey, Mrs. Joseph, 151
Cassatt (family), 47, 351
Cassini, Igor, 532-533
Casson, Herbert, 387
Castellane, Count Boniface de, 230,
    452
Castle, Irene, 111-112
  Vernon, 112
Caton, Arthur, 400
  Mrs., 400
"Caumsett," 401
Cecil, John Francis Amherst, 492
  Mrs. Cornelia Vanderbilt, 492
Celebrity Register, 143, 214
"Celebrity Service," 143
Celebrity Society, 118
Century Magazine, 137
Century Club, 200, 201, 202-203, 207,
    209, 214-215, 226, 227, 366
Cerutti, Marquise de, 456
Chabot (family), 257
Chamberlain, Henrietta, 407-408
Chandler (family), 49
  Mrs. Norman, 527
Chanler (family), 473
  Margaret Astor Ward, 473

Chanler (family)—*Cont.*
  Mrs. Winthrop, 121
Chappel (family), 407
Charleston, S. C., 35, 53, 62, 88 *ff.*,
    125, 283, 300, 329, 335, 340, 433
Charleston *News & Courier*, 35
Charleston: The Place and the People,
    89
Chase, Mary Ellen, 374, 376
Chatfield-Taylor, Robert, 184
  Mrs. Brenda Frazier Kelly, 184
Chattanooga, 461, 462
Chattanooga *Times*, 462
Chesterfield, Lord, 9, 77
Chew (family), 47, 85, 340, 343
  Benjamin, 342, 344
  John, 284, 344
  Peggy, 340-341
Chicago, 13, 48, 81, 104, 122, 127, 156,
    161, 213, 215, 218, 232, 234, 237,
    380 *ff.*, 527, 530
Chicago Club, 201, 212, 399
Chicago *Daily News*, 382, 392, 403
Chicago *Sun*, 402
Chicago *Tribune*, 389, 390, 402
Child, Dick, 111
Chilton Club, 218
Chisholm, Hugh, 493
  Mrs. Rosie Warburton Gaynor, 493
Chmay of Belgium, 234
Choate, Jonathan, 86
  Joseph H., 86, 194-195
  Joseph H., Jr., 86
    Mrs., 244
  Joseph H. III, 86
Choules, J. O., 486
Chouteau (family), 48
  Auguste, Jr., 48
  James M., 48
  Pierre, 48
Christian of Denmark, 175
Christian, Linda, 365 *n.*, 541
"Christiana Hundred," 336
Christie, Harold, 547
Chrysanthemum Ball, 88
Chrysler (family), 48, 104, 537
  Jack, 129
  Walter P., 46, 406
  Walter P., Jr., 129

Church, Frederick, 493
  Mrs. Muriel Vanderbilt, 493
Churchill, Ivor Charles Spencer, 492
Churchill, Randolph, 232
  Mrs. Jennie Jerome, 232
Churchill, Winston, 42, 52, 108, 232,
    240
Cincinnati, 48, 74, 125, 148-151, 443,
    444, 462
Cincinnati *Enquirer*, 148
Cincinnati *Gazette*, 414
Clark (family), 387 *n.*
  Edward, 387 *n.*
  Horace, 485
  Maurice, 373
Clarke, Mrs. Lewis L., 132
Clarke, Thomas B., 209-210
Clarkson (family), 319
Clay, Henry, 81 *n.*, 271, 281, 300-301,
    486
Clayton (family), 282
Clemm, Virginia, 351 *n.*
Clemmons, Katherine, 452
Clendenin, Genevieve, 133
Cleopatra's Barge, 136
Cleveland, 48, 125, 161, 162-163, 165,
    213, 368 *ff.*, 405, 501
Cleveland, Grover, 99, 222, 280, 305 *n.*,
    414, 416, 460, 461, 501
  Mrs., 501
Cleveland Club, 212
Cleveland *Plain Dealer*, 54
Clews, Henry, 450 *n.*, 489
  Mrs., 11-12, 132
"Cliveden," 475
"Cliveden Set," 477
Clothier, Isaac, 350
Coats, Audrey, 401
Coats, Dudley, 401
Cobb (family), 283
  Elaine, 184
  Henry Ives, 394, 522
"Cobb's Hall," 305
Cochrane, Lucy "Cee-Zee," 365 *n.*
Codman (family), 255
Coffee House Club, 139, 215, 226
Coffin (family), 256
Cogswell, Elinor, 431
Cogswell, Joseph Green, 471
Coker, Elizabeth Boatright, 88

Colby, Anne, 498
Colby, Mrs. Kimball, 12-13
Coleman (family), 197
Colford, Mrs. Sydney J., Jr., 132
Collier's, 22, 108
Collins, Elizabeth, 415
Collis, Maurice, 476
Colonial Dames, 67
Colonial Daughters of the Seventeenth Century, 72
Colonial Families of Philadelphia, 342
Colonial Order of the Crown, 99
Colonial Wars Society, 67
Colony Club, 222-223, 224, 226
Colton, David, 427
Comstock Lode, 434, 435
Comus Club, 228
Conant, F., 256
Connelley, Joanne, 186-187
Conniff, Frank, 88
Conroy, Tom, 151
    Mrs., 151
Constable, William, 194
Constantine of Russia, 486
Constitution, 243
Contentment Club, 218
Conway, Gen., 346
Conway, Gertrude, 492
Conway, Mass., 397, 399, 500
"Conway Cabal," 345, 346
Cooke, Barclay, 214
Coolidge, Calvin, 14, 99, 108, 183, 263, 363
Coolidge, Mrs. John Gardner, II, 529
Cooper, Duff, 239
Cooper, Gary, 518
    Mrs., 518
Cooper, James Fenimore, 30, 64, 110-111
Cooper, J. F., 348
Cooper, Peter, 484
Cooper, Mrs. Sheldon, 436
Copley, Mary Sibbet, 366-367
Corbett, Lenore, 131
Corbin (family), 284, 306
Corrigan, "Captain," 162
Corrigan, James, 162-163
    Mrs. Laura Mae Whitrock MacMartin, 108, 132, 135, 161-165, 242
Corsair, 82 n., 83

Cortlandt Manor, 317
Cosden, Joshua, 135
    Mrs., 132, 135
Cosmopolitan Club, 223, 224-225, 226, 227
Cosmos Club, 215
Coumantauros (family), 523
Council Bluffs, Iowa, 380
Country Club, 206
Couzens, James, 406
Coward, Noel, 55, 76, 145-146
Cowles, Gardner, 56
Cowles, Mrs. William (Anna Roosevelt), 326
Cox, Marceline, 66 n.
Coxe (family), 343
    Charles, 344
Craig, Jane, 340
Crane (family), 104
Cranmer (family), 407
Craven, Lord, 520
Crawford, Miss Frank Armstrong, 486
Cresap, Mark, 357 n.
Crichton, Kyle, 185
Crittenden (family), 281
    May, 425
Crocker (family), 49, 421-424, 518
    Aimée, 422
    Clark, 421
    Charles, 421-422, 423, 424, 427
        Mrs., 421, 422
    Charles Frederick, 422
    Charles Templeton "Colonel," 423
    Diana, 423
    Edwin B., 421, 422
    Henry, 421
    Henry J., 423
    Isaac, 421
    William H., 422-423, 530
        Mrs. Ethel Sperry, 422, 423
    W. W., 423
Crockett, Albert Stevens, 519
Cromwell, James H. R., 170
    Mrs. Delphine Dodge, 170
    Mrs. Doris Duke, 170
Crosby, Bing, 530
Crosby Boys, 530
Crowell, Ann Eden, 130, 549-551
Crowell, J. C., 551

Crowninshield (family), 136, 256, 315
　Benjamin, 136
　Frank, 20, 24, 77, 108, 136-140, 490
Crown Prince of Norway, 108
Crugger (family), 449 n
Cryder Triplets, 12
Cudahy (family), 392-393
　Mrs. Edward A., 392 n.
Cuevas, Marquis de, 380
Cunard, Bache, 242
Cunard, Lady Emerald (Maude)
　Burke, 135, 239, 241
Curran, Pamela, 187
Curtis (family), 316
　Frederick, 97, 98
　George William, 116
　Holbrook, 122
　Laura, 160
Curzon, George, 232, 233, 396
　Mrs. Mary Leiter, 232-233
Cushing, Betsey, 507
Cushing, Mary, 480
Cushing Sisters, 18
Cushman (family), 322
Cutler, Robert, 254, 255 n.
Cutting, Bayard, 79
Cutting, Mrs. Charles Suydam, 52
Cutting, R. Fulton, 132
Cutting, Mrs. W. Bayard, 132
Cuyler, Cornelius C., 353

d'Abbadie (family), 101
Daggett, Stuart, 431
Dali, Salvador, 160
Dallas, 48, 53
Dalmas, Sophia Madelaine, 330
Dana, Paul, 120
d'Anterroches (family), 101
Daughters of the American Revolu-
　tion, 40, 67, 68-69, 71, 87
Davenport, Charles Benedict, 280-282
Davenport, John, 264
Davidson (family), 49
Davies, Emily, 498
Davies, Marion, 131, 158, 418-419
Davis, Dwight F., Jr., 214
Davis, Henry Gassaway III, 493
　Mrs. Consuelo Vanderbilt II Smith,
　493
　Mrs. Grace Vanderbilt, 498

Davis, Mrs. James B., 38
Davis, Jefferson, 283, 298, 464
　Mrs., 42
Davis, Joseph, 283
Davis, Kate, 463-464
Davis, Louise, 54
Davis, Mrs. Loyal, 392 n.
Davis, Noah, 195, 196
Davison, Eliza, 371
Daw, Mae, 130
Dayton, 125
Dean, Gordon, 207 n.
Dedham, Mass., 218
Dedmon, Emmett, 122, 201, 381-382
Deering, William, 387
De Eresby, Willoughby, 478
Deering (family), 104
DeGolyer, E., 370, 413
DeGolyer, Mrs. Everette, 53
De Jong (family), 443
Delano (family), 321
　Franklin H., 472
　Mrs. Laura Astor, 472
Delaware State Journal, 331
DeLeon, David Camden, 444
Delmas, Delphin M., 367
Delmonico, Charlie, 166
Delmonico's, 22, 166, 167
Del Monte, Calif., 422
Delphian Club, 351 n.
Delray Beach, Fla., 241
De Marigny, Alfred, 547-548
　Mrs. Nancy Oakes, 547-548
Deming, Mary Ann, 421
Democracy, 277
Democracy in America, 29
Denver, Colo., 156, 215, 218, 406-407
Denyer, Ronald, 496
Depew, Chauncey, 192
De Peyster (family), 25, 47, 115, 319
　Gerard, 319
　Nicholas, 319
Derby (family), 256
Derby, Elias Haskett, 136
Derby, Lord, 112
De Reuter (family), 25
De Rham, William, 50, 537-540
　Mrs., 538
De St. Cyr, Mrs. Jean, 132

Desha (family), 491
Deshais, Athlyn, 392
Desloge (family), 48, 104 *n.*
Dessel, Jean, 54
"Destiny Farm," 112
De Surnay, Gwendolyn Detre, 154
De Tocqueville, Alexis, 29
De Toina, Count Festeils, 231
Detroit, Mich., 48, 81, 95, 125, 172, 213, 221, 234, 403 *ff.*
Detroit *Free Press,* 405
Dever, Joseph Xavier, 141
Devereux, Marion, 148-151
De Voie, Bessie, 453
Dewey, Thomas, 129
Dewey, Adm. George, 326
De Wolfe, Elsie, 21, 132, 140, 502
D'Hauteville, F. G., 120
Diary in America, A, 28
Diary of Philip Hone, 27
Di Bonaventura, Anthony, 508
  Mrs. Sara Delano Roosevelt, 508
Di Cicco, Pat, 498
  Mrs. Gloria Vanderbilt, 498
Dick, Fairman, 325
Dickson, David Augustus, 35 *n.*
  Mrs., 35 *n.*
Dickson, Louise Ann, 35 *n.*
Dictionary of American English, 75
Dictionary of American Family Names, 315
Dictionary of American Biography, 349
Dietrich, Marlene, 135
Di Frasso, Dorothy, 146
DiMaggio, Joe, 142
"Dinner Party, The," 113
Disston, Mrs. William, 132
"Ditchley," 305
Dixon, Dorinda, 356
Dobbs Ferry, N.Y., 156
Documentary History of the United States, 444
Dodge (family), 48, 104, 170
  Delphine, 170
  Frances, 406
  Horace, 406
  John, 406
Dodge, Marcellus Huntly, 377

Dodworth, Allen, 537
"Dog's Dinner," 519
Doheny (family), 49
Doherty, Helen Lee Eames, 167
Doherty, Henry L., 167
Dolan, Thomas, 350
"Dolly Madison," 131
Dolly Sisters, 112
Dominguez (family), 49
Donahue, James, 172
  Mrs. Jessie, 146, 172, 177
Don Juan, 57
Dorchester, Mass., 397
Dorelis, José Rex Holstein, 241
Dorrance (family), 351
Dorsey (family), 351
Douglas (family), 412, 518
  Elizabeth, 412
  James, 412, 413
  James Stuart, 412, 413
  James Stuart II, 413
  Katherine, 412
  Lewis, 413
  Lewis, Jr., 413
  Naomi, 412
  Robert Bell, 412-413
  Sharman, 413
  Walter, 412
  Walter II, 412
Douglas, Ariz., 412
Douras, Cecelia, 418
Dowdey, Clifford, 44, 284
Dowling, Father Edward, 54
Downtown Association, 212
Drake, Maud Lord, 432
Drake Hotel, 55, 146
Draper, Dorothy, 458
Draper, Ruth, 130
Drayton, James Coleman, 479
  Mrs. Charlotte Astor, 479
Dresser, Edith Stuyvesant, 490
Dress magazine, 137
Dress & Vanity Fair, 137
Dresser, Marion Snowden Rospigliosi Reed, 135
Drew, Uncle Dan'l, 82
Drexel (family), 47, 134, 344, 547
  Anthony J., 344, 546
  Mrs. John R., Jr., 132
  Marjorie Gould, 521

Drummond (family), 400
  Maldwin, 400
Dry Fable of a Dry Crowd at Dry Island, The, 162
Dryfoos, Orvil E., 462
Dudley (family), 255
  Eric, 239
Duer (family), 319, 351
  Katherine Alexander, 440-441
Duke (family), 167-168, 517
  Doris, 129, 142, 167-171, 173, 176, 178, 551
  James Buchanan, 167-168
  Mrs. William McCredy, 168
  Mrs. Nanaline Holt Inman (mother of Doris), 168-169, 171
Duke University, 167, 168
Dulles, John Foster, 253
  Mrs., 224-225
Duncan, Isadora, 387 *n.*
Duncan, Mary, 128
Duncan, Raymond, 140
Duncan, William Butler, 120
Dunne, F. Peter, 111, 139
Du Pont (family), 84, 87, 104, 213, 315, 328, 362, 518
  Alexis, 332, 333
  Alfred Irénée, 336-337, 338
  Mrs. Bessie Gardner, 337
  Mrs. Alicia Bradford Maddox, 338
  Mrs. Jessie Ball, 338
  Alfred Victor, 332, 333, 336
  Amélie, 329
  Annie, 336
  Charles Irénée, 329
  Eleuthère Irénée, 328, 330-332, 333, 336
  Mrs. Sophia Dalmas, 331
  Ethel, 328
  Eugene, 334, 336
  Henry, 332-333, 334, 336
  Mrs. Louise Gerhard, 332
  Henry Algernon, 335-336
  Henry B., 333
  Henry Francis, 336
  Irénée III, 335
  Lammot, 333, 334
  Mrs. Mary Belin, 334
  Lammot II, 335
  Maurice, 339 *n.*
  Pierre I, 329, 331

Du Pont (family)—*Cont.*
  Pierre II, 335
  Mrs., 221
  Pierre III, 333-334, 337, 338
  Samuel Francis, 335
  Sophie Madeleine, 335
  T. Coleman, 337, 338
  Victor Marie, 328, 329, 331, 333
  Mrs. Gabrielle Pelleport, 329
  William, 334
Duquesne Club, 212, 358
Durant, William, 406
Durham, N. C., 168
Dutton, William, 330, 332
Dux, Claire, 392
Dyer, Elisha, 111

Earl, N. Clarkson, Jr., 493
  Mrs. Consuelo Vanderbilt II Smith Davis Warburton, 493
Early Memories, 23
East, Mrs. Tom, 410
Eastmond, Bertha, 4, 125
Eaton, Elizabeth, 457
Eckenrode, H. J., 293, 295-296, 297
Edgar, Elizabeth, 464 *n.*
Edison, Charles A., 111
Education of Henry Adams, The, 272-273, 274, 275, 278
Edward VII, 401, 476
Edward VIII, 165; *see also* Windsor, Duke of
Edwards (family), 279-280
  Jonathan, 280
  Richard, 280
  Mrs. Elizabeth Tuttle, 280, 281
  Mrs. Mary Talcott, 280
  Russell, 53
  Timothy, 280
Eisenhower (family), 316
  Dwight D., 11, 103, 152, 206, 254, 279, 403, 414 *n.*
  Mrs. Mamie Doud, 69
Eliot, Charles William, 266
Eliot, Elizabeth, 230
Elizabeth II, 185, 363, 544
Elizabeth, Queen Mother, 165, 241, 242-243, 412
Elkins, William L., 349
Ellet, Mrs. E. F., 26

Elliman, Lois, 178
Ellis, Havelock, 258
Elmhirst, Leonard K., 503
  Mrs. Dorothy Whitney Straight, 503
Eltring, Carol, 381 n.
Elwell, Joseph, 545
Emancipation of Massachusetts, The, 273
Embiricos, Nicholas, 179
  Mrs., 179
Emerson, Margaret, 10, 146, 179-180, 223, 494
Emerson, Ralph Waldo, 113
  Mrs., 42
Emmett, Richard Stockton, 369 n.
  Mrs., 369 n.
Endecott, Gov., 256
English Traits, 113
Enzinger, Mrs. George (Irene Castle McLaughlin), 111-112
Esquire, 142
Esty, William, 528, 529
Etiquette, 19-20
Eulalie, Infanta of Spain, 395
Eureka Springs, Ark., 112
Evans, John, 406
Evanloff, Prince Michael, 241
  Elizabeth Arden, 241
Fabric of Memory, The, 448
Fair (family), 434, 436-437
  Charles, 437
  James, 437
  James Gordon, 436-437, 438
  Theresa, 145, 437
  Virginia, 437, 492
  Senator, 145
Fairbank, Janet, 381 n.
Fairbanks, Douglas, 110
Fairbanks, Douglas, Jr., 239
  Mrs., 239
Fairbanks, Flobelle, 110
Fairchild, Mrs. B. Tappen, 220
Fairfax (family), 43-44, 283, 305
"Fairland Farms," 159
"Falcon's Lair," 171
Falkenburg, Jinx, 186, 222
Fall, Albert, 159
Familiar Quotations, 64
Family Circle Dancing Class, 120
Famous Families of New York, 314

Fanevil (family), 255
Fanshawe, Jessie Jerome, 52, 128, 224
Farley, James, 129, 448
Farlow-Nettleton, Denys King, 456
Farrell, Frank, 141
Far Side of Paradise, The, 531
Fathers of New England, The, 41
Father Struck It Rich, 155
Fauchet, M., 297
Federal Republican, 312
Fell, Dorothy Randolph, 414 n.
Fell, John R., 546-547
  Mrs. Dorothy Randolph, 546
  Mrs. Mildred Santrey, 546
  Mrs. Martha Enderton, 546-547
Field (family), 213, 253, 393, 397-403, 463, 518, 527
  Barbara, 401, 403
  Bettine, 401
  Ethel, 399, 400-401
  Fiona, 401
  Frederick, 403
  Gwendolin, 400
  Henry, 400
  Joanne, 403
  Katherine, 403
  Marshall I, 393, 397-399
    Mrs. Nannie Douglas Scott, 397-398, 399-400
    Mrs. Arthur Caton, 400
  Marshall II, 399, 400
    Mrs. Albertine Huck, 400
  Marshall III, 400, 401-403
    Mrs. Evelyn Marshall, 401
    Mrs. Audrey Coats, 401
    Mrs. Ruth Pruyn Phipps, 401
  Marshall IV, 401, 403, 414
    Mrs. Joanne Bass, 403
    Mrs. Katherine Woodruff, 403
  Marshall V, 403
    Phyllis, 401
  Mrs. W. B. Osgood, 132
  Zachariah, 397
Figueroa (family), 49
Filene (family), 393 n.
Firestone, Harvey, 406
Finletter, Mrs. Thomas K., 224
First Families of Virginia, 40, 43, 44, 45, 292, 304

Fish (family), 315, 320
  Hamilton, 122, 320
    Mrs. Hamilton, Jr., 529
  Stuyvesant, 122-123, 132
    Mrs., 320, 511, 519, 534
Fisher, Mrs. Joel Ellis, 132
Fisher Brothers, 406
Fishers Island, 522
Fish House, 197
Fish House Punch, 197
Fishwick, Marshall, 44 n., 68, 75 n., 291
Fisk, Gwendolyn, 178
Fiske, John, 282
Fitzgerald, F. Scott, 20-21, 523, 531
  Mrs. Zelda, 531
Fitzgerald, "Honey Fitz," 255 n.
Fitz-Gerald, Margery May, 340 n.
Fitzgerald, Scottie, 20-21
Fitzhugh (family), 283, 284, 285, 305
Flagler (family), 369
Flagstaff, Ariz., 265
Flair, 56
Flood (family), 434
  James C., 435
  James L., 436
  Jennie, 435-436
  Jimmie, 436
"Florham," 109-110
Florimond, Joseph, Duc de Loubat;
    see Loubat, Count
Folger (family), 256
Fonda, Henry, 221-222
Forbes (family), 47, 255, 257
Force, Madeleine, 480
Ford (family), 48, 104, 213, 406, 537
  Charlotte, 518
  Edsel, 519
  Henry I, 129, 406, 519 n.
  Henry II, 13, 56, 403, 414
    Mrs. Anne McDonnell, 13, 221
Fortnightly Club, 218
Fortune, 4, 163, 323, 524
Fort Worth, Tex., 187
Fosburgh, Mrs. James (Mary Cushing
    Astor), 480
Fosdick, Harry Emerson, 129
Fosdick, Raymond, 374
Foster, John W. S., 197
Founders and Patriots Society, 71
"Four Hundred," 6, 20, 52, 65, 98, 99,
    108, 114, 115, 120-123, 128, 137,
    139, 203, 233, 366, 464, 478, 479,
    480, 502, 519, 549
Four Seasons Hotel, 122
Fowkes (family), 285
Fowler, Nancy, 387-388, 389
Fox, Mrs. Byron, 129
Fox, John, Jr., 139
Foxcroft School, 14, 542-544
"Foxland," 524

Foy, Mrs. Byron, 529
Francis, Arlene, 534
Franco, Nathan, 234-235
Franklin, Benjamin, 70, 345, 462-463,
    486
Franklin (family), 319
Fraunces' Tavern, 71
Frazier, Brenda, 18, 166, 178, 181-184,
    187
Frazier, Frank Duff, 181
  Mrs. Brenda Williams-Taylor, 181
Freeman, Douglas Southall, 92
  Mrs., 53
Frelinghuysen, Mrs. Frederick T., 132
French, Ellen, 480
French, Elsie, 496
Frick (family), 84
  Henry, 356, 358, 365
Friday Club, 218
Friedlander, Isaac, 444
Friendly, Alfred, 158
"Friendship," 157, 158
"Fruit Garden Path, The," 261
Fuller, Thomas, 75-76
Fullman, Dolores, 480
Fulton, Robert, 386
Funk, Charles Early, 37
Funk, Wilfred, 540
Furness, Thelma, 160

Gabor, Eva, 18
Gabor, Jolie, 18
Gabor, Magda, 18
Gabor, Zsa Zsa, 18, 176
Gallatin (family), 253
  Albert, 270, 470
  Albert Eugene, 217
Galitzin, Prince, 422
Gamal, Samia, 11

Gambrill, Mrs. Richard, 132
Ganz, Joan, 411
Garbisch, Mrs. Edgar, 129
Garbo, Greta, 55, 181, 498
Gardiner (family), 315, 370
  Mrs. David Lion, 370
  Robert David Lion, 370
Gardner (family), 315
  Bessie, 337
  Mrs. Jack, 41
Garnier (family), 49
Garosche (family), 48
Garrett, Robert, 489
Garson, Greer, 186
Gary, Judge, 351
Gates, Frederick T., 374
Gaynor, William, 493
  Mrs. Rosie Warburton, 493
Generall Historie of Virginia . . . , 32
George, Henry, 326
George II of England, 288
George VI of England, 164, 165, 238, 241
Georgetowner, The, 153
"Georgian Court," 452
Gerard, Mrs. Sumner, 50
Gerhard, Louise, 332
Gerry (family), 115, 537
  Elbridge, 122
  Elbridge T., 132
Gershwin, George, 137
Gerstle, Albert, 455
Getty, J. Paul, 541
Gibbons, Floyd, 140
Gibbons, Sarah T., 118
Gibbs (family), 473
  Charlotte, 473
Gibson, Charles Dana, 12, 111, 229, 476
  Mrs. Irene Langhorne, 12, 15, 111, 113, 114, 476
Gibson, Mrs. Preston, 132
Gibson Girl, 12, 111, 166
Gilbert, W. S., 255
Gilder, Richard Watson, 111, 264
Gilmor (family), 351
Gimbel (family), 393 n.
Gimbel, Adam, 393 n.
Gimbel, Bernard, 443
Gish, Dorothy, 534

Gizycka, Felicia, 351 n.
Glamour Girls, 18, 166, 178 ff., 518
Glen Cove, N.Y., 172
"Glenlyvar," 299
Gluck, Alma, 140
Glyn, Elinor, 112, 139
Goelet (family), 188, 319, 512, 537
  Ogden, 493
  Mrs., 132, 134
  Peter, 319, 484
Goicouria, Alice Wall de, 448 n.
Gold (Gould), Nathan, 449
Goldfine, Bernard, 279
Goldman (family), 442
Goldsborough (family), 283
Goldwater (family), 411
  Barry, 445
Goldwyn, Samuel, 142, 239
  Mrs., 239
Gomez, Johnny, 171
Gone With the Wind, 507, 509
Gooch (family), 101
Goodhue, C. C., 120
Goodrich, James J., 101
Goodsell, Almira Geraldine, 376-377
Goodyear, Charles, 386
Gordon, Richard, Jr., 130
  Mrs. Kyle McDonnell, 130
Gore (family), 255
Gore Roll, 96
Gorsuch (family), 101
Goshen, N.Y., 503
Goulandris (family), 523
Gould (family), 49, 134, 316, 354, 439, 446, 448-453, 517
  Anna, 230, 450, 451, 452, 453
  Anne Douglass, 529
  Dorothy, 452 n.
  Edith, 452 n.
  Edwin, 450, 451, 453
  Edwin Jay, 452 n.
  Frank Jay, 450, 451, 452-453
    Mrs. Helen Kelly, 453
    Mrs. Edith Kelly, 453
    Mrs. Florence La Case, 453
  Frank Miller, 452 n.
    Mrs. Florence Bacon, 452 n.
    Mrs. Helen Canan, 452 n.
  George, 450, 451-452, 453
    Mrs. Edith Kingdon, 452

Gould (family)—*Cont.*
  Mrs. Guinevere Jeanne Sinclair,
    452
  George Jay, 135, 521
  Mrs., 134
  George Jay, Jr., 452 *n.*
  Helen, 451, 453
  Helen II, 452 *n.*
  Howard, 450, 451, 452, 453
  Mrs. Katherine Clemmons, 452
  Jay, 162, 449-450, 451, 463
  Mrs. Helen Day Miller, 132, 450
  Jay II, 452 *n.*
  Kingdon, 452 *n.*
  Kingdon, Jr., 452 *n.*
  Marianne, 452 *n.*
  Marjorie, 452 *n.*, 521
  Sylvia, 452 *n.*
  Vivian, 452 *n.*
Gourielli-Tchkonia, Prince Artchill,
    241
  Princess Gourielli (Helena Rub-
    instein), 241
Gouverneur (family), 319
Grace (family), 537
Grace, Eugene, 523 *n.*
Grace, Princess of Monaco, 130, 243-
    245, 349
Grace Church, 116, 117
Gracie, Archibald, 319
Graham, Florence Nightingale (Eliza-
    beth Arden), 53
Graham, Philip, 403
Graham, Mrs. William Miller, 132
Grand Hotel (Mackinack), 16
Grand Hotel, 434
Grand Union Hotel (Saratoga), 445-
    446
Grant, Cary, 176
  Mrs. Barbara Hutton Mdivani Haug-
    witz-Reventlow, 176
Grant, Matthew, 183
Grant, Robert T., 265
Grant, Ulysses S., 42, 99, 103, 280, 394
Grant, Ulysses S., Jr., 435
Gray, Adeline, 412
Gray, Audrey, 178
Great Barrington, Vt., 371, 425
Great Fortunes, 100
Great Neck, N.Y., 365

Greeley, Horace, 81, 414, 528
Green, Hetty, 522
Green Book, 152, 153
Greenbrier Hotel, 56
Greene, Nathanael, 312, 347
Greenewalt, Crawford, 338
Greenough, Peter, 48
Greenslet, Ferris, 263
Greentree Stables, 505
"Greentree Team," 507
Greenwich, Conn., 140, 377
Gregory, Eliot, 121
Gretch, Gertrude, 480
Griess, William, 150
Griffin, Thelma, 549
Grigsby, Hugh Blair, 301-302
Grimes (family), 285
Griswold, Rufus Wilmot, 60, 341
Grosse Pointe, 405
Grund, Francis J., 251-252
Grymes, Lucy, 311
Guest, "Cee-Zee," 18
Guest, Raymond, 365
Guest, Winston, 365, 551
Guest (family), 315
Guggenheim (family), 453-459, 517
  Barbara, 456
  Benita, 456
  Benjamin, 454, 455-456, 457
  Cora, 454, 455
  Daniel, 454, 455, 457, 458
  Daniel, II, 457
  Edmond, 457
  Gladys, 458
  George Denver, 457
  Harry, 457, 458-459
  Mrs. Alicia Patterson, 390, 391
  Isaac, 454, 455, 457
  Jeannette, 454, 455
  Joan, 458
  John Simon, 457
  Marguerite, 456
  Meyer, 453-455, 458
  Mrs. Barbara Myers, 453-454
  Murry, 454, 455, 457
  Nancy, 459
  Robert, 454, 457, 458
  Robert, Jr., 457
  Rose, 454, 455, 457
  Simon, 453

Guggenheim (family)—*Cont.*
Simon, 454, 455, 457
Solomon, 454, 455, 457
William, 454, 455, 456, 457
William, Jr., 455 *n.*, 457
Guinness (family), 361, 362
Guinness, Peter, 361
Gutherz, Lina, 460
Gwin (family), 49
Gwynne, Alice, 493
Gwynne, Foxie, 239

Habits of Good Society, 536
Haddad, William, 508
Mrs. Kate Roosevelt (Whitney), 508
Haggin, Ella, 231
Haggin, James Ben Ali, 415
Haig, George, 479
Mrs. Charlotte Astor Drayton, 479
Half Moon, 32
Hall, Basil, 29
Mrs. Margaret Hunter, 29
Hall, Florence, 218
Hall, Major, 231
Hall, Mary Ann, 386
Halle (family), 393 *n.*
Halleck, Fitz-Greene, 471-472
Hallowell (family), 37-38
N. Penrose, 534-536
Mrs., 534-535
Hamersley, John W., 120
Hamilton, Alexander, 40, 63, 97, 297
Hamm, Margherita Arlina, 314-315, 317
Hammond, Harriet, 389
Hammond, John Henry, 181
Mrs. Esme O'Brien Sarnoff, 181
Hampton, Hope, 19
Hampton (family), 281
Hancock (family), 47, 103, 264
John, 62
Hand, Phebe, 483
Handy, Helen Parmalee, 405
Handy, Truman Parmalee, 405
Hanna (family), 48
Marx, 389
Ruth, 389
Hanson, Alexander, 312

Harbeson, John Frederick, 215
"Harbor Point," 440
Harding, Warren G., 363
Mrs., 158
Harkness (family), 368, 369-370
Edward Stephen, 369-370
Mrs. Mary Stillman, 369
Harkness, Stephen, 369
Mrs., 506
Harkness, William Hale, 130
Mrs. Elizabeth Grant, 130
Harlow, Alvin, 148-149, 443
Harmonie Club, 226
Harper's Bazaar, 51, 113, 129, 170
Harper's Magazine, 77, 261 *n.*, 300
Harriman (family), 84, 308, 315, 474
Averell, 129
Mrs. Marie Norton Whitney, 509
E. H., 219, 428, 451
Mrs., 132
J. Borden, 222
Mrs. J. Borden, 151, 153, 222, 224, 529
Margaret Case, 131
Mary, 219
Mrs. Oliver, 528-529
Harris, Corra May, 76
Harrison (family), 44, 62-63, 284
Harrison, Benjamin, 295
Harrison, Mrs. Burton, 122, 229
Harrison, Frederic, 80
Randolph, 299
Ruth, 151
William Henry, 414, 488
Hartford, Conn., 82, 280
Hartford (family), 393
George Huntington, 393 *n.*
Huntington, II, 86
John, 86
Harvard, John, 103
Harvard Club, 196, 207, 225, 227
Harvard *Lampoon*, 198, 417
Harvard University, 77, 258-259, 264, 275-276, 279, 370
Harvey, 375
Harvey, George, 159
Harvey, Fred, 393 *n.*
Harvey, Jacob, 303
Harvey, Jean, 498

Haugwitz-Reventlow, Count Kurt von, 174
Countess Barbara Hutton Mdivani, 175
Hasty Pudding Club, 198
Hatzfeldt, Prince, of Germany, 427
Haverhill, Mass., 389
Hay, Helen, 504
Hay, John, 276-278, 504
Hayes, Rutherford B., 263, 328
Hayne, Edmund Shubroch, 89
Hayworth, Rita, 541
Hearst (family), 129, 415-420, 463, 527, 537
  David, 419
  George, 16-17, 415, 417, 525
  Mrs. Phoebe Apperson, 416, 417
  George, II, 419
Hearst, John, 419
  Randolph, 419
  William G., 415
  William Randolph, Sr., 17, 131, 225, 367, 415, 416-419
  Mrs. Millicent Willson, 144, 146, 418, 527
  William Randolph, Jr., 419-420
Heath, Charles Monroe, 455 n.
Heath, General, 40
Heathcote, Caleb, 317
Heine, Alice, 230
Heinz (family), 358
Heinz, Henry John, 358
Heiresses and Coronets, 230
Helenita, 451
Hellman, Geoffrey, 140
Hemenway, Mrs. Augustus, 11
Hemingway, Ernest, 523
Heminway, Mrs. John, 522
Hempelmann, Mrs. Louis H., 464 n.
Hendrick, Burton, 101, 305, 306
Hendrick, Mrs. Ellwood, 223
Henrici, Mrs. Jacques, 127
Henry, Mrs. Barklie McKee, 506
Henry, Patrick, 281, 295, 296, 299
Hepburn, Katharine, 130, 532
Hepburn, Thomas, 532
  Mrs., 532
Heraldry Simplified, 97
Herbert, George, 76

Herbert, Grace Brown, 455
Heredity in Relation to Eugenics, 280
Herrick, Ambassador, 531
Herrick, Mrs. Robert, 51
Herter, Christian, 254-255
Hesilrigge (family), 101
"Hever Castle," 475
Hewitt, Abram S., 326
Hewitt, Peter Cooper, 492
Heyward, Dubose, 283
Heyward, Edward, 447
Heyward, Nathaniel, 283
Hibbard, Lydia, 381 n.
Hichens, Robert, 139
Higgins, Carlisle, 546
Higginson, Teresa, 381 n.
Higginson (family), 257
Higham, John, 444, 445
"Highland Falls," 83
Highland Ranch, 366
Hill (family), 407
Hill, Crawford, 156
  Mrs., 407
Hill, Louisa Sanborn, 127
Hilton (family), 49
  Conrad, 210
Hinchman (family), 404
Hirsch, Olga, 455
History of the Navy, 348
History of Philadelphia, 342
Hitchcock, Tommy, 507
Hobart, Ruth, 423
Hobe Sound, 522
Hodge, Martha, 243
Hoffman (family), 315, 322
  Mrs. Francis Burrall, 132
Hoit, Alice Marie, 389
Holbrook, Stewart, 416
Holiday magazine, 339
Holland, Captain, 407
Holland Society, 72
Holloway, Mrs. William Grace, Sr., 216, 524
Holloway, Mrs. William Grace, Jr., 524-525
Hollywood, 17, 110, 113, 137, 185, 186, 243, 244, 507, 548
Holman, Libby, 545-546
Holmes (family), 255
  Oliver Wendell, 74, 82, 250-251

Holmes (family)—*Cont.*
  Oliver Wendell, II, 250, 265
  Ralph, 546 *n.*
Holmsen, Mrs. Nicholas, 135
Homestake, 415, 525
"Home, Sweet Home," 351 *n.*
Hone, Philip, 27-28
Honoré, Bertha, 381 *n.*, 394
Honoré, Henry, 391, 394
Hooper (family), 276
  Marian, 276
  Maryland Mathison, 391
  Samuel, 123
Hoover, Herbert, 103, 108, 206, 363, 414 *n.*, 432, 512
Hope Diamond, 155, 157, 158
Hopkins, Gwladys "Gee" Crosby, 509
Hopkins (family), 49, 421, 424-426
  Johns, 350-351
  Mark, 422, 424-425, 426, 427
  Mrs. Mary Sherwood, 424-426
  Moses, 425
  Timothy Nolan, 424-425
Hopkinson (family), 343
Hopper, Hedda, 141
"Horseback Dinner," 519-520
"Horse Fair, The," 490
"Horseshoe," 549
Horsmandel, Warham, 287
Hosford, Mary Lou, 509
Houston, 11, 48, 212
Hovey, Carl, 82-83
Howard, Anita, 498
Howard, Charles, 498
Howard, John Eager, 340
  Mrs. Peggy Chew, 340
Howard, John Eager of B., 352
Howard (family), 102-103, 129, 351, 527
  Ted, 187
Howe, Elias, Jr., 387 *n.*
Howe, Helen, 225
Howells, William Dean, 9, 81
Hoyt, Mrs. Henry Reese, 132
Hoyt, Rosina Sherman, 132
Hubbard, Anna Joan Dyer, 385
Hubbard, Elisha Dyer, 385
  Mrs. Muriel McCormick, 385
Hubbard, Elisha Dyer, Jr., 385
Hubbard, John Rockefeller, 385

Hubbard, Kim, 78, 82
Huck, Albertine, 400
Hudson, Henry, 32
Hudson, Manuela, 498
Huger (family), 88, 115
Hughes, Charles Evans, 215
Huguenot Society, 72
Human Heredity, 66 *n.*
Humphrey (family), 48, 213
Humphreys, Mrs. Arents, 132
Hunt, James Ramsey, 369 *n.*
  Mrs., 369 *n.*
Hunt, Richard, 399
Hunter, General, 336
Hunter, Margaret, 29
Huntington (family), 49, 50, 421, 426-429
  Archer, 427, 428
  Collis Potter, 421, 424, 426-429, 431, 432, 433
  Mrs. Elizabeth T. Stoddard, 427
  Mrs. Arabella Duval Worsham, 427-428
  Helen Dinsmore, 480
  Henry E., 428
  Mrs. Mary Alice Prentice, 428-429
  Mrs. Arabella Duval Worsham, 429
  Solon, 426, 428
Hurd, Charles, 157
Hurst, John E. of W., 352
Hutchinson (family), 255
  Foster, 264
Hutton (family), 171 *ff.*
  Barbara, 18, 129, 130, 142, 167, 170, 171-178, 319, 551
  Edward F., 172
  Mrs., 132
  Franklyn Laws, 171
  Mrs. Edna Woolworth, 171
  Mrs. Irene Curley Bodie, 172
  James Morgan, Jr., 150
Hyde, James Hazen, 495, 520, 527
Hyde Park, 50

India House, 212
Indianapolis *News*, 35
I Never Grew Up, 184-185

Ingersoll (family), 281, 343, 344
  Ralph, 401
Increase, 320
Inman (family), 49, 168
  Walker Patterson, 169
  Walter, 168, 169
  Mrs. Nanaline Holt, 168-169
In Praise of Gentlemen, 79-81
International Celebrity Register, 142
Invincible, 451
Irish, James Theodore, Jr., 35 *n.*
  Mrs., 35 *n.*
Iron Age, 358
Irving, Washington, 311, 316, 470, 502
Irwin, Annie de Houle, 391
Irwin, Hélène, 423
Irwin, Mrs. Richard, 222
Irwin, Wallace, 64
Iselin, Mrs. Adrian, 50, 132
Iselin, Mrs. Adrian II, 529
Iselin, Mrs. C. Oliver, 50, 132
Isham, Helen, 381 *n.*
Isham, Henry Royall, 292
"It Is Spoken," 382
Izard (family), 88
  Ralph, 61, 62

"Jack Horner Pie" dinner, 520
Jackson, Andrew, 28, 304, 312 *n.*
Jackson, James, Jr., 369 *n.*
  Mrs., 369 *n.*
Jackson, Levi, 198
Jackson (family), 257
James (family), 277 *n.*
  Mrs. Arthur Curtis, 132
  Henry, 24, 111
  Marquis, 334, 340 *n.*
  Mrs. Walter B., 132
Jay (family), 47, 48, 253, 510
  John, 114-115
    Mrs. Sarah Van Brugh Living-
    ston, 114-115, 117
  William, 122
Jazz and Gin, 22
Jazz Festival, 19, 523
Jefferson, Martha, 293-294, 298
Jefferson, Peter, 293
Jefferson, Thomas, 281, 293, 294, 295,
    296, 297, 309, 330
Jelke, Frazier, 393

Jennings, Brewster, 213
Jerome, D. A., 367
Jerome, Jennie, 232
Jerome, Leonard, 232
Jersey, Pat, 239
Johnson, Howard, 535-536
Johnson, Howard, Jr., 535
Johnson, "Josie," 186
Johnson, Louisa Catherine, 271
Johnson, Owen, 184
  Mrs. Elaine Cobb, 184
Johnson, Mrs. Robert, 135
Johnson, Samuel, 308
Johnson, Sophie, 480
Jonas, Joseph, 443
Jones, Benjamin Franklin, 358
Jones (family), 101, 134, 358, 437
  F. S., 254 *n.*
  Jacob Aik, 358
  John Paul, 29
  Lewis Colford, 120
Jordan, David Starr, 98, 99, 432
Jordan, John W., 342
Jorgenson, Christine, 35
Journal of a Young Lady of Virginia,
    310
Joy (family), 404
  Henry B., 405-406
  Mrs., 405
Jubilee Ball, 221
Judah, Theodore, 426
Judge, Arline, 180
Jumbo, 507
Jung, Carl G., 381
Junior League, 218-222

Kahn (family), 134
  E. J., Jr., 182
  Margaret, 355-356
  Otto, 355, 443 *n.*, 521
Kane, De Lancey, 120
Kaufman, Louis G., 130
  Mrs., 132
Kaufman, Mae Daw, 130
Kaufmann (family), 393 *n.*
Kenne, Foxhall, 492
Kenne, James R., 502
Kenne, Nancy, 476
Keese, William Linn, 69

Kelland, Clarence Budington, 411
Keller, Godfrey, 288
Keller, Greta, 548
Keller, Helen, 223
Keller, Louis, 5, 7, 12, 123-125, 127, 130, 144
Kelly (family), 18, 47, 281, 316
  George, 244
  Grace, 130, 243-245, 349
  John Brendan, 244, 245-246, 349
  Mrs., 244
  Walt, 244
Kelly, Edith, 453
Kelly, Brenda Victoria, 183
Kelly, Helen, 452
Kelly, John "Shipwreck," 183-184
  Mrs. Brenda Frazier, 183-184
Kemp (family), 282
Kempner, Sigmund, 456
Kendall, Lyman, 134
Kenedy, Mifflin, 407
Kennedy (family), 18, 101 n., 225 n., 281, 308, 316, 474
  John Fitzgerald, 255 n.
  Joseph P., 18, 142, 255 n.
Kent, A. Atwater, Sr., 186
  Mrs., 13, 522
Kent, Duke of, 108, 164
Kent (family), 47, 443 n.
Kerr, Mrs. E. Coe, 73
Keteltas (family), 319
Kettering, Charles, 406
Key, Francis Scott, 351 n.
Khan, Aly, 146, 534, 541
Kilborne, Mrs. William S., 221
Kilgallen, Dorothy, 19
Kimball, Sara Louise, 98
Kimbrough, Emily, 223
King, Alice, 409
King, Archibald Gracie, 22, 120, 166
King, Charles B., 406
King, Mrs. Charles Garfield, 392 n.
King, Clarence, 276
King, Ella, 409
King, Mrs. James Gore, 50
King, Lee, 409
King, Marjorie, 381 n.
King, "Mimi Bird," 11
King, Nettie, 409

King, Richard ("Captain"), 407-409
  Mrs. Henrietta Chamberlain, 407-410
King, Richard, Jr., 409
King, Sheppard, 11
King-Kleberg (family), 407-411
King Ranch, 407-411
Kingdon, Edith, 452
Kinnaird, Lady Elizabeth, 230
Kinsolving, Arthur Lee, 129
Kinsolving (family), 351
Kip, Leonard, 319
Kirkeby (family), 49
Kissam, Marie Louisa, 487
Kleberg, Alice Gertrudis, 410
Kleberg, "Caesar," 410
Kleberg, Richard, 410
Kleberg, Robert Justus, III, 409, 410, 411
  Mrs. Alice King, 409, 410, 411
Kleberg, Robert J., IV, 410
Knickerbocker, Cholly, 17, 108, 131, 141-142, 184, 338-339, 468, 533
Knickerbocker Ball, 187
Knickerbocker Club, 139, 200, 201, 203, 211, 212
Knight, Tom, 87
Knopf, Alfred, 22, 129
Knox, General, 40
Knoxville, 462
Knoxville Chronicle, 462
Knudsen, William, 406
Kohlsaat, Pauline, 395
Kountze, Mimi, 178
Kountze, Natalie, 178
Kountze (family), 407
Krenn, Edwin, 383-384

La Case, Florence, 453
Ladenburg, Mrs. Adolph, 132
Ladies' Home Journal, 530
La Farge, John, 277, 277 n., 502
La Flamme, Mrs. Frank, 88
Lake Forest, Ill., 237
Lakewood, N.J., 452
Lambert, Thomas, 345
Lambs Club, 215
Lamont, Thomas, 54 n., 259
Lamont (family), 49
Land, Mrs. Fort Elmo, 73

Landon, Alfred, 414 *n.*
Lane, Wheaton, 486
Lange, J. Carvel, 211
Langdon, Walter, 120, 471
Langhorne (family), 87
  Chiswell Dabney, 476
  Irene, 12, 15, 166
  Nancy, 15
Langley, William C., 128
  Mrs. Jane Pickens, 128
Latham, Milton, 425, 430
Lathrop, Jane, 429
Lauder, Polly, 129
Laughlin, James, 358
Lavanburg, Sarah, 460
Lavelle, Monsignor, 204
Law, T. N. Jr., 406
Law (family), 406
Lawrence, Bishop, 11
Lawrence, William, 265
Lea, Tom, 408, 409
Leary, Beth, 135
Leadville, Colo., 454
Lee (family), 44, 115, 284, 285, 304 *ff.*,
    315, 327, 360
  Arthur, 307-308
  Charles, 311
  Francis Lightfoot, 309
  Hannah, 310-311
  Harold, 305
  Henry, 304 *n.*, 311
  Henry, II, 311
  Henry ("Black Horse"), 311 *n.*
  Ivy, 370, 374
  Joseph, 304 *n.*
  "Light Horse" Harry, 311, 312
    Mrs., 312, 313
  Lucinda, 310
  Matilda, 311
  Molly, 310-311
  Nancy, 310
  Philip Ludwell, 309
  Richard, 101, 305
  Richard, II, 305-306, 311
  Richard Bland, 311
  Richard Henry, 60, 61, 296, 309-310
  Robert E., 92-94, 101, 207 *n.*, 257,
    283, 284, 293, 313, 407
  Stephen, 68

Lee—*Cont.*
  Thomas, 306-307, 311
    Mrs. Hannah Harrison Ludwell,
    306, 307
  Thomas Ludwell, 309, 310
  William, 307-308
Leech, Margaret, 464 *n.*
"Leesylvania," 311
Legaré (family), 88
Lehman (family), 140, 442, 461, 518,
    537
  Arthur, 461
  Herbert, 461
  Irving, 461
  Meyer, 461
Lehr, Harry, 123
Leiter (family), 393
  Joseph, 396-397
  Levi, Ziegler, 232, 393, 396-397, 398
    Mrs., 396
  Margaret, 396
  Mary, 232-233, 396
  Nancy, 396
  Thomas, 396-397
LeJeune (family), 443
Leland, Henry, 406
Lentilhon, Julie, 132
Leopold, King of Belgium, 353
Le Petit Salon, 218
LeRoy, Herman R., 194
Lespinasse, Dr., 383
Letters of the Federal Farmer, 309
Leupp, Charles, 449
Levant, Oscar, 396 *n.*
Levering, Enoch, 351
Levering, Mary, 351
Levin, Robert, 187
Levy, Bertha, 462
Levy, Uriah Phillips, 444
Lewis, Oscar, 430
Lewis, Mrs. William Meade, 86-87
Lewis (family), 86, 282
Lewisohn, Walter, 545
Lexington, Ky., 159
Lexington, Va., 335
Libertyville, Ill., 403
Lieber, Francis, 81
Life, 4, 39-40, 186, 187-534
Life With Father, 507
Lightfoot (family), 282

Ligonier, Pa., 357-358
Lincoln, Abraham, 46, 99, 263, 272, 273, 276, 281, 504
Lincoln, Florence, 379
Lincoln, Robert T., 390
Lindbergh, Charles A., 129, 531-532
Mrs. Anne Morrow, 223
Links Club, 200, 202, 212, 213, 226
Linn, Mrs. Howard, 392 n.
Lippmann, Walter, 52-53
Lispenard (family), 25, 318-319
Litchfield, Conn., 427
Littleton, Rachel, 498
Livingston, Belle, 140
Livingston (family), 25, 47, 114, 115, 317, 318, 319, 471
Eugene A., 120
Mrs. Goodhue, 132
Maturin, 120
Mrs. Oscar, 98
Robert, 317
Sarah Van Brugh, 114
Livingston Manor, 317
Lloyd, Thomas, 343
Lloyd (family), 37, 283, 343
Lloyd-Smith (family), 368
Loder, Eleanor, 146
Lodge (family), 47, 101
Henry Cabot, Sr., 23, 47, 230, 267-268, 275
Henry Cabot, Jr., 23, 255
John Davis, 255
Loeb (family), 442, 537
Adeline, 396 n.
Albert, 455, 457
Carl, 396 n.
Edwin, 457
Harold, 457
Nina J., 443 n.
Solomon, 443 n.
Loew, Arthur, 396 n.
Loew, William Goadby, 533
Mrs., 132
Logan, Mary Weir, 498
London Spectator, 366
London Times, 121, 468, 477
Long, 326
Longfellow, Henry Wadsworth, 42
Longworth, Nicholas, 74, 85

Mrs. Alice Roosevelt, 13-14, 151, 153, 327, 529, 541, 542
Look, 56, 126
Lord, James Brown, 353
Lorillard, Elaine, 523
Lorillard, Louis, 523
Lorillard, Pierre, 132, 168, 523
Los Angeles, 49, 87, 524, 527
Los Angeles Times, 35, 527
Lothrop (family), 404
Lotos Club, 215, 226
Loubat, Count, 189 ff.
Louis XVI, 40
Louis Philippe, 341
Louisiana Club, 228
Louisville, 344, 394
Lounsbery, Richard, 16-17, 525-527
"Love," 382
Lowell (family), 47, 254, 257, 260 ff., 315, 351, 360, 518
Abbott Lawrence, 264
Amy, 260, 261
Charles Russell, Jr., 262-263
Mrs., 262, 263-264
Edward Jackson, 260
Francis Cabot, 85 n., 260, 261-262
Guy, 260
James Russell, 82
Mrs. James R., 529
John, 261
John Amory, 262
John "Judge," 260, 262
Lawrence, 265-266, 370
Percival, 260, 264-265
Robert, 260
Robert Traill Spence, 260
Robert Traill, Jr., 255
Lowle, Percivall, 260
Loundes (family), 283
Lucci, Annunziati, 452 n.
Luce, Henry, 17, 225, 411
Luce (family), 527
Ludwell (family), 284
Hannah Harrison, 306
Philip, 284
Thomas, 284
Lumet, Sidney, 498
Mrs. Gloria Vanderbilt Di Cicco Stokowski, 498
Lunch Club, 212

Lundberg, Ferdinand, 369
Lusitania, 401, 496
Lykiardopolos (family), 523
Lyman (family), 32
Lynchburg, 92
"Lyndhurst," 451
Lynes, Russell, 74
Lyon, Mrs. Denniston, 531-532
Lyons, Leonard, 141
Lyons, Louis, 266 *n.*

MacArthur, Douglas, 210
MacArthur (family), 537
Mackay (family), 434
  Ada, 440
  Clarence H., 132, 440
  Ellin, 440-441
  Eva, 440
  John William, 437-440,
    Mrs. Louise Hungerford Bryant,
    438-439
  Katherine, 440
  William, 440
MacMartin, Duncan R., 161-162
  Mrs. Laura Mae Whitrock, 161-162
Macy, Mrs. V. Everett, 223
Macy (family), 256, 393 *n.*
Maddox, George Amory, 337
Madison, James, 136, 345
Magazine of American Genealogy, 96
Magazine of History and Biography,
  282
Magee, Dick, 436
Mager, Ruth, 178
Mangel, Anna Christina, 433
Manhattan Club, 200, 202, 203, 447
Manigault, Peter, 35
Manigault (family), 88
Mann, William D'Alton "Colonel,"
  25, 139, 502, 542
Manners for the Metropolis, 138-139
Manners, John, 65
Manning, Bishop, 512
Manufacturer's Club, 350
Manville, Tommy, 367
Manville (family), 393
Marble, Mantin, 225
Marbury, Elisabeth, 222, 140, 502
Marcus (family), 393 *n.*
Mardi Gras, 228-229

Mardi Gras Ball, 221
Margaret, Princess of England, 413
Marie, Queen of Rumania, 140, 530
Marie Antoinette, 157
Marina, Princess of Greece, 164
Marlborough, Duke of, 230, 234, 492
  Duchess of (Consuelo Vanderbilt),
  50, 234, 448, 503
Marlborough, John, Marquis of Bland-
  ford, 492
Marquand, John, 129
Marquis, Albert Nelson, 96
Marquis, Don, 9
Marriott, Mrs. John, 443 *n.*
Marryat, Frederick, 28
Marshall, Evelyn, 401
Marshall, George Catlett, 93 *n.*
Marshall, John, 293, 294, 299
Marshall, Mary Brooke Russell, 480
Marshall (family), 281
Martin, Alistair, 214
Martin, Bradley, 520
  Mrs., 520
Martin, Frederick Townsend, 24, 520
Martineau, Harriet, 403-404
Mary, Dowager Queen of England,
  241
Maryland Club, 196, 197
Maryland Gazette, 196
Massey, Raymond, 221
Masters, Mayme Cook, 355
Mather, Cotton, 291
Mather, Samuel, 48
Mather (family), 48
Mathison, Maryland, 391
Maugham, Somerset, 78
Mauzé, Jean, 380
  Mrs. Abby Rockefeller Milton Par-
  dee, 380
Maxwell, Elsa, 15-16, 18, 33, 113, 129,
  144-147, 148
Maxwell, James, 149
Maxwell, George, 354
May, Frederick deCourcy, 190
May, Lilian, 231
May, Marjorie Merriweather Post
  Close Hutton Davies, 151
May (family), 393 *n.*
Mayer, Edward B., 456
Mayer, Louis B., 418

Mayflower, 40-41, 42, 45, 67, 103, 254, 257, 305, 500
Mayflower Club, 218
Mayflower Hotel, 167
Mayflower Society, *see* Society of Mayflower Descendants
McAllister, Hall, 123
McAllister, Matthew Hall, 118
  Mrs. Sarah T. Gibbons, 118
McAllister, Ward, 20, 46, 114, 115, 118 ff., 191, 206
McAllister (family), 197
McAlpin, David Hunter, 377
McCabe, James D., 100
McCann, Charles, 172
  Mrs., 172
McCarthy, Julia, 141
McCarty, Daniel, 311 *n.*
McCormick (family), 103, 385 ff., 463, 527
  Alice, 389
  Anita, 389
  "Bazy," 151
  Chauncey, 391-392
    Mrs., 392
  Cyrus Hall, 380, 385, 386-389
    Mrs. Nettie Fowler, 387-388, 389, 394
  Cyrus Hall, Jr., 389
    Mrs. Harriet Hammond, 389
    Mrs. Alice Marie Hoit, 389
    Edith Rockefeller, 377, 380 ff.
  Fowler, 380, 385
    Mrs. "Fifi" Stillman, 385
  Harold Fowler, 380, 383, 384, 385, 389
    Mrs. Edith Rockefeller, 377, 380-384
    Mrs. Ganna Walska, 383
    Mrs. Adah Wilson, 383
  Harold Fowler III, 385
  John Rockefeller, 380
  Leander, 389
  Mathilde, 380, 385
  Mary Virginia, 389
  Medill, 389
  Muriel, 380-381, 385
  Robert, 386
  Robert Hall, 389

McCormick (family)—*Cont.*
  Robert R. "Colonel," 389-392, 402
    Mrs. Annie de Houle Irwin Adams, 391
    Mrs. Maryland Mathison Hooper, 391-392, 403
  Robert Sanderson, 389-390
  Ruth Hanna, 389
  Stanley, 389
  Thomas, 385
  William S., 389
McCrary, Tex, 130, 180
McCredy, Mrs. William, 168
McCutcheon, Mrs. John T., 392 *n.*
McDonnell, Anne, 13
McDonnell, Kyle, 130
McDonnell (family), 281
McEwen, Arthur, 427
McGraw, Mrs. William A., 125
McKean, Thomas, 60
McKean (family), 343
McKenna, Irene, 354
McKim, Margaret Emerson, 496
McKim (family), 351
McKinley, William, 263, 326, 460, 504
McKinlock, Mrs. G. Alexander, 13, 385
McKinlock, G. Alexander, Jr., 385
McKinney, Price, 162-163
McKinnon, Mrs. Harold, 436
McLane, Mrs. Pratt, 369 *n.*
McLane (family), 351
McLean, Edward Beale "Ned," 156-159
  Mrs. Evalyn Walsh, 151, 155-159, 501, 520
McLean, Evalyn, 157, 158
McLean, Jock, 157
McLean, Ned, Jr., 157
McLean, Vinson, 157-158
McMaster, John, 95
McMillan, James, 405
McMullen, Nora, 361-362
McNeil, Mrs. Charles M., 132
McSweeney, Terence, 204
Mdivani, Alexis, 173, 174-175
  Mrs. Louise Van Alen, 174, 241
  Mrs. Barbara Hutton, 174-175
Mdivani, Serge, 241
  Louise Van Alen Mdivani, 241
Meade, George, 344

Meade, William, 289-290
Meadowbrook Club, 87, 365
Medalic History . . . , 190
Medill, Katharine, 389
Medill (family), 390
Meeker, Arthur, 384, 530-531
Meeker, Mary, 381 *n.*
Mele, Pietro, 183-184
Mellon (family), 84, 213, 357, 358-362, 518
  Ailsa, 361, 363
  Andrew W., 156, 359, 360, 361-363, 364
  Cassandra, 364
  Constance, 364
  Paul, 361, 363
  Richard, 150
  Richard II, 364
  Richard King, 363-364
  Seward, 364
  Thomas, 358-361
Memorial History of New York, 318
Mencken, Helen, 130
Mencken, H. L., 74
Mendl, Lady (Elsie de Wolfe), 21, 135, 222, 241-242, 502
Merle-Smith (family), 368
Merryman, John of J., 352
Mesta, George, 153-154
  Mrs. Perle, Skirvin, 18, 53, 142, 151, 153-154
Metropolitan, 137
Metropolitan Club, 200, 202, 203, 210-211, 212, 216, 366
Metropolitan Opera Guild, 448
Meyer, T. Montague, 56
  Mrs. Fleur Cowles, 56
Meyer, Eugene, 403
Miami, 54
Miami *Herald*, 54
Micor, Naranna, 385
Middendorf, J. William of H., 352
Middleburg, Va., 14, 534, 542
Middleton, Henry Augustus, Jr., 89
Middleton (family), 88
"Mikado Ball," 399
Milbank, Sheila, 238
Milburn, N. J., 7
Milford, Conn., 449
Military Order of Foreign Wars, 72

Miller, Dora, 435
Miller, Mrs. Gilbert, 135
Miller, Mrs. G. MacCulloch, 506
Miller, Helen Day, 450
Miller, Hope Ridings, 155
Miller, Mrs. Roswell, 253
Miller, W. Starr, 503
Mills, C. Wright, 144
Mills, Darius Ogden, 414, 434-435
Mills, Elizabeth, 414
Mills, Ogden, 98, 132, 363, 546
  Mrs. Dorothy Randolph Fell, 114, 546
Mills, Ogden Livingston, 414 *n.*
Mills, William Stowell, 99
Milne, Berkeley, 475
Milton, David, 380
  Mrs. Abby Rockefeller, 380
Milton, Mass., 11, 331
Milwaukee, 54
Minneapolis, 125, 213, 445
Minton, Mrs. Charles, 124
Minton, Maurice, 124
Minton, Telfair, 205
Minturn, Robert, 79
Missouri Traveler, The, 509
Mitchell, Broadus, 331
Mitchell, John Clark, 407
Mithras Club, 228
Mizener, Arthur, 531
Mizner, Addison, 387 *n.*
Moale (family), 351
Modern Manners, 153
Moffett, Adelaide, 178
Molyneux, Edward, 112-113
Momus Club, 228
Monaco, Prince of, 230
"Monkey Dinner," 519
Monroe, James, 136, 345, 349
Monroney, Sen., 154-155
Montagu, Ashley, 66 *n.*
Montague (family), 235
Montgomery, Ala., 461
Montgomery, Robert, 130, 225-226
  Mrs. Elizabeth Grant Harkness, 130
"Monticello," 298
Mont-Saint-Michel and Chartres, 274
Moore, George, 165
Moravia, N. Y., 372
Mordaunt, Charles, 288

Morgan (family), 49, 134, 253, 316, 320-321
 Anne, 222
 Elizabeth Hamilton, 448
 Gloria, 135, 496
 J. P., 42, 82-84, 92, 98, 99, 101, 121, 203, 320, 321, 344, 368, 389, 422-423, 506, 527
 Mrs., 132
 Nan, 355
 Thelma, 135
Morgan, E. D., 98
Morgenthau, Mrs. Henry, 226
Morgenthau (family), 442
Morley, Christopher, 159
Morris (family), 317-318, 342, 343
 Anthony, 342, 343, 344
 Cadwalader, 344
 Gouverneur, 299, 318
 Mrs. Nancy Randolph, 50, 318
 Isaac, 344
 Lewis, 317, 318
 Lloyd, 107
 Newbold, 318
 Robert, 342
 Samuel, 344
"Morrisania," 317, 318
Morse, Nannie, 353 n.
Morton, Caroline, 457
Morton, Helen, 230
Moses, Robert, 87
Mottey, Jane, 218
Mt. Kisco, 533
Mount Tremblant, 354 n.
Movius, Rose Saltonstall, 395
Muhlenberg, Gen., 61
Mulligan, Suzie, 178
Munn, Charles, 76, 121
Munsey's magazine, 137
Munson, Charles, 213
Murphy, Clifton, 525
Murray, Jeanne, 498
Murray (family), 281, 319
Muscogee (Ga.) Herald, 27
Muybridge, Eadweard, 431
Myers, Barbara, 453

"Nagirroc," 162, 163
Nahant, Mass., 23
Nairne, Violet Mary Elliot, 477

Nantucket, 256
Napoleon, 231
Napoleon III, 486
Nash, Eleanor Arnett, 52
Nash, Ogden, 52
"Nashua," 549
Nashville, 462
Nassau, 181
Nast, Condé, 137, 138
Nast, Natica, 443 n.
National Geographic, 219
National Isolation—an Illusion, 447
National Society of Colonial Dames, 70
Naushon, 257
Negley, Sarah Jane, 359
Neilson, Cathleen, 496
Needham, Anne Bernadette, 498
Nelson, Lord, 347
"Nemours," 338 n.
Nesbit, Evelyn, 366, 367
Nevin (family), 38
Nevins, Allan, 363, 414
Newbolt, Janet, 355
Newark, N. J., 5
Newberry (family), 48, 404
 Helen, 405
 John, 405
 John Stoughton, 404-405
 Mrs. Harriet Newell Robinson, 405
 Mrs. Helen Parmalee Handy, 405
 Oliver, 404
 Truman, 405-406
 Walter Loomis, 404
Newbury, Mass., 260
Newburyport, 257
Newcastle, Duke of, 116 n.
New England Historic Genealogical Society, 100, 101, 104, 105
Newgass, Babbette, 461
Newman, Cardinal, 76
New Orleans, 45, 218, 228-229, 352, 408, 445, 528
Newport, 15, 19, 21, 23, 24, 40, 50, 51, 107, 109, 154, 156, 167, 169, 171, 179, 234, 241, 320, 330, 437, 447, 448, 474, 497, 501, 506, 510, 512, 521, 523, 541
New Republic, 265

Newsday, 457
Newsweek, 481
New York City Telegraph, 204
New York Club, 190
New York *Daily News*, 182, 390
New York *Dramatic Mirror*, 145
New York *Herald*, 216
New York *Herald Tribune*, 136, 403, 508
New York *Journal American*, 141, 378-379
New York *Mirror*, 180
New York *Morning Journal*, 417
New York *PM*, 402
New York Society on Parade, 464 ff.
New York *Sun*, 120, 186
New York Times, 34, 53, 86, 120, 362, 462, 508
New York *Tribune*, 27, 414, 474
New York *World*, 225, 366, 450, 463
New York *World Telegram and Sun*, 141
New Yorker, The, 182, 440
Niagara, 451
Niarchos, Stavros, 210
Nicola, Lewis, 60
Nicholas, Betsy, 297
Nicholas, Robert Carter, 297
Nichols, Rev. Dr., 98
Nichols (family), 368
Nicoll, De Lancey, 353
Nicoll, Mary T., 353
Nicoll (famliy), 353
Nieu Nederlandt, 46
Nolan, Timothy, 424
Noland, Charlotte, 14, 236, 542-544
Norfolk, 292
Norris, Isaac, 342
Norris (family), 342
North, John Ringling, 142
North Haven, Me., 256-257
North Star, 82, 485-486
Norton, Marie, 509
Nourmahal, 481

Oakes, Harry, 547-548
Oakes, Nancy, 547-548
Oak Spring Farm, 363
Obolensky, Serge, 18, 55, 480
  Mrs. Alice Astor, 480

O'Brien, Esme, 181
O'Brien, William S., 435
O'Brien (family), 434
Ochs (family), 442, 461-462
  Adolph, 461-462
  Julius, 461-462
  Oakes, George Washington, 462
O'Connor, Harvey, 357, 359, 362-363, 456, 477
Odingselle (family), 101
Odlum, Floyd, 210
Oelrichs, Hermann, 437
  Mrs. Jessie Fair, 11, 132, 134, 437
Ogden, William B., 387
Ogilvy, David, 356
O'Keeffe, Georgia, 179
Oklahoma City, 153
Old Guard, 8, 34, 50, 53, 132-133, 135, 151-152, 518, 521-522
Old Time Belles and Cavaliers, 289
Olds, Ransom E., 406
Olin, Stephen, 79
Oliver, Henry, 357
Oliver, John L., 403, 404, 405
Olmsted, Denison, 500
Omaha, 227
O'Malley, Austin, 39
Onassis, Aristotle, 18
Oneonta, N.Y., 426, 428
Order of Colonial Lords of Manors in America, 72
Order of the Founders and Patriots, 70
"Original Costume Ball," 436
Orme (family), 49
Oswego, N.Y., 372
Ortiz-Patino, Jaime, 188
  Mrs. Joanne Connelley Sweeny, 188
Osborn, Carter, 236
Osgood (family), 49
Otis (family), 47, 49, 255
Otis, Harrison Gray, 62
  Mrs., 41
Our First Men . . . , 254
Outspoken Letters, 29

Paar, Jack, 17, 534
Pablos, Feliza Loraine, 498
Pacific Club, 197

Pacific Union, 197
Pacific Union Club, 435
Paderewski, Jan, 111
Page (family), 282
Paget, Almeric Hugh, 503
  Mrs. Pauline Whitney, 503
Paine, Robert Treat, 67 n., 85 n., 280
Palace Hotel, 434
Paley (family), 129, 537
Paley, Mrs. Jay, 396 n.
Paley, William, 73, 396 n., 527
  Mrs., 73, 129
Palfrey (family), 256
Pall Mall Budget, 475
Pall Mall Magazine, 475
Pall Mall Observer, 475
Palm Beach, 13, 15, 21, 76, 135, 158,
  159, 172, 179, 180, 241, 385,
  387 n., 521, 522, 537
Palmer (family), 393, 517
  Bertha, 395
  Gordon, 395
  Honoré, 394, 395
  Honoré, Jr., 395
  Pauline, 395
  Potter, 48, 393-396, 397, 399
  Mrs. Bertha Honoré, 156, 380,
    394-395, 529 n.
  Potter, II, 395
  Mrs. Pauline Kohlsaat, 395
  Potter, III, 395
  Potter D'Orsay, 395
  Mrs., 529
"Palmer Castle," 394
Palmer House, 394
Pálmerston, Lord, 82
Palo Alto, 431
Panz, Hubert, 56
Papanti, Lorenzo, 537
Pardee, Irving, 380
  Mrs. Abby Rockefeller Milton, 380
Parke, Daniel, 287-288
Parker, Suzy, 222
Parr, Howell, 197
Parrott, Abby, 234
Parrott (family), 49
Parsons, Louella, 142
Parsons, Lucille, 498
Parsons, Schuyler Livingston, 15
Parsons (family), 237

Parton, James, 50
"Party of the Century," 518
Pasadena, 110
"Patriarchs," 119-120, 123
Patriarch's Ball, 111
Patterson (family), 151, 390
  Alicia, 390, 457
  Betsy, 231-232, 235
  Eleanor "Cissy," 390, 391
  "Joe," 390-391
Patton, Elizabeth, 280, 281
Patton, George S., 263 n.
Paul, James, 520
Paul, Mary Astor, 520
Paul, Maury (Henry Biddle), 108,
  131-133, 136, 137, 138, 141, 146,
  159, 160-161, 163, 165, 178, 208,
  211, 338-339, 468, 496, 520, 533
Paulekiute, Jievute "Bobo," 380
Paxson, Frederic Logan, 437
Payne (family), 281, 369
  Flora, 501
  Henry B., 501
  John Howard, 351 n.
  Oliver, 501
Payson, Charles Shipman, 506
  Mrs. Joan Whitney, 506
Payson, Payne Whitney, 506
Peabody (family), 136, 256
  Endicott, 85, 411-412
  George, 100, 350-351, 486
Peacocks on Parade, 519
Peale, Norman Vincent, 129
Pearson, Mrs. Frederick, 132
Pegler, Westbrook, 142, 411
Pell, Thomas, 317
Pell (family), 47, 134
Pelleport, Gabrielle Joséphine de la
  Fite de, 329
Pelham Manor, 317
Pemaquid, Me., 364
Pemberton (family), 342, 343, 344
  Israel, 342, 344
  James, 344
  Joseph, 342
Penington (family), 343
Penn, William, 343, 346
Penn (family), 342
Pennoyer (family), 368

Penrose (family), 350
  Bartholomew, 350
  Boies, 350
  Charles Bingham, 350
  James, 344
  Spencer, 350
  Thomas, 344
Pepper, Henry, 344
Pepper (family), 344
Peralta (family), 420-421
  Luis, 420
  Pedro, 420
Perine (family), 351
Perkins, Thomas Handasyd, 62
  Mrs., 222
Perkins (family), 255
Perling, J. J., 328
Perrine, William, 116 n.
Perry, Caroline Slidell, 447
Perry, Commodore Oliver H., 447
Perry, Henry Pierrepont, 182
  Mrs. Brenda Williams-Taylor Frazier Watriss, 182
Pershing, General John J., 108, 402
Pershing, Mrs. Warren (Muriel Richards), 135
Peterborough, Lord, 288
Petroleum Club, 212
Peugnet (family), 48
Pew (family), 47, 213
Peyton (family), 43-44, 197, 281, 282
Pfeffer, Johan Heinrich, 344
Phelps, Henry, 493
  Mrs. Muriel Vanderbilt Church, 493
Phelps, Royal, 120
Phelps, William Lyon, 77
Philadelphia, 9, 13, 47, 52, 60, 62, 70, 85, 125, 131, 170, 197, 213, 215, 218, 243, 245, 251, 261, 304, 324, 326, 329, 331, 335, 340, 354, 362, 453, 479, 495-496, 519 n., 546, 520, 522, 537
Philadelphia Assembly, 90, 198
Philadelphia Club, 198, 343
Philadelphia Gentlemen, 343
Philadelphia Times, 131
Philip, Prince, of England, 185
Philippe, Claudius, 55-56
Philipsborough, 317

Philipse, Frederick, 317
Phipps (family), 184, 364-366, 537
  Henry, 364-365
  Hubert, 365
  Lawrence C., 365-366
  Lawrence C., Jr., 366
  Michael, 365
  Ogden, 214, 401
  Ruth Pruyn, 401
Phoenix, 412, 416, 509
Pickens, Jane, 128
Pickering (family), 256
Pickett, Sallie, 126
Pickwick Club, 228
Pico (family), 49
Pierre Hotel, 167, 176, 210
Pierrepont, R. Stuyvesant, Jr., 212
Pilgrims of the U. S., 67, 72
Pillsbury (family), 213
Pinckney, George Coffin, 89
Pinckney (family), 88, 115
Pinchon (family), 255
Pingree, Sumner, 127
Pinnacle Club, 212-213
Pittsburgh, 38, 81, 150, 153-154, 162, 197, 212, 213, 355, 356, ff.
Pittsfield, Mass., 397
Playdell-Bouyerie, Bartholomew, 480
  Mrs. Nancy Astor Obolensky Von Hofmannsthal, 480
Players Club, 215, 226
Plaza Hotel, 55
Plimpton, George, 210
Plymouth, O., 509
Pocahontas, 163, 292, 298
Poe, David, 351 n.
Poe, Edgar Allan, 351 n.
Poe, John Prentiss, 351 n.
Poe (family), 351
Polk, James K., 345
Poole, Ernest, 388, 394-395, 397
Poor, Nannie, 126
Poor Little Rich Girls, 18, 167, 518, 551
Poor Richard, 462-463
Pope, Mrs. George A., Jr., 436
Porcellian Club, 85, 198, 210, 213
Porgy and Bess, 283
Portago, Marquis de, 76-77
Porter, Benjamin, 121

Porter, Cole, 146, 159
Porter, H. N., 121
Porter (family), 281
Port Huron, 87
Portland, Ore., 219
Post, Edwin A., 120
Post, Emily, 19-20, 129
Post, George, 121
Post, Mrs. Langdon, 529
Post, Mrs. Price (Emily), 19-20
Potter, James Brown, 122
    Mrs. Cora Urquhart, 528
Poulteney, Walter de Courcey, 123
Poulterer (family), 49
Powel (family), 342
Powers, W. A., 356, 451
Pratt (family), 369
    Charles, 369 n.
        Mrs., 369 n.
    Mrs. Charles M., 369 n.
    Edwin, H. P., 369 n.
        Mrs., 369 n.
    Elliott, 369 n.
        Mrs., 369 n.
    Enoch, 350-351
    Frederic Bayley, 369 n.
        Mrs., 369 n.
    Mrs. George Dupont, 369 n.
    George D., Jr., 369 n.
        Mrs., 369 n.
    Harold Irving, Jr., 369 n.
        Mrs., 369 n.
    Helen, 369
    Herbert L., Jr., 369 n.
        Mrs., 369 n.
    John T., 369 n.
        Mrs., 369 n.
    Richardson, 369 n.
        Mrs., 369 n.
    Ruth Baker, 369 n.
    Sherman, 369
    Theodore, 369 n.
        Mrs., 369 n.
    Walter Merriam, 43
    Zadock, 449
Prentice, Clara, 427
Prentice, Ezra Parmalee, 379-380
    Mrs., 377
Prentice, Mrs. John Rockefeller, 392 n.

Prentice, Mary Alice, 428-429
Prescott, Ariz., 411
Prescott, William Hickling, 411
Preston, John, 280
    Mrs. Elizabeth Patton, 280, 281
Preston, May Wilson, 138
Preston (family), 280-281
"Price of Prestige, The," 21
Princeton Club, 222
Pringle, Mrs. Carmen, 481
Pringle (family), 88
Prioleau, Charles Edwin, 89-90
Prioleau (family), 88
Pritchett, Florence, 130
Proceedings of the New York Historical Society, 46
Prosser, Constance, 364
Prosser, Seward, 364
Providence, R.I., 125, 374
"Publi-ciety," 143-144, 151, 153, 155, 159, 170, 176, 178, 180, 181, 187, 518, 519, 536, 541, 546, 549, 550, 551
Publishers' Weekly, 542
Pulitzer (family), 48, 463-464
    Elinor, 464 n.
    Herbert, 464
    Joseph, I, 463-464
    Joseph, II, 464
    Joseph, III, 464 n.
        Mrs., 463
    Joseph, IV, 464 n.
    Kate Davis, 464 n.
    Michael Edgar, 464 n.
    Ralph, 464
        Mrs. Margaret Leech, 464 n.
    Ralph, Jr., 464 n.
    Seward Webb, 464 n.
Pullman, George, 399 n.
Pusey, Nathan Marsh, 259
Putnam, Mrs. James Lowell, 133
Pyne, Percy R., II, 208-209

Queen Mary, 164
Queens of American Society, 26
Quesada, Mrs. Elwood R., 464 n.
Quick, 56
Quigg, Lemuel, 353
Quincy, Mass., 271, 278
Quincy (family), 47, 255

Racquet and Tennis Club, 200, 202, 208, 212, 214, 226
Racquet Club (St. Louis), 212
Raffray, Mary Kirk, 237
Rainier, Prince, of Monaco, 243, 244-245, 246
Rainsford, Mrs. W. S., 222
Ralston, William, 434
Randolph (family), 44, 281, 283, 285, 292 ff.
　Bishop, 292
　Dorothy, 546
　Edith Sibyl May, 504
　Edmund, 132, 296-298
　　Mrs. Betsy Nicholas, 297
　Edmund, II, 298, 300
　Edward of Bremo, 293
　Elizabeth, 293
　Epes, 292
　George Wythe, 298
　Harold, 292
　Harrison, 292
　Henry of Chatsworth, 293
　Hollins, 292
　Isham, 292
　Isham of Dongeness, 293
　Jane, 293
　Jennings, 292
　John I, 298
　　Mrs. Frances Bland
　John, II, 296, 298, 299, 300-304
　John of Tazewell Hall, 293, 294-295
　Judith, 299-300
　Mary, 293
　Nancy, 299, 318
　Peyton, 295-296
　Philip, 414 n.
　Richard of Bizarre, 299
　Richard of Curles, 293, 298
　Robert Lee, 292
　Sarah Nicholas, 292
　Theodoric, 299
　Thomas Jefferson, 298
　Thomas Mann, I, 294, 298
　Thomas of Tuckahoe, 293
　William I of Turkey Island, 292-293, 294, 298
　William II of Turkey Island, 293
　William Mann, 292
Randolph, 348

Random Reminiscences, 373
Rasmussen, Ann Marie, 130
Ravenal, Mrs. St. Julien, 89, 90
Ravenal (family), 88
Rea, Margaret Moorhead, 355
Recess Club, 212
Redington (family), 49
Redskins, 64
Reed, Thomas B., 76
Regency Club, 216, 226
Register, Samuel Croft, II, 369 n.
　Mrs., 369 n.
Reid (family), 413-415, 508
　Elizabeth, 414
　Ogden, 403, 414-415
　　Mrs., 51
　Whitelaw, 413-414
　　Mrs., 132, 414
　Whitelaw, Jr., 403, 414
Remington, Frederic, 418
Reminiscences of an American Loyalist, 285
Remsen, Robert G., 120
Rensselaer Polytechnic Institute, 317
"Rensselaerwyck," 316
Republican Court, The, 60
Reventlow, Lance, 142, 175, 176
Reynal, Eugene, 494-495
Reynolds (family), 545, 546
　Christopher, 546 n.
　John, 227
　Richard J., Jr., 545
　　Mrs. Anne Cannon, 545
　　Mrs. Libby Holman, 545-546
　Richard N., 546
　Robert, 158
　　Mrs. Evalyn McLean, 158
　Zachary Smith, 545-546
"Reynolds," 545
Rhett, Robert Woodward, 89
Rhinebeck, N.Y., 481
Rhinelander, Philip, 132
Rhinelander (family), 46-47, 318
Ribblesdale, Lady (Ava Willing Astor), 479
Rice, Alexander Hamilton, 201, 211, 521
Rice (family), 393 n.
Richard, George, 130
　Mrs. Helen Mencken, 130

Richards, Muriel, 135
Richelieu, Duchess de, 528
Richmond, 53, 92, 125, 287, 304, 445
Ridgeley (family), 283
Ridgely, John of H., 352
Riggs, Lawrason of J., 352
Riggs (family), 351
Ritchie (family), 49
Ritz Hotel, 182, 521
Rivera, Diego, 365 n.
River Club, 216, 226
Rives, Francis R., 120
Rives, George, 79
Roanoke, 304
Robb, Inez, 141
Robbins, Douglas, 150
Robbins, Jessie, 447
Roberts, Jeannie, 178
Robertson, Mrs. T. Markoe, 529
Robinson, Harriet Newell, 405
Robson, Eleanor, 448
Rockaby Stables, 363
Rockefeller (family), 104, 134, 211, 308, 315, 368 ff., 474, 517, 519, 522
  Abby, 380
  Abby Aldrich, 42, 223, 370, 374-376
  Almira, 377
  Alta, 377-378
  Avery, 377
  Bessie, 377-378
  Bobo, 18, 380
  Christina, 371
  David, 371, 376
  Edith, 377-378; see also McCormick, Edith Rockefeller
  Emma, 377
  Faith, 377
  Francis, 372
  Frank, 372
  Geraldine (Ethel), 377
  Gladys, 377
  Godfrey, 371
  Godfrey of W., 377
  Isabel, 377
  James of W., 377
  Johann Peter, 371
  John the elder, 371

Rockefeller (family)—Cont.
  John D. (Davison) I, 84, 99, 103-104, 211, 362, 368, 370, 371-372, 373, 376, 377, 380, 522
  Mrs. Laura Celestia Spelman, 373
  John D., Jr., 370, 371, 373-374, 375, 376, 377-378, 380, 384, 402
  Mrs. Abby Aldrich, 42, 223, 370, 374-376
  John D. III, 371
  John of W., 377
  Laurance, 371, 522
  Lucy, 371-372
  Mary Ann, 372
  Nelson, 201, 211, 371, 518
  Percy, 377, 378
  Steven, 130
  Mrs. Ann Marie Rasmussen, 130
  William, 372, 376-377, 378-379
  William Avery "Big Bill," 371-372, 377
  Mrs. Eliza Davison, 371-373
  Mrs. Florence Lincoln, 379
  William G., 377
  Winifred, 377
  Winthrop, 142, 371, 372 n., 380
  Mrs. Bobo Paulekiute Sears, 18, 380
Rockefeller Brothers, 371, 374, 376
Rodgers, Mrs. Richard, 223
Roebuck, Alvah Curtis, 393 n.
Rogers, Helen, 414
Rogers, Herman, 50, 237, 320
Rogers, H. H., 369, 377
Rogers, Will, 45
Roley, Raymond, 481
Rolfe, John, 163 n., 292
Rolling Rock Hunt Club, 358
Romanov, Alexis Alexandrovitch, 228-229
Rooney, Theresa, 437
Roosevelt (family), 50-51, 103, 207, 308, 315, 318, 321 ff., 391, 517
  Alice, 13-14, 85, 327
  Anna, 326
  Archie, 327
  Betsey Cushing, 507
  Elbert, 322
  Eleanor (Anna Eleanor), 18, 129, 226, 323, 327
  Elliott, 129

Roosevelt (family)—*Cont.*
  Elliott the elder, 323
  Franklin D. (Delano), 17, 42, 57, 207, 321, 413, 481
    Mrs. Anna Eleanor Roosevelt, 18, 129, 226, 323, 327
  Franklin D., Jr., 129, 328
    Mrs. Ethel du Pont, 328
  Henry L., 323
  Hilborne Lewis, 324
  Isaac, 27, 319, 322
  James, 129, 322, 323, 507
  James I (Jacobus), 27, 322
  James Roosevelt, 479
    Mrs. Helen Astor, 322, 479
  James II the elder, 322
    Mrs. Sarah Delano, 322
  James Henry, 323-324
  John, 18, 129
  John Ellis, 325
  John J., 322
  Kate (Whitney), 508
  Kermit, 326, 327
  Nicholas, 322
  Philip, 325
  Quentin, 327
  Robert Barnwell, 324-325
  Robert Barnwell, Jr., 325
  Sarah Delano, 322
  Sarah Delano (Whitney), 508
  Theodore II "Teddie" (Pres.), 14, 84, 85, 108, 152, 321, 322, 323, 325, 326, 328, 414, 460, 504
    Mrs. Alice Hathaway Lee, 327
    Mrs. Edith Carow, 327
  Theodore I (the elder), 325
  Theodore, Jr. (III), 323, 327, 328 *n.*
  Theodore Douglas Robinson, 323
Roosevelt Boys, 18, 327
Root, Elihu, 192
Rose, Billy, 533-534
Rosenberg, Helen, 457
Rosenwald, Julius, 393 *n.*
Rospigliosi, Princess, 133
Ross, Ishbel, 394, 528
Rothschild (family), 103, 315, 446, 447
  Irene, 455
  Louis, 455
"Rough Point," 169
Round Hill, 522

Roxbury, N.Y., 449
Royal (family), 255
Rubinstein, Helena, 241
Rubicam (family), 411
Rubirosa, Porfirio, 170-171, 176-177, 188
  Mrs. Doris Duke Cromwell, 170-171
  Mrs. Barbara Hutton Mdivani Haugwitz-Reventlow Grant Troubetzkoy, 176-177
Ruhl, Margaret, 54
Ruiz, Agnes O'Brien, 496
Rumpf, Vincent, 471
Rumsey, Mrs. Charles Cary (Mary Harriman), 219
Runnells, Mrs. Clive, 392 *n.*
Rush (family), 47, 343, 344
  Benjamin, 344-345
  James, 345
  Richard, 302, 345
  William, 344
Rutger (family), 318-319
Rutherford, "Jack," 133
Rutherford, Lewis M., 120
Rutherford, Lewis Morris, 511
Rutherford, Mrs. Walter, 132
Rutherford, Winthrop, 233
Rutherfurd, Stuyvesant, 512
Rutledge (family), 88
Ryan (family), 352-356, 501 *n.*, 517
  Adele, 355
  Allan, 353, 354, 356
  Allan, Jr., 354, 355
  Barry, 354-355
  Basil, 355
  Caroline, 356
  Clendenin, 353, 354, 356
  Clendenin, Jr., 356
  Donald, 355
  Dorothy, 355
  Elinor, 353 *n.*
  Fortune Peter, 354
  George, 356
  John Barry, 353, 354, 355
    Mrs. Nan Morgan, 355
  John Barry, Jr., 355-356
    Mrs., 443 *n.*
  John Barry III, 356
  Joseph, 353
  Joseph, Jr., 353 *n.*

Ryan (family)—*Cont.*
  Miriam, 354
  Natalie, 355
  Nina, 355
  Richard, 356
  Sally, 354
  Theodore, 354
  Thomas Fortune, 84, 352-354, 356, 378, 501
  Mrs. Ida Barry, 352, 353
  Mrs. Mary T. Nicoll, 353
  Thomas Fortune II, 355
  Virginia, 355
  Virginia Fortune, 356
  William, 355
  William Kane, 353
Ryerson, Mrs. Edward L., 392 *n.*

Sabbatical Club, 223
Sacco, Nicola, 265
Sacco-Vanzetti case, 265
Sachs (family), 442
Sacramento, 422, 429, 431
Saint Augustine, Fla., 45, 88
St. Cecilia Ball, 90-91
St. Cecilia Society, 90-91
St. Francis Hotel, 424
Saint-Gaudens, Augustus, 277
St. George, Katherine, 74
St. George, Priscilla, 355
St. Louis, 48, 212, 228, 352, 409, 463, 534
St. Louis *Post-Dispatch*, 54, 463
St. Nicholas Society, 67, 72
St. Paul, Minn., 125, 445
St. Regis Hotel, 55, 481
St. Simon's Island, 15
Sale, Edith Tunis, 289
Salem, 85, 136, 256, 257, 425
Salomon, Louis, 445
Saltonstall (family), 37-38, 41, 47, 254, 255-256, 258
  Elizabeth Lee, 448 *n.*
  Leverett, 255
  Richard, 41, 500
  William Gurdon, 255
San Antonio, 87-88, 409
San Diego, 237, 434
Sands, Mrs. Emory, 237
Sands Point, 185

Sanford, John, 128
  Mrs. John, 133
Sanford, Stephen ("Laddie"), 128
  Mrs. Mary Duncan, 128
San Francisco, 6, 49, 81, 110, 118, 127, 145, 197, 213, 215, 234, 298, 352, 416, 423 *ff.*, 444, 445, 530
San Francisco *Argonaut*, 530
San Francisco *Examiner*, 415, 427, 428
"San Simeon," 418
Santa Barbara, 87, 110, 411
Saratoga, 121
Sargent, A. A., 428
Sargent, Joan, 111
Sarnoff (family), 129, 537
  David, 527
  Robert, 181
  Mrs. Esme O'Brien, 181
Satterlee, Herbert Livingston, 84, 320-321
  Mrs., 98
Satterwhite, Mrs. Preston Pope, 133
Saturday Evening Post, 13
Saunders, George, 176
Saunders, Lucy, 178
Savannah, Ga., 118, 125, 300
Scaife (family), 357
Scarsdale, N.Y., 317
Schappes, Morris, 444
Schermerhorn (family), 25, 319, 473
  Caroline Webster, 473
  William C., 120
  Mrs., 24
Schieffelin, Mrs. William Jay, 132
Schiff, Frieda, 443 *n.*
Schiff, Jacob, 443 *n.*
Schiff, John, 443 *n.*
Schiff (family), 442
Schindler, Raymond, 547-548
Schlee, George, 55
  Mrs. Valentina, 55
Schlesinger, Harry, 159
  Mrs. Mona Strader, 159
Schloss, Florence, 455
Schneider, Thelma Tevis, 101 *n.*
Schriftgiesser, Karl, 271, 322, 325, 456
Schuyler (family), 46-47, 317, 318, 319, 510
Schwartz, Mrs. Morton L., 133

Scofield, Helen, 372 *n.*
Scott, Nannie Douglas, 397-398
Scranton, Pa., 219
Scribner, Charles, 129
Scriven, Betty, 381 *n.*
Scriven, Jane, 381 *n.*
Scudder, Townsend, 87
Scull (family), 347
  Mrs. Barclay, 13
  Capt., 345
  Mary, 347
  Nicholas, 347
Searchers, The, 509
Searle, Eleanor, 16, 500, 509
Searles, Edward, 425-426
Sears, Richard, Jr., 380
  Mrs., 380
Sears, Sally, 178
Sears (family), 380
Seattle, 221
Sedgwick, Henry Dwight, 79-81
Seely, Herbert Barnum, 520
Selfridge, Henry Gordon, 393 *n.*
Seligman, Fleurette, 455
Seligman, Joseph, 445-446
Seligman (family), 442
Selkirk, Lord, 29
Sepulveda (family), 49
Seton, Celeste Andrews, 451
Seton (family), 319
Severance, Mrs. Mark, 426
Sewall (family), 264
Sewickley, Pa., 38, 357
Shaffer, Anne Childs, 365
Shaffer, Blackwell, 150
Shaker Heights, 162
"Shangri-La," 170
Shannon, Homer, 364
Sharon, William, 434
Sharon (family), 437
Shattuck, Albert R., 492
Shaw, Mrs. Alfred P., 392 *n.*
Shaw, Bobbie, 476
Shaw, Carolyn Hagner "Callie," 152-153
Shaw, Robert Gould, 262, 476
  Mrs. Nancy Langhorne, 476
Shedd (family), 393
Sheldon, Frederick, 120

Shepard, Elliott F., 489
  Mrs. Margaret Louisa Vanderbilt, 489
Shepard, Mrs. Finley, 451
Shepard, Hannah, 348
Shepherd, Howard, 213
Sheridan, Philip, 262
Sheridan, Wyo., 355
Sherman, Mrs. John, 223
Sherman, Mildred, 521
Sherman, Mrs. W. Watts, 133, 521
Sherry-Netherland Hotel, 55
Sherry's, 519, 520, 521
Sherwood, Gregg, 142
Sherwood, Mary, 424
"Sherwood Hall," 425
Shippen (family), 342, 343
  Edward, 60
  Peggy, 340
  Rebecca Nicholson, 37
  Thomas Lee, 307
Shoemaker, Michael Myers, 150
Shoemaker (family), 150
Silsbee (family), 256
Simpson, Ernest, 134, 237, 238
  Mrs. Parsons, 237-238
  Mrs. Wallis Warfield Spencer, 134
Sinclair, Guinevere Jeanne, 452
Sinclair, Isaac Merrit, 386 *n.*
Singer, Paris, 387 *n.*
Sinton Hotel, 149
Skinner, Cornelia Otis, 130
Skirvan, Billy, 153
Skirvan, Pearl, *see* Mesta, Perle
Skouras, Spyros, 142, 210
Skull and Bones, 198
Slader, Matthew, 75 *n.*
Slater, Mrs. Denniston, 525
Slater, Mrs. Lyon, 550
Sloan, Alfred P., 526
Sloan, James Todhunter, 502
Sloan, William D., 489
  Mrs. Emily Thorn Vanderbilt, 489
Smalley, George, 121
"Smart Set," 137, 167, 208
Smith, Abigail, 269
Smith, Adam, 60
Smith, Alfred E., 87
Smith, Alva, 447-448, 490, 491, 493
Smith, Bradford, 42-43

Smith, Earl E. T., 130
  Mrs. Consuelo Vanderbilt II, 130,
    493
  Mrs. Florence Pritchett, 130
Smith, Elsdon D., 315
Smith, Captain John, 32, 33, 44 n.,
    163 n., 292
Smith, Matthew Hale, 472
Smith, William, 269
Snelling, E. Templeton, 120
Snow, Carmel, 51
Snow, George Palen, 210
Sobol, Louis, 136
Social Ladder, The, 22
Social Register, 3 ff., 12, 124 ff., 134,
    143, 152, 161, 224, 380, 508
Social Secretary, 125
Society as I Have Found It, 122
Society in America, 403
Society-List and Club-Register, 124
Society of California, 68
Society of the Cincinnati, 39-40, 67, 69
Society of Colonial Dames, 70
Society of Colonial Wars, 70
Society of the Colonial Wars, 95
Society of the Descendants of the Ille-
    gitimate Sons and Daughters of
    the Kings of England, 106
Society of Mayflower Descendants,
    40, 43, 67, 71
Society of the War of 1812, 67, 70-71
Soley, Mrs. James Russell, 133
Somers, Mrs. Willard, 436
Somerset Club, 196, 197, 210
Somerville, N.J., 371
Sonnenberg, Ben, 534
Sonneborn, Carrie, 455
Sons of the American Revolution, 68
"Sorrento," 475
Southampton, 15, 19, 209, 537
Souther, Miss, 537
Spelman, Laura Celestia, 373
Spencer, Earl Winfield, Jr., 236-237
  Mrs. Wallis Warfield, 237
Spencer, Nicholas, 284
Spencer-Churchill, Charles, 518
Spencer-Clay, Herbert, 475
Sperry, Ethel, 422
Spotswood, Governor, 291

Spreckels (family), 433-434
  Adolph, 434
  Bernard, 433-434
  Charles Augustus, 434
  Claus, 433-434
  Rudolph, 434
  John Diedrich, 434
Springs, Elliott White, 88
Stamford, Conn., 221, 355
Standish, Myles, 103
Stanford (family), 49, 421, 429-433
  Leland, 415, 422, 424, 428, 429-433
    Mrs. Jane Lathrop, 429, 431-433
  Leland, Jr., 431-432
  Thomas Welton, 433
Stanford University, 432-433
Starbuck (family), 256
Star of the East, 157
"Star-Spangled Banner, The," 351 n.
Stegg, Thomas, 284, 287
Steinberger, Aimée Lillian, 455 n.
Steuben, General, 40
Stevens, May Brady, 231
Stevens, Mrs. Paran, 24
Stevens, Robert L., 498
  Mrs. Grace Vanderbilt Davis, 498
Stevenson, Elizabeth, 276
Steward, Margaret, 513
Stewart (family), 351, 397, 437, 445,
    446
  A. T., 350
  Ami, 153
  Lispenard, 98
  Mary Louise, 414
  William Rhinelander, Sr., 133, 263
    Mrs. Janet Newbold, 135, 161, 355,
      541
  William Rhinelander, Jr., 133
Stillman (family), 369
  Anne "Fifi," 385
  Elsie, 377
  Isabel, 377
  James, 377, 385
  Mary, 369
Stirling, Lord, 319
Stockman, Frank Rockefeller, 372 n.
Stoddard, Elizabeth T., 427
Stoddard, Frank, 41 n.
Stokes, Anson Phelps, 318

Stokowski, Leopold, 498
  Mrs. Gloria Vanderbilt Di Cicco, 498
Stoney, Samuel Gaillard, 53, 88-89
"Stony Ford Farm," 503
Stotesbury, E. T., 344, 519 n.
  Mrs. E. T., 133, 170, 344
Stotesbury (family), 47, 443 n.
Strader, Mona, 159
Straight, Willard, 503
  Mrs. Dorothy Whitney, 503
Strange, Michael, 181
Strassburger, Perry, 129
Strassburger, Ralph M., 129
"Stratford," 306, 307
Stratford, Pa., 509
Stratford Club, 228
"Stratford Hall," 338 n.
Stratton, of M.I.T., 265
Straus (family), 316, 393 n., 442, 459-461, 518
  Donald, 461
  Hermina, 459
  Isidor, 459-460, 461
  Lazarus, 459
  Nathan, 443, 459-460
  Oscar, 458, 459, 460
  Percy, 461
  Percy, Jr., 461
  R. Peter, 443
  Ralph, 461
  Roger W., 458
    Mrs. Gladys Guggenheim, 458
  Roger W., Jr., 458
Strawbridge, Justus, 350
Streeter, Edward, 215
Strelsin, Alfred, 523 n.
Strong, Austin, 215
Strong, Mrs. Charles Augustus, 377
Strong, George Templeton, 27
Strong, Margaret Rockefeller, 380
Strongville, Ohio, 372
Stuart, Robert L., 502
Study of British Genius, 258
Stumpf, Mrs. Franz, 87
Sturges (family), 276
Sturgis, Mich., 153
Stuyvesant (family), 25, 47, 315, 509-514, 518
  Anne, 511, 512

Stuyvesant (family)—Cont.
  Augustus Van Horne, Sr., 510
  Augustus Van Horne, Jr., 509-510, 511-514
  Peter, 47, 320, 509, 510, 511, 512
    Mrs. Judith Bayard, 511
Suarez, Diego, 401
Suffolk, Lord, 396
Sullivan, Frank, 321
Sullivan, Mrs. James Francis, 98
Sullivan, John L., 76
Sullivan, Mark, 159
Sulzberger, Arthur Hays, 129, 462
  Mrs., 462
Sulzberger, Ellen, 443
Sulzberger (family), 442
Summit, N.J., 4, 5, 7
Sunday Observer, 475
Sunshine Club, 416
Sutherland, Eileen, 241
Sutherland, Gordie, 239
Sutro, Adolph, 434
Suydam (family), 25
"Swamp Hall," 336, 340 n.
Sweeny, Brenda, 187
Sweeny, Sharon, 187
Sweeny, Robert, 187-188
  Mrs. Joanne Connelley, 187-188
Sweetser, Jesse, 150
Swift, Charles, 392
Swift, Lindsay, 276
Swift (family), 392
Symington, John Fife, 352
Symington, Mrs. Stuart, 178
Symington, William, 352
Symington (family), 351
Széchényi, Alice, 497
Széchényi, Cornelia, 497
Széchényi, Gladys, 497
Széchényi, Nadine, 497
Széchényi, Sylvia, 497
Széchényi, Count László, 497
  Countess, Gladys Vanderbilt, 497, 219

Tack, Sally, 354
Taft, Robert, 414 n., 460
Taft, William Howard, 42, 99
Tailer, T. Suffern, 214
Talcott, Mary, 280

Taliaferro (family), 285
Tallahassee, 549
Tallant, Robert, 45
Talleyrand-Périgord, Duc de, 452
Tams, J. Frederick, 204
Tangeman, Mrs. Cornelius Hoagland, 133
Tankersley, Mrs. Garvin ("Bazy" McCormick), 151
Tanner, Louise, 172, 177, 183
Tappin, Mrs. Huntington, 50
Tavern Club (Boston), 215
Tavern Club (Chicago), 215
Taylor, Francis Henry, 215
Taylor, Frederick, 147-148
Taylor, Mrs. Henry A. C., 133
Taylor, Mrs. L. Mulford, 52
Taylor, Moses, 484
Taylor, Myron, 211-212
Taylor, Mrs. W. R. K., Jr., 178
Taylor, Zachary, 275, 281
Taylor (family), 147
Tebbel, John, 390-391, 397-398, 399, 402
Temple, Shirley, 130
Tew, Mrs. William H., 52
Thackeray, William Makepeace, 58
Thaw, Alice, 230
Thaw, Harry K., 366-367, 545
Thaw (family), 366-367
Thayer, Molly, 136
Thayer, Robert H., 369 n.
  Mrs., 369 n.
Theory of the Leisure Class, The, 37
Theory of Social Revolutions, 273
Theriot, Charles, 436
Things I Remember, 24
Thomas, Augustus, 140
Thompson, Mrs. Griswold, 133
Thompson, Jack, 521
Thompson, J. Walter, 528
Thompson, Lydia, 228-229
Thorne, Mrs. James Ward, 392 n.
Thorne, Mrs. Oakleigh (Bertha Palmer), 395
Thornton, Dan, 49
Thornton (family), 285
"Thou," 382
Throckmorton (family), 43-44, 282
Thurlow, Lord, 268

Tiffany, Marion, 133
Tilghman (family), 283
Tilton, Newell, 15, 209
Timpson, Lawrence, 205
Titanic, 456, 461, 480, 481
To Catch a Thief, 244
Today, 481
Todd, Sarah, 469-470
Tolles, Frederick B., 343
Tolstoi, Leo, 305 n.
Tombstone, Ariz., 411
Toombs, Robert, 76
Topping, Alice, 541
Topping, Dan, 180
Topping, Henry J., 180
  Mrs. Gloria "Mimi" Baker, 180
Torrance, Alfred, 490
Torrance, Louise Anthony, 490
Toussard, Colonel, 330
Tower, Charlemagne, 67
Tower, Lawrence Phelps, 67
Town and Country, 453
Townsend, Reginald, 217
Town Topics, 8, 12, 25, 124, 474, 502, 541-542
Travelling Bachelor, The, 30, 110-111
Travels in North America, 30
Travers, May, 231
Travers, William R., 120, 193
Tree, Arthur, 400, 401
Tree, Arthur Ronald, 401
Tree, Gladys, 401
Tree, Lambert, 401
Tree, Ronald, 478
Trenton, N.J., 346
Trippe, Juan, 508
Troubetzkoy, Prince Igor, 176
  Princess, Barbara Hutton Mdivani Haugwitz-Reventlow Grant, 176
Troy, N.Y., 253, 397, 421, 520
Trudeau, Dr., 414
Truman, Harry S., 17, 103, 152-153, 154, 207, 208, 413, 509
Truth about the Pilgrims, The, 41 n.
Tryon, N.C., 525
Tubbs, Tallant, 436
Tucker, Father, 245
Tucker, St. George, 298-299, 300
  Mrs. Frances Bland Randolph, 298-299

Tuckerman, Mrs. Walter, 126
Tulsa, Okla., 406
Tunney, Gene, 129
    Mrs. Polly Lauder, 129
"Turkey Island," 292, 293
Turnbull, Henry, 190 *ff.*
Turner, Lana, 186
Tuttle, Elizabeth, 280, 281
Tuxedo Park, 15, 74, 168, 528
Twain, Mark, 36, 78
Twombly, Hamilton McKown, 489
    Mrs., 109-110, 114, 133

Ultra-Fashionable Peerage, The, 98
Union Club, 28, 123, 189 *ff.*, 197, 198,
    199-200, 202, 203-205, 207, 209,
    210, 212, 216-217, 226, 485
Union League Club, 200, 201-202, 203,
    208, 212, 225
Union Suit, 194-196
United Confederate Veterans, 68
United Daughters of the Confederacy,
    68
University Club, 200, 202, 207-208, 212
Untermeyer, Samuel, 84
"Uplands," 423
Urquhart, Cora, 528

Vail, Barrie, 355
Vaile, Eugene, 456
Valeccay, Duc de, 230
Valentina, 55
Valentine, Mrs. Patrick A., 392 *n.*
Valentino, Rudolph, 171, 531
    Mrs., 531
Valhalla, 451
Vallee, Rudy, 173
Van Alen (family), 537
    James J., 478-479
        Mrs. Emily Astor, 479
    James Lauren, 98
    General, 478-479
    Louise, 174, 241
Van Blatherskite (family), 25
Van Buren, Augustus, 46
Van Buren, Martin, 328
Van Buren (family), 47, 537
Vance, Nannie, 325

Van Cortlandt, Stephanus, 317
Van Cortlandt (family), 25, 47, 314,
    315, 318, 319
Van de Maele, Albert, 458
    Mrs. Joan Guggenheim, 458
Vanderbilt (family), 25, 47, 49, 50-51,
    100-101, 109, 134, 140, 142, 234,
    253, 316, 448, 467-468, 482 *ff.*,
    499, 501, 512, 517
    Alfred Gwynne, I, 179, 212, 493,
        495-496, 497
        Mrs. Elsie French, 496, 497
        Mrs. Margaret Emerson McKim,
        179, 496
    Alfred Gwynne, II, 10, 128, 494, 497,
        498
        Mrs. Manuela Hudson, 498
        Mrs. Jeanne Murray, 498
        Mrs. Jean Harvey, 212, 498
    Alice Gwynne, 493
    Amy, 129, 529
    Consuelo, 50, 130, 230, 233-234, 448,
        492, 503
    Consuelo, II, 493
    Cornelia, 492
    Commodore Cornelius, I, 82, 108,
        109, 387, 409, 483-488, 504
        Mrs. Sophia Johnson, 133, 181,
        480
        Mrs. Frank Armstrong Crawford,
        486
    Cornelius, II, 140, 489-490, 492, 496,
        504
        Mrs. Alice Gwynne, 493
    Cornelius, III, 493, 495
        Mrs. Grace Wilson, 493-495 (*The
        Mrs. V.*), 11, 50, 98, 108, 109,
        114, 134, 137, 139, 148, 498, 541
    Cornelius, IV, 493, 494 *n.*, 498
        Mrs. Rachel Littleton, 498
        Mrs. Mary Weir Logan, 498
        Mrs. Helen Varner Anderson, 498
        Mrs. Feliza Loraine Pablos, 498
        Mrs. Patricia Wallace, 498
        Mrs. Anne Bernadette Needham,
        498
    Cornelius, V, 18
    Cornelius Jeremiah, 487, 488
    Eliza Osgood, 489

Vanderbilt (family)—*Cont.*
Emily Thorn, 489
Florence Adèle, 489
Frederick, 489, 490
  Mrs. Louise Anthony Torrance, 490
Frederick W., 169
  Mrs., 133
George, 497, 498
  Mrs. Lucille Parsons, 497, 498
  Mrs. Anita Howard, 497, 498
George Washington, I, 487
George Washington, II, 489, 490, 492
  Mrs. Edith Stuyvesant Dresser, 490
Gertrude, 234, 493, 495, 504-505
Gladys, 219, 493, 497
Gloria, 18, 129, 182, 186, 497, 498, 505-506
Gloria Morgan, 496-497, 505-506
Grace Wilson. *See* Mrs. Cornelius IV
Grace, II, 498
Harold, 211
Harold Stirling, 492
  Mrs. Gertrude Conway, 492
Margaret Emerson. *See* Emerson, Margaret
Margaret Louisa, 489
Muriel, 493
Phebe Hand, 483
Reginald, 133, 135, 493, 496-497
  Mrs. Cathleen Neilson, 496
  Mrs. Gloria Morgan, 496-497
Theresa Fair, 145
William Henry, 108, 487-489
  Mrs. Emily Davies, 498
  Mrs. Anne Colby, 498
William Henry, II, 487
  Mrs. Marie Louisa Kissam, 487
William Henry, III, 497
  Mrs. Emily Davies, 497
  Mrs. Anne Colby, 497
William Kissam, 448, 489-490, 492
  Mrs. Alva Smith, 448, 490
  Mrs. Anne Harriman Sands Rutherford, 414 *n.*, 491

Vanderbilt (family)—*Cont.*
William Kissam, II ("Willie K."), 437, 492-493
  Mrs. Virginia "Birdie" Fair, 437, 492
  Mrs. Rose Warburton, 133, 492
Van Der Bilt, Cornelius, 50
Van Der Bilt, Jan Aertson, 482
Vanderbilt University, 486, 489
Vanderbilt Hotel, 495
Van de Water, Frederic, 22
Van Dolsen, Tuenis, 46
Van Doren (family), 277 *n.*
Van Duke (family), 315
Van Horne (family), 115
Vanity Fair, 20, 77, 137, 139
Van Rensselaer (family), 47, 115, 319-320, 510
  Alexander, 120
  Charles, 319
  Mrs. John King, 9, 22, 29, 49-50, 132
  Kiliaen, 316, 317
  Philip, 130, 177-178, 317, 319
Van Rosenvelt, Klaes Martensen, 321
Van Rotterdam, Ten Broek, 25
Van Vorst, Hooper C., 194, 195
Van Wenckum (family), 101
Van Zandt (family), 319
Vanzetti, Bartolomeo, 265
Vassall (family), 255
Vauclain, Louise, 464 *n.*
Vaux, Richard, 341
Vaux, Mrs. Roberts, 341
Veblen, Thorstein Bunde, 37
Veiled Prophet's Ball, 228
Venable (family), 281
Vernon, Ernest, 510, 513, 514
Verplanck (family), 319
Victoria, Queen, 341, 433
Villard (family), 49
Virginia: A New Look at the Old Dominion, 44 *n.*
Virginia City, Nev., 135, 434, 438
Virkus, Frederick, 96
"Vita Serena," 13
Vogue, 4, 51, 78, 129, 137
Von Cramm, Baron Gottfried, 177
  Baroness, Barbara Hutton Mdivani Haugwitz-Reventlow Grant Troubetzkoy Rubirosa, 177

Von Hofmannsthal, Raimund, 480
Mrs. Nancy Astor Obolensky, 480
Voorhees, Enders McClumpha, 213-214

Wagner, Patricia, 167
Wainwright, Stuyvesant, Jr., 214
Waite, Morris, 280
Waldman, Milton, 456
Waldorf-Astoria Hotel, 470
Waldorf Hotel, 146, 178, 474, 520
Wales, Prince of, 108, 115, 347, 438,
    440, 475, 530
Walker, "Ab," 545-546
Wall, Evander Berry, 121
Wallace, Patricia, 498
"Walnut Grove," 386
Walsh, Evalyn, 155-156
Walsh, Tom, 155-156
Walsh, Vinson, 156
Walska, Ganna, 383
Walters, William, 350-351
Wanamaker (family), 47, 537
    John, 350, 446
    Mrs. John, Jr., 133
    Mrs. Rodman, 529
Warburg (family), 442
    Felix, 443 n.
    Gerald, 443 n.
    Paul, 443 n.
Warburton, Rose, 492
Warburton, Rosie, 493
Warburton, William John, 493
    Mrs. Consuelo Vanderbilt II Smith
    Davis, 493
Ward, Clara, 234
Ward, Eber, 234
Ward, Edgar, 212
Ward, Maria, 300
Warfield, Bessie Wallis. See Warfield,
    Wallis
Warfield, Sol, 236
Warfield, Wallis, 163, 165, 231, 235-240
Warfield (family), 235, 282
Warren, George Henry, 120
    Mrs., 51, 133
Warren, Lloyd, 492
Warren, Mrs. Whitney, 133
Warren, Whitney, Jr., 108
Warren (family), 320
Warrenton, Va., 179

Washburn, Caroline, 127
Washington, D.C., 13-14, 52-53, 71,
    74, 118, 126-127, 129, 151 ff., 167,
    215, 232, 237, 255 n., 276, 302,
    304, 330, 335, 393, 396, 501, 520,
    529
Washington, George, 29, 30, 40, 60-61,
    62, 68, 70, 71, 75, 103, 297, 304,
    311, 312, 342, 345, 346, 486, 542
Washington (family), 105, 281, 285
Washington and Lee University, 94
Washington Post, 158, 403
Washington Times-Herald, 390
Washoe Club, 439
Watch Hill, 522
Watervliet, N.Y., 429
Watriss, Frederick, 182
    Mrs. Brenda Williams-Taylor Fraz-
    ier, 182
Watson, John, 371
Watson, Thomas J., Jr., 210, 519
Watts, M. S. Huntington, 187
Waupaca, Wis., 161
Webb, Clifton, 112-113, 135
Webb, Mrs. F. Egerton, 133
Webb, Frederica Vanderbilt, 464 n.
Webb, Mrs. W. Seward, 133
Webb, William H., 438
Webb, William Seward, 489
    Mrs. Eliza Osgood Vanderbilt, 489
Webster, Daniel, 301, 303, 486
Wecter, Dixon, 40, 65, 198, 252-253,
    318, 392, 395, 435, 446
Weed, Roger, 259
Weekes, Arthur, 204
Weeks, Sinclair, 254
Welles, Benjamin S., 120
Welles, Sumner, 201, 211
Welles, Mrs. B. Sumner, 52
Wellman, Mrs. Allen Gouverneur,
    108, 133
Wells, Helen, 54
Wellsville, Ohio, 434
Welton, Louis, 409
Wendell, Mrs. Barrett, 218
Wendell (family), 320
Wentworth, Lord, 231
Wertenbaker, Thomas, 282, 287
West, Mrs. Allen Terwater, 534

West, George Cornwallis, 232
Mrs. Jennie Jerome Churchill, 232
"Western House," 475
Westinghouse, George, 357
Mrs., 520
"Westmoreland," 310
"Westover," 289
Wetmore, Mrs. Ambrose, 133
Wetmore, Seth, 320
Wetmore, Mrs. William, 529
Wetmore (family), 320
Wetmore Sisters, 320
Weyler, Margaret, 457
Weymouth, Mass., 269
Wharton, Charles, 344
Wharton, Edith, 26, 78-79, 86, 111, 121, 139, 531
Wharton, John, 344
Wharton, Thomas, 344
Wharton (family), 343, 344
Wheelright, Mary C., 257
Whidden, Floyd, 549
Mrs., 549
Whisper, 4
White, Andrew Dixon, 432
White, Henry, 489
Mrs. Emily Thorn Vanderbilt Sloan, 133, 489
White, Stanford, 140, 210, 277, 366, 545
White (family), 319, 320, 343
Whiteford, Lucille, 354 *n.*
Whitehouse, Norman, 521
Mrs. J. Norman de R., 133, 521
Alice, 521
"White Marsh," 519 *n.*
Whitney (family), 41, 47, 86, 100-101, 134, 315, 456, 467-468, 499 *ff.*, 512, 537
Cornelius Vanderbilt (Sonny), 18, 142, 499, 506, 508-509
Mrs. Marie Norton, 509
Mrs. Gwladys "Gee" Crosby Hopkins, 509
Mrs. Eleanor Searle, 16, 509
Mrs. Mary Lou Hosford, 509
Daniel, 506
Dorothy, 503
Eleanor, 18

Whitney (family)—*Cont.*
Eli, 386, 500
Elizabeth, 18
Harry Payne, 234, 495, 503-505, 506, 508
Mrs. Gertrude Vanderbilt, 133, 234, 495, 504-505, 506
Joan, 506
John, 499, 500
John Hay ("Jock"), 86, 128, 402, 414, 506-508
Mrs. Mary Elizabeth ("Liz") Artemis, 507
Mrs. Betsey Cushing Roosevelt, 507
Josiah, 500
Mary Lou Hosford, 18
Pauline, 503
Payne (Miss), 506
Payne, 84, 378, 503-505, 506
Mrs. Helen Hay, 504-505
Richard, 499, 500
Sandra, 506
Sarah Swan, 447
Steven, 537
Thomas, 499
William C., 352, 353
William Collins ("W.C."), 500-503, 506
Mrs. Flora Payne, 501, 503
Mrs. Edith Sibyl May Randolph, 504
Whitrock, Laura Mae, 161
Who's Who, 46, 96, 214, 257, 292
Wickersham, Mrs. George, 50
Wickes, Mrs. Forsyth, 133
Wickham, Elinor, 464 *n.*
Wickliffe (family), 281
Widener, Joseph, 108
Mrs., 133
Widener, Peter A. B., 349, 352, 501
Widener (family), 47, 501 *n.*, 537
Wilcox, Ella Wheeler, 75
Wilde, Oscar, 76
Wilhelm, Kaiser, 85, 234
William Guggenheim, 455 *n.*
Williams, Mrs. Clark, 51-52
Williams, Francis, 183
Williams, Gatenby, 455 *n.*

Williams, Harrison, 160, 161
    Mrs. Mona Strader Schlesinger
        Bush, 135, 159-161
Williams, Josephine Leah, 413
Williams, Juliette, 396
Williams-Taylor, Brenda, 181
Willing, Anne, 341
Willing, Ava, 479, 480
Willing, Thomas, 342, 344
Willing (family), 47, 342, 343
Willis, N. P., 116
Willys, Mrs. John N., 133
Wilmerding, David R., 369 n.
    Mrs. 369 n.
Wilmington, Del., 52, 125, 213, 221,
        328, 331, 332, 339, 362
Willson, George, 418
Willson, Millicent, 418
Wilson, Adah, 383
Wilson, Grace, 493
Wilson, Mrs. Marshall Orme, 133
Wilson, Orme, Jr., 479
Wilson, Richard T., 493
    Mrs., 133
Winburn, Jay Te, 182
Winbush, Julian, 157-158
"Windborne," 547
Winchell, Walter, 17, 141
Windsor, Duke of, 17, 56, 129, 140,
        147, 179, 187, 214, 235, 238-240,
        529, 551
    Duchess of (Wallis Warfield Simp-
        son), 15, 17, 102, 129, 134, 140,
        147, 179, 187, 235-240, 529, 549,
        550
Winkler, John, 169, 332, 337, 415
Winn, Charles, 212
"Winrock," 372 n.
Winslow (family), 103, 264, 285
Winston, Louise Victor, 448 n.
"Winterthur," 336
Winthrop, Egerton, 79
Winthrop, H. Rogers, 492
Winthrop, John, 260, 500
Winthrop (family), 103, 225, 319
Winwood, Estelle, 532
Wise, Isaac Meyer, 443, 462
Wise, Isidor, 443
Wister, Daniel, 344
Wister, John, 344

Wister, Owen, 111
Witherbee, Mrs. Frank S., 98
Wolcott, Oliver, 62, 67 n.
Wolf, Mrs. Walter B., 392 n.
Wood, Mrs. Arthur W. (Pauline Pal-
        mer), 395
Wood, Fernanda, 116 n.
Wood, Mrs. Robert E., 392 n.
Wood, Sidney B., Jr., 76-77, 129-130
Woodbury (family), 256
Woodfill, W. Stewart, 16
Woodhull, Victoria, 486
Woodruff, Katherine, 403
Woodruff (family), 49
Woodward, William, 130
    Mrs., 11, 12
Woodward, William, Jr., 549-551
    Mrs. Ann Eden Crowell, 130, 549-
        551
Woollcott, Alexander, 274
Wooley (family), 281
Woolworth, Edna, 171
Woolworth, Frank W., 171-172, 177,
        393 n.
    Mrs., 171, 172
Woolworth (family), 393 n., 517
Worden, Helen, 136
Workum (family), 443
Worsham, Arabella Duval (Yarring-
        ton), 427
Wren, Anna, 381 n.
Wright, Cobina, Sr. (Elaine Cobb),
        130, 141, 184-186
Wright, Cobina, Jr., 130, 184, 185-186
Wright, Louis B., 43, 284-285
Wright, Frank Lloyd, 411
Wright, Louis, 287
Wright, William May, 184, 185
    Mrs. Cobina Johnson, 184, 185
Wyatt, Jane, 130
Wyatt (family), 282
Wyllie, Irwin G., 81
Wyllys (family), 101
Wynne (family), 343
Wysong, Mrs. John J., 133

Xenia News, 413

Yacht Club, 216, 226, 499
Yale, Elihu, 103

Yale Club, 227
Yale University, 198, 370
Yarmouth, 348
Yarmouth, Earl of, 230
Yeomans, Henry, 265
Young, Eleanor "Cookie," 178-179
Young, Robert R., 178-179
Your Family Tree, 98-99
Yurka, Blanche, 545-546

Zeng (family), 101
Zerbe, Jerome, 136
Ziegfeld *Follies*, 418
Zilboorg, Gregory, 401
Zinsser, Peggy, 413
Zouch (family), 101
Zouilla (family), 523
Zukor, Adolph, 140
   Mrs., 140

ABOUT THE AUTHOR

The Proper Bostonians, Cleveland Amory's first book, published in 1947 when he was 29, not only added a new phrase to the language but was also, as of 1960, in its sixteenth printing. The career of *The Last Resorts* (the second in a trilogy of which *Who Killed Society?* is the third and final volume) has also been a phenomenal one.

Although Amory is the son of a long line of Boston merchants and Harvard graduates, the Amory family originally settled, in the Seventeenth Century, in Charleston, South Carolina. Amory himself has lived in Boston, Philadelphia, Washington, and Arizona—the latter the locale of his only novel, also a best-seller, *Home Town*. Now living in New York, Amory married in 1952 Martha Hodge, daughter of the late actor-playwright William Hodge and, in her own right, an actress and writer.

In 1955 Amory made the decision to withdraw from writing the Duchess of Windsor's autobiography, a decision which was generally applauded. In the year 1959, he was editor-in-chief of the widely hailed international *Celebrity Register,* and in 1960 he was co-editor (with Frederic Bradlee) of *Vanity Fair,* an anthology of that famous magazine.

A regular contributor to *Holiday* and the *New York Times Book Review,* as well as conductor of a monthly column for the *Saturday Review,* Amory is also a syndicated newspaper columnist, a lecturer and a television commentator. His hobbies are chess and book collecting.

Coats of Arms (Registered and Proved)*

D'ABBADIE	319	BARLOWE	431	BLACKWELL	409
ABELL	168	BARRETT	490	BLAKE	354
ABERCROMBIE	107	BARTENBACH	512	BLAND	445
ADAMS	23	BARTHE	302	BOLLES	16
AGASSIZ	382	BASKERVILLE	344	BONYTHON	53
ALEXANDER	158	BATE(S)	285	BOURCHIER	451
ALSOP	169	BATTE	298	BOWDEN	437
ALTENKLINGEN	460	BEATTY	226	BOWDITCH	22
AMHERST	128	BECKWITH	392	BOWEN	3
ANDROS	253	BEEKMAN	95	BOWES	119
D'ANTERROCHES	260	BELCHER	283	BRACEY	55
APPLETON	2	BELLINGHAM	259	BRADBURY	139
APSLEY	439	BERGMAN	359	BRADSTREET	145
ASFORDBY	381	BERKELEY	263	BRENTON	91
ASTON	308	BERNARD	195	BREWER	514
AVERY	268	BERNARD	130	BRIDGER	287
BACON	472	BERNON	78	BRIGGS	221
BAINTON	508	BEVERLEY	300	BRINLEY	248
BANCROFT	338	BICKLEY	500	BROMFIELD	410
BARCLAY	124	BIGGE	428	BROUGHTON	109
BARHAM	457	BILLINGSLEY	520	BROWNE	54

* There are, of course, other genuine coats of arms, but only these had, as of 1960, been submitted for registered proof. The numbers indicate the order in which they were submitted for registry to the New England Historic and Genealogical Society, easily the country's outstanding authority on coats of arms.

COATS OF ARMS (REGISTERED AND PROVED)

Name	Page	Name	Page	Name	Page
BRUEN	106	COE	337	DIXON	175
BUEK	63	COGGESHALL	10	DIXWELL	18
BULKELEY	4	COLEPEPER	98	DONGAN	322
BULL	418	CONNEY	17	DONK, VAN DER	468
BURROUGH	220	COLLETT	343	DONNELL	444
BYFIELD	137	COOKE	181,209	DORMER	471
BYRD	174	COOTE	161	DOWNING	131
CALDER	100	COPE	395	DRAKE	36
CALTHORP	492	CORNETTE	329	DRAKE	447
CALVERT	147	CORNWALLIS	481	DUDLEY	87
CAMMOCK	176	DE COURCY	358	DUMARESQ	5
CAMPBELL	306	COVENTRY	371	DUMMER	227
CAMPBELL	396,400	COXE	230	DUNCAN	94
DE CARPENTIER	424	COYTMORE	408	DUNCH	273
CARROLL	234	CRANSTON	27	DUNGAN	322
CARTERET	117	CRISPIN	155	EDEN	247
CARVER	198	CRONLUND	488	EDGECOMB	66
CARY	458	CROSBY	388	ELLIS	421
CASTEEL	459	CROWNE	328	ELWYN	207
CAYNE	205	CUMMING	301	ERRINGTON	222
CHAMPERNOWNE	138	DADE	398	EVEN	489
DU CHASTEL	459	DAKIN	379	EVERARD	217,231
CHATFIELD	134	DANIEL	497	EXMOUTH	503
CHAUNCY	86	DAUBENY	366	FAIRFAX	347
CHESTER	48	DAVENPORT	20	FARLEY	324
CHETWOOD	246	DAVIE	150	FARRAR	342
CHUTE	46	DELAFIELD	170	FAUNTLEROY	470
CLAIBORNE	466	DELFAU	453	FAWKNOR	26
CLARKE	33	DENN	154	FEAKE	402
CLARKSON	503	DEODATE	504	FELTON	15
CLEMENT	37	DICKSON	397	FENWICK	34
CLINTON	224	DIGGES	320	FIELD	420
CLINTON	80	DIGHTON	111	FILMER	423
CLOPTON	341	DINWIDDIE	353	FISKE	19
COCQUIEL	506	DIODATI	504	FITCH	62

COATS OF ARMS (REGISTERED AND PROVED)

FITZHUGH	360	GRESHAM	442	HULL	133
FONES	407	DE GROUCHY	516	HUME	14
FOOTE	405	GURDON	219	HUMFREY	113
DE FOREST	270	HALLET	171	HUNLOCK	153
FOSTER	245	HALLOWELL	517	HURD	261
FRANKLAND	132	HANBURY	140	HUTCHINSON	42
FREEHOF	473	HANCOCK	229	HYDE	293
FREESTONE	76	HARLAKENDEN	144	HYDE	413
FRIEDLAND	212	HAWARDEN	180	INNES	475
GADE	491	HAWES	197	ISELIN	496
GAGE	165	HAYDOCK	72	ISHAM	309
GALE	334	HAYNES	191	JAQUET	443
GALLATIN	498	HEAD	330	JEFFRAY	249
GATES	104	HEATHCOTE	85	JEFFRIES	251
GAYER	67	HELME	348	JOHNSON	162
GIBBON	136	HELMERSHAUSEN	9	JOHNSON	167
GIBBS	74	HENDERSON	467	JOHNSON	272
GOETCHIUS	486	HENSHAW	365	JOHNSON	326
GOLDING	173	HERNDON	501	JOHNSON	485
GOOCH	255	HESILRIGGE	284	JOHNSTONE	82
GOOKIN	39	HEYMAN	456	JONES	476
GORDON	313	HEYWARD	455	DE JONGH	336
GORDON	480,519	HICKS	148	JOSSELYN	99
GORE	6	HIGGINSON	73	KALTENBORN,	
GORGES	93	HOHENZOLLERN,		VON	433
GORSUCH	193	VON	440	KEAYNE	205
GORTON	65	HOLSTEIN	110	KENNEDY	327
GOSNOLD	430	HOOKE	123	KENYON	79
GÖTTSCHI	486	HOOKER	213	KING	68
GRAFFENRIED, DE	464	HORSMANDEN	325	KINSOLVING	115
GRAHAM	511	HOUGHTON	419	KNAUTH	61
DE GRASSE	377	HOUSTON	289	KYLE	237
GRAY	206	HOWARD	265	LABADIE	303
GREENE	97	HUGER	243	LAFAYETTE	157
GREGORY	125	HUIDEKOPER	127	LAKE	41

LANE	454	MANNING	305	NICOLL	186
LANG, VON	478	MANNINGHAM	403	NISBET	114
LANYON	432	MANWARING	32	NOAILLES, DE	483
LATHAM	69	MARBURY	81	NORTON	200
LAWRENCE	393	MARSHALL	60	NORTON	279
LEA	339	MASCARENE	232	NOYES	434,435
LECHMERE	363	MASON	50	O'BRIEN	294
LEE	105	MASTER	250	ODINGSELLE	278
LEEDS	88	MAYHEW	126	OGLETHORPE	282
LEER, VAN	362	MCCAFFREY	387	OLIVER	240
LEETE	143	MCCLAIN	166	OLYPHANT	355
LEIGH	258	MCGEE	208	ORR	112
LEIGH	339	MERCER	506	OWINGS	384
LEWIS	52	LE MERCIER	506	OXENBRIDGE	452
LIGON	415	MERING, VON	438	PADDOCK	199
LINDESAY	276	MILDMAY	281	PALGRAVE	401
LINDSAY	296	MILLET	262	PALMER	465
LINKER	499	MINER	24	PALMES	77
LINKLETTER	406	MITCHELL	304	PARRY	58
LISLE	242	MONTAGUE	350	PASTORIUS	116
LITTLETON	484	MONTEJOYE	236	PAYNE	70
LIVINGSTON	96	MONTGOMERY	477	PECK	202
LLOYD	179	MOODY	274	PELHAM	43
LORD	159	MOODY	411	PELL	40
LOVELACE	194	MORIARTY	118	PELLEW	502
LOWELL	30	MORRIS	101	PEMBERTON	356
LOWNDES	380	MORRIS	449	PENHALLOW	135
LUCAS	394	MORRISON	495	PENINGTON	386
LUDLOW	156	MOSELEY	45	PENN	177
LYNCKER	499	MULLERY	493	PEPERELL	28
LYNDE	211	MURRAY	264	PERCY	214
MACKARTY	352	NANFAN	510	PERKINS	233
MACKENZIE	351	NELSON	317	PERNAY, DE	497
MACKWORTH	295	NEWTON	316	PEYSTER, DE	375
MALLORY	299	NICHOLSON	507	PHIPPEN	12

COATS OF ARMS (REGISTERED AND PROVED)

PHIPPS	469	
PICOLET	121	
PLUMB	391	
PLUMSTED	345	
POLE	57	
DU PONT	332	
POOLE	75	
POOLE	291	
POTIER DE LA MORANDIÈRE	389	
POWNALL	256	
POYEN DE ST. SAUVEUR, DE	436	
PRICE	390	
PUTNAM	35	
PYNCHON	8	
PYNE	513	
QUARLES	286	
RAINSBOROUGH	376	
RANDOLPH	178	
RAWSON	120	
RAWSON	239	
READE	196	
REMINGTON	203	
RENSSELAER, VAN	378	
RICHARDS	204	
ROBINSON	412	
ROBINSON	474	
ROCKWELL	187	
RODNEY	292	
ROME	160	
ROOSA	335	
ROWE	238	
RUSSELL	267,277	
RUTHERFURD	92	
SAFFIN	149	
ST. JOHN	182	
SALTONSTALL	13	
SALTZA, VON	244	
SANDERS	290	
SANDOZ	494	
SANFORD	38	
SAVAGE	141	
SCARBOROUGH	364	
SCARBURGH	364	
SCHUYLER	163	
SCOT	83	
SCOTT	288,297	
SEGAR	164	
SETON	505	
SEYMOUR	275	
SHAPLEIGH	307	
SHARPLESS	383	
SHEPPARD	448	
SHERMAN	216	
SHIRLEY	254	
SIEMERS	90	
SILLE, DE	331	
SKINNER	215	
SKIPWITH	183	
SLICHTENHORST, VAN	416	
SMITH	190,218	
SMITH	370	
SMITH	441	
SMITH, CAPT. JOHN	151	
SMITH, WILLIAM	84	
SNELLING	142	
SOUTHWORTH	152	
SPENCER	461	
SPOTSWOOD	31	
STACY	223	
STANDISH	102	
STERLING	333	
STEUBEN, VON	56	
STILEMAN	427	
STOCKMAN	188	
STORM	228	
STOUGHTON	385	
STRATTON	425	
STUYVESANT	414	
SYMONDS	271	
TALBOT	372	
TALCOTT	189	
TAYLOR	225	
THACHER	59	
THOMPSON	29	
THORNDIKE	11	
THOROLD	71	
THROCKMORTON	21	
THROCKMORTON	103	
TILGHMAN	368	
TIMPSON	482	
TOUTEVILLE	373	
TOWNLEY	269	
TRAFFORD	450	
TRAPP	399	
TRYON	266	
TYLER	429	
UNDERHILL	108	
UPDIKE	252	
VANBRUGH	184	
VANE	129	
VASSALL	357	

COATS OF ARMS (REGISTERED AND PROVED)

VERNON	280	WEST	201	WINSLOW	185
VINCENT	509	WETMORE	422	WINTHROP	7
VLECK, VAN	518	WHALLEY	122	WOODHULL	235
WADDELL	367	WHARTON	426	WREFORD	346
WADE	315	WHITE	172	WRIGHT	257
WALLER	462	WHITE	340	WYATT	192
WARREN	479	WHITFIELD	241	WYATT	515
WASHBOURNE	311	WHITING	210	WYLLYS	47
WASHINGTON	1	WILKES	522	WÜST	463
WATSON	487	WILLIAMS	51	YALE	146
WELD	64	WILLOUGHBY	49	ZENG	374
WENCKUM, VAN	417	WILSON	25	ZINZENDORF	521
WENTWORTH	44	WILSON	404	ZOLLIKOFER	460
WESSELHOEFT	89	WINGFIELD	446	ZOUCH	318